AFRICAN AMERICAN PERSPECTIVES
ON
POLITICAL SCIENCE

African American Perspectives

on

Political Science

Edited by

WILBUR C. RICH

With a Foreword by

CHARLES V. HAMILTON

TEMPLE UNIVERSITY PRESS
Philadelphia

Temple University Press
1601 North Broad Street
Philadelphia PA 19122
www.temple.edu/tempress

∞

The paper used in this publication meets the requirements
of the American National Standard for Information Sciences—
Permanence of Paper for Printed Library Materials,
ANSI Z39.48–1992

Library of Congress Cataloging-in-Publication Data

African American perspectives on political science / edited by Wilbur C. Rich ;
foreword by Charles V. Hamilton.
p.   cm.
Includes bibliographical references and index.
ISBN 1-59213-108-5 (hardcover : alk. paper)   ISBN 1-59213-109-3 (pbk. : alk. paper)
1. Political science.   2. Racism—Political aspects.   3. Racism—Political aspects—
United States.   4. African American political scientists—Attitudes.
I. Rich, Wilbur C.

JA76.A355 2007
320.01—dc22   2006015922

2   4   6   8   9   7   5   3   1

CONTENTS

Foreword • CHARLES V. HAMILTON   *ix*

Acknowledgments   *xi*

Introduction • WILBUR C. RICH   *1*

PART ONE   Race and Political Scientists   5

CHAPTER 1   Still at the Margins: The Persistence of Neglect of African American Issues in Political Science, 1986–2003 • ERNEST J. WILSON III AND LORRIE A. FRASURE   *7*

CHAPTER 2   The Race Variable and the American Political Science Association's *State of the Discipline* Reports and Books, 1907–2002 • HANES WALTON JR. AND ROBERT C. SMITH   *24*

CHAPTER 3   African American Political Scientists in Academic Wonderland • WILBUR C. RICH   *38*

PART TWO   Globalization and Transnational Politics   53

CHAPTER 4   Black Politics in Latin America: An Analysis of National and Transnational Politics • OLLIE A. JOHNSON III   *55*

CHAPTER 5   Globalization and the Study of Development • VERNON D. JOHNSON   *76*

PART THREE   Civic Engagement and Voting   105

CHAPTER 6   Political Science and the Study of African American Public Opinion • MELISSA V. HARRIS-LACEWELL   *107*

CHAPTER 7   A Black Gender Gap? Continuity and Change in Attitudes toward Black Feminism • EVELYN M. SIMIEN   *130*

CHAPTER 8   Going It Alone: Black Women Activists and Black Organizational Quiescence • ANDREA Y. SIMPSON   *151*

CHAPTER 9   Political Scientists and the Activist-Technocrat Dichotomy:
The Case of John Aubrey Davis • MARTIN KILSON   169

PART FOUR   **Political Institutions**   193

CHAPTER 10   Dimensions of Representation and the Congressional Black
Caucus • KENNY J. WHITBY   195

CHAPTER 11   Toward a Critical Race Theory in Political Science:
A New Synthesis for Understanding Race, Law, and Politics •
BARBARA LUCK GRAHAM   212

CHAPTER 12   Presidential Leadership and the Politics of Race:
Stereotypes, Symbols, and Scholarship • WILBUR C. RICH   232

PART FIVE   **The Subfields**   251

CHAPTER 13   Comparative Politics and Asia: Contesting Hegemonic
Inter- and Intra-Disciplinary Boundaries •
GERMAINE A. HOSTON, PHD   253

CHAPTER 14   Race and the Problem of Equity in the Administrative State:
Implications for Political Science Theory and Methods •
LENNEAL J. HENDERSON JR.   285

CHAPTER 15   Race and the City: The View from Two Political
Science Journals • MARION ORR AND VALERIE C. JOHNSON   308

CHAPTER 16   Navigating the Muddy Waters of the Mainstream:
Tracing the Mystification of Racism in International Relations •
ERROL A. HENDERSON   325

CHAPTER 17   A Critical Review of American Political Institutions:
Reading Race into the Constitutional "Silence" on Race •
KATHERINE TATE, KEVIN L. LYLES, AND LUCIUS J. BARKER   364

CHAPTER 18   Political Science Confronts Afro-America:
A Reconsideration • JERRY G. WATTS   398

Contributors   434
Index   438

LIST OF TABLES AND FIGURES

Tables

1.1 Search Totals for Full-Length Articles (FLAs), 1970–1985   14

1.2 Search Totals for Full-Length Articles (FLAs), 1986–2003   15

1.3 Search Totals for Full-Length Articles (FLAs) by Titles and Abstracts, 1970–1985   16

1.4 Search Totals for Full-Length Articles (FLAs) by Titles and Abstracts, 1986–2003   17

1.5 Search Totals for Full-Length Articles (FLAs) by Select Political Science Journals   18

2.1 APSA-Sponsored *State of the Discipline* Reports and Books   26

5.1 Typology of Paradigms of Development   99

7.1 Characteristics of the Sample, 2004–2005 NBFS versus 1993–1994 NBPS   137

7.2 Support for Black Feminist Consciousness in 2004–2005   141

7.3 Support for Black Feminist Consciousness in 1993–1994   142

7.4 Determinants of Black Political Behavior, Estimated Separately for Gender   143

7.5 Determinants of Various Modes of Political Behavior, Estimated Separately for Black Women   145

7.6 Determinants of Various Modes of Political Behavior, Estimated Separately for Black Men   146

10.1 African American Members in Congress, 92nd–108th Congresses   198

10.2 African American Members in 109th Congress by Party, State, and Year Elected   204

14.1   Department of Defense Spending for Goods, Services,
       and Research and Development in Selected Metropolitan
       Areas (Excluding Military Payroll), 1992   296

14.2   Number of Minority Firms Participating in SBA's 8(a) Program,
       1985–2000   297

14.3   Budget of the Office of Minority Economic Impacts,
       U.S. Department of Energy, 1985–1991   297

14.4   Percentage Change in Federal Taxes, 1991   299

14.5   Tax Increase Borne by Various Income Groups, 1991   300

14.6   EITC Benefit Structure, 1993   301

15.1   Articles in Two Premier Journals   309

15.2   Percentage of Articles in Five Substantive Research Areas   311

Figures

8.1   Women in Congress, State Elective Office, and State
       Legislatures, 2004   161

12.1   Respondents' Attitudes about Black Presidential Candidates,
       1999   243

15.1   Urban Articles in PSQ and APSR, 1886–2002   310

FOREWORD

Charles V. Hamilton

F IFTY YEARS AGO, this book likely would not have been published or even conceived of as necessary to the study of the discipline of American political science. This is understandable, but regrettable. I suggest that it is regrettable because this volume is no more valuable today than it would have been in the immediate post–World War II years. There were, indeed, several African American political scientists at that time with perspectives relevant to the study of race and American governance. They were trained by well-respected scholars at highly regarded universities. But most of those professionally established scholars had not the slightest notion of the woefully limited perspectives they were expounding about race policy in this country and abroad. Not entirely wrong perspectives, for sure, but certainly limited ones. They worked from paradigms that were simply not in sync with the experimental realities of many "minority" political scientists. Challenging these models—in PhD dissertations, refereed professional journals, and hiring and tenure committees—was near nigh impossible.

In the discipline of political science, conceptualizations, methodologies, and research proposals were set. Thus, we were presented with disciplinarily sanctioned research premises: the American Creed and the American Dilemma; African Americans as appendages to the big-city political machines; the ethnic political succession theory and the ultimate assumption that it would apply to Black Americans; and, of course, the ever-present theoretical notion of class as the overriding factor supplanting the "significance" of race in the American socio-political-economic dynamic.

Then, seemingly, of a sudden, Black Americans were boycotting, protest marching, yelling, burning, and becoming more mass involved than merely as plaintiffs raising major constitutional issues. And equally abruptly, the American political discipline was caught with its paradigms down. The 1968 Kerner Commission Report opened the door to a raft of grant proposals from political scientists pursuing the "two nations" theme of that report. It took upheavals on the ground, not in the discipline's comfortable confines of its limited lectures and seminars, to broaden the intellectual input regarding this most important issue in society.

This is the value of this book: It provides new perspectives. Some of us always understood that the African American struggle in this society was aimed, fundamentally, at broadening the arena of participation to include electoral participation, educational access, economic opportunity, etc. Neither was and is the struggle's intent to usurp the old and established, but rather to make it more legitimate by opening up a closed society.

This is another reason why this book is so valuable. It challenges the discipline of American political science to broaden its intellectual insights by considering even more perspectives not previously thought worthy of pondering.

ACKNOWLEDGMENTS

E ACH OF THE ESSAYS has been written expressly for the book. Accordingly, I would express my appreciation to each of the contributors. I wish to acknowledge the advice and thoughtful comments of several of my friends and colleagues at Wellesley College. I would particularly like to thank Lawrence Hanks, Theophilus Herrington, Toni-Michelle Travis, Michael Hanchard, Mary Stuckey, Craig Murphy, and Michael Nelson for taking the time to read the drafts of individual essays and provide thoughtful feedback. I also wish to thank Peter Wissoker and Alex Holzman of Temple University Press. They had the insight and patience necessary for such a project. In addition, I want to thank the anonymous reviewers for their time, criticisms, and suggestions. They have helped make this a better volume. My family was, as usual, supportive and willing to listen to me talk about the uniqueness of this book. Without their generosity, this book would not have been possible. Finally, this anthology is dedicated to all political scientists who love the profession of teaching and the discourse about politics and democracy.

INTRODUCTION

Wilbur C. Rich

T HIS COLLECTION OF ESSAYS is about political science as seen through the eyes of African American political scientists—their assessment of the subfields, their views about the quality of race-related research and their regrets about the omissions in the literature. The central theme is that race matters in politics, not only nationally but internationally. Because we do not understand race in our own politics, it makes it difficult to comprehend ethnic and racial disputes in other countries. Accordingly, the discipline needs multiple perspectives to keep expanding its blind spaces and to prevent it fom becoming too comfortable with itself. Although not all African American political scientists agree with the Perestroika group's critique of the discipline, most agree that there is a danger of unconscious insularity in methodology and outlook. For this reason we African American political scientists have a special responsibility to rethink the norms, canons, and directions of the discipline.

This collection of essays reflects the concerns of African American political scientists who teach and investigate political behavior. The idea for the volume came to me as I walked through the exhibit hall at an annual meeting of the American Political Science Association (APSA). In many ways, the exhibit hall is one of the most interesting parts of the annual meeting. Attendees get a chance to meet old friends, network with new ones, pitch book ideas to editors, and thumb through books. As I was thumbing through the latest version of *Political Science: The State of the Discipline (The State)*, it occurred to me that it is time that African Americans evaluate the discipline. We have been in the profession long enough to assess whether the discipline is headed in the right direction. At meetings of the National Conference of Black Political Scientists (NCOBPS) we often commiserate about the discipline going off track and not dealing with the critical issues facing the nation. I thought it was time to share these ideas. I approached Temple University Press with the idea, and Peter Wissoker encouraged me to send him a proposal.

The first task was to select the essay writers. I asked both European and African American political scientists for suggestions. One senior political scientist thought the idea would not work because so many senior African American political scientists were too busy writing books, serving on committees, and taking on administrative assignments in their universities. Another complained about the lack of diversity in subfields focused on by African American political scientists. In his opinion, they were stacked in American government. I discovered that the first reservation had some merit, as some potential writers turned me down for those reasons, but the second reservation was groundless. There are several African Americans in comparative and international relations. Granted these political scientists are not very active in APSA or NCOBPS, but they are very involved in area studies associations. It is true, however, that there are few African Americans with primary university appointments as political theorists.

Unexpectedly, the selection process gave me the chance to meet new people. Senior scholars who had never contributed to the earlier versions of *The State* seemed like a good choice for contributors. Of course, one should never pass up an opportunity to engage younger scholars. The strategy of mixing senior and junior scholars is not without its problems. Some senior scholars were too deep into other projects to write an essay. Others accepted but withdrew as their schedules overwhelmed them. Some young scholars were too busy preparing for tenure to write an essay. After I submitted the first set of names and their abstracts to the publisher, the reviewers suggested other names and topics. A new round of invitations went out to potential contributors. I am recounting the selection process because readers may be interested in the genealogy of this volume.

African American Perspectives on the Political Science Discipline is aimed at the growing interest in diversity in higher education and how African Americans fit into academic departments, as well as the overall purpose of the university. The discourse on the future of political science can no longer be left to European American scholars of whom we minority scholars refer to as the "usual suspects." There is simply too much at stake to do that. These "usual suspects" have been missing too many nuances, following too many circuitous arguments, and reverting the discipline around its relevant past.

African American Perspectives on the Political Science Discipline intends to make political scientists aware of the vast changes in the demographics of academia and its potential impact on classroom teaching. All of the earlier *State of the Discipline* volumes have been reference books. None attempted to examine the discipline from a minority perspective. The earlier volumes contain reviews of the literature in the various subfields. Usually they were rather congratulatory essays suggesting that the state of the discipline was good but could be better. The writers in this anthology have promised not to replicate the practice.

Editing a volume about one's profession can be as narcissistic as it is revealing. Choosing the contributors to this book reminded me of a short essay written by Patrick Dunleavy entitled "So, What Do Political Scientists Do?" He was asked that question at a cocktail party and found himself fumbling for an answer. For me, it is the occasional fellow airline seat passenger who asks that question. On learning that I am a political scientist, most immediately ask me about national politics. Others ask me if I know some politician, and still others whether I plan to run for office. A few just turn away and stay quiet through the trip. I agree with Dunleavy's observation that

> [l]ike other disciplines, political science covers a big canvas. At the well-established end of the subject are philosophical and normative thinking about politics or straight political history, or the semi-zoological collection of information about exotic foreign political systems. Some political scientists sit and think hard about dilemmas that have been with us for as long as human societies have existed. Some pound computers all day long and read brain-aching books on statistical methods. Other people work in dusty archives, or do participant observation at party conferences. All of this work focuses on states, how to control them, or how states interact with each other or with their citizens.[1]

Like Dunleavy I want to defend all approaches to political science and their subjects. Political scientists do a variety of things and hold a variety of views. The essays in this volume demonstrate some of this diversity.

Overview of the Essays

In assembling this collection of essays, I have solicited a diverse group of contributors who represent different subfields, departments, and generations. One can see that their writing styles are different as are their intellectual agendas. Yet, although they do not necessarily agree with one another, all are concerned about the future of political science and the society that depends on our analysis.

The essays are organized into four sections. The purpose of Section One is to delve into the racial isolation of the field. Ernest J. Wilson III and Lorrie A. Frasure's "Still at the Margins: The Persistence of Neglect of African American Issues in Political Science, 1986–2003," is a discussion of the lack of political science attention to race. Hanes Walton Jr. and Robert C. Smith's "The Race Variable and American Political Science Association's *State of the Discipline* Reports and Books 1907–2002" surveys the history of APSA-sponsored volumes entitled *The State of the Discipline* and their treatment of race. Finally, Wilbur Rich discusses African American political scientists as newcomers to academe and tries to put their problems in organizational context.

Section Two examines transnational black politics and its implications. It also discusses the impact of globalization on developing countries. Ollie A. Johnson's "Black Politics in Latin America: An Analysis of National and Transnational Politics" explores race politics in Latin America. Vernon D. Johnson's "Globalization and the Study of Development" analyzes the meaning of globalization for developing countries.

Section Three addresses questions of civic engagement and participation. Melissa Harris-Lacewell's "Political Science and the Study of African American Public Opinion" reviews the methodology and literature on black public opinion. Evelyn M. Simien's "A Black Gender Gap? Continuity and Change in Attitudes toward Black Feminism" analyzes data from the 1993–1994 National Black Politics Study and 2004–2005 National Black Feminist Study. Andrea Y. Simpson's

"Going It Alone: Black Women Activists and Black Organizational Quiescence" discusses the political participation of black women. Martin Kilson's "Political Scientists and the Activist-Technocrat Dichotomy: The Case of John Aubrey Davis" examines the career of Professor Davis as a prototype of the activist/analyst quandary.

Section Four reviews race and American political institutions. Kenny J. Whitby's "Dimensions of Representation and the Congressional Black Caucus" examines the role of the Congressional Black Caucus and representation. Barbara Luck Graham's "Toward a Critical Race Theory in Political Science: A New Synthesis for Understanding Race, Law, and Politics" looks at critical race theory as a possible way for the courts to address the race question. Wilbur C. Rich's "Presidential Leadership and the Politics of Race: Stereotypes, Symbols, and Scholarship" reviews the presidential literature and its neglect of the presidential responsibility in race relations.

Section Five presents overviews of the various subfields of political science. Germaine Hoston's "Comparative Politics and Asia: Contesting Hegemonic Inter- and Intra-Disciplinary Boundaries" examines why African American political scientists should study comparative politics. Lenneal Henderson's "Race and the Problem of Equity in the Administrative State" links race with resource allocation and equity. Marion Orr and Valerie C. Johnson's "Race and the City: The View from Two Political Science Journals" is an examination of the political science journals and their neglect of urban issues. Katherine Tate, Kevin L. Lyles, and Lucius J. Barker's "A Critical Review of American Political Institutions" raises questions about blacks and the political system. Examining the role that political theory plays in the discourse on race is Jerry Watts' "Political Science Confronts Afro-America: A Reconsideration."

Finally, this volume attempts to expose some of the glaring gaps in the field as well as raise new questions for future research. Comments and reactions are welcome.

Note

1. Dunleavy, Patrick, "So, what do political scientists do?" New Stateman 127 (October 9, 1998).

PART I

Race and Political Scientists

T HE DISCOURSE ABOUT RACE and politics continues. Race is so important because it defines so much of our political culture. Although polls show that white Americans are less prejudiced than they were in the 1940s, the races are becoming more socially isolated. Douglas S. Massey and Nancy Denton's *American Apartheid* reported this when they discovered housing segregation after the 1990 U.S. Census. The 2000 Census did not reveal any lessening of this isolation. Yet as I suggested in *The Politics of Minority Coalitions*, watching individual blacks queue-jump their collective group does not mean that the overall situation for them has improved. There have been three African American presidents of the American Political Science Association (APSA), but this has not triggered a mad rush by departments to recruit more African American political scientists.

The essays in Part I attempt to explain the barriers to the incorporation of political scientists of African descent into the profession. This is not to say that all African Africans feel alienated, but on a whole, most do not feel fully a part of the discipline. If this was not the case, why does the National Conference of Black Political Scientists (NCOBPS) continue to draw participants who do not attend APSA meetings? Why does the APSA's Committee on Blacks in the Profession events draw mostly blacks during APSA national meetings? This is not to deny the effort by the APSA to increase the overall level of minority participation. Nor does it suggest the disappearance of the NCOBPS would signal the end of black isolation in the discipline. However, the professional careers of African American political scientists are a microcosm of the internal intellectual and power struggle within this historically white association. Part I also hopes not only to capture the angst of African American political scientists but also, more importantly, provide their critique of the research in political science.

CHAPTER ONE

Still at the Margins

The Persistence of Neglect of African American Issues in Political Science, 1986–2003

ERNEST J. WILSON III AND LORRIE A. FRASURE

A CADEMIC DISCIPLINES are grids that provide scholars a way to divide up the world and to impose order and consistency on unruly reality. Each discipline presents a slightly different grid such that the "same" topic—for example, family, power, or equality—will be defined and situated differently relative to other topics and relative to its centrality or distance from core disciplinary concerns. For political scientists *power, choice, and the state* are given pride of place at the center of the field (Katznelson and Milner, 2002), whereas the study of families is more peripheral. The structure and behavior of families are far more central to sociology and anthropology.

Disciplines also guide their members to study some topics more than others by providing varying constraints and rewards. In this chapter, we examine the differential treatment of race and ethnicity by the discipline of political science, comparing and contrasting it to its sister disciplines of sociology, history, and economics, with a specific focus on topics related to black issues.[1] This chapter revisits and extends an earlier examination by one of the authors for the time period 1970–1985 (Wilson 1985), which was published in the political science journal *PS*. Wilson found that political science ranked third after sociology and history in its treatment of black topics, and the original essay offered several explanations for this hierarchy across disciplines.[2] In this more comprehensive review, we extend the analysis to cover the 1986–2003 period and add the discipline of economics to determine whether the relative rankings of the disciplines have changed or largely remained the same.

Our evidence, drawn from JSTOR computer-generated evaluations of mainstream journal citations covering more than three decades in each of the four disciplines, still finds significant differences across the fields in their treatment of black issues. The extent of these differences raises sharp questions about our understandings of the varying disciplinary frameworks used to study race in America, particularly as they relate to the investigation of African American issues in political science.

In the third edition of *Political Science: The State of the Discipline*, Katznelson and Milner (2002) observe these concerns broadly and their effect on the discipline:

> The character of the founding of political science further helped shape its contours by pushing certain areas of inquiry into the margins. Demarcating itself from history, political science showed a greater concern for current events. To differentiate itself from sociology, it became relatively disinterested in the social basis of political action and inequality. In distinguishing itself from economics, it mainly left issues of political economy to other scholars, at least until recent decades. Further, born in the heyday of segregation, political science initially treated race as mainly beyond its ken. Later, each of these areas became contentious inside the discipline, as dissatisfied scholars sought to bring history, social analysis, political economy, and the studies of race into its core (2002, 4–5).

As Katznelson and Milner point out above, political science has been relatively apathetic toward topics like the politics of race and inequality (and arguably the politics of gender and sexuality as well). Long before Katznelson and Milner's assessment, numerous scholars in the field have examined the implications of this "disciplinary factionalism" related to the study of racial politics (see Dawson and Cohen 2002; Dawson and Wilson 1991; Prestage 1979; Walton and McCormick 1997; Walton, Miller, and McCormick 1994; Warren 2005 ; Wilson 1985). For example, Dawson and Wilson (1991) examined how different social science paradigms address African American politics. They refer to the study of African American politics as the "step child of the discipline" (1991, 192). They further contend, "The major journals usually do not feature articles on the subject. Black politics is marginalized in graduate studies programs, in American politics textbooks, and in the research priorities of agencies like the National Science Foundation" (Dawson and Wilson 1991, 190–91).

Walton and McCormick (1997) examined the marginalization of black topics in the political science discipline as a form of "social danger," arguing that "the study of the black experience is seen by the larger culture as socially unacceptable and therefore socially dangerous" (1997, 230). They draw on extensive empirical evidence from the review of materials in two journals, *Political Science Quarterly* and *The American Political Science Review*. They find evidence for their social danger hypothesis, which suggests in part that personal, political, and professional fears limit the discipline and its members in studying the African American experience (1997, 240).

Perhaps this tendency has shifted to some extent in recent years. Dawson and Wilson (1991) observed that, although the 1983 volume, *Political Science: The State of the Discipline* (edited by Ada Finifter), devoted nineteen chapters to the study of various topics in political science, there was no chapter on race, few references to race, and even fewer African American scholars cited for their work on black politics (192–93). Ten years later, the 1993 edition included a chapter by McClain and Garcia entitled "Expanding Disciplinary Boundaries: Black, Latino, and Racial Minority Groups in Political Science" (247–79). The 2002 edition of *Political Science: The State of the Discipline* (edited by Katznelson and Milner) includes a chapter by Dawson and Cohen entitled "Problems in the Study of the Politics of Race" (488–510). In their essay, Dawson and Cohen state, "The possible existence of racial orders should have profound consequences for the conduct of empirical and theoretical research within political science. . . . Unfortunately, that is not the case, and indeed research on race enjoys less status in this field than in any other discipline in the social science with the probable exception of economics" (Dawson and Cohen 2002, 497).

In this chapter, we build on these earlier works, particularly Wilson's 1985 findings, to determine whether the relative treatment of race across four disciplines has changed in twenty years. More broadly, we use this chapter to engage an ongoing debate about the discipline's recent record in bringing race "into the core." Why should one care about the cross-disciplinary treatment of race and ethnicity in the social sciences? Does it matter to what degree the varying disciplines treat race? We believe this exercise is important for several reasons. First, the study of topical exclusion and inclusion can illuminate the ways in which formal institutionalized structures for knowing the world—disciplines—bring some topics to their center even as they marginalize others. Why do these inclinations persist, and what does this persistence tell us about how such biases are introduced and sustained over time? Within any given discipline, what is the process—personnel changes, institutional reforms, or strictly intellectual shifts in paradigms and models—through which once-marginal topics are brought closer to the core?

Second, scholars should be more aware of which topics and perspectives they exclude or include in their analytic and theoretical repertoire of most accessible issues. Arguably, the exclusion of certain terms may affect the thoroughness of their explanations of the world. This may be especially true at a moment in history when the underlying social and political conditions seem to be changing rapidly in the "real world," when the traditional structures of the disciplines are challenged from *within* the academy, and when the technologies for knowledge creation and diffusion have improved so radically that we can very easily juxtapose old knowledge and its categories to the new; that is, we can "google" and hyperlink our subjects as never before and find unanticipated connections. Thus, the exclusion of a key set of political dynamics and actors poses concerns about the overall adequacy of contemporary models of politics.

This topic also brings institutionalized issues to the fore. In what ways do material and non-material incentives in graduate training, promotion, and tenure and the rejection and acceptance of journal articles shape the contours and content of the discipline? If a topic like race is marginalized in one institutional setting, but promoted in another, are the "appropriate" cues transmitted from teacher to student in the formal (classroom) or informal (during office hours) setting? Moreover, these issues in the American politics subfield raise parallel issues for comparative politics, international relations, political theory, and other subfields. Finally, the relative inclusion and exclusion of race in the disciplines raise key questions of both citizenship and pedagogy. How well are we training the next generation of young people to be informed citizens?

Thus, we claim that studying the centrality or marginality of race in the discipline poses difficult, complex questions of theory, methodology, and subsequent analysis. To impose greater order on these questions and to begin to address some of them, we proceed by offering the following hypotheses derived from the find-ings and conjectures of Wilson's earlier work from which the current chapter developed (Wilson, 1985).

Hypotheses

Wilson (1985) suggested that the paradigmatic and methodological orientations of the political science discipline might account for why political science ranked third behind history and sociology in the publication of mainstream journal arti-cles on African American topics. He explained the relative disciplinary differences as being partially due to the pressure to do large-scale voter studies; this pressure placed those interested in African American politics at a severe disadvantage because the relevant empirical data on the black population were insufficient to render external validity and generalizability of the findings. Wilson's second expla-nation pointed to the discipline's traditional focus on elite politics and elite decision-making processes (arenas in which blacks have historically been denied access), thereby limiting the types of research articles favored in the mainstream journals. Based on these two explanations, we developed several hypotheses to guide our study.

Hypothesis One

Wilson (1985) noted that many contributions in such disciplines as sociology and history share several features: They use a bottom-up rather than a top-down approach, emphasize the role of non-formal institutions, and employ methods that permit data collection from non-traditional sources such as ethno-graphies and other qualitative methods. Drawing on a simple syllogism from Wilson (1985), political science, unlike its sister disciplines, *typically* studies elite decision makers, voting, and other formal channels of participation; yet blacks have historically been excluded from elite status and the decision-making process.

The earlier essay also concluded that the relative exclusion of African Ameri-can materials in political science reflected its traditional focus on the exercise of power by the powerful and its lack of attention to the powerless. Dawson and Wil-son (1991) observed, "Black politics now has gone well beyond the black church and the black voluntary associations like the NAACP and the Urban League. Now the meaning of black politics includes participation in a much wider array of political arenas, at the federal, state and local levels, including executive, judi-cial, and legislative bodies" (191; see also Barker, Jones and Tate 1999; Bobo and Gilliam 1990). Although this wider participation allows for greater systematic investigation of the new reigns of power and political entrepreneurship in polit-ical science, the central focus on elite politics has not changed in a manner that would shift the relative rankings of the disciplines. Therefore, we do not expect the relative rankings of political science, history, and sociology to have changed substantially from the first period, 1970–1985, to the second, 1986–2003.

Hypothesis Two

Although we do not expect the comparative ranking of history, sociology, and political science to change, we do expect that the gap between political science and its sister disciplines in the first period (1970–1985) was greater than that gap in the second period (1986–2003). As noted above, a plausible reason for the absence of African American topics in top-tier journals resulted from professional pressure to do large-N voter studies. This methodological orientation disadvantaged those interested in black politics because the study of African American politics (and more generally racial and ethnic politics) has long faced an "insufficient data" problem. As Dawson and Cohen (2002) point out, concerning the American National Election Study and the General Social Survey, "Neither important study is designed to provide adequate coverage of minority communities or the survey instrumentation necessary for probing the political beliefs and behaviors of communities with their own significantly distinct political histories and outlooks" (506).

However, these and other scholars also note that these conditions are changing with the introduction of new data collection efforts tailored to suit the study of racial and ethnic politics, such as the 1984 and 1988 National Black Election Study, the 1993–1994 National Black Politics Study, the Latino National Political Survey of 1989–1990, the Pew Hispanic Center/Kaiser Family Foundation 2002 National Survey of Latinos, and the Pilot National Asian American Political Surveys, and more recently the Latino National Survey. Given these improvements, we expect that articles on or about African Americans would fare better in the major journals of political science in the second time period, decreasing the gap between political science and its sister disciplines.

Finally, we also anticipate that reform movements within the discipline would more readily take up the issue of race and ethnicity as a central component of their platforms, leading to greater scholarly visibility. In the 1990s a reformist movement named "Perestroika" emerged in political science to challenge several core disciplinary orthodoxies, including what the reformers saw as inappropriate and exclusionary behaviors in the field's top journals, especially *The American Political Science Review*. We anticipate that, although the rankings of the disciplines will remain the same, the gap between political science and other disciplines would decrease. We believe these changes may be advanced in large part through the efforts of the Perestroika reform movement. In the next section, we describe the methods employed to address these hypotheses, followed by an examination of our findings.

Methods and Limitations

In 1985, Wilson examined journal materials on African Americans published between 1970 and 1985 in three leading journals in each discipline of political science, history, and sociology, finding that political science ranked third after sociology and history in its treatment of African American subject matter. To confirm or disconfirm the hypotheses laid out above, we recalculated the previous findings from 1970–1985 and extended the analysis to cover the 1986–2003 period, using the same journals. The political science journals were *The American Political Science Review*, the *American Journal of Political Science*,[3] and *The Journal of Politics*; for history, we analyzed *The American Historical Review*, *American Quarterly*,[4] and the *Journal of American History*; and for sociology we examined *Social Forces*, the *American Sociological Review*, and the *American Journal of Sociology*. In addition, we also included three economics journals—the *American Economic Review*, the *Journal of Political Economy*, and *The Quarterly Journal of Economics*—for both the 1970–1985 and 1986–2003 periods.

To determine whether the relative rankings of political science, history, and sociology have changed or remained the same, we employed several JSTOR computer-generated searches using the key words "black" or "African American" or "Negro" or "Afro-American."[5] In each of the three mainstream journals selected by discipline, we searched full-length articles (FLAs) from 1970–1985 and then from 1986–2003.[6]

Let us clarify a few additional points about our data collection and limitations. First, this analysis excludes reviews, opinion pieces, books reviews, and other items in its concentration on FLAs published within the time periods 1970–1985 and 1986–2003. Second, we realize that using the word "black" in the search causes "connotation limitations." Although our search was refined to exclude author names (eliminating the possibility that an author whose name is Black was included in the results), the word search could have included some journal articles that use colloquial language that merely refers to the color black. We recognize this as a genuine limitation of the study. However, given that the word "black" is commonly used to describe our subject, we believe that it is imperative to continue to include this term, but with caution. We assume that a similar sampling limitation is likely to be consistent across the other disciplines as well. JSTOR does not yet have the technology to conduct a mass filter for colloquial verbiage, given the current design of its search engine and the quality of JSTOR data available.

Given this limitation and anticipating the potential of our "text" search of FLAs to yield results that significantly overestimate the number of articles related to black topics in each discipline, we also conducted a "title only" search as well as an "abstract only" search using the key words "black" or "African American" or "Negro" or "Afro-American." The "text only" search excludes titles, abstracts, author names, or captions. The "title only" search excludes text, abstracts, author names, or captions. The "abstract only search" excludes text, title, author names, or captions. Finally, to refine the search of political science journals further, we conducted a search using the terms "Negro politics" or "black politics" or "African American politics" or "Afro-American politics to examine the relative change, if any, in the number of journal articles related to black politics that were published between 1970–1985 and 1986–2003 in three of the discipline's mainstream journals.

Another limitation is that some journals in JSTOR do not extend to the year 2003. Again, we suspect that this limitation is consistent across the disciplines.[7]

Finally, we recognize that a fuller evaluation of these materials should pay qualitative attention to the content of the articles and not just the number of citations. Indeed, the most interesting questions do not necessarily concern how many articles are published on a particular topic, but what they reveal and connote for broader currents of intellectual and political life in America. For example, are there interpretative or normative differences between mainstream journals and African American-oriented publications, such as the *National Political Science Review* and *The American Political Science Review*? Providing a critical analysis of this sort can contribute to a critical discourse on race in political science. However, our analysis is a systematic step in evaluating the treatment of topics related to blacks in mainstream journals over time.

Findings

This chapter addresses three questions about the treatment of race in mainstream journals of four disciplines:

1. whether the relative rankings of the disciplines have changed or largely remained the same,
2. whether the gap between the disciplines has lessened from the first (1970–1985) to the second period (1986–2003), and
3. if so, to what extent.

Tables 1.1 and 1.2 indicate the name of the journal in the first column, the total number of full-length articles (FLAs) for the journal in the second column, and the total number of FLAs for the journal including the key words "*black*" or "*African American*" or "*Afro-American*" or "*Negro*" in the third column. The final column represents the percentage of total FLAs with these key words for each time period: Table 1.1 for 1970–1985 and Table 1.2 for 1986–2003.

From 1970–1985, Table 1.1 indicates that in *The American Political Science Review*, the *American Journal of Political Science*, and *The Journal of Politics* a total of 2,272 articles were published; of these publications 711 or 31 percent concerned black topics. In the sociology journals reviewed there were 3,122 articles published during this time period, of which 1180 or 38 percent related to blacks. In the history journals reviewed there were 1,463 total articles published in this time period, of which 679 or 46 percent pertained issues concerning blacks. Finally, we examined three mainstream journals in economics, finding that of the 5,447 articles published from 1970–1985, 534 articles or 10 percent pertained to black topics. As we expected, economics ranked well below the other disciplines. However, in agreement with Wilson (1985), political science (31%) ranked third after history (46%) and sociology (38%).

In our similar search of the same journals for 1986–2003, we found that the percentage of FLAs on black topics in the top political science journals fell slightly from 31 percent in the first time period to 30 percent. In contrast, for history, sociology, and economics, the percentage of FLAs in the three mainstream journals on black issues increased. In sociology, the percentage of citations rose 11 per-

TABLE 1.1 Search Totals for Full-Length Articles (FLAs), 1970–1985

	Total FLAs†	Text Only‡	% of Total FLAs
Political Science			
The American Political Science Review	813	279	34.31
American Journal of Political Science	649	191	29.42
The Journal of Politics	810	241	29.75
Political Science Total	2,272	711	31.29
Sociology			
American Journal of Sociology	768	336	43.75
American Sociological Review	1,388	493	35.51
Social Forces	966	351	36.33
Sociology Total	3,122	1180	37.79
History			
The American Historical Review	664	262	39.45
American Quarterly	481	257	53.43
Journal of American History	318	160	50.31
History Total	1,463	679	46.41
Economics			
American Economic Review	3,099	320	10.32
Journal of Political Economy	1,432	144	10.05
The Quarterly Journal of Economics	916	70	7.64
Economics Total	5,447	534	9.80

Source: Author's compilation of JSTOR computer-generated citations by discipline.

†Key word search for "black" or "African-American" or "Afro-American" or "Negro" in FLAs, excluding reviews, opinion pieces, and other items.

‡Key word search for black" or "African-American" or "Afro-American" or "Negro" in text only, excluding titles, abstracts, author names, and captions.

centage points from 38 to 49 percent, and in economics it increased 5 percentage points from 10 to 15 percent. For history the percentage of citations rose from 46 to 50 percent. For sociology and economics, the percentage of citations in each of the mainstream journals increased from the first time period to the second, and two of the economics journals showed a substantial increase over the earlier time period. For example, the citations in the *Journal of Political Economy* rose from 10 to 17 percent and those in *The Quarterly Journal of Economics* rose from 8 to 17 percent from the first to the second time periods.[8] In history two of the mainstream journals showed an increase from the first time period to the second, but the percentage of FLAs on black topics decreased in *American Quarterly* from 53 to 43 percent.

For political science, although *The Journal of Politics* showed a percentage increase from 29 to 32 percent from the first to the second time period, *The American Political Science Review* had a decrease from 34 to 29 percent, and the *American Journal of Political Science* remained about the same. Overall, we expected that the comparative rankings of history, political science, and sociology would not have changed considerably from the first to the second time period. Our expectations were confirmed. We also expected that the gap between political science and its sister disciplines would decrease. This expectation largely holds up, although a significant gap persists, particularly between history and political science. Interestingly, the gap between history and sociology appears to have lessened in the 1986–2003 time period.

Let us be clear, we strongly believe that the very high percentages of FLA citations in Tables 1.1 and 1.2 on black topics are an artifact of the methodology used and do not accurately reflect reality. Obviously, none of the mainstream journals in political science devotes a third of its articles to topics related to blacks. We believe this measurement problem holds true for other disciplines as well, considerably overestimating the attention paid to black topics by each disciplines' mainstream journals.

Dissatisfied with the quality of these findings, we limited our search in several ways to examine further whether the *relative* rankings of the disciplines have changed or largely remained the same and whether the gap between the disciplines has lessened over time. We conducted a "title only" and an "abstract only" search using the key words "black" or "African American" or Afro-American" or "Negro" for 1970–1985 and 1986–2003, by discipline. Although searches by titles or abstracts remain problematic, it is easier to manually filter out citations that

TABLE 1.2   Search Totals for Full-Length Articles (FLAs), 1986–2003

	Total FLAs†	Text Only‡	% of Total FLAs
Political Science			
The American Political Science Review	845	249	29.46
American Journal of Political Science	942	279	29.61
The Journal of Politics	767	243	31.68
Political Science Total	2,554	771	30.18
Sociology			
American Journal of Sociology	552	267	48.36
American Sociological Review	1,050	491	46.76
Social Forces	963	504	52.33
Sociology Total	2,565	1,262	49.00
History			
The American Historical Review	730	324	44.38
American Quarterly	371	160	43.12
Journal of American History	586	365	62.28
History Total	1,687	849	50.32
Economics			
American Economic Review	3,028	439	14.49
Journal of Political Economy	857	146	17.03
The Quarterly Journal of Economics	659	111	16.84
Economics Total	4,544	696	15.31

Source: Author's compilation of JSTOR computer-generated citations by discipline.

†Key word search for "black" or "African-American" or "Afro-American" or "Negro" in FLAs, excluding reviews, opinion pieces, and other items.

‡Key word search for black" or "African-American" or "Afro-American" or "Negro" in text only, excluding titles, abstracts, author names, and captions.

do not directly relate to the subject, decreasing but not eliminating the likelihood of overestimating the publication of articles related to black topics in the mainstream journals.

Both Table 1.3 (1970–1985) and Table 1.4 (1986–2003) indicate the name of the major journal in the first column, the total absolute number of citations for the journal in the second column, and the total absolute number of citations for the titles containing the key words in the third column. The fourth column represents the percentage of total FLAs with titles containing the key words. The fifth column contains the total absolute number of citations for the abstracts containing the key words. The final column represents the percentage of total abstracts with the key word.

TABLE 1.3 Search Totals for Full-Length Articles (FLAs) by Titles and Abstracts, 1970–1985

	Total FLAs†	Title Only‡	% of Total FLAs	Abstract Only	% of Total FLA
Political Science					
The American Political Science Review	813	58	7.13	13	1.59
American Journal of Political Science	649	7	1.07	19	2.92
The Journal of Politics	810	28	3.45	7	0.86
Poli Sci Total	2,272	93	4.09	39	1.71
Sociology					
American Journal of Sociology	768	78	10.15	72	9.37
American Sociological Review	1,388	45	3.24	79	5.69
Social Forces	966	79	8.17	76	7.86
Sociology Total	3,122	202	6.47	227	7.27
History					
The American Historical Review	664	234	35.24	NA	NA
American Quarterly	481	30	6.23	NA	NA
Journal of American History	318	204	64.15	NA	NA
History Total	1,463	468	31.98	NA	NA
Economics					
American Economic Review	3,099	31	1.00	1	.03
Journal of Political Economy	1,432	1	.06	5	.34
The Quarterly Journal of Economics	916	7	.76	4	.43
Economics Total	5,447	39	.71	10	.18

Source: Author's compilation of JSTOR computer-generated citations by discipline.

†Key word search for "black" or "African-American" or "Afro-American" or "Negro" in FLAs, excluding reviews, opinion pieces, and other items.

‡Key word search for black" or "African-American" or "Afro-American" or "Negro" in titles only, excluding text, abstracts, author names, and captions.

Key word search for black" or "African-American" or "Afro-American" or "Negro" in abstracts only, excluding text, titles, author names, and captions Abstract information is not available for the history journals selected (except *American Quarterl* beginning in 2003).

TABLE 1.4   Search Totals for Full-Length Articles (FLAs) by Titles and Abstracts, 1986–2003

	Total FLAs†	Title Only‡	% of Total FLAs	Abstract Only	% of Total FLA
Political Science					
The American Political Science Review	845	52	6.15	19	2.24
American Journal of Political Science	942	7	0.74	22	2.33
The Journal of Politics	767	38	4.95	43	5.60
Poli Sci Total	2,554	97	3.79	84	3.28
Sociology					
American Journal of Sociology	552	62	11.23	30	5.43
American Sociological Review	1,050	24	2.28	83	7.90
Social Forces	963	104	10.79	119	12.35
Sociology Total	2,565	190	7.40	232	9.04
History					
The American Historical Review	730	245	33.56	NA	NA
American Quarterly	371	50	13.47	NA	NA
Journal of American History	586	342	58.36	NA	NA
History Total	1,687	637	37.75	NA	NA
Economics					
American Economic Review	3,028	30	0.99	6	0.19
Journal of Political Economy	857	2	0.23	10	1.16
The Quarterly Journal of Economics	659	3	0.45	7	1.06
Economics Total	4,544	35	0.77	23	0.50

Source: Author's compilation of JSTOR computer-generated citations by discipline.

†Key word search for "black" or "African-American" or "Afro-American" or "Negro" in FLAs, excluding reviews, opinion pieces, and other items.

‡Key word search for black" or "African-American" or "Afro-American" or "Negro" in titles only, excluding text, abstracts, author names, and captions.

Key word search for black" or "African-American" or "Afro-American" or "Negro" in abstracts only, excluding text, titles, author names, and captions. Abstract information is not available for the history journals selected (except *American Quarterly* beginning in 2003).

Table 1.3 shows title and abstract data for the first time period, 1970–1985. History journals had the most titles related to black topics at 32 percent, followed by sociology at 6 percent and political science at 4 percent. In the percentage of abstracts related to black topics, political science journals significantly trailed sociology, 1.71 versus 7.27 percent.[9] Table 1.4 shows data for the second time period, 1986–2003. For each discipline there is an increase in the number of titles related to black topics from the first period to the second. The number of abstracts related to black topics for both sociology and political science also increased from 1970–1985 to 1986–2003.

Our results clearly show that regardless of the coding schema used—text only, title only, or abstract only—the relative rankings of political science, history and sociology have not changed over this period. Political science trails behind history and sociology in both the first and second time periods.

Finally, to target the prevalence of articles related to the study of black politics in political science journals we conducted a search using the terms "Negro politics" or "black politics" or "African-American politics" or "Afro-American politics." We examined the relative change (if any) in the number of journal articles published related to black politics between 1970–1985 and 1986–2003 in *The American Political Science Review*, *American Journal of Politics*, and *The Journal of Politics*. Table 1.5 shows that of the 2,272 FLAs published between 1970–1985 only 34 or 1.49 percent included topics directly related to black politics. This also held true for the second time period. Between 1986–2003, of the 2,554 journal articles published in the mainstream journals selected, only 38 or 1.48 percent included topics directly related to black politics.

We are continuing to review these three political science journals to improve our evaluation of their treatment of black topics. To arrive at a more accurate count of the materials concerning black topics, we are manually evaluating each of the three journals using JSTOR or hard copies for the last five years (2000–present). We also seek to move beyond the numbers and to provide a qualitative assessment of the content of the articles published.

Discussion and Implications

Implications for the Research and Study of Politics

This analysis raises a central question: How do we define American politics and what units of analysis are *allowed* into the "melting pot"? It seems ironic that

TABLE 1.5   Search Totals for Full-Length Articles (FLAs) by Select Political Science Journals

	1970–1985			1986–2003		
	Total FLAs†	Text Only‡	% of Total FLAs	Total FLAs	Text Only	% of Total FLAs
Political Science						
The American Political Science Review	813	10	1.23	845	11	1.30
American Journal of Political Science	649	8	1.23	942	11	1.16
The Journal of Politics	810	16	1.97	767	16	2.08
Political Science Total	2,272	34	1.49	2,554	38	1.48

Source: Author's compilation of JSTOR computer-generated citations for political science.

†Key word search for "black" or "African-American" or "Afro-American" or "Negro" in FLAs, excluding reviews, opinion pieces, and other items.

‡Key word search for black" or "African-American" or "Afro-American" or "Negro" in text only, excluding titles, abstracts, author names, and captions.

research topics concerning blacks appear to have gained little prominence in mainstream political science outlets, even though African Americans as an electoral group have made the most headway of any minority in joining the American political system. This lack of prominence is particularly paradoxical given the advances in the study of African Americans; it speaks volumes about the power of long-standing disciplinary filters to exclude important political conditions from analysis, description, and theorizing.[10]

As Dawson and Cohen (2002) observe, "One consequence of not having the study of race more central to political science is the failure not only to fully contribute to these debates but also to examine some of the most interesting intellectual problems of our time. Fortunately some are standing on the margins and engaging such questions" (496). As Dawson and Cohen further contend, "Without any attention to the historical and current context of these interactions or phenomena we may be severely misinterpreting the meaning of the data. Instead, we must utilize frameworks that acknowledge the processes of radicalization and categorization that are embedded in social interactions where groups are assigned places within changing social structure" (491).

Walton and McCormick (1997) argue, "By excluding or omitting the black political experience, a political scientist adopts a noncritical stance toward the political system. The very tools of the political scientist's craft are not used to describe and fully analyze the political processes and experiences" (231). In the United States, structurally induced racial and ethnic impositions are the nucleus from which cultural, social, political, and economic institutional arrangements spring forth, influencing preference formation, public opinion, as well as individual and collective group interests.

Furthermore, if the study of politics in America excludes political conditions of the *least* wealthy and *least* powerful then these theories may be flawed. This is particularly troublesome because America is becoming ever more diverse— culturally, socially, politically, and demographically.

Implications for Advancement in the Academy

These findings pose important implications for young scholars who choose to pursue the fields of racial and ethnic politics as they attempt to make their mark in the discipline. James Garand (1990) summarizes how these findings might affect tenure and promotion decisions:

> Some political scientists, administrators or departments will be interested in making assessments based on how journals are perceived by the (sometimes narrow) audiences with exposure to the journal. For instance, in hiring, promotion, and tenure decisions some faculty and administrations may be concerned with whether a candidate is publishing in journals that are highly regarded by the experts in the field, regardless of the profession-wide visibility. . . . On the other hand some in our profession will want to make assessments based on both the evaluations and profession-wide visibility of a journal. In these cases, a publication in *The American Political Science Review* . . . may be perceived as reaching a wider audi-

ence and therefore, contributing more broadly to the visibility and or national reputation of the individual or department in question (Garand 1990, 451).

Walton and McCormick (1997) also describe professional limitations in the study of racial/ethnic politics. They contend, "The professional fear revolves around the political scientists' understanding of the risks involved in researching and writing about the African-American political experience, which is considered marginal. . . . Doing so can result in fewer academic opportunities, lowered professional standing, and greater difficulty in obtaining grants and awards" (231).

Our findings also have consequences for the ways in which the next generations of students are introduced to the intersections of race and politics. Negative disciplinary biases may shape how the next generations of political scientists understand the meaning and significance of race, influencing their training in colleges, as well as in graduate and professional schools. Such biases may also divert graduate students from the study of racial and ethnic politics, because they may feel that they will be "pigeon-holed" if they choose to study African American politics or another facet of racial and ethnic politics. Do white students and professors believe that the study of African American politics is, or should be, mainly the domain of black students and faculty? Are some black students steered away from the study of black politics for fear that they will not get a "good" job? Clearly, racial barriers to entry might operate in both directions. If this is true we are compromising the quality of our graduate students and the future of the professoriate. We contend that it is important to encourage all students, regardless of race/ethnicity, to become well versed in a variety of paradigmatic and methodological approaches, including the study of racial/ethnic politics.

Conclusion and Next Steps

In this chapter, we considered the persistent neglect of black topics in the study of American politics and noted some reasons why African American perspectives continue to be marginalized in the top journals. Based on our analysis of the cross-disciplinary treatment of black issues in mainstream journal outlets for political science, history, sociology, and economics, we conclude that political science still does not hold up well when measured against history and sociology. History and sociology still rank number one and two respectively, with political science third. In the 1986–2003 time period, economics finished last.

Institutional elements are associated with this paradox in political science. The Perestroika movement's lack of attention to racial dynamics is especially disappointing, given methodological advancements in the study of racial and ethnic politics, an increased prevalence of outlets for the study of formal political participation among African Americans, and the reformers' greater sensitivity to the problems of methodological and topical marginalization. In our review of the literature related to the reform movement, most political scientists who were writing on methodological pluralism in journals and graduate education did not address adequately the issues related to the cross-disciplinary treatment of research topics, particularly those related to race and ethnicity. In fact, there has been little consideration of issues related to the marginalization of the study of racial and ethnic politics. One notable exception is an essay by Dorian Warren (2005), which examines the debate in the reform movement within the context of race and ethnicity.

Our research focuses on the treatment of African American politics in the discipline. However, we believe our approach could be applied fruitfully to other groups as well. We do not know whether the treatment of other minorities of color in the United States—Latinos or Asian Americans—follows the patterns we describe here. It would also be revealing to study the treatment of white ethnics—Poles, Irish, Italians—by political scientists, both today and in earlier years when their political participation was more problematic and was tied to higher rates of immigration and greater inter-group conflict during their assimilation process.

What can be done to address these institutional issues with the seriousness they deserve? The leadership of the American Political Science Association (APSA) and its constituent groups, as well as the leadership of the National Conference of Black Political Scientists (NCOBPS), need to engage these matters more seriously through panels at their annual meetings, in articles in their publications, and in organizations, such as the American Council on Education and the Social Science Research Council, with a wider scope. Other bodies, such as the National Science Foundation, the National Research Council, and others, should also become involved in such a discourse. Political science departments should reconsider their course offerings and the structures of their programs to examine ways to expand their coverage. Journals in the political science discipline should also take steps to ensure greater pluralism, perhaps recruiting or urging authors to submit work in underrepresented areas. This is not a call to lower standards but rather to solicit essays in substantive yet underrepresented issue areas.[11]

On a more personal level, those of us who are genuinely concerned with the state of the discipline must also take personal responsibility for its advancement. How many times are we given an opportunity to press the issue while serving on editorial boards and department committees, and engaging in other professional activities, and yet we have been reluctant to do so? We need to urge others to engage with their colleagues and their graduate students about the role of race and ethnicity in the study of politics. We also should invite scholars to seize the time and to engage in a thorough discussion of these findings in order to design concrete mechanisms of inclusion to enhance pluralism in American political science.

Notes

Acknowledgments: The authors would like to thank Michael Krot and Kristen Garlock at JSTOR, University of Michigan, Ann Arbor for their data collection assistance and Sheree Bennett for her assistance on this chapter. We also thank those who gave their advice and suggestions concerning this chapter, including panel participants at the 2004 NCOBPS Roundtable entitled "The Cross-Disciplinary Treatment of African American Issues" including Cathy Cohen, Shelby Lewis, Aldon Morris, Dianne Pinderhughes, and James Steele. Any errors of fact or judgment are our own.

1. In this analysis "black" includes the study of individuals in the Diaspora of African descent.

2. We selected the disciplines of history, sociology, and political science in an effort to duplicate the previous study conducted in 1985.

3. This journal was formerly entitled *Midwest Journal of Political Science*.

4. The original analysis examined the *Journal of Social History*, but it is not available through JSTOR. For consistency in methodology, we decided to examine *American Quarterly* instead. This journal is consistent with the other journals by discipline examined in this study.

5. JSTOR, housed at the University of Michigan, was established as an independent not-for-profit organization in August 1995. Originally conceived by William G. Bowen, president of the Andrew W. Mellon Foundation, JSTOR began as an effort to ease the increasing storage problems faced by libraries. The basic idea was to convert the back issues of paper journals into electronic formats, thereby saving space (and the capital costs associated with that space) while simultaneously improving access to the journal content. It was also hoped that the project might offer a solution to preservation problems associated with storing paper volumes. See http://www.jstor.org/about/background.html.

6. During the initial phase of this study, the information necessary to conduct this research was not immediately available through the public (Internet) JSTOR interface (there was a "ceiling" for viewing the journal entries using the public database). Therefore, JSTOR generously agreed to provide the data from their home base at the University of Michigan, in the form of an Excel spreadsheet. However, in early 2005 JSTOR improved its public search engine, thereby allowing us to conduct and refine our own search of the twelve journals selected. Thus, the data presented in the tables are the author's compilation.

7. JSTOR available coverage by discipline at the time of this study: Political science—*The American Political Science Review* (1906–2001), *American Journal of Political Science*, formerly *Midwest Journal of Political Science* (1957–2003), and *The Journal of Politics* (1939–2001); history—*The American Historical Review* (1895–1999), *American Quarterly* (1949–2004) and the *Journal of American History* (1964–1999); sociology—*Social Forces* (1925–2004), the *American Sociological Review* (1936–2002), the *American Journal of Sociology* (1895–2000); and economics—the *American Economic Review* (1911–2002), the *Journal of Political Economy* (1892–2000) and *The Quarterly Journal of Economics* (1886–1999).

8. It is important to reiterate our previous contention concerning the limitations of our data and methodology, which also call for a subsequent contextual analysis of the nature of articles published concerning African American issues. For example, some economists would caution against optimism concerning the apparent increase in economic journal citations on African American topics, noting that African Americans as a substantive research area remain understudied in the mainstream economics journals. Thus, our findings may be a reflection of applied versus theoretical relevance in economics, whereas more favorable outlets for substantive analysis of African American topics are still more likely to be found in such publications as the *Review of Black Political Economy*.

9. Abstract information is not available for the history journals selected (except *American Quarterly* beginning in 2003).

10. Notably, Hardy-Fanta and Gerson (2002) acknowledge a significant increase in the political science literature on Latino politics from about ten references from the 1970s to over seventy from 1990 to 1999. Moreover, recently, an Asian American Politics Symposium in *PS* 2001 provided six articles by scholars examining Asian American politics.

11. The new political science journal, *Perspective on Politics*, edited by Jennifer Hochschild, is one notable effort.

References

Barker, Lucius, Mack Jones, and Katherine Tate. 1999. *African Americans and the American political system*, 4th ed. Englewood Cliffs, NJ: Prentice Hall.

Bobo, Lawrence, and Franklin D. Gilliam Jr. 1990. Race, sociopolitical participation, and black empowerment. *The American Political Science Review* 84 (June): 377–93.

Dawson, Michael C., and Cathy Cohen. 2002. Problems in the study of the politics of race. In *Political science: The state of the discipline*, edited by Ira Katznelson and Helen V. Milner, 488–510. New York: W. W. Norton.

Dawson, Michael C., and Ernest J. Wilson III. 1991. Paradigms and paradoxes: Political science and African American politics. In *The theory and practice of political science*, edited by William Crotty. Evanston, IL: Northwestern University Press.

Garand, James C. 1990. An alternative interpretation of recent political science journal evaluations. *PS: Political Science and Politics* 23 (3): 448–51.

Hardy-Fanta, Carol, and Jeffrey N. Gerson, eds. 2002. *Latino politics in Massachusetts*. New York: Routledge.

Katznelson, Ira, and Helen V. Milner. 2002. American political science: The discipline's state and the state of the discipline. In *Political science: The state of the discipline*, edited by Ira Katznelson and Helen V. Milner, 1–26. New York: W. W. Norton.

McClain, Paula D., and John D. Garcia. 1993. Expanding disciplinary boundaries: Black, Latino, and racial minority groups in political science. In *Political science: The state of the discipline II*, edited by Ada Finifter, 247–79. Washington, DC: American Political Science Association.

Prestage, Jewel L. 1979. Quelling the mythical revolution in higher education: Retreat from the affirmative action concept. *The Journal of Politics* 41:763–83.

Walton, Hanes, Jr., and Joseph P. McCormick, II. 1997. The study of African-American politics as social danger: Clues from the disciplinary journals. In *Race & Representation: The National Political Science Review* 6:229–44.

Walton, Hanes, Jr., Cheryl Miller, and Joseph McCormick, II. 1994. Race and political science: The dual traditions of race relations politics and African American politics. In *Political science and its history: Research programs and political traditions*, edited by John Drysek et al, 144–74. New York: Cambridge University Press.

Warren, Dorian T. 2005. Will the real Perestroikniks please stand up? Race and methodological reform in the study of politics. In *Perestroika! The raucous rebellion in political science*, edited by Kristen Renwick Monroe, 218–29. New Haven, CT: Yale University Press.

Wilson, Ernest J. 1985. Why political scientist don't study black politics, but historians and sociologist do. *PS: Political Science and Politics* 3:600–607.

CHAPTER TWO

The Race Variable and the American Political Science Association's *State of the Discipline* Reports and Books, 1907–2002

HANES WALTON JR. AND ROBERT C. SMITH

Introduction

MATTHEW HOLDEN JR. has written that the study of race has been viewed as an "academic graveyard" for any young scholar who sought "academic respectability" because white political scientists did not perceive it as raising "critical intellectual problems."[1] This essay addresses a simple research question: How has the race variable been explored and analyzed in the official reports and books of the American Political Science Association's *State of the Discipline* studies? These official reports and books, which cover the period from 1907 to 2002, can tell us how the Association both defined the "state of the discipline" and how it developed a vision for the discipline from these official studies, as well as the relationship of the race variable to the definition and vision of the state of the discipline. Herein lies the testable hypothesis of this work.

If researchers are to develop an African American perspective on the state of the discipline, it goes without saying that one must of necessity know what the official professional portrait of the discipline is and how it has evolved during the first hundred years (1903–2003) of its existence. Once that is established, then it follows that, from this official portrait(s), readers and researchers can discern what the unofficial portraits of the state of the discipline are. These unofficial portraits are the ones emanating from the official ones, and they act like an update and extension of them. They are the journal articles and single and multivolume studies that are published in the periods and time frames between the official reports and books. By providing addendums and updates, these unofficial scholarly studies highlight the limitations, weaknesses, and omissions of the official studies. These outsider perspectives are thus helpful in assessing and evaluating the official studies and are needed to construct the holistic portrait of the state of the discipline.

But we are not simply interested in these official *State of the Discipline* reports and books in and of themselves. We are searching these official documents for their discussion of the race variable and its relationship to the definition and vision of the discipline. What do they tell us about the role and function of the race variable as an independent factor shaping the political behavior of individuals, groups, organizations, institutions, the state, and the global political system? Or do they tell us anything at all? Has the race variable been considered at all? Is it one of the independent variables in the study of the science of politics? Is it a variable that tells us about the very essence of the state of the discipline? And finally, has the state of the discipline even been conceptualized to include this variable, and if so, how does it factor into the very vision of the discipline itself? Thus, we want to know about the official portrait of the discipline for what it can reveal about the role and function of the race variable. Only when we know that can we effectively determine an African American perspective about the state of the discipline. In this study, the role and function of the race variable and the state of the discipline are intimately linked and related. Our task is to uncover, delineate, and assess this linkage and relationship.

Data and Methodology

Several of the contemporary studies of political science as a discipline reflect its intellectual evolution from a "science of the state" to a "science of group political behavior" to a "science of individual political behavior" to currently a "science of institutional political behavior."[2] And in each of these eras, there is at least one, if not more, *State of the Discipline* reports and sponsored books by the American Political Science Association (APSA). In this material is contained the discipline's official portrait and story.

Table 2.1 identifies the five committee reports, two of which would later become monographs, and the four sponsored books of APSA. Although the last three books are numbered as Volume I, II, and III, this is incorrect because the first book, which came out in 1939, was not acknowledged by the editor of Volume I, Ada W. Finifter. However, the 1939 volume, a reprinting of Anna Haddow's doctoral dissertation, was the first APSA-sponsored book. One can learn from reading its prefatory section that in December, 1938 at the Columbus, Ohio Association's annual meeting "a committee of five" had been appointed by the Association President to examine and report on the merits of the dissertation. At the December meeting, the committee of five recommended that "the Association sponsor and . . . subsidize it"[3] and was even subsidized by the American Council of Learned Societies. Even though it was the first work in the series, it was overlooked in the so-called Volume I except as a reference and footnote in the first chapter dealing with political theory as a subfield.[4] Although some might say that this 1939 book dealt solely with the existence of the discipline in America's colleges and universities, that defense is not valid because it also focused on the material of a "science of politics."[5] The best that can be said about this matter is that Volume I is the first of the APSA-sponsored books to be entirely published by the Association. Nevertheless, the editor of the so-called initial volume wrote in her prefatory note that: "if the volume is successful, a continuing series of this type may be authorized by the Council."[6]

TABLE 2.1   APSA-Sponsored *State of the Discipline* Reports and Books

Year Published	Title	Discussion of the Race Variable
	COMMITTEE REPORTS	
1907/1908	"What Do Our Students Know about American Government before Taking College Courses in Political Science?"	No
1910	"Is Sufficient Time Devoted to the Study of Government in Our Colleges?"	No
1916	"The Teaching of Government"†	No
1923	"Report on the Committee on Political Research"	No
1951	"Goals for Political Science"†	No
	BOOKS	
1939	*Political Science in American Colleges and Universities 1636–1900*	No
1983	*Political Science: The State of the Discipline*‡	No
1993	*Political Science: The State of the Discipline II*	Yes
2002	*Political Science: The State of the Discipline III*	Yes

Source: Adapted from J. Peter Meekison, "A Bibliographic Essay," in Robert Connery, ed., *Teaching Political Science: A Challenge to Higher Education* (Durham, NC: Duke University Press, 1965), 266.

†These reports were later issued as monographs.

‡A chapter on the race variable was commissioned for this volume, but was not included at the last minute.

Collectively, these nine works in Table 2.1 constitute the official, APSA-sponsored studies on the state of the discipline. They span the ninety-five years from 1907 until 2002. The last three numbered volumes seem to have been deliberately scheduled for publication a full decade a part. The first committee reports were published about a decade apart, but there was a hiatus between 1923 and 1951, broken only by the 1939 publication of *Political Science in American Colleges and Universities 1636–1900*. This substantial gap was filled in by several annual reports of the "National Conference on the Science of Politics," unofficial reports that stemmed from the 1923 official APSA report.

In fact, it was the 1923 "Report of the Committee on Political Research" that would have the greatest impact and influence of all of these nine studies in shaping both the definition and the vision of the state of the discipline. Simply put, the 1923 report's characterization of the state of the field, its vision, and its definition is, with few exceptions, still true today.

In addition to these nine official reports and books, this study uses, as both reference and comparison works, the major unofficial reports and books. As defined here, the unofficial books are those works by individual scholars produced on their own without the support or sponsorship of the APSA or any other professional political science organization. Such works tended to appear in the gaps between the official ones.

This study focuses on four such works that focused on the official *State of the Discipline* publications. The first is *Handbook of Political Science*, the eight-volume series edited by Nelson Polsby and Fred Greenstein. Its first volume was published in 1975 just before the appearance of the so-called Volume I and the last official APSA committee report, and it was clearly intended to fill a gap in the thirty-year hiatus of official publications. It attempted a comprehensive assessment of the state of the discipline in nearly every subfield and category, yet it somehow omitted the race variable.

Political Science: The Science of Politics, a single-volume work edited by Herbert Weisberg and published in 1986, is the second unofficial work, coming a decade after Polsby and Greenstein's series and three years after APSA's Volume I. Although its stated goal was to cover areas not found in the official volume and to update some of those that had been covered, it did not offer an analysis of the race variable; this is despite the fact that Volume I had not covered this topic. In this case, one omission built on the preceding one.

Third is the much-used and notable four-volume series edited by William Crotty, *Political Science: Looking to the Future*. The first volume appeared in 1991, five years after the Weisberg volume and two years before APSA's Volume II. Unique to this four-volume study is that Crotty's conceptualization included the race variable in the state of the discipline.

He observes, in his introductory essay to the chapter on the race variable, that its two African American authors find "that the exploration of race as a part of American politics is separated from mainstream disciplinary concerns, receives relatively limited attention, and, while important in real-world politics, is treated by political scientists in such manner that it adds little to an understanding of political life."[7] Crotty indicates that this lack of attention to race would be the wrong thing for the discipline as it charts its new future.

Finally, the fourth volume looks at a specific subfield, judicial behavior and public law; because this area is so much less quantitative than the other subfields, it is not always included in the official and unofficial reports. Nancy Maveety edited *The Pioneers of Judicial Behavior*, a single-volume work published in 2003. It is the most comprehensive work on the area of judicial behavior and public law. And although this book does include a judicial behaviorist who has analyzed the race variable, it somehow manages not to discuss this aspect of her work. This work appears one year after the APSA's Volume III.[8]

Combining these four unofficial *State of the Discipline* works with the official ones not only permits us to compare and contrast the two types of studies but also allows us to show how the two types of studies relate and influence each other. Thus, these unofficial studies give us the context for this study and enrich the portrait of the field.

There is one other data source that is central to our study. It is the literature on the race variable. Without this literature, we would not know or understand the African American perspective. It is both vital and central to the analysis. We have shown that the race variable has been omitted, overlooked, ignored, and suppressed in both the official and unofficial *State of the Discipline* studies. Hence, the question is, did this just happen because there was an absence of any literature on this variable, or had the entire profession, in its official and unofficial sectors, been uninformed about the variable?

According to Crotty in political science, "there is a division by race in the study of black/white politics more pronounced than in related disciplines such as sociology or history. In addition, when political scientists engage in crossover research, and more specifically when white political scientists study African-American political questions, they produce distinctively different types of research. They ask different questions and employ different criteria to judge the significance of what they uncover."[9]

A longitudinal (1886–1990) study of the premier political science journals, *American Political Science Review* and the *Political Science Quarterly*, found that two dominant research traditions have developed around the race variable. One research tradition categorized as "race relations politics" tended to "emphasize an implementation strategy to obtain peaceful and consensual relations between the two races, even if the result is the domination of one and subordination of the other."[10] This was the tradition favored by white political scientists and black political conservatives.

The second research tradition, categorized as "African American politics," tended to emphasize "parity and empowerment. Here, blacks would seek to eradicate white dominance, to empower themselves."[11] This one was favored by African American political scientists. Data from the literature on African American politics were taken to structure, highlight, and underpin this study's discussion of the race variable in the *State of the Discipline* official and unofficial studies.[12]

Thus, our database comprises (1) the official and unofficial *State of the Discipline* reports and books and (2) the basic literature on the race variable. These different and at times overlapping data sources provide the empirical materials for our analysis of the research question and allow us to test our research hypothesis.

Having explained our different data sources for the work, let us describe the research methodology. It combines textual and content analysis of these official and unofficial reports and books to determine whether a discussion of the race variable exists, what the nature of that discussion is, and, when such a discussion appears, how it influences the definition and vision of the state of the discipline. After identifying the race variable and analyzing the discussion about it, the identified sections are categorized and counted, which allows us to analyze the majority of white scholars who excluded the race variable and the minority who included it as seen in the official and unofficial reports. These empirically based findings will enable us to develop an African American perspective on the state of the discipline.

Definition of the State of the Discipline in APSA's *State of the Discipline* Reports and Books

In 1965, J. Peter Meekison wrote, "The continuing concern of the Association about the 'state of the discipline' is demonstrated by five studies, which it has sponsored over the last fifty years. Indeed there has been approximately one study in each decade since 1900."[13] Yet, in every official study up to 1965 and since then, one is hard pressed to find a single acceptable definition of the "state of the discipline."

All the major concepts in political science have a standard definition or at least some type of consensual definition or, failing that, a working definition. However, neither the APSA committee reports nor the books by individual scholars define or explicate clearly the meaning of the term "state of the discipline." Primarily, the official reports and books simply assert it as a term and pick up a meaning from its usage within the text. As a quick review of Table 2.1 reveals, these reports and books give six different meanings for this concept, including student knowledge about American government, the amount of time spent on this subject matter, the teaching of the subject matter, and then political research in the discipline, evolution of the discipline in colleges and universities, and finally its goals. However, on closer inspection of the official reports and books, particularly the books, a pattern and trend become clear. Volumes I, II, and III and parts of the initial book define, without a doubt, the state of the discipline as meaning a scientific approach. Further, one sees that the 1923 report also dealt with a scientific approach and that it has somehow come to dominate and shape the state of the discipline much more so than any of the other official studies. One therefore must ask what was it about this official report that gave it such an impact and influence on the conceptual definition of the state of the discipline and later on the nature of the unofficial reports. Thus, the 1923 report demands closer analysis.

A look into that report's background and origins reveals that at the APSA's meeting in December 1921 it created a Committee on Political Research comprising four men and chaired by Charles Merriam at the University of Chicago. This committee was charged with the task of looking into the "scope and methods for political research" for the discipline. Both the committee and its charge were driven essentially by Merriam's desire to create a scientific approach to the study of politics. The committee held four meetings, one in Pittsburgh and Cleveland and two in Chicago.

Merriam, in his initial preliminary report after the first meeting in Pittsburgh, began the effort to define the state of the discipline. He wrote, "When something like exact measurement of recurring processes begins, we are on the way to exact knowledge; to scientific verifiable inference."[14] In his concluding remarks in this preliminary report, he added more to the definition by stating, "I had hoped to develop, namely . . . the grave necessity of constant revision of our methods and processes, . . . [so that we can] . . . calculate and measure more accurately than we have thus far been able to do, the desirability of minute, thorough, patient, intensive studies of the detail of political phenomena . . . and open the way to a deeper and more scientific understanding of political relations."[15] In this initial report we see that the "constant revision" of methods and techniques is identified strongly with the concept, "state of the discipline."

The final report of the Committee on Political Research, which was published by the APSA as its 1923 official report, made recommendations regarding techniques

and methods for adopting a scientific approach, and the APSA accepted these recommendations. Merriam, in speaking for the committee, told the APSA that the discipline should tend toward "more general use of quantitative measurement of political
phenomena. On the one side this took the form of statistics or the mathematical analysis of political processes. . . . Two disciplines in particular were able to apply the quantitative methods with especial success."[16] Thus, here were the seeds of the evolving
definition of the state of the discipline, but the matter did not end there.

Reaction to the committee report was not only strong but also led to the creation of a National Conference on the Science of Politics, in which Merriam was
a mover and shaker. The Conference held several annual meetings and reported
its findings and recommendations each year to the members of the editorial board
of the *American Political Science Review*.[17] Each of these annual conference reports
had a section entitled "Political Statistics," which trumpeted the need for ever
more advanced quantitative research methods and an increased number of techniques. In the end, these conference reports helped move the evolving definition
of the state of the discipline in a single direction and that was toward methods
and techniques.[18]

Another outcome of the 1923 report was the creation of the Social Science
Research Council in which Merriam and his disciples sought to coordinate and
assist all of the social sciences in moving toward quantitative methods and techniques. Hence, there would be no way to escape the movement and revolution
in the scientific study of society and politics. And like the National Conferences on the Science of Politics, this new funding organization for social science research channeled the concept of the state of the discipline into one
meaning and definition.[19]

There was one other major outcome from the fourth official APSA report,
and Merriam was intimately involved with this development as well. At the University of Chicago under Merriam's direction, a new generation of empirically
trained political scientists emerged under the leadership of two men. One leader
was not only Merriam's own student but subsequently a colleague and co-author,
Harold Gosnell.[20] The other was a University of Chicago graduate and Gosnell's
own student, V. O. Key Jr. The writings, research methods, and techniques pio-
neered by these two men would become by the 1960s the very essence of the concept of the "state of the discipline"[21] in both the official and unofficial books. And
outside of the discipline, Merriam helped influence Stuart A. Rice, a sociologist,
whose book became the bible for the science of politics.[22] After the publication
of the Rice volume, there would be no other primary definition for the state of
the discipline than the science of politics.

In the final analysis, the fourth APSA report, published in 1923, with its recommendations echoed in national conferences, journal reports, the Social Science Research Council, and a new generation of quantitative-oriented scholars
who dominated the discipline, became the defining feature of the discipline. The
1923 report and the state of the discipline literally became one and the same thing.
And this reality had severe consequences for a vision of political science. This
final definition shaped not only the state of the discipline but also limited the
vision of what the discipline should be.

Vision in the APSA's *State of the Discipline* Reports and Books

Before the publication of the 1923 report, the ill-defined and loosely structured concept of the state of the discipline made it difficult for the field to develop a vision. Even after the concept started to take on the meaning of scientific methods and techniques a vision still remained elusive. The reason is that such a meaning is quite narrowly limited and circumscribed, making the act or power of seeing and imagination extremely difficult if not sightless. For a vision fixed and focused on methods and techniques is an inward-looking vision that is microscopic, rather than macroscopic in nature. With such a focus, vision is refracted to the minute levels, rather than at the systemic level, and little is therefore captured about the whole. In this type of vision, parts become more important than the entire canvas.

Therefore, if we want to see a larger vision for the state of the discipline we need to look for efforts to develop such a vision that were made before publication of the 1923 official Report on Political Research or shortly after it was made and became so pervasive on the discipline. In a history of such an early effort to develop a vision for the discipline, Stephen Leonard writes, "Between the end of the Civil War and the turn of the century, the founders of the discipline advanced three distinct yet related pedagogical missions for the discipline: to educate citizens and political leaders for civic life, to reproduce scholars and researchers for the discipline and to train bureaucrats for state administration."[23] Simply put, in the nineteenth century, the discipline was envisioned to undertake civic education and thereby solve human and social problems in the polity. Leonard expands on the concept of civic education, as follows:

> In the discourse of American republicanism, political science was the mode of knowledge that served to cultivate and reinforce the virtues of republican morality and politics, a fact that made the educational mission of academic political science particularly central to the discipline's identity. Not just education in general, but *civic* education was the responsibility of political science. Civic education was important if only because for many republicans 'the problem of good government' was a 'problem of good men' and this meant making both *good citizens* and *good leaders*.[24]

However, with the publication of Merriam's reports, both the preliminary and final ones, and the subsequent transformation under his strong leadership of the concept of the state of the discipline and the discipline itself, this early vision of a civic educational mission to achieve a good society literally disappeared. Leonard notes that the promotion of the scientific study of politics, which made methods *the* tool for the achievement of this science, eventually "authorized a wholesale retreat back into the academy."[25] This action divorced the discipline from society's problems and practical politics and thereby pushed concerns about moral questions to the margins while elevating methodology to the core of the discipline. Scientism made the discipline value neutral and moved moral questions and concerns outside of the discipline's concerns. Leonard writes, "All of this suggested that there was a need to detach the discipline's intellectual identity from the American experience and to develop a science of politics that could account for all manner of political experiences regardless of their historical or geographical location."[26]

This focus on the universal meant that the race variable could be dropped from most research efforts because it was not seen as a global concern. In fact, Merriam mentioned race specifically in the final 1923 report, writing that "significant defects in the scientific development of the study of government are as follows . . . (2) tendency toward race, class, nationalistic bias in the interpretation of data available."[27] Therefore, to correct the "significant defects in the scientific . . . study of government," one should drop or omit the race variable.

However, shortly after World War II, the APSA's fifth official report entitled "Goals for Political Science" suggested the need once again for a greater vision than an emphasis on methods. In the 1950s two APSA presidents, Ralph Bunche and V. O. Key Jr. offered in their presidential addresses new visions for the discipline. However, the Bunche and Key visions were strikingly different, and Key's vision would come to define the field and the state of the discipline until today.

On September 9, 1954, Ralph Bunche delivered his presidential address on the APSA's fiftieth anniversary, telling its members that the nation-state and the global community had certain human and social problems "which merited greater attention than the discipline was giving them." As he saw it, these concerns included "the problem of colonialism, and more particularly of colonial Africa" and the "fear, intolerance, suspicion and confusion emanating from racial demagogues and the second class citizenship emerging from racial segregation, white supremacy and disenfranchisement" in the nation-state.[28] The discipline had ignored these grave and difficult realities. Hence, Bunche's vision for the state of the discipline was not of a political science transfixed by methods and procedures but one that also embraced human problem solving. It was the latter to which Bunche argued that the discipline should rededicate itself.

On September 4, 1958, V. O. Key Jr. delivered his presidential address entitled "The State of the Discipline." In that address, Key offered a very different vision to the APSA membership from that proposed by Bunche, stating that "the burden of my argument may be stated briefly and bluntly. It is that the demands upon our profession have grown more rapidly than has the content of our discipline. . . . We must devote greater resources in manpower and ingenuity to the systematic analysis of the phenomena of politics. . . . A critical need of our discipline is for more, and for more rigorous, research training. . . . A second area . . . is that of recruitment of . . . genuinely creative scholars to push back the frontiers of knowledge."[29] Key's vision echoes that of Merriam almost totally. For Key methods and techniques are what the discipline is and ought to be about. In fact, he said in the address that "method without substance may be sterile, but substance without methods are only fortuitously substantial."[30] Thus there is nothing in Key's vision about human and social problem solving, only intellectual problem solving. And that can only occur with quantitative methods and techniques.

Of these two attempts at vision building for the discipline, the one first promoted by Merriam and pushed after World War II by one of his students, Key, is now the dominant one in the discipline. It is no surprise, then, that this vision of methods and techniques is literally synonymous with the last three official *State of the Discipline* APSA-sponsored books. Definition and vision have caught up with each other and are now one and the same thing in both the official and unofficial publications.

The Race Variable and the APSA Reports and Books

In the nine official reports and books shown in Table 2.1, the race variable is treated only in the last two. Although a chapter for the race variable was commissioned for the 1983 book, *Political Science: The State of the Discipline*, it never appeared. Neither was the race variable discussed in three of the four unofficial books used in this study—those of Polsby and Greenstein, Weisberg, and Maveety.

Of all the unofficial and official books and reports, the 1991 edited volume by Crotty, *Political Science: Looking to the Future, is the only one to discuss the race variable*. His introductory comment about the chapter on race that "the exploration of race as a part of American politics is separated from mainstream disciplinary concerns [and] receives limited attention"[31] is not only poignant but instructive and profound. Yet Crotty fails to point out that the official reports and books of the discipline defined race as being outside the very vision of the field. In fact, his own comments never reflect how the race variable became invisible— and this in a field in which the scientific approach requires the identification of major and important independent variables to make the quantitative approach work. Without the identification of independent variables there is no way to determine what influences the dependent ones. Thus, the very objective science that the APSA sought to guide the discipline was biased in and of itself.

Moreover, and perhaps most important, there was never any intellectual need to discount or eliminate the race variable. In fact, at the University of Chicago, Merriam's own disciple, Gosnell, took on the variable first in article form and later in his pioneering book, *Negro Politician*.[32] This book became a major foundational work in the evolution of the African American politics subfield. In addition, the classic work by another Chicago alumnus, Key, made the race variable central in explaining Southern political behavior. But these exceptional and award-winning works failed to get this variable into the official portrait of the state of the discipline.

In addition to these pioneering and classic works by the University of Chicago scholars, there was the ever-evolving literature by both African American political scientists like Bunche and whites of considerable prestige and statute. Yet, the official reports and books managed to define the state of the discipline without this variable in all but nineteen of the ninety-five years they covered. Some seven decades went by before this variable entered into the official vision of the state of the discipline.[33]

The African American Perspective on the State of the Discipline

At this writing, there are two African American perspectives on the state of the discipline. The initial one was advanced first by Ralph Bunche and later by Samuel DuBois Cook in his presidential address in 1964 to the Southern Political Science Association in remarks entitled "Democracy and Tyranny in America: The Radical Paradox of the Bicentennial and Blacks in the American Political System."[34] Cook made this same definitional and visionary argument earlier in his essay, "Introduction: The American Liberal Democratic Tradition, The Black Revolutionary and Martin Luther King Jr."[35] published in the 1971 book, *The Political Philosophy of Martin Luther King, Jr.* This vision of the state of the discipline includes the race variable as a major independent variable that will help guide the discipline in its efforts to solve human and societal problems. Methods and techniques do not take priority over the moral and ethical concerns.

In contrast, the second African American perspective on the state of the discipline sees methods and techniques as the number one priority and eschews moral and ethical considerations. Values in this perspective are neutral, and value judgments are unscientific. Writing about the race variable in his edited book, Crotty indicates that the authors of that chapter found "a number of deficiencies" in the current research on Afro-American Politics that disturbed and motivated them. He continues,

> There is evidence of a general failure to employ theoretical models as a starting point or for explaining the behavior under investigation. They also find a lack of attention to rules of evidence and scientific (or other) criteria as standards against which to judge the value of outcomes or to test propositional inventories relevant to an understanding of black political behavior. The research undertaken can be rudimentary. The authors find little formal modeling or sophisticated quantitative analysis available in this field.[36]

Thus, this lack of methods and techniques has forced some African Americans to promote the Merriam, Gosnell, and Key vision over that of Bunche, Cook, and other humanistic scholars in their efforts to gain respect and acceptance from their white colleagues and enter the mainstream of discipline scholarship. As these scholars see it, methods and techniques are synonymous with the state of the discipline."[37]

Although the first African American perspective on the state of the discipline has been largely ignored, the second one has come under searing criticism.[38] In fact, one of the African American political scientists who promotes this perspective has recently attacked his white colleagues for failing to read the works not only of the empirical African American political scientists but also of any African American political scientists.[39] The reality here is that there is no safety in being like the white empiricists.

There is also a much different and more telling criticism. In a pioneering and seminal work, Vincent L. Hutchings and Nicholas A. Valentino, in a massive review article in Volume 7 (2004) of the *Annual Review of Political Science* (this annual review is an unofficial continuation of the *State of the Discipline* work that omitted the race variable in its first six annual volumes), analyzes nearly every major journal article and book on racial attitudes and public opinion, voting behavior, policy opinions, and partisanship. Previous literature reviews on the race variable had only surveyed books and not journal articles. In addition to finding that the white and black studies are currently done in "relative isolation" of each other, Hutchings and Valentino assert that more than a few of these opinion and attitudinal studies using the race variable are racially biased. Many of the scholars on white public opinion and the black conservatives using cutting-edge techniques to analyze this opinion and attitudinal data seek a rollback of governmental programs and policies that advance democratic equality. Hence, this brilliant review essay reveals without a shadow of a doubt that many of these "scientific studies of politics," with all of their refined techniques and methods, have failed to achieve what Merriam promised for the profession in his 1923 report: Racial bias, even in this age of quantitative analyses, has not abated.[40] Thus, there is no safety in methods and techniques or the "science of politics."

Our hope is that the Bunche vision and perspective will resurface and refocus the discipline toward solving human and social problems in both domestic and global polities. Of the two perspectives, this is the one related most closely to the democratic spirit and promise of liberty and justice for all.

Notes

1. Matthew Holden Jr. *Moral Engagement and Combat Scholarship* (McLean, VA: Court Square Institute, 1983), as quoted in Paula McClain and John Garcia, "Expanding Disciplinary Boundaries: Black, Latino and Racial Minority Group Politics in Political Science," in *Political Science: The State of the Discipline*, ed. Ada Finifter, 247 (Washington, DC: American Political Science Association, 1983).

2. For the two best overview works see two books by Albert Somit and Joseph Tanenhaus: *American Political Science: A Profile of the Discipline* (New York: Atherton, 1964), and Somit and Tanenhaus, *The Development of American Political Science* (New York: Irvington, 1982). For an analysis of the "science of group political behavior" see David Truman, *The Governmental Process* (New York: A. Knopf, 1951); Jack Walker Jr., *Mobilizing Interest Groups in America* (Ann Arbor: University of Michigan Press, 1991); and Hanes Walton Jr., "Protest Politics," in *African Americans and Political Participation*, ed. M. K. C. Morrison, 63–116 (Santa Barbara, CA: ABC–CLIO, 2003). Although there are numerous works on the "science of individual political behavior," two very informative efforts are: Robert Dahl, "The Behavioral Approach in Political Science: Epitaph for a Monument to a Successful Protest," *American Political Science Review* 55 (1961): 763–72; and the more recent work, James Farr, "Remembering the Revolution: Behavioralism in American Political Science," in *Political Science in History: Research Programs and Political Traditions*, ed. James Farr, John Dryzek, and Stephen Leonard, 198–224 (New York: Cambridge University Press, 1995). For works on the "science of institutional political behavior," see two book chapters by Rogers Smith, "Science, Non-Science, and Politics," in *The Historic Turn in the Human Sciences*, ed. Terrence McDonald, 119–59 (Ann Arbor: University of Michigan Press, 1996); and Smith, "Still Blowing in the Wind: The American Quest for a Democratic, Scientific Political Science," in *American Academic Culture in Transformation*, ed. Thomas Bender and Carl Schorske, 123–36 (Princeton, NJ: Princeton University Press, 1997).

3. Anna Haddow, *Political Science in American Colleges and Universities, 1636–1900* (New York: D. Appleton-Century, 1939), vii.

4. Finifter, ed., *Political Science*, 6, 41.

5. William Anderson, "Political Science Enters the Twentieth Century," in Finifter, ed., *Political Science*, 257–66.

6. Finifter, *Political Science*, v.

7. William Crotty, "Introduction: Setting the Stage," in *Political Science: Looking to the Future*, by *William Crotty* (Evanston, IL: Northwestern University Press, 1991), 12.

8. Nancy Maaveety, ed., *The Pioneers of Judicial Behavior* (Ann Arbor: University of Michigan Press, 2003).

9. Crotty, *Political Science*, 12

10. Walton, Cheryl M. Miller, and Joseph P. McCormick, II, "Race and Political Science: The Dual Traditions of Race Relations Politics and African American Politics," in Farr, Dryzek, and Leonard, eds., *Political Science in History*, 145–74.

11. Ibid., 151.

12. See these works by Walton: *The Study and Analysis of Black Politics: A Bibliography* (Metuchen, NJ: Scarecrow Press, 1973); Walton, "The Recent Literature on Black Politics," *PS: Political Science and Politics* (Fall 1985): 769–80; and Walton, "The Current Literature on Black Politics," *National Political Science Review* (1989): 152–68. See also Walton, Leslie Burl McLemore, and C. Vernon Gray, "The Pioneering Books on Black Politics and the Political Science Community, 1903–1965," *National Political Science Review* (1990): 196–218; and Walton, Marion E. Orr, Shirley M. Geiger, and Mfanya Tryman, "The Literature on African American Politics: The Decade of the Nineties," *Politics & Policy* (December 2001): 753–82.

13. J. Peter Meekison, "A Bibliography Essay," in *Teaching Political Science: A Challenge to Higher Education*, ed. Robert Connery, 266 (Durham, NC: Duke University Press, 1965).

14. Charles Merriam, "Political Research," *American Political Science Review* (May 1922): 319.

15. Ibid., 321.

16. Merriam, "Progress Report of the Committee on Political Research," *American Political Science Research* (May 1923): 274. See also Merriam, "Report of the Committee on Political Research: Political Science in Great Britain and France," *American Political Science Review* (August 1924): 574–600.

17. See these works by Arnold Bennett Hall, "Report of the National Conference on the Science of Politics," *American Political Science Review* (February 1924): 119; Hall "Report of the Second National Conference on the Science of Politics," *American Political Science Review* (February 1925): 104–62; and Hall et al., "Report of the Third National Conference on the Science of Politics," *American Political Science Review* (February 1926): 124–70.

18. See Lent Upson, "Round Table V: Political Statistics," *American Political Science Review* (February 1924): 46–148.

19. See Merriam, "The Social Science Research Council," *American Political Science Review* (August 1924): 594–99.

20. See Harold Gosnell, "Statisticians and Political Scientists," *American Political Science Review* (June 1933): 392–403.

21. See V. O. Key Jr., *A Primer of Statistics for Political Scientists* (New York: Crowell, 1954). See also Andrew Lucker, *V. O. Key Jr.: The Quintessential Political Scientist* (New York: Peter Lang, 2001).

22. Stuart A. Rice, "Some Applications of Statistical Methods to Political Research," *American Political Science Review* (May 1926): 326–29. After this article appeared in the *American Political Science Review*, Rice was asked to write the work for the discipline. This article became the basis for his ever influential book, *Quantitative Methods in Politics* (New York: Knopf, 1928).

23. Stephen Leonard, "The Pedagogical Purposes of a Political Science," in Farr, Dryzek, and Leonard, eds., *Political Science in History*, 67. For a recent return to this civic educational mission see Farr, "The Science of Politics as Civic Education Then and Now," *PS: Political Science & Politics* (January 2004): 37–40.

24. Leonard, "The Pedagogical Purposes," 69. Emphasis original.

25. Ibid., 79.

26. Ibid., 80.

27. Merriam, "Progress Report," 287.

28. Ralph Bunche, "Presidential Address," *American Political Science Review* (December 1954): 961–71. See also Walton, "The Political Science Educational Philosophy of Ralph Bunche: Theory and Practice," *Journal of Negro Education* (Spring 2004): 147–58.

29. Key, "The State of the Discipline," *American Political Science Review* (December 1958): 961–71.

30. Ibid., 967.

31. Crotty, *Political Science*, 12.

32. See two works by Harold Gosnell, "Political Meeting in Chicago's Black Belt," *American Political Science Review* (January 1934): 254–58; and Gosnell, *Negro Politician: The Rise of Negro Politics in Chicago* (Chicago: University of Chicago Press, 1935).

33. It is worth noting that race did not enter the "state of the discipline" because the profession finally recognized its intellectual worth. Rather it entered because of protests and the increasing presence of blacks in the discipline. On the growing presence of blacks in the discipline after the 1960s, see Sheila Ards and Maurice Woodard, "African Americans in the Political Science Profession" in *American Government and Politics*, ed. Alice Jackson and Maurice Woodard, 267–73 (Boston: Pearson Custom, 2002). And it is still not clear that white scholars recognize the intellectual worth of research on race. For example Michael Dawson and Ernest Wilson in the early 1990s reported "anecdotal evidence that black and white graduate students are steered away from the study of black politics by their faculty advisors. There seems a bias against the field that suggests that if you work on African-American materials, then by definition you are not as good as those who work on other materials." See Michael Dawson and Ernest Wilson, "Paradigms and Paradoxes: Political Science and African American Politics," in Crotty, *Political Science*, 227.

34. Samuel DuBois Cook, "Democracy and Tyranny in America: The Radical Paradox of the Bicentennial and Blacks in the American Political System," *Journal of Politics* (August 1976): 276–80. For more on Cook's vision for political science see Walton, "Moral Man and a Moral Journey," in *Politics, Morality, and Higher Education: Essays in Honor of Samuel DuBois Cook*, ed. F. Thomas Trotter, 1–9 (Franklin, TN: Providence House, 1997).

35. Cook, "Introduction: The American Liberal Democratic Tradition, The Black Revolutionary, and Martin Luther King Jr.," in *The Political Philosophy of Martin Luther King Jr.*, ed. Hanes Walton Jr., i–xxviii (Westport, CT: Greenwood, 1971).

36. Crotty, *Political Science*, 13.

37. This focus on method and technique is a principal concern of Cathy Cohen and Michael Dawson's contribution to the *State of the Discipline III*. See Cohen and Dawson, "Problems in the Study of the Politics of Race," in *Political Science: State of the Discipline*, ed. Ira Katznelson and Helen Milner, 506–7 (New York: W. W. Norton, 2003).

38. See Adolph Reed, "Reflections on Atlanta University Political Science," *National Political Science Review* 9 (2003): 243.

39. Dawson, "Slowly Coming to Grips with the Effects of the American Racial Order on American Policy Preferences," in *Racialized Politics: The Debate about Racism in America*, ed. David Sears, Jim Sidanius, and Lawrence Bobo, 344–57 (Chicago: University of Chicago Press, 2000).

40. For more on this point see Vincent Hutchings, "The Complexity of Racial Attitudes: Continuing Progress or the Calm Before the Storm?" *DuBoisois Review: Social Science Research on Race* 1 (2004): 203–8.

CHAPTER THREE

African American Political Scientists in Academic Wonderland

WILBUR C. RICH

Introduction

THIS ESSAY EXAMINES African American political scientists' encounters with the academic workplace environment. The "Wonderland" analogy comes from Lewis Carroll's *Alice in Wonderland* and its sequel *Through the Looking Glass.* As a newcomer to this odd world, one can understand why some African Americans might think that they have fallen down a rabbit hole and entered a bewildering universe where nothing is quite as it seems. In this chapter the emergence of African Americans in the discipline, tenure dynamics, and networking opportunities are examined. I will also discuss academic superstars and the lure of prestigious universities.

As a discipline, political science has come a long way since the turn of the 20th century when most colleges and universities did not have separate political science departments. In many institutions political science and history were combined into one department. Today, by contrast, political scientists in most institutions are housed in free-standing departments of political science, government, and politics. These departments are grouped with other social sciences, such as sociology, anthropology, psychology, and economics in liberal arts colleges or public affairs schools. Today, political science scholars focus on understanding governments, political actors, and public policies.

Political scientists play a critical role in framing the interpretative construction of American politics—they write the books and articles that explain political events and their meanings. Writing books about political power can have a curious effect, causing some political scientists to identify, consciously and unconsciously, with the government of the day or the establishment. Martin Kilson has called these individuals "establishment pretenders." They operate under the illusion of being intimately involved in the governing of the nation and are what Loren Baritz calls "servants of power." In *The Servants of Power* Loren Baritz chronicles how industrial psychology and sociology were placed in the service of capitalism. He concludes,

> Many industrial social scientists have put themselves on auction. The power elites of America, especially the industrial elite, have bought their services—which, when applied to areas of relative power, have restricted the freedom of millions of workers. Time was when a man knew that his freedoms were being curtailed. . . . A major characteristic of twentieth-century manipulation has been that it blinds the victim to the fact of manipulation. Because so many industrial social scientists have been willing to serve power instead of mind, they have been themselves a case study in manipulation by consent.[1]

Andrew Stark makes an interesting argument that political scientists do not interact with what he calls "practitioners and identifiable clients" and so are in less danger of co-optation than are psychologists and sociologists.[2] What about the role of political scientists in misinforming the American public? Are political scientists engaging in the manipulation of the public when they downplay the saliency of racial cleavage in American politics? Do they provide solace to political leaders when they make light of declining voter turnouts—offering methodological solipsism that suggests that this decline does not matter? In making their work unreadable by the general public, are they denying their insights to the masses? Or are they comfortable within the walls of the university teaching middle-class aspirants and writing notes to the elite? Or are they trapped in the structural hard place, as Stark suggests?[3]

As Stark points out, some political scientists are public intellectuals, but the majority are not. This is not to deny that some political scientists are committed and public critics of the establishment. Some are, but they are the exceptions. These distinctions are important because each type of political scientist serves as a role model for new groups entering the discipline.

African American political scientists entered the discipline at a time when the nation was undergoing profound social transformation. The late sixties brought the issue of race to the forefront of American politics. It was a time of boundless optimism about solving the nation's festering race problem. However, history shows that the nation's white leading political scientists did not assert themselves during this historical and social transformation. These political scientists left no legacy to their progeny. Part of the explanation for this "flat-footedness" on the part of political science of that era is the extant organizational culture of universities. African Americans were the newcomers to this culture.

The Wonderland of Academia

American colleges and universities have distinct organizational cultures and idiosyncratic governing norms, which may or may not reflect the location of the university or its resources. However, location does matter. Colleges and universities located in urban settings behave differently than those in rural settings. Life in a college town is different from life in the big city. Commuter institutions behave differently than residential ones, state institutions behave differently than private ones, and schools with substantial endowments behave differently than those with fewer resources. The history of the institution also plays a role in the development of the campus culture. For any newcomer, understanding academic cultural nuances is extremely difficult; making sense of the culture requires one to become a student of organizational behavior. Van Maanen and Schein outline the content of an organizational culture as follows:

> Any organizational culture consists broadly of long-standing rules of thumb, a somewhat special language, an ideology that helps edit a member's everyday experience, shared standards of relevance as to the critical aspects of the work that is being accomplished, matter-of-fact prejudices, models for social etiquette and demeanor, certain customs and rituals suggestive of how members are to relate to colleagues, subordinates, superiors, and outsiders, and a sort of residual category of some rather plain "house sense" regarding what is appropriate and "smart" behavior within the organization and what is not.[4]

Academic culture, with its self-absorbed insularity, log-rolling ethics, platitudinous liberalism, and propensity to inflate its own importance, is perpetuated by its members or "insiders." There are all types of insider-interest groups in the academy, but the important ones are the tenured professors. They are charged with keeping the traditions.

These cultural imperatives may come as a surprise to a first-generation black professor. Edgar Epps, then a young black professor in an elite university, tried to make sense of the tenets of this new culture in his 1989 article, "Academic Culture and the Minority Professor." Basically, he agrees with my assessment of the anxiety-producing nature of this bittersweet encounter. However, he attributes the inequalities to a system that tracks potential scholars from prep school to graduate school. The tracking system determines who gets into the elite colleges and university and who gets recruited as professors. He asserts, "The relative paucity of minority scholars in doctoral programs of highly prestigious institutions assures that minority scholars will encounter difficulty when they apply for faculty positions at elite schools."[5] I call this the fear and trembling explanation. This explanation assumes that the system needs to be more altruistic and humanistic if blacks are to participate effectively. It accepts the notion that a system of merit is entrenched and that whites are waiting for a few black PhDs from elite universities to become available in the marketplace.

I agree that some tracking is inherent in the system, but the tracking system as an institution has been subverted by the improvement in quality of the great state universities, such as the University of Michigan and the University of California, Berkeley. Similarly, the democratization of the publishing process has allowed scholars at North Texas University to become leaders in their field.[6] I agree that having a PhD from an Ivy League university helps one gain a first job, but opportunities even out in the middle years of an academic career. Increasingly, Ivy League universities have had to mix their faculty with scholars from non-Ivy League schools. Today, most leading schools are mixers.

The problem with most elite faculties is not excessive inbreeding, but rather overspecialization by scholars. Black newcomers, who expect to find an inquiring community of scholars, find instead colleagues who are narrowly invested in a single line of interest. Many scholars are not knowledgeable about anything beyond their work and what they read in the *New York Times* or saw on PBS. Russell Jacoby's *The Last Intellectuals* laments the passing of the great white scholars who wrote for an educated public.[7] Now, academics are writing for other academics. Black newcomers may be surprised and chagrined by the celebration of this so-called splendid cocooning. Many will have to resist the lure of becoming public intellectuals because at tenure review time their white colleagues may not value their visibility and activities outside of academia.

Another aspect of the organizational culture is its tendency to attract people who seek relatively risk-free and conservative lives. In 1958 George Williams' *Some of My Best Friends Are Professors* described what he called the professorial personality. The professorial personality stems from a life of being expected to live apart from the general society. A life with books is by nature a neurotic one, and Williams comes close to saying that neurotics populate the academic community. He observes the following:

> The personality that eventually emerges from all this is, typically, underlain with a deep sense of inferiority, fear, and maladjustment, yet overlain by an almost frantic sense of superiority. This deep sense of inferiority is further complicated by a latent hostility to that which is nonbookish and nonintellectual, and a fluttery insecurity that creates morbid fear of any criticism that may endanger a hard won academic place.[8]

In this respect political scientists are like other academics. They want to protect their hard-won laurels. They want to believe that they are part of an independent elite, and they enjoy the splendid isolation that some campuses afford. The academic culture, reinforced by bureaucratic rules, allow insiders almost total freedom to work within their specialization after receiving tenure. The security of academic tenure allows one to take a hostile and arrogant attitude toward the outside world. It is a "the world is a mess and I am pure" attitude.

The same culture that allows considerable independent work and personal freedom tolerates racial solipsism. Some black newcomers have reported their surprise at learning that so-called experts on minority issues do not know any minority individuals personally. Some have never spent time in the black community. Most derive their insights about minorities from analyzing a large database assembled by professional interviewers. White colleagues often rely on liberal opinion journals for insight about minorities in America.

Professorial careerism has transformed the university into a highly complex but insular organization.[9] Part of this insularity can be traced to the tradition of recruiting individuals on the basis of their dissertations to teach subjects they know. Many have never worked outside the university. University life is a comfortable place where research/writing is rewarded and political action is not. The university remains one of the few institutions that relies on status ambition to manage individual behavior. Although the rewarding and punishing of individuals is highly decentralized, the system works extremely well. Professors are easily organized around issues of tenure, promotion, titled academic chairs, research center directorships, and reduced teaching loads.

One of the most solemn obligations of tenured professors is their recruitment responsibility, but it is hampered by one of the most venerated norms in the academy, departmental autonomy. Such autonomy has functioned as a barrier to recruitment of minorities and of women; as one professor put it, "Department autonomy is a license to discriminate." This may explain why white insiders can ignore black applicants with impunity. Although such practices result in rampant nepotism and favoritism in the recruitment process, it is tolerated because it fosters organizational loyalty.

Academic departments should be thought of as laboratories of small group behavior. Scholars relate to each other in a highly informal manner that belies the rigid differentiation among colleagues. Senior professors are treated differently than junior ones. Researchers are rewarded differently than pure teachers. Old-timers are handled differently than newcomers. At first glance, these differences may not be apparent.

In elite universities the process of watching and herding newcomers has a long history. In 1938 the great sociologist A. B. Hollingshead began the first study of the making of white professors. He concluded that outsiders, in his case non-WASPs, faced a series of formidable social barriers.[10] The newcomers at that time, particularly Jews and Catholics, underwent a complete socialization before being accepted as full-fledged and unambiguous members of the university's professorial class. In the thirties, very few, if any, black political scientists held professorships at historically white universities.

Stages of Entry

African Americans came into the discipline in three stages. In the first stage, they were isolated in historically black institutions, burdened with few financial resources and heavy teaching loads. Relatively large historically black institutions like Howard University and Atlanta University (now Clark Atlanta University) employed black political scientists, whereas small ones housed them in history and social studies departments. The civil rights movement, the black power movement (and its spin-off demands for black studies departments), and the affirmative action initiative triggered the second stage. Although historically white colleges and universities were literally forced to hire black faculty, the cocoons of the historically black colleges and universities (HBCUs) did not yield many academic butterflies. The HBCUs, most of which were underfunded, had smothered the research careers of many of these professors. Accordingly, many universities made a conscious decision to recruit more black graduate students or to grow their own professors. This strategy worked fairly well in the 1960s and 1970s ,but it failed quickly and notably in the 1980s.[11]

We are currently in the third stage of faculty appointments or what sociologists called the "post-compliance period."[12] I prefer the term "the post-guilt period."

Assistant professors recruited after the civil rights era found that universities had retained their organizational culture. More astonishingly, their post-1980s successors faced much the same social isolation and alienation as did their predecessors of the sixties and seventies. Total integration of these post-1980s newcomers continued to be complicated by a silent Negrophobia among white colleagues.

Despite the proliferation of court cases, student protests, and target of opportunity initiatives, progress in desegregating academia has been uneven. Is it a problem of supply and demand? Many elite institutions have reduced the numbers of black scholars in their pipeline, and Howard and Atlanta University have become the largest producers of black PhDs.[13] By getting out of the business of training black PhDs, institutions created a scarcity that serves the interest of white insiders who do not want African Americans in their department. The practice is not exactly price fixing, but it is close to it.

The process of training and recruiting black professors is reminiscent of the protracted struggle over the desegregation of schools in the South in the fifties. It seems as if several hundred George Wallaces were standing in the schoolhouse door. Why?

Apparently, the entry of African American professors into the workplace represents a status crisis for the white insiders. Whites, holding on to every imaginary claim to status and power, resist the idea of a color-blind department. Some whites apparently believe that having one black professor in their department would lower the reputation of the department or their concomitant status. Following this line of thinking, two or more blacks threaten the continued ability of a department to build its scholarly reputation and standing in the discipline. This is a curious notion about the prestige hierarchy or what sociologist C Wright Mills called the "petty hierarchy" of university departments.[14] This notion holds that the academic reputation of a department is based partly on demonstrated exclusivity and the ratio of research-productive superstars to pure teachers. Academic departments, like most of American society, place a high value on organizations that exude exclusivity. To acquiesce to black entry in a legal sense is one thing, but to allow these "intruders" to make fundamental decisions within the university is unacceptable. Accordingly, white insiders regard granting full membership to black newcomers as evidence they have lost control, real or imagined, over the distribution of prestige within the university.

Except for departments of black studies or Africana studies, no liberal arts department in any elite white university has an all-black faculty. It is hard to imagine an all-black political science department at Stanford. This line of thinking explains why a white professor felt comfortable telling a black colleague "a law school of our caliber and tradition simply cannot look like a professional basketball team."[15] These "this is not the NBA" comments are quite common even at low-prestige universities. The one attribute the University of Mississippi and Harvard University's Department of Political Science share is that they both employ a single black faculty member.[16]

The unstated assumption is that white members got their jobs the old-fashioned way, they earned them. As such they do not need to explain or justify their presence. As true believers, white insiders seldom admit that recruitment of some white department members was based on something less than merit. The cherished and operative myth is that the academic marketplace has worked for them. For many, the recruitment of black professors interferes with that market and, more importantly, makes a mockery of the merit myth. Because the employment of blacks is thought to be the result of pressure from the outside, they are regarded as intruders.

Armed with the notion of blacks as "intruders," white insiders feel justified in engaging in silent civil disobedience and not cooperating with the university's stated goals of recruiting, integrating, and assimilating black faculty. This new racism differs only in form from the old, insulting racism. David Messick and Diane Mackie call it *aversive racism*.[17] Whites continue to hold negative views of blacks, but they suppress anti-black statements (self-governing speech) and behavior because it is considered crude even in all-white situations. By keeping their views to themselves and avoiding appearing to be racists, white insiders who oppose black recruitment can avoid detection.

Five years into the twenty-first century, all-white political science departments are still common. Political science departments in many colleges and universities have not even interviewed a single African American job applicant. The excuse given by smaller departments is that an African American may not fit into the family-like environment, and in larger ones, the pretext is that black applicants do not measure up to their white counterparts. Because of these attitudes black applicants have a smaller chance of being successful in the tenure process.

Turnover and Tenure Games

The prevailing attitude is that blacks are not ready for the vigorous demands of a scholarly life or that the departments do not want to disappoint aspiring black political scientists by denying them tenure. We do not have exact data on the turnover of blacks in political science or evidence that they receive tenure any more or less easily than whites. Although universities keep data on hires and minorities in academic positions, they rarely highlight those who do not get tenure or leave the university voluntarily. Monique Clague's research on African American faculty was hampered by the lack of historical records. She discovered the "faculty who resigns or retires are zapped from the records."[18]

The norm is to hire blacks at the assistant professor level and advise them not to apply for tenure since their research record is inadequate. It is often suggested that they can start over again at a lower ranked institution or seek employment outside of academia. Some are encouraged to take administrative jobs that deal with diversity issues or public relations. There is also a pattern of not granting tenure to the first set of black assistant professors in a department, but to accord more consideration to the next set of applicants. This does not mean that the second wave of black assistant professors will be granted tenure but rather that whites feel their departments have learned something from the first experience.

Despite these discouraging patterns, expectations are high among newly minted black PhDs. They believe that they will be the ones who will be granted tenure, particularly those who are employed in all-white departments with no minority members. Psychologically speaking, it is not hard to understand why they feel that, because they were chosen to integrate the department, they are quite deserving of tenure. Recruitment by an elite department after graduate school can be extremely flattering and legitimizing.

The promised seven years of probation before a tenure review seems a long time. Some newcomers have no idea that course preparations and dissertation rewriting/revising can eat up three to four years of the tenure clock. In addition, most elite schools consider publication of the dissertation a given and expect those who apply for tenure to have a new project on a publisher's desk.

Disillusionment can also set in when an assistant professor begins to deal with the misleading representations of the department that recruited them. New-comers are given one tenure scenario at recruitment time and another at their third-year review. For example, newcomers are told to publish, but not told that some journals have more value than others. They are told that service on uni-versity and department committees would be considered in the tenure decision process, only to discover that it plays a lesser role than scholarly production and teaching.

The entire tenure process can be a Catch-22 situation in which standards of quantity and quality are appropriate for one candidate and not for another, shift-ing unpredictably. The tenure review process becomes whatever the tenured department members decide it is. Social compatibility pays a larger role than the insiders will admit. Despite all the folklore about professors having a high toler-ance for dissent, diversity, and idiosyncratic behavior, most are more comfortable with people with whom they share a racial, religious, and class affinity.[19] Homo-geneity facilitates networking, which is so necessary to build a successful career.

Networks and the Marketplace

The academic community is a network of supportive relationships. It was once described as an informal exchange market where participants use barter to accu-mulate IOUs and to promote their careers. It is not uncommon for young white scholars to put their energy into helping superstars with their research for the sake of a simple publication acknowledgment. White scholars often edit the work of colleagues before publication as a mechanism for building obligations within the profession. Black newcomers will discover instead that they are not asked to read papers or do things that will incur obligations. Black colleagues are rarely asked to be co-principal investigators, even in large research projects on blacks.

To be blunt, very few whites will incur obligation from blacks. Hence blacks are seldom allowed to participate in the ongoing exchange process. Without cur-rency, blacks cannot negotiate in the academic marketplace. Trying to break into this circle of supportive and reciprocal relationships is difficult, if not impos-sible. As one white colleague put it, "Black grapes don't grow on the same vine as white grapes." There is no mechanism that the university can use to graft these relationships.

Black newcomers may also find the power array within the university bureaucracy confusing. At first glance university administrators appear to have considerable power, but newcomers discover that they are often relatively powerless in tenure matters. Only presidents and deans have any real power over senior professors in tenure matters. High-level black administrators are simply extensions of the president and cannot help when black professors come under attack within departments. Perhaps the most surprising and puzzling aspect of the academic culture is how the possibility of an appointment at an elite university serves to discipline the behavior and research of professors at lesser known universities.

The Lure of Academic Heavens

The most prestigious universities are considered academic heavens. A professor can ascend to these institutions once he or she is acknowledged to be the best scholar in his or her field. Such universities can confer added prestige and visibility. The myth is that these universities, after surveying the field, only recruit the best. Professors there have titled chairs, big offices, bright graduate students, and high salaries—perks not available in lesser-known institutions. Obviously only a few colleges and universities qualify as academic heavens.

The operating culture of colleges and universities varies from region to region and within regions, but there are three basic types: *research, teaching, and uplift*. In a research culture the emphasis is on finding and discovering. Professors are expected to look for new theories, reinterpret old findings, and write about them. Students in this culture are viewed as the audience. They listen to those who discover and write. In a teaching culture, the emphasis is on describing what others have discovered and reported. Students are viewed as a service constituency. Pure teachers act as ambassadors from the scholarly world. Occasionally they report insights, but their primary goal is to decode scholarly research for students. In the uplift institutions, the emphasis is on facilitating class mobility among students. Teachers seek to compensate for inadequacies of a poor high-school education and erase whenever possible working-class markings (speech patterns, writing, and manners). Students are considered clients, and the services provided are mainly socio-psychological.

This typology does not suggest that these institutions are mutually exclusive or that the location of institutions in the academic hierarchy is fixed. Obviously not all universities and colleges with research cultures are considered elite institutions. It is equally true that the research culture is not adverse to having first-rate teaching staffs. Correspondingly, uplift colleges and universities teach and grant procurement credentials. One of the great myths of academe is that all higher educational institutions are equal at some level. Academia is a world that espouses egalitarianism, but practices elitism. All academics believe that first-rate minds can be found in what they call "Podunk U." In other words, the winnowing process is neither absolute nor fair. In a homogenized academic world, the cream does not always rise to the top. Therefore it is difficult to say which type of institution is best at what.[20]

Ask any seven political scientists what are the seven best political science departments in the country, and you will get at least seven different answers. Granted, there will be departments that are frequently named, but the mixes will vary. The reason for this lack of consensus is that ranking departments is a purely subjective process. Some departments have more productive Americanists, others have professors who are more visible in international relations, and still others have "stars" in political theory and comparative politics. The annual rankings of such publications as *U.S. News & World Report* provide favorable publicity and reassure alumni, but the discipline has its own standards for rankings. Some people judge departments on the productivity of the members and others on the prestige of the institutions.[21]

Prestige seems to carry weight in the magazine and in the practitioner ranking process based on two assumptions. The first assumption is that prestigious universities can always attract or raid productive scholars from lesser-known institutions. The second assumption is that such scholars will come because being granted tenure at a prestigious institution means that one is obviously at the top of his or her field. As in most fields some professors are more equal than others.

White Superstar Political Scientists

An academic superstar is a person whose reputation for scholarship extends beyond the bounds of his or her host institution. Such individuals have made what is considered to be a "defining contribution" to their field; they are the so-called names in the field. Graduate students are required to read their work. Journalists refer to them repeatedly as sources of expertise. They may be known for a particular approach or school of thought. Their work is engaged in the verifying and revising of the major paradigms of the discipline, and some of it is seminal. These are the men—and women—of knowledge who create the research agenda of the discipline and announce the death of a paradigm. As one superstar has described himself, "I am the straw that stirs the drink." Stirring the drink implies power. Power as defined by scholars is the ability to occupy an academic space; that is, no one can address the issues on which they have written without mentioning their names.

With stardom come the perks. Citations in books and articles are important, but the real recognition comes at discipline conventions.[22] Fawning over superstars is not uncommon. In such meetings the hierarchy of social status is established and reified. Stars are given single billing on the program. They are invited to special and sometimes secret gatherings.

Superstar professors operate in a fiercely competitive environment. As innovators, discipline builders, and paradigm challengers, they write the books that others feel compelled to respond to, review, and quote. Their networks are filled with rumors about outside offers, salaries, and perks. Superstars are comfortable with controversy and the spotlight. Although some of the most powerful discipline superstars are not known to the general public, their views are taken seriously within academia and solicited by public intellectuals and other members of the discipline.

The rank and status of white superstars in their disciplines allow them tremendous flexibility and mobility. Their home universities are prepared to exempt them from all types of organizational rules to keep them happy. Their host institutions will accept behavior that they would not tolerate from other professors. The names of superstars always appear on nationwide search lists for distinguished professorships and titled chairs. Their best graduate students are considered extensions of superstardom and are preferred by research universities. This national visibility allows the home university to claim that it maintains a distinguished faculty. This reputation attracts graduate students, foundation and government grants, and media attention. The departure of a superstar from his or her home university usually causes a stir within the entire discipline. It may cost the departed institution some prestige and standing within the university department ranking system.

Obviously not all white professors are superstars or what sociologist Alvin Gouldner refers to as "cosmopolitans." Most are "locals," professors with less outside visibility that do the housekeeping for their institutions.[23] What is less obvious is why the non-superstars enjoy so much local authority within the university. They have gained power by becoming students of university politics. They have invested their time and energy in university committee service and in administrative positions. A professor who has not written anything in twenty years can still hold his or her own in a department committee meeting. For this reason such a person may wield as much clout as a superstar in matters of granting tenure and recruitment. Yet within the scholarly community at large they are not taken seriously.

Are There Black Superstars?

What is a black superstar? How are they different from lesser-known colleagues? Are black superstars accorded the same deference as their white counterparts? It is difficult to answer these questions because there is no empirical research on the subject. Part of the argument in this essay is that black political scientists are not treated equally but that the discipline still has a few black superstars. Some of their work is cited in this volume. The key indicator of superstardom is visibility outside of one's home department. In political science, academic status is accorded to individual work that demands citations. If black superstars' work "demands" citation, why aren't they leaders in their subfield? Why can't they exercise authority within the university or home departments? Herein lies the difference between white and black superstars. Whereas white superstars usually dominate the discourse in their subfield, a black superstar needs only to be a productive and high profiled participant. Black superstars are considered exceptions to the rule that blacks are not productive scholars. Being able to come up with a black person's name is not to be confused with total acknowledgment. White scholars may concede that these black scholars are good but not great. Despite media recognition for a being an expert on black political behavior, black superstars cannot escape the "exception" label. Accordingly, black superstars can be divided into two subgroups: discipline stars and intellectual celebrities. For discipline stars the real capital in academia is an award-winning book. Frank Westie observed:

> One can, however, seek other forms of capital: permanent ensconcement in the bound journals, those dead sea scrolls which our faith tells us will forever occupy an important place on the shelves of libraries as long as there are libraries; recognition in the form of footnotes and citations, both now and in future; and the satisfaction that one's having lived made a difference, and more of a difference than the lives of those who gathered more worldly treasures.[24]

Since scholarly reputation is so critical to becoming a discipline superstar, one is obligated to write at least more than one major book or critical article in one's subfield. Ironically a black political scientist can become a well-known political scientist by writing books or articles that criticize the so-called black civil rights leadership. This is particularly true for intellectual celebrities. After these individuals make appearances in the media and on talk shows, they achieve celebrity or pundit status.

Because the entire business of evaluating superstars is based on reputation, it is difficult to discuss the topic of black superstars with any certainty. There is no published ranking of black political scientists. We don't know whether black and white political scientists would rank each other differently. Would blacks rank other blacks differently than whites? Would whites rank each other differently? Generally speaking, political scientists do not like to rank colleagues publicly, but ranking is widely used informally in appointments and tenure decisions. Outside tenure reviewers are often asked to rank the tenure applicant against scholars in the subfield. Since the letters are usually confidential, we do not know whether blacks are routinely ranked against whites. It would not be surprising to find that blacks are graded against other blacks and not compared with their white colleagues.

The real issue is whether superstars have equal status. Can black and white superstars demand the same salaries, titled professorships, research opportunities, and association honors? I believe such racial parity is a goal yet to be achieved. As the Kilson chapter suggests, a rigid activist/technocrat dichotomy is difficult for black political scientists. They are often forced into the role of activist because they are troubled by the injustice in the outside world. White scholars have the luxury, if they choose to take advantage of it, of avoiding controversial racial issues. As a white colleague once said to this writer, he was not expected to do anything other than write books and articles. Many black scholars feel compelled to do something about political life in their communities. Political science as a discipline celebrates democracy and extols civic participation, but it does not reward scholars who are activists. Political activists are not the leaders in their subfield. Indeed, being perceived as being too close to politicians and "real politics" is frowned upon. We write books suggesting that participation improves democracy, but we often eschew colleagues who actually get involved in politics. In *Through the Looking Glass*, Alice walks through a mirror into a strange land populated by chess pieces, where everything happens backward, and newcomers are confused. It is no wonder that newcomers are confused.

Possibilities for Life in Academia

Is there space for a scholar who is not trying to serve power, but is committed to creating work that helps the public understand government? Yes. There are scholars who question authority, attack government bureaucracies, lambaste the press, and excoriate wrongdoings of powerful politicians. Can these politicians have credibility and visibility with the attentive public? Yes. However the majority of successful professors could not be described in those terms. There is a quota on these types of critics.

Many black political scientists chafe at being called servants of power. Most do not find the old university jokes that "academics are the court jester of the advanced capitalist society" or "you can't start a revolution with a Ford Foundation grant" funny. Like their white colleagues they see themselves trying to understand the human condition and to report it as it is. Most seek to describe the positive aspects of the human condition. Whether that is rescuing black people from stereotypes, calling attention to their misery, documenting historical oversights, or interpreting the pathos of black writers, the pattern of their work is not to overthrow the system but to enlighten it.

Black political scientists cannot make a difference in departments unless they have the needed numbers. No group can change the working environment without large numbers. Therefore, the energy of tenured black professors should be directed toward consolidating a power base within the university. This requires an entrepreneurial spirit and a passion for recruiting black colleagues. Simultaneously, they must demand that the university allocate more prestige and status to black professors in the form of titled chairs and research support. Most elite colleges and universities have a surplus of prestige value. They can easily absorb many more blacks and minorities without forfeiting any rung on the prestige ladder.

The best survival strategy for a black newcomer is to accumulate as much academic capital as soon as possible. Not every black newcomer will become a superstar, but he or she should work extremely hard until a judgment is made otherwise.

Why should black professors strive toward superstardom? The short answer to this question is that marginality is the purgatory of academia. The longer answer is that they should do so to acquire more status. Status is the currency of university life. With status one can demand that certain things be done. One can also threaten to leave if one doesn't get one's way. Without status, one can expect a less than sympathetic hearing before administrators. Without academic capital one cannot mentor or sponsor another minority professor's career or insist on tenure for him or her. Without the ability to replicate oneself, there is no cumulative organizational power. Besides, it is difficult to imagine that universities would tolerate large numbers of black locals.

Undermining white male-centeredness in academia may take another generation of alert scholars, but it will happen. The first step in this dismantling process is to understand the university and its culture.

Conclusion

This review of the academic community does not reflect every university or political science department. It is by necessity a composite portrait. A few political science departments have not been afraid to recruit and grant tenure to more than one black political scientist. It is important also to point that a few black political scientists have not faced the types of tactics reported in this essay.

This essay is aimed at those departments who believe that their stalling and blocking tactics have gone undetected. Its other purpose is to alert readers to the challenges faced by African American political scientists. Changing this culture is not the sole responsibility of these newcomers; it is an assignment for all members of this Wonderland.

Notes

Acknowledgments: The authors would like to thank Michael Krot and Kristen Garlock at JSTOR, University of Michigan, Ann Arbor for their data collection assistance and Sheree Bennett for her assistance on this chapter. We also thank those who gave their advice and suggestions concerning this chapter, including panel participants at the 2004 NCOBPS Roundtable entitled "The Cross-Disciplinary Treatment of African American Issues" including Cathy Cohen, Shelby Lewis, Aldon Morris, Dianne Pinderhughes, and James Steele. Any errors of fact or judgment are our own.

1. Loren Baritz, *The Servants of Power: A History of the Use of Social Science in American Industry* (Middletown, CT: Wesleyan University Press, 1960), 210.

2. Andrew Stark, "Why Political Scientists Aren't Public Intellectuals," *Political Science and Politics* (September 2002): 578.

3. Ibid., 579.

4. John Van Maanen, and Edgar H. Schein, "Toward a Theory of Organizational Socialization," in *Research in Organizational Behavior*, ed. Barry Staw, 209–64 (Greenwich, CT: JAI Press, 1979), 210.

5. Edgar G. Epps, "Academic Culture and the Minority Professor," *Academe* 36 (September/October 1989): 23–26.

6. See Michael Ballard and Neil Mitchell, "The Good, the Better, and the Best in Political Science," *PS: Political Science and Politics* 31 (1998): 826–28; see also James M. McCormick and Tom W. Rice, "Graduate Training and Research Productivity in the 1990s: A Look at Who Publishes," *PS: Political Science and Politics* 34, no. 3 (September 2001): 675–80.

7. See Russell Jacoby, *The Last Intellectuals: American Culture in the Age of Academe* (New York: Basic Books, 1987).

8. George Williams, *Some of My Best Friends Are Professors* (New York: Abelard–Schuman, 1958), 50.

9. Talcott Parson and Gerald Platt, *The American University* (Cambridge, MA: Harvard University Press, 1973); Neil Smelser and Robin Clement, *The Changing Academic Market* (Berkeley: University of California Press, 1980).

10. A. B. Hollingshead, "Ingroup Membership and Academic Selection," *American Sociological Review* (December 1938): 826–33.

11. See Maurice Woodard and Michael Preston, "The Rise and Decline of Black Political Scientists in the Profession," *PS: Political Science and Politics* 17, no. 4 (Autumn 1984): 787–92. See also Woodard and Preston, "Black Political Scientists: Where Are the New Ph.Ds?" *PS: Political*

Science and Politics 18, no.1 (Winter 1985): 80–88. The number did not improve much in an article written in 1992 that showed many schools had gotten out of the black PhD-producing market. See Sheila Ards and Woodard, "African Americans in the Political Science Profession," *PS: Political Science and Politics* 25 (June 1992): 252–59.

12. Smesler and Clement, *The Changing Academic Market.*

13. Ards and Woodard, "African Americans."

14. C. Wright Mills, *White Collar* (New York: Oxford University Press, 1956).

15. Derrick Bell, *And We Are Not Saved* (New York: Basic Books, 1979), 144.

16. In 1998 Theodore Cross did a survey of twenty-five prestigious schools and was surprised to find no black political science professors in some leading schools. Some of the schools he included in this survey still have no black professors. See Theodore Cross, "The Black Faculty Count at the Nation's Most Prestigious Universities," *Journal of Blacks in Higher Education* 19 (1998): 109–15.

17. David Messick and Diana Mackie, "Intergroup Relations," in *Annual Review of Psychology* 40 (1989): 45–81.

18. Monique Weston Clague, *Hiring, Promoting and Retaining African American Faculty: A Case Study of an Aspiring Multi-Cultural Research University* (Washington, DC: ASHE–ERIC Report, 1992), 77.

19. See Anne S. Tsui, Terri D. Egan, and Charles A. O'Reilly III, "Being Different: Relational Demography and Organizational Attachment," *Administrative Science Quarterly* 37 (1989): 549–79.

20. See McCormick and Rice, "Graduate Training and Research."

21. See Ballard and Mitchell, "The Good, the Better."

22. Having multiple publications in the discipline's premier journal, the *American Political Science Review*, is one type of superstar certification. See Arthur Miller, Charles Tein, and Andrew Peebler, "The American Political Science Review Hall of Fame: Assessment and Implication for the Evolving Discipline," *PS: Political Science and Politics* 29, no.1 (March 1996): 73–83.

23. Alvin Gouldner, "Cosmopolitans and Locals: Toward an Analysis of Latent Social Roles, Part I," *Administrative Science Quarterly* 2 (December 1957): 281–306. See also Gouldner, "Cosmopolitans and Locals: Toward an Analysis of Latent Social Roles, Part II," *Administrative Science Quarterly* 2 (March 1958):444–80.

24. Frank Westie, "Academic Expectations of Professional Immortality: A Study of Legitimation," *American Sociologist* 8 (1973): 23.

PART II

Globalization and
Transnational Politics

T HE TERM "GLOBALIZATION" is perhaps the most overused, misunderstood, and contested term in the discipline. We live in what William Knoke's *Bold New World* calls a "Placeless society." Everything is everywhere. There is an old saying that nothing is certain but death and taxes. Globalization may be added to these two inevitabilities.

There are a variety of articles and books written about how this phenomenon affects the nation's economy and culture. Paul Kennedy's *Preparing for the Twenty-First Century* questions whether we have the political structures for a global society. James Mittleman's *The Globalization Syndrome: Transformation and Resistance* also raises questions about globalization's process and impact on nations.

Regardless of where one stands on the issue of globalization, the world economies and demographics are shifting so discernibly that internal national isolation is an extremely difficult policy to maintain. Political scientists are devoting more time to analyzing the impact of these changes on politics. It would be too inward looking to organize a volume on the state of the discipline without paying attention to this critical discourse. Black Americans will not be spared from the impact of globalization on our economy or our politics. The essays in Part II concern the impact of globalization throughout the African Diaspora.

Television has taught ordinary African Americans that there are individuals with the same ancestry living over the world. There are black Arabs, Brazilians, and Fijians. The Diaspora is huge, but do we share more than skin color and hair texture? As the world gets smaller, these are questions we will be forced to confront.

CHAPTER FOUR

Black Politics in Latin America

An Analysis of National and Transnational Politics

OLLIE A. JOHNSON III

Introduction

IN THE LAST 25 YEARS, scholars have made significant contributions to our understanding of race and ethnicity and, more specifically, of Black populations in Latin America. Most of these books and articles have come from historians (Andrews 2004; Appelbaum, Macpherson, and Rosemblatt 2003; Davis 1995a), anthropologists (Wade 1993, 1997; Whitten and Torres 1998; Yelvington 2001), and sociologists (Hasenbalg 1986; Twine 1998; Winant 2001). As a result, we have a better sense of the central roles that Africans and their descendants have played in shaping Latin America. Contemporary Latin American religion, cuisine, music, style, language, and social relations all bear the marks of African influence. However, in the area of government and politics, intellectuals have paid far too little attention to Afro-Latin American movements, organizations, and struggles for justice, equality, and democracy.[1]

For example, in *Utopia Unarmed: The Latin American Left after the Cold War* (1993), Mexican political scientist Jorge G. Castañeda argues that the post–cold war period represented a great opportunity for the Latin American Left to influence the direction of social and political change. He maintains that the economic crises and processes of democratization opened political space throughout the region for leftist policies that could promote economic growth and reduce inequality. Like most progressives, Castañeda identifies poverty and social inequality as the key problems to be overcome. Unfortunately, he fails to examine how these fundamental problems are directly related to race and ethnicity.

Castañeda is hardly the only political scientist to ignore Afro-Latin American political activity. Centrist, conservative, and other leftist political scientists who study Latin America have also neglected this area of inquiry. Scholars must investigate Blacks in Latin America as political actors to increase our understanding of Latin American politics. A few political scientists such as Hanchard (1994), Nobles (2000), and Thorne (2003) are beginning to join historians, anthropologists, and sociologists in highlighting the roles of Blacks in Latin America. These scholars are following the initiatives of Afro-Latin American intellectuals and activists (Fontaine 1980; Moore 1989; Mosquera 2000; Nascimento 1978; 1982) who have been condemning pervasive racial inequality and discrimination and documenting Black political action for decades. In this tradition, this chapter examines Black political participation in several Latin American countries and discusses the development of Black transnational advocacy networks in the Americas. I conclude by highlighting ongoing Black political activity in the Americas.

In the last two decades, Black Latin Americans have made progress in publicizing their political agendas. Black groups have become more politically active. This progress has highlighted several challenges for Black political struggle that vary by country and often within countries. First, after Blacks gain government recognition and formal support for specific public policies, the crucial question becomes how to implement those policies, laws, and programs. Frequently, policy implementation does not follow policy formulation. Second, Blacks are divided by various political, economic, social and cultural cleavages. One of the most important is the ideological debate over autonomy. Should Blacks work primarily within their own communities to build strong organizations, movements, and identities? Or should Blacks struggle primarily in alliance with sympathetic White, Mestizo, and Indigenous groups to improve their socioeconomic and political conditions? Generally, Afro-Latin Americans have pursued both strategies. Third, political context greatly shapes Black political activity in Latin America. Socialist revolution in Cuba and civil war in Colombia are two clear examples of major events and processes impacting the evolution of Black politics.

Where Are Blacks in Latin America?
Questions of Identity and Visibility

People of African ancestry represent approximately 30 percent of the more than 500 million Latin Americans (Minority Rights Group 1995; *Race Report* 2003, 1–2; Rout 1976). Most Latin American governments have not attempted to count the number of Blacks or African descendants as part of their regular censuses. This failure has created a situation of official invisibility for Blacks in many government reports, studies, and policies. Some argue that Latin American population groups have mixed so much over the years that categorizing them by race or ethnicity would be impossible or extremely difficult to do accurately. Other scholars have argued that race and ethnicity are of limited relevance in Latin America because these group identities are weak and rarely politically relevant. In contrast, Black Latin American leaders generally state that race does matter, that there is a sense of Black or Afrodescendant group identity, and that Blacks are victims of discrimination and neglect in education, employment, housing, health care, and other sectors of social life (*Alianza Estrategica*; Cowater International Inc. 1999; Hasenbalg 1986).

Blacks live in all Latin American nations, though they tend to be most visible in the Caribbean and coastal areas of Central and South America. Haiti, the Dominican Republic, Cuba, Brazil, Colombia, Panama, Venezuela, and Puerto

Rico have the largest and most visible Black populations. Ecuador, Peru, Mexico, and the other Central American countries have smaller African descendant communities. Uruguay, Argentina, Chile, Paraguay, and Bolivia generally have the smallest Black populations in Latin America (Cowater International Inc. et al 1996; Minority Rights Group 1995; *Race Report* 2003).

In *Shades of Citizenship: Race and the Census in Modern Politics* (2000), political scientist Melissa Nobles has argued persuasively that racial censuses are not neutral and objective instruments of scientific study. Rather, they are fundamentally political means by which the state classifies and categorizes its population. Although most Latin American countries have not regularly conducted racial, ethnic, or color censuses, Black activists have been encouraged by recent political developments in Brazil, Colombia, and Ecuador.

Afro-Brazilian intellectuals and organizations have advocated for inclusion and worked with the census bureau, scholars, and other groups to influence the process of census taking. Brazil stands out in Latin America in that most of its censuses since 1872 have nominally included a color question. The census currently allows individuals to identify as *Branca* (White), *Preta* (Black), *Parda* (Brown), *Amarela* (Yellow), and *Indigena* (Indigenous) or not to identify. Black Brazilian leaders consider it a victory that Afro-descendants are counted. But they generally do not endorse the division between Blacks and Browns. Most Black leaders and groups use terms like *Negros* (Blacks) and *Afro-Brasileiros* (Afro-Brazilians) to refer to Blacks and Browns or people of African ancestry.

The Colombian national government has been inconsistent and ineffective in conducting a racial census. Government and private sector estimates of the Black population vary widely. Black groups are working with the census bureau, DANE (*Departamento Administrativo Nacional de Estadistica* [National Administrative Statistics Department]) to ensure an accurate count of Afro-Colombians in the next census. This author attended public meetings in Cartagena and Bogota, Colombia, in 2003 and 2004, in which Black leaders expressed their fear that if DANE conducts the census without outside participation it will undercount Afro-Colombians. Dr. Cesar Augusto Caballero Reinoso, DANE director, acknowledged these concerns. Nevertheless, many Afro-Colombian leaders remained skeptical that DANE would discover the true Afro-descendant percentage of the Colombian population (Thorne 2003, 315).

Although the Colombian constitution of 1991 defines the nation as pluri-ethnic and multicultural, Colombia's many Black elected officials and activists have been protesting the Black population's exploitation and neglect by the state. These leaders have also been working to guarantee implementation of Law 70, which recognizes the Afro-Colombian population as an ethnic group with certain territorial, economic, political, and cultural rights. Black activists also question the effectiveness of the Office of Black Community Affairs (*Direccion de Asuntos para las Comunidades Negras*) formed in 1994 within the Interior Ministry to develop public policies to assist Black communities in attaining their full constitutional rights (DACN 1997).

The Ecuadorian constitution of 1998 defines the country as pluri-cultural and multiethnic among other characteristics. There is also specific reference to "*los*

pueblos negros o afroecuatorianos" (Black peoples or Afro-Ecuadorians) having collective rights (*Constitución Política* 2002). Although the Indigenous movements in
Colombia and Ecuador have led the campaigns for officially recognizing racial and
ethnic diversity, Black groups in both countries and throughout the region have used
these constitutions to call attention to their cultural uniqueness.

Throughout Latin America, Black politicians and social movement leaders
often invoke historical struggles against racial oppression to give a positive connotation to Black racial identity. This strategy attempts to counter the negative
image of Blackness as intrinsically related to poverty and backwardness and the
alleged political irrelevance of Blackness in societies dominated by notions of mis-
cegenation, *mestizaje*, and racial democracy. To increase their potential constituency, Afro-Latin American leaders have tended to adopt a broad and flexible
view of Black identity. These leaders have demanded that national censuses
include race or color questions to determine the national racial composition.
Moreover, Black leaders have supported efforts to define their countries as multicultural, multiethnic, and pluri-national. In addition, these leaders and activists
have developed ties with Blacks in other countries as a way of strengthening a
transnational Black identity. Together these efforts are consolidating a subnational Black identity, a national identity that includes people of African ancestry, as well as a Pan-African identity in the international sphere (*Alianza
Estrategica*; Cowater International Inc. 1999; de la Torre 2002; Nascimento and
Nascimento 1994; Moore et al 1995).

Black National Politics in Latin America

*The most intractable problem for both the state and society in the matter of Afro-
Latin Americans is how, for the first time in their collective history, to incor-
porate demands of nondominant groups into the system of governance.
(Dzidzienyo 1995, 346)*

The literature on race and politics has recently begun to address the causes and
consequences of Black political struggles in Latin America. Black Latin Americans have organized themselves, allied with other political groups and politicians,
and demanded recognition as political actors, as well as the implementation of
government initiatives to improve their living conditions. The confluence of
Black political activism, democratization, and alliances with major politicians
has led to a series of racially explicit state agencies and policies that are unprecedented in postslavery Latin American politics (Andrews 1991; Conniff and Davis
1994; Guimarães 1995).

Throughout Latin America, democratization over the last two decades has
brought about a change in the political opportunity structure for groups traditionally marginalized from power. In the 1960s and 1970s, most countries experienced some type of authoritarian rule. Military dictatorships routinely violated
the rights and liberties of the people and often cancelled and manipulated elections. Since the 1990s, most countries have made the transition to civilian rule,

and this process has increased opportunities for partisan electoral competition and popular participation.

In this more democratic environment, Black political organizations and social movements have been more successful in calling attention to the political existence of Black Latin Americans as citizens (Hanchard 1994; Wade 1997, 95–110; Walker 2001, 284–347). This is no small achievement. Activists have changed the political debate in Latin American societies in three main ways. First, they have hammered at the point that racism and racial discrimination exist. This view contradicts the popular perspective that racism does not exist in Latin America and instead is a problem unique to societies that experienced rigid racial segregation, such as the United States and South Africa. Black activists have also emphasized that Afro-Latin Americans tend to trail White Latin Americans in practically every country on the standard indicators of socioeconomic status, such as income, education, and health. Second, they have argued that because racism and racial inequality exist, it is the government's responsibility to improve the situation through institutional measures, policies, and programs. Third, Black leaders and groups have been most responsible for challenging negative scholarly and public opinion about Blacks and Blackness in Latin America (Bello and Rangel 2002; Cowater International Inc. 1999; Minority Rights Group 1995).

Blacks have been elected to executive and legislative offices throughout Latin America, but at rates well below their proportion of the population. Given this political underrepresentation and the economic marginalization of their communities, Afro-Latin American politicians and activists often support race-specific public policies. They argue that these policies are necessary to combat racial discrimination, Black subordination, and racial inequality. The public policies vary considerably by country. A brief review of several countries demonstrates this diversity.

Brazil

Brazil is the most populous country in Latin America with more than 180 million people. Forty-five percent of the population is of African ancestry. In the 1970s, Afro-Brazilian activists founded the Unified Black Movement (MNU [Movimento Negro Unificado]), the Black Cultures Research Institute (IPCN [Instituto de Pesquisas das Culturas Negras]), and other groups to protest against racial discrimination, police violence, and poverty. Blacks also participated actively in the leading labor union, community, and student groups fighting against the Brazilian military dictatorship (1964–1985). Over the last thirty-five years, many Black activists and intellectuals have formed organizations to mobilize Blacks to improve all areas of Black life. One of the most significant developments is the emergence of Black women's groups, such as the Black Women's Institute (Geledes–Instituto da Mulher Negra) and the Black Women's House of Culture (Casa de Cultura da Mulher Negra). These groups work to reduce sexism and domestic violence and advocate for human rights (Fontaine 1985a, b; Gonzalez 1985; Hanchard 1994; Reichmann 1999). Although all these groups and others continue to fight against Brazilian racism, much of the literature emphasizes their organizational and ideological weaknesses (Burdick 1995; Marx 1998; Twine 1998).

Leading Black politicians and activists, including Abdias do Nascimento, Lelia Gonzalez, Helio Santos, and Benedita da Silva, worked consistently to convince their political parties and party leaders to recognize the ongoing negative influence of racism within the country. Eventually, Nascimento and da Silva became the strongest and most visible Afro-Brazilian advocates in the Brazilian Congress. During the 1980s and 1990s, they criticized the "myth of racial democracy" within the national Chamber of Deputies and Federal Senate, and da Silva attempted to organize fellow Black elected officials and educate the nation about the specific difficulties still facing Afro-Brazilians (da Silva et al. 1997; Nascimento and Nascimento 1994). One of the problems Nascimento and da Silva faced was the underrepresentation of Blacks in Congress. In a country in which Afro-Brazilians (Blacks and Browns) make up almost 50 percent of the population, they comprise less than 5 percent of congressional representatives (Johnson 1998; Valente 1986). Continuing the efforts of Nascimento and da Silva, Deputy Luiz Alberto from Bahia and Senator Paulo Paim from Rio Grande do Sul are working with other politicians and Black movement activists to pressure political parties and the state to address more effectively the issue of race.

In the Latin American context, Black Brazilian leaders have been successful in getting government officials to acknowledge their concerns. At the state and local levels in São Paulo, Rio de Janeiro, Minas Gerais, and Rio Grande do Sul, such government agencies as the Council for Participation and Development of the Black Community (*Conselho de Participação e Desenvolvimento da Comunidade Negra*) and the Special Office for Afro-Brazilian Affairs (*Secretaria pela Promoção e Defesa Afro-Brasileira*) were created to incorporate Blacks into the policymaking process. Nationally, the Brazilian government in 1988 created the Palmares Foundation (*Fundação Cultural Palmares*), whose purpose is to work with educational, governmental, and private institutions and the public to increase awareness of Afro-Brazilian contributions to Brazilian society and culture. The foundation publishes materials by and about Afro-Brazilians and sponsors educational forums. More recently, the foundation has become involved in assisting traditional rural Black communities in gaining legal title and ownership of their communal lands. Moreover, the Fernando Henrique Cardoso presidential administration (1995–2003) created the Interministerial Working Group with representatives from all cabinet ministries to develop public policies to improve the situation of Blacks (Santos 1999). By the end of the Cardoso administration, the national government and some state governments began passing affirmative action legislation. The most controversial is the affirmative action policy in education. The state government of Rio de Janeiro and several others have adopted fixed percentages or quotas for Black public university admissions (Heringer 2002; Htun 2004).

The administration of President Luiz Inácio Lula da Silva (2003–present) has also been formally responsive to the demands of the Workers Party's Black activists and elected officials. The Lula government created the Special Office for the Promotion of Racial Equality (SEPPIR [*Secretaria Especial de Politicas de Promoção da*

Igualdade Racial]) on March 21, 2003. This unit was designed to advocate for racial equality throughout all policy areas. The head of the Special Office is Matilde Ribeiro, a Black activist from São Paulo who has been given cabinet minister status to recognize the government's commitment to pursuing pro-racial equality policies. Minister Matilde Ribeiro has had to struggle for resources to staff and structure her office. She sees her mission as one of building support within the government and the public for affirmative action and other public policies that will reduce racial inequality and improve the socioeconomic situation of Afro-Brazilians. In an interview with this author in November 2003, Minister Ribeiro stated that she has already been successful in working with the ministries of Education, Health, and Culture. A lack of resources to fully implement its agenda represents the main challenge for Minister Ribeiro's Special Office.

In an unprecedented move, President Lula appointed three additional Afro-Brazilians, Marina Silva (Environment), Gilberto Gil (Culture), and Benedita da Silva (Social Welfare), to cabinet minister positions. Despite her close relations with President Lula, da Silva was forced to resign early in Lula's administration because of her questionable use of public funds for personal travel. It is unclear whether other cabinet ministers, agency heads, and thousands of government workers fully embraced the government's policies of reducing racial inequality and Black poverty while giving Blacks more educational and employment opportunities. To what degree did government officials support, resist, or ignore Minister Ribeiro's efforts? New research is necessary to answer this question.

Ecuador

Ecuador is politically unstable and economically vulnerable. A large percentage of its population of 13 million is poor and lacks access to quality education and employment. At 5 percent of the national population, Afro-Ecuadorians are virtually absent from the country's political and economic elite. For many years, leftist Jaime Hurtado was the most visible Afro-Ecuadorian politician. Hurtado was assassinated on February 17, 1999, in Quito near the national Congress building. Hurtado's political party, the Democratic Popular Movement (MPD [*Movimiento Popular Democratico*]), a leftist party that doesn't prioritize racism generally has been successful in the majority Black province of Esmeraldas. Rafael Erazo, an outspoken leader of Hurtado's party from Esmeraldas, is a first-term member and the only Black deputy in Congress.

In Ecuador, there has been less governmental attention paid to the concerns of Black political groups than in Brazil and Colombia. However, the powerful Indigenous social movement has forced the Ecuadorian government to create a range of policies and agencies for that population. PRODEPINE (*Programa de Desarrollo de los Pueblos Indigenas y Negros del Ecuador*) is a foundation that has distributed government funds to Indigenous and Black communities for diverse development projects. The Afro-Ecuadorian Development Corporation, a government agency, has recently begun operation. It has a mandate to develop policies and programs to improve the living conditions of Blacks. Moreover, there have been specific government initiatives in the cities of Esmeraldas and Quito directed toward the Black population (de la Torre 2002).

Cuba

Cuba is a crucial case for examining the role of Blacks in Latin American politics. The Cuban Revolution of 1959 brought Fidel Castro and his brother Raul Castro to power, where they remain almost 50 years later. This Caribbean socialist revolution transformed social relations, political institutions, and culture. The revolutionaries created a more egalitarian society with an emphasis on free education and health care, and a comprehensive social welfare state. On its own terms, the revolution endures despite the counter-revolutionary activities of the U.S. government and the Cuban exile community concentrated in southern Florida. As the poorest segment of the country, Blacks have benefited from the revolutionary government's policies (De la Fuente 2001; McGarrity and Cardenas 1995; Perez Sarduy and Stubbs 1993; 2000).

The demise of the Eastern European socialist regimes and the Soviet Union devastated the Cuban economy. Cuban trade with and aid from these governments declined dramatically in the 1990s and forced President Castro to declare a "Special Period" of sacrifice. In response, the Cuban government opened the country to foreign investment, promoted tourism, and allowed Cubans to open small businesses. Despite tremendous pain and suffering resulting from the economic crisis and decreased governmental support in the areas of health and social services, the government survived when some commentators thought it would not (Centeno and Font 1997; Oppenheimer 1992). However, Afro-Cubans experienced a new level of racism as they were discriminated against in the revitalized tourist industry. They also had fewer relatives abroad to send them cash remittances (De la Fuente 1998, 2001). This reality created new tensions in race relations and necessitates a review of the Cuban Revolution's impact on Blacks, despite the assertions of the government and its supporters of its positive characteristics.

This author spoke with various Cuban diplomats from the Cuban Interests Section in Washington, DC, during the 1990s and with Cuban government and Communist party officials in Havana, Cuba, in January 2000. These representatives highlighted the brutality of the old Batista regime and the social progress of the revolution. For example, Felix Wilson, Afro-Cuban diplomat and then First Secretary of the Cuban Interests Section in Washington, DC, lectured at the University of Maryland, College Park, in September 1997, emphasizing the improvement in literacy and life expectancy and the decline in infant mortality and racial and gender discrimination between 1959 and 1997. He also pointed out that in 1997 there were five Black government ministers and several Black ambassadors and that Afro-Cubans were one-third of the parliament. In the face of ongoing hostility from the most powerful government in the world, Wilson offered a strong defense of the revolution in terms of human development and Black progress.

Not all Afro-Cubans have such a positive evaluation. Carlos Moore, a promi-
nent ethnographer, has offered the most sustained critique of the Cuban Revolution from an Afro-Cuban perspective. Moore, an initial supporter of the
Revolution, had an early falling out with the new government and has since conceptualized Fidel Castro and the Revolution as perpetuators of White supremacy.
He argues that Castro, his brother Raul Castro, and most political leaders are
White and have refused to allow an open national discussion of race in Cuba.
Moore acknowledges that the government's commitment to national integration
appealed to all Cubans, especially Black Cubans, but maintains that the government's closing of all independent organizations and its failure to allow organized
dissent prohibits Blacks from fully protesting racial discrimination and creating
groups to promote their collective cultural and political interests (Moore 1989;
1995, 199–239).

Few have studied the evolution of Cuba's racial question in the depth and
nuance of Cuban scholar Alejandro de la Fuente (2001). One of his main points
is that too many scholars have examined Cuban and Latin American race relations through North American eyes. De la Fuente argues that this has led to mis-
understandings of Latin American racial discourse and dynamics. He calls for
renewed attention to the concept of racial democracy. He argues that White
Cubans have tended to accept this idea as descriptive and have used it to prevent a full debate on Cuba's racial reality. On the other hand, Afro-Cubans have
more often embraced racial democracy as an ideal or goal to be achieved. These
divergent interpretations have led to Cubans generally embracing independence
hero José Martí's formulation of Cuban identity as "more than mulatto, black, or
white" but differing substantially over the meaning of that identity.

De la Fuente has argued that Cubans have often worked together across racial
and class lines in the army, political parties, labor movements, and other areas.
His defense of the Cuban myth of racial democracy and other "Latin American
paradigms of racially mixed, integrated nations" highlights the positive characteristics of these ideologies in restraining racist elite behavior, providing an inclusive and participatory vision of the nation, and criticizing the brutal segregationist
and White supremacist patterns of race relations in the United States. Moreover,
these ideologies provided a stronger basis for Black social mobility and political
leadership in Latin America than is found in the United States. De la Fuente
maintains that scholars, especially those using the North American model, have
assumed incorrectly "that blacks should mobilize separately and that racially based
political mobilization is the legitimate—perhaps even only—way to fight racism
effectively" (2001, 9). He concludes by noting that, because formal racial segregation was not the norm in postslavery Latin America, Afro-Latin American
political participation and social action usually assumed nonracial forms.

De la Fuente's analysis tends to minimize the negative aspects of Latin American myths of racial democracy. These myths often serve to cover up and defend
manifestations of racism. The 1912 massacre of Afro-Cubans in the name of
defending the nation against racist Blacks is an important case in point (Helg
1995). The fact that Brazilian, Venezuelan, Cuban, and other Latin American

officials have condemned acts of racial discrimination and their governments have passed laws banning such discrimination means little if political leaders then fail to actively fight against racial prejudice and enforce antidiscrimination laws. Finally, myths of racial democracy are usually actively hostile to independent Black political organization. Black Latin American activists and intellectuals, such as Brazilian Abdias do Nascimento, Venezuelan Jesús "Chucho" García, Colombian Juan de Dios Mosquera, and Cuban Carlos Moore, have consistently made this point.

Summary of Black National Politics in Latin America

Major obstacles remain to the development of Black politics in Latin America and public policies that address specific Black concerns. Despite the formal transition to democracy in most Latin American countries, political instability, violence, and poverty have led to ongoing human rights violations and limited opportunities for Blacks and other groups to participate in politics. For example, Colombia continues to suffer from civil war, and Ecuador has experienced major government instability in recent years. As Latin America's largest country, Brazil has achieved political and economic stability, but at a tremendous cost. Socioeconomic and racial inequality, crime, and violence are widespread in Brazil's urban centers and rural areas. In addition, there remains the widespread political and social belief that Latin Americans have transcended race. This idea delegitimizes race-specific initiatives to overcome Black poverty and racial inequality.

Black political activists continue to overcome obstacles in their struggle to improve Afro-Latin American living conditions. They work in political parties, labor unions, community groups, professional associations, and their own Black movement organizations. Slowly, they are gaining more visibility in public debates and the mass media. Some Afro-Latin American activists have drawn on earlier Pan-African experiences and recent Indigenous campaigns to internationalize their struggle by establishing relationships with each other across borders and taking their concerns to major international financial and government institutions.

Black Transnational Politics

Afro-Latin American Conferences and Meetings

> Perhaps the most important contemporary phenomenon in the African world is the emergence and re-assertion of the African people of South and Central America within the context of Pan-Africanism. (Nascimento 1980, 1)

During the last thirty years, leading Afro-Latin American activists and intellectuals have organized across national borders and worked continuously to unify their forces and overcome various obstacles. These leaders have succeeded in meeting regularly, exchanging information, outlining common problems, and proposing solutions. However, they have not been able to implement many of their proposals. Still, the totality of their efforts has created a transnational advocacy network committed to working to improve the situation of Blacks in the Americas.

The network began in the 1970s and has gone through several phases. The key events in the creation of this network were the four Congresses of Black Culture in the Americas. They were held in Cali, Colombia (August 1977); Panama City, Panama (March 1980); São Paulo, Brazil (August 1982); and Quito, Ecuador (1984). The outstanding achievement of the Congresses was the recognition that Blacks had to unite across national boundaries to affirm their culture and identity as people of African ancestry. Scholars and activists presented papers and offered analyses on diverse aspects of Black life in the Americas. Hundreds of Blacks from many countries in the Americas and several representatives from African countries participated in each Congress along with non-Black activists and scholars. The lead organizer of each Congress was a citizen of the host country. The first three host leaders were Colombian Manuel Zapata Olivella, Panamanian Gerardo Maloney, and Brazilian Abdias do Nascimento (*AfroDiaspora* no. 1, 3, 4, 1983–1984; Davis 1995b; Nascimento 1980; *Primer Congreso* 1988).

The Congresses evolved over time in substance and form, maintaining the organizational structure of dividing into working groups and having all delegates approve resolutions and recommendations in the concluding sessions. Although the working groups varied, together they debated the central cultural, socioeconomic, and political issues facing Blacks in the Americas. The Congresses approved resolutions condemning racism, racial discrimination, and White supremacy. More important, they asked individual participants and their organizations to do everything possible to improve the Black condition.

Congress leaders considered each gathering to be successful and created an organizational structure to continue the work, which nonetheless was not maintained for various reasons. First, the leadership of the host government was supposed to assume primary responsibility for the meeting arrangements. In Brazil, Don Rojas of Grenada agreed to host the fourth Congress. However, before it could be held, the Grenadian Revolutionary Government of Maurice Bishop was overthrown and the U.S. government invaded and occupied the country. This U.S. intervention interrupted activities of the Congress and required that it be moved to a new location, Ecuador. The main problem leading to the demise of the Congress was an inability to raise sufficient funds from Black individuals and groups, thereby creating a dependency on outside governmental and civic institutions, such as the Organization of American States. Abdias do Nascimento described in depth his difficulties in getting financial support for the 3rd Congress in Brazil (*Afrodiaspora* 1983, 42, 71–82).

Nevertheless, the Congresses of Black Culture in the Americas represented a tremendous achievement. For the first time Black leaders from throughout the Americas united to discuss problems and propose solutions to the serious challenges facing Blacks in the hemisphere. Congress participants were usually already activists and leaders in their respective countries, but the debates, discussions, and activities helped them educate each other about their collective reality. Many participants continued their work in their home countries, realizing the importance of maintaining ties with their brothers and sisters throughout the Americas.

After the last Congress was held, numerous meetings and gatherings throughout the Americas have emphasized various aspects of Black life. Perhaps most important was the First Seminar on Racism and Xenophobia held in Montevideo, Uruguay, on December 8–10, 1994. This meeting was hosted by *Mundo Afro*, a prominent Afro-Uruguayan organization. Participants divided themselves into five major commissions and agreed that a permanent network of organizations and activists would be necessary to maximize their effectiveness. Although *Mundo Afro* would maintain a coordinating role, the network was divided into geopolitical regions: North America, the Caribbean and Central America, and South America (*Alianza estrategica*; Davis 1995b, 364–69).

Black legislators from Latin America organized three unprecedented meetings that laid the foundation for a new Black transnational network. On November 21–23, 2003, in Brasília, Brazil, on May 19–21, 2004 in Bogota, Colombia, and on August 28–31, 2005 in San José, Costa Rica, Black elected officials from the Caribbean and Latin America met to examine the situation of Afro-descendants in the Americas. The deputies, representatives, and senators agreed that Black people in different countries often face similar hardships. They decided to continue meeting and discussing how they as elected officials can best work to improve the living conditions of their people. They summarized and distributed their views in two documents: *Carta de Brasília* and *Carta de Bogota*.

Afro-Brazilian–African American Network

A key component of the internationalization of Afro-Latin American politics involved U.S.-based institutions. Over the past twenty-five years, African Americans have made numerous efforts to improve their relationship with Afro-Brazilians, working through the U.S. government, nongovernmental organizations, political organizations, and individual contacts. As a result, there is currently an informal network of African Americans who travel regularly to Brazil; host Black Brazilians when they visit the United States; teach African Brazilian history, culture, and politics at the university and community levels; and in general advocate strengthening pan-African ties between the two largest groups of the African diaspora. Other Americans interested in racial issues have also contributed to and are part of this network in key ways.

This section illuminates the immediate history, recent development, and current status of this network by focusing on key events, organizations, individuals, and activities in the 1970s, 1980s, and 1990s. Clearly, there has been much controversy, conflict, and relationship-building over the years. However, as a result of numerous factors, African Americans and African Brazilian leaders have not yet been able to build the formal and lasting organizational ties that they desire.

The 1970s
In the early 1970s, Afro-Brazilians were suffering with the rest of the country under the most repressive period (1968–1973) of the twenty-one years of military authoritarian rule (1964–1985). Leading Black political activists like Abdias do Nascimento were severely constrained in their work, and some radical Black leaders

such as Joel Rufino were tortured. Nascimento eventually went into exile, and Rufino and others spent time in prison. In general, publicly discussing racism in Brazil, attempting to organize Blacks for political action, and drawing inspiration from the racial struggles of Blacks around the world were considered subversive activities (Hanchard 1994; Nascimento and Nascimento 1994).

In contrast to the Nixon administration's support of the brutal Médici administration, some U.S.-based institutions working in Brazil were not supportive of authoritarian rule. Two in particular played important roles in assisting Brazilian Blacks. The Ford Foundation and the Inter-American Foundation (IAF) established a presence in Brazil in the early 1960s and early 1970s, respectively, and since then have made numerous grants to Afro-Brazilian political organizations and individuals. The IAF was created in 1969 as an independent agency of the U.S. government to provide development assistance to organizations active in Latin America and the Caribbean. The Ford Foundation is a private philanthropic foundation created in 1936 and has had a worldwide mission to improve human welfare.

Although the IAF had been funding diverse groups throughout Brazil since the early 1970s, it made a grant on February 4, 1977, that would have serious consequences. On that day, the IAF gave $82,000 to the Research Institute of Black Cultures (IPCN [*Instituto de Pesquisas das Culturas Negras*]) to buy office space and support various community outreach programs. IPCN was a leading Black political organization founded in 1975 to raise Black consciousness and organize and mobilize Blacks against racial discrimination. In an interview with this author on September 15, 1997, Carlos Medeiros revealed that IPCN founders emphasized academic and cultural concerns to prevent drawing unwanted attention from the military government and its repressive intelligence agencies to their political activities. Nonetheless, the government did take notice of the grant and protested to the IAF. The IAF refused to rescind the award and was asked by the Brazilian government to leave the country. In 1978, the IAF did so and suspended its operations in Brazil for five years, until 1983.

The conflict between the IAF and the Brazilian government coincided with President Jimmy Carter's criticism of military dictatorships in Latin America and their long record of human rights violations. The Brazilian military president, Ernesto Geisel, did not appreciate Carter's blunt remarks and considered them attacks on Brazilian sovereignty. Diplomatic relations improved enough for the IAF to return only after Ronald Reagan came to power in the United States and General João Figueiredo became Brazil's president. On its return, the IAF initially made fewer grants to Black political groups in Brazil.

As a result of the IAF grant, IPCN was able to purchase a building in the Lapa neighborhood near downtown Rio de Janeiro. IPCN remains one of the few Black Brazilian groups to own its meeting space. The organization developed an extensive program of activities related to the racial question in Brazil. IPCN held numerous meetings, educational classes, lectures, and cultural events and was a hub of Black movement activities in the late 1970s and throughout the 1980s. In addition, the IPCN office became an obligatory stop for African Americans with an interest in race and politics. In the author's interview with Carlos

Medeiros, he noted that some of the personal and political relationships between Black Brazilians and Black Americans developed through IPCN in the 1970s and 1980s still continue today.

The 1980s

The Ford Foundation opened its Brazil office in Rio de Janeiro in 1961 and has maintained an uninterrupted presence in the country since then (Brooke and Witoshynsky 2002). As did the IAF, the Ford Foundation awarded money to various Black intellectuals and activists in the 1970s, 1980s, and 1990s. In the last few years, Ford has given millions of dollars to Afro-Brazilian groups, including the Black Women's Institute (Geledes–*Instituto da Mulher Negra*) for its innovative and respected legal and educational programs. The Casa Dandara National Association received $30,000 for an international conference on African Brazilian rights and citizenship. Geledes and Casa Dandara are led by African Brazilians Sueli Carneiro and Diva Moreira, respectively. These Black women have visited various cities in the United States and met with African American intellectuals and activists, such as Professor Ronald Walters and Gisele Mills.

The Ford Foundation's generous funding of Afro-Brazilian scholarship and community activism can be traced to its generally liberal and racially tolerant mission and to two important Black American program officers in Rio de Janeiro, Michael J. Turner and Patricia Sellers, in the early 1980s (Brooke and Witoshynsky 2002, 426). Before joining the Ford Foundation, Turner was a scholar on Brazil and professor of African and Latin American history from New York, and Sellers was a criminal defense lawyer and activist from Philadelphia. Turner and Sellers recommended the generous funding of Afro-Brazilian scholarship and community activism. The foundation provided significant grants to one of the leading Brazilian academic units on race relations and the situation of Blacks, the Center of Afro-Asian Studies (*Centro de Estudos Afro-Asiáticos*), based at Candido Mendes University in Rio de Janeiro. During the tenure of Turner and Sellers, the Ford Foundation also funded numerous community and economic development programs in shantytowns and other low-income areas.

While working as Ford program officers, Turner and Sellers developed an extensive range of Afro-Brazilian contacts. In numerous formal and informal settings, these African Americans described and discussed the situation of Blacks in the United States with Afro-Brazilian leaders, students, and professionals. A tremendous cross-fertilization and exchange of ideas, experiences, and future plans occurred. African Brazilians became connected indirectly to the Black U.S. experience. Afro-Brazilians who wanted to visit the United States often received advice and contacts from Turner and Sellers. Similarly, the two were visited in Brazil by their family and friends from the United States, who would then be introduced to African Brazilians.[2]

In the 1980s, political events occurred in the United States that had repercussions in Afro-Brazil. In 1984 and 1988, the Reverend Jesse Jackson campaigned for the Democratic Party's nomination for president. In his campaigns, Rev. Jackson questioned the elitist and Eurocentric aspects of U.S. foreign policy. He called for more attention to Africa and the Caribbean, better relations with Fidel

Castro's Cuba, and more Black participation in international affairs (Stanford 1997). Jackson's rescue missions to the Middle East and other regions, as well as his dramatic campaign and speaking style, caught the attention of African Brazilian leaders. Jackson's strong campaigns for one of the most important political positions in the world inspired several Black Brazilians to greater political activism (da Silva et al, 1997, 134–36).

Brazilian military rule ended in 1985. One of the important results of this transition has been the election of more Black members to the national Congress. Several of these politicians have an interest in learning from the Black American political experience and developing ties between African Brazilians and African Americans. Abdias do Nascimento is a key figure for understanding relations between Blacks in Brazil and the United States. Nascimento lived part of his exile in the United States, where he met with a broad spectrum of the African American community: artists, professionals, Black Panthers, intellectuals, members of Congress, and students. Nascimento always respected and admired the level of organization and political activity in the U.S. Black community. At the same time, he found that African Americans had little knowledge of, but great interest in, the situation of Blacks in Brazil. Consequently, he has consistently devoted significant time to educating African Americans on the racial situation in Brazil. In 1980 and 1983, Nascimento spoke to members of the Congressional Black Caucus. In his speeches, he shocked American audiences by describing the reality of Afro-Brazilians as more oppressive than that of American Blacks. He invited U.S. Blacks to visit Brazil and witness this racial oppression for themselves (Nascimento and Nascimento 1994, 49–53, 56–57).

The 1990s
Several times during the decade, politician Benedita da Silva and a group of Black Brazilian leaders visited the United States and met with Congressional Black Caucus members and other Black leaders. Appalled by their lack of knowledge about Brazil in general and Afro-Brazil in particular, the Brazilians commissioned an English-language video on Blacks in Brazil for U.S. audiences. This excellent documentary, *Images of the Heart*, was made by Afro-Brazilian filmmaker Joel Zito Araújo in 1995. Furthermore, these Afro-Brazilian leaders created *VisBrasil* (*Centro AfroBrasileiro de Informação, Cooperação, e Capacitação* [Afro-Brazilian Center for Information, Cooperation and Training]). Based in Rio de Janeiro, this organization was formed to increase the visibility of Brazilian Blacks who were notoriously underrepresented in Brazilian mass media and usually stereotyped when they were presented.

VisBrasil illustrates well the dilemma of many Black groups. Regina Domingues and Judith Rosario, Afro-Brazilian researchers and activists, were chosen to run the Rio de Janeiro office along with a very small support staff. Domingues and Rosario were in the process of establishing the office and collecting demographic data on the Afro-Brazilian population when they faced serious financial difficulties. They both worked other full-time jobs and were unable to secure sufficient funds from the sponsoring individuals and groups or to raise adequate funds from other sources. Although *VisBrasil* had the backing of da Silva, João Jorge (leader of *Olodum*, a popular Black cultural group in Bahia), and many notable Black political and cultural figures, it folded after less than two years because of a lack of financial resources and a clear plan of action.

In the 1990s, three national African American figures visited Brazil and met with top African Brazilians. Lee Brown, drug czar of the first Clinton administration, traveled to Brazil to discuss the country's increasing use as a shipment point for drugs on their way to the U.S. market. Commerce Secretary Ron Brown also visited Brazil in an official capacity to discuss commercial relations between the two countries. He also visited a *favela* (shantytown) and met with Black Brazilian political figures. Finally, in an interview with this author, former member of Congress Adalberto Camargo explained that Jesse Jackson visited Brazil and met with a broad range of Black politicians and activists, primarily to engage in dialogue about problems shared with African Americans.

African American Political Exiles in Cuba

For the last forty years, prominent Black progressives, radicals and revolutionaries from the United States have visited or moved to Cuba. Some have gone out of curiosity. Others have gone out of solidarity. Still others have gone out of necessity. Fidel Castro and his government have consistently encouraged African Americans to visit (Reitan 2001; Tyson 1999; Brock and Castañeda Fuertes 1998). Some African Americans, and Americans in general, continue to visit Cuba despite the recent measures to restrict travel and limit relations between the American and Cuban peoples.

The Cuban Revolution triumphed at a critical time in American history. Formal, explicit White supremacist segregation in the United States had been declared illegal by the Supreme Court's *Brown v. Board of Education* decision in 1954. However, because many White Americans in the South disagreed with this decision, widespread segregation and brutal racial oppression still existed in the late 1950s and throughout the 1960s. Robert Williams was one of the most dynamic grassroots leaders fighting against White racism. Forced from his leadership position in the NAACP because of his outspoken activism and embrace of armed self-defense in Monroe, North Carolina, Williams argued vigorously that Blacks should defend themselves against White terrorism and violence. He had expressed early interest in the Cuban Revolution, visited Cuba, and met Fidel Castro. Williams was impressed with Castro's denunciation of racial discrimination. Williams also perceived that Afro-Cubans were supportive of the revolution (Tyson 1999, 220–43).

In the United States, Williams continued to denounce racism and segregation as illegal and un-American. He traveled throughout the country speaking and organizing against White terrorism. Williams, believing that segregationists in Monroe would unite with White racists in the state and national government to kill him and his family, left the country through Canada and eventually settled in Havana in October 1961. Castro and the Cuban government treated him as a fellow revolutionary fighting for freedom. Initially, the Cuban government assisted Williams in producing "Radio Free Dixie," a progressive radio program broadcast to the United States. Radio Free Dixie combined music and commentary to criticize American racism and encourage Black Americans to fight against it (Tyson 1999, 287–92).

After four years in Cuba, Williams and his family left Cuba for China in 1965 for two main reasons. First, never one to engage in self-censorship, Williams had spoken out publicly on the lack of racial diversity among Cuban leadership. This commentary was unwelcome. As Carlos Moore has noted, the revolutionary Cuban government has never allowed a full, open, and democratic debate on the role of Blacks in Cuban society and government. Second, after the U.S.-government-sponsored Bay of Pigs invasion in 1961, the Cuban government was becoming increasingly concerned about its national security. More violent intervention was a definite possibility. Cuban leaders felt that allowing Williams to continue to antagonize its big neighbor to the north might hasten more violent intervention. Consequently, Williams's ability to speak his mind about what was happening in the United States and Cuba became increasingly limited (Reitan 2001; Tyson 1999, 292–94).

After the departure of Williams, other Black American leaders received political asylum in Cuba. Black Panther leader Eldridge Cleaver arrived in Cuba in December 1968, hoping to train Black American militants in guerrilla warfare in preparation for waging revolution in the United States. However, by that time, the Cuban situation had become even more restrictive. Airplane hijackers from the United States had forced the Cuban government to become extremely cautious because it was uncertain whether the hijackers were legitimate revolutionaries or U.S. government spies. Cleaver also left Cuba unsatisfied (Reitan 2001, 172–73).

William Lee Brent, a former Black Panther, hijacked an American plane to Cuba in June 1969. After spending almost two years in a Cuban jail, Brent was granted political asylum and remains in Cuba today (Brent 1996). Brent was one of the first African American activists who fled to Cuba beginning in the late 1960s to avoid legal charges related to their political activism in the United States. He was followed by Black Panther Party cofounder Huey P. Newton, who lived in exile in Cuba from 1974 to 1977. Former Black Panther and Black Liberation Army soldier Assata Shakur arrived in Cuba in 1986. Nehanda Abiodun, a grassroots Black nationalist from New York, also fled the U.S. and lives in exile in Cuba. These activists have been supported by the Cuban government. Some like Huey P. Newton returned to face their charges. Others like Brent, Shakur, and Abiodun have refused to return to the United States and have experienced the triumphs and tragedies of Cuban socialism (Brent 1996; http://www.afrocubaweb.com).

Conclusion: Black Politics in the Americas

Despite their significant presence throughout Latin America, Blacks have not had much power and influence on government policies. However, since the 1970s, Afro-Latin Americans have renewed their historic struggle for political inclusion and social justice. Their efforts have been partially successful. Latin American leaders and the general public are more aware that Blacks exist as political actors and that racial discrimination and inequality are problems that cannot be reduced to poverty and social inequality. Throughout the region, governments have passed and begun to implement race-specific policies and initiatives that respond to Afro-Latin American demands.

Afro-Latin American leaders, activists, and intellectuals have protested continuing racial discrimination, pervasive poverty and hardship, and the lack of governmental attention to their specific problems. These activities have contributed to projects that illustrate both the successes and the challenges facing Blacks. In 2000, international development agencies and private groups (largely based in the United States) founded the Inter-Agency Consultation on Race in Latin America (IAC). The IAC is an effort to coordinate the activities of important institutions in addressing the concerns of Afro-Latin American groups. The first director of the IAC and the Inter-American Dialogue (IAD) Race Program was Afro-Brazilian scholar and activist, Luiz Claudio Barcelos. For four years, Barcelos was based in IAD's office in Washington, DC, working with representatives from international governmental organizations, Latin American governments, the U.S. government, Black activist groups, and scholars (*Race Report* 2003). Barcelos helped organize the meetings of Black elected officials in Brazil in 2003 and Colombia in 2004. He also worked with Afro-Costa Rican leader Epsy Campbell in her capacity as an elected official and as a leader of the Afro-Caribbean and Afro-Latin American Women's Network (*La Red de Mujeres Afrocaribeñas y Afrolatinoamericanas*). The Network has given Black women a forum to organize against racism and sexism (Campbell Barr and Careaga 2002).

Judith Morrison became the new executive director of the IAC in 2004. An African American scholar, activist, and management/foundation executive, Morrison has continued and expanded the IAC's work. She has traveled throughout the United States and Latin America lecturing on the situation of Afro-Latin Americans, organizing visits and exchanges among Black leaders, and encouraging governments and other institutions to do more to reduce poverty, racial discrimination, and racial inequality.

The activities of Judith Morrison and the IAC, Epsy Campbell and the Black women's network, and Black politicians from Latin America are among the many initiatives that demonstrate the urgent need for political scientists to document and analyze contemporary Black politics in Latin America. At the local, national, and international levels, Afro-Latin Americans are continuing their struggle against racial oppression. One aspect of that struggle is convincing non-Blacks that formal and informal racial discrimination is wrong. Finally, there is the unfinished task of building strong political, cultural, financial, and social organizations and institutions to defend Black interests. Mapping the main trends of Afro-Latin American political activity and researching the most important Black political leaders and organizations are jobs that have only just begun.

Notes

1. I would like to thank Lori S. Robinson for extensive comments and Kelli Morgan for research assistance. The Race and Democracy in the Americas research group within the National Conference of Black Political Scientists (NCOBPS) provided and continues to offer stimulating debate on the issues discussed in this chapter. Some of the ideas and formulations in this chapter were presented at Arizona State University at the Consortium on Qualitative Research Methods (CQRM) in January 2003 and received constructive criticism from several participants. The anonymous reviewers for Temple University Press also offered important suggestions for revisions.

2. In addition to research on the Ford Foundation at the Library of Congress in Washington, DC, the author lived in Rio de Janeiro, Brazil for extended periods in the 1980s and 1990s, and observed and participated in various activities organized by Turner and Sellers.

References

Afrodiaspora 1, no. 1 (January–April 1983).

Afrodiaspora 2, no. 3 (October 1983–January 1984).

Afrodiaspora 2, no. 4 (1984).

Alianza estrategica Afrolatinoamerica y Caribena 1a and 2a Etapa. Montevideo, Uruguay: Organizaciones Mundo Afro.

Aliança estrategica Afrolatinoamericanos e Caribenhos 2000–2002. Montevideo, Uruguay: Organizaciones Mundo Afro. [Portuguese version of *1a Etapa*]

Andrews, George Reid. 1991. *Blacks and whites in São Paulo, Brazil, 1888–1988*. Madison: University of Wisconsin Press.

———. 2004. *Afro-Latin America, 1800–2000*. New York: Oxford University Press.

Appelbaum, Nancy P., Anne S. Macpherson, and Karin Alejandra Rosenblatt, eds. 2003. *Race and nation in modern Latin America*. Chapel Hill: University of North Carolina Press.

Bello, Alvaro, and Marta Rangel. 2002. La equidad y la exclusión de los pueblos indígenas y afrodescendientes en America Latina y el Caribe, *Revista de la CEPAL* 76 (April): 39–54..

Brent, William Lee. 1996. *Long time gone: A Black Panther's true-life story of his hijacking and twenty-five years in Cuba*. New York: Times.

Brock, Lisa, and Digna Castañeda Fuertes. 1998. *Between race and empire: African Americans and Cubans before the Cuban Revolution*. Philadelphia: Temple University Press.

Brooke, Nigel, and Mary Witoshynsky, eds. 2002. Os 40 anos da Fundação Ford no Brasil: Uma parceria para a mudança social. In *The Ford Foundation's 40 years in Brazil: A partnership for social change*. São Paulo: Editora da Universidade de São Paulo.

Burdick, John. 1995. Brazil's black consciousness movement. In *Fighting for the soul of Brazil*, by John Burdick, 174–83. New York: Monthly Review Press.

Campbell Barr, Epsy, and Gloria Careaga, eds. 2002. *Poderes cuestionados: Sexismo y racismo en América Latina*. San José: Diseno Editorial.

Castañeda, Jorge G. 1993. *Utopia unarmed: The Latin American left after the cold war*. New York: Alfred A. Knopf.

Centeno, Miguel Angel, and Mauricio Font. 1997. *Toward a new Cuba? Legacies of a revolution*. Boulder, CO: Lynne Rienner.

Conniff, Michael L., and Thomas J. Davis. 1994. *Africans in the Americas: A history of the black Diaspora*. New York: St. Martin's.

Constitución política de la República del Ecuador: Comentarios, legislación conexa, concordancias, Índice Temático. 2002. Quito: Corporacion de Estudios y Publicaciones.

Cowater International, Inc., ed. 1999. *Forum proceedings on poverty alleviation for minority communities in Latin America: Communities of African ancestry*. Washington, DC: Inter-American Development Bank.

Cowater International, Inc., Margarita Sanchez, and Michael J. Franklin. 1996. *Communities of African ancestry in Costa Rica, Honduras, Nicaragua, Argentina, Colombia, Ecuador, Peru, Uruguay, Venezuela*. Washington, DC: Inter-American Development Bank.

da Silva, Benedita, Medea Benjamín, and Maisa Mendonca. 1997. *Benedita da Silva: An Afro-Brazilian woman's story of politics and love.* Oakland, CA: Institute for Food and Development Policy.

Davis, Darien J., ed. 1995a. *Slavery and beyond: The African impact on Latin America and the Caribbean.* Wilmington, DE: Scholarly Resources.

————. 1995b. Postscript to *No longer invisible: Afro-Latin Americans today.* London: Minority Rights Publications.

De la Fuente, Alejandro. 1998. *Recreating racism: Race and discrimination in Cuba's "Special Period."* Georgetown University: Cuba Briefing Paper series, no. 18, July.

————. 2001. *A nation for all: Race, inequality, and politics in twentieth-century Cuba.* Chapel Hill: University of North Carolina Press.

De la Torre Espinosa, Carlos. 2002. *Afroquiteños: Ciudadanía y racismo.* Quito: Centro Andino de Acción Popular.

Dirección de Asuntos para las Comunidades Negras (DACN). 1997. *Visión, gestión y proyección de la Dirección de Asuntos para las Comunidades Negras–DACN.* Santa Fe de Bogotá: Oficina Asesora de Publicaciones–Ministerio del Interior.

Dzidzienyo, Anani. 1995. Conclusion to *No longer invisible: Afro-Latin Americans today.* London: Minority Rights Publications.

Fontaine, Pierre-Michel. 1980. Research in the political economy of Afro-Latin America. *Latin American Research Review* 15, no. 2:111–41.

————, ed. 1985a. *Race, class, and power in Brazil.* Los Angeles: Center for Afro-American Studies.

————. 1985b. Blacks and the search for power in Brazil. In *Race, class and power in Brazil,* ed. Pierre Michel Fontaine, 56–72. Los Angeles: Center for Afro-American Studies.

Gonzalez, Lélia. 1985. The Unified Black Movement: A new stage in black political mobilization. In *Race, class and power in Brazil,* ed. Pierre Michel Fontaine, 120–34. Los Angeles: Center for Afro-American Studies.

Guimarães, Antonio Sergio Alfredo. 1995. Raça, racismo e grupos de cor no Brasil. *Estudos Afro-Asiáticos* 27 (April): 45–63.

Hanchard, Michael George. 1994. *Orpheus and power: The Movimento Negro of Rio de Janeiro and São Paulo, Brazil, 1945–1988.* Princeton, NJ: Princeton University Press.

Hasenbalg, Carlos. 1986. Racial inequalities in Brazil and throughout Latin America: Timid responses to disguised racism. In *Constructing democracy: Human rights, citizenship, and society in Latin America,* ed. Elizabeth Jelin and Eric Hershberg, 161–75. Boulder, CO: Westview.

Helg, Aline. 1995. *Our rightful share: The Afro-Cuban struggle for equality, 1886–1912.* Chapel Hill: University of North Carolina Press.

Heringer, Rosana. 2002. Ação afirmativa, estrategias pos-Durban. In *Observatorio da Cidadania.* Rio de Janeiro: Ibase.

Htun, Mala. 2004. From "racial democracy" to affirmative action: Changing state policy on race in Brazil. *Latin American Research Review* 39, no. 1:60–89.

Johnson, Ollie A., III. 1998. Racial representation and Brazilian politics: Black members of the National Congress, 1983–1999. *Journal of Interamerican Studies and World Affairs* 40, no. 4 (Winter): 97–118.

Marx, Anthony. 1998. *Making race and nation: A comparison of the United States, South Africa, and Brazil.* New York: Cambridge University Press.

McGarrity, Gayle, and Osvaldo Cardenas. 1995. Cuba. In *No longer invisible: Afro-Latin Americans today.* London: Minority Rights Publications.

Minority Rights Group, ed. 1995. *No longer invisible: Afro-Latin Americans today.* London: Minority Rights Publications.

Moore, Carlos. 1989. *Castro, the blacks and Africa.* Los Angeles: Center for African American Studies, University of California Los Angeles.

————. 1995. Afro-Cubans and the communist revolution. In *African presence in the Americas.* Trenton, NJ: Africa World Press.

Moore, Carlos, Tanya R. Sanders, and Shawna Moore, eds. 1995. *African presence in the Americas.* Trenton, NJ: Africa World Press.

Mosquera, Juan de Dios. 2000. *Las comunidades negras de Colombia hacia el siglo XXI: Historia, realidad y organizacion.* Bogota: Docentes Editores.

Nascimento, Abdias do, ed. 1982. *O negro revoltado*. Rio de Janeiro: Editora Nova Fronteira.
———. 1978. *O genocídio do negro brasileiro: Processo de um racismo mascarado*. Rio de Janeiro: Paz e Terra.
Nascimento, Abdias do, and Elisa Nascimento. 1994. *Africans in Brazil*. Trenton, NJ: Africa World Press.
Nascimento, Elisa Larkin. 1980. *Pan-Africanism and South America: Emergence of a black rebellion*. Buffalo, NY: Afrodiaspora.
Nobles, Melissa. 2000. *Shades of citizenship: Race and the census in modern politics*. Stanford, CA: Stanford University Press.
Oppenheimer, Andres. 1992. *Castro's final hour: The secret story behind the coming downfall of communist Cuba*. New York: Touchstone.
Perez Sarduy, Pedro, and Jean Stubbs, eds. 1993. *Afrocuba: An anthology of Cuban writing on race, politics and culture*. Melbourne, Australia: Ocean.
———. 2000. *Afro-Cuban voices: On race and identity in contemporary Cuba*. Gainesville: University Press of Florida.
Primer Congreso de la Cultura Negra de las Americas. 1988. Bogotá: UNESCO–Fundación colombiana de investigaciones folclóricas.
Race Report. January 2003. Washington, DC: Inter-American Dialogue.
Reichmann, Rebecca, ed. 1999. *Race in contemporary Brazil: From indifference to inequality*. University Park: Pennsylvania State University Press.
Reitan, Ruth. 2001. Cuba, the Black Panther Party, and the U.S. black movement in the 1960s: Issues of security. In *Liberation, imagination, and the Black Panther Party: A new look at the Panthers and their legacy*. New York: Routledge.
Rout Jr., Leslie B. 1976. *The African experience in Spanish America: 1502 to the present day*. Cambridge: Cambridge University Press.
Santos, Helio. 1999. Políticas públicas para a população negra no Brasil In *Observatorio da cidadania, no. 3*. Rio de Janeiro: Ibase.
Stanford, Karin L. 1997. *Beyond the boundaries: Reverend Jesse Jackson in international affairs*. Albany: State University of New York Press.
Thorne, Eva. 2003. Ethnic and racial political organization in Latin America. In *Social inclusion and economic development in Latin America*, ed. Mayra Buvinic, Jacqueline Mazza, and Ruthanne Deutsch. Washington, DC: Inter-American Development Bank.
Twine, France Winddance. 1998. *Racism in a racial democracy: The maintenance of white supremacy in Brazil*. New Brunswick, NJ: Rutgers University Press.
Tyson, Timothy B. 1999. *Radio Free Dixie: Robert F. Williams and the roots of black power*. Chapel Hill: University of North Carolina Press.
Valente, Ana Lucia E. F. 1986. *Política e relações raciais: Os negros e as eleições paulistas de 1982*. São Paulo: Faculdade de Filosofia, Letras e Ciências Humanas, University of São Paulo.
Wade, Peter. 1993. *Blackness and race mixture: The dynamics of racial identity in Colombia*. Baltimore: Johns Hopkins University Press.
———. 1997. *Race and ethnicity in Latin America*. London: Pluto.
Walker, Sheila, ed. 2001. *African roots/American cultures: Africa in the creation of the Americas*. Lanham, MD: Rowman & Littlefield.
Whitten, Norman E., Jr., and Arlene Torres, eds. 1998. *Blackness in Latin America and the Caribbean: Social dynamics and cultural transformations*. Bloomington: Indiana University Press.
Winant, Howard. 2001. *The world is a ghetto: Race and democracy since World War II*. New York: Basic Books.
Yelvington, Kevin A. 2001. Patterns of race, ethnicity, class, and nationalism. In *Understanding contemporary Latin America*, 2nd ed., ed. Richard S. Hillman, 209–36. Boulder, CO: Lynne Rienner.

CHAPTER FIVE

Globalization and the Study of Development

Vernon D. Johnson

T HIS ESSAY DISCUSSES THE evolution of development studies in the contemporary period, which has come to be called the era of globalization. The study of development, with economics as the lead discipline, became a preoccupation of the social sciences after World War II. The postwar international setting was structured by three forces: the rise of the United States and the Soviet Union as global superpowers, the collapse of the European colonial empires as a consequence of metropolitan enervation resulting from the war effort, and the emergence of a host of sovereign postcolonial countries. The United States and the Soviet Union were heirs to the Old European-based balance of power and became engaged in a global struggle for hegemony in the international state system. That strategic conflict was not only military and political but it was also ideological. It was a competition between democratic capitalism and state socialism, each of which purported to be better for the world than the other. Because dozens of new countries were emerging from colonialism, it became necessary for each side to compete for their allegiances by attempting to incorporate them into its power bloc and transfer its social system to them. The concern for bringing development to the new countries, thus, was motivated more by strategic interests than humanitarian considerations.[1]

Globalization can be seen as the spread of social forces and structures that link peoples around the world in ways that are beyond the control of national states and societies.[2] The language of globalization has animated the imagination of policymakers and publics since the downfall of the Soviet bloc and with it, the end of the possibility for command economies and Leninist party–states. Two issues are of importance here. First, from a Western perspective, what became global after 1991 was the inexorable diffusion of market economies and democratic polities. Development, henceforth, has come to mean evolving in those economic and political directions. With economics, as usual still the driving force behind the pursuit of development, globalization has also been synonymous with the incorporation of national economies everywhere into a world-economy and the homogenization of economic structures and practices everywhere in compliance with capitalist norms of efficiency and economic growth. Second, what we have termed globalization after 1991 is only the most recent phase of forces that have been in motion since 1492 and earlier. The last fifteen years can merely be seen as the latest chapter of what began as the "expansion of Europe" after the voyages of Columbus.[3] From this vantage point, American leadership in the surge toward globalization simply represents the further evolution of forces animated by World War II, when the United States picked up the mantle of leadership for liberal democratic capitalism, first to defeat the reactionary capitalism manifested by fascism, and finally to defeat state socialism during the cold war. So the industry of development studies after 1945 was emergent in a world where globalization had already been going on for centuries.

Against that backdrop this chapter has several aims. It briefly discusses the major paradigms for the study of development in the West since the 1940s. In the process it offers a new typology of development paradigms, and it argues that what one finds in moving from the original paradigm to its competitors is an increasing acknowledgment of the reality that development occurs in a global context. Finally, it provides an in-depth overview of the latest of these paradigms, localglobalism, as part of an argument concerning the blind spots of mainstream political science and development studies in this period of globalization."[4] It concludes by giving some attention to the continuing relevance of scholarship under each paradigm.

Three Paradigms for Development Studies

According to standard treatments of the evolution of development studies, two major worldviews have dominated the field. The dominant paradigm has usually been dubbed either modernization or political development, or the liberal or mainstream paradigm; the opposing paradigm has been referred to as the paradigm of dependency or underdevelopment, or the neo-Marxian, radical, or Eastern paradigm.[5] Alvin So broke with this tendency in his text *Social Change and Development*, in which he posited that there were three paradigms for development: modernization, dependency, and world-system theory. Whereas most treatments of development saw Wallerstein's world-system theory as a derivative of the dependency paradigm, So thought it was different enough in crucial ways to allow it to stand alone.[6] Wallerstein himself had been arguing that he was up to something distinct and was no doubt pleased by the acknowledgment by So, but few other scholars bought into that distinction. However, So's text was also noteworthy because the narrative is structured very tightly. The historical context in which each paradigm arose, its main assumptions, the classical studies done under each, and the way in which each was revised in response to critics are all sectioned off in a way that is helpful for students new to the field and seasoned professionals as well.

So was not alone in seeing the academic differences among the paradigms as ideological divisions reflecting the cold war context in which they were spawned. But he concludes by arguing that, by the late 1980s, a growing number of scholars working under each paradigm were beginning to agree on what issues needed to be emphasized in development studies. First, although all three perspectives were initially guilty of being overly abstract and ahistorical in critical ways, by the late 1980s they had all moved toward "bringing history back in" to their analyses. Moreover, after being wedded to particular variables said to be important, each paradigm began to examine "how the family, religion, ethnic groups, classes, the state, social movements, transnational corporations, the interstate system, and the world-economy interact to shape the historical development of Third World countries."[7] Finally, the polemics over whether the contemporary structure and direction of the world were good or bad were suspended. Therefore, by the late 1980s the beginnings of a convergence among competing worldviews were rendering them less ideological and more useful in the enterprise of science.[8] Along the way So provided subtypologies comparing and contrasting modernization to dependency, dependency to world-system, and all three regarding issues of convergence.

Now that more than a decade has passed since he developed this analysis and we are in the era of globalization, it might be beneficial to offer a new typology of development paradigms that borrows from So, but goes beyond what he advanced. I argue that there are still three paradigms for development, but now the categories are modernization, world-system and a new one, localglobalism.

The Modernization Paradigm

It is not a stretch to say that the modernization paradigm, which emerged as World War II was being fought, represents the Western model for development.[9] The genesis of modernity lies in Renaissance Europe at some time during the last half-millennium, give or take a couple of centuries. Armed by the growing evidence that scientific rationality could allow humankind to understand and then seek to control the natural environment, the seminal idea of modernity was that "progress" was possible. Progress entailed advancement to an improved or more advanced stage of human existence on both the material and spiritual planes, but in that nexus the material plane was considered to be primary. That is, material progress, which was manifest in the alleviation of scarcity and personal insecurity, was thought to create hospitable conditions for human spiritual well-being and peace of mind. The political revolutions framing the Enlightenment (English, American, and French), and the economic revolution stimulated by industrialism created social models for economies producing ever more goods and services in a context of polities that were moving toward ever greater levels of popular participation in governance. By the time of World War II, the philosophy and ideology of liberalism, featuring economic and political liberty, was viewed widely as having been the intellectual and cultural framework in which that human well-being had been achieved. The structure of this liberal society revolved around the democratic *state* and the market *economy*, both of which employed rational-legal *bureaucracies* run by rational, achievement-oriented *individuals*.

As we stated at the outset, Western policymakers, facing rumblings for self-determination in the colonies and an energetic adversary in the Soviet Union, sought to export the Western model for development to the new countries as they gained independence. As intellectual underpinning for the modernization paradigm, evolutionary and functional theories from sociology and social psychological theories proved to be useful tools.[10] The unit of analysis, the structure that was the centerpiece in development in modernization thinking, was the nation-state or national society, and the focus of research was the developing countries. The problem plaguing premodern societies was that they were held back by their traditional cultures and institutions.

Using a conceptualization derived from the work of Max Weber and Talcott Parsons, a typology of traditional versus modern societies was constructed. In the economic realm traditional societies lacked a class of modernizers who could provide the scientific knowledge and capital needed for industrialization. Politically, they needed bureaucracies capable of providing incentives for industrialization and adapting the populace to the disruptions of economic and social life. And civil society increasingly needed to be transformed from collective orientations, such as ethnicity or religion, to an individual achievement orientation.

In economics the classical modernization statement of the forces involved in development and the trajectory it took was W. W. Rostow's five stages of growth. For the political system the structural functionalism of Gabriel Almond became the model on which research agendas were launched. And sociologists and social psychologists were influenced by the work of people like David McClelland and Alex Inkeles who were concerned with the emergence of "achievement"-oriented "modern men."[11]

By the late 1960s critiques were being leveled against the assumptions of the modernization paradigm. First, the categories of traditional and modern were said to be inadequate for rigorous scientific inquiry. Tradition was seen to be mutually exclusive to modernity. Therefore, the assumption was that traditional values and ways of life had to be liquidated for modernization to take place. Traditional societies themselves were too often seen as static and homogeneous. Although the ideal for modern society was pitched in universal terms, concrete descriptions of it tended, inexorably, to mirror the economic and political development of Western societies. Against this backdrop modernization studies were accused of being ahistorical in character. One of the major elements of the history of developing countries that was left out was the role of colonialism and the continuing influence of former colonizers and other international forces. Finally, the paradigm was criticized for being glibly optimistic about the prospects for modernization.[12]

Armed with these powerful critiques a generation of "modernization revisionist" scholars came to the fore in the late 1960s. These researchers undertook in-depth case studies of the internal dynamics of developing countries that highlighted the shortcomings of the traditional versus modern typology.[13] Ethnicity, religion, caste, the military, and patron-clientism were prominent among the domestic sociopolitical forces that began to be analyzed. Cultural forces, such as religion, ethnicity, and caste, were found not to recede, but to adapt to, and in some circumstances, become agents of modernization.[14] Whether under the rubric of patron-clientism or patrimonialism, other scholars highlighted the enduring importance of hierarchical networks of personal connections between individuals in determining who gets what, when, and how.[15]

Another major trend in modernization revisionism, led by Samuel P. Huntington, controverted the facile assumptions of earlier work regarding the evolution of Western-styled democracy alongside a capitalist economy. The wave of military coups and the emergence of either military dictatorships or one-party regimes in the 1960s raised questions about the viability of Almondian structural functionalism. Interventionist states often sporting socialist ideologies subverted predictions regarding the emergence of free market economies. In 1965 Samuel Huntington observed that in most of the developing countries political decay was more salient than political development. At the end of the decade his argument that political order was the *sine qua non* for all other positive political and economic developments signaled a new research agenda under which scholars were identifying the "crises of political development."[16]

Finally, Warren Uphoff and Norman Ilchman derided political science for employing abstract models that see politics in isolation and do not account for the real situations in which rulers in developing countries make policy. They called on political scientists to incorporate economic understandings into their study of development in order to advance "the achievement and improvement of public purposes."[17] This work accelerated an already apparent move, stimulated by Almond and others, toward employing rational choice models to "make political theory more relevant to public policy."[18]

Countering the specious assumptions of the first generation of theory, modernization revisionists brought history into their analysis, and they began to research a multiplicity of micropolitical phenomena. The optimism of the 1950s and early 1960s, however, was soon replaced by a mood of pessimism, as it was conceded that the context for development outside the West was different enough that change and development would not be smooth or easy. Much of the Western-centric character of the paradigm was diminished. Strong political institutions that could ride herd over the forces unleashed by development were seen as more important than popular participation in governance. In the 1980s, in response to the massive debts accumulated by developing states, the International Monetary Fund began to impose draconian structural adjustments on those states in exchange for assistance in redressing their balance of payments problems. In the 1990s communism collapsed, and the world witnessed a surge toward democratization that was especially profound in Eastern Europe and Latin America but was also felt in Asia and Africa. Together, these changes seemed to suggest that Western free markets and polities were the only options for developing states.

With capitalism supreme, the underpinnings for a unique development economics or Marxian structural analysis were demolished. As Barbara Geddes has shown, the center of gravity in the study of development in political science shifted toward frameworks from neoclassical economics. Likewise, with the explosion of democratic regimes, large-scale cross-national studies employing survey research and quantitative methods could be employed in studying the politics of development, just as they had been used in the Western world.[19] The optimism of the 1960s may not have been recaptured, but there is now the widespread sense that the scientific study of development has become more rigorous.

The World-System Paradigm

As we have noted, the modernization paradigm expressed the orientation of the majority of scholars of development during the first decades of the cold war. In the 1950s, a smaller but significant group of scholars emerged who were from the developing countries and who began to analyze modernization from the perspective of the concrete experience of their countries. In a parallel fashion, a group of Western scholars emerged who were critical of capitalist modernization and frequently (though not always) advocated socialism. This structuralist school of development studies evolved from the perceived failings of the UN Economic Commission for Latin America (ECLA) in the early postwar period. As articulated by Raoul Prebisch and others, this school argued that some of the most imposing obstacles to modernization lay not in the internal dynamics of developing countries, but rather in the structure of their economic relations with the advanced capitalist economies of the West. These scholars claimed that autochthonous development and industrialization were inhibited when those in power applied the principles of neoclassical economics to late developing economies. Those countries had been encouraged to ascertain their economy's "comparative advantage" in order to produce commodities to earn the foreign exchange needed to finance industrialization. But in a global setting in which dozens of other countries were pursuing the same policies and exporting the same mix of commodities, accelerated global competition for scarce markets generated declining terms of trade, falling export earnings, and huge debts to the international lending community.[20]

Prebisch and other scholars of his generation highlighted these issues to alert policymakers to the need to devise ways of improving the competitive situation for their economies. However, by the late 1960s, at about the same time modernization revisionism emerged, a group of scholars led by Andre Gunder Frank took the ECLA analysis several steps further. They were deeply influenced by the Cuban and, to a lesser extent, the Chinese revolutions. In the debate over the role of the national bourgeoisie, these scholars asserted that the bourgeoisie in Latin America were actually junior partners in the project of Western-centered capitalist globalization. Local capitalists, therefore, were not thought to share nationalist aspirations of industrialization and uplifting the poor masses. Frank described them as "compradors," those who were bought by external capitalist interests. Further, the advanced capitalist countries were termed as the "metropole" of the global economy, whereas Latin American countries along with the rest of the developing world were called economic "satellites."[21]

Theorizing in a similar vein and at about the same time, but in the real world of politics, Kwame Nkrumah, the first president of Ghana, assailed neocolonialism. It is not clear that Frank and the Latin Americanists ever read Nkrumah, but his work influenced a number of Africans who came to work under the early dependency framework; it undoubtedly, prompted Immanuel Wallerstein in his journey from African studies through dependency and into analysis of a world-system.[22] The conclusion of dependency theorists, generally, was that the satellite countries had to break their economic and political ties to the metropole and establish stronger links to other underdeveloped states in order to achieve development. For some of them, inspired by events in Cuba, that meant socialist revolution.[23]

Out of the debates over dependent development a new research program evolved. The world-system approach made more explicit what the dependency theorists had declared as part of their overarching argument. Dependency theory, in juxtaposing itself to modernization, argued that structural economic arrangements between metropolitan and satellite states in an international division of labor forestall meaningful economic advancement in the latter states. In focusing on national development in satellite states, it provided the outlines for the argument that one world-economy existed. This new approach took the leap of positing that what is really developing is the capitalist world-economy. Immanuel Wallerstein is usually credited with initiating the world-system school of scholarship, but in a volume of this kind one must acknowledge the work of the Trinidadian American sociologist Oliver Cox, who toiled beneath the mainstream radar screen, mostly at historically black universities, throughout the middle decades of the twentieth century. In three books during that period Cox outlined the origins and evolution of the world-economy "beginning with the city-state of Venice in the sixth century A.D."[24]

Important historical developments influencing Wallerstein's thinking were the remarkable growth of East Asian economies and the crisis of state socialism, both discernible by the 1970s. These occurrences, inexplicable under the dependency framework, compelled Wallerstein to move beyond it. Along with his debt to Lenin's theory of imperialism and the dependency school itself, Wallerstein incorporated the approach of the Fernand Braudel and the French Annales school of history and social science into his project. The Annales school called for the integration of history and the social sciences in the pursuit of a "total history." Further, it argued for the study of "la longue durée" (the long term). In this way history could become less event-driven, and social science could historicize its attempts to establish covering laws of societal development. Finally, the Annales school advanced a problem-oriented approach that exhorted scholars to ask the big questions, such as why have the East Asian countries, generally, been successful at development, whereas African states, by and large, have failed? Or what role does racial stratification play in the comparative historical development of Africa, Asia, and Latin America?[25]

In lobbying for a world-system perspective Wallerstein replaced the bimodal model of metropole and satellite with a trimodal structure featuring a core, periphery, and an intermediary level he termed the semiperiphery. This last sphere served as a haven for capital investment when production costs grew too high at the core. It also acted to ameliorate the potentially explosive consequences of economic polarization and superexploitation of the periphery by creating a middle-income sphere that was relatively better off than the poor peripheral regions.[26] Additionally, the world-system approach enabled more in-depth analysis of political forces, such as the role of states, the military, and state–class alliances at the core, semiperiphery, and periphery. Most significantly perhaps, it conceded that structural dependency could be overcome, that economic development was possible for semiperipheral and peripheral states, and that the movement of states and regions within the world-system could be upward toward core status or downward toward peripheralization.[27]

Even with the refinements made by Wallerstein, neo-Marxian structural theories were said to be pitched at too high a level of abstraction. Despite their sweeping historical interpretations, both the dependency and the world-system approaches were criticized for lacking empirical historical grounding. From both perspectives agency seemed to emanate exclusively from the center. Missing were analyses of concrete cases of the internal dynamics of dependency or how regions or states at differing levels of the world-system really were produced out of the workings of that system.[28]

By the mid-1970s a number of revisionist studies had been offered from the dependency perspective that answered its critics. Cardoso demonstrated that development could occur alongside economic dependency. O'Donnell and Evans, building on Cardoso's insights, portrayed the dynamics of the alliance of forces around the state that constitute dependency.[29] Those working from a more orthodox Marxist orientation explained the role of the state and the evolution of social classes in development.[30] World-systems scholars also responded by producing research on concrete cases of national development within the evolving world-system.[31]

Of greater interest here is the voluminous literature spawned partly by Wallerstein, but also by scholars working in the traditions of international relations and international political economy, which attempts to further delineate the features of the world-system. These structuralist approaches to the study of development have certainly not "all but disappeared" as Geddes would have us believe.[32] Wallerstein's notion of the world-system has also been criticized for being economically determinist. But the idea that a world-system existed and that national development both produced and was a product of that system was not earth-shattering news to students of international relations. For most of those working in the mainstream of academia, of course, that system was essentially political. It was composed of states and dominated by the struggle for power among the strongest of them. A group of scholars working around John Meyer and Michael Hannan also argued that the world-system was primarily political, but emphasized the pressures exerted by international human rights norms in compelling states to pursue social welfarist policies.[33] Roland Robertson was perhaps foremost among those advancing the argument that globalization is essentially a cultural phenomenon.[34] Simultaneously, a group of international political economists working from a neo-Gramscian perspective appeared. Led by Robert Cox, these transnational historical materialists began to posit that there is a global system with several interconnected and overlapping spheres.[35] These elaborations of the dynamics of the world-system were part of the intellectual underpinning for the localglobalist paradigm, which is discussed below.

From the 1950s to the 1990s structuralist scholars can be seen as having come full circle. In the 1950s Prebisch and company had pointed to the structure of the world-economy as an obstacle to development that could be overcome with appropriate policy orientations. By the late 1960s radical dependency theorists led by Frank countered that capitalism was bad and meaningful development was impossible within the structural arrangements bequeathed by the world-economy. The world-system analysis of Wallerstein added sophistication to Frank's often crude formulations by clearly positing the existence of a trimodal historical world-economy in which states and regions experienced both upward and downward movement over time. Though world-system theorists, like proponents of dependency, have tended to be socialist-oriented, their flexibility allowed for the possibility that development could occur for peripheral states, though they were not sanguine about those possibilities. Finally, in the best places in the academy, students have at least been exposed to structural arguments. This has given rise to an eclecticism in scholarship directed toward reflecting more accurately the concrete realities facing developing countries since the 1970s.[36] This eclecticism has been made even more salient as a third paradigm, localglobalism, has entered into the debate.

Localglobalism and the Postmodern Sensibility

History, it would seem, has decreed that we in the postcolonial world shall only be perpetual consumers of modernity. Europe and the Americas, the only true subjects of history, have thought out on our behalf not only the script of colonial enlightenment and exploitation, but also that of our anticolonial resistance and postcolonial misery. Even our imaginations must remain forever colonized.

—Partha Chatterjee[37]

In the Third World, modernity is not "an unfinished project of Enlightenment." Development is the last and failed attempt to complete the Enlightenment in Asia, Africa, and Latin America.

—Arturo Escobar[38]

Despite the success of the East Asian countries and evidence that some industrialization had occurred in the large Latin American economies, most of the developing countries were experiencing economic decline by the early 1980s. The second "oil shock" in 1979, the debt crisis of the early eighties, and the imposition of draconian IMF-led structural adjustments had precipitated huge cutbacks in government social services and in protections for domestic producers. The collapse of the Eastern bloc in the early nineties and the disappearance of socialism both as a model and as an alternative source of financial and military support acted not only to accelerate the power of this "capitalist globalization" but also to deepen the resistance to it from the global South. From peasants, workers, and even sections of the elite and intelligentsia, calls for an economic orientation away from the mandates of the World Bank and the IMF began to be heard.

As I suggested at the outset, this surge of integration of the world-economy is merely the latest phase of developments since the fifteenth century. But the drive toward globalization and the attendant international organization and law undergirding it fly in the face of a half-century of international law and discourse supporting the sovereignty of nation-states in choosing their economic and political direction. They also seem to those in the global South to be unabashedly in the interest of northern hemispheric capital and indifferent to the plight of the masses of people in southern countries.[39] If modernity involved a universal drive for progress regarding the human condition, then from the perspective of the developing countries, the modern era has surely come to a close.

The ideas that we have entered a postmodern world and that a postmodern analysis of this world is required have both made a dramatic entry into the academy in the last generation. Introduced into philosophy through the work of Michel Foucault, Jacques Derrida, and others, postmodernism spread rapidly into literary and cultural criticism, anthropology, and the other social sciences. Modernity, as we have noted, is generally considered to be coextensive with the age of European expansion since roughly 1492. Philosopher Cornel West has provided one of the clearest statements of the characteristics of the shift to the postmodern world. He places that shift at 1945 and sees three major changes in the structure of the world: the end of the epoch of European preeminence and dominance, the beginning of an era of American dominance, and the self-determination of the former colonial countries.[40] As political theorist Stephen White observes,

> Four interrelated phenomena constitute this problematic: the increasing incredulity toward metanarratives, the growing awareness of new problems wrought by societal rationalization, the explosion of new information technologies, and the emergence of new social movements.[41]

A full treatment of the impact of postmodern analysis in political science is beyond the scope of this chapter, but it does address its impact on the study of development.

One kind of postmodern analysis of the developing world originated with the late literary critic and activist Edward Said. His book *Orientalism* applied the discourse analysis of the French philosopher Michel Foucault to the study of European colonialism and postcolonial relations between the West and the former colonial world. In contrast to the modern Western urge to seek universal knowledge and truth through rationality and science, Foucault argued that, far from universal or objective, knowledge and truth were simply subjective constructions of the powerful. Discourse was the explanation of what was known and also the rationale for institutional arrangements. In this way knowledge was always political, subjective, and biased and never universal or pure. Power and knowledge were in a circular arrangement, with one producing the other successively, throughout history. "Genealogy" was the term Foucault used for this method of analyzing how discourse unfolds across history in concert with organizational evolution as the handmaidens of efforts to accrue power and control.[42]

Said used Foucault's analytical framework to examine the manner in which the Orient was constructed as an inferior "other" in the European mind and, further, how that construction rationalized the imposition of a system of domination over the peoples of the East:

> Orientalism can be discussed and analyzed as the corporate institution for deal-
> ing with the Orient—dealing with it by making statements about it, authorizing
> views of it, describing it, by teaching it, settling it, ruling over it: in short Orien-
> talism as a Western style for dominating, restructuring, and having authority over
> the Orient.

and

> Without examining Orientalism as a discourse one cannot possibly understand
> the enormously systematic discipline by which European culture was able to man-
> age—even produce—the Orient politically, sociologically, militarily, ideologi-
> cally, scientifically and imaginatively.[43]

Under Said's reading European historical and social scientific discourse toward the
Orient is exposed as the ideological superstructure supporting an imperial project, rather than as the expression of the universal, rational urge for knowledge
about the world. As Arturo Escobar puts it, "Genealogy is concerned with the
formation of discourse by nondiscursive practices, such as socioeconomic factors,
institutions, (or) administrative requirements."[44] Moreover, Said's attention to discourse as a cultural mechanism for ideological and psychological domination
turns Foucaldian methodology toward relations of inequality between the global
North and South and heralds the beginnings of cultural studies, of which postcolonial studies is a subset.

   This focus on culture as opposed to economics or politics is another feature
of the postmodern sensibility. The disbelief in metanarratives mentioned above
leads to the rejection of the rationalist explanations of the Enlightenment. The
new social movements in existence since at least the 1960s can be seen, above
all, as cultural movements eschewing hierarchy, individualism, scientism, and
materialism in favor of egalitarianism, communitarianism, human experience,
and (often) spiritualism.[45] In the modern era the great structural entities poised
against one another were the state and the economy. The debate between liberals and socialists has been over which of the two was to be dominant in the march
toward progress.[46] The new social movements are based on an active citizenry in
civil society as the cutting edge in determining the direction for both the state
and economy. Cultural values, not the technically driven discourses of politics and
economics, have been posited as the guiding force for change.[47] That modernist
ideological divide, as we have shown, penetrated development studies, with modernization theorists favoring development led by market forces and dependency
and world-system proponents favoring state-led development.

   The alienation from large bureaucratic structures of power common to postmodernism generally has been manifested in the development field in two ways.
On the ground a wave of localized grassroots movements attempting to seize the
initiative in development has developed in opposition to global capital and states
in the global South, and in the academy a generation of scholarship attuned to
these "subaltern" forces has emerged.

In the early nineties three texts appeared that signaled movement toward this postmodernist paradigm in development studies. *Rethinking Third World Politics* brought together political scientists from northern and southern countries who felt dissatisfied with the state of the field. In the introductory essay, editor James Manor argued that the old paradigms were teleological and tended "to begin studies with the script half-written." This group of scholars shared a bias toward "studying how things actually work in third world political systems." Their work focused on three sets of concerns. First, they were interested in "the theatrical and imaginary dimensions of politics" that emphasized the constructions of the political by elites and the understandings of those constructions by citizens. Second, they saw that processes of hybridization of local and Western political, economic, and cultural forms were more common than transformations from tradition to modernity or from peripheral capitalism to socialism. Finally, they advocated a need "to reassert the importance of politics" in determining the course of development while retaining an interdisciplinary approach to research.[48]

At roughly the same time another anthology, similarly titled *Rethinking the Third World*, and with a parallel set of concerns, was produced by a group of Western scholars from across the social sciences. The lead article by anthology editor Rosemary Galli questioned the environmental and human sustainability of both modern capitalism and socialism.[49] In one of the more compelling articles in the anthology entitled "In Defense of the Primitive," K. P. Moseley called for the "delegitimization of the ideologies of progress, development and growth for growth's sake."[50] She notes that, despite a half-millennium of being ravaged, primitive communities still exist, want to exist, and as a human right ought to be allowed to continue existing. These communities should be sustained, Moseley said, not only because of their humanity but also because their approach to social relations is more humane than that of modern industrial societies. Therefore, they need to be available as models for humanizing the so-called advanced societies.[51]

Both of these *Rethinking* anthologies advanced a more idiographic and narrative kind of research than did the old paradigms. Manor's book foregrounds the fictive in the politics of development in ways that amount to a fresh way of looking at political culture. Galli and company lend integrity to the cultural lives and aspirations of the masses, who are often left faceless and voiceless in modernist analyses. Both texts move away from the economic determinism of the old paradigms while making culture and politics more salient. In doing so they point us in new paradigmatic directions.

At about the same time the British economist Paul Ekins offered the outlines of the new paradigm in a more concrete fashion in his *A New World Order: Grassroots Movements for Global Change*. Ekins identified militarism, poverty, environmental degradation, and human rights abuses as four crises that, taken together, constitute a "global problematique." He acknowledged the work of major UN commissions on these issues in the 1970s and 1980s, but lamented the general lack of commitment from the world body toward addressing human rights issues. This came despite the fact that the Universal Declaration of Human Rights is widely considered to be the foundation for the vision of the future that the

founders of the UN aspired to after World War II. Ekins attributed this paradoxical lack of commitment to human rights to the structure of the UN. It is composed of states, and most states in the world were involved in the systematic
repression of some portion of their populations. Thus they could not counte-
nance a global regime on human rights that had real substance. Even the handful of liberal democracies, although they focused on human rights abuses of states
they opposed, routinely ignored those shortcomings in states with which they had
important economic or security ties. For these reasons Ekins doubted the capacity of international institutions or states to do much more than pay lip service to
human rights problems, including the issue of meaningful development.

Because national and international institutions had failed to bring about
development, Ekins called for grassroots movements in every corner of the world
to seize the initiative in bringing development for themselves. He advanced a new
set of values, derived from the Dag Hammarskjold Foundation, around which
"another development" might be pursued:

> *Need oriented*, . . . being geared to meet human needs, both material
> and non-material
> *Endogenous*, . . . stemming from the heart of each society, which defines
> in sovereignty its values and the vision of its future
> *Self-reliant*, . . . each society relies primarily on its own strength and
> resources in terms of its members' energies and its natural and cul-
> tural environment
> *Ecologically-sound*, . . . utilizing rationally the resources of the biosphere
> in full awareness of the potential of local ecosystems as well as the
> global and local outer limits imposed on the present and future gen-
> erations
> *Based on structural transformation*, required, more often than not, in
> social relations, in economic activities and in their spatial distribu-
> tion, as well as power structure[52]

Having charted a new trajectory for development, Ekins went on to identify
movements in every corner of the world that were already operating proximately
according to the principles that he laid out. His case studies included the micro-
financing movement initiated by the Grameen Bank in Bangladesh, which was
serving over one million people by 1990 (80% of whom were women), and the
Six S federation of 4,000 peasant organizations, across nine West African countries working to bring "culturally appropriate" development there.[53]

Ekins's observations were noteworthy for several reasons. First, they lent visibility to the emergence in processes of globalization of a third sector that illustrates the postmodern urge. Modernist studies of development had identified the
world-economy and the global system of states as the key international forces
motivating development. Ekins's analysis added a third force—the global civil
society comprising citizens in grassroots movements organizing for a more humane
kind of development than that offered by the other two spheres. In their analysis of interest group involvement in the foreign policy arena, Augelli and Murphy

define "international civil society" as "the realm in which politics first emerges from the international economy."[54] These citizens' movements are cases in point.

Elsewhere, I have argued that each of the three spheres of the global system has an ideological logic that animates action at its site. The ideology of the global economy dominated by multinational corporations is capitalism, the ideology of the global polity centered around the UN and the system of states is realism, and the ideology of global civil society embodied in these grassroots movements is humanism, or human rights. In my research on African guerrilla movements, I show how the ideological logic of the three spheres is contradictory and how African revolutionaries mobilized support across global civil society on the basis of the human-rights-based claims of self-determination of nations. That global pressure, at its zenith in the struggle against South African apartheid, caused actors in both other sectors to accede to the values of a mobilized global civil society, and apartheid was dismantled.[55]

What Ekins described, likewise, was a contradictory situation. He depicted a gathering consensus from every corner of the globe that citizens at the grassroots of global civil society should dictate the terms of development discourse and policies, rather than political elites atop the world polity or the corporations and wealthy strata who dominate the world-economy. The impetus for this emergent movement was the differing values it held vis-a-vis the most powerful actors in the world-economy and polity.

Another important arena in which Ekins moved beyond the conceptual log-jam of modernity is in his views toward the economy. Most leftists have seen the state as the only set of institutions capable of neutralizing the power of capital in the quest to provide social welfare. Because Ekins distrusted both states and the market economy, he introduced the notion of the "progressive market" wherein "economic activities are undertaken through the market for specific ethical, social, or environmental purposes as well as for financial return or in pursuit of self-interest."[56] He identified the components of this economy as progressive (or socially responsible) businesses, investors, and consumers and provided examples of increasing activity along all of these lines from around the world. This use of the capitalist market to achieve "socialistic" ends is an example of an ideological pragmatism that sidesteps the rigidity of the modernist left and right while creating new principles that embrace the best of both ideological poles.[57] The third sphere of civil society is thus given primacy, but is still dependent on citizen action in a democratic polity and market economy for achieving its aspirations.

Ekins's research had pointed the way toward movements that possessed knowledge of the logic of capitalism, could harness parts of the local economy toward humane ends and network with like-minded actors to address the same agenda globally. In 1994 three events spurred a qualitative leap in localglobal activism and in scholarship under this emerging paradigm. Two of the events were linked organically. On January 1, 1994 the North American Free Trade Agreement (NAFTA) between the United States, Canada, and Mexico went into effect. On the same day native Mayans led by the Zapatista front in Chiapas state in Mexico began a rebellion against their government and NAFTA. Later in the year, the Uruguay Round of the General Agreement on Tariffs and Trade (GATT) ended with the establishment of the World Trade Organization (WTO). The WTO sought to bring to the world what NAFTA promised for North America: the nearly total elimination of all barriers to trade and investment among states in the world-economy.

Thus, at the same time that economic globalization was making its most important strides since World War II, local indigenous peoples in the south of Mexico were mounting a bold challenge to its principles. By declaring their griev- ances in local cultural terms the Zapatistas turned the elitist economic emphasis of the development debate on its head. By anticipating negative outcomes for indigenous peoples with the implementation of NAFTA, they questioned the morality of economic globalization and the basis of sovereignty of the Mexi- can state.[58]

Expert at propaganda and the use of the media, the Zapatistas quickly gained national and international attention and support; all to the embarrassment of the Mexican government. International activism in opposition to NAFTA among activists from the three countries involved had already sprung up as the treaty was being debated, and concerns had been raised regarding the treaty's weak envi- ronmental and labor standards. To those grievances the voice of indigenous peo- ples was now added as the anti-globalization movement of the turn of the century began to take shape.[59]

In 1996 Jerry Mander and Edward Goldsmith edited a volume featuring a group of scholars associated with the International Forum on Globalization (IFG), entitled *The Case Against the Global Economy*. IFG brings together scholars from all over the world who share Ekins's view that the world-economy is dysfunctional regarding the satisfaction of human needs. Its membership included several promi- nent Southern scholars representing the voice of the poor from those regions. The IFG's emphasis on localism offered a venue for those voices to be heard. *The Case Against the World Economy* critiques economic globalization from several per- spectives. Korten questions the efficacy of Bretton Woods institutions and calls for economic structures that meet basic human needs, maintain biodiversity, and leave ecologically sustainable practices for posterity. Shiva and Holla-Bhar cite the tyranny of trade-related intellectual property rights because of their dismissal of local traditional knowledge and practices. Bello argues that IMF structural adjustment programs regularized debt payments and further entrenched the South into the world-economy, but brought neither sustained growth nor development to those countries. Heredia and Purcell show how structural adjustments precip- itated increased poverty and economic polarization in Mexico. Khor points out that the world-economy transfers wealth from the South to the North via the con- tinuous decline in the terms of trade and via debt. He suggests that a restructured world-economy is necessary and that it might be achieved through force either by a unified Southern bloc or by a "physical collapse" of the present order because it is ecologically and humanly unsustainable.[60]

The final section of the text echoed Ekins in advancing relocalization as an alternative to globalization. Norberg-Hodge promotes limited and voluntary trade between relatively self-sufficient localities. Berry declares the need for locally based political parties to advance localist practices against the big government politics of the traditional left or the big business leanings of the traditional right. Kumar advocates Gandhi's conceptualization of *Swadeshi*, meaning local self-sufficiency. He envisions the nation-state as a "confederation of self-governing, self-reliant, self-employed people living in village communities."[61]

In 2000 IFG collaborated with the Food First/Institute for Food and Development Policy to produce *Views from the South: The Effects of Globalization and the WTO on Third World Countries*. As the title suggests, the volume includes several scholars from across the global South, and it trumpets many of the themes from *The Case Against the Global Economy*. Khor points out that the Uruguay Round of GATT talks wrenched disproportionate concessions from the South in the rush to make a set of trade rules advantageous to more powerful northern economies.[62] Shiva terms the initial structure of WTO proceedings "economic totalitarianism"; the WTO was not only an undemocratic global forum denying meaningful input from developing countries, but it also subverted democracy at home by eliding the particular characteristics and economic histories of differing countries that might make them petition for a more flexible global trade regime.[63] Larrain and Douglas provide short case studies of Chile and Nigeria, two countries that have been very compliant with the trend toward globalization. Chile in particular rushed headlong into free markets under Pinochet in the 1970s and 1980s. But Larrain concludes that the economic miracle of those years brought economic polarization along with growth, and she describes Chile as "a corporate state with no concept of a social contract" left.[64] Douglas summarizes Nigeria's economic development in the colonial and postcolonial eras, focusing on the plunder of palm oil and petroleum industries. He describes Nigeria as a nation "designed by corporations for corporations (that) simply disregards the people who live there."[65] The final chapter written by Anuradha Mittal of the Food First Institute outlines thirteen principles for "selective or negotiated integration into the global economy." Prominent among them are unconditional debt cancellation, national sovereignty over economic policy, and the movement of humans as freely across national borders as goods, services, and capital.[66]

At about the same time, African scholars, largely outside of the IFG network, were theorizing in a parallel fashion about the fate of their beleaguered continent. Under the auspices of the Council for the Development of Social Science Research in Africa (CODESRIA) and the International Development Research Centre (Canada), Thandika Mkwandawire and Charles Soludo wrote *Our Continent, Our Future: African Perspectives on Structural Adjustment*. The volume delivers a damning assessment of how sub-Saharan Africa suffered under the IMF conditions imposed on the continent since the early 1980s to induce the payment of international debts. They illustrate how the IMF, in the rush to get debts paid, was already denying any historical-structural specificity to African states. They cite a whole range of factors that the IMF tends to dismiss, such as:

> per capita income; the development of human capital; the natural resource base; the levels and structure of production; the degree of the economy's openness and its form of integration into the world system; the development of physical infrastructure; and institutional variables such as governance, and tenure, and property rights.

but also including

> the nature of colonial rule and the institutional arrangements it bequeathed the
> former colonies, the decolonization process, and the economic interests and poli-
> cies of the erstwhile colonial masters.[67]

Eschewing the technocratic approach of the IMF, Mkwandawire and Soludo assert
that economic development is fundamentally political. And referencing Peter
Evans's work, they call for an "embedded autonomy" in which the developmental state is "embedded in the social fabric that constitutes the nation."[68] This is,
latently at least, an endorsement for the subordination of economic policy to cultural
values and political processes in much the same way called for by the IFG people.

In 2002 the IFG published *Alternatives to Economic Globalization*, which presents "Ten Core Principles for Sustainable Societies." The principles mirror those
of Ekins, but go beyond them, advancing a "new," more substantive democracy,
cultural diversity, food security, and human rights.[69] The people associated with
the IFG are a diverse group. Most have some academic training, and many have
or presently hold academic positions and have conducted mainstream field
research. Others left academia to form or join think tanks, foundations, or advocacy groups. Some are simply activist intellectuals. Their work is not value-free
and most of them are probably beyond concerning themselves about scientific
standards, but their positions are based on first-hand experience of the pitfalls of
development over the past half-century. Like the contributors to the books edited
by Galli and Manor, this research is idiographic and theoretical. These scholars
are trying to tell stories that illuminate the problems of the global system and to
speculate about how to create new institutions and ways of living.

In the African American intellectual tradition this kind of activist scholarly
commitment is much more mainstream, being embodied in the life and work of
W. E. B. Du Bois and followed by legions of African American scholars since his
time. The competing demands of scholarship and activism are difficult to do justice to simultaneously, but many African Americans pursue postgraduate studies
as a means of gaining additional skills and credentials that can be lent to the cause
of social justice. In this regard, the work of those under the localglobalist paradigm is both familiar and laudable.

I have focused on research produced by IFG-based scholars, but they are representative of a whole generation of academics connected to progressive think
tanks and social movements around the world. In the last ten years millions of
people have engaged in street demonstrations at numerous times and places in
opposition to the direction of development advocated by existing global institutions. For example, the Cancun Ministerial summit of the WTO in the fall of 2003
failed in its goal of creating freer trade for agricultural commodities because the
United States refused to decrease its farm subsidies. The massive street demonstrations in Cancun in response to the summit were accompanied by a walkout
of developing countries led by Brazil, China, South Africa, Egypt, and Indonesia. These large economies are at the forefront of the "Group of Twenty-One," a
nascent bloc of Southern states formed to extract concessions from the North over

the direction of the global economy. The IFG and a whole host of scholars involved in grassroots organizations were present at those meetings.[70]

The list of researchers and organizations associated with the IFG is too long to mention here, but many can be found in the network surrounding the World Social Forum, which began meeting in 2001 in Porto Alegre, Brazil. By 2003 the Forum was drawing over 100,000 activists from all over the world. Working from the premise of "globalization from below," the Forum has promoted grassroots forces emanating from civil society over states, multinational corporations, or existing global economic institutions such as the WTO or the IMF.[71] This world forum has been organized as a conscious alternative to the World Economic Forum held annually at Davos, Switzerland, which is organized by those who support the dominant forces directing globalization as we have known it thus far.

In addition to the large throngs that gather to protest economic globalization or to attend international meetings, large numbers of people from grassroots movements have waged protests against national or local government policies or seized power democratically and begun to govern based on a different set of priorities. In India "literally millions" of people have taken to the streets "in protest against the World Trade Organization's Trade Related Intellectual Property Rights agreement" since the late 1990s. In Brazil a movement of the landless "has won actual title to over fifteen million acres of farmland that are able to serve 250,000 families."[72] In Venezuela the populist President Hugo Chavez withstood months of massive street demonstrations trying to topple him, because demonstrations supporting him were even larger. Chavez had incurred the wrath of the Venezuelan upper classes by instituting political and economic reforms that would empower poor citizens. Conversely, the indigenous majority in Bolivia drove President Gonzalo Sanchez de Lozada from power after a month of demonstrations protesting his pro-U.S., natural resource and trade policies. In Africa Nigeria is worth watching. Local ethnic communities have fought the environmental degradation of the oil industry in the Niger River delta. Protests have been continual and government repression has been consistent. However, the situation gained international attention when foreign oil workers were held hostage and had to be rescued by British forces in early 2003.[73] The point of all of this is not to engage in a journalistic overview of global social movements, but to highlight the importance of scholarship that chronicles them and gives voice to the people involved in them.

Most of the scholars reviewed under the localglobalist paradigm thus far have mounted their arguments based on a critique of mainstream economics and development policymaking. Another strain of localglobalist research is engaged more actively in a more postcolonial kind of genealogical approach to studying development. The work of two scholars, Arturo Escobar and Partha Chaterjee, is perhaps the most incisive of a whole range of work using this methodology.

The Colombian anthropologist Arturo Escobar applies Foucault's genealogical method to the evolution of the discourse on development after World War II. We said earlier that genealogy attempts to examine the way that discourse as a representation of knowledge is enunciated by those with power to rationalize the deployment of resources through institutional mechanisms that serve to stabilize or extend that power. Escobar shows how the Western powers' concern for the allegiances of newly independent countries in the early cold war period spawned the production of a new language. Until World War II, colonial discourses had offered the natives civilization but not progress in terms of material wealth. With the advent of a communist bloc offering progress under state socialism, it was necessary to generate a discourse tendering a Western liberal alternative to communism. For Escobar and any postmodernist, that discourse was created not from a sense of concern for the plight of the peoples emerging from colonialism, but rather from the global security dilemma for capitalism facing a powerful communist bloc. Because the West was rich and the South was poor, the elimination of poverty became a central concern for development from the very beginning, but attacking poverty opened up an entire Pandora's Box for Western policymakers. As Escobar points out, "Not only poverty, but health, education, hygiene, (and) employment . . . were constructed as social problems, requiring extensive knowledge about the population and appropriate modes of social planning."[74] These social problems became "fields of intervention" around which an entire industry and set of institutions and professions geared toward development were elaborated. Also noteworthy is the fact that, although development discourse was clothed in compassionate language, the eventual designation of societies as "backward" and "underdeveloped" mirrored earlier racist categories, such as savage, pagan, and uncivilized, in suggesting that something was wrong with those people and that Europeans could fix them. Escobar emphasizes the fact that before colonization Third World areas did not often experience modern poverty. Although they frequently lived close to a subsistence level, they organized economic production and distribution communally in ways that addressed basic human needs for all. Colonialism generally eroded traditional collectivist values while introducing (European) market incentives, individual initiative and achievement, and the gap between rich and poor. This point was ignored by Western policymakers, although in all fairness, it was probably not part of their socialization or general understanding of the Third World. Poverty and the attendant "problems" now existed and they had to be addressed.

Escobar also emphasizes the economic fundamentalism of development discourse. Economics has achieved the status of a science that offers an objective representation of the way a part of the natural world operates, but Escobar avers that the economy is not a natural phenomenon. Rather, it is socially, and indeed politically constructed by powerful interests with the resources to make and enforce its rules of operation. In this sense the economy is a cultural phenomenon. From this vantage point Western capitalism can be seen as a construct comprising systems of power, production, and signification. In other words, it is a cultural form in which human beings are made into rational producing subjects.[75] This analysis is part of Escobar's mission to "anthropologize" the study of development by identifying "Western modernity as a culturally and historically specific phenomenon . . . produced by historical practices combining knowledge and power."[76]

In succeeding chapters, Escobar examines hunger and malnutrition as early fields of Western intervention, and peasants, women, and the environment as "others" not originally accounted for in development discourse, which then required intervention as well. He notes that, although the scientific knowledge about and attention to each of these issue areas increased, the problems failed to be stemmed. This is in large part because the people that were to be improved were not considered to have relevant knowledge regarding their predicament and were never consulted. In that way the technical application of scientific knowledge acts not only to depoliticize policymaking but also to deny the human subjects agency and voice in the improvement of their circumstances. Escobar also calls attention to peasant resistance and validates the creation of spaces where the politics of that resistance can be mobilized.

In his closing chapter "Imagining a Postdevelopment Era," Escobar asserts that after several centuries of European domination, including a half-century of development, Latin America is "neither on the way to the lamentable eradication of all traditions nor triumphantly marching toward progress and modernity." He calls instead for a "hybrid modernity" that melds local traditions with the modern in ways negotiated between locals and the national state, and lastly, with global economic forces.[77] Writing in the mid-nineties he could allude to the already numerous examples of local resistances to Western modernity.

Ongoing work by Escobar and his colleagues investigates these local social movements throughout Latin America with sensibilities akin to IFG scholars.[78] Development for Escobar and colleagues is first a cultural question of how life can be improved without doing fundamental violence to people and their ways of life. Second, it involves a politics of holding conversations within communities about what they value and negotiating with national and international power holders to sustain their ways of life. Economics is determined by culture and politics. In Escobar's world the job of the scholar is to engage in "participatory action research" to involve the locals directly in research and policy implementation.[79] If development has traditionally meant that the ultimate means and ends were economic, and modernity entailed bringing progress from above, then Escobar is postmodern in turning all of these orientations and practices on their heads.

The Indian political theorist Partha Chatterjee is a student of nationalism in the postcolonial tradition. His project is to unpack Western discourses on nationalism, the state, and civil society to discern their relevance for the postcolonial world. He demonstrates that European philosophical debates about the relative purviews of state and civil society came to be contained within the modern liberal state. He views European nationalism, following Benedict Anderson, as the product of the alliance between print-capitalists and state rulers.[80] At the same time that powerful princes were bringing broader geographic territories under their dominion, standardized forms of languages were spread via the print media. In addition, capitalist social relations of production spread throughout the countryside, undermining feudal and other traditional forms of production and the community life and identities based on them. These processes unfolded unevenly across Europe.[81]

But by the twentieth century, alongside the expansion of European influence via colonialism, the liberal capitalist state with an autonomous realm in civil society regulated by that state was the modular framework for nationalism and political community. The nation then became the reservoir for feelings "of love, duty, welfare, and the like."[82] Anderson calls nations "imagined communities," because they existed in the minds of print capitalism and rulers and then were constructed politically, economically, and culturally. Anderson pitches his argument in universal terms. As we see in every other sphere of life in this era of globalization, the West has provided the models for human activity and behavior. This leads Chatterjee to ask what people in the postcolonial world "have left to imagine."[83]

Chatterjee's question sits at the core of localglobalist critiques of development. He argues that in the colonial world the discourse on nationalism arises not in the context of trade-offs between the state and civil society, but rather as the mode of resistance to colonialism and the capitalist destruction of communal life. He shows that Indian nationalisms emerged culturally, at least a generation before modern political nationalism. As political nationalism came to the fore in the generation before independence, it built on the autonomous identities buttressed by cultural nationalism, but sought to benefit from the scientific and organizational know-how of the West. In this "material domain of the outside . . . the West had proven its superiority and the East had succumbed." However, political nationalism was the vehicle for achieving independence so that "the spiritual inner domain bearing the essential marks of the cultural identity" could remain insulated from Western contamination and be allowed to develop autonomously.[84] The precolonial Indian polity was culturally pluralistic, and colonialism brought together several communities in most other places. Chatterjee analyzes the evolution of postcolonial India, lamenting the way that political nationalists used the state to pursue Western-styled industrialization and suppressed, often violently, local communities along the way. They used as their model the classical national ideas from the West, which posit the homogeneity of the nation under the state.[85]

In a closely argued concluding chapter, Chatterjee asserts that the European philosophical discourse on state-civil society relations may not even apply to the whole of Europe, and it certainly does not apply to the rest of the world. What is really universal is the narrative of capital and its relentless effort to destroy communities, as he writes

> What then, are the true categories of universal history? State and civil society? public and private? Social regulation and individual rights?—all made significant within the narrative of capital as the history of freedom, modernity and progress? Or the narrative of community—untheorized, relegated to the primordial zone of the natural, and denied any subjectivity that is not domesticated to the requirements of the modern state, and yet persistent in its invocation of the rhetoric of love and kinship.[86]

Communities other than the national state are left untheorized, invalidated, and indefensible before the technical rationality of the state and capital.

Modern political and economic discourse has no place for a narrative fundamentally based on affective relations or love for one's fellows. Nigerian anthropologist Ifi Amadiume enlarges this theme in her research on rural social structures in postcolonial Africa. Working from the Afrocentric perspective charted by Cheik Anta Diop, she argues that traditional African communities were matriarchal.

Although a great deal of institutional variety was found from locale to locale, women controlled religion, production, distribution, and exchange, and they were politically organized, often in structures parallel to men's organizations. Thus, African systems of checks and balances existed, but with woman as mother, provider, nurturer and foundation of the cultural cosmology. The encroachment of the international state system and the world-economy over the centuries fragmented and in many places completely destroyed matriarchal institutions. Amadiume was able to show that vestiges of those older social systems featuring matrifocality abound in contemporary Africa, though they have been inaccurately analyzed by Northern scholars.[87] These matrifocal structures, where they still exist, continue to be the repository for compassion and love vis-a-vis patrifocal institutions that valorize competitiveness, force, and violence. In *Reinventing Africa* Amadiume calls for the reinvigoration of matriarchal values "as the basis of affective relationships so badly needed as an alternative to the present political culture of violence underlying all the current problems of Africa."[88]

In a manner similar to Chatterjee, Amadiume gives voice to communities other than the nation-state that are based on the irrational rhetoric of affection and love. Modern states may appropriate the love of nation to manipulate their citizens, but they are almost always under the control of a modernizing national political elite, who themselves are handmaidens for global capital. The supremacy of capital and the myth of progress are made stronger by the absence of a narrative that links them to violence, misery, sociopsychological dislocation, and the cultural death of communities. Some of the black communities that Escobar works with alluded to this discursive lacuna in 1994:

> We don't know exactly when we started to talk about cultural difference. But at some point we refused to go on building a strategy around a catalogue of "problems" and "needs." The government continues to bet on democracy and development; we respond by emphasizing cultural autonomy and the right to be who we are and have our own life project. To recognize the need to be different, to build an identity, are difficult tasks that demand persistent work among our communities, taking their very heterogeneity as a point of departure. However, the fact that we do not have worked out social and economic alternatives makes us vulnerable to the current onslaught by capital. This is one of the most important political tasks at present: to advance in the formulation and implementation of alternative social and economic proposals.[89]

From this vantage point scholars like Escobar, Chatterjee, and Amadiume are able to valorize the right of communities to defend their autonomy from their national states and globalizing capital. They offer us an episteme for completely reconfiguring our understanding of the politics of what is going on outside of the global North. They interrogate the forces of Westernization and Americanization driving the world system from a powerful culturalist perspective that demands our attention. Although Escobar and Amadiume are more concerned with the plight of indigenous communities and Chatterjee focuses more on the construction of the nation, all are interested in the articulation of the local to the national in ways that affirm sovereignty from a Western-biased globalization. The analyses of

Chatterjee and Escobar in particular are based on countries that are "democratic" and can be studied with neoclassical economic theories and quantitative research methodologies and not only on authoritarian countries to which those theories and methods cannot be fruitfully applied. But Chatterjee might say that mainstream scholarship, despite its claims of objectivity, is uncritically serving the grand narrative of capitalist modernity and conveniently overlooking those who have not had "voice" or "positionality" within that narrative. This is an oversight that postcolonialists like Escobar, Chatterjee, and Amadiume are struggling to address.

Conclusion

This chapter has reviewed the major paradigms in the study of development since the beginning of the cold war and the era of decolonization over fifty years ago.

TABLE 5.1   Typology of Paradigms of Development[90]

	Modernization	World-System Dependency	Localglobalism
Unit of Analysis	nation-state	nation-state, world system	sub-nation-state forces, world-system
Research Focus	underdeveloped states	underdeveloped states, spheres of world system	social movements, spheres of world-system
Theoretical Heritage	liberalism, functionalism, evolutionary theories	ECLA program, Neo-Marxism	poststructuralism, Neo-Gramscianism
Theoretical Structure	bimodal tradition—modernity	bimodal, trimodal metropole—satellite, core—semiperiphery—periphery	bimodal local—global
Civilizational Genealogy	Eurocentric, Enlightenment Eurocentric, Enlightment-pluralist, globalist, post-Enlightenment		
Sociological Basis	economic determinism	economic determinism	cultural determinism
Leading Social Strata	capitalist-oriented economic and political elites	socialist-social democratic political elites	new social movements
Main Classical Thinkers	Weber, Parsons, Rostow, Easton, AlmondLenin, Prebisch, Frank, O. Cox, Wallerstein	Said, Escobar, Ekins, Chaterjee	
Some Main Revisionist Thinkers	Huntington, Powell, Apter, Roett, Rodrik, and Hannan, R. Cox, Laitin	Cardoso and Faletto, Meyer Amadiume Robertson	Goldsmith and Mander,

It has argued that a new paradigm of development emerged in the 1990s that has been overlooked by other recent overviews of development. Table 5.1 shows a revised typology for development that incorporates the localglobal paradigm. I hope that, given the foregoing discussion, no extended explanation of this typology is essential for the reader. It is merely offered here as a heuristic device in our ongoing debates about development.

No attempt was made in this chapter to review work over the last decade done under the modernization paradigm, and very little attention was given to recent research from the world-system or dependency perspective. Such research is amply addressed elsewhere.[91] However, having argued vigorously on behalf of local-globalism, we must at the same time acknowledge the enduring relevance of research under the older paradigms. The modernization paradigm's observations of elections, parties, and institution building in the new democracies and the advances made in our understanding of how ethnicity operates in politics are of continuing importance. And it is obvious that the drama of an emerging "anti-Western-styled globalization" historical bloc fueled by new social movements from below reminds us of the lingering salience of the question of dependent development in a capitalist world system. As Alvin So found over a decade ago, the most significant research in the new millennium will probably employ concepts and methodologies popular under each of these newly configured paradigms in an eclectic fashion.

Notes

1. Arturo Escobar makes this argument regarding the postwar Western orientation toward development. "Discourse and Power in Development: Michel Foucault and the Relevance of His Work to the Third World," *Alternatives* (Winter 1984–1985): 384–86. For insight into similar considerations from the Soviet side during the cold war, see Jerry Hough, *The Struggle for the Third: Soviet Debate and American Options* (Washington, DC: The Brookings Institution, 1986).

2. This definition is similar to that of Tony McGrew, "A Global Society?" in *Modernity and its Futures*, ed. Stuart Hall, David Held, and Tony McGrew, 6–66 (Cambridge: Polity, 1992).

3. Phrase borrowed from Henry Bernstein and Ben Crow, in Ben Crow and Mary Thorpe, eds., *Survival and Change in the Third World* (New York: Oxford University Press, 1988), 9–29.

4. Mainstream political science in the era of globalization has tended to ignore both localglobalism and the world-system dependency perspective. For comprehensive overviews of recent mainstream literature, see Frances Hagopian, "Political Development Revisited," *Comparative Political Studies* (August–September 2000): 880–911; and Barbara Geddes, "The Great Transformation in the Study of Politics in Developing Countries," in *Political Science: State of the Discipline*, ed. Ira Katznelson and Helen V. Milner, 343–70 (New York: W. W. Norton, 2002).

5. Some of the better overviews of the field that structure the debate in these terms include the following: Richard Higgot, *Political Development Theory: The Contemporary Debate* (Kent, UK: Croom Helm, 1983); Vicky Randall and Robin Theobald, *Political Change and Underdevelopment: A Critical Introduction to Third World Politics* (Durham, NC: Duke University Press, 1985).

6. See Alvin Y. So, *Social Change and Development: Modernization, Dependency and World System Theories* (Newbury Park, CA: Sage, 1990).

7. Ibid., 267.

8. Ibid., 266–68.

9. David Korten, "The Failure of Bretton Woods," in *The Case Against the World Economy*, ed. Jerry Mander and Edward Goldsmith, San Francisco: Sierra Club Books, 1996), 21.

10. So, *Social Change*, 18–23; Randall and Theobald, *Political Change and Underdevelopment: A Critical Introduction to Third World Politics*, 2nd rev. ed. (Durham, NC: Duke University Press, 1998), 20–24.

11. W. W. Rostow, *The Stages of Economic Growth: A Non-Communist Manifesto* (Cambridge: Cambridge University Press, 1962); Gabriel Almond and James Coleman, eds., *The Politics of Developing Areas* (Princeton, NJ: Princeton University Press, 1960); David McClelland, *The Achieving Society* (Princeton, NJ: Van Nostrand, 1961); Alex Inkeles, "Making Men Modern: On the Causes and Consequences of Individual Change in Six Developing Countires," in *Social Change*, ed. Amitai Etzioni and Eva Etzioni (New York: Basic Books, 1964), 342–61.

12. So, *Social Change*, 54–58; Randall and Theobald, *Political Change*, 45–47.

13. Joseph Gusfield, "Tradition and Modernity: Misplaced Polarities in the Study of Social Change," *American Journal of Sociology* (January 1967): 351–62; Alejandro Portes, "On the Sociology of National Development: Theories and Issues," *American Journal of Sociology* (September 1976): 55–85.

14. For ethnicity and modernization, see Donald Rothchild and Victor Olorunsola, eds., *State Versus Ethnic Claims: African Policy Dilemmas* (Boulder, CO: Westview, 1983); Donald Horowitz, *Ethnic Groups in Conflict* (Berkeley: University of California Press, 1985). Regarding caste, see Lloyd Rudolph and Suzanne Rudolph, *The Modernity of Tradition: Political Development in India* (Chicago: University of Chicago Press, 1967).

15. A good summary of the dynamics of patron-clientism is provided by J. D. Powell, "Peasant Society and Clientelistic Politics," *American Political Science Review* (June 1970): 411–25. Riordan Roett's work on Brazil is representative for patrimonialism; see *Brazil: Politics in a Patrimonial Society* (New York: Praeger Publishers, 1972). Christopher Clapham shows the role of patron-clientism within what he terms neopatrimonial political systems, in *Third World Politics: An Introduction* (Madison: University of Wisconsin Press, 1985), Chapter 3.

16. See Samuel P. Huntington, "Political Development and Political Decay," *World Politics* (April 1965): 386–430; see also Huntington, *Political Order in Changing Societies* (New Haven, CT: Yale University Press, 1968). Also see Leonard Binder, Lucian W. Pye, James S. Coleman, Sidney Verba, Joseph LaPalombara, and Myron Weiner, *Crises and Sequences in Political Development* (Princeton, NJ: Princeton University Press, 1971).

17. Norman T. Uphoff and Warren F. Ilchman, *The Political Economy of Change* (Berkeley: University of California Press, 1969), viii; and Uphoff and Ilchman, *The Political Economy of Development* (Berkeley: University of California Press, 1972).

18. Gabriel A. Almond, "Political Theory and Political Science," *American Political Science Review* (December 1966): 877. See also David E. Apter, *Choice and the Politics of Allocation* (New Haven, CT: Yale University Press, 1971).

19. Geddes, "The Great Transformation," 343–46.

20. Raoul Prebisch, *The Economic Development of Latin America and Its Principal Problems*. New York: United Nations, 1950.

21. Andre Gunder Frank, *Capitalism and Underdevelopment in Latin America: Historical Studies of Chile and Brazil* (New York: Monthly Review, 1967).

22. Kwame Nkrumah, *Neo-Colonialism: The Last Stage of Imperialism* (New York: International Publishers, 1966). Those using the dependency framework for Africa include Walter Rodney, *How Europe Underdeveloped Africa* (Washington, DC: Howard University Press, 1974); Claude Ake, *A Political Economy of Africa* (New York: Longman, 1981). For Wallerstein's own exposition about his journey into the analysis of the world-system, see his *The Modern World-System I: Capitalist Agriculture and the Origins of the European World—Economy in the Sixteenth Century* (San Diego, CA: Academic, 1974), 4–6.

23. Ronald Chilcote and Joel Edelstein, *Latin America: The Struggle with Dependency and Beyond* (New York: John Wiley and Sons, 1974).

24. Vernon Damani. Johnson, *The Structural Origins of Revolution in Africa* (Lewiston, NY: Edwin Mellen, 2003), 8–9. Oliver Cox's trilogy on the evolution of the world-economy includes Oliver Cox, *The Foundations of Capitalism* (New York: Philosophical Library, 1959); Cox, *Capitalism and American Leadership* (New York: Philosophical Library, 1962); and Cox, *Capitalism as a System* (New York: Monthly Review, 1964).

25. So, *Social Change*, 171–73.

26. Wallerstein believes that the stark core-periphery (or metropole-satellite) polarization would have created an untenable political situation between a small number of rich countries and a large number of very poor ones, which would generate political instability and uprisings. See Immanuel Wallerstein, "Dependence in an Interdependent World: The Limited Possibilities for Transformation Within the Capitalist World-Economy," in *The Capitalist World-Economy*, ed. Immanuel Wallerstein (Cambridge: Cambridge University Press, 1979), 69–70.

27. On states, alliances, and political forces in the world-economy, see Wallerstein, *The Modern World-System I* (San Diego, CA: Academic, 1974), Chapters 3 and 5. For the potential for overcoming dependency, see Wallerstein, *The Capitalist World-Economy*, 69–70. Regarding movement both toward and away from core status, see Wallerstein, *The Modern World-System I*, 102–3.

28. For a critique of dependency theory along these lines, see Bill Warren, "Imperialism and Capitalist Industrialization," *New Left Review* (September–October 1973): 3–44. For a similar critique of the world-system approach, see Maurice Zeitlin, *The Civil Wars in Chile (Or the Bourgeois Revolutions that Never Were)* (Princeton, NJ: Princeton University Press, 1984), 222–37.

29. Fernando Henrique Cardoso, "Associated-Dependent Development: Theoretical and Practical Implications," in Alfred Stepan, ed., *Authoritarian Brazil: Origins, Policies, and Future* (New Haven, CT: Yale University Press, 1973), 142–76; Guillermo O'Donnell, *Modernization and Bureaucratic-Authoritarianism: Studies in South American Politics* (Berkeley: University of California Press, 1973); Peter Evans, *Dependent Development: The Alliance of Multinational, State and Local Capital* (Princeton, NJ: Princeton University Press, 1979).

30. For the role of the state see Thomas E. Skidmore, *Politics in Brazil, 1930–64: An Experiment in Democracy* (New York: Oxford University Press, 1967). Ernesto LaClau is representative of a Marxian class analysis featuring "modes of production"; see Ernesto LaClau, "Feudalism and Capitalism in Latin America," *New Left Review* (May–June 1971): 19–38.

31. See So, *Social Change*, Chapter 10.

32. Geddes"The Great Transformation," 351.

33. John W. Meyer and Michael T. Hannan, eds., *National Development and the World-System: Educational, Economic and Political Change, 1950–70* (Chicago: University of Chicago Press, 1979); John W. Meyer, "The World Polity and the Authority of the Nation-State," in *Studies in the Modern World-System*, ed. Albert Bergesen (New York: Academic, 1980), 109–37.

34. Roland Robertson, *Globalization: Social Theory and Global Culture* (London: Sage, 1992); Stephen K. Sanderson, ed., *Civilizations and World-Systems: Studying World-Historic Change* (Walnut Creek, CA: Altamira, 1995).

35. Robert W. Cox, *Production, Power and World Order: Social Forces in the Making of History* (New York: Columbia University Press, 1987); Stephen Gill and David Law, *The Global Political Economy: Perspectives, Problems and Policies* (Baltimore: Johns Hopkins University Press, 1991); Leslie Sklair, *Sociology of the Global System* (Baltimore: Johns Hopkins University Press, 1991).

36. For analysis employing this eclecticism, see Christopher Clapham, *Third World Politics: An Introduction* (Madison: University of Wisconsin Press, 1988); and Howard Handelman, *The Challenge of Third World Development* (Upper Saddle River, NJ: Prentice-Hall, 1996).

37. Partha Chaterjee, *The Nation and its Fragments: Colonial and Postcolonial Histories* (Princeton, NJ: Princeton University Pess, 1993), 5.

38. Arturo Escobar, *Encountering Development: The Making and Unmaking of the Third World* (Princeton, NJ: Princeton University Press, 1995), 221.

39. For elaborations of this argument see Handelman and Werner Baer, *Paying the Costs of Austerity in Latin America* (Boulder, CO: Westview, 1989); and D. R. Fraser Taylor and Fiona MacKenzie, *Development from Within: Survival in Rural Africa* (NewYork: Routledge, 1992).

40. Cornel West, *The American Evasion of Philosophy: A Genealogy of Pragmatism* (Madison: University of Wisconsin Press, 1989), 235–36.

41. Stephen K. White, *Political Theory and Postmodernism* (Cambridge: Cambridge University Press, 1992), 4.

42. For Foucault's the initial formulation of discourse analysis, see *The Archaeology of Knowledge* (London: Tavistock, 1972). For his evolution toward genealogy, see Foucault, *Discipline and*

Punishment: The Birth of the Prison (New York: Random House, 1977), and Foucault, *The History of Sexuality* (New York: Pantheon, 1980).

43. Edward W. Said, *Orientalism* (New York: Vintage, 1979), 3.

44. Arturo Escobar, "Discourse and Power in Development," 379.

45. Barbara Epstein provides a thorough analysis of the centrality of cultural values to American new social movements in the 1960s in *Political Protest and Cultural Revolution: Nonviolent Direct Action in the 1970s and 1980s* (Berkeley: University of California Press, 1991).

46. Regarding the twentieth-century debates over state-led, market-led, or a balanced economic strategy, see Kenneth R. Hoover, *Economics as Ideology: Keynes, Laski, Hayek and the Creation of Contemporary Politics* (Lanham, MD: Rowman and Littlefield, 2003).

47. Jurgen Habermas, "New Social Movements," *Telos* 49 (Fall 1981): 33–37.

48. James Manor, introduction to *Rethinking Third World Politics*, ed. James Manor, 2–6 (New York: Routledge, 1991).

49. Rosemary Galli, "Winners and Losers in Development and Antidevelopment Theory," in *Rethinking the Third World: Contributions Toward a New Conceptualization*, ed. Rosemary Galli et al., 1–28 (New York: Taylor Francis, 1992).

50. K. P. Moseley, "In Defense of the Primitive," in Galli et al., eds., *Rethinking the Third World*, 102.

51. Ibid., 94.

52. Taken from Paul Ekins, *A New World Order: Grassroots Movements for Global Change* (New York: Routledge, 1992), 99–100.

53. Ibid., 112–26.

54. Enrico Augelli and Craig Murphy, *America's Quest for Supremacy and the Third World* (London: Pinter, 1988), 179.

55. In the book I argue that the ideology of global civil society is liberalism, but on further consideration, I define it as humanism, which can have the capacity for including non-Western humanist traditions (Confucian, Islamic, etc.) as well as Western liberalism. See Vernon D. Johnson, *The Structural Origins of Revolution in Africa* (Lewiston, NY: Edwin Mellen, 2003), 12–17.

56. Ekins, *A New World Order*, 127.

57. West, *The American Evasion of Philosophy*, 57.

58. George Yudice, "The Globalization of Culturre and the New Civil Society," in *Cultures of Politics, Politics of Cultures: Re-visioning Latin American Social Movements*, ed. Sonia E. Alvarez, Evelina Dagnino, and Arturo Escobar, 364–72 (Boulder, CO: Westview, 1998).

59. Mexican Action Network on Free Trade, Alliance for Responsible Trade, and the Citizens Trade Campaign, with Action Canada, "A Just and Sustainable Trade and Development Initiative for North America," in *Global Backlash: Citizen Initiatives for a Just World Economy*, ed. Robin Broad (Lanham, MD: Rowman and Littlefield, 2002), 129–34.

60. Martin Khor, "The Global Economy and the Third World," in *The Case Against the Global Economy and For a Turn Toward the Local*, by Jerry Mander and Edward Goldsmith (San Francisco: Sierra Club Books, 1996), 57.

61. Ibid., 419.

62. Martin Khor, "How the South is Getting a Raw Deal at the WTO," in *Views from the South: The Effects of Globalization and the WTO on Third World Countries*, ed. Sarah Anderson, (Oakland, CA: Food First, 2000), 19–20.

63. Vandana Shiva, "The War Against Nature and the People of the South," in S. Anderson, ed., *Views from the South*, 123.

64. Sara Larrain, "The Case of Chile: Dictatorship and Neoliberalism," in S. Anderson, ed., *Views from the South*, 158.

65. Oronto Douglas, "The Case of Nigeria: Corporate Oil and Tribal Blood," in S. Anderson, ed., *Views from the South*, 159.

66. Anuradha Mittal, "The South in the North," in S. Anderson, ed., *Views from the South*, 172–75.

67. Thandika Mkwandire and Charles C. Soludo, *Our Continent, Our Future: African Perspectives on Structural Adjustment* (Trenton, NJ: Africa World Press, 1999), 1.

68. Ibid., 132.

69. International Forum on Globalization, *Alternatives to Economic Globalization* (San Francisco: Berrett–Koehler, 2002), 56–78.

70. Elizabeth Becker, "Coming U.S. Vote Figures in Walkout at Trade Talks," *New York Times*, September 16, 2003.

71. In addition to the IFG, other research and advocacy organizations present at Porto Alegre included Institute for Policy Studies, Sierra Club, Food First Institute, Public Citizen, International Society for Ecology and Culture, Center for Food Safety, Climate Initiative Fund, Global Exchange, Protect the Local Globally, People-Centered Development Forum Focus on the Global South, and Third World Network. This list does not even begin to be exhaustive!

72. For India, see International Forum on Globalization, *Alternatives to Economic Globalization*, 96. On Brazil, ibid., 178.

73. For Bolivia, see Larry Rohter, "Outsider Mesa Inherits Bolivia's Long-Simmering Rage," *Seattle Tmes (from New York Times)*, October 19, 2003, A16; on Nigeria, see Ike Okonto and Oronto Douglas, *Where Vultures Feast: Shell, Human Rights and Oil in the Niger Delta* (San Francisco: Sierra Club Books, 2001).

74. Escobar, *Encountering Development*, 23.

75. Ibid., 58–63.

76. Ibid., 11–12.

77. Ibid., 218.

78. Sonia E. Alvarez, Evelino Dagnino, and Arturo Escobar, eds., *Culture of Politics, Politics of Cultures: Re-Visioning Latin American Social Movements* (Boulder, CO: Westview, 1998).

79. Escobar, "Discourse and Power in Development," 391.

80. Benedict Anderson, *Imagined Communities: Reflections on the Origins and Spread of Nationalism* (London: Verso, 1983).

81. Partha Chaterjee, *Nationalist Thought and the Colonial World* (Minneapolis: University of Minnesota Press, 1993), 20.

82. Chaterjee, *The Nation and its Fragments*, 235.

83. Ibid., 5.

84. Ibid., 6

85. Chaterjee, *Nationalist Thought*, 20, refers to linguistic creole and linguistic nationalism as the major models of nationalism proffered by the West to the world. One might cogently argue that pluralistic European polities like Belgium and Switzerland represent a model more useful for Southern countries. But except for Belgium in the Congo, the two were not great colonial powers, and it can be argued that their models of government were not seriously considered in many of the new countries.

86. Chaterjee, *The Nation and its Fragments*, 238–39.

87. Ife Amadiume, *Reinventing Africa: Matriarchy, Religion, Culture* (London: Zed, 1997), 81. Her definition of matrifocality as "the moral primacy of biological motherhood in the definition of social relations" comes from Wendy James, "Matrifocus on African Women," in *Defining Females: The Nature of Women in Society*, ed. Susan Ardener (London: Croom, Helm, 1978), 150.

88. Ibid., 24. Amadiume examines how matriarchal values might be exercised in contemporary African politics in a subsequent book, Amadiume, *Daughters of the Goddess, Daughters of Imperialism: African Women, Culture, Power and Democracy* (London: Zed, 2000).

89. Escobar, *Encountering Development*, 212

90. Work of thinkers included in the typology, but not in the narrative of the text. David Easton, *A Systems Analysis of Political Life* (New York: John Wiley and Sons, 1965); Fernando Henrique Cardoso and Enzo Faletto, *Dependency and Development in Latin America* (Berkeley: University of California Press, 1979); David Laitin, *Identity in Formation: The Russian-Speaking Populations in the Near Abroad* (Ithaca: Cornell University Press, 1998); Dani Rodrik, *Has Globalization Gone Too Far?* (Washington, DC: Institute for International Economics, 1997).

91. See Geddes "The Great Transformation"; and Hagopian, "Political Development Revisited."

PART III

Civic Engagement and Voting

A S THIS VOLUME WAS BEING EDITED, the nation was anticipating the 2008 presidential elections. Clearly the vote is the most critical political resource available to African Americans. Because it has become so predictable, does it lose some of its significance? In recent national elections, blacks have voted as a bloc. Most black voters did not vote for President George W. Bush even though he made a relatively weak appeal to black voters at the annual Urban League Conference. He reminded blacks that the Democratic Party takes their vote for granted and that they should leverage their vote to exact benefits from both parties. However, this did not deter blacks from voting overwhelmingly for John Kerry. The large turnout of black voters indicated that they saw the election as critical. The 2008 national elections will present a new set of candidate options. Will black voters play a similar role to the one they played in 2004? Will the issues change? Do racial issues trump those of gender for the black community? Do the increased number of minority candidates stimulate more civic engagement among blacks? The essays in Part III discuss African American public opinion and voting behavior.

Some African American organizations are nonpartisan but are still engaged in political activities. Citizen groups also provide opportunities for political participation. Blacks are involved in a variety of interest groups ranging from self-help organizations to advocacy associations. Involvement in these groups increases the social capital in the black community.

Political participation poses a special problem for African American political scientists. Many of them live in communities with few highly educated individuals and they cannot afford to stay on the sidelines and take notes. They feel obligated to get involved politically. A number of them become community activists, candidates, and pundits. In some cases, this involvement has enriched the political process, and in other cases, it has sidetracked an academic career. One of the essays in Part III examines these career choices.

CHAPTER SIX

Political Science and the Study of African American Public Opinion

MELISSA V. HARRIS-LACEWELL

H ANES WALTON'S FOUNDATIONAL TEXT, *Black Politics*, asserts that "black politics in America is continually changing" (1972, 15). His assertion confirms observations that black political leadership has grown, diversified, and taken on new shadings in the past half-century. This assertion of a diverse black politics is less transparent in the study of black public opinion. Marked by a striking homogeneity of electoral preferences dominated by Democratic partisan affiliation, African American political thought is often wrongly assumed to be unidirectional and to lack the internal complexity of white American political attitudes. Despite the assumption that there is little surprising to uncover in African American attitudes, political scientists have spent the last several decades developing the field of black public opinion into an important contribution to our understanding of black American politics.

Political science scholarship has convincingly demonstrated a wide and persistent gap between the political attitudes of white and black Americans. The discipline also draws connections between specific elements of black cultural life and collective psychological predispositions that contribute to the particular shape of black public opinion. This research on black public opinion demonstrates that African Americans are engaged members of the political system, rather than apolitical, uninvolved participants at the margins. However, although it lays the groundwork for understanding black political thought, the emphasis of much of this work on a unique black politics obscures the heterogeneity of black public opinion. This scholarship inadequately captures the ways that politics is a contested terrain within blackness. More recent work challenges the notion of unitary black politics, drawing attention to the cross-cutting identities and communities within African American politics. This chapter both reviews the accomplishments of several decades of scholarship on black public opinion and offers a critique of the shortcomings that often mark this work. It also takes up the issue of methodology, questioning how scholars of public opinion can continue to do their work in the face of a shortage of survey data. The chapter then sets out a number of thematic and methodological items for a new research agenda of black public opinion.

Conclusions in the Study of Black Public Opinion

In their 1993 chapter for *Political Science: State of the Discipline*, McClain and Garcia trace the study of African American politics through four generations. The study of black public opinion emerges most forcefully in the fourth generation of their history of black politics within political science. In the early-to-mid-twentieth century, black politics was engaged with questions of political theory (Bunche 1935; Myrdal 1944), regional politics (Gosnell 1935; Key 1949), leadership studies (Dunbar 1961; Ladd 1966; Matthews and Prothro 1966; Walker 1963; Wilson 1960, 1961), power relations (Carmichael and Hamilton 1967; Jones 1972), and political participation (Holden 1973; Walton 1973). Although these issues continued to be studied throughout the twentieth century, the study of mass-based public opinion only emerged as a subfield within the study of black politics in the early 1970s. This intellectual interest was spurred in part by the historical realities of black political life.

The Voting Rights Act of 1965 and the urban riots of the late 1960s forced political scientists to consider the opinions of the masses of African Americans, both because Southern blacks entered the electorate and because urban blacks entered the American consciousness. The urban riots of the 1960s, the emergence of youth-led black power organizations, and the growing prominence of racial politics in the American Midwest, Northeast, and California exposed the fault lines between the black political leadership and the black masses. As it became clearer that elites did not necessarily speak for whole communities, it likewise became clearer that understanding the goals, ideas, and tactics of African American political leadership was insufficient for understanding mass opinion. As a result of these changes in the political world and the increasing availability of African American samples in national public opinion data, political scientists increasingly turned their eye to the study of black political thought. Political science makes fewer claims to cumulative knowledge than other social science disciplines. Still, after thirty years of concentrated effort studying the public opinions of African Americans, two questions are worth asking: *what have we learned,* and *what findings about black public opinion are reasonably stable and consistent?*

What we have learned can be grouped into two broad categories: First, political science scholarship has convincingly demonstrated the existence of a wide and persistent gap between the political attitudes, ideological positions, partisan affiliations, and policy preferences of white and black Americans. Using statistical analysis of national survey instruments, political scientists show that African Americans perceive and exist in a political world very different from that of whites. Second, political science has drawn the connections between specific elements of black cultural life and collective psychological predispositions that contribute to the particular shape of black public opinion. These scholars have argued for the importance of African American institutions like the church in shaping political attitudes and have identified racial heuristics that guide policy preferences.

Black Thought is Different from White Opinion

Black American public opinion is substantially different from that of white Americans (Kinder and Sanders 1996). Perhaps the most consistent finding of black public opinion research is that African American partisanship differs from that of whites in its overwhelming support for the contemporary Democratic Party. African American allegiance to the Republican Party of Lincoln was solid for the half-century between emancipation and the New Deal, but "by 1936 blacks had moved overwhelmingly into the Democratic column" (Weiss 1983, xiii). Contemporary black voting patterns and self-assessments of partisan identification reflect consistent attachment to the Democratic Party (Dawson 1994, Tate 1993). Democratic partisanship makes African Americans unique both in terms of the direction of their affiliation and in the homogeneity of the attachment. This difference in how blacks perceive the Democratic Party is substantive and not just affective. "The movement of African Americans into and out of the Republican party was never blind or random, but was based on a realistic assessment of which party would best further black political and economic interests" (Dawson 1994, 106). African Americans have supported the Democratic Party because they perceive it as the party most interested in pursuing policies that advance racial group interests. This attachment to the party based on racial interests leads some scholars to believe that black attitudes are more sophisticated than that of other racial groups because of the ability to perceive partisan differences (Glaser 1995).

Despite the strength of this attachment, black Democratic partisanship is not a simple dimension of black public opinion. The Democratic Party itself is fraught with a racial division of public opinion in which black Democrats differ greatly from white Democrats; for example a "virtual gulf exists between black and white Democrats" on issues of economic redistribution, affirmative action, and attitudes toward the presidents (Hadley 1994, 597). In summary, political science scholarship finds that black public opinion differs from white public opinion both because of the broad attachment of blacks to the Democratic Party and in terms of more liberal policy preferences by blacks within the party.

In addition to these differences in partisanship, public opinion research shows a substantial racial divide in attitudes toward public policy, particularly with respect to policies associated with issues of race (Kinder and Winter 2001). Sigelman and Welch (1991) demonstrate that throughout the 1980s African Americans and whites differed dramatically on their perception of the existence of prejudice and discrimination and their assessment of the potential for realizing a racially fair society. Generally, whites were nervous that blacks were pushing too hard, whereas blacks believed that they were still forced to battle a biased system (Sigelman and Welch 1991). These differing perceptions of racial discrimination translated into enormous gaps between blacks and whites in support for race-based public policies.

One of the most comprehensive studies of change in U.S. racial attitudes, Schuman, Steeth, Bobo, and Krysan's *Racial Attitudes in America* (1997), uncovers "large differences in the perspectives of blacks and whites about the causes of black disadvantage. Blacks emphasize continuing discrimination; whites stress low motivation on the part of blacks. This disagreement in perceptions of causality sets the stage for many other differences" (Schuman, Steeth, Bobo, and Krysan 1997, 275) Blacks continue to support affirmative action, school integration, preferential hiring, open housing laws, and a number of other racial policies at levels far exceeding those of whites. An increase in white support for certain race-targeted government policies and a slight attenuation in black support for these same policies have led to a marginal narrowing of the gap between black and white attitudes in the 1990s; however, the racial gulf in public opinion persists (Bobo and Kleugel 1997; Shipler 1997; Sigelman and Welch 1991)

The racial gap in public opinion is equally deep around attitudes toward political leaders. African American animosity toward Presidents Reagan and Bush, who were well liked by most whites, was a salient feature of black public opinion throughout the 1980s (Barker 1989; Dawson 1994; Tate 1993; Walters 1988). Black respondents to national surveys in the 1980s reported very cool affect toward Presidents Reagan and George H. W. Bush. When asked to rate their warmth toward Reagan on a scale from 0 to 100, black respondents averaged a rating of 29 points in 1984. Michael Dawson's 1994 text on contemporary black politics finds that "having consistently bypassed and denounced the recognized leadership of the black community, [Reagan] was viewed as extraordinarily hostile to black aspirations" (Dawson 1994, 117). In a 1984 volume on blacks in America, Pinkney goes as far as to argue that "the Reagan administration has given increased impetus to the conservative movement in the United States, ranging from such neofascist groups as the Ku Klux Klan to the Moral Majority" (Pinkney 1984, 178). Initially received somewhat more warmly than Reagan, the first President Bush ultimately fared poorly within black public opinion. Black attitudes toward President Clinton were quite different. In 2000, black respondents reported an average warmth rating toward Clinton of 79 points, a score that outstripped even the ratings for Jesse Jackson. Thus whereas Presidents Reagan and Bush were widely liked among whites, they were reviled by blacks. Alternately, whereas Clinton enjoyed only moderate warmth among white voters he was beloved among African Americans (Harris-Lacewell and Albertson 2004; Wickham 2002).

New research in political science demonstrates that the racial divide in public opinion extends beyond the statistically significant gaps in support for parties, policies, and leaders. It also is manifest in processes of political reasoning. Evidence shows that blacks respond differently from whites to race-laden messages in the media, suggesting that the racial gap is a matter not only of different streams of information but also of differing processes of reception and interpretation (Gilliam and Iyengar 2000). In recent decades, political science research has demonstrated a renewed interest in the effects of social trust on political ideas and action (Putnam 2001). Findings show both a substantial racial gap in trust (Aberbach and Walker 1970; Abramson 1972; Howell and Fagan 1988; Rodgers 1974) and racial differences in how trust influences policy preferences. African Americans are considerably less trusting of both fellow citizens and of many social and political institutions than whites (Aberbach and Walker 1970; Brehm and Rahn 1997; Kramer 1994). This lack of trust has important but different implications for blacks and whites. Those whites who are less trusting of government are less likely to support affirmative action, school integration, and education quotas (Hetherington and Globetti 2002). For African Americans political trust is responsive to the presence of black political leadership. Those blacks who live in cities with black mayors or who have black representatives are more likely to trust the government (Abney and Hutcheson 1981; Howell and Fagan 1988). These trust findings demonstrate that white and black citizens maintain very different attitudes about their government and about their fellow Americans. They also suggest that blacks and whites use trust differently with respect to formulating policy positions.

The gap in public opinion between whites and blacks is a widely agreed-on conclusion in the field. Public opinion surveys dating to the middle of the twentieth century indicate that African Americans and whites perceive different political realities, support different political parties, assess political leaders differently, and stake out different positions on matters of policy. This divide emerges from differences in class position, self-interest, and tradition, but there is also a deeper basis for this gap: "The racial divide is, as we've seen partly philosophical disagreement between African Americans and white Americans over the importance of equality and the proper scope of government" (Kinder and Winter 2001, 451). Among the things that political science has learned is that black public opinion as a whole is distinctive from white opinion in content and direction.

Distinctive Racial Culture and Experiences Affect Black Opinion

Political science scholarship has not only documented the ways that African American public opinion is distinct from white attitudes, but it has also mapped the unique contributions of black cultural practices, psychological processes, and political traditions in shaping this distinctive constellation of public opinion. First, we have learned that black public opinion is deeply affected by racial consciousness, solidarity, and identity. Second, we know that black cultural and social traditions play complicated but critical roles in shaping black political attitudes and directing black political action. Finally, we know that the expression of black public opinion is affected by racial context.

Research on African American political participation throughout the 1960s and 1970s convincingly demonstrated that African Americans participated in politics at surprisingly high levels despite being overrepresented among those with lower socioeconomic status (Olsen 1970; Verba and Nie 1972). Part of the explanation for these higher levels of political action was the acknowledgment that racial consciousness operated as a resource for political action. Verba and Nie (1972) argue that black consciousness makes African Americans aware of their subordinate status and encourages political participation. Shingles (1981) shows that racial consciousness combines political mistrust with political efficacy in a potent participatory combination. Although this stream of research suggests the ways that racial consciousness influences political action, it only hints at its influence on the shape and direction of black attitudes.[1] It was Michael Dawson's decisive text, Behind the Mule (1994), which articulated the role of racial consciousness in the development of black political attitudes.

Dawson's work intervenes in a debate about the relative importance of class in shaping black political attitudes. Responding to Wilson's (1987) assertion that economic bifurcation among black Americans has created distinctively classed communities within black America and that these communities did not necessarily share common experiences, interests, and opinions, Dawson offers an alternative analytic framework for understanding how African Americans use group interests as a heuristic for assessing individual political interests. Dawson's black utility heuristic provides a convincing mechanism that connects black public opinion to a sense of linked fate among African Americans based on the historical and structural realities of their position as a subordinate racial group (Dawson 1994). Research in the 1970s and 1980s demonstrated that black consciousness was a "missing link" (Shingles 1981) capable of explaining African American political participation despite the challenges of socioeconomic status. Dawson's account articulates the role of racial consciousness in shaping African American public opinion in spite of the shifting economic realities that distinguish middle-class black experiences from the realities facing the black poor. In the decade of research that has followed Dawson's contribution, the role of black-linked fate has been debated and challenged, but grappling with the idea of the black utility heuristic is a necessary element of all contemporary black public opinion research. Those who want to map black attitudes must consider the ways that an assessment of racial group interests shapes and defines individual political attitudes. We may not know precisely how collective psychological predispositions influence individual ideas, but political science has clearly shown that public opinion among blacks is not just an aggregation of individual, self-interested individuals; black opinion is connected to assessments of the welfare of the collective (Davis and Brown 2002; Dawson 2001; Harris-Lacewell 2004).

In addition to knowing that racial consciousness is at work at the level of individual psychology, we also know that aggregate features of culture, tradition, and institutions operate to shape black public opinion. Levine (1977) and Henry (1990) provide evidence that black politics in the United States is rooted in cultural traditions, such as folklore, blues, and the church. This research draws out elements of black cultural traditions, such as defiance, orality, collectivism, and redemptive suffering, and ties them to the unique ways that African Americans think about and perform politics. For example, Davis and Davenport (1997) find that the film *Malcolm X* and the media attention surrounding it had an influence on black political attitudes, making African Americans more racially conscious, knowledgeable, and racially concerned. Their findings reinforce the importance of shared cultural experiences in the development of African American attitudes.

Political science scholarship has also used our understanding of black cultural practices to explain the explosive popularity of Jesse Jackson during his mid-1980s presidential bids. Jackson's primary candidacies were critical for invigorating work on black public opinion because they revealed the tensions within the Democratic Party and prompted the collection of national survey data[2] that made the quantitative study of mass opinion possible in new ways (Dawson 1994; Tate 1993). Further, Jackson's style and popularity encouraged discussion of how black cultural practices shape opinion (Reed 1986; Walters 1988). Jackson's moral fervor and church-based oratorical style were important elements in his explosive popularity among black voters (Dawson 1994; Henry 1990; McCormick and Smith 1989; Washington 1985). Black voters assessed Jackson as more intelligent, compassionate, moral, inspiring, knowledgeable, and honest than either Dukakis or Bush in 1988 (Dawson 1994, 142). In the 1980s Jackson was perceived as a true leader who was deeply concerned with addressing racial inequality. Black support for him in the 1980s further emphasized the connection among black consciousness, black cultural practices, and public opinion.

Research on Jackson's candidacies can also be linked to the work of political scientists who study public opinion and political action in the church. In turn, their work links them with scholars who claim that the black church was crucial in initiating and sustaining the modern civil rights movement (Genovese 1974; McAdam 1982; Morris 1984). Reed (1986) critiques the connection between the church and progressive, racial, social movements as a myth, but such scholars of the black church as Lincoln and Mamiya (1990) and researchers of black political behavior such as Tate (1993) continue to find empirical evidence linking black churches to the political mobilization of African Americans. Whether in the mid-century civil rights movement or the 1980s presidential bids of Jesse Jackson, the black church seems to have provided organizational resources for black political involvement (Dawson 1994; Nelsen, Madron, and Yokley 1975).

Important new contributions in this field find that both macro- and micro-level resources support a variety of political activities by African Americans. Macro resources include "indigenous leadership, communication networks, easy availability of mass memberships, and social interaction of political actors" (Harris 1999, 28). Micro-level resources include the psychological and cultural factors that help individuals do the work of politics, including religiously inspired efficacy and oppositional civic culture (Calhoun-Brown 1996; Ellison 1993; Harris 1999). "Religion's psychological dimensions could potentially empower individuals with a sense of competence and resilience, inspiring them to believe in their own ability, with the assistance of an acknowledged sacred force, to influence or affect governmental affairs, thus—in some instances—to act politically" (Harris 1999, 82). Although there is still debate about whether the black church discourages political action by encouraging followers to focus on the rewards of an afterlife (Drake and Cayton 1962; Frazier 1974; Marx 1967; Orum 1966; Reed 1986; Silberman 1964), there is a good deal of respected, empirical evidence that many black churches are actively committed to providing worshipers with the organizational and psychological resources necessary for political action.

Whereas those who study political participation have drawn convincing linkages to the black church, researchers of black public opinion have articulated the connections between religiosity and political attitudes. It is clear that African Americans are among the most religious members of American society. Following in the tradition of Holden (1973), Levine (1977), and Stuckey (1987), Smith and Seltzer (1992) provide evidence that a high level of personal religiosity is one of the distinguishing characteristics of black public opinion. They also uncover a complex role for religiosity in shaping black political attitudes. Religiosity encourages greater social and moral conservatism among African Americans without generating concomitant political conservatism (Smith and Seltzer 1992, 129).

The church stands out as the most extensively studied black institution. Research on the church demonstrates the centrality of black cultural practices to encouraging political action and shaping political attitudes and opinions among blacks. We have learned that black culture matters to black opinion and that the church is among the most important sites of the reproduction of black cultural practices.

In addition to knowing that collective psychological predispositions, such as the black utility heuristic, and black cultural practices, such as the church, influence black opinion, we also know that context affects the expression of black public opinion. Some researchers have demonstrated that blacks living in certain racial environments have distinct racial opinions. Bledsoe, Welch, Sigelman, and Combs (1995) explore the influence of residential segregation on feelings of racial solidarity and find support for a social density hypothesis that blacks living in cities and black neighborhoods have greater racial solidarity. Cohen and Dawson (1993) find that living in communities with high concentrations of poverty (over 30%) increases feelings of political efficacy but decreases the sense of community efficacy. They also find that "living in a neighborhood with over 30% poverty has a chilling or isolating effect" (Cohen and Dawson 1993, 291) on organizational involvement; thus African Americans from economically devastated communities express a greater sense of "political isolation" (Cohen and Dawson 1993, 295) in opinion surveys. In an increasingly economically bifurcated black community, not all African Americans build their political views within the same structural context. Some live in relatively more economically and racially marginalized communities than others. Political science scholarship offers convincing evidence that these structural contexts of race and class affect the shape and content of public opinion among African Americans.

The influence of context on the shape and expression of black public opinion is also evident in the findings on how black public opinion is affected by perceptions of the race of the interviewer in survey research. Because our knowledge of public opinion relies heavily on empirical evidence gathered in surveys, it is important to know how the effects of racial context in surveys direct the expression of black political views. More than thirty years of research have found that the expression of black public opinion depends in part on the perceived racial context of the interview. When respondents believe that they are in an interracial survey environment their views are different from those expressed when they believe themselves to be in an intraracial interaction. Schuman and Converse (1971) find that African American respondents give differing responses to white and black interviewers when asked about protest and feelings toward whites. Anderson, Silver, and Abramson (1988) find that blacks interviewed by whites express more warmth and closeness to whites. Davis (1997) concludes that black respondents acquiesce to white interviewers on a number of contradictory evaluations of parties, leaders, and racial political position. These effects are more than simply empirical realities that complicate the task of studying public opinion. They are also markers of the ways that the expression of black attitudes is marked by racial context. Davis (1997) links this deference to white interviewers to the tradition of racial accommodation that is a necessary feature of African American life, given the subordinate status of the group. Similarly, Harris-Lacewell (2004) argues that intraracial contexts provide unique opportunities to study the development of black political attitudes because these contexts are free from the surveillance by whites that often constrains expression of black attitudes.

The systematic study of African American public opinion within political science is now more than thirty years old. During these decades scholars have contributed importantly to our understanding of the contours of black public opinion. The firm conclusions we have in this field can be summarized as follows:

- Black attitudes are different from white attitudes.
- This distinctiveness exists across a wide range of political realms including partisanship, policy stances, and assessments of political leaders.
- Black public opinion is shaped by distinct psychological processes, cultural practices, and racial contexts.
- Black consciousness, identity, and the sense of linked fate are critically important to understanding the contours of black opinion.
- African American cultural tropes and practices influence political thought. The church and black religiosity are among the most important elements of this distinct racial culture.
- Structural context affects both the content and expression of black political views.

Untested Models and Unasked Questions

Two important weaknesses continue to plague the study of black public opinion. Much of the scholarly work in this area has emphasized the unique elements of African American thought. This research has not only demonstrated the distinctiveness of black public opinion relative to white attitudes, but it has also shown the ways that collective racial attitudes and experiences shape black politics. Whether it is Levine's (1977) assertions of a single black cultural tradition or Dawson's (1994) description of a single heuristic for black political decision making, these scholars have often inadequately captured the ways that politics is a contested terrain within blackness. Although this research has taught us a great deal about African American thought, this focus also has obscured the heterogeneity *within* black public opinion.

In addition to the discipline's failure to investigate intraracial diversity in attitudes, the study of black public opinion has been hampered by a kind of "drunkard's search" that has limited the range of topics investigated in the field. In the allegory of the drunkard's search, the drunk looks for his lost keys beneath the streetlight not because it is the most likely location for the keys, but because the light is best there. Similarly, the study of black public opinion has focused almost exclusively on the study of African American attitudes about racial issues and policies not because these areas are most inherently varied or interesting, but because data and previous literature exist on these topics. The result is that we have very little information about other dimensions of black political thought.

Intersectionality and Heterogeneity of Opinion

Despite the titular assertion of Wilson's (1980) volume, the significance of race has not declined in the role that it plays in shaping black political attitudes. African Americans demonstrate stunning agreement across class, sex, age, region, and urbanity on many important political attitudes. For example, it is a robust finding that African Americans of all classes share political attitudes that are more like African Americans of other class positions than like non-blacks of the same class (Huckfeldt and Kohfeld 1989). In 1993, Dawson and Cohen found that "most black people, regardless of poverty status, agreed on the evaluation of the president, the need for a strong state, redistributive economic politics, and choices for elected office" (Dawson and Cohen 2002, 298). Smith and Seltzer (1992) find important differences between middle-class and poorer African Americans, but they still concede a spectacular similarity across educational and income divisions.

These empirical findings mask the sites of heterogeneity in black public opinion, discouraging researchers from complicating their investigations of black attitudes with a thorough intersectional approach. To the extent that political scientists have sought heterogeneity in black opinion, it has been through narrowly empirical means, most frequently through the use of various demographic regression equations. Research on black public opinion has used measures of education, income, sex, urban dwelling, Southern identity, and age to uncover cleavages in African American thought. These standard socioeconomic and demographic variables are placed in complex regression equations. Sometimes they reach statistical significance, offering additional explanatory power to models of black opinion (Schuman, Steeh, Bobo, and Krysan 1997; Sigelman and Welch 1991). Scholars report, for example, that black women tend to be more religious than black men (Smith and Seltzer 1992); that young African Americans are more connected to black popular culture than older African Americans (Davis and Davenport 1997); or that poor blacks remain under the spell of the American dream while middle-income blacks are succeeding more and enjoying it less (Hochschild 1995). These studies dispute the notion of an entirely unitary black politics by demonstrating the ways that various personal characteristics have an independent effect even after accounting for race. However, they have not led to a comprehensive or cumulative base of knowledge about the role of difference in shaping black opinion. This approach acknowledges that some diversity exists within African American attitudes, but it rarely offers fully theorized investigations of how internal divisions within the black community might shape black politics and opinion.

By thinking about intraracial diversity in attitudes as individual variables to be analyzed for their independent effect, political scientists are missing the value of a truly intersectional analysis. "Scholars must move away from individualist models where respondents and their political views and actions are examined or counted independent of the historical and social context in which their racial and ethnic identities are given meaning. . . . Without any attention to the historical and current context of these interactions or phenomena we may be severely mis-interpreting the meaning of the data" (Dawson and Cohen 2002, 491). A com-prehensive intersectional approach to the study of black public opinion would borrow from black feminist theorizing about the ways that race is part of an inter-locking system of identity and subordination. Gender, class, sexual orientation, and age are not simply variables. These concepts represent socially constructed realities that have material consequences for the lives of those who are at their intersections. Feminist scholars (Collins 1991); sociologists (Gilroy 2000; Pattillo-McCoy 1999); historians (Holt 2000), and critical race theorists (Roberts 1995) have theorized and demonstrated empirically the ways that race has very differ-ent influences on individuals when it intersects with gender, class, age, and sex-ual identity.

Some innovative studies within political science have made contributions to an intersectional analysis. Cohen's (1999) *Boundaries of Blackness* is a definitive text that uncovers the ways that traditional African American political strate-gies, centered on a narrow politics of respectability, marginalize and silence sub-ordinate groups within the black community. As an example, Cohen traces the unresponsiveness of the African American political machinery to the AIDS cri-sis. She cites the realities that the disease was linked in the public imagination with homosexuality and drug use and traces the unwillingness of black leaders to acknowledge its impact on African American communities. This text forces a reevaluation of notions of a single black identity and unitary black politics, but it is not primarily a text about pubic opinion.

The field of black public opinion continues to await multiple contributions of intersectional analyses. One promising article by Gay and Tate (1998) does make inroads into theorizing on the complicated relationship between race and gender that influences the ways that black women form opinions on political matters. Although they demonstrate that both racial and gendered identities are important to black women, they also find that racial identification exerts a more powerful influence on political attitudes than does gender identification (Gay and Tate 1998). Their work attempts to think about the multiplicative effect of black womanhood, but it remains nearly unique in this attempt.

Not only does political science scholarship know little about the intersections of gender, sexual identity, and class within black opinion but it has also failed to investigate the effects of black ethnic identity. Blackness is a socially constructed category that includes not only the descendants of African slaves from the Amer-ican South but also black people of multiple ethnic backgrounds, including recent immigrants from Africa and the Caribbean. Although blackness is a complex social category, most public opinion research assumes a single black ethnic iden-tity. Public opinion surveys from the 1980s and 1990s rarely asked respondents about their ethnic heritage or identity and assume that a model of black public opinion could be equally applied to all black ethnic groups. Sociologist Mary Waters (1999) argues that we must complicate the notion of blackness itself by recognizing that black people comprise many ethnic groups, including more recent immigrants to the United States from the black Diaspora. Her research details the experiences, identities, and expectations of West Indian immigrants and their children. She traces both their shared and distinct interpretations of America when compared with those of native-born blacks. Waters's research is an invaluable contribution to understanding blackness at the intersection of ethnic identity, but this is a contribution made by a sociologist, not a political scientist. There are still many unanswered questions within the study of public opinion. How do the political attitudes of first-generation Caribbean or African blacks compare with those of native-born blacks? Are they guided by the same sense of linked fate? How is linked fate made more complicated by ethnic identity?

A review of the literature suggests that the study of public opinion has remained largely silent on the investigation of intersectional identities and political attitudes. As we move into the second half-century of research on black public opinion, political science scholarship must be willing to confront a number of unanswered questions in this arena. How are the contours of public opinion different for African American gays and lesbians than for heterosexual blacks? How might the utility heuristic be deployed differently for a group that is marginalized within blackness? Can racial linked fate still stand as a reasonable shortcut for assessing individual interests if the racial group itself is hostile toward the marginal community, as is sometimes the case with black women, black gay men and lesbians, and other groups labeled as "deviant"? How might assumptions about gender, class, ethnicity, and sexual orientation influence the questions that public opinion researchers ask? How do public opinion researchers influence findings by assuming a male, straight, native-born respondent to our surveys, interviews, and focus groups?

Related to the failure of public opinion research to adequately offer an intersectional approach to the study of black public opinion is its inability to move beyond the black-white paradigm in the study of political attitudes. The United States is becoming a more multiracial society. The relationship between a powerful white majority and a subordinated black minority has been the guiding structure for research in African American politics, but this paradigm is quickly becoming a less useful way of thinking about racial politics in the United States. It is therefore less useful as a structure for the study of black public opinion, yet political science scholarship knows little about black attitudes toward and in relation to other racially marginalized groups.

The field of political science does know something about blacks in multiracial contexts, however. Multiracial electoral coalitions in American cities in the 1980s and 1990s prompted research in the subfield of urban politics that situated African Americans within a strategic, multiracial electoral environment. (Browning, Marshall, and Tabb 1984, 1997; Gilliam 1996; Jackson, Gerber, and Cain 1994; Sonenshein 1993) More recently in this tradition Kim (2000) offers an analysis that goes beyond the black-white paradigm of American racial politics with an urban study of the conflict between African American and Korean communities in New York City. All of these studies demonstrate the ways that African Americans position themselves within urban contexts that require sharing power

through coalitions of racial minorities. We know from the urban politics literature that African American officeholders and voters share some concerns, styles,
and political practices with Hispanic and Asian American communities; and we
also learn that they are unique from and even hostile to other issues that arise in
these minority communities. Although this work has made valuable contributions to our understanding of black politics, it has rarely focused on public
opinion and the intersections of black public opinion with that of other minority groups.

To the extent that we do know something specifically about black public
opinion in a multiracial context, political science scholarship has tended to take
the models of black-white attitude cleavages and simply tried to extend them to
include other racial minorities (Jackson, Gerber, and Cain 1994; Lien 1998; Thorton and Mizuno 1999; Welch and Sigelman 1992). This approach is similar to
the one that adds variables like income, sex, and region to models of public opinion and then analyzes the coefficients on these variables without entering into a
full intersectional analysis. Similarly, the research on multiracial attitudes has
tended to add Latinos and Asians to models that were originally generated to test
differences in attitudes among blacks and whites.

Another model for studying black attitudes in context with other minorities
is to ask black people what they think of immigrants, of Latinos/Hispanics, of
Asians, or of policies that affect other minority communities. These studies seek
to validate or repudiate an inter-minority conflict theory by determining whether
blacks view other minorities in the ways that whites view blacks (Morris 2000).
These public opinion studies tend to be narrowly empirical and fail to contribute
to a comparative racial framework theory that would illuminate the role of power,
privilege, history, and attitudes in shaping a complicated racial society. To date,
political science's study of black public opinion has not produced a comparative
racial theory that will situate African American political attitudes in a complex
global society and help us understand how black attitudes respond to and help
generate this new racial politics.

Unexplored Dimensions of Black Public Opinion

Although it has outlined the contours of black political thought, the discipline
of political science has not provided significant insight into our understanding of
black public opinion at the intersection of other relevant identities or beyond
the black-white paradigm. Further, the discipline has done little to expand our
knowledge of black public opinion beyond a very narrow range of issue domains.
Nearly everything that political science scholarship has learned about black political attitudes has been in the realm of racial attitudes, opinions toward policies
that disproportionately affect African Americans, and assessments of national
candidates, officeholders, and parties. Very little is known about black public
opinion in other political areas.

In a post–September 11 America, perhaps the most glaring omission in our
knowledge of black public opinion is our failure to learn anything meaningful
about black public opinion toward foreign policy. Terrorism, war, immigration, and

globalization are making domestic politics an increasingly global affair. For example, it would be impossible to discuss American attitudes toward President George W. Bush without attention to issues of war, foreign aid, and involvement in international conflicts. Yet political science scholarship implies that the only attitude dimensions of interest in black political thought are those that revolve around narrowly constructed racial concerns. In an increasingly global society, political science must understand the shape and direction of black people's opinions on matters of foreign policy. Otherwise the discipline will both promote the notion that African Americans are parochial and will limit our own understanding of the multiple forces affecting black thought.

The few research endeavors that have sought to investigate black attitudes toward foreign policy have demonstrated that black opinion in this realm may be different from black opinions on other attitude dimensions. For example, Gartner and Segura (2000) examine black and white support for the Vietnam War as a function of war casualties, paying attention to the proximity and the race of the casualties. They find that it is proximity, not racial similarity, that affects black and white attitudes toward the Vietnam War. This is important because that it is a very different conclusion from findings on domestic issues. Gartner and Segura show that in this arena race does not emerge as the single most powerful indicator of attitudes. We know so little that it is difficult to hypothesize in what directions this research might take political science or what insights it might provide about African Americans as political beings. It is clear, however, that political science's failure to investigate other issue dimensions is a significant shortcoming. When Martin Luther King Jr. spoke out against the Vietnam War, he was vilified in the American press. Many journalists suggested that this Nobel Peace Prize recipient did not have the expertise or right to speak about international warfare and that he should remain focused on domestic issues of racial inequality. King, of course, recognized the interconnection between racial inequality at home and unjust war abroad, and he spoke out against the war until the end of his life. African American public opinion does not stop at the shores or borders of the United States, yet we know little about the shape of or influences on black political attitudes beyond a narrowly defined domestic, racial agenda.

Foreign policy, war, and international affairs stand out as glaring examples of how little we know about African American public opinion outside a narrowly defined realm of racial policy issues. Even in well-researched domains, political science scholarship still has not mapped important areas. For example, although we know that African Americans express a high level of religiosity and we know that black churches are important sites of political mobilization, we know relatively little about how the theological content of black religious belief might inform political positions. The current debate on gay marriage has revealed this hole in the literature because scholars of public opinion are unsure whether black religious ideas can be deployed for or against a constitutional ban on gay marriage. While pundits conjecture, public opinion researchers are unable to provide empirical evidence about the content of black religious ideas and their connection to political and policy positions.

Over the past fifty years, the study of African American public opinion has taught us a great deal about the shape and development of black political attitudes. But, like any field, it has shortcomings that can be summarized as follows:

- The discipline lacks a comprehensive intersectional approach to the study of intraracial differences in black public opinion.
- Among the most important areas needing investigation are the intersections of race with gender, sexual identity, and black ethnicity.
- Political science research on black public opinion is mired in a black-white paradigm for understanding political attitudes.
- The study of black public opinion has focused on a narrow set of domestic, racial policy issues and has not asked questions across a wide array of other attitude dimensions, most notably foreign policy.

Methodology, Publishing, and Other Structural Constraints

Many of the limitations in public opinion research can be traced in part to methodological constraints, rather than attributed entirely to a lack of imagination or insight on the part of researchers. For example, an important reason for the discipline's failure to construct an intersectional framework or an international focus in its study of black public opinion is the reliance on national survey data. These data have shortcomings even in the field of white public opinion, but their limitations are infuriating in the study of black political attitudes. In their chapter on racial politics for *Political Science: The State of the Discipline* Dawson and Cohen write, "For a number of years researchers interested in conducting public opinion or elections studies of people of color have labored under the handicap of using the American National Election Studies or the General Social Survey. Neither important study is designed to provide adequate coverage of minority communities or the survey instrumentation necessary for probing the political beliefs and behaviors of communities with their own significantly distinct political histories and outlooks" (Dawson and Cohen 2002, 506). This handicap is a significant one accounting for many of the weaknesses in the field. Without adequate samples or uniquely crafted surveys, researchers of black public opinion face substantial obstacles to producing scholarship that is sophisticated, replicable, and capable of making unique contributions to the field.

Researchers in black public opinion not only face a shortage of reliable survey data but they also suffer implicit and explicit discrimination when attempting to publish in refereed journals in the discipline. The political science discipline continues to reward a narrowly constructed concept of race and to insist on a limited menu of methodological approaches. In a discipline in which publication in one of three journals remains the gateway for professional success, the study of black public opinion is hampered by the inability of innovative researchers to publish in those journals.

Data: Feast or Famine

The Jackson presidential primary bids of the mid-1980s prompted support for collecting data on black voters. With Jackson making a serious bid for the American presidency, it suddenly seemed worth the investment to do professional, academic surveys on the order of the American National Election Studies (ANES) that had been repeated every four years since the mid-twentieth century. The two election-year panel studies of black public opinion, the 1984 and 1988 National Black Election Studies, laid the groundwork for a whole new generation of scholars interested in black public opinion (Dawson 1994; Tate 1993). These studies provided adequate black samples and replicated questions commonly asked in ANES studies. Their two-wave panel procedures seemed to open up the possibility of time-series analysis among black respondents for the first time. But just as quickly as they appeared, they disappeared. Although the 1992 election of Bill Clinton represented only the second time in more than three decades that the presidential candidate preferred by a majority of African Americans secured the White House, there was no 1992 National Black Election Study.

Even in the booming financial times of the nineties, when foundations and government increased funding for social scientific endeavors, it was difficult to field national surveys of black Americans. In 1994, Dawson and Brown secured support for the 1994 National Black Politics Study (NBPS).[3] This unique study has provided the basis for research in black public opinion for the last decade. But in the nineties only one other national, random digit telephone survey was completed. In 1996 the National Black Election Study was finally replicated,[4] but it was less well funded and could not provide the continuity of the 1984 and 1988 studies. Still, the 1996 study is an important contribution to data collection efforts, and though it is nearly ten years old, it is the most recent, comprehensive survey of black political attitudes. No academic surveys of a national sample of African Americans on this scale have been completed in the twenty-first century. The ANES and General Social Survey (GSS) still fail to offer oversamples of black populations sufficient for testing statistical models, and neither survey organization has accounted for new findings in the field that would alter the question wording or issue domains around topics of race and politics.

The utter lack of contemporary survey data is an enormous structural constraint for researchers of black public opinion. These researchers are forced to rely on media-collected data that are notorious for sampling failures and problematic question wording. Because surveys have not been replicated among black samples, it is nearly impossible to complete a time-series analysis of black public opinion, making it difficult to trace dynamic change in black attitudes. The lack of survey data traps political scientists in a study of snapshots of black thought that are often a decade old before they are published. Further, these studies are often constructed around the narrow, parochial racial policy issues that framed black politics thirty years ago. Those collecting new data must always decide between replicating older questions to provide opportunities to study attitude change or asking questions about innovative new areas of opinion. This trade-off is one that has severely handicapped our understanding of black public opinion.

Committed scholars are working to collect national samples of African Americans through new surveying technologies. Most notable is the 2000 election study fielded by Lawrence Bobo and Michael Dawson of Harvard University. This study was collected in partnership with an innovative new firm, Knowledge Networks. Knowledge Networks employs a random digit dialing (RDD) telephone methodology to develop a representative sample of households for participation in its panels. Once a Knowledge Networks household is selected, members are contacted first by an express delivery mailing and then by telephone for enrollment in the panel. The panel structure enables clients to conduct surveys of low-incidence populations, such as African Americans, more efficiently and inexpensively than would otherwise be possible. Every participating Knowledge Networks household receives free hardware, free Internet access, free e-mail accounts, and ongoing technical support. Participants receive a short multimedia survey about once a week. Surveys are delivered by e-mail on the same standardized hardware through the television set. Although the 2000 election study is an important contribution to publicly available data, it cannot replace the large-scale, national telephone surveys that are the discipline's standard.

Publishing: The Anecdotes That Tell the Story

Lack of survey data not only hinders intellectual progress for the discipline but it also affects the professional goals of scholars who study black public opinion. Statistical analysis of national survey data remains the gold standard for publication in the discipline's major journals. There is no systematic, empirical evidence demonstrating that studies of black public opinion are rejected more frequently than other kinds of American politics manuscripts when submitted to the discipline's leading peer-reviewed journals. But in recent years a group of political scientists became concerned about hegemonic methodological practices in political science, and to address these concerns they created a "Perestroika movement" in the discipline. This movement resulted in, among other actions, the creation of a new journal, *Perspectives*, launched in 2001. *Perspectives* maintains explicitly and self-consciously that its role is to offer more substantively and methodologically diverse perspectives than are currently available in the discipline. The existence of the Perestroika movement and the emergence of *Perspectives* provide anecdotal evidence that the intellectual assumptions that underlie political science have made it difficult for scholars working on communities of color to publish in political science journals. The Perestroika movement prompted discussions in the panel rooms and lunch tables at the American Political Science Association meetings where black public opinion researchers shared the stories of their personal difficulty with finding an audience for their work in political science.

With only unsystematic, narrative evidence it would be easy to overstate this issue, but it is at least worth taking note of a nearly universal impression among emerging and established scholars of black public opinion that it is difficult for them to publish in the top journals in political science. Like data shortages, lack of publishing opportunities represents a second structural constraint on the study of black public opinion. If it is difficult to publish in their field and journal publications are necessary for tenure and promotion at the nation's top research institutions, then the subfield of black public opinion will find it difficult to attract and retain the most innovative, exciting, and ambitious young scholars.

Toward a New Agenda

The study of black public opinion enjoys decades of contributions by established researchers, but it also faces deficiencies in research knowledge and data availability and structural constraints. The future of the study of black public opinion lies in addressing the intellectual shortcomings in the field and developing innovations to overcome the structural constraints facing researchers.

As political science moves into the twenty-first century, black public opinion researchers must reorient the study of African American political attitudes to a more complicated racial and political world. This means that scholars must grapple with the intersections of race with other social cleavages and identities. A new agenda for the study of black public opinion must begin with a comprehensive intersectional approach to the study of race that acknowledges its shifting dynamics and meanings in marginal communities. This new agenda must also employ a comparative racial framework that situates African American opinion within a broader multiracial context. Finally, the new agenda for black public opinion research must shed parochial assumptions about what constitutes the appropriate areas for study of black opinion. African Americans are complicated political beings with attitudes that extend across multiple political domains. It is the job of public opinion researchers to discover, map, and analyze those opinions.

In addition to broadening the substantive focus of the field, public opinion research must also use methodological innovations. This means not only demanding more responsiveness from the ANES and GSS to survey racial oversamples and to include relevant batteries of questions but also thinking creatively about sources of knowledge. Experimental work offers one largely untapped methodological possibility. Those who study white racial attitudes have made extensive use of experimental findings to test mechanisms of racial reasoning among white citizens, but very few researchers of black public opinion have followed suit. Experiments are relatively inexpensive when compared with national surveys and offer the possibility of making causal statements and exploring mechanisms of change and reproduction in black attitudes (Harris-Lacewell 2004). Black public opinion researchers can also potentially form a vanguard in counter-hegemonic movements in political science by questioning the epistemological assumptions that elevate statistical evidence over other ways of knowing.

African American political thought can be studied in many ways. Dawson's (2003) *Black Visions* provides a rich historical account of the nuances of black political thought. Harris-Lacewell's (2004) *Barbershops, Bibles, and BET* combines survey data, experimental research, and ethnographic research to map constellations of contemporary black opinion. Historian Barbara Savage (1999) has pointed the way to using an analysis of media outlets to understand influences on public opinion. Taeku Lee (2002) uses correspondence to the President as a site for understanding race and public opinion. These projects represent some of the innovations that are possible for challenging the ways that political scientists claim to understand the attitudes and ideas of the mass public. These are the thematic and methodological concerns that will shape the study of black public opinion in the years to come.

Notes

1. After the high participation periods of the 1960s and 1970s black political participation began to look more consistent with expectations of socioeconomic status, but researchers did continue to find populations of African Americans who defied participatory expectations. For example, Bobo and Gilliam (1990) find that African Americans living in areas of high black empowerment are more likely to participate politically.

2. The 1984 and 1988 National Black Election Studies (NBES) were prompted by the presidential bids of Jesse Jackson. These national surveys spawned a generation of research by young black political scientists. I discuss these studies in more length in a section below. The 1984 NBES included telephone interviews with 1,150 blacks of voting age respondents prior to the presidential election and postelection re-interviews with 872 of the original respondents. The 1988 NBES attempted to re-contact all 1,150 original respondents and was successful in completing 473 pre-election interviews and 392 post-election interviews. The sample was drawn using a random-digit dialing design that selected disproportionately from geographic areas representing varying densities of black populations. Respondents were selected randomly from all eligible households. The 1984 and 1988 NBES were administered through the Interuniversity Consortium for Political and Social research (ICPSR) at the University of Michigan–Ann Arbor under principal investigator James Jackson.

3. The data from the National Black Politics Study (NBPS) come from a probability sample of all African American households, yielding 1,206 observations of African Americans 18 years or older. The survey was conducted by telephone between November 20, 1993 and February 20, 1994, with a response rate of 65 percent. The survey was administered through the University of Chicago with principal investigators Ronald Brown of Wayne State University and Michael Dawson of the University of Chicago. NBPS respondents ranged in age from 18 to 88, with 43 being the average age. Sixty-five percent of NBPS respondents were women. Eighty-six percent had completed at least a high school diploma.

4. The 1996 NBES was administered through the Interuniversity Consortium for Political and Social research (ICPSR) at the University of Michigan–Ann Arbor under principal investigator Katherine Tate. This survey was modeled after the original 1984 NBES. Telephone interviewing began July 19 and ended on November 4, 1996. The data included telephone interviews with 1,216 voting-eligible blacks. Immediately following the election, 854 respondents were re-interviewed; the post-election re-interviewing ended January 6, 1997. Sixty-three percent of the sample was female. The 1996 NBES sample was very similar to the original 1984 sample. Both overrepresent women, middle-income and educated blacks, and blacks in the labor force and working.

References

Aberbach, Joel D., and Jack L. Walker. 1970. Political trust and racial ideology. *American Political Science Review* 64, no. 4 (December): 1199–219.

Abney, F. Glenn, and John D. Hutcheson. 1981. Race, representation, and trust: Changes in attitudes after the election of a black mayor. *Public Opinion Quarterly* 45, no 1 (Spring): 91–101.

Abramson, Paul R. 1972. Political efficacy and political trust among black school children: Two explanations. *Journal of Politics* 34, no. 4 (November): 1243–75.

Anderson, Barbara A., Brian D. Silver, and Paul R. Abramson. 1988. The effects of the race of the interviewer on race related attitudes of black respondents in SRC/CPS national election studies. *Public Opinion Quarterly* 52, no. 3 (Autumn): 289–324.

Barker, Lucius. 1989. *New perspectives in American politics*. New Brunswick, NJ: Transaction.

Bledsoe, Tim, Susan Welch, Lee Sigelman, and Michael Combs. 1995. Residential context and racial solidarity among African Americans. *American Journal of Political Science* 39, no. 2 (May): 434–58.

Bobo, Lawrence, and James Kleugel. 1993. Opposition to race-targeting: Self-interest, stratification, ideology, or racial attitudes? *American Sociological Review* 58, no. 4 (August): 443–64.

Brehm, John, and Wendy Rahn. 1997. Individual-level evidence for the causes and consequences of social capital. *American Journal of Political Science* 41, no. 3 (July): 999–1023.

Browning, Rufus P., Dale Rogers Marshall, and David H. Tabb. 1984. Protest is not enough. The struggle of blacks and Hispanics in urban politics. Berkeley: University of California Press.

———, eds. 1997. *Racial politics in American cities*. 2nd. ed. New York: Longman.

Bunche, Ralph. 1935. A critical analysis of the tactics and programs of minority groups. *Journal of Negro Education* 4, no. 3 (July): 308–20.

Calhoun-Brown, Alison. 1996. African-American churches and political mobilization: The psychological impact of organizational resources. *Journal of Politics* 58, no. 4 (November): 935–53.

Carmichael, Stokely, and Charles Hamilton. 1967. *Black power: The politics of liberation in America*. New York: Vintage.

Cohen, Cathy J. 1999. *The boundaries of blackness: AIDS and the breakdown of black politics*. Chicago: University of Chicago Press.

Cohen, Cathy J., and Michael C. Dawson. 1993. Neighborhood poverty and African American politics. *American Political Science Review* 87, no. 2 (June): 286–302.

Collins, Patricia Hill. 1991. *Black feminist thought: Knowledge, consciousness, and the politics of empowerment*. New York: Routledge.

Davis, Darren W. 1997. The direction of race of interviewer effects among African Americans: Donning the black mask. *American Journal of Political Science* 41, no. 1 (January): 309–22.

Davis, Darren W., and Ronald E. Brown. 2002. The antipathy of black nationalism: Behavioral and attitudinal implications of an African American ideology. *American Journal of Political Science* 46, no. 2 (April): 239–52.

Davis, Darren W., and Christian Davenport. 1997. The political and social relevancy of Malcolm X: The stability of African Americans' political attitudes. *Journal of Politics* 59, no. 2 (May): 550–64.

Dawson, Michael C. 1994. *Behind the mule: Race and class in African-American politics*. Princeton, NJ: Princeton University Press.

———. 2001. *Black visions: The roots of contemporary African-American political ideologies*. Chicago: University of Chicago Press.

Dawson, Michael, and Cathy J. Cohen. 2002. Problems in the study of the politics of race. In *Political science state of the discipline*, edited by Ira Katznelson and Helen Milner. Washington, DC: W. W. Norton.

Drake, St. Clair, and Horace R. Cayton. 1962. *Black metropolis: A study of negro life in a northern city*. New York: Harper & Row.

Dunbar, Leslie. 1961. Reflections on the latest reform of the South. *Phylon* 22 (Fall): 249–57.

Ellison, Christopher G. 1993. Religious involvement and self-perception among black Americans. *Social Forces* 71, no. 4 (June): 1027–55.

Frazier, E. Franklin. 1974. *The negro church in America*. New York: Schocken.

Gartner, Scott Sigmund, and Gary Segura. 2000. Race, casualties and opinion in the Vietnam War. *Journal of Politics* 62, no. 1 (February): 115–46.

Gay, Claudine, and Katherine Tate. 1998. Doubly bound: The impact of gender and race on the politics of black women. *Political Psychology* 19, no. 1 (March): 169–84.

Genovese, Eugene. 1974. *Roll, Jordan, roll the world the slaves made*. New York: Vintage.

Gilliam, Frank. 1996. Exploring minority empowerment: Symbolic politics, governing coalitions and traces of political style in Los Angeles. *American Journal of Political Science* 40, no. 1 (February): 56–81.

Gilliam, Franklin D., and Shanto Iyengar. 2000. Prime suspects: The influence of local television on the viewing public. *American Journal of Political Science* 44, no. 3:560–73.

Gilroy, Paul. 2000. *Against race: Imagining political culture beyond the color line*. Cambridge, MA: Harvard University Press.

Glaser, James. 1995. Black and white perceptions of party differences. *Political Behavior* 17, no. 2 (June): 155–77.

Gosnell, Harold. 1935. *Negro politics: The rise of negro politics in Chicago*. Chicago: University of Chicago Press.

Hadley, Charles D. 1994. Blacks in southern politics: An agenda for research. *Journal of Politics* 56, no. 3 (August): 585–600.

Harris, Frederick C. 1999. *Something within: Religion in African-American political activism*. Oxford: Oxford University Press.

Harris-Lacewell, Melissa V. 2004. *Barbershops, Bibles, and BET: Everyday talk and black political thought*. Princeton, NJ: Princeton University Press.

Harris-Lacewell, Melissa V., and Bethany L. Albertson. 2004. Good times? Understanding African American misperceptions of racial economic fortunes. *Journal of Black Studies* 35, no. 5: 650–83.

Henry, Charles. 1990. *Culture and African American politics*. Bloomington: Indiana University Press.

Hetherington, Marc J., and Suzanne Globetti. 2002. Political trust and racial policy preferences. *American Journal of Political Science* 46, no. 2 (April): 253–75.

Hochschild, Jennifer. 1995. *Facing up to the American dream: Race, class and the soul of the nation*. Princeton, NJ: Princeton University Press.

Holden, Matthew. 1973. *The politics of the black "nation."* New York: Chandler.

Holt, Thomas. 2000. *The problem of race in the 21st century*. Cambridge, MA: Harvard University Press.

Howell, Susan E., and Deborah Fagan. 1988. Race and trust in government: Testing the political reality model. *Public Opinion Quarterly* 52, no. 3 (Autumn): 343–50.

Huckfeldt, Robert, and Carol Kohfeld. 1989. *Race and the decline of class in American politics*. Chicago: University of Illinois Press.

Jackson, Byran O., Elisabeth R. Gerber, and Bruce E. Cain. 1994. Coalitional prospects in a multiracial society: African-American attitudes toward other minority groups. *Political Research Quarterly* 47, no. 2 (June): 277–94.

Jones, Mack. 1972. A frame of reference for black politics. In *Black political life in the United States*, edited by Lenneal Henderson, <~?~Q: page numbers?>. San Francisco: Chandler.

Key, V. O. 1949. *Southern politics*. New York: Vintage.

Kim, Claire. 2000. *Bitter fruit: The politics of Black-Korean conflict in New York City*. New Haven, CT: Yale University Press.

Kinder, Donald, and Lynn Sanders. 1996. *Divided by color: Racial politics and democratic ideals*. Chicago: University of Chicago Press.

Kinder, Donald, and Nicholas Winter. 2001. Exploring the racial divide: Blacks, whites, and opinion on national policy. *American Journal of Political Science* 45, no. 2 (April): 439–56.

Kramer, Roderick. M. 1994. The sinister attribution error: Paranoid cognition and collective distrust in organizations. *Motivation & Emotion* 18:199–230.

Ladd, Everett. 1966. *Negro political leadership in the South*. Ithaca, NY: Cornell University Press.

Lee, Taeku. 2002. *Mobilizing public opinion: Black insurgency and racial attitudes in the civil rights era*. Chicago: University of Chicago Press.

Levine, Lawrence. 1977. *Black culture and black consciousness: Afro-American folk thought from slavery to freedom*. New York: Oxford.

Lien, Pei-Te. 1998. Does the gender gap in political attitudes and behavior vary across racial groups? *Political Research Quarterly* 51, no. 4: 869–94.

Lincoln, C. Eric, and Lawrence Mamiya. 1990. *The black church in the African American experience*. Durham, NC: Duke University Press.

Marx, Gary T. 1967. *Protest and prejudice: A study of belief in the black community*. New York: Harper & Row.

Matthews, Donald, and James Prothro. 1966. *Negroes and the new southern politics*. New York: Harcourt, Brace, and World.

McAdam, Doug. 1982. *Political process and the development of black insurgency, 1930–1970*. Chicago: University of Chicago Press.

McClain, Paula D., and John Garcia. 1993. Expanding disciplinary boundaries: Black, Latino, and racial minority group politics in political science. In *Political science: The state of the discipline II*, edited by Ada Finiftner, 246–79. Washington, DC: American Political Science Association.

McCormick, Joseph, and Robert Smith. 1989. Through the prism of Afro-American culture: An interpretation of the Jackson campaign style. In *Jesse Jackson's presidential campaign: Challenge and change in American politics*, edited by Lucius J. Barker and Ronald W. Walters, 96–107. Urbana: University of Illinois Press, 1989.

Morris, Irwin. 2000. African American voting on Proposition 187: Rethinking the prevalence of interminority conflict. *Political Research Quarterly* 53, no. 1 (March): 77–98.

Myrdal, Gunnar. 1944. *An American dilemma*. New York: Harper and Brothers.

Nelsen, Hart M., Thomas W. Madron, and Raytha L. Yokley. 1975. Black religion's Promethean motif: Orthodoxy and militancy. *American Journal of Sociology* 81, no. 1 (July): 139–46.

Olsen, Marvin E. 1970. The social and political participation of blacks. *American Sociological Review* 35, no. 4 (August): 682–96.

Orum, Anthony. 1966. A reappraisal of the social and political participation of negroes. *American Journal of Sociology* 72, no. 1 (July): 32–46.

Pattillo-McCoy, Mary. 1999. *Black picket fences: Privilege and peril among the black middle class*. Chicago: University of Chicago Press.

Pinkney, Alphonso. 1984. *Red, black and green: Black nationalism in the United States*. New York: Cambridge University Press.

Putnam, Robert. 2001. *Bowling alone: The collapse and revival of American community*. New York: Simon and Schuster.

Reed, Adolph. 1986. *The Jesse Jackson phenomenon: The crisis of purpose in Afro-American politics*. New York: Greenwood.

Roberts, Dorothy. 1995. Punishing drug addicts who have babies: Women of color, equality, and the right of privacy. In *Critical race theory: The key writings that formed the movement*, edited by Kimberle Crenshaw, Neil Gotanda, Gary Peller, and Kendall Thomas, 384–425. New York: New Press.

Rodgers, Harrel R., Jr. 1974. Toward explanation of the political efficacy and political cynicism of black adolescents: An exploratory study. *American Journal of Political Science* 18, no. 2 (May): 257–82.

Savage, Barbara Dianne. 1999. *Broadcasting freedom: Radio, war, and the politics of race, 1938–1948*. Chapel Hill: University of North Carolina Press.

Schuman, Howard, and Jean Converse. 1971. The effects of black and white interviewers on black responses in 1968. *Public Opinion Quarterly* 35, no. 1 (Spring): 44–68.

Schuman, Howard, Charlotte Steeh, Lawrence Bobo, and Maria Krysan. 1997. *Racial attitudes in America: Trends and interpretations*. Cambridge, MA: Harvard University Press.

Shingles, Richard D. 1981. Black consciousness and political participation: The missing link. *American Political Science Review* 75, no. 1 (March): 76–91.

Shipler, David. 1997. *A country of strangers: Blacks and whites in America*. New York: Knopf.

Sigelman, Lee, and Susan Welch. 1991. *Black Americans' views of racial inequality: The dream deferred*. New York: Cambridge University Press.

Silberman, Charles. 1964. *Crisis in black and white*. New York: Vintage.

Smith, Richard, and Robert Seltzer. 1992. *Race, class, and culture*. Albany: State University of New York Press.

Sonenshein, Raphael. 1993. *Politics in black and white: Race and power in Los Angeles*. Princeton, NJ: Princeton University Press.

Stuckey, Sterling. 1987. *Slave culture: Nationalist theory and the foundations of black America*. New York: Oxford University Press.

Tate, Katherine. 1993. *From protest to politics: The new black voters in American elections*. New York: Russell Sage.

Thorton, Michael, and Yuko Mizuno. 1999. Economic well-being and black adult feeling toward immigrants and whites, 1984. *Journal of Black Studies* 30, no. 1 (September): 15–44.

Verba, Sidney, and Nie, Norman. 1972. *Participation in America: Political democracy and social equality*. Chicago: University of Chicago Press.

Walker, Jack L. 1963. Protest and negotiation: A case study of negro leadership in Atlanta, Georgia. *Midwest Journal of Political Science* 7, no. 2 (May): 99–124.

Walters, Ronald. 1988. *Black presidential politics in America: A strategic approach*. Albany: State University Press of New York.

Walton, Hanes. 1972. *Black politics: A theoretical and structural analysis*. Philadelphia: J. B. Lipppincott.

———. 1973. *The study and analysis of black politics*. Metuchen, NJ: Scarecrow.

Washington, James Melvin. 1985. Jesse Jackson and the symbolic politics of black Christendom. *Annals of the American Academy of Political and Social Science* 480 (July): 89–105.

Waters, Mary. 1999. *Black identities: West immigrant dreams and American realities*. Cambridge, MA: Harvard University Press.

Welch, Susan, and Lee Sigelman. 1992. A gender gap among Hispanics? A comparison with blacks and Anglos. *The Western Political Quarterly* 45, no. 1 (March): 181–99.

Weiss, Nancy. 1983. *Farewell to the party of Lincoln: Black politics in the age of FDR*. Princeton, NJ: Princeton University Press.

Wickham, DeWayne. 2002. *Bill Clinton and black America*. New York: Ballantine.

Wilson, James Q. 1960. *Negro politics*. New York: Free Press.

———. 1961. The strategy of protest: Problems of negro civic action. *Journal of Conflict Resolutions* 5, no. 3 (September): 291–303.

Wilson, William J. 1980. *The seclining significance of race: Blacks and the changing American institutions*. Chicago: University of Chicago Press.

———. 1987. *The truly disadvantaged: The inner city, the underclass, and public policy*. Chicago: University of Chicago Press.

CHAPTER SEVEN

A Black Gender Gap?

Continuity and Change in Attitudes toward Black Feminism

Evelyn M. Simien

USING DATA FROM the 1993–1994 National Black Politics Study and the 2004–2005 National Black Feminist Study, I observe a gender gap in attitudes toward black feminism among African Americans. The male-female difference is attributable to an attitudinal shift on the part of men that has persisted and widened over time. The attitudes of African American men are, on the whole, more liberal and progressive than the attitudes of African American women. In this chapter, I consider whether black feminist consciousness affects political behavior in general and various modes of political behavior in particular. I find that black feminists have been successful at galvanizing a mass following that actively participates in politics.

Introduction

One thing about African American public opinion is clear. Both the women's liberation and black civil rights movements have had a profound effect on attitudes toward gender equality and feminist priorities among African Americans. It is not so much the case that black civil society has come to embrace feminisms, nor has it come to identify with the goals and objectives of the women's liberation movement per se. Rather, the effect is seen in the controversy that black feminism has engendered within African American communities concerning the simultaneity of oppression and the belief that such co-dependent variables as race, class, gender, and sexuality cannot be separated (or ranked) in lived experience.

Time and time again, African American women have felt forced to choose between their commitments to women's liberation and to black civil rights. The Anita Hill/Clarence Thomas and Desiree Washington/Mike Tyson episodes have made this much clear. In 1991, U.S. Supreme Court Justice Clarence Thomas was accused of sexual harassment. His accuser, Anita Hill, was a black female law professor at the University of Oklahoma. Despite her testimony, the Senate voted 52 to 48 to confirm Thomas's nomination to the Supreme Court. In 1992, the former heavyweight boxing champion, Mike Tyson, went on trial for the rape of Miss Black Rhode Island, Desiree Washington. Tyson was convicted on February 10, 1992. Both controversies drew critical attention to issues of vital concern to black women—sexual harassment and rape. However, the interests of black women and black men were pitted against each other, and many in black communities across this country lined up on the side of black men (Gay and Tate 1998; White 1999). Supporters saw Clarence Thomas and Mike Tyson as high-profile victims of racial discrimination. Anita Hill and Desiree Washington, on the other hand, were considered part of a larger conspiracy to sabotage the successful careers of upwardly mobile black men (White 1999). In light of these two examples, the gender gap in attitudes toward black feminism has real-world implications for the conduct of legislative proceedings and outcomes of judicial decisions.

An understanding of the gender gap in attitudes toward black feminism can alert us to issues relevant to racial group consensus that black politicians and civil rights activists can use for the purpose of mobilizing the electorate and organizing the grassroots. Hence, the role of political scientists in raising consciousness and awareness about those circumstances that impinge on the lives of black women—sexual harassment and rape—cannot be overestimated, as they are not divisive issues but matters of vital concern to all people committed to social justice within and outside black communities.

The formation of African American public opinion takes place constantly as individual members of the race react to the world around them. African Americans are bombarded with persuasive communications daily from media outlets and information networks, local black leaders and civil rights activists, and voluntary organizations and religious spaces, as well as friends and family (Harris-Lacewell 2004). This flood of incoming information has a tremendous impact on the way African American men and women think about the simultaneity of oppression, which makes it especially difficult to predict the nature of African American public opinion and how it changes. To date, the aggregate patterns and trends in race and gender (or feminist) consciousness have not received considerable attention. Relatively little is known about the level of support for black feminist consciousness among African Americans, particularly over time.

Utilizing data from the 1993–1994 National Black Politics Study (NBPS) and the 2004–2005 National Black Feminist Study (NBFS), I update findings published in earlier work on attitudes toward black feminism among African Americans (Simien 2004; Simien and Clawson 2004). More specifically, I examine whether male and female respondents display a different level of support for black feminism than they did a decade ago. Along the way, I discover an important trend in African American public opinion that clearly attests to the fact that certain political attitudes are more persistent and consequential than others. For instance, I observe a gender gap in black feminist attitudes that points to a process whereby men are, in some cases, more likely to support black feminist tenets than are women. The male-female difference is attributable to an attitudinal shift on the part of men that persists over time. This finding is consistent with evidence reported in prior work, which suggested that a gender gap in African American public opinion toward gender equality and feminist priorities might become more pronounced in the future (Simien 2004). Item analysis reveals both the distinctiveness and heterogeneity of African American public opinion. The attitudes of African American men are, on the whole, more liberal and progressive than the attitudes of African American women toward black feminist tenets.

Here I also consider whether black feminist consciousness affects political behavior in general and various modes in particular—for example, voting in presidential elections, contacting public officials and signing petitions, attending protest meetings or demonstrations, giving someone a ride to the polls, aiding a voter registration drive, and donating money to a campaign. I find that black feminist thinkers have been successful at disseminating their beliefs about the matrix of domination and galvanizing a mass following that actively participates in politics. Therefore, I conclude that black feminists have had a recognizable impact on the constituency they aim to serve.

Previous Research

Much of the literature on African American public opinion ignores the issue of male-female differences or the gender gap in attitudes toward gender equality and feminist priorities among African Americans. To date, only two political scientists have tracked male-female differences in public opinion toward feminist belief systems over a long period of time using a comparative approach that included both African American men and women in their analyses—namely, Fulenwider (1980) and Simien (2004). Using data from the 1972–1976 American National Election Studies, Fulenwider (1980) discovered a startling trend in minority attitudes toward feminism. In 1972 minority men were almost twice as likely as minority women to oppose feminism, but by 1976, the reverse became true. Whereas 29 percent of minority women opposed feminism, only 13 percent of minority men opposed feminism. Item analysis revealed that minority women were more opposed both to the women's liberation movement when asked to rate the movement according to a feeling thermometer and to its tactics for social change that involved women—of any race—organizing and working together.

Given that the women's liberation movement reflected the aims and objectives of white middle-class women, its leadership treated the interests of black women as less important. Therefore, it is not particularly surprising that many black women organized separately around their own interests during the years of 1972–1976 (Roth 2004; Springer 2005). Since then, however, Simien (2004) discovered a like trend in attitudes toward black feminism among African Americans. From 1984 through 1988, African American men were less likely to exhibit an awareness of sex-role socialization and the comparative influence of women in society, but by 1993 and 1994, African American men were equally and, in some cases, more likely than African American women to exhibit such awareness. More specifically, Simien (2004) found that there was a significant difference in the responses to three items by African American women and men using data from the 1984–1988 National Black Election Study (NBES). One item asked respondents whether men were better suited emotionally for politics. Another asked whether men possess too much influence, just about the right amount of influence, or too little influence; a third item asked the same question about women. This analysis indicated that roughly 39 percent of black women strongly disagreed with the statement that men are better suited for politics versus 27 percent of black men. And although less than half of the male respondents (45 percent) indicated that men have too much power, the majority of women (60 percent) indicated that men did in fact possess too much power. Finally, just under one-third of black women (30 percent) believed that women have far too little power, in contrast with less than a quarter of black men (24 percent). Although these items do not capture the full essence of black feminist thought, they do successfully capture some component of feminism. In prior research, scholars used similar items that tapped perceptions of sex role socialization and the comparative influence of women in society. In fact, Fulenwider (1980, 44) identified such items as "basic to the core belief structure of a feminist belief system."

Using data from the 1993–1994 NBPS, Simien (2004) found that African American men were more likely to recognize that the problems of racism, poverty, and sexual discrimination are linked together; that black feminist groups help the black community; and that they share a common fate with black women. However, African American men were somewhat less likely to support the idea that black women should share equally in the political leadership of the black community and to acknowledge that black women suffered from both sexism within the black movement and racism within the women's movement. Although these differences were not statistically significant in 1993 and 1994, this does not imply homogeneity on the part of African American women and men in their attitudes toward black feminism. When Simien (2004) examined only those who "strongly agreed" with the position that there should be more black women clergy, a twelve-point difference existed between African American women and men. African American men, in this case, were far more likely to take a progressive stance on the issue of black women clergy.

One view has emerged to explain this trend in attitudes toward black feminism among African Americans. Although the objective condition of African American women seemingly warrants the development of black feminist consciousness, as they occupy the lower stratum of the social hierarchy, the idea that racism is the sole cause of black female subordination has inhibited its development. Many African American men and women continue to hold the view that feminism is the cultural property of white women and that black women who identify with it are less authentically black. That is to say, the acute awareness of "interlocking systems of oppression" on the part of African American women cannot be assumed. When some African American women still feel that black feminist groups do little more than divide black communities by working to advance their position, being both black and female does not automatically lead to support of black feminist tenets. According to the 1993–1994 National Black Politics Study, just under one-third of its female respondents (31 percent) held this view.

A long-standing debate exists within the black community about the relationship between black feminist consciousness and race loyalty. Black civil rights organizations and their predominately male leadership have argued that feminism detracts from race loyalty and divides its membership into separate camps. From this perspective, a focus on sex discrimination inhibits, or even precludes, the development of racial awareness and black empowerment. Robert Staples avers, "Any Movement that augments the sex-role antagonisms extant in the black community will only sow the seed of disunity and hinder the liberation struggle. Whether black women will participate in a female liberation movement is, of course, up to them. One, however, must be cognizant of the need to avoid a diffusion of energy devoted to the liberation struggle lest it dilute the over-all effectiveness of the movement" (1970, 15-16). That is to say, the need to subordinate matters of vital concern to African American women for the sake of black liberation should take precedence, so as to protect African American men from the forces of racism. Despite this position, many black feminist activists have spoken out against patriarchy in their communities only to find themselves sharply criticized by both African American men and women alike who argued that airing "dirty laundry" only fed white efforts at racial domination.

Given that African American women are targeted and, to some extent, mobilized by women's liberation and black civil rights organizations, controversies like that of Anita Hill/Clarence Thomas and Mike Tyson/Desiree Washington only exacerbate their unique situation of occupying a subordinate position within two marginalized groups for which they must forge alliances (Gay and Tate 1998; Mansbridge and Tate 1992; Simien 2005; Simien and Clawson 2004). During the highly publicized confirmation hearings for Supreme Court nominee Clarence Thomas, black feminists published a statement in support of Anita Hill that appeared November 17, 1991, in the *New York Times*, as well as in six black newspapers. Black feminists also launched an anti-rape campaign in the wake of the appeals case of Mike Tyson, which involved obtaining signatures in support of a full-page ad that appeared April 15-21, 1993, in the *St. Louis American* and included educational workshops, radio interviews, and television appearances, as well as flyers and mailings debunking racist and sexist myths about rape. Working in this way, black feminists participated in a process that wedded black feminist theory with various modes of political behavior.

Such political acts on their part are significant because, at the very least, they attest to the lengths at which black feminists are willing to resist patriarchal power aimed at their families and communities. Black feminists are situated at the center of two political movements that, when cast as diametrically opposed, create uneasy alliances. Therefore, the ability to adopt a dispassionate, objective stance toward such cross-cutting issues as sexual harassment and rape that so obviously affect them personally is virtually impossible. By virtue of their intense and passionate advocacy, black feminists have found a voice, and this new-found voice is unwilling to be dismissed, belittled, or rejected by other members of the adult African American population who refuse to recognize the simultaneity of oppression.

Significance of the Research

Although the above evidence seems somewhat mixed and contradictory, the fact remains that African American men were equally and, in some cases, more likely to endorse black feminist tenets than African American women in 1993–1994. In keeping with this trend, I anticipate a growing divide or gender gap in attitudes toward black feminism among African Americans with the understanding that prior research has paved the way for this analysis. Although the results cited above are neither absolute nor fixed in time, my expectation is that the male-female differential will *not* be attributable to any attitudinal shift on the part of African American women but rather to growing liberalism on the part of African American men that has persisted over time. Here, I pick up where Fulenwider (1980) and Simien (2004) left off. Using data from the 1993–1994 NBPS and the 2004–2005 NBFS, I extend their work by determining the level of support for black feminist consciousness in recent years and investigating whether black feminist consciousness stimulates active participation in politics.

Until recently, black feminist consciousness had not been defined and measured formally, let alone incorporated into empirical investigations of black political behavior (notable exceptions being Dawson 2001; Simien 2004; Simien and Clawson 2004). The present analysis of survey data allows me to investigate the extent to which black feminist thinkers have been successful at disseminating their core beliefs and galvanizing a mass following of African American men and women who actively participate in politics. To date, the question that remains unanswered is whether black feminist thinkers can realistically compete in the ideological marketplace amidst nationalist and liberal formations. Assuming that black feminist thinkers wish to translate their ideas into mass political behavior, they must make their intellectual pursuits available to non-elite actors. Ideally, black feminist thinkers must merge theory and practice so as to affect the lives of those most vulnerable to oppression. Otherwise, the study of black feminist thought and praxis will remain largely limited, with little prescriptive utility for individuals and groups that confront interlocking systems of oppression.

Research Questions

At the heart of this chapter are answers to the following questions: Does the level of support for black feminism differ across gender and persist over time? Given that African American women are often asked to choose between their commitments to women's liberation and to black civil rights, my expectation is that African American women will support black feminist consciousness to a lesser extent than African American men. Does black feminist theorizing translate into political behavior generally and various modes specifically? Given that black feminists have used various mobilization strategies to recruit both male and female supporters for collective action, my expectation is that black feminist consciousness will serve as an impetus for political behavior in general and various modes in particular. Answers to these questions speak to whether black feminist thinkers have made their intellectual work accessible to those outside of academe and have mobilized successfully the constituency they aim to serve.

Data

The present study requires that attitudes toward black feminism among African Americans be measured on two separate occasions. To assess continuity and change in these attitudes. I compare two distinct samples of the adult African American population. The 1993–1994 NBPS is a unique study in that it contains questions that measure black feminist consciousness with multiple survey items that address the core of black feminist thought. It was conducted between December 1993 and February 1994. The data for the NBPS were obtained from a national probability sample of all black households: 1,206 telephone interviews were completed, each one with an African American respondent who was eligible to vote. Modeled after the NBPS, the data for the 2004–2005 NBFS was obtained from a national probability sample of all black households: 500 telephone interviews were completed, each one lasting about fifteen minutes. To be eligible, respondents had to be both African American and eligible to vote. The survey was conducted between November 2004 and January 2005 and administered by the Center for Survey Research (CSRA) at the University of Connecticut. Like the NBPS, the NBFS provides general information about the public attitudes and political preferences of voting-eligible African Americans. However, the focus of the NBFS is on black feminist consciousness and its effect on various modes of political behavior. To facilitate comparisons, the survey includes several of the questions that measure black feminist consciousness from the 1993–1994 NBPS (Dawson, Brown, and Jackson 1993). Demographic information on respondents included sex, age, education, marital status, income, and employment status.

The Samples

Table 7.1 compares several important demographic characteristics in the NBFS and the NBPS samples. When each sample is considered separately, one of the most noticeable features is their remarkable degree of similarity to the demographic characteristics of the overall African American population. This similarity is important for drawing inferences to African Americans generally. As is often the case with telephone surveys of the adult African American population, both samples were disproportionately female. However, the figure of 56 percent female in the NBFS is closer to the proportion of women in the overall African American population than the 65 percent figure in the NBPS. As usual in telephone surveys of African Americans that correlate census tract density information with directory-listed telephone households using a computer-assisted telephone interviewing (CATI) system, the sample population was relatively older (Dawson 2001). The mean age for respondents was 37 for the NBFS and 43 for the NBPS. These samples were also biased upwardly in terms of socioeconomic status in that high school dropouts make up 21 and 17 percent of respondents, respectively. In addition, the NBFS was slightly better at picking up the high end of the income

TABLE 7.1 Characteristics of the Samples, 2004–2005 NBFS versus 1993–1994 NBPS

2004–2005 NBFS		1993–1994 NBPS	
Percent	N=500	Percent	N=1206
79	High School Graduate	83	High School Graduate
Income		*Income*	
11	Less than $10,000	12	Less than $10,000
15	$11,000–$20,000	22	$11,000–$20,000
11	$21,000–$30,000	20	$21,000–$30,000
26	$31,000–$50,000	23	$31,000–$50,000
22	More than $50,000	15	More than $50,000
15	DK/Refused	8	DK/Refused
Marital Status		*Martial Status*	
37	Married	36	Married
63	Not Married	64	Not Married
Sex		*Sex*	
44	Male	35	Male
56	Female	65	Female
Age		*Age*	
16	18–24	13	18–24
20	25–34	23	25–34
29	35–49	33	35–49
21	50–64	20	50–64
11	65 & over	11	65 & over
3	DK/Refused	0	DK/Refused
61	Employed	64	Employed

Source: 2004–2005 National Black Feminist Study (NBFS) and 1993–1994 National Black Politics Study (NBPS).

distribution and the NBPS the low end. Of course, this difference might be attributable to inflation.

Operational Definitions and Measurement

Black feminist consciousness refers to the recognition that African American women are status-deprived because they face interlocking systems of oppression on the basis of race and gender (Collins 2000; D. King 1988; M. King 1975; Simien 2004). A complex concept, black feminist consciousness includes several interrelated attitudes and beliefs derived from the ideas and experiences of African American women. Several recurring themes delineate the contours of black feminist thought and appear in black feminist intellectual work: intersectionality, gender inequality, black feminism as benefiting the black community, and the linked fate of black women (Simien 2004; Simien and Clawson 2004). The first, intersectionality, involves an acute sense of awareness that the struggle to eradicate racism and sexism is rooted in other "isms" that plague humanity—namely, classism and heterosexism (Crenshaw 1993, 1995; D. King 1988). It is measured by two survey items: The first question asked whether racism, poverty, and sexual discrimination were linked together and should be addressed by the black community (Address All Discrimination), and the second question asked whether black women suffered from both sexism within the black movement and racism within the women's movement (Both Movements). The second theme is the acceptance of the belief that gender inequality and patriarchal practice exist within black communities, and the third is the acceptance of the belief that feminism benefits the black community by advancing the agenda of black women (Collins 2000; Harris 1999; hooks 1984, 1989; Robnett 1997; Stone 1979). The second theme is measured by two survey items: The first question asked whether black women should share equally in the political leadership of the black community (Black Women Leadership), and the second question asked whether more women should become members of the clergy in black churches (More Women Clergy). The third theme is measured by one survey question that asked respondents whether black feminist groups help the community by advancing the position of black women (Feminist Help Community). The fourth theme, linked fate, involves an acute sense of belonging or conscious loyalty to the group in question (i.e., black women) on account of having a shared experience. In this instance, the individual who identifies with the group label has come to realize that individual life chances are inextricably tied to the group (Dawson 1994). This theme is measured by one survey item that asked whether respondents thought that what generally happens to black women in this country will have something to do with what happens in their own lives (Linked Fate with Black Women).

The same six items were asked of African American women and men. All items were rescaled to a zero to one format with 1 indicating high black feminist consciousness. Using factor analysis, I determined whether all six items were closely related and equally effective measures of black feminist consciousness. On the basis of factor scores, I created an acceptable scale for which to measure black feminist consciousness. See Appendix A for exact question wording and response choices.

The measurement items chosen for political behavior have been examined previously (see, for example, Timpone 1998; Verba and Nie 1972; Verba, Schlozman, and Brady 1995). They have been tested and retested over the course of the landmark National Election Studies (NES) and the NBES. Comprised of those questions that best measure political behavior, this project replicates operational definitions that typically set the standard in political science survey research. Political behavior refers to those efforts by citizens to influence the selection of elected officials or public policy outputs (Beckwith 1986; Conway 1991; Guterbock and London 1983; Rosenstone and Hansen 1993; Verba and Nie 1972; Verba, Schlozman, and Brady 1995). It is important to note that there are several types or modes of political behavior and that voting is merely one type. Here, I consider an array of political activities that can be distinguished in terms of difficulty or desired impact on government. It is also the case that some activities require more initiative than others and that black citizens will engage in activities requiring the least amount of motivation because of their lack of resources—money, civic skills, and time—that have been shown to influence the likelihood of political participation (Angus et al. 1960; Rosenstone and Hansen 1993; Timpone 1998; Verba and Nie 1972; Verba, Schlozman, and Brady 1995). Thus, citizens who participate in electoral and governmental politics tend to come from the most advantaged sectors of society. Typically, they are wealthy, well-educated Americans. They also tend to be more informed, politically interested, and efficacious than others (Bobo and Gilliam 1990; Rosenstone and Hansen 1993).

Of all types of political behavior, presidential election turnout is thought to be the easiest to engage in because political parties, media outlets, and campaign organizations try the hardest to mobilize the electorate during national elections (Beckwith 1986; Verba and Nie 1972; Wolfinger and Rosenstone 1980). The basic argument is that voting does not require much attention to politics (Campbell et al. 1960; Rosenstone and Hansen 1993; Verba and Nie 1972; Verba, Schlozman, and Brady 1995). Signing a petition is another political activity that is among the least difficult to engage in because it requires little personal initiative on the part of the citizen (Rosenstone and Hansen 1993; Verba and Nie 1972). Both voting and signing a petition yield collective outcomes through cooperative behavior among citizens (Rosenstone and Hansen 1993; Verba and Nie 1972; Verba, Schlozman, and Brady 1995). It is assumed here that voting, signing a petition in support of a specific candidate, and signing a petition in support of or against some issue are indirect forms of communicating messages to government officials (Verba and Nie 1972; Verba, Schlozman, and Brady 1995).

Direct contact behavior, on the other hand, constitutes a more difficult political activity to engage in because it requires much initiative on the part of the citizen. As Verba and Nie (1972) have suggested, citizens have to decide whom to contact, when to contact the person, and why to do so by certain means—namely, writing a letter and making a phone call. Communal and campaign activities are also among the most difficult participatory acts because such political engagement involves volunteerism on the part of the citizen—devoting hours to the campaign, contributing dollars to the candidate, dispatching communications to various media outlets, and attending protests (Beckwith 1986; Conway 1985; Guterbock and London 1983; Rosenstone and Hansen 1993; Verba and Nie 1972; Verba, Schlozman, and Brady 1995).

Respondents were asked whether they had voted in the last presidential election, contacted a public official, provided transportation to the polls, attended a protest rally or fundraiser, signed a petition, helped in a voter registration drive, donated money to a political candidate, or handed out campaign material. Using factor analysis, I determined whether thirteen items were closely related and equally effective measures of political behavior. On the basis of factor scores, I created a scale by which to measure black political behavior in general, as well as separate scales for voting, indirect and direct contact behavior, and communal and campaign activity by which to measure various modes of political behavior in particular. See Appendix A for exact question wording and response choices.

Results

The first goal was to determine who supports black feminist tenets and whether the level of support for black feminist consciousness differs by gender. Cross-tabulation was the method of choice to organize, describe, and summarize observations. I compared the proportion of black women who possess black feminist consciousness to the proportion of black men who support its fundamental tenets. Tables 7.2 and 7.3 present the results from the 2004-2005 NBFS and the 1993–1994 NBPS. The data show that black feminist attitudes did change somewhat over time, though there are some areas of striking stability. It appears that black feminist intellectuals have been successful in disseminating their beliefs about the matrix of domination.

Analysis of the 2004–2005 NBFS shows that roughly 72 percent of all respondents believe that racism, poverty, and sexual discrimination are linked together. Another 68 percent report that black feminist groups are beneficial to the black community. Even more respondents endorse the notion that black women should share equally in the political leadership of the black community and express that what generally happens to black women in this country will have something to do with their own lives—96 percent and 75 percent, respectively. Although there is less support for black female clergy, the majority (67 percent) indicate that more black women should be allowed to become members of the clergy. These numbers reflect an upward trend in the level of support for black feminist consciousness for both sexes.

Analysis of the 1993–1994 NBPS showed that 70 percent of all respondents believe that racism, poverty, and sexual discrimination are linked together. Another 68 percent report that black feminist groups are beneficial to the black community because they advance the position of black women. An even greater proportion, 78 percent, endorse the notion that black women should share equally in the political leadership of the black community and 71 percent agree that what generally happens to black women in this country will have something to do with their own lives. Although there was less support for black female clergy, the majority, 55 percent, indicate that more black women should be allowed to become members of the clergy.

The results from the 2004–2005 NBFS bear a striking resemblance to those of the 1993–1994 NBPS in that black feminist consciousness appears to be widespread for both sexes when African American women and men are studied together. The gender gap in African American public opinion becomes apparent when we examine African American men and women separately. When we examine those who agree that problems of racism, poverty, and sexual discrimination are linked together, a twelve-point difference exists between African American women and men. Whereas an eleven-point difference exists when we examine those who agree with the statement that black feminist groups help the black community, a nine-point difference exists when we examine those who agree with the statement that black churches or places of worship should allow more women to become members of the clergy.

TABLE 7.2 Support for Black Feminist Consciousness in 2004–2005

	Black Women N=278	Black Men N=222	TOTAL N=500
The problems of racism, poverty, and sexual discrimination are all linked together. (Address All Discrimination)	67**	79**	72
Black feminist groups help the black community by advancing the position of black women. (Feminist Help Community)	63**	74**	68
Black women should share equally in the political leadership of the black community. (Black Women Leadership)	95	96	96
Black churches or places of worship should allow more women to become members of the clergy. (More Women Clergy)	63*	72*	67
Strongly agree	47	49	48
What generally happens to black women in this country will have something to do with your life. (Linked Fate with Black Women)	74	75	75
Black women have suffered from both sexism within the black movement and racism within the women's movement. (Both Movements)	75	72	74

Source: 2004–2005 National Black Feminist Study.

Note: For all of the items, except for the linked fate item, table entries are the percentage of respondents who indicated that they strongly agreed or somewhat agreed with that statement. For the linked fate item, the table entry is the percentage of respondents who indicated that they thought what generally happens to black women will affect them a lot or some.

*p < 0.05; **p < 0.01; for 2–tailed test

The fact that African American men are equally and, in some cases, more likely than African American women to support black feminist tenets in 2004-2005 clearly bolsters prior research. Based on data from the 1984–1988 NBES and the 1993–1994 NBPS, Simien (2004) reported a similar trend in black attitudes toward gender equality and feminist priorities. Moreover, the 2004–2005 NBPS contains enough respondents to allow us to be confident that these changes are real—they are no accident. The data show that support for black feminist tenets increased from 1993–1994 to 2004–2005 and that many of the differences in male-female attitudes reached statistical significance.

To date, scholars have debated the societal effects of such interrelated trends as increased female participation in the paid labor force, better educational opportunities for women, the breakdown of the traditional family unit, and the transformation of gender roles in the home (Klein 1984). Perhaps the rise of single-parent female-headed households in African American families might explain contemporary attitudes toward black feminism. Of course, more work

TABLE 7.3   Support for Black Feminist Consciousness in 1993–1994

	Black Women N=781	Black Men N=425	TOTAL N=1206
The problems of racism, poverty, and sexual discrimination are all linked together. (Address All Discrimination)	71	68	70
Black feminist groups help the black community by advancing the position of black women. (Feminist Help Community)	69	65	68
Black women should share equally in the political leadership of the black community. (Black Women Leadership)	77	79	78
Black churches or places of worship should allow more women to become members of the clergy. (More Women Clergy)	54	59	55
Strongly agree	41**	53**	47
What generally happens to black women in this country will have something to do with your life. (Linked Fate with Black Women)	70	72	71
Black women have suffered from both sexism within the black movement and racism within the women's movement. (Both Movements)	55	49	53

Source: 1993–1994 National Black Politics Study.

Note: For the first three items, table entries are the percentage of respondents who chose that option when presented with two choices. For the More Women Clergy item, the first table entry is the percentage of respondents who indicated that they strongly agreed or somewhat agreed with that statement, and the second table entry is the percentage of respondents who indicated that they strongly agreed with that statement. For the linked fate item, the table entry is the percentage of respondents who indicated that they thought what generally happens to black women will affect them a lot or some.

*p < 0.05; **p < 0.01; for 2–tailed test

must be done to conclusively link the rising incidence of single-parent female-headed households among other factors to liberal attitudes toward gender equality and feminist priorities. Unfortunately, no survey items were available in either the 1993–1994 NBPS or the 2004-2005 NBFS to make this determination.

The second goal was to determine the effect of black feminist consciousness on political behavior in general. Table 7.4 presents the estimates for the regression model of political behavior separately for black women and men. The first important finding is that black feminist consciousness stimulates political behavior among black women. Both educational attainment and church attendance have a positive effect on black female political behavior. Marital status is also a significant predictor of political behavior for black women, indicating that single women are more likely to participate in American political processes. However, such variables as income, home ownership, age, and urban residence are not significant predictors of political behavior for black women. Table 7.4 also

TABLE 7.4 Determinants of Black Political Behavior, Estimated Separately for Gender

Independent Variables	Black Women	Black Men
Group Consciousness		
Black Feminist	0.207**	0.226**
	(0.069)	(0.079)
Socioeconomic Status		
Education	0.326**	0.224**
	(0.088)	(0.094)
Income	0.017	0.067
	(0.054)	(0.053)
Other Predictors		
Urban Residence	0.081	0.077
	(0.043)	(0.048)
Age	0.035	0.101
	(0.064)	(0.071)
Home Ownership	0.010	0.022
	(0.032)	(0.035)
Marital Status	–0.071*	–0.049
	(0.030)	(0.034)
Church Attendance	0.026**	0.050
	(0.040)	(0.046)
Constant	–0.100	–0.147
	(0.079)	(0.084)
Adjusted R^2	0.169	0.115

Source: 2004–2005 National Black Feminist Study.

Table entries are unstandardized OLS regression coefficients, followed by the associated standard error.

*p < 0.05; **p < 0.01; for 2–tailed test

presents the estimates for the regression model of political behavior for black men, and the findings here differ from those reported above. Although black feminist consciousness stimulates black male political behavior, such predictors as marital status and church attendance do not. Especially striking is the fact that only two variables—black feminist consciousness and educational attainment—predict black male political behavior.

Next, I determine the effect of black feminist consciousness on various modes of political behavior in particular. Tables 7.5 and 7.6 present the estimates for the regression models of voting, indirect and direct contact behavior, and communal and campaign activity separately for African American women and men. With regard to voting in presidential elections, black feminist consciousness is statistically significant for both sexes. Other standard predictors of presidential voting include age, education, home ownership, and marital status for women, whereas income, urban residence, and church attendance are significant predictors for men. Given that the core themes of black feminist consciousness emphasize the importance of political activism, a particularly interesting finding is that black

TABLE 7.5   Determinants of Various Modes of Political Behavior, Estimated Separately for Black Women

Independent Variables	Voting	Indirect	Direct	Communal	Campaign
Group Consciousness					
Black Feminist	0.528**	0.491**	0.280**	0.042	0.126
	(0.123)	(0.120)	(0.118)	(0.106)	(0.081)
Socioeconomic Status					
Education	0.419**	0.502**	0.608**	−0.222	0.360**
	(0.156)	(0.152)	(0.149)	(0.134)	(0.103)
Income	−0.087	0.082	0.025	0.076	0.031
	(0.096)	(0.094)	(0.092)	(0.082)	(0.064)
Other Predictors					
Urban Residence	0.104	0.152*	0.145*	0.131*	0.008
	(0.077)	(0.075)	(0.074)	(0.066)	(0.051)
Age	0.234**	0.043	0.057	−0.199*	0.115
	(0.114)	(0.111)	(0.109)	(0.098)	(0.076)
Home Ownership	0.121*	0.010	−0.001	0.003	0.018
	(0.056)	(0.055)	(0.054)	(0.048)	(0.037)
Marital Status	−0.175**	−0.071	−0.106*	−0.152**	−0.024
	(0.054)	(0.053)	(0.052)	(0.047)	(0.036)
Church Attendance	0.085	0.003	0.055	0.015	0.028
	(0.072)	(0.070)	(0.069)	(0.062)	(0.048)
Constant	0.088	−0.214	−0.270*	0.209	−0.108
	(0.140)	(0.137)	(0.134)	(0.120)	(0.093)
Adjusted R^2	0.188	0.158	0.159	0.072	0.073

Source: 2004–2005 National Black Feminist Study.

Table entries are unstandardized OLS regression coefficients, followed by the associated standard error.

*p < 0.05; **p < 0.01; for 2-tailed test

feminist consciousness does not predict communal behavior for either sex. However, it clearly serves as an impetus for indirect and direct contact behavior among black women—that is, signing a petition in support of some issue or someone running for elective office, as well as contacting a public official or agency. It also serves as an impetus for campaign activity among black men—that is, donating money, helping in a voter registration drive, giving people a ride to the polls, attending fundraisers, and handing out campaign material. In this analysis, communal behavior was limited to taking part in a neighborhood march and attending a protest meeting. Considering that communal behavior was defined by only two political activities, it seems reasonable to assume that an expanded model of communal behavior inclusive of either non-political or additional political activities might yield different results.

I contend that black feminist consciousness and its effect on communal behavior warrant further investigation, especially when considering that such other variables as urban residence, age, and marital status constitute the driving force behind communal activity for black women. Whereas younger, single black

TABLE 7.6 Determinants of Various Modes of Political Behavior, Estimated Separately for Black Men

Independent Variables	Voting	Indirect	Direct	Communal	Campaign
Group Consciousness					
Black Feminist	0.321*	0.296	0.145	0.064	0.294**
	(0.143)	(0.156)	(0.157)	(0.129)	(0.095)
Socioeconomic Status					
Education	0.070	0.419*	0.470*	0.357*	−0.005
	(0.170)	(0.185)	(0.186)	(0.153)	(0.112)
Income	0.284**	0.020	0.013	0.112	0.091
	(0.097)	(0.105)	(0.106)	(0.087)	(0.064)
Other Predictors					
Urban Residence	0.185*	0.131	0.215*	0.066	0.006
	(0.087)	(0.095)	(0.095)	(0.079)	(0.058)
Age	0.009	−0.003	0.141	0.055	0.147
	(0.129)	(0.141)	(0.142)	(0.117)	(0.085)
Home Ownership	0.017	0.058	0.062	−0.089	0.036
	(0.063)	(0.069)	(0.069)	(0.057)	(0.042)
Marital Status	−0.019	−0.096	0.044	−0.071	−0.059
	(0.061)	(0.067)	(0.067)	(0.055)	(0.040)
Church Attendance	0.198*	−0.075	0.065	−0.066	−0.165*
	(0.084)	(0.092)	(0.092)	(0.076)	(0.071)
Constant	0.148	−0.056	−0.248	−0.007	−0.198*
	(0.153)	(0.167)	(0.167)	(0.138)	(0.101)
Adjusted R^2	0.120	0.064	0.063	0.080	0.091

Source: 2004–2005 National Black Feminist Study.

Table entries are unstandardized OLS regression coefficients, followed by the associated standard error.

*p < 0.05; **p < 0.01; for 2–tailed test

women living in urban areas are more likely to engage in neighborhood marches and attend protest rallies, highly educated black men are more likely to participate in such activities because educational attainment constitutes the single predictor of communal behavior for black men. All in all, the effects of black feminist consciousness, socioeconomic status, and other standard predictors, such as age, urban residence, marital status, home ownership, and church attendance, on various modes of political behavior often differ across gender.

Conclusion

For years, African American men and women have exhibited similar aggregate patterns and trends in policy preferences and political partisanship. In fact, the search for a black gender gap was considered futile when studies revealed no appreciable differences in African American public opinion toward a series of issues ranging from military spending to social welfare (see, for example, Welch and Sigelman 1989). Not surprisingly, political scientists paid little attention to these seemingly inconsequential findings as they were not extensively reported and summarized in subsequent research. For this reason, I expect the findings cited here to stimulate additional scholarly work when the obvious question that emerges is why a black gender gap surfaced in the last two decades. Future research must consider the theoretical importance of contextual factors. More specifically, future empirical investigations should continue to focus on intragroup differences by paying close attention to gender role socialization and generational effects. Such a focus on how messages of gender role socialization are transmitted from mother to daughter, as well as from father to son, and how such information influences the development of black feminist consciousness would likely result in better models of black feminist support and predict the conditions under which black feminists of both sexes might support collaborative efforts to end patriarchy today.

It is also important to bear in mind that changes in aggregate attitudes may be at least partially the result of intergenerational differences. Younger generations have very different life experiences and values from those of older generations. Unlike the previous generation that came of age during the 1960s and 1970s, when attitudes toward traditional sex roles were changing, those who came of age during the 1980s and 1990s were more like to grow up in a single-parent household. That is to say, political scientists must clarify the theoretical bases for expecting black men to be more supportive of gender equality and feminist priorities than are black women by identifying several factors not investigated in prior research-specifically, gender role socialization and generational effects.

Notably, this research identifies a gender gap in attitudes toward black feminism among African Americans. It dispels the notion that African American men have not supported or have had no engagement with black feminism. Updating prior analysis, I show that the male-female differential in African American public opinion is attributable to growing liberalism on the part of African American men toward gender equality and feminist priorities. I recognize some striking stability in African American public opinion, which means that the present study provides additional evidence to support the claim that African American men have truly progressed in their thinking about traditional gender roles and have supported black feminist tenets for longer than many realize. African American women are similarly supportive of black feminist tenets, but to a lesser extent than African American men.

Although many African American women may be aware of the ways in which male privilege and white privilege operate to erase their lives and perspectives, some African American men and women continue to hold the view that feminism is the cultural property of white women and that black women who identify with it are less authentically black. For this reason, African American women often feel that they must reject feminism to avoid being labeled a traitor to the race (Gay and Tate 1998; Mansbridge and Tate 1992; Simien 2005; Simien and Clawson 2004). The dilemma of having to choose between women's liberation and black civil rights constitutes a crisis for most African American women as they are uniquely situated at the center of these respective movements.

Given that prior studies have neglected the importance of such intragroup relations in determining African American public opinion and political behavior, additional research is necessary to examine this phenomenon in more detail. The present study represents a step forward in this regard, especially when considering that black feminist consciousness is significantly related to black political behavior. Black citizens who recognize that the problems of racism, poverty, and sexual discrimination are linked together; that black feminists are beneficial to black communities; that black women should share equally in the political leadership and take on a more prominent role in the black church; and that they share a common fate with black women are more likely to actively participate in politics than those who do not subscribe to these core beliefs. To the extent that black politicians and civil rights activists value consensus issues over cross-cutting issues, the study of the gender gap in attitudes toward black feminism and its over-time variation alerts us to issues relevant to gender that promote racial group consensus and, at the same time, stimulate various modes of political behavior.

Appendix A: Variables and Coding

Items Tapping Black Feminist Consciousness

All of the variables were coded on a 0 to 1 scale, with 1 indicating greater support for black feminist consciousness.

"People have different ideas and opinions about politics. We would like to know what you think about the following matters. For the next several questions I'm going to give you two choices. Please tell us which choice is most true for you." (Some respondents volunteered "both"; those respondents were coded as a 0.5.)

Address All Discrimination: The problems of racism, poverty, and sexual discrimination are all linked together and must be addressed by the black community or blacks should emphasize the struggle around race.

Black Feminist Help Community: Black feminist groups help the black community by working to advance the position of black women or black feminist groups just divide the black community.

Black Women Leadership: Black women should share equally in the political leadership of the black community or black women should not undermine black male leadership.

Common Fate with Black Women: Do you think that what generally happens to black women in this country will have something to do with what happens in your life? Will it affect you a lot, some, or not very much?

"I'm going to read some questions and please tell me if you strongly agree, somewhat agree, somewhat disagree, strongly disagree."

More Women Clergy: Black churches or places of worship should allow
   more women to become members of the clergy.
Both Movements: Black women have suffered from both sexism within
   the black movement and racism within the women's movement
   or black women mostly suffer from the same type of problems as
   black men.

Items Tapping Political Behavior

All of the variables were coded on a 0 to 1 scale, with 1 indicating greater political engagement.

Political Activity

"As I read from a list of political activities that people sometimes do, please tell
me whether or not you have engaged in these activities in the last TWO years?
Have you..." Respondents who replied yes were coded 1, and respondents who
replied no were coded 0.

Voting
Presidential: Did you vote in the past presidential election?

Indirect Contact Behavior
Signed Petition Supporting Candidate: Signed a petition supporting a candidate who was running for office.
Signed Petition Supporting Something: Signed a petition in support of
   something or against something

Direct Contact Behavior
Contacted Public Official: Contacted a government agency.
Contacted Elected Official: Have you ever contacted an elected official
   about a concern or problem that you have had?

Communal Activity

"Now, I'm going to read you a list of things people have done to address such problems as neighborhood crime, drug trafficking, the quality of education or the
safety of children. Please tell me if you have done any of these things in the last
2 years."

Attend Protest Meeting: Attended a protest meeting or demonstration
Take Part In March: Taken part in a neighborhood march

Campaign Activity

Helped in Voter Registration: Helped in voter registration drive.
Give Ride to Polls: Given people a ride to the polls on Election Day.

Give Money: Given money to a political candidate
Attend Fundraiser: Attended a fundraiser for a candidate
Hand out Campaign Material: Handed out campaign material or placed
   campaign material on cars.

References

Beckwith, Karen. 1986. *American women and political participation: The impact of work, generation, and feminism.* Westport, CT: Greenwood.

Bobo, Lawrence D., and Franklin D. Gilliam Jr. 1990. Race, sociopolitical participation, and black empowerment. *American Political Science Review* 84, no. 2 (June): 377–94.

Campbell, Angus, Philip E. Converse, Warren E. Miller, and Donald E. Stokes. 1960. *The American voter.* New York: Wiley.

Collins, Patricia Hill. 2000. *Black feminist thought.* 2nd ed. New York: Routledge.

Conway, Margaret. 1991. *Political participation in the United States.* Washington, DC: CQ Press.

Crenshaw, Kimberle. 1993. Demarginalizing the intersection of race and sex: A black feminist critique of antidiscrimination doctrine, feminist theory and antiracist politics. In *Feminist legal theory,* edited by D. Kelly Weisberg, 383–95. Philadelphia: Temple University Press.

———. 1995. Mapping the margins: Intersectionality, identity politics, and violence against women of color. In *Critical race theory,* edited by Kimberle Crenshaw et al. New York: New Press.

Dawson, Michael. 1994. *Behind the mule: Race and class in African-American politics.* Princeton, NJ: Princeton University Press.

———. 2001. *Black visions.* Chicago: University of Chicago Press.

Dawson, Michael, Ronald Brown, and James S. Jackson. 1993. National Black Politics Study Codebook (ICPSR 2018). Ann Arbor, MI: Inter-university Consortium for Political and Social Research.

Fulenwider, Claire Knoche. 1980. *Feminism in American politics.* New York: Praeger.

Gay, Claudine, and Katherine Tate. 1998. Doubly bound: The impact of gender and race on the politics of black women. *Political Psychology* 19, no. 1 (March): 169–84.

Guterbock, Thomas M., and Bruce London. 1983. Race, political orientation, and participation: An empirical test of four competing theories. *American Sociological Review* 48, no. 4 (August): 439–53.

Harris, Fredrick C. 1999. *Something within: Religion in African American political activism.* New York: Oxford University Press.

Harris-Lacewell, Melissa V. 2004. *Barbershops, Bibles, and BET: Everyday talk and black political thought.* Princeton, NJ: Princeton University Press.

hooks, bell. 1984. *Feminist theory: From margin to center.* Boston: South End.

———. 1989. *Talking back.* Boston: South End.

King, Deborah. 1988. Multiple jeopardy, multiple consciousness: The context of black feminist ideology. *Signs* 14, no. 1 (Autumn): 42–72.

King, Mae. 1975. Oppression and power: The unique status of black women in the American political system. *Social Science Quarterly* 56, no. 1:117–28.

Klein, Ethel. 1984. *Gender politics: From consciousness to mass politics.* Cambridge, MA: Harvard University Press.

Mansbridge, Jane, and Katherine Tate. 1992. Race trumps gender: The Thomas nomination in the black community. *PS* 25, no. 3 (September): 488–92.

Robnett, Belinda. 1997. *How long? How long? African American women in the struggle for civil rights.* New York: Oxford University Press.

Rosenstone, Steven J., and John Mark Hansen. 1993. *Mobilization, participation, and democracy in America.* New York: Macmillan.

Roth, Benita. 2004. *Separate roads to feminism.* Cambridge: Cambridge University Press.

Simien, Evelyn M. 2004. Gender differences in attitudes toward black feminism among African Americans. *Political Science Quarterly* 119, no. 2 (Summer): 315–38.

———. 2005. Race, gender, and linked fate. *Journal of Black Studies* 35, no. 5 (May): 529–50.

———. 2006. *Black feminist voices in politics.* Albany: State University of New York Press.

Simien, Evelyn M., and Rosalee A. Clawson. 2004. The intersection of race and gender: An examination of black feminist consciousness, race consciousness, and policy attitudes. *Social Science Quarterly* 85, no. 3 (September): 793–810.

Springer, Kimberly. 2005. *Living for the revolution: Black feminist organizations, 1968–1980.* Durham, NC: Duke University Press.

Staples, Robert. 1970. The myth of the black matriarchy. *Black Scholar* 1 (January–February): 8–16.

Stone, Pauline Terrelonge. 1979. Feminist consciousness and black women. In *Women: A feminist perspective*, edited by Jo Freeman, 607–16. Palo Alto, CA: Mayflower.

Timpone, Richard. 1998. Structure, behavior, and voter turnout in the United States. *American Political Science Review* 92, no. 1 (March): 145–58.

Verba, Sidney, and Norman H. Nie. 1972. *Participation in America: Political equality and social equality.* Chicago: University of Chicago Press.

Verba, Sidney, Kay Lehman Schlozman, and Henry E. Brady. 1995. *Voice and equality: Civic voluntarism in American politics.* Cambridge, MA: Harvard University Press.

Welch, Susan, and Lee Sigelman. 1989. A black gender gap? *Social Science Quarterly* 70, no. 1 (March): 120–33.

White, Aaronette. 1999. Talking black, talking feminist: Gendered micromobilization processes in a collective protest against rape. In *Still lifting, still climbing*, edited by Kimberly Springer. New York: New York University Press.

Wolfinger, Raymond E., and Steven J. Rosenstone. 1980. *Who votes?* New Haven, CT: Yale University Press.

CHAPTER 8

Going It Alone

Black Women Activists and Black Organizational Quiescence

ANDREA Y. SIMPSON

Introduction

THE DOMINANT CULTURE perceives African American women as aggressive in both public and private life (Bell 2004; Childs 2005; Givens and Monahan 2005). On the one hand, the characterization of Black women as aggressive suggests high levels of self-confidence and agency. On the other hand, it may suggest social pathology or learned impertinence. This perception of high levels of confidence and agency is in contrast with other realities of Black women's lives—overrepresentation in the ranks of single parenthood, high levels of underemployment, and political invisibility. This reality, expressed in essays, commentaries, literature, popular novels, magazines, and talk shows, raises questions about how we address political and social issues that affect Black women (Meyers 2004a, 2004b). Mainstream political actors marginalize Black women, and this marginalization affects how Black women respond politically. They relate to the political realities of their lives from the space where race, class, and gender intersect. This intersectionality of identities, discussed in the literature of critical race feminists, determines the extension of rights and the availability of opportunities for Black women (Austin 1995; Cohen 1999; Crenshaw 1995; Roberts 1995). How multiple marginalized identities interact to constrain the Black woman's life determines if she votes and for whom, and what party she supports. They also determine whether or not she organizes and how she organizes to address challenges.

One of the tasks of political scientists is to research, organize, and analyze the different realities of Black women to obtain a deeper understanding of the dynamics of all citizens—regardless of gender and race. To some extent, White female political scientists are beginning to tease out the differences between the political attitudes of White males and White females, but this process is still in its nascent stages for Black male and Black female political scientists (Flammang 1997).

In an effort to inspire new discourses in African American politics this chapter attempts to marry issues of intersectionality and Black organizational agenda-setting using critical race theory and the scholarship of Kevin Gaines on racial uplift ideology. These new discourses would place working-class women at the center of analyses, perhaps yielding new strategies for expanding the rights of all oppressed groups, especially African Americans. African American politics is not limited to electoral politics—it includes life issues, such as access to jobs, child care, environmental justice, crime, and affordable housing. However, we know that it is not just about race or just about gender. The junction where race, class, and gender meet and intersect is fraught with political challenges. Residential segregation, familial and community responsibility, health issues, criminal justice, and welfare are some issues that take on new meaning from this junction. Occupying the space where working-class status meets marginalized racial and gender identities might require one to do battle with those who represent Black elite interests, as well as with those representing White elite interests. The struggle for political agency is at the heart of democratic politics and needs exploration by scholars.

The New Frontier of Political Activism

Research on the nature of Black politics includes studies of electoral politics, identity and political attitudes, religion and efficacy/mobilization, public policy, and ideology, among other topics. We need further research on the enduring nature of gender bias in Black politics; the diverging interests of Black Americans along class and gender lines; the development of gender consciousness in Black civil society; Black organizations; and new movements in social justice. We need to explain and analyze how Blacks are responding to the global movements for economic, environmental, and gender equity. Collapsing Black males and females into a single political category—Blacks—erases the critical differences between the genders. Tate and Gay's characterization of Black females being "doubly bound" (i.e., constrained by race and gender status) captures the presence of a sense of shared fate among Black women (Gay and Tate 1998). It is imperative that political science as a discipline recognize these differences and shape a discourse aimed at understanding both the Black gender divide and the racial divide among all Americans.

In our efforts to understand gendered perspectives on political agendas and strategies, many social science researchers have relied on survey data, much of which is inadequate for answering these questions. We know that it is inadequate because issue cleavages among Black Americans are difficult to locate using surveys. Gender differences also elude us in most studies. Scholars have established that, thus far, race trumps gender when it comes to political priorities in the Black community (Mansbridge and Tate 1992).

Contemporary economic and political life encourages a single-issue focus and the formation of professional, civic, and social organizations. Where does that leave the community without access or membership to these mostly middle-class circles? Stepping into this political gap is the working-class Black woman, who seeks political redress through entrepreneurial political activities in her community. As Todd Shaw demonstrates so eloquently in his article on welfare rights

activism, declining resources and a shift in public opinion on the merits of welfare forced activists and grassroots organizers out of the civil rights tradition and
into restructuring and reshaping their organizations (Shaw 2003).

Why is it important to understand the activities of Black women and of
working-class Black women in particular? Given the objective policy interests
of this group—education for their children, crime and the criminal justice system, housing, environmental justice, and other issues—it is worth understanding
what compels some to act in the face of tremendous odds. If rates of participation are linked to socioeconomic status, which determines the policy issues that
make it onto the national agenda, then the work that these women do in their
communities is vital to changing this process.

Recent U.S. Census statistics reveal that 26 percent of African American
women are in managerial and professional specialty occupations as compared
with 18 percent of African American men.[1] At the same time, 19 percent of
Black men are in the service sector compared with 27 percent of Black women.
This is indicative of the complex status of the Black woman. She is a professional
and a service worker—a boss, a mother, and a sole provider. Black women are key
factors in our understanding of the feminization of poverty (Northrop 1990). The
Black woman's misunderstood position is partly the result of society's continuing
negotiations on the role of all women. Research on women indicates that for
career advancement, employers must perceive women as both feminine and able
(Rudman and Glick 2001). If notions of femininity and agency encourage per-
ceptual distortions, these distortions may create particularized obstacles to political power and incorporation. Black women need representation for the kinds of
issues that emerge from the multiple stigmatized identities carried by this group.

The political behavior of African American women is perhaps the least understood in political science. Data with substantial numbers of Blacks and nearly
equal numbers of Black men and Black women are difficult to obtain, which
means that social scientists do not have as many tools with which to extract
intraracial differences along gender lines. However, some studies have addressed
the competing identities of sex and race in the African American community.
Most find that racial group identity eclipses gender identity (Gay and Tate 1998;
Wright 1999); however, we know little about the variety of attitudes and activities of the African American woman and her role in the community. A number
of policies disproportionately affect this group. Abuse by partners or other loved
ones, issues of crime and punishment, HIV/AIDS—all affect the African American woman. Black women between the ages of 20 and 24 are more likely to be
victims of domestic violence than White women or Latinas.[2] Black women
have an incarceration rate of 205 per 100,000, which compared with the rate for
White women (34 per 100,000), and Latinas (60 per 100,000), is staggering. We
can look to the mandatory minimum sentencing laws associated with the "War
on Drugs" as the primary culprit for the ever-increasing number of Black women
behind bars.[3] The Centers for Disease Control reports that 64 percent of new HIV
infections among women in the United States affect African American women,
compared with 18 percent of White women and 18 percent of Latina women.[4]
Yet, political scientists rarely reference these data. The issues confronting Black

women are not on the political agenda of the political parties, political candidates, or national Black organizations.

Black Organizations and Racial Uplift Ideology

The work of Kevin Gaines is crucial to understanding the failure of Black organizations to set agendas that reflect the needs of working-class and poor Black women. Gaines identifies an ideological framework that he calls "racial uplift ideology." According to Gaines, one can recognize such an ideology in an agenda that "emphasizes self-help, racial solidarity, temperance, thrift, chastity, social purity, patriarchal authority, and the accumulation of wealth" (Gaines 1997, 2). Gaines argues that this ideology dominated Black social and political thought after Reconstruction and into the 1920s in response to virulently racist attitudes and policy (Gaines 1997). The hope was that if Black elites could promote "American" values among poorer Blacks, White attitudes and public policies would become more favorable. It was an effort to "earn" full-fledged citizenship. The current racial climate continues to support Gaines's theory that opposition to racial equality inspires racial uplift ideologies.

The post–civil rights era ushered in a rollback of efforts to guarantee opportunities to Blacks and other minorities. The retreat from affirmative action programs is evident in the anti-affirmative action initiatives passed by the states of California and Washington. So-called "Minutemen" or citizen volunteers troll the border between Arizona and Mexico, creating a dangerous and hostile atmosphere for immigrants seeking employment in this country. Most recently, the events in the aftermath of Hurricane Katrina are painful reminders of the continuing second-class citizenship of Blacks. Black residents of the Ninth Ward of New Orleans were left to fend for themselves during the post-hurricane flooding. Levees that protected the ward broke, and there was no plan to evacuate these residents. The federal agency responsible for rescuing citizens in emergencies, FEMA, was astoundingly slow in responding to the crisis. As of this writing, the death toll is 1,100 in Louisiana alone, and 2,700 people are on a "Missing Persons" list kept by the state.[5]

The most important ideological components of racial uplift theory for the purposes of this chapter are the linkage of this ideology to patriarchy and its power in locating the source of the oppression of Blacks within Blacks themselves. Embedded in racial uplift ideology is the placement of patriarchy, middle-class respectability, and economic advancement at the center of strategies for achieving racial equality (Gaines 1997). In uncertain times, Black organizations are loathe to associate themselves with issues of prison abuse, incarceration, drug laws and mandatory minimum sentencing, welfare rights, affordable housing, HIV prevention programs, or any issues that are tinted or tainted with the image of Blacks as morally deficient, lazy, or incompetent. The problem is that these issues are precisely the ones that strike at the heart of the Black community. How we respond to these issues reveal whether or not we are moving toward a true democracy. The democratic ideal must have equality as its cornerstone. Equality allows citizens to live, work, and participate in communities confident in the knowledge that the rights enjoyed by the the most socioeconomically privileged among us are theirs, too. The difficult issues named above are not rooted in Black "pathology"—they are rooted in democratic inequality. When, how, and where they appear on the agendas of Black organizations should matter for political scientists.

In the next section, a review of the agendas of Black social, civic, and political organizations illustrates how racial uplift ideology drives their agendas. The orientation of these agendas in a patriarchal and middle-class ethos is apparent. There is no doubt that many of these organizations contribute positively to the Black community. This chapter only seeks to point out the need for more research on Black organizational efforts, politics, and policy with the hope that such research encourages an expansion and enlargement of those efforts.

Social and Civic Organizations

A search for national Black civic and political organizations on the World Wide Web using three search engines—Google, Yahoo, and Teoma—resulted in the following Web sites: 5,822 sororities and fraternities (these include all of the local chapters); 92 academic, research, or historical organizations or sites;16 religious organizations or church denominations; 28 professional organizations; 9 organizations for women; and numerous chapters of large organizations such as the NAACP and the Urban League. Professional organizations are those associated with a profession—engineers, attorneys, and physicians, for example. One might argue about whether fraternities and sororities are social or civic organizations, but one cannot argue about the strength of their numbers in Black communities.

Black Greek organizations can be socially oriented and civic-minded; however, these kinds of organizations, as are organizations such as Jack and Jill of America, Inc. and The Links, Inc., are not centers of political engagement. Jack and Jill of America's membership is by invitation only and admission is based on the evaluation of current members. The dues for this organization, whose main goal is to provide activities for young African American preteens and teenagers, range from $200 to $600 annually, and chapters sponsor an annual service project in November each year.[6]

Links, Inc. has over 274 chapters and a membership of 10,000 "professional women of color."[7] Education, civic, and cultural service are the three goals identified by the national organization that guide the activities of the chapters. On the Web site for the Los Angeles chapter of The Links, the organization lists the Achiever Program as one of its major projects designed to fulfill its educational service goal. This program has granted $1,190,000 in scholarships to over 673 young men since 1981.[8] The fact that this organization of professional Black women prioritized the needs of young Black men, not young Black women, indicates that central to its ideology are conservative and traditional notions that the education of young Black men is key to the progress of Black people.

Not all Links chapters function in the same way. One of the Chicago chapters participates in the Chicago Community Trust, which supports a range of community agencies serving people in public housing and the arts, as well as ex-felons.[9] However, it, like many chapters, also organizes cotillions or formal balls as fundraising and social events for the middle- and upper-middle-class Black community.

The point here is that these organizations, which have many resources at their disposal, have agendas that, for the most part, meet the social and networking needs of the middle- to upper-middle-class Black community. To become a member of a Greek organization, one joins either a college chapter or a graduate chapter. The requirement for a college or graduate school education serves as a barrier to the inclusion of members from a range of socioeconomic levels. The cost of joining Jack and Jill of America and The Links, Inc. require financial investments, as well as social capital in the form of professional power and authority, and friends or associates in positions of power and authority. This power and authority may be limited to Black civil society, but it remains one of the criteria for entry into these organizations. Social position is currency, and the right associates and contacts enhance one's currency. These organizations serve to enhance the individuals' social capital through membership and any social or business relationship that may develop.

Political and Civic Organizations

An Internet examination of a few of the major political and civic organizations' Web sites reveals mission statements that neglect some of the more pressing problems of the working class. Such organizations as the National Council for Negro Women have broad goals, as in "promote community empowerment, build on the rich heritage, traditional values, and historic strengths of the African-American family, and celebrate the legacy of Mary McLeod Bethune,"[10] but they do not address the specific needs of the Black community. The National Political Congress of Black Women lists six areas of interest in its mission statement, including[11] to "encourage African American women to engage in political education, voter registration, forums, and seminars" and to advocate for public policy issues. There is nothing about mandatory minimum sentencing laws, health, or Blacks as crime victims. For example, more Whites use cocaine than Blacks, yet 65 percent of Blacks in federal prison are convicted on drug charges, as opposed to 54 percent of Whites.[12] Black adolescents are more likely to be uninsured than White adolescents and are four times more likely to have public health insurance, which offers substandard coverage.[13] Although the Web site does state that a project to fight AIDS among women and children is underway, it describes the organization's "assault against 'Gangsta Rap' and 'misogynistic lyrics'" as a primary activity.

In general, many of the organizations whose roots were formed before and during the civil rights movement are ineffectual in combating problems of abuse, incarceration, and HIV/AIDS. The NAACP, in 1999, chose to focus its energies on the representation of Blacks in sitcoms and dramas on the major television networks. Right now, HIV/AIDS is the number one cause of death for Black men and the second leading cause of death for Black women ages 25 to 44—before heart disease, cancer, and homicide. African Americans account for 57 percent of new infections of HIV and 60 percent of AIDS cases. It took the NAACP until October 1999 to launch an AIDS awareness campaign—and that campaign took a back seat to its negotiations with the networks for more Black actors in net-work sitcoms.

The NAACP does list a prison program as one of its activities. However, this program does not address sentencing inequities, HIV/AIDS risk in prison, or prison overcrowding. Instead it focuses on establishing NAACP branches in pris-ons, working to re-enfranchise former felons through voter education and regis-tration, and addressing unequal treatment of inmates and disparities in the criminal justice system. It also is interested in "collaborative partnerships to assist in providing services to inmates."[14]

However, the NAACP lists only 22 prison branches on its Web site, which represents a fraction of the 1,668 state and federal prisons throughout the nation.[15] Moreover, one could argue that this NAACP program fails to take into account the underlying causes of incarceration and focuses on post-incarceration issues, such as voting and skills training. A vast literature chronicles problems of pris-oner abuse in this country, and the NAACP could make its efforts noteworthy by including prisoner abuse in its agenda (Abramsky 2002; Beckett and Sasson 2004; Herivel and Wright 2003.) It is unlikely that prisoners could effect much change from within the institution, even in the form of organizational branches, without considerable commitment from the national organization. Moreover, skills training programs should be combined with taking action against the dis-crimination that many ex-felons face on their return to their communities.

Finally, the NAACP Image Awards program, which is nationally televised, is a major medium through which the organization could send messages, politi-cal and otherwise, to the entire nation. In 2004, of 37 total awards, 35 went to movie actors and R&B and hip-hop entertainers, and over half went to men. Only one literary writer received an award, Toni Morrison, and there were no awards for public service, community organization, or political activism.[16] Contrast this awards program to the Essence Awards program, which is sponsored by the fash-ion magazine, but issued awards in 2003, as in previous years, to "street warriors"—people who have devoted their time to causes in their communities, often at great sacrifice. Angela Dawson, a woman who fought drug dealers in her community in Baltimore, received an Essence award in 2003. Her activities had resulted in the firebombing of her home and the deaths of her husband and five children. Janice Ferebee, the founder of GIGO (Got It Goin' On Foundation), an organization to help young Black women in Washington, DC, also received an award.

Why do these kinds of awards matter, and why are they more important than the NAACP Image Awards and the myriad awards given out by other civic and social organizations? These awards matter because they provide a way for the entire country, especially African Americans, to recognize the activities of grass-roots women activists who are improving the living conditions in their commu-nities. People are empowered by the stories of activists who are not entertainers, athletes, or men. If organizations are going to sponsor media events that high-light individuals of merit, an emphasis on the real struggles in our communities is a preferable centerpiece for such events.

The Urban League's programs seem almost quaint when scrutinized in the current climate. Its mission statement lays out a "three-pronged strategy" for pursuing economic self-reliance, parity, power, and civil rights. These strategies promote "good jobs, homeownership, entrepreneurship, and wealth accumulation." Blacks can obtain equal rights by "eradicating all barriers."[17] These goals are laudable, but they fall short of addressing the needs of Black Americans in the urban trenches. Programs sponsored by the Urban League encourage home ownership and promote the acquisition of technical knowledge—all positive endeavors. However, an individualist and conservative ethos drives these goals. There is no program for building political skills and knowledge or for community empowerment or assessment of community needs.

In a ground-breaking book on the AIDS crisis in the Black community, Cathy Cohen argues that the NAACP, along with the Urban League and the Southern Christian Leadership Conference, has done little to address the problem:

> We need to recognize that not all Black institutions can effectively organize the most vulnerable, alienated, and stigmatized groups of African Americans. Established organizations and leaders such as the NAACP and the Urban League may be so distanced—physically, culturally, and normatively—from certain subpopulations in Black communities that the provision of truly inspired transformative leadership may be beyond their reach. Moreover, traditional leaders, incorporated into dominant institutions to fulfill, in part, managerial roles, may view the transformational demands of those in the second tier of Black communities as working against their specific interests and mobility (Cohen 1999, p.291).

The new economy, new political landscape, and the complex interplay of race, class, and gender may be confounding to older organizations such as the Urban League and the NAACP. How do the programs of more recently organized groups, such as the 100 Black Men and 100 Black Women of America, compare with those of older organizations? The 100 Black Men of America, Inc. comprises eighty-three chapters in twenty-four states and the District of Columbia. Their mission statement is to improve the quality of life in Black communities and enhance educational and economic opportunities for Blacks: "to serve as a beacon of leadership by utilizing our diverse talents to create environments where our children are motivated to achieve, and to empower our people to become self-sufficient shareholders in the economic and social fabric of the communities we serve."[18] Again, the mission statement of this organization reinforces the conservative and traditional message of educational and material advancement as the way to full citizenship.

Regarding HIV/AIDS, the 100 Black Men sponsor the "Black Church Week of Prayer" in an outreach effort specifically to Black men. During this week, they suggest that chapters encourage Black churches and pastors to do the following:

Deliver a sermon on HIV and the role of the church on the designated Sunday.

Hold a special prayer for the healing of AIDS during the worship service.

Disseminate information on HIV/AIDS educational material to the church community on Sunday and throughout the designated week.

Invite members infected with, or affected by, HIV/AIDS to testify
about their experiences.

Invite a guest speaker who has been involved with HIV/AIDS issues
and services.

Distribute red ribbons and other items for members to wear on Sunday
and during the week.

Invite HIV/AIDS activists from a service or advocacy organization in
your community.

Invite an elected official to make remarks.

This organization is a serious one and worthy of our respect. However, this nod
to an overwhelming problem in the community is, to put it mildly, inadequate.
This program ignores the special vulnerability of Black women to HIV/AIDS
(Hawkins 2005; Johnson 2005). One week of superficial activities for the
scourge of the twenty-first century is not enough. The fight against HIV/AIDS
must become part of the fabric of our political, civic, and community agendas
and activities.

The National Coalition of 100 Black Women of America, Inc. states as its
purpose the empowerment of the Black woman and the recognition of her unique
status among minority groups. Toward that end, this group sponsors leadership
programs, literacy and reading programs for young single mothers, and mentor-
ship programs. In addressing reproductive and health rights, its Web site states
that an awareness program was launched in 1989 and "addresses a range of topics related to reproductive health: values, economics, religion, public policy, abor-
tion, teen pregnancy, drug addiction, AIDS, stress and nutrition."[19] Note that
AIDS comes almost at the bottom of the list and that "values" and economics
are listed first. Again, the emphases on reading, literacy, and values are all positive. However, these emphases flow from a conservative perspective that implies that all of the responsibility for the conditions of marginalized groups belongs
with that group—and that this group is unprepared intellectually and morally to
compete in the world.

Are these organizations out of touch with the needs of the working-to-lower
class members of the African American community, or is it more likely that they
are simply more in touch with the needs of the middle-to-upper class members,
which now have a combination of class-based and race-based needs? Cohen calls
this *advanced marginalization*, which is evident in the examples above. Black elites
use organizational resources to "[expand] integration into the dominant society"
(Cohen 1999, 64). If organizations reward those who have "made it" by majority
society standards and emphasize "values" in moral, religious, and economic terms,
the goal must be to demonstrate that with the "right" attitude, individuals can
succeed. This approach, rooted in racial uplift ideology, dismisses all consideration of systemic inequality as the root of suffering.

It is not my intent to demean the work of these organizations or to cast their
mission statements, goals, and programs in a negative light. There is no claim
being made here that this essay contains the full spectrum of good works done by
the organizations discussed. Rather, my intent is to cast a critical eye on the

underlying ideologies of these organizations. Rarely do these organizations mount challenges to mainstream political ideologies. In the next section, I chronicle the activities of Black working-class grassroots activists. What are their agendas, and how are they attempting to address the issues absent from the agendas of Black organizations?

Working-Class Black Women and Spheres of Political Activism

Although it is true that grassroots mobilization has always been a catalyst for change, one has only to look at one of the most successful social movements, the civil rights movement, to see that one of the most efficient ways to effect change is for grassroots mobilizers to work in partnership with middle-class organizers (Robnett 1997). Social movements have undergone a significant transformation since the civil rights movement. Although successful movements require organizational infrastructure and benefit from the resources and skills of more-established national organizations, many grassroots leaders cannot access or develop relationships with national organizations that might provide them with structural resources. I argue that established Black civic and social organizations could increase their utility for improving conditions in the Black community by reaching out to these grassroots activists. The Internet and other technologies have increased the ability of citizens to create virtual communities that are not geographically close, but share certain interests. However, these new ways of organizing and creating multiple political identities potentially leave out groups that do not have as much access to these technologies and for whom the geographic community is the locus of desired change.

Why are so many women serving as grassroots activists today? A brief look at census data explains part of the reason. Women head nearly 30 percent of the 14 million Black households in the United States, and almost 40 percent of these Black households are below the poverty line.[20] We know that poverty is concentrated in urban areas, which is why we find numerous anecdotal stories of Black women at the frontlines of community organization and activism, fighting for better housing, schools, a reduced crime rate, and a cleaner environment.

Given the limited opportunities for Black women to run for elective office, grassroots organizing becomes a viable alternative. Why are these opportunities limited? As other scholars have argued, it takes resources to run for public office, and we hold women to different standards than men when running for office. The public holds women accountable for the actions of their family members and friends, and they must balance their public image so that they do not appear too feminine or too masculine (Takash 1997; Witt et al. 1994). If all women face the resistance of voters when running for elective office, it makes sense that Black women would encounter even more resistance. Figure 8.1 compares the percentage of women in Congress, state elected office, and state legislatures in 2004 to the percentage of African American women.

This chart indicates that women comprise 24 percent of Senators and members of Congress. Of these, Black women comprise only 15 percent of the women

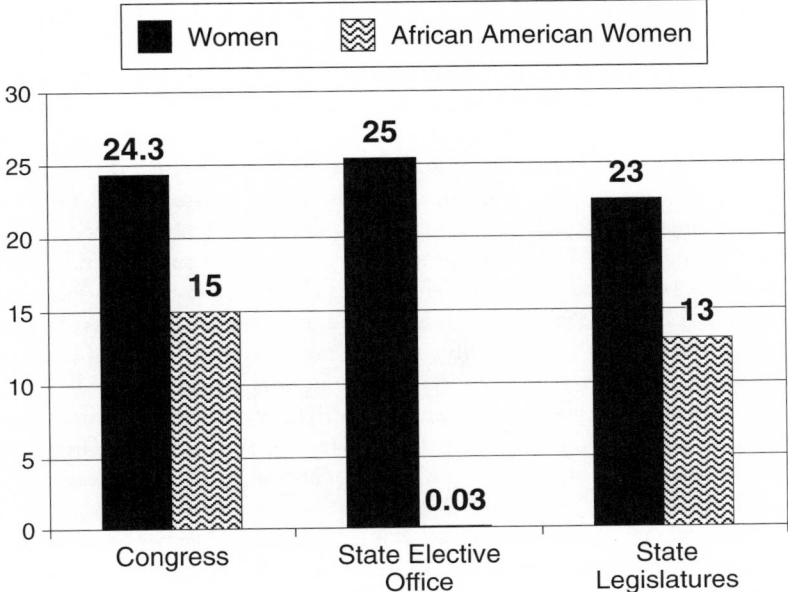

FIGURE 8.1 Women in Congress, State Elective Office, and State Legislatures, 2004
The percentage for women is the percentage of total members of the House and Senate,
all state elective offices, and all state legislatures. The percentage for *Black women is a*
percentage of the total number of women.
Source: Center for American Women in Politics, Rutgers University, Women of Color
in Elective Office, 2004, http://www.cawp.rutgers.edu/FACTS/Officeholders/cawpfs.html.

in the House of Representatives and there are no Black women in the Senate.
Black women are less than 1 percent of women holding statewide elective office
compared to White women who hold 25 percent of those positions. White
women comprise 23 percent of state legislators, and of that group of women,
Black women comprise only 13 percent. African American women hold less
than 1 percent of statewide elective executive offices, and only one mayor is a
Black woman—Shirley Franklin of Atlanta. We all recognize that running for office
requires resources—one needs financial and political backing to make a successful
bid for elective office. So what are other ways of engaging in civic and political life?

One such way is to employ grassroots organizing as a means of empowerment.
Black mothers' children face violence, substandard public education, and high levels of lead exposure. Yet, where are the voices of Black leaders on these issues?
They are mute. These grassroots activities are fundamentally different in form and
emphasis from those of the national civic and political organizations discussed in
the previous section, which serve primarily as networking and single-issue groups.
Grassroots activists work with small groups and are loosely organized with few
material resources. They are involved and seeking to change undesirable conditions in everyday living rather than access to higher education and policy issues

on a national scale. It is no wonder that Black women everywhere are staking out political territory in their own backyards.

One area in which we find significant grassroots organizing efforts is in the environmental justice movement. This movement is an informal collective of local, and mostly urban, movements throughout the nation. Led primarily by women of color, with a significant African American presence, this movement seeks policy redress for the unjust distribution of toxic waste sites and industries with toxic emissions. A number of studies have found evidence that locally undesirable land uses (LULUs) are disproportionately located in poor and minority communities (Boer et al. 1997; Bowen et al. 1995; Davidson and Anderton 2000; Stretesky and Lynch 1999). One study showed that ethnic minorities are 47 percent more likely than Whites to live near a toxic waste facility (Ember 1994).

Black women serve at the center of the most publicized local movements for environmental justice. In Warren County, North Carolina, Dollie Burwell led the fight against the dumping of toxic PCB-laden fuel along the highway in her community. The struggle of women who live in Cancer Alley, the stretch of land between Baton Rouge and New Orleans, against the building of the chemical plant, Shintech, made national news and was made into a *Lifetime* network movie. Black women are fighting for clean air and water in East St. Louis, Richmond, Los Angeles, Houston, Seattle, and Chicago.

Renee Morrison of Oakland, California has been fighting toxic waste in her West Oakland community for years. A leader of the Chester Street Block Club Association and Citizens for West Oakland Revitalization, Morrison fights plants that produce air toxins such as the Red Star Yeast/Lasaffre Yeast Corporation.[21] In Memphis, Tennessee, Doris Bradshaw leads the fight against buried toxins at the South Memphis Army Depot. In North Memphis, Balinda Moore leads the struggle against toxic emissions from the Velsicol Chemical Plant (Simpson 2004).

Grassroots organizing is alive and well in working-class Black communities. Two years after the Million Man March was held in October 1995, the Million Woman March was held in Philadelphia. Unlike the Million Man March, which was organized by the Nation of Islam and supported by a wide network of organizations and leaders, the Million Woman March was organized by two grassroots activists, Asia Coney and Phile Chionesu. Coney had been a housing activist in Philadelphia, and Chionesu ran a store that also served as a cultural center (Fletcher and Brown 1997). Attendance estimates for the march ranged from 500,000 to two million. Participants cut across socioeconomic lines, much like the participants in the Million Man March.

The platform developed by the founders and organizers of the Million Woman March lists education concerns as the second point.[22] The platform is as follows:

Support a probe into the CIA's participation in the drug trade
Support the development of Black independent schools
Address the development of Black women who leave the penal system
Support the development of health facilities
Support the formation of Rites of Passage centers and academies

Support the development of Black women who wish to become
    professionals, entrepreneurs, and politicians
Support the development of facilities to help Black women in
    transition
Examine human rights violations of African Americans
Support the development of a better environment for Black youth
Combat homelessness
Halt gentrification of Black communities
Reclaim Black elders' rights

More formal Black women's organizations have not addressed these issues. Although there has been little follow-up coverage of the Million Women March, individual working-class women continue to struggle for issues that affect their communities.

In Boston, Candelaria Silva works to improve Roxbury, a poor and predominantly Black community, through arts and culture initiatives. As director of the Arts, Culture, and Trade (ACT) Roxbury Consortium she struggles to build community interest in the work of artists, thereby creating economic opportunities. Her organization sponsors workshops for artists on legal issues, negotiating in the music industry, and writing. Talks have begun of building an arts and entertainment complex in the area, which will lead to employment opportunities and increased numbers of customers for businesses already in the area (Coleman 1999). In October 2001, ACT moved to a new building in the Dudley Square Business District in Boston.[23]

In Chicago, Jamesetta Harris has received national recognition for her efforts to reduce the level of terror inflicted on her community by drug dealers and gang members. She lobbied for additional police patrols and planted grass and flowers, inspiring other neighbors to plant gardens and clean vacant lots (Lawrence 1997). She is still a community activist and works with CAPS, the Chicago Alternative Police Strategy, a community policing program.

Margaret Madden of Long Beach, California, heads the Safe Streets Now! program for the city and is a veteran of community activism around gang and drug activity. After relatives visiting from Arizona witnessed a drive-by shooting in the community, she decided to confront wrongdoers (Shuit 1997). Madden even set up lawn chairs so that she and others could sit and stare drug dealers down while they conducted their business. Madden was, as of 2006, a board member of Neighborhoods USA or NUSA, a nonprofit national organization dedicated to building communities through networking and information sharing.[24]

In Milwaukee, Annette Polly Williams led the fight for school vouchers. She was an early advocate for educational reform from the ranks of the working class and is now a state representative. Williams believed that the magnet school plan so popular in many school districts was "private education at public expense." Williams justifies the support of vouchers, saying, "I simply say that my Black parents want the same choice they do. None of the people who oppose my plan [vouchers] lack choice in education themselves. They have no idea what the lack of choice in education means, the damage it does when you have to go to an inferior school that will trap you for life."[25] Although the use of school vouchers is considered a conservative strategy for improving public education, Annette Polly Williams shares support for school vouchers with other working-class women of color.

The House Judiciary Committee held a hearing on the effectiveness of mandatory busing in September 1996. At the hearing, Genevieve Mitchell, a Cleveland, Ohio, activist and proponent of school vouchers, had this to say: "We have, in the Black community, been placed at a serious disadvantage because we have been censored, Black women's voices and solutions have been determined by those who do not speak for us. Black women have some important messages for this world, and our voices must be heard!"[26]

In October 1997, Nina Adams was named president of the Queensbridge Housing Tenant Association, the largest public housing project in North America. One of the tenants was quoted as saying, "Finally, a Public Housing Tenant Association that will start kicking a-- instead of kissing a--."[27] Under her leadership a tenants' association that represented the interests of the housing authority changed to one that represented the tenants' interests. Adams had a seven-year history of activism in the Queensbridge Housing development before becoming the leader of the tenants' association.

Earlier in this chapter, I offered the aftermath of Hurricane Katrina as evidence of a more hostile racial climate in the United States. On Tuesday, December 6, 2005, a Select Bipartisan Committee to Investigate the Preparation for and Response to Hurricane Katrina sponsored a hearing entitled "Hurricane Katrina: Voices from Inside the Storm."[28] Testifying at the hearing were individuals representing different perspectives on the effects of Hurricane Katrina. Three of the four men represented organizations or were professionals—Charles Allen, vice mayor of Newport News, Virginia; Harry C. Alford, president and CEO of the Black Chamber of Commerce; and Ishmael Muhammad, a staff attorney for the Advancement Project, a political action group in Washington, DC. Four of the women—Dyan French, Patricia Thompson, Leah Hodges, and Doreen Keeler—were citizens of New Orleans and gave eyewitness testimony regarding the devasting aftermath of Katrina. The voices of the people in the community came from the women, while the men had no organic connection to the community. It was a tense hearing as these women put racism and classism on the agenda. These women represented the dispossessed of New Orleans, as they testified to the brutality of the New Orleans Police Department and the failure of the Federal Emergency Management Agency (FEMA) to address their needs in good faith. Leah Hodges called the area on the Causeway where people were waiting for relief the "Causeway Concentration Camp." Representative Jeff Miller (R-Florida), repeatedly asked her not to use the term "concentration camp." She replied, "I am going to call it what it is. If I put a dress on a pig, it's still a pig." Some media implied that the most celebrated of these witnesses, Dyan French, or "Mama D," might be a "conspiracy theorist" because of her assertion that the levees protecting the Ninth Ward were dynamited intentionally to redirect water away from some White areas (Alpert 2005; Goldblatt 2005). "Mama D's" testimony regarding the ineptness of FEMA and her community's determination to survive and rebuild was powerful and persuasive. However, one could not help but notice that there were four women there representing the people of the Ninth Ward, but only one man.

The ideology of racial uplift cannot adequately support opposition to the forces that left the people of the Ninth Ward stranded. All of the signs of Black "pathology" are there—poverty, dependency on government, and most definitely too many "Mothers." Yet, we must go beyond appearances and ask the hard questions: What created the Ninth Ward? Why did the New Orleans Police Department fail the people? Why is New Orleans both a treasure and a trial? In spite of a significant Black middle class in this country, negative Black stereotypes endure. Clearly, heroic efforts to pass through the racial uplift ideological tunnel have failed to lead Black folks to the light. Although many people, both White and Black, have donated funds and goods to the victims of Katrina, there is an absence of concentrated organizational efforts to address the systemic causes of this tragedy. Black women activists are going it alone, and many Black organizations are silent on the politics of this event.

There are many other women who, like "Mama D" and Leah Hodges, have the courage to tell their stories and represent the interests of the people in the working-class communities. If we uncover, document, and analyze cases of local triumphs by people bound by gender, race, and class constraints, it will help transform narrow views of political participation and power. A more inclusive research agenda for political scientists must address these issues, or it will fail to understand fully the politics it professes to know.

Notes

1. U.S. Census Bureau. March 2002. Current Population Survey at http://www.census.gov/population/socdemo/race/Black/ppl-164/tabl1.pdf.

2. Bureau of Justice Statistics. October 2001. *Intimate Partner Violence and Age of Victim, 1993–1999*. U.S. Department of Justice, Office of Justice Programs at http://www.ojp.usdoj.gov/bja/pub/pdf/ipva99.pdf.

3. Bureau of Justice Statistics. 2001. Prisoners in 2000 at http://www.ojp.usdoj.gov/bjs/abstract/pOO.htm

4. Centers for Disease Control and Prevention (CDC). *HIV and AIDS—United States, 1981–2001*. MMWR 2001:50, 430–34.

5. "FEMA Workers Arrested on Fraud, Bribery Charges: Death Toll Rises After Body Found in Rubble," retrieved February 7, 2006, from http://cnn.worldnews.com.

6. Lee Anna Jackson, *Climbing Up the Hill*, retrieved September 26, 2004, from http://www.Blackenterprise.com.

7. *The Links, Inc.*, retrieved September 26, 2004, from http://www.linsinc.org.

8. *Angel City Chapter, The Links, Inc., History*, retrieved September 26, 2004, from http://angelcitylinks.org/aboutlinks.com.

9. *The Chicago Community Trust*, retrieved September 26, 2004, from http://www.cct.org/donors.

10. *National Council of Negro Women*, retrieved September 21, 2004, from http://www.ncnw.com/centers/centersbody.html.

11. *National Political Congress of Black Women, Inc.*, retrieved September 21, 2004, from http://www.npcbw.org.

12. *Sourcebook of Criminal Justice Statistics*, retrieved August 24, 1999, from http://www .albany.edu/sourcebook/19995/ind/CRIME.ind.html.

13. *Joint Center for Political and Economic Studies*, retrieved August 24, 1999, from http://www .jointctr.org/factshts/access.html.

14. *Prison Project*, retrieved September 23, 2004, from www.naacp.org/programs/prison/ prisonproject.shtml.

15. *Department of Justice*, Census of Sate and Federal Correctional Facilities, 2000, retrieved February 5, 2006, from http://www.ojp.usdoj.gove/bjs/abstract/csfcf00.htm.

16. *NAACP Image Awards*, retrieved September 23, 2004, from http://www.infoplease.com.

17. *National Urban League*, retrieved September 23, 2004, from http://www.nul.org/about/ mission.htm.

18. *100 Black Men of American, Inc.*, retrieved September 23, 2004, from http://www.100 Blackmen.org.

19. *National Coalition of 100 Black Women, Inc.*, retrieved September 23, 2004, from http://www.ncbw.org/programs/programs4.html.

20. *U.S. Census Bureau*, retrieved February 5, 2006, from http://www.census.gov.

21. *Greenaction*, retrieved October 1, 2004, from http://www.greenaction.org/westoakland/ redstar/pr121902.shtml.

22. *Million Woman March*, retrieved August 19, 1999, from http://members.aol.com/_ht_a/ lilbitz/pl-atform.htm.

23. *ACT*, retrieved September 24, 2004, from http://www.actroxbury.org.

24. *NUSA*, retrieved September 14, 2006, from http://www.nusa.org/who.htm.

25. *Reason Online*, retrieved August 20, 1999, from http://www.reasonmag.com/william-sint.html.

26. *Hearing on the Effectiveness of Mandatory Bussing in Cleveland*, retrieved October 1, 2004, from http://www.house.gov/judiciary/257.htm.

27. Press release, retrieved August 22, 1999, from http://pluto.informatik.uni-oldenburg.de/ ~also/welar170.html.

28. Information on both the hearings and parts of the transcript from New Orleans Evacuees and Activists Testify at Explosive House Hearing on the Role of Race and Class in Government's Response to Hurricane Katrina, retrieved February 7, 2006, from http://www.democracynow .org/print.pl?sid=05/12/09/1443240.

References

Abramsky, Sasha. 2002. *Hard time blues: How politics built a prison nation*. New York: St. Martin's.

Alpert, Bruce. 2005. Racism costs lives, N.O. evacuees say. *Times-Picayune*, December 7, http://www.nola.com.

Austin, Regina. 1995. Sapphire bound! In *Critical race theory*, edited by Kimberle Crenshaw, Neil Gotanda, Gary Peller, and Kendall Thomas. New York: New Press.

Beckett, Katherine, and Theodore Sasson. 2004. *The politics of injustice*. Thousand Oaks, CA: Sage.

Bell, Ella Louise. 2004. Myths, stereotypes, and realities of black women: A personal reflection. *Journal of Applied Behavioral Science* 40, no. 2:146–59.

Boer, J. Tom, Manuel Pastor Jr., James L. Sadd, and Lori D. Snyder. 1997. Is there environmental racism? The demographics of hazardous waste in Los Angeles County. *Social Science Quarterly* 78, no. 4:793–810.

Bowen, William M., Mark J. Salling, Kingsley E. Haynes, and Ellen J. Cyran. 1995. Toward environmental justice: Spatial equality in Ohio and Cleveland. *Annals of the Association of American Geographers* 85, no. 4:641–63.

Childs, Erica Chito. 2005. Looking behind the stereotypes of the 'angry black woman': An exploration of black women's responses to interracial relationships. *Gender & Society* 19, no. 4 (August): 544-61.

Cohen, Cathy. 1999. *The boundaries of blackness: AIDS and the breakdown of black politics*. Chicago: University of Chicago Press.

Coleman, Sandy. 1999. Groups in Roxbury unite to link arts and economic growth. *The Boston Globe*, June 20, p. 13.

Crenshaw, Kimberle Williams. 1995. Mapping the margins: Intersectionality, identity politics, and violence against women of color. In *Critical race theory*, edited by Kimberle Crenshaw, Neil Gotanda, Gary Peller, and Kendall Thomas. New York: New Press.

Davidson, Pamela, and Douglas L. Anderton. 2000. Demographics of dumping II: A national environmental equity survey and the distribution of hazardous materials handlers. *Demography* 37, no. 4 (November): 46.

Ember, Lois. 1994. Minorities still more likely to live near toxic sites. *Chemical and Engineering News*, 72, no. 36 (September): 19.

Flammang, Janet. 1997. *Women's political voice: How women are transforming the practice and study of politics*. Philadelphia: Temple University Press.

Fletcher, Michael A., and DeNeen L. Brown. 1997. Anticipation, hopes build for million woman march. *Washington Post*, October 24, p. A03. Retrieved August 19, 1999, from http://www.freerepublic.com/forum/a18142.htm.

Gaines, Kevin. 1997. *Uplifting the race: Black leadership, politics, and culture in the twentieth century*. Chapel Hill: University of North Carolina Press.

Gay, Claudine, and Katherine Tate. 1998. Doubly bound: The impact of gender and race on the politics of black women. *Political Psychology* 19, no. 1 (March): 169–84.

Givens, Sonja M. Brown, and Jennifer L. Monahan. 2005. Priming mammies, jezebels, and other controlling images: An examination of the influence of mediated stereotypes on perceptions of an African American woman. *Media Psychology* 7, no. 1:87–106.

Goldblatt, Mark. 2005. Race, reason, and reaching out. *The American Spectator*, http://www.spectator.org.

Hawkins, Denise B. 2005. On the frontline of the HIV/AIDS epidemic. *Black Issues in Higher Education* 22, no. 3 (March): 24-29.

Herivel, Tara and Paul Wright, eds. 2003. *Prison nation: The warehousing of America's poor*. New York: Routledge.

Johnson, Jason B. 2005. Secret gay encounters of black men could be raising women's infection rate. *San Francisco Chronicle*, May 1, p. A1.

Jones, Jacqueline. 1985. *Labor of love, labor of sorrow*. New York: Basic Books.

Lawrence, Curtis. 1997. S. Sider takes on gangs and wins. *Chicago Sun-Times*, October 13, p. 14.

Mansbridge, Jane, and Katherine Tate. 1992. Race trumps gender: The Thomas nomination and the black community. *PS: Political Science and Politics* 25, no. 3 (September): 488–92.

Meyers, Marian. 2004a. African American women and violence: Gender, race, and class in the news. *Critical Studies in Media Communication* 21, no. 2 (June): 95-118.

———. 2004b. Crack mothers in the news: A narrative of paternalistic racism. *Journal of Communication Inquiry* 28, no. 3 (July): 194-216.

Northrop, Emily. 1990. The feminization of poverty: The demographic factor and the composition of economic growth. *Journal of Economic Issues* 24 (March): 145-60.

Roberts, Dorothy. 1995. Punishing drug addicts who have babies: Women of color, equality, and the right of privacy. In *Critical Race Theory*, edited by Kimberle Crenshaw, Neil Gotanda, Gary Peller, and Kendall Thomas, 384-425. New York: New Press.

Robnett, Belinda. 1997. *How long? How long? African-American women in the struggle for civil rights*. New York: Oxford University Press.

Rudman, Lauri A., and Peter Glick. 2001. Prescriptive gender stereotypes and backlash toward agentic women. *Journal of Social Studies* 57, no. 4 (Winter): 743–63.

Shaw, Todd. 2003. We refused to lay down our spears: The persistence of welfare rights activism, 1966–1996. In *Black political organizations in the post-civil rights era*, edited by Ollie A. Johnson and Karin L. Stanford, 170–79. New Brunswick, NJ: Rutgers University Press.

Shuit, Douglas P. 1997. Getting involved. *Los Angeles Times*, June 10, p. 1.

Simpson, Andrea. 2002. Public hazard, personal peril: The impact of non-governmental organi-
    zations in environmental justice claims. Presented at the Annual Meeting of the American
    Political Science Association, August.
Smith, Eric L. 1996. United they stand: Church-based business corporation 'reveals' new way to
    bring black dollars together. *Black Enterprise* 26, no. 11 (June): 36.
Stretesky, Paul, and Michael J. Lynch. 1999. Environmental justice and the predictions of distance
    to accidental chemical releases in Hillsborough County, Florida. *Social Science Quarterly* 80,
    no. 4:830–47.
Takash, Paule. 1997. Breaking barriers to representation: Chicana/Latina elected officials in Cal-
    ifornia. In *Women transforming politics*, edited by Cathy J. Cohen, Kathleen B. Jones, and Joan
    C. Tronto. New York: New York University Press.
U.S. Bureau of the Census. 1998. *Selected economic characteristics of people and families, by sex and
    race.* Washington, DC: U.S. Government Printing Office.
Witt, Linda, Karen M. Paget, and Glenna Matthews. 1994. *Running as a woman.* New York: Free
    Press.
Wright, Sharon D. 1999. Black women in congress during the post-civil rights era. In *Still lifting,
    still climbing: African-American women's contemporary activism*, edited by Kimberly Springer,
    149–63. New York: New York University Press.

CHAPTER NINE

Political Scientists and the Activist-Technocrat Dichotomy

The Case of John Aubrey Davis

MARTIN KILSON

Introduction

BY THE 1930s a small cadre of African American professionals had emerged with full-fledged graduate school training in the social science professions, and in this chapter I want to discuss the fascinating career of one such African American who gained graduate school training in the field of political science.

Just a handful of African Americans had attained professional degrees at the doctoral level in political science by the end of the 1940s; prominent among them were Ralph Bunche (PhD, Harvard University), Robert Martin (PhD, University of Chicago), Merze Tate (PhD, Radcliffe College), and Robert Brisbane (PhD, Harvard University).

So when John Aubrey Davis—the younger brother of Allison Davis, the prominent African American anthropology and psychology scholar and author of the landmark study, *Deep South* (1940)—enrolled at the University of Wisconsin to study international politics and comparative politics after graduating from Williams College in June 1933, he was preparing to join a small subgroup within the evolving twentieth-century African American professional stratum. He was raised in Washington, DC, in a well-to-do, fair-skinned African American household that was oriented to activism in the civil rights movement. His sister, Dorothy, attended Wellesley College in the 1920s and 1930s; along with his attendance at Williams College, this college-attendance pattern was extremely rare for African Americans in that high-noon era of Jim Crow in American society, when over 95 percent of college-going African Americans attended Negro colleges.

Davis completed requirements for the master's degree by the summer of 1934 and returned to his hometown, Washington, DC. There the new head of the political science department at Howard University—the newly minted Harvard PhD, Ralph Bunche—hired Davis as an instructor in political science. However, it would be twelve years before Davis completed the graduate studies that led to his PhD degree in political science, studies that he began on a Rosenwald Foundation

Fellowship at Columbia University in 1936. As Davis observed in a letter to me, he "majored in American Government and Constitutional Law, a standard combination at Columbia [in that era], and minored in labor economics, across department and against all advice about too tough a program." At the same time, Davis married a young African American librarian and English scholar, Mavis Wormley, and embarked on a rather long academic association with Lincoln University (Pennsylvania), where he was appointed an assistant professor in political science in 1935 and where he continued to teach—except for several years during World War II—until 1953.

Davis submitted his doctoral dissertation in 1946. It probed the administrative arrangements, rules, procedures, styles, and citizen impact of the New Deal's Social Security policies embodied in the Social Security Acts of 1935 and 1939. Davis's dissertation earned a high-distinction evaluation, which led to a special publication niche as Study Number 571 in Columbia University Press's coveted series, Studies in History, Economics, and Public Law. The published version of Davis's dissertation was titled *Regional Organization of the Social Security Administration: A Case Study (1950)*. To my knowledge, before the publication of Davis's dissertation by Columbia University Press, the only other Columbia dissertation by an African American scholar to be published in the same series was Ira de Augustine Reid's *Negro Immigrants*, published in 1939.

The foregoing constitutes the core features of the academic-groundwork background to Davis's intellectual odyssey. One additional feature should be added to this background, however. In 1953, Davis was wooed away from Lincoln University to become one of several African American scholars to gain full professorships in the main colleges in New York City's college system. He joined the faculty of City College, Hylan Lewis (a sociologist at Howard University) joined Queens College, and John Hope Franklin (an historian at Howard University) joined Brooklyn College.

But we are now some 20 years ahead of the core story of John Aubrey Davis's intellectual and professional odyssey as a member of that small cadre of first-generation African Americans in the political science field. So let us return to the time frame of our core story.

Role of Civil Rights Activism in John Aubrey Davis's Professional Odyssey

Formation of the New Negro Alliance Movement, 1933

John Aubrey Davis was only a few months out of Williams College with his BA degree when he joined a street protest against a White-owned fast-food shop located in the heart of the Negro community in Washington, DC. In response to the Hamburger Grill's firing of several Negro workers and replacing them with White workers, the protesters insisted that the fired Negro workers be rehired immediately and asked the local Negro neighborhood to boycott the White-owned fast-food shop until this occurred. A boycott ensued and was successful.

This neighborhood boycott in August 1933 was Davis's baptismal experience with civil rights activism. The historian of Washington, DC, Michele Pacifico, describes this experience as follows:

> Monday morning, August 28, 1933. The Great Depression has reached all regions and all levels of American society. In Washington, three African-American employees of the white-owned Hamburger Grill on 12th and U streets, N.W. are fired and three whites hired in their places. The business is in a black neighborhood and depends entirely upon black patronage. Almost immediately after the three are fired, John Aubrey Davis, 21, a recent graduate of Williams College, organizes a group of young neighborhood men, most of whom frequent the grill, to picket the business. Their signs urge fellow community members to boycott the restaurant. The protest proves effective: the following day the Hamburger Grill closes. On Wednesday the three black workers are rehired, business returns to normal, and the informal group of neighbors savor their first victory in a battle to open up African-American economic opportunity.[1]

As Davis has related to me in numerous conversations, his participation in boycotting the Hamburger Grill in August 1933 awakened in him his first awareness of the broader political possibilities of street-level civil rights activism among African Americans. He pondered and discussed the possible political implications of the boycott against the Hamburger Grill with a group of young Black professionals in the Washington, DC, area; among this group were several lawyers— William Hastie and James Nabrit (faculty members at Howard Law School), Belford Lawson (a lawyer in private practice), Naylor Fitzhugh (professor of accounting at Howard University), Doxey Wilkerson (professor of education at Howard University), Thurman Dodson (a lawyer in private practice), and Charles Houston (Dean of Howard Law School), among others. By the late fall, Davis's discussions with his peers resulted in the idea that street-level civil rights activism could be translated into public policy mobilization against the American White supremacist edifice. What was required, however, was an organized agency to make that possible. Several members of Davis's discussion circle gained insight into how they might proceed by probing the linkage between trade union activism and public policy mobilization among White workers; this linkage had earlier produced prolabor legislation at both the state and federal level—such as the Wagner Act in the 1920s that legalized the right to strike—as well as federal court decisions that advanced the rights of working-class Americans.

The organization formed in the fall of 1933 by John Aubrey Davis and his peers was named the New Negro Alliance (NNA). In ideological terms, Davis and his peers adhered to a kind of "pragmatic activism," rather than a "radical activism," which is to say that the policy goals of the New Negro Alliance were conceived along incremental, not revolutionary lines. As William Hastie observed in an article titled "The Way of the Alliance," which appeared in *The New Negro Alliance Yearbook* (1939), the sociological character of the Black population in Washington was hardly conducive to the application of "radical activism" by the NNA. As Hastie observed,

The colored population of Washington was divided into two socio-economic groups; one composed principally of salaried white-collar workers, a large number of them in public employment, and the other composed principally of skilled and unskilled workers whose services were employed in the commercial domestic activities of a non-industrial city. [So] when the New Negro Alliance was beginning its activities [in 1933 more than one-third of the Negroes in Washington were dependent upon some form of relief, while less than one-twentieth of the whites were similarly situated.[2]

There were, however, competing visions of political activism that diverged from the "pragmatic activism" of the NNA. One competing vision was associated with the Universal Negro Improvement Association of the Garvey movement. It was a "Black nationalist" vision that supported an all-Black communitarian activism. Hastie, Davis, and other members of the NNA rejected this type of activism. They also rejected another variant of "radical activism" that was associated with one of their prominent intellectual peers among Washington's activist Black professionals in the 1930s, namely, Ralph Bunche, a political scientist like John Aubrey Davis and chair of the political science department at Howard University. As Charles Henry notes in his brilliant biography, *Ralph Bunche: Model American or American Other* (1999), Bunche adhered to a Marxist vision of Black activism that differed from the NNA's "pragmatic activism." Bunche believed that the racist oppression of African Americans should not be challenged merely along the lines of Black-ethnic activism and mobilization. Rather, he saw an alliance with the White American working class and its trade unions as a precondition for effective Black American civil rights activism. John Aubrey Davis, Hastie and other NNA members rejected this position because there was no serious evidence that White workers were ready to challenge American racism; rather they were among its core practitioners. As Davis put it in correspondence to me, "Bunche was never a member [of the New Negro Alliance], only a critic. . . . Bunche attacked the NNA because he feared the division of the labor movement on the basis of race. He saw the only good in the [Alliance] organization was that it taught public protest, solidarity, and direct action."[3]

Leadership Styles in the New Negro Alliance

There were some tactical or methodological differences among leading figures in the NNA in regard to the styles of civil rights activism. For instance, William Hastie, a lawyer and budding legal scholar, favored a kind of "institutionalist activism," which meant a leadership-hierarchic mode of civil rights activism. As Hastie wrote in an article in *The New Alliance Yearbook 1939*, "The neighborhood petition and, where necessary, the neighborhood boycott were the effective weapons of struggle. It was contemplated that in the course of many efforts of this sort, organization would be developed throughout the city. Such organization would permit an extension of program with appropriate variation of tactics to the end that racial proscriptions and restrictions might be removed in public as well as private employment."[4]

On the other hand, John Aubrey Davis, the budding political scientist, held a leadership vision with a distinctly populist bent. As Davis put it in correspondence to me, in the early days of the NNA he emphasized street-level political mobilization, reaching out to the grassroots through Black evangelist-oriented clergymen, including Reverend Elder Micheaux of the Apostolic Church of God. Davis described the involvement of Rev. Elder Micheaux as follows:

In 1933 I recruited personally at his [Eider Micheaux's] home, 1700 block of "C" St., N.W. Washington, DC, the Rev. Elder Micheaux ("Happy Am I In My Redeemer").[5] He had a strong image where he had been successful in Newport News and Philadelphia. In 1933 the A & P opened an all-white store at 9th and "S" Streets, and I put up a picket line (including my sister—Wellesley '29). Micheaux supported us and took up money for us at his big rallies in Griffith Stadium. I addressed one of these. We had the camp meeting as well as the regular (black) church on our side. You may remember Micheaux's Radio Church of God in Philly.[6]

Furthermore, the first historical analysis of the NNA, which was presented by Michele Pacifico in a 1994 article in *Washington: Magazine of the Historical Society of Washington, DC*, gave similar emphasis to what I call Davis's "street-level activist mobilization" methodology. For instance, Pacifico describes Davis's role in the founding events that shaped the NNA movement as follows:

The "Jobs for Negroes" campaigns, also known as "Don't Buy Where You Can't Work," relied on visible, even confrontational actions. They used negotiation [too but especially] mass protests, and boycotts to force white businesses in black communities to employ African Americans, and to employ them in non-manual labor positions. Leaders exhorted black citizens . . . to boycott local businesses that refused to employ African Americans in clerical and managerial positions. They also worked to prevent black expenditures on goods or services in black neighborhoods where inequitable employment practices prevailed. The campaigns galvanized both poor and middle-class blacks to action.[7]

In short, in contrast with William Hastie's "institutionalist mobilization" perspective, Davis's "street-level activist mobilization" methodology had a broad impact on the modus operandi of the NNA throughout the 1930s. It particularly influenced its continuing effort to expand the range and type of job market reforms demanded from both private and public employers in Washington throughout the 1930s. For example, in its annual yearbook for the year 1939 can be found a protest-skewed graphic portrayal of the racial-caste patterns in Washington's social system as they related to public employment in Washington's Fire Department. According to *The New Alliance Yearbook 1939*, whereas Blacks made up 27 percent of the population they held a mere 2 percent of the Fire Department jobs as of 1939. This was just 17 out of 871 Fire Department jobs—the same number as in 1918, in fact—which meant that by 1939 African Americans experienced a deficit of 240 firemen jobs. Similarly, whereas Washington Whites received 98 percent of the Fire Department payroll in 1939 ($2.2 million), Blacks claimed just 2 percent, which translated into a Black payroll deficit of nearly $600,000.

The contrasting mobilization styles of William Hastie and John Aubrey Davis during the NNA's formative days can be characterized in still yet another way. If

Hastie's institutionalist-mobilization mode can be classified as a variant of *bourgeois-establishmentarian activism*, then Davis's street-level mobilization mode can be labeled a variant of *bourgeois-progressive activism*. The key differentiation between the Hastie and Davis modes was that the former exhibited more faith in middle-class status persons functioning as Black activist mobilizers, whereas Davis's mode was willing to reach outside the ranks of Black middle-class or professionally trained persons to the working-class leadership sector in urban African American communities. The populist dynamic was at work in Davis's bourgeois-progressive activism.

For Davis, moreover, the roots of his bourgeois-progressive activism reached back to his boyhood years around World War I and the 1920s, to the solid Black middle-class neighborhood he grew up in on the northeast side of DuPont Circle. There the most progressive and activist district branch of the NAACP was located, the branch in which his father played a role. Davis recalls as a nine- and ten-year-old boy joining his parents in street demonstrations on behalf of an early antilynching bill before Congress, a bill stemming from the brilliant and courageous antilynching activist career of the African American journalist Ida Wells-Barnett. "My father used to carry me on his strong shoulders at those anti-lynching demonstrations," Davis once remarked to me during the many conversations we had on these developments.

Let me make one additional observation on the Hastie-Davis mobilization stances at the start of the NNA. Although the bourgeois-establishmentarian activism mode of Hastie often coalesced sympathetically with aspects of Booker T. Washington's accommodationist strategy of forging ties with paternalistic White conservative elites, John Aubrey Davis's bourgeois-progressive activism mode did not. For Davis, White capitalists especially were, as we say today, part of the problem, not part of the solution. Or rather, White business elements had to be made part of the solution through all manner of populist-thrusted Black protest activism. For Davis, moreover, there was even a kind of higher order benefit for African Americans associated with progressive activism—*namely, the fashioning of a sense of Black ethnic efficacy*, of Black ethnic honor, if you will.

John Aubrey Davis first suggested the idea of a formalized boycott of the fast-food restaurant to the NAACP district branch in his old neighborhood, assuming it was still the activist-minded NAACP chapter his parents had participated in during the World War I era and the 1920s. He discovered, to his dismay, that the NAACP chapter had gone "establishment" since his boyhood years, "completely dominated by the respectable, well-off, and stuffed-shirt residents of the city," as Davis told Michele Pacifico.[8] That his boyhood-era NAACP chapter by 1933 would not, in Pacifico's words, "offer assistance to those struggling to obtain and keep jobs" simply "outraged Davis." He was outraged "that [NAACP] leaders were patronizing White businesses, especially chain stores, that did not employ any neighborhood African-Americans except in the most menial jobs. No one was acting to change these conditions."[9]

It was, then, the establishmentarianization of a once bourgeois-progressive NAACP chapter in Washington that initially radicalized along Black-populist lines the young political scientist John Aubrey Davis. Michele Pacifico describes this formative event and activism in this way:

> When events presented the opportunity that hot August day in 1933, Davis was prepared and launched the New Negro Alliance with the highly successful Hamburger Grill Boycott. Davis gave the new organization its name. He used the words "New Negro" to separate it from the previous [Leadership] generation of African Americans whom he deemed too content and apathetic. Yet Davis did not embrace Alain Locke's "New Negro" movement of the 1920s, noting that "Dr. Locke and the followers of his philosophy believed that racial prejudice would soon disappear before the altar of truth, art, and intellectual achievement."
>
> Davis argued that the black people's problems in the 1930s could not be solved by saying," "I'm culturally worth something." He stressed that African Americans had contributed to American cultural life since the time of the slave boats, but their situation had not improved. Overtly founded to win economic rights for African-American Washingtonians, the New Negro Alliance was an organization "with a new vision, a new thought and spirit, fearless in its undertakings and willing to sacrifice and fight for its own principles, even if it meant being thrown in jail," according to Davis. The New Negro Alliance would surpass the "New Negro" movement in its direct fight for economic progress.[10]

Organizational Dynamics of the New Negro Alliance

Black Intellectuals Challenge Racist Capitalism

It was in the summer of 1935—two years after the original demonstration against the Hamburger Grill—that Davis, Hastie, Fitzhugh, George Rycraw, Albert DeMond, Belford Lawson, James Nabrit, and other inner-circle activists formally fashioned the NNA into a mechanism for challenging White businesses in the Washington area patronized by African Americans that either refused to employ Blacks or, if they did employ Blacks, failed to treat them at parity with their White employees. Some ten committees were created as the day-to-day operating units of the NNA. Four committees—the Civil Rights Committee, the Public Utilities Committee, the Legal Committee, and the Case Committee—were especially concerned with tailoring the NNA's activism so as to maximize its public policy impact. George Rycraw, law partner of John Aubrey Davis's closest friend Belford Lawson, headed up the Civil Rights Committee; Doxey Wilkerson, a sociologist and Howard University faculty member, chaired the Public Utilities Committee; Thurman Dodson, another colleague of Belford Lawson, headed up the Legal Committee; and Rolandus Cooper, a lawyer, headed up the Case Committee.

There was a synergistic interaction among these four day-to-day operating committees from 1935 onward. For example, when the Public Utilities Committee identified utility companies that might be the object of an NNA boycott, it had to mobilize the other three committees around its concern before involving the executive officers, who were called Administrators. The Case Committee played a key early role in this decision-making process, for its members developed the analysis as to whether a given business, if chosen as object of activism, would produce good dividends on the public policy impact side of the ledger. The boycott and picketing aspects of the NNA's activism might not in fact be initiated if the Case Committee decided to send a suspected business a preliminary request to hire Black employees and that request was honored. For instance, in a study of the activity of the Case Committee during 1938 can be found the following report of a request to hire Black employees that was sent to a Washington area business:

> Case No. 163—Brown's Corner Store—Seventh & T Streets N.W. Case: (Noting a part-time clerk only.) We feel that your business being supported 100% by Negroes demands, in all fairness to the policy you state that you subscribe to, a full-time clerk as well as a part-time clerk. Result: Suggestion accepted and complied with by proprietor.

On the other hand, in the following report on job requests sent to several White businesses, a rather different outcome ensued. In two instances, the White businesses refused even to enter into discussions with the NNA:

> Case No. 290—Capital Shore Store/Case No 297—Bonnett's Shoes:
> These stores having ignored three regular form letters, used by the Case Committee in its approach for a conference and also having ignored a registered letter, received as a last resort our Picket Line.[11]

The clear tone of pragmatism apparent in these instances of the NNA's dealings with White businesses in 1938 was, in fact, a central modus operandi basic to all of its operations. Although Davis and other leading figures in the NNA were firm about the long-run goal of smashing White supremacist practices by White businesses that African Americans patronized, they were not committed ideologically to any one method for achieving this goal; rather they were fully experimental and pragmatic. For instance, the NNA was willing to make all kinds of accommodations to a given business where required, as illustrated in a report on negotiations between it and three businesses during 1938. The report observed,"All three stores [will] hire a week-end clerk to start and will increase by filling vacancies until majority of clerks are Negroes. These stores could not afford full week clerks."[12]

It is notable, however, that although quite attuned to the needs of specific businesses as they attempted to incorporate integrationist practices, the Black intellectuals who shaped the affairs of the NNA did not shirk from exercising a kind of normative surveillance in regard to the personal treatment accorded Black employees by White businesses. Its leaders were firm about their progressive sense of interpersonal relations between Whites and Blacks, and they were willing to pressure White businesses along these lines. This can be seen in the following report contained in the files of the Case Committee:

Case No. 303—Harry Kaufman Department Store—Case Committee: We respectfully wish to state that our Alliance very definitely views the practice of having Negro clerks relieve the elevator operator and pressing articles for window display a vicious discriminatory policy unless all clerks, both white and Negro, are compelled to take regular turns at this work. We also take this opportunity to suggest that now is the opportune time to employ the promised third Negro clerk.

Result: Discontinuance of the discriminatory policy. No more non-clerical work. On account of Union affiliations which must be adjusted, a Negro Shipping Clerk (male) is to be employed by August 15th, 1939.[13]

Thus, both in pressuring White businesses to engage in integrated hiring and fair interpersonal treatment of their Black employees, the NNA was clearly breaking new ground in the matter of civil rights activism. It should also be noted that it broke new ground by demonstrating that a progressive-tilted Black activist organization could succeed at achieving a broad mobilization among middle-class African Americans, not just among working-class Blacks who suffered most from American racist practices.

John Aubrey Davis was a veritable true believer in the activist potential of middle-class African Americans—a belief cultivated in him by his civil rights activist parents—and his closest professional peer, Belford Lawson, equally shared this belief. In this regard, Davis and Lawson differed from some activist-oriented Black intellectuals in the Washington community during the 1930s, especially Ralph Bunche and E. Franklin Frazier. Bunche and Frazier were more Marxist in their progressive outlook and thus looked more favorably on trade-union working-class Blacks as soldiers of civil rights activism among African Americans, viewing middle-class Blacks as intrinsically more bourgeois and self-serving. So Davis and Lawson were ahead of their generally leftist and progressive cohorts in their optimism about the activist potential of middle-class Blacks, and Davis in particular initiated numerous linkages between the NNA and the relatively sizeable middle-class population in the Washington African American community during the 1930s. In correspondence to me, Davis observed, "In 1935 I established, as part of the New Negro Alliance, the New Negro Forum, which met in the Berean Baptist Church at 11th and 'V' Streets, N.W. Speakers included a DC Commissioner, Jiggs Donahue, one of the three who ran the city, and John Sullivan, head of the American Federation of Government Employees."[14]

Accordingly, by mid-1935 onward, a broad sector of Washington's middle-class African American civic and professional associations, such as the National Association of Negro College Women, a variety of fraternities and sororities, and Black civic associations of all sorts, joined forces with the NNA. Above all, nearly all of the leading Black churches in Washington similarly joined forces with the NNA, as was recorded by James Nabrit in the *New Negro Alliance Yearbook.* Among the leading Black churches and clergymen mentioned by Nabrit were the following: Rev. Walter Brooks of the Nineteenth Street Baptist Church, Rev. R. W. Brooks of the Lincoln Memorial Temple, Rev. E. C. Smith of the Metropolitan Baptist Church, Rev. G. O. Bullock of the Third Baptist Church, Rev. C. T.

Murray of the Vermont Avenue Baptist Church, Rev. R. Douglas Grimes of the
Salem Baptist Church, Rev. Josiah Elliott of St. Luke's Protestant Episcopal
Church (the first all-Black Episcopal congregation organized by White Episco-
palians), Rev. H. B. Taylor of Fifteenth Street Presbyterian Church, Rev. A. F.
Elmes of Peoples Congregational Church, and Rev. Thomas W. Wallace of the
African Methodist Episcopal Zion Church.[15]

Alliance Activism and the Courts

Between 1935 and 1940 the NNA's use of boycotts was typically met with court
injunctions that charged it with activity that served as an illegal impediment to
free commerce. Although the U.S. Congress enacted the LaGuardia-Norris Anti-
Injunction Act of March 1932, which gave unions the right to use picketing and
boycott tactics, it was not at all clear whether federal courts would permit these
activism methods to be used by a pressure group whose members were not directly
employed by the businesses they were picketing or boycotting. At some point, then,
it was almost inevitable that the NNA's activism would clash with federal courts.

However, this clash did not occur all at once, but rather evolved slowly. During its first eighteen months of operation the NNA was met by injunctions initiated by several Washington businesses that it had boycotted and picketed, but
each time the courts refused to bear bids by the NNA to appeal the injunctions.
All this suddenly changed in late 1936, when it mounted a broad-based boycott
against a major Washington area supermarket chain, the Sanitary Grocery Company. This company asked for and received an injunction, which was appealed
by the NNA to and accepted by the U.S. Supreme Court, a decision that had a
major two-fold political impact on the African American community. First, it
sparked a fissure between the upstart NNA and the older Washington NAACP
chapter. That chapter, still smarting from the initial emergence and success of the
NNA and not certain yet of the viability of its activism modalities, remained aloof
from the injunction dispute. This NAACP aloofness proved politically disastrous
because quite the opposite response was taken by the grassroots Washington
African American community. The major historian of the NNA movement,
Michele Pacifico, records the events surrounding the NNA's appeal of its injunction, which amounted to a Black community-wide mobilization:

> The black press publicized the story. It was a heady time for the young African-
> American legal team set up [separate from the NAACP Branch] to fight this bat-
> tle. If the New Negro Alliance could win the case, then all "Jobs-For-Negroes"
> picketers [nationwide] would have the force of law behind them. While the
> NAACP doubted that the Alliance could win its case and offered little support,
> the black community of the District of Columbia rallied behind the organization.
> The NNA declared Sunday, December 17, 1937, New Negro Alliance Day. Pas-
> tors invited NNA representatives to their churches to discuss NNA program and
> the legal case, and to raise funds. Capping New Negro Alliance Day was an
> evening church service with music and speeches at the John Wesley A. M. E. Zion
> Church at 14th and Corcoran Streets, N.W. John Aubrey Davis was the guest
> speaker with other presentations by Belford Lawson, Thurman L. Dodson, church

pastor Reverend Stephen G. Spottswood, and John Zuker, the national representative of the Retail Clerks Association. The community turned out, donating a critical $500 toward the expenses of the Supreme Court case. . . . Belford Lawson and Thomas Dodson presented the Alliance's arguments, researched and prepared by William Hastie, Thurgood P. Marshall, Edward P. Loyett, Theodore M. Berry, and James M. Nabrit Jr.[16]

Noteworthy in Pacifico's account is that, among the young activist lawyers who presented the case to the Supreme Court in 1937, were future leading figures in the African American legal profession in general and, in particular, key figures who were to direct the national-level NAACP desegregation cases in federal courts a generation later, during the 1950s and 1960s. These early legal warhorses for the NNA who later became major national figures included William Hastie (the first Black federal justice), James Nabrit (dean of Howard Law School in the 1950s who argued the school desegregation cases before the Supreme Court in the 1950s along with Thurgood Marshall), and Thurgood Marshall (head lawyer for the NAACP Legal Defense Fund in the 1940s, chief of the NAACP legal staff that argued the school desegregation cases in the 1950s, and the first Black member of the U.S. Supreme Court, appointed by President Lyndon Johnson).

In returning to the 1937 case of *New Negro Alliance v. Sanitary Grocery Company*, the brief produced by Belford Lawson, Thurman Dodson, William Hastie, James Nabrit, Edward Lovett, and Thurgood Marshall was argued before the Supreme Court on March 5, 1938. The brief's core thesis was that the NNA, in pressuring White businesses to employ Blacks was, in legal terms, the equivalent to a trade union in pressuring industrial firms on behalf of fair working conditions for trade union members. Whereas trade unions were the key instrument for ensuring economic security and egalitarian social rights—for protecting White workers against economic discrimination in short—the NNA's use of boycotts and picketing functioned similarly as a guarantee against racial-caste discriminatory practices faced by African American citizens. As the NNA's brief put it, the NNA was the "only defense [available] against a discriminatory policy which jeopardizes [Blacks'] economic security."[17] As such, the brief characterized its pressuring activities as the functional equivalent of a genuine "labor dispute" under the language and terms of the LaGuardia-Norris Act of 1932, which gave trade unions the right to utilize boycotts and picketing.[18]

To the enormous surprise of Lawson, Nabrit, Davis, Hastie, and other inner-circle members of the NNA, the U.S. Supreme Court, on March 28, 1938, ruled in favor of its brief. Michele Pacifico records the Court's decision this way:

> In a 6–2 decision, the Supreme Court, led by Chief Justice Charles Evans Hughes, decided that "those having a direct or indirect "interest" in the employment of certain people should have the freedom to disseminate information and "'peacefully persuade others" to take action against such injustices. The climax of a four-year battle, the Supreme Court decision gave African Americans an effective method for fighting discriminatory hiring practices. African Americans now had a weapon they could lawfully use nationwide to combat discrimination in the work place!"[19]

Elaborating on the decision, one of the NNA lawyers, Leon Ransom, proffered the following formulation:

> Mr. Justice Roberts read the history-making decision which reversed the lower courts and dismissed the injunction [against the NNA]. In the course of the decision, the Court pointed out that the employer-employee relations did not have to exist in order for a '"labor dispute" to arise, and that an organization such as the Alliance, striving to obtain employment from employers who discriminated against them on account of race and color, could be a '"person interested" in a labor dispute and so within the protection of the law prohibiting court interference.[20]

The immediate impact of the Supreme Court's ruling was an expansion of NNA's activism in the Washington area. Michele Pacifico describes this stepped-up activism as follows: "For the next three years, until 1941, the Alliance used its newly won right to secure more jobs for Black Washingtonians. In the wake of the Supreme Court decision, the struggle eased; White employers preferred compromise to boycotts and picket lines. . . Old opponents such as *Kaufman's* Department Store and High's Ice Cream finally hired African American clerks."[21]

At the same time however, developments at the national level set into motion a chain of events that eventually led to the dissolution of the NNA. One of these developments was America's entry into World War II in 1941. The second development, also related to the war, was the issuance on June 25, 1941, by President Franklin Roosevelt of an Executive Order (No. 8802). This set into motion a brand new and totally unforeseen set of events that would recalibrate the political activism that the inner-circle members of the NNA had grown accustomed to between 1933 and 1940. These events would recalibrate that activism from what I have called street-level political activism to technocratic-policy activism practiced within federal government decision-making agencies. What Executive Order No. 8802 did, with the stroke of President Roosevelt's pen, was to extend to the federal level the right to equal or fair employment that the young John Aubrey Davis and other inner-circle NNA members spent nearly a decade seeking to apply simply to the District of Columbia.

Young Black Administrators Enter the Fair Employment Practices Committee

John Aubrey Davis was 31 when the second chairman of the Fair Employment Practices Committee (FEPC)—Father Haas, an economist at Catholic University who succeeded Mark *Etheridge*—asked him in the summer of 1943 to assume the post of director of the FEPC Division of Review and Analysis. With this appointment, John Aubrey Davis first encountered the issue of how to sustain intact the synergistic interaction between what I have called the two strands of his intellectual persona; namely, the activist-intellectual strand and the technocrat-intellectual strand. Fortunately for Davis, this activist-technocrat dilemma or tension was equally shared by virtually all of the dozen or so Black professionals who also gained key administrative appointments in running the FEPC-professionals like George Crocket (a lawyer), George Johnson (a lawyer and the highest-ranking Black FEPC administrator during the War), Clarence Mitchell (Urban League activist), and Elmer Henderson (a lawyer), among others. The issue they faced was plain enough: would the day-to-day rule-management and rule-allocating tasks associated with guaranteeing a fair degree of job integration for Black workers in America's massive wartime industries (tasks that inevitably demanded a lot of strategic-pragmatic bargaining and thus strategic-pragmatic concessions or tradeoffs) whittle away at and perhaps even nullify the ideology of civil rights activism that formatively fashioned the intellectual persona of John Aubrey Davis and his Black professional peers in the FEPC?

However this issue was to be resolved for Davis and his Black professional peers, they received some measure of assurance from the fact that the very processes that sparked the issuance of Executive Order 8802 by President Roosevelt were themselves rooted in civil rights activism. Civil rights realities were at the birth of the FEPC in 1941, in other words. Perhaps the account of the founding of FEPC that best evokes the primacy of civil rights realities in this event is that by Denton Watson, a former journalist and public relations officer of the NAACP national office, which he offers in his brilliant biography of Clarence Mitchell, the NAACP's public policy lobbyist in Washington during the 1950s and 1960s. Here is Watson's characterization of the FEPC's founding events:

> President Roosevelt's issuing of Executive order 8802 on June 25, 1941 was the most celebrated act in the battle against discrimination in war industries. That date marked the launching of the modern civil rights movement. The struggle for the executive order was led by A. Philip Randolph, president of the International Brotherhood of Sleeping Car Porters. Walter White, since early 1940, had been mobilizing the NAACP branches to fight discrimination in the defense program, but Randolph became the driving force in the movement. The idea dated back to 1917–18, when the NAACP [sparked by W. E. B. Du Bois] began calling for equal opportunity in employment. Randolph threatened to lead a march on Washington of ten thousand blacks (White increased the number to one hundred thousand) if Roosevelt did not issue the order barring discrimination in the armed services and defense industries. Roosevelt issued the order to stave off the march, which was to have been held on July 1. . . . Executive Order 8802 was a compromise that [left] untouched discrimination in the armed services, but Executive Order 8802 met *Randolph's* basic demands and created the Fair Employment Practices Committee (FEPC) as an administering agency to implement the directive.[22]

Although Denton Watson's portrayal of the birth of the FEPC refers only to the goal of nondiscrimination in defense industries, Executive Order 8802 had additional goals as well. In one of the most authoritative analysis of these goals, which appeared in *The Annals of the American Academy of Political and Social Science* in 1946, John Aubrey Davis observed that, in addition to outlawing discrimination in defense industries," Executive Order 8802 . . . forbade discrimination in Government [jobs] on account of race, creed, color and national origins, or in vocational and training programs carried on by Federal agencies for defense purposes. The same prohibition was repeated in Executive Order 9346 on May 27, 1943 [which required agency heads to report violations of the original Order directly to the President's office]. These orders were issued under the powers of the President as bestowed by Congress and the Constitution."[23]

Of course, explicit public policy goals like those laid out in Executive Order 8802 and Executive Order 9346 are one thing—formalistically legal things, that is—and the actual realization of the purposes of such policy goals is quite another thing altogether. This is to say that the day-to-day task of advancing Black employment under the FEPC proved to be inevitably problematic; it was a process involving some gains, yes, but gains that were often quite marginal too, and there were numerous outright defeats as well. An important factor underlying the FEPC's problematic outcome pattern was that it initially lacked independent authority status; instead, it was saddled with a dependent authority status. Between June 1941 and July 1942, the FEPC operated as a unit of the Office of Production Management, possessing neither its own office space nor its own operational staff. As the biographer of Clarence Mitchell (who was an early Black field administrator among the African American technocrats in FEPC), Denton Watson has informed us, "[FEPC] was required [between 1941 and 1942] to share staffs of the Negro Employment and Training Branch and the Minority Groups Branch [within the Office Of Production Management]. The FEPC served [initially] as a board of appeal for those two units, which certified [discrimination] cases to it."[24]

But in the summer of 1942 these structural limitations on FEPC changed. President Roosevelt transferred FEPC to a new war-related agency, the War Manpower Commission, one of whose officials was a young African American civil rights activist and economist, Dr. Robert Weaver. Weaver had already played a role in wartime antidiscrimination policy when he was hired to serve in the Office of Production Management in early 1940, making him the first African American administrator of consequence in the wartime Roosevelt administration. So in July 1942 the FEPC gained a bona fide parallel authority status with the War Manpower Commission in the sphere of antidiscrimination policy, though the line of command required the FEPC staff to communicate through two War Manpower Commission officials, Robert Weaver and Will Alexander, who was a White American.

Above all, the new operational autonomy provided the FEPC in July 1942 was fleshed out through the appointment of several African American administrators who had been linked to Robert Weaver through their civil rights activism, which took place under the auspices of the National Urban League, the NAACP, and the NNA movement during the 1930s. One of these early FEPC Black administrators was Clarence Mitchell, who was appointed associate director of the Division of Field Operation, a position that Mitchell had prepared for when he functioned as a deputy to Robert Weaver in the Office of Production Management from the middle of 1940 to mid-1942. In early and middle 1943, several additional Black administrators were appointed to the FEPC. Elmer Henderson, a Baltimore-Washington area lawyer, was appointed head of its Chicago regional office; George Crocket, a labor activist lawyer from Detroit, was made Deputy Legal Analyst; George Johnson, former dean of Howard University Law School, was made Deputy Director of the Division of Review and Analysis; and John Aubrey Davis was appointed Director of the Division of Review and Analysis.

Maneuvering FEPC for Black Workers

Following quite closely on the FEPC's gaining of a relatively viable administrative infrastructure of its own by the end of 1942, President Roosevelt issued an amending set of administrative arrangements under a new Executive Order 9346 in May 1943. These new administrative arrangements gave FEPC the authority to police discriminatory practices within federal government agencies. According to Professor Desmond King's authoritative study of the FEPC years in his volume, *Separate and Unequal: Black Americans and the U.S. Federal Government* (1995), Executive Order 9346 directed federal agencies, under the authority of FEPC, to "make a thorough examination of their personnel policies and practices to the end that they may be able to assure me [President Roosevelt] that in the Federal Service the doors of employment are open to all loyal and qualified workers regardless of creed, race or national origin."[25]

With these words President Roosevelt went a long way to helping remove the glaring contradiction that obtained under the 1941 Executive Order 8802, namely, a federal government that was practicing discrimination in its own ranks while legally mandating the end of discrimination in wartime-related private job markets. Thanks to a 1943 memorandum sent in early 1943 from the third chairman of the FEPC, Malcolm Ross, President Roosevelt had this issue clarified for him vividly and candidly. "Very early in its official life," observed Malcolm Ross to the President, "the Committee came to the conclusion that its chances of success in securing cooperation from private employers would be lessened if the government's own employment practices were open to serious criticism."[26]

However, even with its new authority to challenge discrimination in federal agencies the FEPC had a tenuous impact on ensuring government job-market access by African American workers during the course of World War II. This issue was addressed by John Aubrey Davis's analytical postmortem on FEPC for *The Annals of the American Academy of Political and Social Science* in 1946. Davis observed that although the "FEPC had the power in government cases to report [discrimination] to the President," it was important to recognize at the same time that "the President personally cannot be concerned with individual cases, and his assistants will not consider anything except general violations of the President's [Executive] orders." Davis continued,

> In government cases the Committee has never been allowed to hold public hearings as in the case of war industries, and thus the sanction of public opinion has not been open to it. As the enforcing agent of the national nondiscrimination policy, Government would perhaps be in an unfortunate position to have to expose its [own] failings to the public.[27]

Thus in this article, John Aubrey Davis provided a rather unfavorable view of the U.S. government's willingness to police job discrimination in its own ranks as compared to private wartime industries. Davis even appended some quantitative findings to his postmortem: "Although government cases have formed 27 percent of its caseload, FEPC has felt constrained to resort to hearing[s] in only three government cases involving three agencies, as opposed to 27 industry hearings involving 102 companies and 38 unions."[28] Davis also observed, with a clear touch of disappointment, that nearly 80 percent of the federal discrimination complaints brought to FEPC (a total of 2,048 complaints) were not acted on for one reason or another. As Davis put it, "[Only] 23 percent [of 2048 complaints] were settled satisfactorily; the rest were dismissed on merits, for lack of jurisdiction, or for insufficient evidence, or continued pending."[29]

Keep in mind, however, that for both John Aubrey Davis and his Black administrator peers, FEPC gave due recognition to the technocratic and pragmatic problem-solving attributes that defined part of their intellectual persona. Thus although the activist orientation kept Davis and his peers attentive to the performance gap between the FEPC's stated goals and their realization in regard to federal jobs for African Americans, they were also attentive to whatever progress was attainable during the war years, and they made every effort to recognize those attainments. A summary of federal and District of Columbia job data is presented by Davis in his postmortem analysis of FEPC as well. More detailed aggregate federal job data relating to African American employment during the war years are also presented in Professor Desmond King's definitive study of FEPC processes. Using data covering pre-FEPC and FEPC years, Davis makes clear that a measure of job advancement for African Americans did indeed occur. Aggregate data on Blacks employed in war agencies (the Army and Navy departments) as of 1944 impressed Davis: Of nearly 2 million employees (1,928,216 to be exact) some 231,438 or 12 percent were African Americans.

Davis viewed Black employment status in the District of Columbia's federal jobs, especially the qualitative attributes of such jobs, quite favorably. As his baseline, Davis used data from a 1938 job survey that showed that African Americans held overwhelmingly custodial-type jobs as federal employees in the governance of the District of Columbia (some 90% of such jobs were held by Blacks); in contrast they held only 9 percent of clerical and administrative-grade jobs and a mere 0.5 percent of professional-grade jobs. However, by 1944 the custodial category of Black employment had declined to 40 percent, and more importantly, in federal jobs servicing the District of Columbia some "49 percent of all Negro employees were classified as Clerical-Administrative and Fiscal."[30] Finally, in regard to independent federal agencies—those organized outside the central cabinet or executive departments—Davis also identified a measure of Black job employment progress. As Davis put it his postmortem survey, "The March 1944 survey [for FEPC] revealed that Negroes were 13.6 percent of all employees in the independent agencies, the highest proportion in the three groups of [federal] agencies. Comparatively good records were noted for the Federal Works Agency, the Federal Security Agency, the Veterans Administration, the General Accounting Office, the Government Printing Office, and the Tennessee Valley Authority."[31]

There was, however, one area of Black employment in federal jobs that left Davis and his Black peers rather pessimistic. It happened that under the Civil Service Act of 1923 a two-fold job classification was set forth—"classified" and "unclassified" federal jobs—and the former happened to "carry the greatest security in Government," as Davis and his colleagues noted in a January 1945 appraisal report on the wartime functioning of FEPC. This report titled *The Wartime Employment of Negroes in the Federal Government* found that only 7 percent of Black federal employees fell in the "classified" category, the category of high job-security workers. This rather startled Davis and his colleagues because as the war was in the process of ending by January 1945, they were especially cognizant of future federal job downsizing—as we call it today—which would more than likely translate into massive job dismissals among African American federal employees. Because Davis understood that this outcome could not be alleviated by new federal job classification rules, he put forth the suggestion that a new post-war federal agency might be created that would have a special responsibility (what today we would call an affirmative action responsibility) to cushion the impact on African American federal employees of massive postwar job downsizing. As John Aubrey Davis put it in *The Wartime Employment of Negroes in the Federal Government*, "For the time being, an independent permanent [anti-job discrimination] agency of Government is needed which can enforce anti-discrimination in [post-war] Government by working with the several agencies and by co-operating with the Civil Service Commission. The wartime experience of the Civil Service Commission and FEPC indicates that this can be a feasible arrangement."[32]

Unfortunately, however, no such FEPC-like agency was established in the immediate post–World War II years. Indeed, giving African Americans access to federal jobs in a proactive manner did not occur until affirmative action policies were promulgated by the Kennedy-Johnson Administrations in the late 1960s and elaborated during the Nixon-Ford Republican Administrations—thanks to liberal and moderate Republican administrators—throughout the 1970s.

The overall outcome of the FEPC experiment in regard to the furtherance of Black employment in the spheres of government and wartime industries was on balance quite positive. On this matter, there is no more authoritative chronicler than Denton Watson, who, in the course of producing the most effective biography we have of that 1930s cohort of African American professionals who were the first to secure full-fledged federal administrative posts, read widely and deeply in the official FEPC records. Thus in Watson's considered appraisal, "The FEPC was the most promising symbol of hope for equal economic opportunity that African Americans had ever had. . . . The best proof that the FEPC was opening doors of opportunity was the increase in the number of minorities employed in war industries, from less than 3 percent in early 1942 to more than 7 percent two years later, and 8 percent by the end of the war. Eighty percent of those benefiting from Executive Order 8802 [and Executive Order 9346] were Black; 14 percent were mostly Mexican Americans."[33] Translated into aggregate terms, nearly one million Blacks were added to the industrial workforce thanks to the FEPC, a figure that represented some 300,000-plus Black males and 600,000 Black females.[34]

The FEPC's impact on African Americans has an elite or leadership dimension as well. According to Denton Watson, the FEPC "gave African Americans their first opportunity to be line officers in the federal government. Though small, that group of African Americans extended their influence by maintaining a close-knit network of interrelationships."[35] In this accounting of the FEPC's Black leadership impact, Denton Watson is very much on target, for I would suggest that there is a direct line of action from the Black policymaking cadre under the FEPC (e.g., Clarence Mitchell, George Crockett, Elmer Henderson, Robert Weaver, John Aubrey Davis, et al.) to the Black policymaking cadre of Black federal lobbyists, administrators, and legislators who emerged from the early 1960s through the 1970s. It was, moreover, this Black policymaking cadre at the federal level in the 1960s through 1970s era who, along with liberal White administrators and legislators, helped fashion the civil rights legislation and multi-layered administrative practices that broke the legal back of American racism. As this post–World War II full-fledged Black political class was evolving, important roles were performed by the ex-FEPC Black cadre. Clarence Mitchell organized a civil rights lobbying office for the NAACP in Washington, George Crockett lobbied for Black trade unionists in Washington and became a congressman for a majority-Black district in Detroit, John Aubrey Davis became a key policy advisor to Roy Wilkins, the head of the NAACP, and Robert Weaver became the first African American to hold a post in the Cabinet when President Johnson appointed him Secretary of Housing and Urban Development.

John Aubrey Davis also produced an accounting of the FEPC's impact on African Americans that dovetailed with Denton Watson's analysis. Though critical of its work in the area of advancing federal jobs for African Americans, Davis nonetheless recognized the significance of FEPC to African Americans' overall status. In his 1946 postmortem appraisal, Davis suggested that FEPC, or some agency like it, be made a permanent federal agency. Like Denton Watson, moreover, Davis also recognized the unique qualitative impact that FEPC had on African American political leadership status. Before the New Deal era, Blacks had almost zero institutionalized authoritative presence at the federal level. The only Blacks in government then secured jobs by what might be called *clientage political appointments*, by which I mean highly personalistic patronage appointments that involved limited policymaking authority for Black officials who gained weak consultative or advisory roles, not administrative policy-managing roles. As John Aubrey Davis remarked on this issue, Blacks' pre-FEPC policy status at the federal level "was characterized by numerous appointments as *advisors* on racial policy in the many agencies which were carrying out economic and social programs." Note that "as advisors" is italicized, for Davis's point was that in the pre-FEPC period, appointments of Blacks at the federal level did not yet include policymanaging functions.

However, the FEPC reversed this situation, propelling Black federal-level officials from "advisory officials" to full-fledged policy-managing and thus policymaking officials. Thanks to a presidential Executive Order promulgating the FEPC and empowering it with the federal task of managing job-advancement policy for African Americans throughout the course of World War II, a glacier-like shift occurred in the operational character of Blacks appointed to staff federal agencies—a shift from "advisory officials" to "policy-managing and policy-making officials." Davis concluded his postmortem analysis of FEPC in 1946 with this observation: "In FEPC Negroes participated as equals in policy formation and administration."[36] And in correspondence, John Aubrey Davis underscored to me the fundamental role of the White House under President Franklin Delano Roosevelt in making possible a revolution in the qualitative status of African American federal-level officials: "The fact is," Davis remarked, "that the thing that broke the back of discrimination in the Federal government was the President's letter [May 25, 1943] to the Department heads [operationalizing anti-discrimination practices] and the requirement that they report to the President on their progress. . . . This was the first 'affirmative action' to remedy [decades-long] discrimination."[37]

One additional thought. Had John Aubrey Davis and his street-level civil rights activist peers in Washington DC during the 1930s left no more than the civil rights activist legacy of the New Negro Alliance movement for African Americans to learn from and build on, they would have indeed left us contribution enough. That they served during the wartime years as key officials in the FFPC to advance on that legacy places John Aubrey and his Black professional peers, to my mind anyway, in a special category. It makes them a very precious and venerated segment of the twentieth-century African American intelligentsia.

Conclusion: The Activist Imperative

As a budding African American professional in the middle 1930s, John Aubrey Davis had a formative encounter with the American racist system that might be called an *activist-encounter*. An *activist-encounter* with American racism is one that endeavors to challenge the edifice of White supremacist pariahization, marginalization, torment, and oppression of Black people in American life. Commencing his intelligentsia career shortly after graduating from Williams College in 1933, John Aubrey Davis was part of the second generation-and-a-half cohort of African Americans who attended college in the twentieth century. This cohort did not have before them many everyday examples of African American professional persons who had fashioned an *activist-encounter demeanor* for themselves.

Instead, Davis's cohort of Black college graduates had before them numerous examples of African American professionals who had fashioned an *accommodationist-encounter* demeanor toward America's racist practices. This demeanor was given prominence from the 1880s into the 1930s by Booker T. Washington and his Tuskegee Institute machine. It was a *Black middle-class conservative demeanor* that emphasized the self-advancement of one's own professional goals, benefits, and compensations, thereby ignoring the vicious American racist systemic barriers to African American citizens' human rights and citizenship participatory rights. The *accommodationist-encounter* orientation among the emergent African American professional sector in the early twentieth century was just the opposite of the *activist-encounter* orientation that John Aubrey Davis and his circle of young Black professionals in the 1930s chose for their own identity.

Growing up as he did in a middle-class Black neighborhood in Washington, DC, in the World War I era into the 1920s, John Aubrey Davis had many examples around him of professional-stratum African American individuals who had adopted the *accommodationist-encounter* demeanor that Booker T. Washington made famous. These were Black professional persons who chose to maximize their ability to cash in on whatever market value a racist American capitalist democracy decided to attach to their middle-class and professional attributes as businessman, businesswoman, pharmacist, seamstress, lawyer, doctor, bookkeeper, dentist, schoolteacher, etc. These were decent, fair-minded Black American citizens, mind you, caring for their families and seeking to do the best by them in social mobility terms. It just happened, however, that those social mobility terms were hemmed in crudely and viciously by America's racist edifice and practices. Therefore, by relating to America's racist practices along the *accommodationist lines* fashioned by Booker T. Washington and his Tuskegee Institute machine, conservative Black middle-class persons in early twentieth-century Washington, DC— and elsewhere in America—were adopting an ideological rationale for their decision to "look out for number one," so to speak, rather than to challenge through civil rights activism the cruel American racist system.

Happily for the status of African American society in contemporary post–civil rights era, the second-generation cohort of evolving twentieth-century African American professionals that John Aubrey Davis was a part of spawned a sizable number of activist-minded personalities. What a probe of John Aubrey Davis's intellectual and professional career teaches today's generation is that the civil rights activist choice made by Davis and his fellow young Black professionals in the 1930s was not the *natural choice* for them to make. Rather it was a *deviant choice*, relative to the choices made in the period of the 1920s and 1930s by thousands of other middle-class and professional African American persons who deferred to the Booker T. Washington leadership model. The deviant choice by John Aubrey Davis and his civil rights activist peers was, therefore, *a heroic Black professional-class identity choice*, one that entailed risks to their future mobility trajectory.

However, in making their deviant choice as civil rights activist African American professionals, John Aubrey Davis and his peers did have some role models to follow. Among several earlier generations there was a small population of African American professionals (e.g., only around 8,000 Blacks had graduated college by 1930) who had courageously laid down guidelines to an *activist-encounter* with American racism. Uncovering these role models required an intellectual effort on the part of John Aubrey Davis and his peers, an effort that was partly associated with the Harlem Renaissance or New Negro Movement in the post– World War I era. While attending Negro colleges in the 1920s most of the Black professional peers associated with John Aubrey Davis's civil rights activism learned about the African American historical record of struggle against racist oppression in American society; about the journey of tears and blood and sweat rooted in American slavery, the Civil War, and Reconstruction; and about the betrayal of Reconstruction on which rested the American White supremacist edifice from the late 1870s onward.

It was this historical quest that enabled John Aubrey Davis and his civil rights activist peers (James Nabrit, Clarence Mitchell, Robert Weaver, Belford Lawson, Doxey Wilkerson, Elmer Henderson, George Crockett, Albert Demond, Naylor Fitzhugh, George Johnson, Charles Houston, and others) to forge their second-generation cohort activism agenda. This historical quest turned up civil rights activist forerunners extending back to the pre–Civil War era, like James W. C. Pennington (a clergyman and abolitionist), Frederick Douglass (a newspaper editor and abolitionist), Lewis Hayden (an abolitionist and legislator in Massachusetts), and John McCune Smith (a medical doctor and abolitionist). There were post-Emancipation era activist forerunners like Alexander Crummell (activist clergyman, scholar, and founder of the American Negro Academy), Francis Grimke (civil rights activist clergyman), Archibald Grimke (civil rights activist lawyer), John Wesley Cromwell (newspaper editor and founder of the American Negro Academy), and Reverdy Ransom (civil-rights activist clergyman and founder of the American Negro Academy). Finally, there were early twentieth-century activist forerunners like W. E. B. Du Bois, Monroe Trotter (newspaper editor and founder of the Niagara Movement), and Ida Wells-Barnett (activist newspaper reporter and antilynching crusader). It was, then, through this historical quest and intellectual probing that John Aubrey Davis and his peers discovered the African American activist forerunners on whose earlier work was the foundation for the "Don't Buy Where You Can't Work" civil rights activism organization in the 1930s.

Probing the core facets of John Aubrey Davis's professional career as a route to remembrance of our civil rights activist Black intelligentsia forebears helps us grasp one core lesson above all. That lesson is that the activist orientation toward the American racist edifice provided a way to withhold legitimacy from that racist edifice. The activist-encounter demeanor toward America's racist patterns that John Aubrey Davis and his 1930s circle of Black professional peers fashioned for themselves empowered them, in turn, to create organizational weapons to maneuver in behalf of African Americans' freedom quest and secure the small participatory space available in our White supremacist democratic nation-state. Davis and his peers already had before them examples of activist organizational weapons fashioned by earlier generations of activist-oriented Black professionals, examples that functioned as cross-generational blueprints for fashioning the New Negro Alliance organization in the 1930s. And the New Negro Alliance would itself become a cross-generational blueprint for the activist sector of African Americans' freedom quest in the 1950s and 1960s. The remembrance of our African American intelligentsia forebears teaches us how much successive activist Black intelligentsia generations stand on each others' shoulders.

Yet important though cross-generational activist blueprints have been and still are something else was required as well. What was also required was acquisition of a variety of technocratic skills through which the institutions of political power, judicial power, and economic power are managed and manipulated in the American system. Teasing out facets of John Aubrey Davis's intellectual career as a route to remembrance of our African American intelligentsia forebears brings front-and-center recognition of what might be called *the other side of the activist imperative* in the African American freedom quest. That other side is the *technocratic imperative*, by which I mean acquisition by the evolving twentieth-century African American intelligentsia of the fulsome quantum of technocratic skills required to penetrate the institutions of political, bureaucratic, judicial, and economic power in the American system.

As I have shown in this probe of John Aubrey Davis's career, he and his 1930s circle of Black professional peers like William Hastie, James Nabrit, Belford Lawson,

Thurman Dobson, George Rycraw, Albert Demond, Naylor Fitzhugh, Doxey Wilkerson, Rolandus Cooper, Clarence Mitchell, and others understood very well the centrality of the technocratic imperative to Black people's freedom quest. To this end, Davis seized on every opportunity available to gain job experience in the workings of city, county, state, and federal bureaucracies—as did his circle of Black professional peers. And Davis and his peers were especially attentive to learning how to translate the rules, procedures, and networks of power structures in the American system into weapons for Black people's freedom quest.

However, crucial though the technocratic imperative was to Black people's freedom quest, John Aubrey Davis and his peers recognized that technocratic skills could not in themselves produce the outcomes they sought. Something else was also required, and that something else was some degree of political alliances with White Americans who managed key power structures in the American system. Fortunately for that second-generation cohort of pragmatic-activist African American professionals of which John Aubrey Davis and his peer were a part, there was a small cadre of White American professionals willing to enter into an alliance with activist Black professionals. The first important demonstration of this willingness occurred during the FEPC years under President Franklin Roosevelt's administration. Davis and his circle of Black professional peers recognized this immediately and flocked to the work of the FEPC. Most of the White chairmen of FEPC were at least moderate liberals who engaged in alliance with activist Black professionals like Davis and his circle, and the last chairman of FEPC, Malcolm Ross, was a veritable progressive liberal.

As an enduring Black intelligentsia legacy Davis and his peers left us a blueprint on how to combine human will, fortitude, courage, discipline, and political savvy with a technocratic-activist challenge to America's racist edifice. This blueprint always exhibited an aura of fidelity to Black people's honor, a fidelity to the view that the Black people's freedom quest is not fulfilled until the plight of the weakest and most oppressed of our African American brethren is redeemed from racist and social oppression.

Notes

1. Michele F. Pacifico, "Don't Buy Where You Can't Work: The New Negro Alliance of Washington," *Washington History: Magazine of the Historical Society of Washington, DC* (Spring–Summer, 1994): 67.

2. William H. Hastie, "The Way of the Alliance," in *New Negro Alliance Year Book 1939* (Washington, DC: New Negro Alliance, 1939), 14.

3 John Aubrey Davis, *Notes for Dr. Martin Kilson re Chapter on Dr. John Aubrey Davis*, n.d. (circa 1987).

4. Hastie, "The Way of the Alliance," 14–15.

5. This was Rev. Elder Micheaux's radio "theme song." During my boyhood in the 1930s in a mill town that was a suburb of Philadelphia, Elder Micheaux's religious radio broadcast aired every Sunday.

6. Davis, *Notes for Dr. Martin Kilson.*

7. Pacifico, "Don't Buy," 68–69.

8. Ibid., 72.

9. Davis, *Notes for Dr. Martin Kilson.*

10. Pacifico, "Don't Buy," 72–73.

11. Rowlandus H. Cooper, "Notes from Alliance Case Book," in *New Negro Alliance Year Book 1939*, 4a.

12. Ibid.

13. Ibid., 25.

14. Davis, *Notes for Dr. Martin Kilson*.

15. See James M. Nabrit, "Civil Rights Endorsers of the Alliance," in *New Negro Alliance Year Book 1939*, 31–33.

16. Pacifico, "Don't Buy," 82–83.

17. Ibid., 83–84.

18. Summaries of the NNA's brief presented to the U.S. Supreme Court in March 1938 are found in B. Rhoden Coward, "The History of the NNA," in *New Negro Alliance Year Book 1939*, 15–16.

19. Pacifico, "Don't Buy," 84.

20 Leon A. Ransom, "The Supreme Court Speaks," in *New Negro Alliance Year Book 1939*, 18.

21. Pacifico, "Don't Buy," 84–85.

22. Denton Watson, *Lion in the Lobby: Clarence Mitchell Jr.'s Struggle for Passage of Civil Rights Laws* (New York: William Morrow, 1990), 130ff. Watson was an African American journalist who covered civil rights activities at the federal level for African American news organs. His brilliant work on Clarence Mitchell's years as a NAACP legislative lobbyist contains major material on the role of African American professionals in the operation of the FEPC. My chapter on John Aubrev Davis is, to my knowledge, the only study that probes the full range of Black professionals' experiences in the FEPC, though Watson's book presents some material on Mitchell's experience in the FEPC. What now cries out for study is Robert Weaver's role as the ground-breaking African American civil rights activist professional involved in policymaking during the Roosevelt Administrations. Weaver was a graduate student at Harvard in economics in the late 1920s to early 1930s when Ralph Bunche was there in political science and John P. Davis was at Harvard Law School. Weaver, Bunche, and John P. Davis interacted with each other at Harvard, where Weaver and Davis created the Negro Industrial League, an organization that gathered data on federal government practices affecting Black workers. Weaver and Davis later folded the Negro Industrial League into the national office of the NAACP as a Black labor research agency. Ralph Bunche and John P. Davis participated, along with A. Philip Randolph, in launching the National Negro Congress from 1935 onward; this was the leading leftist organization among the Black intelligentsia in the period. On the activity of Weaver and John P. Davis in founding the Negro Industrial League, see Kenneth Janken's biography on Walter White: Janken, *White: The Biography of Walter White, Mr. NAACP* (New York: New Press, 2003), 213ff.

23. John A. Davis, "Non-Discrimination in the Federal Services," *The Annals of the American Academy of Political and Social Science* (March 1946): 66.

24. Watson, *Lion in the Lobby*, 132.

25. Quoted in Desmond King, *Separate and Unequal: Black Americans and the U.S. Federal Government* (Oxford: Clarendon, 1995), 75. Professor Desmond King's work contains valuable material on FEPC's interface with African Americans.

26. Malcolm Ross, "*The President's Committee on Fair Employment Practices: Beginning and Growth, undated memorandum,*" *The Wartime Employment of Negroes in the Federal Government*, memorandum, January 1945, National Archives Record Group Number 228 of FEPC. Box 358. Quoted in King, *Separate and Unequal*, 75.

27. John Aubrey Davis, "Non-Discrimination," 67.

28. Ibid., 68.

29. Ibid., 71–72.

30. Ibid., 72.

31. Ibid., 73.

32. Davis, C. L. Golightly, and I. W. Hemphill, *The Wartime Employment of Negroes in the Federal Government*, memorandum, January 1945, National Archives Record Group Number 228 FEPC. Box 358. Quoted in Davis, "Non-Discrimination," 75.

33. Watson, *Lion in the Lobby*, 147–48.

34. See Jesse Pankhurst Guzman, ed., *Negro Year Book: A Review of Events Affecting Negro Life* (Tuskegee, AL: Tuskegee Institute Department of Records and Research, 1947), 136.

35. Watson, *Lion in the Lobby*, 147–48

36. Davis, "Non-Discrimination," 65.

37. Davis, *Letter to Martin Kilson* (October 26, 1992).

PART IV

Political Institutions

AMERICANS HAVE A RIGHT to be proud of their venerated political institutions. These institutions have evolved considerably since
the first edition (1910) of Charles A. Beard's *American Government and
Politics* textbook. These institutions have stood the test of time and have adapted
under pressure. The interaction of these institutions with the race question is particularly fascinating. On the road to achieve racial equality, blacks have engaged
all three branches of government. In the fifties and sixties, the U.S. Supreme
Courts played a critical role in the desegregation of our society. Blacks have considered the Supreme Court their ally in the fight for freedom, but with the advent
of the Berger and Rehnquist Courts there has been a shift to the center, if not to
the right. There is no doubt that the judicial reasoning of members has changed.
Because the Court is taking up issues once considered moral ones, more and more
attention is accorded to the nuances of its decisions.

In responding to racial issues, the Congress has been slightly behind the
Court, but its role in implementing and institutionalizing remedies for blacks continues to be important. Not since Reconstruction have we had so many blacks
serving in the Congress. The increase in the number of black representatives in
the Congress is one of the byproducts of the 1965 Voting Rights Acts. The Congressional Black Caucus began as an effort to pool resources and to present a collective agenda; it has since become highly visible and institutionalized. Although
this is a remarkable achievement, many scholars have raised questions about the
efficacy of the group. Are black interests being effectively represented by this

organization? Does the fact that there are no Republican members make its job difficult in a Republican-dominated government?

More than the other two branches of government, the presidency looms at the center of American politics. The president sets the political agenda and is the official who can speak for the nation. Race has been an issue for most of our presidents. Presidential statements on race have the potential to shape attitudes about race. The point is that the president is not a neutral actor in the struggle for equal opportunity for blacks. Beginning with the Lyndon Johnson administration, several African Americans have served in the Cabinet. Although the nation may be several election cycles away from an elected African American president, the prospect of such an event continues to fascinate pundits.

CHAPTER TEN

Dimensions of Representation and the Congressional Black Caucus

Kenny J. Whitby

T HE CURRENT DEBATE over African American representation in the political science profession runs parallel to the debate over the value of racial diversity in legislative institutions. Both debates center around an important question: What are the appropriate mechanisms to ensure that racial minorities will have an adequate voice in the decision-making process? In both cases, decision makers have struggled to find the appropriate remedy for the underrepresentation of racial minorities in governing bodies.

Nowhere is the debate over African American representation more evident than in the controversy surrounding the significance of racial diversity in Congress. The current maelstrom over racial representation is in large measure a function of redistricting aimed at increasing minority representation in Congress. Indeed, after the 1990s round of redistricting, the size of the Congressional Black Caucus (CBC) grew by nearly one-third in the 103rd Congress (see Table 10.1). Since then, the size of the CBC has remained relatively constant, largely as a byproduct of affirmative racial redistricting.

Students of legislative and minority politics have taken note of these developments and have expended much energy examining the effects of race on minority representation. The number of papers, articles, and books on black representation in Congress has grown considerably. Since the early 1990s, for example, several influential books have been published on the topic (Canon 1999; Fenno 2003; Lublin 1997; Singh 1998; Swain 1993; Tate 2003; Whitby 1997). In addition, William Clay, former congressman and co-founding member of the CBC, offers a good insider's account of its birth and internal operations in his 1993 work, *Just Permanent Interests: Black Americans in Congress, 1870–1991.*

Furthermore, special conferences have been devoted exclusively to exploring the dynamics of minority political representation. In May 2003, for instance, the Center for the Study of African American Politics at the University of Rochester sponsored a conference on racial representation. In part, the conference focused on the contributions of Richard Fenno and his seminal work on representation.

Fenno's research on the different representational styles of House members in *Home Styles: House Members in Their Districts* (1978) has served as the foundation for many subsequent studies on black congressional representation (e.g., Canon 1999; Swain 1993; Tate 2003). Twenty-five years after the publication of *Home Styles*, Fenno published *Going Home: Black Representatives and Their Constituencies* (2003), further testimony to this lively and important area of research.

This chapter offers an assessment of the CBC from the perspective of three dimensions of representation: *descriptive, substantive,* and *symbolic* representation. This approach represents a departure from previous assessments that detail the origins, evolution, operations, organizational structure, and accomplishments of the Caucus (Barnett 1975, 1982; Champagne and Rieselbach 1995; Clay 1993; Henry 1977; Jones 1987; Poinsett 1973; R. Smith 1981). The objective here is to use this analysis of dimensions of representation to point out some of the strengths and weaknesses in the literature in the hopes that this overview will serve as blueprint for future research on this important topic.

The chapter proceeds in the following manner. The first section discusses the theoretical framework for this overview of the Caucus. In the second part, the CBC is evaluated in the context of each dimension of representation. The chapter concludes by offering a broad assessment and points to areas for future research.

Framework

The study of the CBC is inextricably linked to the concept known as representation. In other words, the CBC is a race-based informal organization seeking to promote the interests of racial minorities within the confines of a representative institution. Researchers have come to understand that representation is a multifaceted concept with different meanings. Three dimensions of representation have commanded particular attention in political science. These dimensions are defined by Hanna Pitkin in her influential book *The Concept of Representation* (1967). They serve as a guide for scholarly analysis on representation and for the assessment of the CBC in this chapter.

The first dimension is *descriptive* representation. This dimension suggests that the social characteristics of those who serve in legislative assemblies ought to reflect the social diversity of the country's population. In the context of this chapter, descriptive representation means that the membership of Congress should approach symmetry with the proportion of African Americans in the general population. Whether legislative assemblies should reflect the racial diversity of the general population is a debatable issue. To a large degree, the answer lies within the relationship between descriptive representation and the other dimensions. As Carol Swain (1993), Katherine Tate (2003), and others (e.g., Guinier 1994) astutely point out, having more black faces in the chambers of Congress may not necessarily result in increased congressional responsiveness to black constituents.

The second dimension is termed *substantive* representation. To use Pitkin's language, this means "acting in the interest of the represented, in a manner responsive to them" (1967, 209). According to this dimension, representatives should be judged primarily on the basis of their activities (i.e., whether they are responsive to their constituents). This viewpoint suggests that Congress may be a truly representative body even if it does not mirror the racial composition of the general population. The substantive significance of member race in Congress is the source of great scholarly debate and is the basis for any investigation of the role of the CBC.

Symbolism is the third dimension of representation. Symbolic representation is the extent to which a representative is accepted as believable by his or her constituents. Put differently, symbolism is the psychology of representing the represented. It is important to note that symbolic representation need not entail descriptive representation. The suggestion, however, is that there are symbolic benefits to black descriptive representation in that African American representatives may serve as role models for black constituents. Moreover, according to this line of reasoning, the presence of racial minorities in Congress may enhance the legitimacy of governmental authority by increasing levels of political efficacy and political trust among disadvantaged social groups (Mansbridge 1999).

Each of these dimensions is discussed in turn with an eye firmly focused on the CBC. Several questions revolve around these dimensions of representation and can be summarized succinctly in the following way: Does the racial identity of the representative matter in the legislative process on both substantive and symbolic grounds? Though we have made considerable progress in answering this question, controversy still remains.

Descriptive Representation

The CBC was formally established in 1971 to promote the legislative interests and needs of African Americans and the poor. Though the formal organizational structure was not created until 1971, black descriptive representation at the federal level began in the Reconstruction era. Between 1870 and 1901, twenty African Americans served in the House of Representatives and two in the Senate.[1]

There are few scientific investigations on the subject during the Reconstruction era,[2] although there is evidence to suggest that black descriptive representation was an important issue (Kousser 1999; Swain 1993). As Morgan Kousser states, black voters' "first preference, then as now, was to be represented by people of their own race" (1999, 20). Previous research also indicates that some black leaders agitated for greater black descriptive representation (Swain 1993, 24), but how they proposed to achieve this goal is unclear.

What is the nature of the relationship between the black population and the number of blacks in Congress? We know very little about the effects of constituency characteristics on the electoral fortunes of black congressional candidates during the Reconstruction period. During this period, did black representatives build biracial coalitions or employ race-based campaign strategies to win their seats in Congress? What accounts for the fact that no African American was elected to Congress outside the South during the Reconstruction period? Obviously, much fruitful research can be conducted in this area. Because most empirical studies on black descriptive representation are confined to the contemporary era, our ability to generalize across different time periods is limited.

Black political gains in Congress diminished once the Jim Crow system began in the fourth quarter of the nineteenth century. No blacks served in Congress between 1901 and 1928, and only four blacks were elected in the three decades to follow.[3] Scholars tend to ignore this period because of the small number of blacks in Congress. The few studies that do exist are confined to biographical and descriptive accounts of individual black congressmen (Gosnell 1967; Hamilton 1991; S. Smith 1940).

The efforts of black protesters during the civil rights movement of the 1950s and 1960s led to the passage of the Voting Rights Act of 1965. After passage of this law, voter turnout among blacks increased and so did black descriptive representation in Congress. Of particular interest here is the growth in the size of the CBC across time and the factors that brought about the increase. As Table 10.1 shows, membership in the CBC grew dramatically in the 103rd Congress after the 1990 redistricting cycle and the 1992 elections.

The chief mechanism for achieving a racially diverse Congress has been the creation of majority-black and majority-minority districts. Racial redistricting as a tool for advancing minority descriptive representation is a major source of controversy in the scholarly literature.[4] Some scholars suggest that, given the high level of racially polarized voting in America, majority-black districts are necessary to increase black descriptive representation (e.g., Cain 1992; Davidson 1992; Grofman and Handley 1989; Kousser 1992).[5] Some critics of majority-minority districts argue that these types of districts are not the most efficient means of electing black representatives; instead, they propose a redistricting arrangement somewhere in the black population range of 40 to 49 percent (e.g., Cameron, Epstein,

TABLE 10.1 African American Members in Congress, 92nd–108th Congresses

Congress	Senate	House
92nd (1971–1972)	1	13
93rd (1973–1974)	1	16
94th (1975–1976)	1	17
95th (1977–1978)	1	17
96th (1979–1980)	0	17
97th (1981–1982)	0	19
98th (1983–1984)	0	21
99th (1985–1986)	0	21
100th (1987–1988)	0	23
101st (1989–1990)	0	24
102nd (1991–1992)	0	27
103rd (1993–1994)	1	39
104th (1995–1996)	1	40
105th (1997–1998)	1	39
106th (1999–2000)	0	39
107th (2001–2002)	0	39
108th (2003–2004)	0	39
109th (2005–2006)	1	42

Note: House totals included nonvoting delegates.

and O'Halloran 1996; Lublin 1997). Another school of thought maintains that black congressional candidates can win elective office by building biracial coalitions (e.g., Swain 1993; Thernstrom and Thernstrom 1997). In effect, this perspective suggests that black congressional candidates would be better off by broadening their base of support to include white voters, rather than concentrating their energies on winning election by appealing primarily to black voters.

To what extent are racial remedies needed to increase black representation in Congress? An answer to this question requires an understanding of the significance of race in American electoral politics. What is clear from a preponderance of the evidence is that race is a major determinant of black descriptive representation (see, for example, Canon 1999; Whitby 1987, 1997). One simply cannot ignore the tendency toward racially polarized voting in America, a practice that tends to disadvantage racial minority candidates. Hence, the surest way of electing African Americans (and other racial minorities) to legislative bodies under America's single-member plurality voting system is to create majority-black or majority-minority districts (Grofman, Griffin, and Glazer 1992; Handley, Grofman, and Arden 1998; Lublin 1997). This mechanism would help counter the effects of racial bloc voting that give white candidates an advantage over black candidates at the voting polls. But there is a catch. Only a small number of these districts can be created because of asymmetrical residential patterns among blacks in the South. In other words, the dispersion of the black population in Southern states makes it difficult to create these types of districts and simultaneously meet the constitutional standards of contiguity (see *Shaw v. Reno* 1993) and fair treatment for all racial groups (see *Miller v. Johnson* 1995).[6]

Clearly, there are risks involved in maximizing black descriptive representation through the creation of majority-black districts. Even so, the evidence suggests that this approach may be the best way at the present time to increase the size of the black congressional delegation. If promoting racial diversity is a desirable goal, then redistricting authorities should weigh the political costs of redistricting by giving careful consideration to such factors as voter registration and voter participation in political jurisdictions, especially in areas where the turnout rate among racial minority groups is especially low. To prescribe a standard such as the "65 Percent Rule" seems to be too simple a solution to a complex and controversial issue.[7]

As a campaign strategy, biracial coalition building by African American candidates is an appealing proposal that should not be abandoned. Although there is the general belief that African Americans who are elected in majority-white districts may not be "authentic" because they will have to acquiesce to the demands of white constituents (Guinier 1994; R. Smith 1996; Walters 1992), there is little empirical evidence to suggest that these fears are warranted. Past research has demonstrated that black Democrats representing these districts have not compromised their efforts to work on behalf of their black constituents (Canon 1999). This optimistic view of coalition building, however, tends to deemphasize the divisive role of race in American electoral politics. To be sure, there are recent examples of liberal black candidates winning in majority-white districts (e.g., Corrine Brown, D-FL; Julia Carson, D-IN; and Cynthia McKinney,

D-GA). The fact remains that there is little scientific evidence to show that they are able to win on a consistent basis. According to one major study, less than 2 percent of black candidates have won a House seat in majority-white districts since the 15th Amendment to the U.S. Constitution was ratified in 1870 (Canon 1999, 10).

A solution to the racial redistricting debate may lie in electoral reform. A promising area for future research would be to examine the effects of alternative electoral systems (e.g., a proportional system) on the electoral fortunes of minority candidates. Alternative voting systems are of increasing interest in the United States because of the controversy surrounding racial redistricting. Civil rights activist and law professor Lani Guinier's failed nomination as Assistant Attorney General for Civil Rights brought greater attention to the possibility of electoral reform legislation.[8] Yet, few studies have been conducted in this area. To some extent, research on the effects of alternative voting systems in the United States is constrained by the limited number of offices for which proportional representation, in some version or another, is used. The few studies that do exist suggest that proportional representation may be a fairer system than the one used in America (Adams 1996; Engstrom 1994; Issacharoff and Pildes 1996). Clearly more research is necessary to draw safe conclusions on this matter. At the very least, racial redistricting becomes a nonissue under a proportional system because governmental authorities would not have to engage in race-conscious redistricting to promote black descriptive representation in legislative bodies.

Descriptive representation is only one dimension of representation. In fact, Pitkin describes this dimension as "passive" because it focuses on "being something rather than doing something" (1967, 67). In other words, this form of representation tells us little about the activities of a representative other than his or her skin color; hence, the analyst cannot determine whether black descriptive representation translates into substantive or symbolic benefits for African Americans. This leads to the conclusion that an eclectic approach in which the investigator draws on the different dimensions of representation would lead more effectively to a full understanding of the value of racial diversity in legislative bodies.

Substantive Representation

By far the majority of work on the CBC has been in the area of substantive representation. In this dimension, representation is defined as an "activity" or, in Pitkin's words, "acting in the interests of the represented in a manner responsive to them" (1967, 209–10). The critical question is, to what extent is descriptive representation linked to substantive representation? Or, does the racial identity of the representative affect the quality of policy representation that African American citizens receive? The question is of critical importance because the rules of inclusion for African Americans and other racial minorities have yet to be clearly defined by legal experts and public policymakers. The underlying premise behind the creation of majority-minority districts is that blacks do a better job than whites of representing the substantive interests of African Americans. But is this assumption true? If there is a tenuous link between passive and active representation, then the case for racial remedies to promote minority representation is seriously compromised.

During the formative years of the CBC, empirical researchers accepted unquestionably the role of the Caucus as the voice of African Americans in Congress. By most accounts, this voice was largely silent on substantive issues primarily because of the relative small size of the CBC and what might be construed as self-inflicted wounds brought on by the organization's legislative strategy of protest actions (Barnett 1982; Henry 1977; Levy and Stoudinger 1976; Loomis 1981). Hence, during the early years of its existence the CBC functioned more as a social organization choosing to engage in protest activities in an attempt to articulate and voice the concerns of African Americans and other disadvantaged groups both inside and outside of Congress (Clay 1993). Since then, the CBC has been in a state of transition, from outsider to insider politics, from protest to accommodation in an effort to increase its chances of winning more victories on substantive matters (Canon 1999; Champagne and Reiselbach 1995).[9]

It is important to note that early studies of the CBC do not address the fundamental question of whether black or white legislators better represent the substantive interests of African Americans in Congress. As noted previously, this question escaped empirical scrutiny because it was largely assumed that blacks do a better job than whites of representing the interests of black constituents. Moreover, there was little reason to investigate the linkage between descriptive and substantive representation because of the small size of the Caucus. As a consequence, researchers focused their attention on understanding the CBC's formation, stages of development (Barnett 1975; Henry 1977), levels of vote cohesion (Gile and Jones, 1995), sources of voting cues (Levy and Stoudinger 1976), and social background characteristics (R. Smith 1981). It was only after the dramatic increase in the size of the black congressional delegation after the 1990 round of redistricting that the substantive significance of race in Congress became the subject of empirical inquiry and investigation.

Does the race of the member of Congress matter in the domain of public policy? There is a growing body of statistical evidence to suggest that it does. Most of these findings are based on roll-call votes (Canon 1999; Hall 1996; Whitby 1997; Whitby and Krause 2001), but they also extend to the agenda-setting, committee, and amending stages of the legislative process (see Canon 1999; Whitby 1997). Overall, these findings contradict the argument that we live in a color-blind society in which race has little consequence for the substantive representation that African Americans receive in our principal lawmaking institution (Swain 1993; Thernstrom and Thernstrom 1997).

A more difficult question to answer is whether the creation of majority-black districts is necessary to maximize black substantive representation. Even though these districts have increased the size of the CBC, some researchers have come to question their utility on substantive grounds. The centerpiece of their argument is that majority-minority districts undermine black substantive representation by diluting black political strength in adjoining districts. In effect, packing districts with black voters is harmful because concentrating black voters in a few districts may result in adjacent districts becoming whiter and more conservative, thereby increasing the probability of electing Republicans who tend to be less sensitive to the policy wishes of many racial minorities (Hill 1995; Overby and Cosgrove 1996). It is debatable as to whether change in voting behavior has actually occurred because of racial redistricting. Bullock (1995) and Whitby (1997) findings reveal that white representatives from the South did not alter their voting behavior in a significant way as a consequence of racial change in their districts in the 1990s.

One possible solution to the dilemma posed by majority-minority districts under the current electoral system is to create as many "influence" districts as possible (i.e., districts with a black population in the range of 40 to 50 percent). This strategy would likely increase Democratic Party strength in surrounding districts, thus increasing the likelihood of electing more Democrats to Congress. But these types of districts may come at the expense of electing black Democrats, who tend to have difficulty winning House seats in majority-white districts. Despite the risks involved, some researchers suggest that influence districts would advance black substantive representation. Cameron, Epstein, and O'Halloran (1996), for example, suggest that the best redistricting strategy for advancing the policy interests of racial minorities would be to create as many districts as possible with an upper threshold of 47 percent of the black population. Lublin (1997) finds a threshold at about 40 percent.

As impressive as these studies are on threshold effects, their findings are open to question because they do not take into account issue heterogeneity. In other words, previous investigations are based on aggregate interest group ratings that do not differentiate between bills of primary and secondary importance to African Americans. A bill, for instance, that would provide funding for historically black colleges and universities may be of primary interest to African Americans, whereas a measure that would offer family and medical leave to workers would be of secondary importance because benefits are more diffuse across racial lines. If this logic is correct, then specific types of issues may magnify (or attenuate) the importance of race. Put differently, past studies on the representational effects of the racial composition of congressional districts on legislative vote choice may underestimate the percentage of blacks needed in a district to advance black policy representation because they fail to take into account race-based differences attributed to the policy substance of legislation.

Indeed, prior research reveals that the racial composition of a congressional district has an influence on the policy content of legislation (Whitby and Krause 2001). As the black population increases across congressional districts, white representatives are less likely than black representatives to support the liberal position on policies that would bring substantive benefits to African Americans. These differences suggest that the optimal redistricting arrangement for black substantive representation may be conditional on the relative weights placed on primary and secondary issues. Unless researchers take into account issue heterogeneity in their analyses, the optimal redistricting strategy for promoting black policy representation will remain unknown.

Much research has been devoted to understanding the dyadic relationship between race (either the racial composition of districts or the racial identity of the representative) and congressional voting behavior on civil-rights–related issues. Indeed, understanding the degree of policy congruence between minority constituents and the policymaking behavior of representatives is one of the major benefits of the study of minority representation. Yet there are additional ways in which policy representation can be understood. As Canon (1999), Fenno (1978; 2003), and Swain (1993) inform us, all policy representation does not occur in the nation's capital. Fenno, in particular, stresses the importance of studying the policy activities of representatives in their home districts. As Fenno notes, "House member activities in their home districts help to shape the decisions of House members in Washington and the decisions of constituents at home" (2003, 253).

The major focus of district-level studies has been participant observation, which allows the researcher to observe firsthand the behavior of black and white representatives and how they interact with their constituents.[10] The small number of cases in these studies, however, makes it difficult to draw strong conclusions about the policy connection between representatives and their constituents. Obviously it would be useful for future researchers to employ a more representative sample to develop more definitive generalizations. Still, field research provides rich insights and a solid foundation for further inquiry on how House members interact directly with their local constituents.

For nearly five decades, survey data have been a valuable instrument for understanding the linkage between constituents' attitudes and their representatives' behavior.[11] Surprisingly, there is relatively little survey research on the topic of racial representation in Congress. Fortunately, the 1996 National Black Election Study (NBES) is available to help fill this lacuna in the literature. The 1996 NBES is designed to learn more about the attitudes of black constituents. As it stands, Katherine Tate's *Black Faces in the Mirror: African Americans and Their Representatives in the U.S. Congress* (2003) is the only major work to employ this valuable data set. She provides corroborating evidence that black constituents do feel that their black representatives do a better job than their white representatives of representing their substantive interests.

The CBC has seen its membership grow from nine members in 1970 to forty-three members in the 109th Congress at the time of this writing (see Table 10.2). As the Caucus approaches a critical mass, its political clout should also increase in Congress. However, the potential for division within the ranks of the organization also accompanies its growth. The CBC is no longer a small group of liberal lawmakers from urban areas in the North. Nearly half of its members come from the South, and some members are more conservative than others in their roll-call voting behavior. Sanford Bishop, for example, a Democrat of the 1992 class and one of the more conservative members of the CBC, has regularly supported the Conservative Coalition (voting alliance between Republicans and southern Democrats). Despite these demographic and ideological differences among members in the Caucus, the group remains cohesive on most issues affecting disadvantaged groups (Canon 1999, 148–54).

TABLE 10.2 African American Members in the 109th Congress by Party, State, and Year Elected

Name	Party	State	Year
Senate			
Barack Obama	D	Illinois	2004
House			
John Conyers	D	Michigan	1964
Charles B. Rangel	D	New York	1970
Major R. Owens	D	New York	1982
Edolphus Towns	D	New York	1982
John Lewis	D	Georgia	1986
Donald M. Payne	D	New Jersey	1988
Maxine Waters	D	California	1990
William J. Jefferson	D	Louisiana	1990
Eleanor H. Norton*	D	Washington, DC	1990
Corrine Brown	D	Florida	1992
Alcee L. Hastings	D	Florida	1992
Sanford Bishop Jr.	D	Georgia	1992
Bobby L. Rush	D	Illinois	1992
Albert R. Wynn	D	Maryland	1992
Melvin L. Watt	D	North Carolina	1992
James E. Clyburn	D	South Carolina	1992
Eddie B. Johnson	D	Texas	1992
Robert C. Scott	D	Virginia	1992
Bennie G. Thompson	D	Mississippi	1992
Bobby L Rush	D	Illinois	1992
Chaka Fattah	D	Pennsylvania	1994
Sheila Jackson Lee	D	Texas	1994
Jesse L. Jackson Jr.	D	Illinois	1994
Donna M. Christian-Christensen*	D	Virgin Islands	1996
Elijah E. Cummings	D	Maryland	1996
Juanita M. McDonald	D	California	1996
Julia Carson	D	Indiana	1996
Danny K. Davis	D	Illinois	1996
Harold Ford Jr.	D	Tennessee	1996
Carolyn Kilpatrick	D	Michigan	1996
Barbara Lee	D	California	1998
Stephanie T. Jones	D	Ohio	1998
Gregory W. Meeks	D	New York	1998
William L. Clay	D	Missouri	2000
Diane E. Watson	D	California	2001
Artur Davis	D	Alabama	2002
Kendrick B. Meek	D	Florida	2002
David Scott	D	Georgia	2002
G. K. Butterfield	D	North Carolina	2004
Emanuel Cleaver	D	Missouri	2004
Al Green	D	Texas	2004
Cynthia A. McKinney	D	Georgia	2004**
Gwendolynne S. Moore	D	Wisconsin	2004

* Representatives are nonvoting delegates.

**Cynthia McKinney was first elected in 1992 and served from 1993–2002.

Can the CBC succeed in responding to black interests at the institutional level? More specifically, can the CBC serve the vital interests of the minority community in a majority-white legislative body? With its increase in size, can the Caucus wield much influence on matters of vital interest to the minority community? These important questions are the source of much debate in the scholarly literature. One school of thought suggests that the answer is no. This viewpoint is expressed in works by Lani Guinier (1991; 1992; 1994). According to Guinier, a majority-rule institution undermines the political power of racial minorities. Even though existing voting rights laws do a relatively good job of protecting the rights of individuals to vote and run for public office, none is able to bring about minority political empowerment. The solution, Guinier contends, is radical reform in the electoral system (e.g., cumulative voting) and in the legislative process (minority veto power on issues of primary interest to the African American community).

Guinier's assertion is a testable proposition that has received scant attention in the extant literature. There is a need to fill this void in the literature. Understanding the nexus between black descriptive representation and favorable policy outputs will further our understanding on whether the CBC is an effective organization in representing black interests. Thus far the findings are favorable for the Caucus. Canon's study (1999, 154–59) of congressional behavior in the 103rd Congress under Democratic Party control finds evidence of black legislative success.

What is the current status of the CBC in the area of black substantive representation? As of the 109th Congress, more than half of the members of the CBC have served in Congress for more than ten years. Their longevity is an opportunity for black representatives to chair more committees and subcommittees, which should place them in a better bargaining position to lobby on behalf of the policy interests of disadvantaged groups. Their political influence, however, is heavily dependent on whether the Democratic Party has majority control of the House. In the 109th Congress, all members of the Caucus are Democrats. Their strong affiliation with the Democratic Party poses a dilemma for members of the group as players in the world of congressional politics. On the one hand, if this trend continues, they will likely have the votes necessary to make them influential players in a House under Democratic Party control; on the other hand, because of their liberal stance and strong allegiance to the Democratic Party, they will likely become bench players in the House under Republican control.

Symbolic Representation and New Frontiers for Research on the CBC and Black Representation

Nearly three decades ago, Heinz Eulau and Paul Karps (1977) astutely pointed out that responsiveness is an elusive concept that has a multidimensional character. Yet empirical researchers have largely ignored this cue to examine dimensions beyond the ones discussed in this chapter. In addition to policy responsiveness, Eulau and Karps (1977, 241–47) identify three more dimensions of responsiveness that constitute representation: *service* (i.e., representatives responding to individual inquiries and problems), *allocation* (i.e., representatives obtaining more public funds or projects for citizens), and *symbolism* (i.e., representatives responding in a manner that would build constituency trust and confidence). These dimensions deserve careful attention from scholars if we are to fully understand the role of the CBC in the representational process.

It is important to note that the focus of past research on policy responsiveness is understandable because public policy is at the epicenter of the representational process. There is no symbolic action, for example, that can ever match the importance of the passages of the Civil Rights Act of 1964 or the Voting Rights Act of 1965. Still, this tendency to equate responsiveness with policy congruence leaves a large gap in our understanding of the value of racial diversity in our legislative assemblies.

There is strong evidence in the congressional literature to show that constituents are relatively uninformed about their representatives' policy records (see, for example, Fenno 1978; Miller and Stokes 1963). Yet incumbents, on average, tend to win reelection with relative ease. This is especially true of CBC members who have been highly successful in retaining their House seats. If constituents are not keenly aware of their representatives' policy records, then logic dictates that representatives must be engaging in other activities to garner citizen support and thus stay in office. But, what are these activities? Does the race of the representative matter in the dimensions of service, allocation, and symbolism? Is it the case that members of the CBC are responsive in one component of representation but unresponsive in another? Research opportunities abound here, and these questions and others should inspire more extensive theory-building and empirical analysis.

There are indications that researchers are beginning to take up this challenge and pay greater attention to dimensions beyond the realm of public policy. In particular, one area that is receiving greater scholarly attention is symbolic responsiveness. The bulk of the literature on symbolic politics has been descriptive in nature and has generally focused on CBC protest activities (e.g., the boycott of President Richard Nixon's State of the Union address in January 1971 and the CBC's protest of President George W. Bush's controversial victory after the 2000 elections held at the official counting of the Electoral College votes in early January 2001).

As noted earlier, prior research has been critical of the CBC for engaging in too much symbolic rhetoric and even dramaturgical politics (Levy and Stoudinger 1976; Loomis 1981; Singh 1998; R. Smith 1996). These criticisms may be too severe. The nature of electoral politics encourages all members of Congress to engage in symbolic politics (Mayhew 1974). As risk-averse actors, virtually all elected officials engage in symbolic acts to optimize their chances for reelection (e.g., making agreeable speeches to constituents, position-taking on popular issues, credit-claiming for particularized benefits, sponsoring symbolic bills regardless of actual results). This is not to suggest that the CBC should abandon its principal role of becoming an effective legislative organization. But one should not underestimate the value of symbolic actions in electoral politics in enhancing the electoral fortunes of incumbents. Other than a few studies on black congressional candidates and their representational styles in majority-black districts (see Canon 1999, Chapter 3; Canon, Schousen, and Sellers 1996; Lublin 1997), there is little known about the use of symbols and whether they are more important for black candidates than for white candidates during the course of congressional campaigns.

The electoral connection is only one consideration in studying the CBC from the standpoint of symbolic politics. There is also the attitudinal component of symbolism, which seeks to understand how constituents feel about their representatives and, in turn, how representatives manage to maintain citizen support. John Wahlke emphasizes the importance of symbolic politics when he states that the "symbolic satisfaction with the process of government is probably more important than specific, instrumental satisfaction with the policy output of the process" (1971, 288).

The symbolic value of descriptive representation may be especially important for racial minority groups as they continue to struggle for full inclusion in mainstream American society.

A growing number of normative theorists now embrace this position (Dovi 2002; Mansbridge 1999; Phillips 1995; Williams 1998; Young 1990). On the subject, Mansbridge (1999, 641, 648, 650) argues that descriptive representation will enhance "communication between constituents and representatives, de facto legitimacy" (i.e., feelings of inclusion), and the perception that members of a disadvantaged social group have the "ability to rule." Thus, what Anne Phillips calls the "politics of presence" (descriptive representation) of racial diversity will help legitimize governmental authority and signal to underrepresented groups that they have an important stake in the American political system.

Empirical research on the symbolic linkage between representative and black constituents has lagged behind the contribution of normative theorists, but fortunately, empirically oriented researchers are beginning to conduct research in this area. The works of Valeria S. Chapman (2002), Richard Fenno (2003), Claudine Gay (1996), and Katherine Tate (2001, 2003) examine some aspect of the effects of political attitudes on black congressional representation. As it stands, their research provides evidence that African American constituents have a better overall assessment of the job performances of black representatives than of white representatives. Although there do appear to be race effects in the dimension of symbolic representation, it is not entirely clear which political attitudes (i.e., confidence, empowerment, efficacy, satisfaction, trust, or voter participation) are influenced. The 1996 NBES has been a valuable data source from which many of these findings are drawn. Unfortunately, survey data at the district level that include a representative sample of black respondents do not exist. If available, longitudinal survey data would be an excellent means to learn more about the effects of race in the dimension of symbolic representation.

In conclusion, racial diversity in legislative assemblies is a vital debate, one that runs parallel to the debates over affirmative action and multiculturalism. It is a debate that turns out to be difficult to resolve. Fortunately, political scientists can help inform the debate. The expansion of research in all dimensions will deepen our general knowledge of racial representation and further our understanding on racial diversity in representative institutions.

Notes

1. For a more detailed biographical and descriptive account of these elected officials, see Bositis (1994); Clay (1993); Bruce A. Ragsdale and Treese (1990); and Swain (1993, 20–34).

2. One notable exception to these descriptive and historical accounts is Cobb and Jenkins (2001). This article is directed toward understanding the relationship between descriptive and substantive representation of black interests. Their analysis reveals that black members during the Reconstruction period were significantly more likely than white members to support black interest legislation. In effect, behavioral difference between black and white lawmakers is not confined to the contemporary period.

3. The four congressmen are Oscar De Priest, R-Ill. (1929), Arthur W. Mitchell, D-Ill. (1934), William L. Dawson, D-Ill. (1942), and Adam Clayton Powell Jr., D-NY. (1944)

4. In the 103rd Congress, for example, thirty-two of the thirty-nine African American representatives came from majority-black districts, and in five of the seven remaining districts, they came from majority-minority districts in which African Americans and Hispanics comprised a majority of the population.

5. As adopted by the U.S. Supreme Court in *Thornburg v. Gingles* (1986), racially polarized voting exists when "black voters and white voters vote differently." In most instances, this means black voters casting their ballots for black candidates and white voters for white candidates. Racial bloc voting systematically prevents racial minorities from electing most of their preferred candidates, a practice known as "minority vote dilution."

6. In *Shaw v. Reno* (1993), the U.S. Supreme Court ruled that racial gerrymandering segregated blacks and whites and thus violated the traditional standard of creating districts built around contiguous communities. In *Miller v. Johnson* (1995), the High Court held that race cannot be the "predominant factor" in drawing district boundary lines.

7. In the case of *Kirsey v. Board of Supervisors of Hinds County, Mississippi* (1977), a federal court advocated a 65 percent minority percentage for blacks to elect candidates of their choice to office.

8. Guinier contends that other methods (e.g., minority veto power on issues concerning racial minorities) and alternative electoral arrangements (e.g., cumulative voting) can provide a more effective voice for minority citizens. According to Guinier, fair representation under the Voting Rights Act of 1965 should be measured in terms of the "extent protected minority groups are provided meaningful voice in government" (1994, 93).

9. For a good summary of studies on the CBC during the early years, see the works of Canon (1999, Chapter 4), Swain (1993, 37–44), Champagne and Rieselbach (1995); Jones (1987), Robert Smith (1996, 105–15), and Tate (2003, 104–10).

10. Fenno (2003), for example, uses participant observation to examine district-level behavior of four CBC members (Chaka Fattah, D-PA; Stephanie T. Jones, D-OH; Barbara Jordan, D-TX; and Louis Stokes, D-OH) in five linkage areas (electoral, personal, policy, organizational, and symbolic).

11. For the seminal study that employs survey data to examine the district relationship between constituents' attitudes and their representatives' perception of constituents' opinions, see Warren E. Miller and Donald Stokes, "Constituency Influence in Congress," *American Political Science Review* 57 (1963): 45–57.

References

Adams, Greg D. 1996. Legislative effects of single-member vs. multi-member districts. *American Journal of Political Science* 40, no. 1 (February): 129–44.

Barnett, Marjorie R. 1975. The Congressional Black Caucus. In *Congress against the president*, edited by Harvey C. Mansfield. New York: Praeger.

———. 1982. The Congressional Black Caucus: Illusions and realities of power. In *The new black politics*, edited by Michael B. Preston, Lenneal J. Henderson Jr., and Paul Puryear. New York: Longman Press.

Bositis, David A. 1994. *The Congressional Black Caucus in the 103rd Congress*. Washington, DC: Joint Center for Political and Economic Studies.

Bullock, Charles S., III. 1995. The impact of changing the racial composition of congressional districts on legislators' roll call behavior. *American Politics Quarterly* 23:141–58.

Cain, Bruce. 1992. Voting rights and democratic rheory: Toward a color-blind society? In *Controversies in minority voting: The Voting Rights Act in perspective*, edited by Bernard Grofman and Chandler Davidson. Washington, DC: Brookings Institution, 1992.

Cameron, Charles, David Epstein, and Sharyn O'Halloran. 1996. Do majority-minority districts maximize substantive black representation in Congress? *American Political Science Review* 90, no. 4 (December): 794–812.

Canon, David T. 1999. *Race, redistricting, and representation: The unintended consequences of black majority districts*. Chicago: University of Chicago Press.

Canon, David T., Matthew M. Schousen, and Patrick J. Sellers. 1996. The supply-side of congressional redistricting: Race and strategic politicians, 1972–1992. *Journal of Politics* 58, no. 3 (August): 837–53.

Champagne, Richard, and Leroy N. Rieselbach. 1995. The evolving Congressional Black Caucus: The Reagan-Bush years. In *Blacks and the American political system*, edited by Huey L. Perry and Wayne Parent. Gainesville: University of Florida Press.

Chapman, Valeria S. 2002. *Presence, promise, and progress: Black representation in the U.S. Congress*. Unpublished manuscript, Ohio State University.

Clay, William L. 1993. *Just permanent interests: Black Americans in Congress, 1870–1991*. New York: Amistad.

Cobb, Michael D., and Jeffrey A. Jenkins. 2001. Race and the representation of blacks' interests during Reconstruction. *Political Research Quarterly* 54, no. 1 (March): 181–204.

Davidson, Chandler. 1992. The Voting Rights Act: A brief history. In *Controversies in minority voting: The Voting Rights Act in perspective*, edited by Bernard Grofman and Chandler Davidson. Washington, DC: Brookings Institution.

Dovi, Suzanne. 2002. Preferable descriptive representatives: Will just any woman, black, or Latino do? *American Political Science Review* 96, no. 4 (December): 729–44.

Engstrom, Richard L. 1994. The Voting Rights Act: Disenfranchisement dilution and alternative electoral systems. *PS: Political Science and Politics* 27:685–88.

Eulau, Heinz, and Paul D. Karps. 1977. The puzzle of representation: Specifying components of responsiveness. *Legislative Studies Quarterly* 2, no. 3 (August): 233–54.

Fenno, Richard F., Jr. 1978. *Home style: House members in their districts*. Boston: Little Brown.

———. 2003. *Going home: Black representatives and their constituents*. Chicago: University of Chicago Press.

Gay, Claudine. 1996. The impact of black congressional representation on the behavior of constituents. Presented at the annual meeting of the Midwest Political Science Association, Chicago.

Gile, Roxanne L., and Charles E. Jones. 1995. Congressional racial solidarity: Exploring Congressional Black Caucus voting cohesion, 1971–1990. *Journal of Black Studies* 25, no. 5 (May): 622–41.

Gosnell, Harold F. 1967. *Negro politicians: The rise of Negro politics in Chicago*. Chicago: University of Chicago Press.

Grofman, Bernard, Robert Griffin and Amihai Glazer. 1992. The effects of black population on electing Democrats and liberals to the House of Representatives. *Legislative Studies Quarterly*, 17, no. 3:365–79.

Grofman, Bernard, and Lisa Handley. 1989. Minority population proportion and black and Hispanic congressional success in the 1970s and 1980s. *American Politics Quarterly* 17, no. 3 (August): 436–45.

Guinier, Lani. 1991. The triumph of tokenism: The Voting Rights Act and the theory of black electoral success. *Michigan Law Review* 89, no. 5 (March): 1077–154.

———. 1992. Voting rights and democratic theory: Where do we go from here? In *Controversies in minority voting: The Voting Rights Act in perspective*, edited by Bernard Grofman and Chandler Davidson. Washington, DC: Brookings Institution.

———. 1994. *Tyranny of the majority*. New York: Free Press.

Hall, Richard L. 1996. *Participation in Congress*. New Haven, CT: Yale University Press.

Hamilton, Charles V. 1991. *Adam Clayton Powell Jr.: The political biography of an American dilemma*. New York: Atheneum.

Handley, Lisa, Bernard Grofman, and Wayne Arden. 1998. Electing minority-preferred candidates to legislative office: The relationship between minority percentages in districts and the election of minority-preferred candidates. In *Race and redistricting in the 1990s*, edited by Bernard Grofman. New York: Agathon.

Henry, Charles P. 1977. Legitimizing race in congressional politics. *American Political Quarterly* 5:149–76.

Hill, Kevin. 1995. Does the creation of majority black districts aid Republicans? An analysis of the 1992 congressional elections in eight southern states. *Journal of Politics* 57, no. 2 (May): 384–401.

Issacharoff, Samuel, and Richard H. Pildes. 1996. All for one: Can cumulative voting ease racial tensions? *The New Republic*, November 18, p. 10.

Jones, Charles E. 1987. An overview of the Congressional Black Caucus: 1970–1985. In *Readings in American political issues*, edited by Franklin Jones, Michael A. Adams, Sanders Anderson, and Tandy Tollerson. Dubuque, IA: Kendall/Hunt.

Kirsey v. Board of Supervisors of Hinds County, Mississippi. 1977. 544 F. 2d 139.

Kousser, J. Morgan. 1992. The Voting Rights Act and the two reconstructions. In *Controversies in minority voting: The Voting Rights Act in perspective*, edited by Bernard Grofman and Chandler Davidson. Washington, DC: Brookings Institution.

———. 1999. *Colorblind injustice: Minority voting rights and the undoing of the Second Reconstruction*. Chapel Hill: University of North Carolina Press.

Levy, Arthur B., and Susan Stoudinger. 1976. Sources of voting cues for the Congressional Black Caucus. *Journal of Black Studies* 7, no. 1 (September): 29–45.

Loomis, Burdett A. 1981. Congressional caucuses and the politics of representation. In *Congress reconsidered*, edited by Lawrence C. Dodd and Bruce I. Oppenheimer. Washington, DC: CQ Press.

Lublin, David. 1997. *The paradox of representation*. Princeton, NJ: Princeton University Press.

Mansbridge, Jane. 1999. Should blacks represent blacks and women represent women? A contingent 'yes.' *Journal of Politics* 61, no. 3 (August): 628–57.

Mayhew, David R. 1974. *Congress: The electoral connection*. New Haven, CT: Yale University Press.

Miller v. Johnson. 1995. 115 S. Ct. 2475.

Miller, Warren E., and Donald Stokes. 1963. Constituency influence in Congress. *American Political Science Review* 57, no. 1 (March): 45–57.

Overby, L. Marvin, and Kenneth M. Cosgrove. 1996. Unintended consequence? Racial redistricting and the representation of minority interests. *Journal of Politics* 58, no. 2 (May): 540–50.

Phillips, Anne. 1995. *The politics of presence*. Oxford: Oxford University Press.

Pitkin, Hanna F. 1967. *The concept of representation*. Berkeley: University of California Press.

Poinsett, Alex. 1973. The Black Caucus: Five years later. *Ebony* (June): 64–73.

Ragsdale, Bruce A., and Joel D. Treese. 1990. *Black Americans in Congress, 1870–1989*. Washington, DC: U.S. Government Printing Office.

Shaw v. Reno. 1993. 509 U.S. 630.

Singh, Robert. 1998. *The Congressional Black Caucus, racial politics in the U.S. Congress*. Thousand Oaks, CA: Sage.

Smith, Robert C. 1981. The Black Congressional Delegation. *Western Political Quarterly* 34, no. 2 (June): 203–21.

———. 1996. *We have no leaders: African Americans in the post–civil rights era*. Albany: State University of New York Press.

Smith, Samuel D. 1940. *The Negro in Congress, 1870–1901*. Chapel Hill: University of North Carolina Press.

Swain, Carol M. 1993. *Black faces, black interests: The representation of African Americans in Congress*. Cambridge, MA: Harvard University Press.

Tate, Katherine. 2001. African Americans and their representatives in Congress. *Legislative Studies Quarterly* 26:623–38.

———. 2003. *Black faces in the mirror: African Americans and their representatives in the U.S. Congress.* Princeton, NJ: Princeton University Press.

Thernstrom, Stephan, and Abigail Thernstrom. 1997. *America in black and white.* New York: Simon and Schuster.

Thornburg v. Gingles. 1986. 478 U.S. 30.

Wahlke, John C. 1971. *Policy demands and systems support: The role of the represented. British Journal of Political Science 1, no. 3 (July): 271–90.*

Walters, Ronald. 1992. Two political traditions: Black politics in the 1990s. *National Political Science Review* 3:198–207.

Whitby, Kenny J. 1987. Measuring congressional responsiveness to the policy interests of black constituents. *Social Science Quarterly* 68 (June): 367–77.

———. 1997. *The color of representation: Congressional behavior and black interests.* Ann Arbor: University of Michigan Press.

Whitby, Kenny J., and George Krause. 2001. Race, issue heterogeneity, and public policy: The Republican revolution in the 104th U.S. Congress and the representation of African-American policy interests. *British Journal of Political Science* 31:555–72.

Williams, Melissa S. 1998. *Voice, trust, and memory: Marginalized groups and the failings of liberal representation.* Princeton, NJ: Princeton University Press.

Young, Iris Marion. 1990. *Justice and the politics of difference.* Princeton, NJ: Princeton University Press.

CHAPTER ELEVEN

Toward a Critical Race Theory of Political Science

A New Synthesis for Understanding Race, Law, and Politics*

BARBARA LUCK GRAHAM

Introduction

THE POST–CIVIL RIGHTS ERA, described as a period of retrenchment that began in the 1980s, scholars of race, law and politics began to reassess the role of race and ethnicity in their understanding of domestic and international subordination, marginalization, and exclusion of people of color. According to Walton and Smith (2000, xvii), "Race is the most important cleavage in American life, with enormous impact on the nation's society, culture and politics." Despite the saliency of race and ethnicity in American law and politics, however, political scientists and law professors continue to articulate their opposition to the lack of serious scholarly attention paid to the structural disempowerment of racial and ethnic groups. Alex-Assensoh (2000, 10) echoes this sentiment by observing that "political science as a discipline has not devoted adequate attention to issues of race and ethnicity, very often relegating minority politics to a stepchild position in the discipline." Delgado, in his seminal law review article, "The Imperial Scholar: Reflections on a Review of Civil Rights Literature," observed the presence of a second scholarly tradition in legal writing (1984, 51), namely, "that it consists of the exclusion of minority writing about key issues of race law, and that this exclusion does matter; the tradition causes bluntings, skewings, and omissions in literature dealing with race, racism, and American law."[1] Political scientists and law professors have sought to bridge this gap by developing new frameworks and directions for understanding multiracial politics and law in domestic, international, and comparative contexts.

The Supreme Court's conservative decision making in the 1980s and 1990s in particular prompted civil rights lawyers and law professors to reconsider the role of law and the courts in eradicating racial hierarchies and oppression of people of color. Critical race theory (CRT) emerged as a form of oppositional scholarship devoted to developing a distinct legal strategy informed by the actual conditions of people of color. Critical race theory offers a harsh critique of traditional liberal principles while at the same time rejecting conservative visions of equality. Critical race theory seeks to uncover how appeals to color blindness, merit, neutrality, and equality of opportunity actually impede racial progress and contribute to the continual oppression of people of color. Critical race theory has been driven largely by legal scholarship; however, its central tenets and ideas have influenced scholarly writings on race and ethnicity in other disciplines, including education, ethnic studies, and feminist studies. In short, CRT, which seeks to challenge rights-based individualism and hierarchy, holds considerable promise for understanding the role of race and ethnicity in America.

Despite the fact that CRT has figured prominently on the intellectual map of law for over two decades, there is a curious absence of mention of critical race theory in political science, particularly in the subfield of public law—the subfield most closely identified with legal studies. This lack of attention from political scientists is indeed puzzling, given that CRT is pervasive in the legal academy and has influenced the discourse on race and the law.[2] What accounts for the scant attention paid to CRT by political scientists who study race, ethnicity and politics? Is this oversight another example of "imperial scholars'" attempts to exclude "outsider" scholarship? Another answer might be that CRT grew out of critical legal theory and has maintained a close alliance with legal scholars. Whatever the explanation for the inattention given to CRT in political science, however, I argue that CRT is consistent with political trends and intellectual developments in the subfield of racial and ethnic politics. Both critical race theorists and scholars of race and ethnicity politics seek to understand how law and politics subordinate marginalized groups. Critical race theorists, also known as race crits and scholars of critical race politics, critique the existing liberal paradigm and the limitations of other extant theories utilized in explaining the nexus between race, law, and politics in the United States.[3]

I argue, however, that the contemporary connection between CRT and the study of race, ethnicity, and politics goes deeper. Both race crits and scholars of critical race politics try to reconcile the same set of tensions between the dominance of the liberal individual rights paradigm and the placement of race at the center of intellectual inquiry. In this chapter I call for a critical race theoretical perspective in political science analogous to that of critical race theory in legal scholarship.[4] My main objective is to show how critical race theory is an important framework for understanding racial and ethnic politics. Law and politics are inextricably linked, and CRT offers an alternative framework for bridging the gap in our quest for a general theory of racial and ethnic hierarchy and oppression. Critical race theory calls for a multidisciplinary approach to understanding the role of race in society, and I argue that both race crits and scholars of critical race politics can advance further by building on each other's work rather than pursuing parallel courses of theory building and research. As I hope to show in this chapter, political scientists may well find that CRT is quite relevant for addressing questions in the study of race, law, and politics.

One point that readers should keep in mind while seeking to acquaint themselves with CRT as an analytic perspective is that the CRT literature is quite substantial, diverse, dynamic, and perhaps eclectic at times. It is not my intention within the confines of this chapter to engage in a thorough literature review or substantive critiques of CRT. With this caveat in mind, in this chapter I present an examination of CRT as an important framework for understanding race, law, and politics. In the following section, I will present an overview of the intellectual genealogy of the CRT movement. Next, I will discuss CRT's central tenets and significant developments over the past decade. Then I will attempt to link CRT to the efforts of scholars of critical race politics to explain racial hierarchy in the domestic and international arenas. I will conclude my discussion by suggesting that CRT can inform political science scholarship on race and ethnicity in that CRT offers scholars an insightful approach to conceptualizing race, politics, and the law that may lead to progressive strategies for reform.

Intellectual Genealogy of the CRT Movement

The legal and political conservatism of the 1980s contributed to the increasing ambivalence and disillusionment of a number of legal scholars and activists with what they viewed as efforts to turn back the clock on previous hard-won advances in civil rights during the 1950s and 1960s. Commitment to racial justice was undercut by initiatives at the local level, several anti–civil rights measures from Congress, and conservative appointments to the Supreme Court by President Richard Nixon and subsequent Republican presidents. Several narrow and restrictive rulings of the Burger and Rehnquist Courts set a more conservative direction in cases involving civil rights for racial and ethnic minorities and the poor. These rulings affected the areas of school desegregation, political participation, employment discrimination, affirmative action, and housing (Davis and Graham 1995). According to Lawrence (2002, xiv), "the *Bakke* case is the doctrinal marker of the times that helped shaped this generation of critical race theorists."[5] This contextual understanding of the current political and legal climate led some scholars to question the effectiveness of past civil rights strategies.

The most influential source of thought critical of traditional civil rights discourse is the legal scholarship of Derrick Bell, who is considered to be the intellectual godfather of CRT. Bell, a former civil rights attorney for the National Association for the Advancement of Colored People (NAACP) Legal Defense Fund and a professor at Harvard Law School during the 1970s and early1980s, advanced several critiques in his early writings on the liberal ideology of the mainstream civil rights movement. Bell's "Serving Two Masters" article (1976) was openly critical of the role of civil rights attorneys in school desegregation cases. He argued that because of increasing resistance to desegregation efforts, the rigidity of these lawyers in their attempts to seek "maximum feasible desegregation" (especially through the use of racial balancing and busing) undermined the interests of their clients, the black plaintiffs. For Bell, "some civil rights lawyers, like their more candid poverty law colleagues, are making decisions, setting priorities, and undertaking responsibilities that should be determined by their clients and shaped by the community" (cited in Crenshaw, Gotanda, Peller, and Thomas, 1995, 17). Bell observed that the civil rights lawyers' commitment to integration overshadowed their "assessment of the economic and political conditions that so influence the progress and outcome of any social reform improvement" (cited in Crenshaw, Gotanda, Peller, and Thomas 1995, 17).

Professor Bell expanded on the problem of subordination of the clients' interest to that of the attorneys' dogmatic commitment to busing and racial balance in a 1980 *Harvard Law Review* article, "*Brown v. Board of Education* and the Interest Convergence Dilemma." Bell's objective in this article was to "offer an explanation of why school desegregation has in large part failed and what can be done to bring about change" (Bell 1980, 519). Bell explicated his interest convergence thesis—that civil rights gains happen solely when the interests of whites would either be advanced or not harmed by recognizing claims for racial justice. Bell (1980, 524–25) asserted:

> I contend that the decision in *Brown* to break with the court's long-held position on these issues cannot be understood without some consideration of the decision's value to whites, not simply those concerned about the immorality of racial inequality, but also those whites in policymaking positions able to see the economic and political advances at home and abroad that would follow abandonment of segregation. First, the decision helped to provide immediate credibility to America's struggle with communist countries to win the hearts and minds of emerging third world people. . . . Second, *Brown* offered much needed reassurance to American blacks that the precepts of equality and freedom so heralded during World War II might yet be given meaning at home. . . . Finally, there were whites who realized that the South could make the transition from a rural plantation society to the sunbelt with all its potential and profit only when it ended its struggle to remain divided by state-sponsored segregation. Thus, segregation was viewed as a barrier to further industrialization in the South.

Related to this thesis is Bell's argument that racial remedies come with a price—that whites will not support civil rights policies that threaten their property right in whiteness that is grounded on a theory of racial supremacy.

Another important figure in the early critique of conventional civil rights discourse was Alan Freeman, who was one of the founders of the critical legal studies (CLS) movement. Freeman (1978) critically analyzed Supreme Court doctrine in the area of antidiscrimination law from two perspectives—those of the victim and the perpetrator respectively—and showed how legal doctrine legitimates racial power. From the victim's perspective, according to Freeman (cited in Crenshaw, Gotanda, Peller, and Thomas 1995, 29), "racial discrimination describes those conditions of actual social existence as a member of a perpetual underclass." From the victim's perspective, the problem of racial discrimination will not be solved until the conditions associated with it have been remedied. The remedies needed to effectuate change would require affirmative efforts to neutralize the wrongful conduct of the perpetrator. In contrast, the perpetrator "sees racial discrimination not as conditions but as actions, or series of actions, inflicted on the victim by the perpetrator" (cited in Crenshaw, Gotanda, Peller, and Thomas 1995, 29). According to the perpetrator's perspective, the law views racial discrimination as the "misguided conduct of particular actors," in which the twin notions of fault and causation are central to understanding the application of antidiscrimination laws. Freeman applied this framework to *Brown* and subsequent Burger Court cases in the areas of school desegregation and employment discrimination litigation. His analysis demonstrated that in an effort to present law as objective and neutral, the courts have adopted the perpetrator's perspective, from which there is no remedy for the victims of racial discrimination.

Richard Delgado, who became one of the CRT movement's founders, took to task what at the time appeared to be an inner circle of white law professors who ignored the writings of minority scholars in civil rights scholarship. In his controversial "Imperial Scholar" article (1984), Delgado's examination of civil rights scholarship led him to question the phenomenon and the explanations of the absence of minority scholarship from the texts and central arenas of legal scholarship dealing with civil rights. For Delgado, scholars of color spoke in a different voice from that of the dominant group, and their perspectives needed to be heard. His article signaled an important break from the traditional civil rights discourse through his assertion that the race of the scholar does matter.[6]

The early writings of Bell, Freeman, and Delgado during the 1970s and 1980s provided the intellectual foundation for legal scholars of color to reject the existing civil rights discourse. During the mid-1970s, the CLS movement emerged as an attack on mainstream ideas of law and legal institutions. CLS, like CRT, is complex and multifaceted; I admit that there is a huge risk of oversimplification in describing its theoretical underpinnings (see Unger 1983; and Altman 1990 for works on CLS). The CLS movement was made up of white leftist law professors and activists whose aim was to fundamentally transform society in order to create a more egalitarian social order rather than one based on illegitimate hierarchies of power. Critical legal scholars were highly critical of the underlying tenets of legal liberalism—namely, the rule of law, formalism, neutrality, abstraction, and individual rights. The CLS movement exposed and challenged the conventional conception of law as rational, apolitical, and technical. In addition, the CLS scholars were critical of rights discourse in bringing about social change. While scholars of color were initially drawn to the conferences and writings of the CLS movement; they became disillusioned with the critical legal scholars' lack of attention to race and racism (Delgado 1987). In a seminal law review article, Crenshaw (1988, 1356–58) offered three major critiques of CLS writings. First, she argued that critical scholars rightly criticized mainstream legal ideology for its legitimation of oppressive policies directed at minorities. The problem was that they did not sufficiently account for the effects or the causes of the oppression. For Crenshaw (1988), the result was legal scholarship that was essentially incomplete because it failed to incorporate racism into its analysis. According to Crenshaw (1988, 1356), this failure led to a second criticism of CLS writings—that is, that the CLS scholars failed "to analyze racism as an ideological pillar upholding American society, or as the principal basis of Black oppression." She goes on to argue that "if racism is just as important as, if not more important than, liberal legal ideology in explaining the persistence of white supremacy, then the Critics' single-minded effort to reconstruct liberal legal ideology will be futile" (Crenshaw 1988, 1357). Finally, Crenshaw (1988, 1357) argued that the critical scholars disregarded the transformative potential of liberalism; that is, "it remains receptive to some aspirations that are central to Black demands, and may also perform an important function in combating the experience of being excluded and oppressed."

Matsuda et al. (1993) and Crenshaw, Gotanda, Peller, and Thomas (1995) identified two key events that led to the genesis of the critical race theory movement. The first event occurred in 1981, when Derrick Bell left Harvard to assume the deanship of the law school at the University of Oregon (see also Bell 1996). A group of law students demanded that Harvard hire a teacher of color to replace Bell, but the administration responded by offering a three-week mini-course on civil rights litigation taught by Julius Chambers and Jack Greenberg. The law students boycotted the mini-course because they viewed it as an inadequate response to their demands to hire minority professors and to reinstate Bell's course.[7] Crenshaw (in Crenshaw, Gotanda, Peller, and Thomas, 1995), who was then a student at Harvard and one of the principal organizers of the protests, notes that the foundation for CRT was being laid. Subsequently scholars of color began to meet in small groups at law school conferences and conventions in the mid-1980s to discuss their views and experiences at the margin of liberal discourse.[8] A key organizing event took place in 1989 at the University of Wisconsin–Madison law school that turned out to be the founding of the Critical Race Theory Workshop. The primary organizers, Kimberlé Crenshaw, Neil Gotanda, and Stephanie Philips, coined the term *critical race theory* to make it clear that the thirty-five law scholars in attendance would locate their work at the intersection of critical theory, racism, and the law. Their task was to synthesize a theory that was "responsive to the realities of racial politics in America" (Crenshaw, in Crenshaw, Gotanda, Peller and Thomas 1995, xxvii).

Cho and Westley (2002) argue that the genesis of CRT went beyond the individualistic strategies that took place at Harvard Law School; rather, these legal scholars emphasize the historic significance of the race-conscious student protests at Berkeley beginning in the 1960s and continuing in the form of student activism for diversity in the 1990s. Although Cho and Westley do not discount Crenshaw's recollection of events, they offer a more contextual political understanding of the rise of CRT. These scholars argue that it was race plus student organizing that "challenged the structure, substance, and culture of U.S. legal education, helping to fertilize the proliferation of institutional-cultural resistance to the reigning (non-)analysis of race and law" (Cho and Westley 2002, 45). In short, they argue that the student movement played a major role in the receptivity of premier student-run law reviews to minority scholarship and for curriculum changes sensitive to diversity. Cho and Westley's (2002, 57) account offers additional insights beyond another genesis of the CRT story—they conclude by arguing that the impact of student activism reveals the necessity to link praxis and theory, and that CRT must be grounded in resistance movements in order to "contend with the continuing and coming storms of backlash and retrenchment against racial and social justice, which already engulf us."

CRT: Basic Tenets and Analytical Framework

Against this brief overview of the history of the CRT movement, I will now explicate the theoretical underpinnings of CRT. CRT, as it is currently situated in the
discipline of law, is best understood as an analytical framework for understanding
race, hierarchy, and power. CRT has a broad ideological trajectory that draws upon
the intellectual traditions of Marxism, liberalism, postmodernism, pragmatism,
and cultural nationalism (Wing 1997, 30).[9] CRT owes an intellectual debt to such
European philosophers as Antonio Gramsci and Jacques Derrida; the thought
and activism of W. E. B. Du Bois, César Chávez, and Martin Luther King Jr.; and
the black power and Chicano movements of the 1960s and early 1970s (Delgado
and Stefancic 2001, 4). No single set of doctrines or methodologies exists to
which all race crits subscribe. Although there is considerable diversity within the
CRT movement, Crenshaw (in Crenshaw, Gotanda, Peller, and Thomas, 1995,
xiii) points out that CRT is unified by two common interests: "The first is to
understand how a regime of white supremacy and its subordination of people of
color have been created and maintained in America, and, in particular, to examine the relationship between that social structure and professed ideals such as 'the
rule of law' and 'equal protection.' The second is a desire not merely to understand the vexed bond between law and racial power but to *change* it."

After a decade of writing, adherents to CRT have advanced three oppositional
stances to mainstream beliefs about racial injustice:

1. the color-blind approach will not eliminate racism;
2. racism is systematic and structural, thus strategies to address individual racism fail to address discrimination and subordination; and
3. antiracist transformation can be achieved only through intersectional analysis by taking into account sexism, homophobia, economic exploitation, and other forms of injustice (Valdez, Culp, and
   Harris 2002, 2).

The utility of CRT is grounded in its placement of race at the center of intellectual inquiry rather than at the margins. It has the potential to become a powerful framework in explaining racial hierarchy and oppression. Listed below are the
major tenets and themes found in the discourse of CRT.

Centrality of Racism

A fundamental tenet of CRT is the centrality and pervasiveness of racism in American society. The observation that racism is normal rather than aberrant
in American society acknowledges the systemic and subtle forms of racism that
oppress people of color. From the perspective of race crits, antidiscrimination law
can remedy only the more extreme forms of racial injustice; it can do very little
about the "business as usual" forms of racism people of color deal with on a daily
basis. This line of thinking exposes racism as an intractable problem because it
is incorporated into a wide range of assumptions and practices. Adherents to

CRT believe that formal equality is incapable of eradicating racism. For example, Bell (1987, 1992) explicates a thesis of continuing racial injustice, failure of civil rights laws, and the permanence of racism. Bell's thesis about the permanence of racism has prompted critics to charge that CRT is overly pessimistic, whereas other race crits seek solutions and remedies through law or through the political process.

Interest Convergence Theory

The interest convergence theory advanced by Derrick Bell is another fundamental tenet of CRT. As stated in the previous section, Bell argues that racial progress in the area of civil rights is inexorably linked to white self-interest; that is, civil rights progress comes about when the interests of whites would be either advanced or not harmed. In order to have progressive civil rights laws according to Bell's thesis, white self-interest must be promoted. Dudziak (2000) developed Bell's interest convergence thesis by offering evidence of the impact of the cold war on domestic civil rights. Dudziak contends that racial justice was not in the the self-interest of whites until the Soviet Union used the race issue in anti-American propaganda. Expanding on Bell's thesis, Delgado (2003) argues that contemporary civil rights law and discourse are used to promote white self-interest rather than improving the condition of people of color. His evidence falls into three categories:

1. material self-interest (in which whites subordinate people of color to either advance or not endanger their own economic self-interest);
2. protection of the psychic comfort of whites (the adoption of legal strategies and modes of discourse that make whites feel comfortable);[10] and
3. the extent to which civil rights discourse has shifted from protecting blacks to protecting whites (color-blind discourse in civil rights).

Critique of Liberalism

For critical race theorists, civil rights strategies have either failed or at best produced limited victories; therefore, the time has come to move beyond existing rights analysis. One explanation for this failed approach is that the classic liberal visions of race have been conscripted by conservatives and the Supreme Court to wage an attack on governmental efforts to remedy racial discrimination. One problem race crits have with liberals is that they profess belief in color blindness and the neutrality of law (Delgado and Stefancic 2001, 21–25). Such legal doctrines as color blindness, meritocracy, and neutrality have been met with skepticism on the part of race crits (see Gotanda 1991, for a critique of the Supreme Court's use of color-blind constitutionalism in perpetuating racial subordination). Liberalism, under this mode of analysis, does not go far enough in eradicating racial subordination.

Charles Lawrence's (2001) analysis of the legal controversy over affirmative action in higher education involving the University of Michigan and a

discrimination suit against the University of California, Berkeley, is a good illus-
tration of the application of the critique of liberalism and the critical race theorist's response. Lawrence (2001) argues that a liberal defense of affirmative action
is the diversity defense—which is grounded in liberal theory because it is based
on the social utility thesis. According to Lawrence's (2001, 940) analysis, the
diversity argument does not go far enough because it preserves the status quo and
"leaves no room for deeper criticisms of the racial hierarchy—a hierarchy that
produces unequal secondary education as well as past and ongoing racism, both
are deliberate and unconscious, at institutions of higher learning." Lawrence
(2001) asserts that the diversity defense is conservative in that it participates in
the production of an ideology that justifies segregation of universities in the name
of equality. In sum, the diversity defense does not address the ways in which
admissions standards, the use of Scholastic Aptitude Test (SAT) scores, and other
criteria maintain white privilege.

Critique of the Black/White Paradigm

Race crit scholars look beyond the struggle between blacks and whites, thus rejecting the black/white paradigm of race and its properties. Perea (1997, 1219), utilizing Kuhn's notions of paradigms, defines the binary paradigm of race as "the
conception that race in America consists, either exclusively or primarily, of only
two constituent racial groups, the Black and the White." For Perea (1997, 1254),
race in America means more than black and white; it also refers to Latinos,
Asians, Native Americans and other racial and ethnic groups. He demonstrates
how the black/white paradigm—which is widely accepted among scholars-
marginalizes other people of color by the implication that other nonwhite
groups are not subjected to racism.[11] Delgado's (2000) critique of Derrick Bell's
(1998) *Afrolantica Legacies* lists seven ways in which the black/white binary model
harms and obstructs the path to liberation. In summary fashion, they are:

1. Under the binary model, society arranges progress for one group to
   coincide with the repression of another.
2. The binary model hides the way in which the dominant society pits
   one minority group against the other to the detriment of both.
3. The binary approach encourages exaggerated identification with
   whites at the expense of other groups.
4. Binary thinking interferes with moral insight and reasoning for
   whites, leading to selective empathy and differentiated racialization.
5. The black/white paradigm warps minorities' views of themselves and
   their relation to whites, thus causing them to believe that they are
   uniquely victimized and entitled to special consideration from iniq-
   uitous whites.
6. Binary thinking impairs the ability to generalize and learn from
   history.
7. The black/white model impairs groups' ability to forge useful
   coalitions.

For Matsuda (2002, 395), going beyond the black/white paradigm means that "we need to know how racism in all its variant forms has played out in our history, how inter- and intragroup oppression makes a people-of-color coalition a fantasy in many contemporary parts of the United States, and as we complexify, we have a challenge." Matsuda (2002, 396) is concerned, however, with the *effects* of any given deconstruction, whether it is of the black/white binary or the notion of race itself. She writes:

> Is the effect of your deconstruction to give aid and comfort to the enemies of racial justice? Is your deconstruction of race further obfuscating deep rooted stratification and white supremacy? If so, you're engaging in reactionary politics, whether you intend to or not. Similarly, when I speak loudly and clearly on behalf of racial justice and I'm attacked, I notice that the same people who are attacking me are attacking Catherine MacKinnon when she speaks loudly and clearly on the subject of the sexual abuse of women. When the same people are attacking us, when we have the same enemies, we are allies.

Asian race crits have also challenged the conventional black/white legal discourse because it implicitly assumes that all minorities are black. Chang (1999), for example, incorporates the tenets of CRT in his examination of the history and discrimination against Asian Americans and to strike out at the myth of "the model minority." Lat Crit and Asian Crit theorists point to the necessity of broadening the paradigm of race because it brings to the forefront issues of bilingual education, immigration, national origin, accent discrimination, and English-only rules that are not largely shared with blacks and do not fit neatly into mainstream liberal civil rights discourse. Johnson (2002, 187) demonstrates the shortcomings of the black/white paradigm in understanding the relationship between race and immigration law. He asserts that the dichotomy obscures the relationships between the subordination of various communities; that is, immigration law is unquestionably central to Asian and Latino subordination. According to Johnson (2002, 196–97), racial exclusions in immigration laws reinforce the subordination of minority citizens; therefore, critical race theorists "must begin to consider how the daily operation of immigration law—and its elaborate system of ceilings, quotas, exclusions, and removal grounds—disparately affect immigrants and communities of color and how this impact relates to domestic racial subordination."

Narrative as Methodology

An essential part of understanding CRT is its use of storytelling, counter-storytelling and narratives to challenge the pervasive hegemony of the dominant voice about racial issues.[12] Critical race theorists assume that whites cannot easily grasp what it is like to be nonwhite; thus they use techniques of narratives and storytelling to build cohesion within a minority group *and* to shatter the negative mindset of the dominant group. Critical race theorists argue that there is *power* in stories, in that writers are able to analyze the myths and presuppositions that make up the common culture about race. Paradigm shifts can occur because of powerfully told stories that may lead to an adjustment in whites' belief system about people of color. For race crits, culture constructs its own social reality in ways that promote its own self-interest; therefore, critical race scholars set out to construct a different reality through narratives, storytelling and counter-storytelling.

The two most prominent examples of writing in this genre include works by Derrick Bell (1987, 1992) and Patricia Williams (1991). Storytelling and narratives are extensively used by critical race theorists and their spin-offs, but by no means are these the only approaches used by race crits. Although there is a tendency to brand the use of personal narratives and stories as "controversial," the use of these methods is not unique to CRT. If we confine our examination to the legal academy, we find that the use of storytelling is quite common in clinical scholarship and practice (Miller 2000). Despite the burgeoning use of storytelling and narratives in various contexts, these methods have been attacked as an illegitimate form of legal scholarship (see Delgado and Stefancic 2001 for a brief discussion of the major criticisms directed at critical race theorists' use of storytelling and responses to the criticisms). Farber and Sherry (1997), for example, brand CRTs as "radical multiculturalists" who use stories to advance their own viewpoints and attack notions of merit (for other critiques, see Tushnet 1992 and Posner 1997).

Intersectional Analysis

Critical race theory is committed to challenging racial hierarchy and subordination in all its intersecting forms (Lawrence 2002, xviii). Intersectionality, that is, "the examination of race, sex, class, national origin, and sexual orientation, and how their combination plays out in various settings," has figured prominently in the writings of critical race theorists (Delgado and Stefancic 2001, 51). At its core, intersectionality challenges the assumption that all minorities are black and indicates the ways in which various movements for racial justice have affected our understanding of subordination and marginalization in America. Intersectionality synthesis allows race crits to turn the critique inward within their respective communities. For example, Latino/a scholars who are dissatisfied with the liberal approach to antidiscrimination law have contributed to a new body of scholarship called LatCrit theory that focuses on Latino/a identity and oppression (see Stefancic 1998 for an annotated bibliography of LatCrit theory). Critical race theorists' critique of the shortcomings of mainstream feminism in its failure to address the oppression of both race and gender when they intersect has created another spin-off, critical race feminism (CRF). Critical race feminists attempt to address the perspectives of women of color in a system of white male patriarchy and racist oppression (see Crenshaw 1989 and Harris 1990 for seminal articles on critical race feminism; also see Wing 1997 and Wing 2000 for anthologies of critical race feminism in both American and international contexts). Asian critical race theorists have made the case for AsianCrit theory, which challenges the legal and social implications of white supremacy and subordination of Asian Americans (Matsuda 1991, Chang 1999). Outsider critical scholarship also includes lesbian, gay, and bisexual scholars, Queer Crits, who seek "to craft an incisive antisubordination legal discourse" (Valdes, Culp, and Harris 1995). Hutchinson

(1997) argues for a "queer interconnectivity" that challenges heterosexist supremacy and takes into account how sex and race are inevitably implicated in sexual minority communities. In sum, race crits believe that "racial justice is a matrix, with the fortunes of all nonwhite groups linked in a complex fashion" (Delgado and Stefancic 1999).

CRT in Comparative and International Law and Politics

Romany (2002, 304) asserts that CRT has considerable potential in shaping our understanding of international law, human rights law and comparative law, yet she does not deny the "complexity of racial, gender and economic subordination in the global landscape." Gunning (2002) relies on a critical race feminism perspective in her examination of the criminalization of female genital surgeries targeting African-born women. Hernández-Truyol (2002) explored the relationship of CRT to international human rights law. CRT has also affected the way in which scholars in other nations view racism's impact on people of color. Carol Aylward's work, *Canadian Critical Race Theory* (1999), seeks to apply CRT to shatter the myth of Canada's lack of racism and to show how Canadian legal scholars are developing critical litigation strategies to address this problem.

Critical White Studies

Critical race theorists recognize that races are not biologically differentiated groups; they are instead social constructions. What role does the law play in the legal construction of race? For race crits, law creates and maintains racial differences. Haney-López (1996, 10) argues that given the centrality of law in society, it is important to understand how law shapes the formation of race. Haney-López's (1996, 10) insightful work goes beyond showing that the law simply codifies race; it also demonstrates that legislatures and courts "define the content of racial identities and to specify their relative privilege or disadvantage in U.S. society." Chang (2002) builds upon Haney-López's analysis by asking about the implications of race being regarded as a social construction. Chang (2002) asserts that race crits must distinguish between the "new racialism" and "scientific racism." Arguments used to counter social-scientific racialism were grounded on the goal of ending de jure segregation and to secure equal treatment under the law. With respect to post-1964 strategies, Chang (2002, 95) writes:

> Today in the era of colorblind jurisprudence and the new racialism, social construction must be argued to establish that individuals and institutions have acted in concert to create differences in the material conditions of racial minorities and that this requires or justifies remedies that necessary entail racially different treatment.

Another important spin-off of CRT is critical white studies—an approach that analyzes what it means to be white. Delgado and Stefancic's edited volume (1997) presents the leading works of scholars who study the white race from a multidisciplinary perspective as a socially constructed concept. In their work, Delgado and Stefancic address a variety of themes: how whites see themselves; how whites see other groups; the historical understanding of whiteness; the role of whiteness in law and culture; white privilege; white upward mobility; multiracial people passing for white; the role of biology and pseudoscience; white power, and the role of whites in improving the condition of people of color.

Applications of CRT in Political Science

A central argument of this chapter is that CRT as an analytical framework for understanding and dismantling racial hierarchy, oppression, and subordination of people of color will be useful to political scientists engaged in a similar research agenda. The goals and agendas of race crits and scholars of critical race politics are compatible, albeit on somewhat parallel courses. For example, scholars of race and ethnicity politics have criticized the dominant theories and methodologies used in political science to explain the politics of racial and ethnic groups for over two decades, just as race crits have critiqued legal liberalism and its manifestations. Walton and Smith (2000) engage in precisely this type of critical analysis in their work on African Americans' quest for universal freedom and the failure of political science theories and approaches to enhance our understanding of racial subordination in various institutional, contextual, and behavioral arenas. A theory of critical race politics advanced by scholars of race and ethnicity could fill this important void in our search for paradigms that place race at the center of intellectual inquiries.

Scholars of racial and ethnic politics have already engaged in critiques of the black/white paradigm for understanding racial oppression for many of the same reasons that have prompted race crits to dismantle its application to explanations of racial oppression, both domestically and internationally. For example, Affigne and Lien (2002) show the limitations of the binary paradigm in their search for a theoretical framework explaining the politics of communities of Asian origin. CRT, especially in its attempt to explain subordination globally, could be extended to their analysis of these communities' "outsider" position in the Americas. Related to this issue is the trend toward intersectionality in the study of racial and ethnic politics. The flowering of outsider scholarship lends support for this trend in racial and ethnic politics, including recent works on Latino/a politics (García, 2003), Asian American politics (Nakanishi and Lai 2003) and American Indian politics (Wilkins 2002).

Although CRT has been criticized for its use of narrative methodology, race crits do not exclude other methodologies. For example, Hutchison (1997) examined the impact of minimum wage laws on low-skilled minority workers against a CRT framework. Hutchison's empirical analysis (1997) found no support for the widely held belief that the minimum wage is a progressive program designed to help the poor; instead, he found that minimum wage regimes are in fact an abuse of power and that the nation should reevaluate its commitment to them. Empirical political research employing a range of quantitative and qualitative methods can only amplify CRT's utility as an explanatory model for understanding the politics and behavior of racialized communities; of course, the appeal to science is a powerful tool in political and legal discourse.

Delgado and Stefancic (2000, 591) point to another vital strand of CRT-critical race praxis, which is an attempt to connect theory to practice. Scholarship in this area is aimed at correcting the dissociation of law from racial justice. Yamamoto (1997), for example, has taken progressive race theorists to task for not joining lawyers and activists behind the scenes in litigation. He explains further (Yamamoto 1997, 829–30):

> Critical race praxis combines critical, pragmatic, socio-legal analysis with political lawyering and community organizing to practice justice by and for racialized communities. Its central idea is that racial justice requires antisubordination practice. In addition to ideas and ideals, justice is something experienced through practice. . . .[C]ritical race praxis requires an understanding of justice in terms of both method—experience-rethinking-translation-engagement-and norm—first principles of antisubordination and rectification of injustice. It requires, in appropriate instances, using, critiquing, and moving beyond notions of legal justice pragmatically to heal disabling intergroup wounds and forge intergroup alliances. It also requires, for race theorists, enhanced attention to theory translation and deeper engagement with frontline practice; and for political lawyers and community activists, increased attention to a critical rethinking of what race is, how civil rights are conceived, and why law sometimes operates as a discursive power strategy.

Critical race theory is transformative in the sense that it seeks strategies for reform. Political scientists have a long-standing relationship with lawyers as expert witnesses in litigation, especially in voting rights litigation—for example, in attacking discriminatory voting practices. Critical race theorists are pragmatic in the sense that during a period of legal conservatism on such civil rights issues as affirmative action, they argue that it makes sense to resort to political strategies of electoral politics, grassroots organizing or economic self-help policies. Race crits advocate the use of multiracial coalitions, but they do not deny the complexity and dynamics of coalition formation and action. Alex-Assensoh (2000) has speculated on the role of multiracial politics and its potential in shaping political outcomes. In sum, the praxis of critical race theory is an area in which political scientists can build upon race crits' work and has the potential for making important contributions to this body of research.

Implications and Conclusions

Race and ethnicity continue to be central in understanding marginalization, disadvantage, and subordination in American society. Critical race theorists have broken away from mainstream liberal ideology and have thus brought a critical perspective and vision to the discourse on race, racism, and the law. Not only have critical race theorists attacked the dominant civil rights paradigm, but they have also pointed out the limitations of liberal and leftist accounts of racial power in law. CRT is not purely theoretical; it has a dominant activist strain in seeking new strategies and approaches to achieving racial justice. The discussion of CRT presented in this chapter should convince scholars of critical race politics that many of the same intellectual currents that preoccupy political scientists are also central to race crits in the legal academy. Political scientists who specialize in the subfield of race and ethnicity politics can play a greater role in the next decade of scholarship on critical race theory. Race crits in the legal academy have articulated strong criticisms of traditional legal scholarship and its tendency to place race at the margins of jurisprudential analysis. Adopting a critical race theory perspective in understanding racial hierarchy, white privilege, and oppression in domestic and international contexts would require political scientists to engage in a similar critical discourse of dominant paradigms that purport to explain political phenomena. Scholarship on race in political and legal contexts will be advanced by looking beyond the confines of the traditional subfields of political science and drawing upon the interdisciplinary work of CRT. The challenge for scholars of critical race politics is to reshape our current models, approaches, and methodologies in ways that find new paths to our understanding of race, law, and politics. I think political scientists have important insights, perspectives, and methodologies to bring to the table in shaping and defining future work in critical race theory.

Critical race theory is not new in the sense that its dominant themes have engaged students of racial and ethnic politics for some time. What *is* new and promising about CRT, however, is that a cadre of law professors have engaged in a critical discourse on race and liberation in law against a politics of retrenchment and resistance. They continue their scholarly pursuits despite highly organized attacks and relentless criticisms of critical race theory. After two decades of scholarly writings about critical race theory, it is time for scholars of critical race politics to become more engaged in analyses, critiques and refinement of CRT and to determine whether CRT offers substantive insights into our understanding of racial subordination. By ignoring this body of work or remaining silent about it, we play a role, whether consciously or unconsciously, in the efforts to silence our colleagues in the law schools who are on a similar quest to transform the status quo and break down racial hierarchy and white supremacy.

Notes

This chapter is a substantially revised version of my 2002 paper presented at the Midwest Political Science Association Meeting, "The Impact of the Rehnquist Court on Second Generation Lawsuits: A Critical Race Theory Perspective," Chicago.

1. Critical race theorists have had considerable success in getting their articles published in leading law reviews, thus reaching the widest potential audience in the legal academy, including judges. There is no similar pattern among political scientists of color who specialize in the subfield of racial and ethnic politics. An examination of political science abstracts published since the emergence of CRT revealed only a handful of articles that referenced CRT. Moreover, very little attention is given to CRT in public law texts and other works. A perusal of the major

political science conference programs online over the past few years indicates only a few papers or panels devoted specifically to CRT.

2. For readers who are not acquainted with the writings of CRT, I would recommend the following anthologies: Crenshaw, Gotanda, Peller and Thomas, eds., *Critical Race Theory: The Key Writings That Formed the Movement* (1995); Delgado and Stefancic, eds., *Critical Race Theory: The Cutting Edge* (2000); Valdes, Culp, and Harris, eds., *Crossroads, Directions, and a New Critical Race Theory* (2002); and Delgado and Stefancic, eds., *Critical White Studies: Looking Behind the Mirror* (1997). Other important works include Delgado and Stefancic, *Critical Race Theory: An Introduction* (2001); Haney-López, *White by Law: The Legal Construction of Race* (1996); and Kevin R. Johnson, ed., *Mixed Race America and the Law: A Reader* (2003). For a casebook, reader, and synthesis of CRT, see Perea, Delgado, Harris, and Wildman, *Race and Races: Cases and Resources for a Diverse America* (1999); Flagg, *Was Blind, But Now I See: White Race Consciousness and the Law* (1998); and Davis, Johnson, and Martínez, eds., *A Reader on Racism, Civil Rights, and American Law: A Multicultural Approach* (2001). For additional perspectives on the flowering of outsider scholarship, see Wing, ed., *Critical Race Feminism: A Reader* (1997); Wing, ed., *Global Critical Race Feminism: An International Reader* (2000); Matsuda, *Where is Your Body?: And Other Essays on Race, Gender, and the Law* (1996); Chang, *Disoriented: Asian Americans, Law, and the Nation-State* (1999); Yamamoto, *Interracial Justice: Conflict and Reconciliation in Post-Civil Rights America* (1999); Delgado and Stefancic, eds., *The Latino/a Condition: A Critical Reader* (1998); and Carbado, *Black Men on Race, Gender and Sexuality: A Critical Reader* (1999).

3. I use the term *scholars of critical race politics* to situate those political science scholars who seek to place race at the center of intellectual inquiry; those who challenge extant paradigms; and those who seek to develop alternative theories and methodologies in explaining racial hierarchy, marginalization, and oppression in the domestic, comparative, and international contexts. See Crenshaw (2002) for a discussion of the tensions inherent in the early discussions of CRT on the question of whether CRT was a product of people of color only or of any scholar engaged in a critical reflection of race.

4. See for example Ladson-Billings and Tate (1995, 47), who make a similar call for a critical race theory of education. See also Parker, Deyhle, and Villenas, *Race Is . . . Race Isn't: Critical Race Theory and Qualitative Studies in Education* (1999).

5. See *Regents of the University of California v. Bakke*, 438 U.S. 265 (1978). In *Bakke*, the Burger Court addressed the issue of affirmative action in education on the merits for the first time. In a 5–4 ruling, Justice Powell struck down the medical school admissions program at the University of California, Davis, as an impermissible fixed quota while at the same time upholding the use of race as part of the university's interest in promoting a diverse student body in its medical school.

6. Delgado's article was originally published in the *University of Pennsylvania Law Review* 132 (1984): 561–78. For an updated version, see Richard Delgado, "The Imperial Scholar Revisited: How to Marginalize Outsider Writing, Ten Years Later." *University of Pennsylvania Law Review* 140 (1992): 1349–72. In the 1992 article, Delgado concluded that although "outsider voices are finding their articles published in leading law reviews, their positions are not being easily interpreted into traditional legal scholarship."

7. See Jack Greenberg's account of the Harvard boycott in *Crusaders in the Courts* (1994).

8. See Greene (1999) for a discussion of the law conferences attended by people of color, including a discussion of the CRT conferences.

9. Whether CRT is modern or postmodern is a matter of contention for some race crits. For example, Hayman (1995 at note 5) argues that CRT is postmodern and is perhaps the most rapidly developing form of postmodern jurisprudence. He defines postmodernism as "the growing sense that the conventional ways of thinking and talking about law are not adequate to describe law as it is practiced and experienced." Other race crit scholars have used the term *reconstructive jurisprudence*, which seeks to critique legal liberalism and does not separate legal scholarship from concrete actions in addresses problems of racial justice. See Harris (1994) for a discussion of this concept.

10. Legal strategies would include the Supreme Court's requirement of showing proof of intent to discriminate in discrimination cases and making it tougher for civil rights plaintiffs to have standing to sue in discrimination litigation. Another example would include the Supreme

Court's differential treatment of whites and minorities in free speech cases; that is, making it tougher for minorities' use of protests and sit-in demonstrations to fall under First Amendment protection while at the same time upholding racist cross burnings as protected speech.

11. Perea (1997, 1223) uses Andrew Hacker's work, *Two Nations: Black and White, Separate, Hostile, Unequal* (1992) as an example of over-reliance on the black/white paradigm. He sees the greatest danger in Hacker's work as "its suggestion that non-White groups other than Blacks are not really subject to racism." Perea (1997, 1224) views Hacker's work as adopting the ethnicity theory, "which posits that non-White immigrant ethnics are essentially Whites-in-waiting who will be permitted to assimilate and become White." Another example that Perea (1997) gives of near-exclusive focus on the black/white paradigm is Cornel West's work, *Race Matters* (1993). Perea (1997) is critical of West's failure to acknowledge the extensive struggles of other minority groups for civil rights and his suspicious view of immigrants and other nonwhites.

12. These terms should be carefully distinguished. A *story* is an account of an event; it typically incorporates personal experience. A *narrative* denotes a broader theme or meaning. Stories add up to narratives (Miller, 2000). *Counter-stories* are used to challenge stories and narratives that perpetuate myths or stereotypes about people of color.

References

Affigne, Tony, and Pei-te Lien. 2002. Peoples of Asian descent in the Americas: Theoretical implications of race and politics. *Amerasia Journal* 28:1–16.

Alex-Assensoh, Yvette M. 2000. Introduction: In search of black and multiracial politics in America. In *Black and multiracial politics in America*, edited by Yvette M. Alex-Assensoh and Lawrence J. Hanks, 1–12. New York: New York University Press.

Altman, Andrew. 1990. *Critical legal studies: A liberal critique.* Princeton, NJ: Princeton University Press.

Aylward, Carol A. 1999. *Canadian critical race theory.* Halifax, NS: Fernwood.

Bell, Derrick. 1976. Serving two masters: Integration ideals and client interests in school desegregation litigation. *Yale Law Journal* 85, no. 4 (March): 470–90.

———. 1980. *Brown v. Board of Education* and the interest-convergence dilemma. *Harvard Law Review* 93, no. 3 (January): 518–33.

———. 1987. *And we are not saved: The elusive quest for racial justice.* New York: Basic Books.

———. 1992. *Faces at the bottom of the well: The permanence of racism.* New York: Basic Books.

———. 1996. *Confronting authority: Reflections of an ardent protestor.* Boston: Beacon.

———. 1998. *Afrolantica legacies.* Chicago: Third World.

———. 2000. *Race, racism and American law.* 4th ed. Gaithersburg, MD: Aspen Law & Business.

Carbado, Devon W. 1999. *Black men on race, gender and sexuality: A critical reader.* New York: New York University Press.

Carbado, Devon W., and Mitu Gulati. 2003. The law and economics of critical race theory. *Yale Law Journal* 112:1757–828.

Chang, Robert S. 1999. *Disoriented: Asian Americans, law, and the nation-state.* New York: New York University Press.

———. 2002. Critiquing "race" and its uses: Critical race theory's uncompleted argument. In *Crossroads, directions, and a new critical race theory, edited by* Francesco Valdes, Jerome McCristal Culp, and Angela P. Harris, 87–96. Philadelphia: Temple University Press.

Cho, Sumi, and Robert Westley. 2002. Historicizing critical race theory's cutting edge: Key movements that performed the theory. In *Crossroads, directions, and a new critical race theory,* edited by Francesco Valdes, Jerome McCristal Culp, and Angela P. Harris, 32–70. Philadelphia: Temple University Press.

Crenshaw, Kimberlé Williams. 1988. Race, reform, and retrenchment: Transformation and legitimation in antidiscrimination law. *Harvard Law Review* 101, no. 7 (May): 1331–87.

———. 1989. Demarginalizing the intersection of race and sex: A black feminist critique of antidiscrimination doctrine, feminist theory and antiracist politics. *University of Chicago Legal Forum* 1989:139–67.

———. 1995. Introduction to *Crossroads, directions, and a new critical race theory*, edited by Francesco Valdes, Jerome McCristal Culp, and Angela Harris, xiii–xxxii. Philadelphia: Temple University Press.

———. 2002. The first decade: Critical reflections, or "a foot in the closing door"? In *Crossroads, directions, and a new critical race theory*, edited by Francesco Valdes, Jerome McCristal Culp, and Angela P. Harris, 9–31. Philadelphia: Temple University Press.

Crenshaw, Kimberlé, Neil Gotanda, Gary Peller, and Kendall Thomas. 1995. *Critical race theory: The key writings that formed the movement*. New York: New Press.

Davis, Abraham L., and Barbara L. Graham. 1995. *The Supreme Court, race and civil rights*. Thousand Oaks, CA: Sage.

Davis, Timothy, Kevin R. Johnson, and George A. Martínez, eds. 2001. *A reader on race, civil rights, and American law: A multiracial approach*. Durham, NC: Carolina Academic Press.

Delgado, Richard. 1984. The imperial scholar: Reflections on a review of civil rights literature. *University of Pennsylvania Law Review* 132:561–78.

———. 1987. The ethereal scholar: Does critical legal studies have what minorities want? *Harvard Civil Rights–Civil Liberties Law Review* 22:301–22.

———. 1992. "The imperial scholar" revisited: How to marginalize outsider writing, ten years later. *University of Pennsylvania Law Review* 140:1349–72.

———. 2000. Derrick Bell's toolkit—Fit to dismantle that famous house? *New York University Law Review* 75, no. 2:283–307.

———. 2003. White interests and civil rights realism: Rodrigo's bittersweet epiphany. *Michigan Law Review* 101:1201–24.

Delgado, Richard, and Jean Stefancic. 1999. Review of *Canadian critical race theory: Racism and the law. The Canadian Journal of Sociology Online*, by Carol A. Aylward. Available at http://www.cjsonline.ca/backiss/cjsseptoct99.html. Accessed on September 23, 2006.

———. 2001. *Critical race theory: An introduction*. New York: New York University Press.

Delgado, Richard, and Jean Stefancic, eds. 1997. *Critical white studies: Looking behind the mirror*. Philadelphia: Temple University Press.

———. 1998. *The Latino/a condition: A critical reader*. New York: New York University Press.

———. 2000. *Critical race theory: The cutting edge*. 2nd ed. Philadelphia: Temple University Press.

Dudziak, Mary L. 2000. *Cold war civil rights: Race and the image of American democracy*. Princeton, NJ: Princeton University Press.

Farber, Daniel A., and Suzanna Sherry. 1997. *Beyond all reason: The radical assault on truth in academic law*. New York: Oxford University Press.

Flagg, Barbara J. 1998. *Was blind, but now I see: White race consciousness and the law*. New York: New York University Press.

Freeman, Alan David. 1978. Legitimizing racial discrimination through antidiscrimination law: A critical review of Supreme Court doctrine. *Minnesota Law Review* 62:1049–119.

García, John A. 2003. *Latino politics in America: Community, culture, and interests*. Lanham, MD: Rowman and Littlefield.

Gotanda, Neil. 1991. A critique of "our Constitution is color-blind." *Stanford Law Review* 44, no. 1: 1–68.

Greenberg, Jack. 1994. *Crusaders in the courts: How a dedicated band of lawyers fought for the civil rights revolution*. New York: Basic Books.

Greene, Linda S. 1999. From tokenism to emancipatory politics: The conferences and meetings of law professors of color. *Michigan Journal of Race and Law* 5:161–84.

Gunning, Isabelle R. 2002. Global feminism at the local level: The criminalization of female genital surgeries. In *Crossroads, directions, and a new critical race theory*, edited by Francesco Valdes, Jerome McCristal Culp, and Angela P. Harris, 337–44. Philadelphia: Temple University Press.

Handler, Joel F. 1992. Postmodernism, protest, and the new social movements. *Law and Society Review* 26, no. 4:697–731.

Haney-López, Ian F. 1996. *White by law: The legal construction of race*. New York: New York University Press.

Harris, Angela P. 1990. Race and essentialism in feminist legal theory. *Stanford Law Review* 42, no. 3 (February): 581–615.

————.1994. Foreword: The jurisprudence of reconstruction. *California Law Review* 82:741–85.

Hayman, Robert L., Jr. 1995. The color of tradition: Critical race theory and postmodern constitutional traditionalism. *Harvard Civil Rights–Civil Liberties Law Review* 30:57–108.

Hernández-Truyol, Berta Esperanza. 2002. Breaking cycles of inequality: Critical theory, human rights, and family in/justice. In *Crossroads, directions, and a new critical race theory*, edited by Francesco Valdes, Jerome McCristal Culp and Angela P. Harris, 345–65. Philadelphia: Temple University Press.

Hutchinson, Darren L. 1997. Out yet unseen: A racial critique of gay and lesbian legal theory and political discourse. *Connecticut Law Review* 29:561–645.

Hutchison, Harry. 1997. Toward a critical race reformist conception of minimum wage regimes: Exploding the power of myth, fantasy, and hierarchy. *Harvard Journal on Legislation* 34:93–134.

Johnson, Kevin R. 2002. Race and the immigration laws: The need for critical inquiry. In *Crossroads, directions, and a new critical race theory*, edited by Francesco Valdes, Jerome McCristal Culp, and Angela P. Harris, 187–98. Philadelphia: Temple University Press.

————, ed. 2003. *Mixed race America and the law: A reader*. New York: New York University Press.

Karst, Kenneth L. 1996. Integration success story: A review of three recent books on critical race theory. *Southern California Law Review* 69:1781–94.

Ladson-Billings, Gloria, and William F. Tate, IV. 1995. Toward a critical race theory of education. *Teachers College Record* 97:47–68.

Lawrence, Charles R., III. 2001. Two views of the river: A critique of the liberal defense of affirmative action. *Columbia Law Review* 101:928–75.

————. 2002. Who are we and why are we here? Doing critical race theory in hard times. In *Crossroads, directions, and a new critical race theory*, edited by Francisco Valdes, Jerome McCristal Culp, and Angela P. Harris, xi–xxi. Philadelphia: Temple University Press.

Matsuda, Mari J. 1991. Voices of America: Accent, antidiscrimination law, and jurisprudence for the lost reconstruction. *Yale Law Journal* 100:1329–407.

————. 1996. *Where is your body?: And other essays on race, gender, and the law*. Boston: Beacon.

Matsuda, Mari J., Charles R. Lawrence III, Richard Delgado, and Kimberlé Crenshaw. 1993. *Words that wound: Critical race theory, assaultive speech, and the first amendment*. Boulder, CO: Westview.

Miller, Binny. 2000. Telling stories about cases and clients: The ethics of narrative. *Georgetown Journal of Legal Ethics* 14:1–54.

Munger, Frank. 2001. Inquiry and activism in law and society. *Law and Society Review* 35:7–20.

Nakanishi, Don T., and James S. Lai. 2003. *Asian American politics: Law, participation, and policy*. Lanham, MD: Rowman and Littlefield.

Parker, Laurence, Donna Deyhle, and Sofia Villenas. 1991. *Race is . . . race isn't: Critical race theory and qualitative studies in education*. Boulder, CO: Westview.

Perea, Juan F. 1997. The black/white binary paradigm of race: The "normal science" of American racial thought. *California Law Review* 85:1213–58.

Perea, Juan F., Richard Delgado, Angela P. Harris, and Stephanie M. Wildman. 1999. *Race and races: Cases and resources for a diverse America*. St. Paul, MN: West Group.

Posner, Richard. 1997. The skin trade. *New Republic*, October 13, p. 40.

Romany, Celina. 2002. Critical race theory in global context. In *Crossroads, directions, and a new critical race theory*, edited by Francesco Valdes, Jerome McCristal Culp, and Angela P. Harris, 303–9. Philadelphia: Temple University Press.

Rosen, Jeffrey. 1996. The bloods and the crits. *New Republic*, December 9, p. 27.

Rubin, Edward L. 1996. The new legal process, the synthesis of discourse, and the microanalysis of institutions. *Harvard Law Review* 109:1393–438.

Spann, Girardeau A. 1993. *Race against the Court: Supreme Court and minorities in contemporary America*. New York: New York University Press.

Stefancic, Jean. 1998. Latino and Latina critical theory: An annotated bibliography. *La Raza Law Journal* 10:1509–84.

Tushnet, Mark. 1991. The degradation of constitutional discourse. *Georgetown Law Journal* 81:251–311.

Unger, Roberto Mangabeira. 1983. *The critical legal studies movement.* Cambridge, MA: Harvard University Press.

Valdes, Francisco. 2002. Outsider scholars, critical race theory, and "outcrit" perspectivity: Post-subordination vision as jurisprudential method. In *Crossroads, directions, and a new critical race theory,* edited by Francisco Valdes, Jerome McCristal Culp, and Angela P. Harris, 399–409. Philadelphia: Temple University Press.

Valdes, Francisco, Jerome McCristal Culp, and Angela P. Harris. 2002. Battles waged, won, and lost: Critical race theory at the turn of the millennium. In *Crossroads, directions, and a new critical race theory,* edited by Francisco Valdes, Jerome McCristal Culp, and Angela P. Harris, 1–6. Philadelphia: Temple University Press.

Walton, Hanes Jr., and Robert C. Smith. 2000. *American politics and the African American quest for universal freedom.* New York: Longman.

Wilkins, David E. 2002. *American Indian politics and the American political system.* Lanham, MD: Rowman and Littlefield.

Williams, Patricia J. 1991. *The alchemy of race and rights.* Cambridge, MA: Harvard University Press.

Wing, Adrien Katherine, ed. 1997. *Critical race feminism: A reader.* New York: New York University Press.

———. 2000. *Global critical race feminism: An international reader.* New York: New York University Press.

Yamamoto, Eric K. 1997. Critical race praxis: Race theory and political lawyering practice in post civil rights America." *Michigan Law Review* 95:821–900.

———. 1999. *Interracial justice: Conflict and reconciliation in post-civil rights America.* New York: New York University Press.

CHAPTER TWELVE

Presidential Leadership and the Politics of Race

Stereotypes, Symbols, and Scholarship

Wilbur C. Rich

T HE GRAND OR META-NARRATIVE of America is its unwavering commitment to freedom and equality.[1] The presidency is the sentinel of these democratic ideals. To be faithful to these ideals, presidents must take on the issue of race straightforwardly. Yet race relations continue to play only an ancillary role in the discourse about the nature of the American presidency. Trying to explain presidential leadership without using race relations as a case study reveals a myopia that is neither fair to presidents nor faithful to the metanarrative. Addressing black civil rights demands cannot be seen as a distraction from the important work modern presidents are required to do. Yet too often scholars treat civil rights as a footnote or ignore the issue altogether. For many political scientists, the road to presidential greatness is best traveled offshore, defending the nation from real and imagined enemies.[2] When the nation is at war, racial reform can be demanded; when it is at peace there is a chance of backsliding.[3] One possible explanation for this attitude can be traced to scholars' preoccupation with what they consider the big issues; that is, external threats to the nation's existence. In any case, the gilding of the history of American presidents is often done in the service of saving the presidency from the *lilliputians*.

There are a variety of theories, typologies, and apologies in the literature on presidential leadership. In this chapter I raise serious questions about the literature on presidential accountability in the context of race relations. I make a distinction between racial acknowledgment gestures (RAGs) and situational improvement policies (SIPs). Presidents, regardless of party or espoused political ideology, have employed RAGs. RAGs are mainly symbolic, individual-specific, or event-specific, and they do not result in any substantive change in the position of blacks as a group. SIPs include major policy shifts that result in substantive race hierarchical changes; they apportion status, power, and resources to blacks as a group.

This chapter will also suggest that the discourse on presidential power—a tradition of comparing weak and strong presidents—obfuscates the critical role that the office plays in the political progress of black Americans. In America, the president represents the state. Burman asserts, "The role of the state, therefore, becomes critical in any evaluation of Black progress because of its property of reflecting, encapsulating, crystallizing, and manifesting the diverse pressures, material and ideal, economic and cultural, whose balance governs the rate of Black progress."[4]

History suggests that presidents play a major role in reinforcing social boundaries (i.e., supporting communal rules) for racial competition between whites and blacks. Some presidents have reassured whites that racial boundaries will remain intact, while others have promised whites that they have little to fear from conceding privileges to blacks or that racial progress will not take place at their expense. These rhetorical reassurances define racial etiquette and political correctness in discussions of the race problem.

Nevertheless, the dynamics of this process has escaped some political scientists; many have ignored or downplayed the president's responsibility for defining racial etiquette. These social scientists assume that the presidency may be neutral on race conflicts or practice what Daniel Patrick Moynihan, in an internal 1970 memo to President Nixon, called "benign neglect." Bachrach and Baratz were correct in pointing out that nondecisions are still decisions.[5] Lack of talk about race by a president is not benign. By not responding to situations that demand a response, presidents send signals about what constitutes acceptable behavior for white Americans. A specific example is Franklin Delano Roosevelt's refusal to support anti-lynching laws, which gave solace to people who committed these crimes. More specifically, presidential signaling engages or disengages the "imagined community" described in Charles Mills' racial contract.[6] Russell Riley makes a similar characterization when he suggests that on the question of African American equality, the presidency is a *nation-maintaining* institution.

> One of the enduring roles each president is required to execute is that of nation-keeper, a protector of the inherited political and social order and a preserver of domestic tranquility. . . . It most commonly promotes presidential behavior intended to ward off or moderate significant social change as a threat to the preferred status of the polity's prevailing interests. Yet nation-keeping presidents may also find, in some uncommon instances, that profound change is a prerequisite of preservation.[7]

Riley's concept of nation-keeping reminds us of Talcott Parsons's definition of *pattern maintenance* as a requirement for system equilibrium. Social systems seek to maintain themselves by replicating social patterns that assure their survival. The absence of internal conflict is considered equilibrium. This notion may explain why presidents use the language of law and order when they defuse racial disturbances. The objective is to stop the riots and once that is done, chief executives are not obliged to do much else. Presidents do not want to be seen as rewarding the participants. If subsequent concessions are made or new resources granted, every effort is made to dissociate presidential action from previous racial disturbances.

In this way scholarly discourse treats addressing black civil rights grievances as an intrusion on presidential time. Presidential papers show presidents carefully balancing long-term answers to the plight of blacks on one hand and reactions from white voters on the other. Presidents prefer to be seen as being forced to act. Harry S. Truman ordered the integration of the military to offset the losses of Southern voters to the Dixiecrats. Dwight D. Eisenhower and John F. Kennedy failed to convince Southern governors to use their offices to ensure the safety of black activists and thus had no other choice to but to send in federal troops. These presidents addressed black grievances as unwanted and unwelcome entanglements;[8] however, their reluctance did not stop journalists from celebrating Truman, Eisenhower, and Kennedy as defenders of freedom.

Telling a good story is something many journalists use to prove that presidents are generally exemplary individuals. Truman's outrage at the mistreatment of uniformed black soldiers was used as a justification for his executive order. Johnson's story about his maid's not being able to use a public restroom while traveling with his daughters on a trip to Washington, DC, from Texas was used as a personal incentive for the 1964 Civil Rights Act. These stories attribute altruistic and sometimes idealistic motives to presidents by insinuation.[9] The Truman and Johnson anecdotes are about shame and embarrassment. The insinuation runs like this: You (white Americans) have a right to your feeling about blacks, but mindless humiliations inflicted on individuals should be beneath you. We (Americans) are better than that.[10] These presidential stories also reinforced early American political socialization into the belief that presidents are sensitive and benevolent.[11]

Revisionist history is also utilized to present the American presidency as an exceptional institution. This description defines the presidency as both unusually powerful and at the same time extremely fragile. Stretching or overusing it can lead to a diminution of its mythical power. Other countries cannot hope to emulate the institution structurally because it grows out of a special context. This revisionism has led scholars to rewrite the nation's history in a way that renders some presidents' indifference toward black grievances superfluous or insignificant.[12]

Scholars of the presidency since World War II seem to be caught in a bind between romantic deference to the Roosevelt years and unease with the unpredictable terrain that presidents now face. Self-tracking among political scientists—aligning oneself with existing thinking about the presidency—makes good sequential reading but it also inhibits creative thinking about the future needs of the modern presidency.[13] This self-tracking explains why contemporary presidential scholars have become worrywarts. A review of five leading seminal works on the presidency may provide insight into whether their anxieties and concerns about the office are justified.

Concerns about Impotency

Richard Neustadt's *Presidential Power*, first published in 1960, informed several generations of presidential scholars.[14] Neustadt regards presidents as having limited constitutional powers. Their real powers are derived from extraconstitutional sources. Because they cannot command, they must persuade. Operational presidential power is obtained from acting in the political environment. For Neustadt, a president must have persuasive skills in order to convince the Washington establishment to do what he wants it to do. This persuasion is not an easy task because the denizens of the Washington power center are fairly entrenched. Accordingly, a president can be overwhelmed if he is not careful. A successful president must understand his limitations and anticipate the needs of the other political players in Washington. Franklin Roosevelt, the role model for Neustadt's entrepreneurial-type president, promoted change, inveigled people, but also incurred obligations.

Neustadt's successful presidents are careful not to overspend their political capital. Being elected president automatically endows them with a ready supply of political capital; however, a single miscalculation can render it useless. This depletion theory holds that power is a bargaining tool to be used strategically. Reputation and image are critical factors in Neustadt's analysis of different presidencies. Scholars who subscribe to Neustadt's views fret about presidents losing power (or wasting it) and being unable to rally the nation in times of crisis. For some of these scholars, exposing the presidency to the conundrum of race relations could potentially squander a considerable amount of political capital with no assurance of results. Depletion theory may help to explain why Neustadt's presidents do not spend precious time solving race problems.

Critics of Neustadt attacked him for not defining a useful purpose for power.[15] What are the ethical implications of a president's indifference to the race issue?[16] Does presidential unresponsiveness leave blacks waiting for a second Lyndon Johnson? Another war? More importantly, given the fragility of racial reform, could such a conservative president as Ronald Reagan reverse the change or embolden latent anti-black attitudes?[17] Could a conservative transformation of American politics take place under a president with a liberal reputation but a keen eye toward his legacy? An example would be Bill Clinton's ease in selling such free trade policies as the North American Free Trade Agreement (NAFTA) and the 1996 Welfare Reform Act, which was backed by conservatives. Those two policies demonstrate the ways in which a president can frame an issue in such a way that people who will be hurt by the policies will nonetheless vote for him. Like other Americans, blacks have been socialized to believe that the president would not deliberately do anything that would hurt them and that any policy with overwhelming bipartisan support cannot be nefarious.

Concerns about Symbols and Substance

Murray Edelman's The Symbolic Uses of Politics is really an expression of concern about the inclination of political leaders to substitute symbols for substance.[18] Symbols affect political action and also affect what people expect from government. There is an inescapable ritual dimension to the relationship between leaders and followers that allows leaders to symbolize the relationship. History suggests that relatively powerless people can be easily manipulated by symbolic gestures. For example, President Theodore Roosevelt's famous 1901 dinner with Booker T. Washington was hailed as an important breakthrough in racial etiquette. Although the dinner invitation consolidated Washington's claims of being the paramount black leader, becoming a presidential confidant amounted to little more than a RAG in race relations. This fact became clear when Washington refused to criticize the President's actions in the Brownville incident.[19]

A president who signs an executive order on fair housing can claim that something is being done. The reality, however, is that such an order cannot be implemented, as in the case of President Kennedy and Executive Order 11063. Another example of symbolic action was the amount of energy put into the Humphrey-Hawkins full employment bill. The bill languished for years, gathering opponents and proponents, spending a considerable amount of political capital, and in the end requiring very little from the government. Although symbolic action is not always intended to be deceptive, it often does in fact deceive, and the public is prepared to give credit to a leader for good intentions. Most presidents have gotten a lot of mileage out of good intentions. This fact suggests that even powerless people can be drawn to a benevolent image of the presidency.

Presidential leadership by definition is about symbols. Presidents have to give the impression that they can cope with any problem presented to them. Edelman asserts,

> When an individual is recognized as a legitimate leading official of the state, he becomes a symbol of some or all aspects of the state; its capacity for benefiting and hurting, for threatening and reassuring. His acts, for this reason, are public in character. They are perceived as having significant, strong, enduring, indirect consequences for a large number of people.[20]

Public acts by a president can send different messages to different groups. Personalizing the race problem is a rather old refuge for a president. By definition, he supports equal rights for all Americans. The message given is that the president is being evenhanded and magnanimous, but the situation for blacks requires quite a bit more than evenhandedness and goodwill.

Presidential action on television raises the ante for symbolic gestures. Television can be both revealing and deceptive. Skowronek admits in his chapter on President Johnson that television helped Johnson with the passage of the 1964 Civil Rights Act. "The use of the media by the civil rights movement in Selma in early 1965 is perhaps the leading example of how television brought new pressure to bear on the task of interest management. The movement refused to be treated as an interest like any other or to accept the Civil Rights Act of 1964 as sufficient recognition of its concerns."[21] The civil rights movement used television to make America aware of the need for a voting rights bill. Skowronek believes that television can magnify "the dissonance between the President's commitment and actual events."[22] It follows that if television can magnify this gap, it can also diminish differences. This concern was the subject of Edelman's book *Constructing the Political Spectacle*. Political spectacles can go either way—to compel presidential action or induce acquiescence. Bruce Miroff observed, "A spectacle does not permit the audience to interrupt the action and redirect its meaning. . . . A spectacle is not designed for mass participation; it is not a democratic event."[23] Edelman warns us about this characteristic but does not offer any way to avoid the charade.[24]

Attending to race grievances seems particularly susceptible to symbolic gestures. A President can often pick his stage. Nixon selected the Philadelphia Plan, the first affirmative action gesture that opened up the building trades to minorities.[25] Kennedy selected the 1961 graduation ceremony at the Coast Guard Academy to ask about the absence of black cadets. Although espousing a doctrine of "constructive engagement" toward South Africa, Ronald Reagan appointed Edward J. Perkins, a black man, as ambassador to that nation at the height of the apartheid regime. Reagan endorsed the Martin Luther King Jr. federal holiday. George H. W. Bush elevated General Colin Powell to the chairmanship of the Joint Chiefs of Staff. Bill Clinton appointed Vernon Jordan, the former president of the Urban League, as co-chair of his transition team. In 1998 Clinton promoted a retired general, Benjamin O. Davis, to the rank of four-star general; a year later he posthumously pardoned Henry O. Flipper, West Point's first black graduate, who had been wrongly accused of embezzlement. These actions not only surprised the black public but also left the impression that the president is their friend. These low-cost activities were symbolic actions that won the president applause but did not change the objective conditions of blacks as a group.

Concerns about Overreaching

Charles Jones's *The Presidency in a Separated System* asserts that the government of the United States is a separated system of governance and that the framers never intended to create a presidential system.[26] The first sentence in Jones's book asserts, "The president is not the presidency. The presidency is not the government. Ours is not a presidential system."[27] For many students of the presidency, Jones's argument is a rebuttal to James McGregor Burns's *Presidential Government*. Burns had argued for expanding the presidency's agenda, one that allows the president to set the national agenda and grant the authority to take action.[28] In many ways Burns continues the argument made by Alexander Hamilton, who had warned against a feeble presidency at the 1787 Constitutional Convention. Jones, following the lead of James Madison, instructed presidents to stay within the lines.

At the same time, the nation keeps piling new responsibilities on the presidency. When expectations exceed the management capacity of the president's office, it becomes what Harold Barger has described as the *impossible presidency*.[29] Others have called it the imperiled presidency.[30] The evolution of presidential government began as far back as the Jacksonian Era in the nineteenth century but was consolidated with the invention of television and culminated in incessant presidential appearances. The president is seen everywhere. Modern presidents are now surrounded by hordes of Secret Service officers, reporters, and cameras. One can easily count the days of the year on which the president is not mentioned, seen, or heard. Apparently this overexposure is what the American people want.

The presidency is not a feeble institution. The record shows that the reach of presidents seems to expand with each administration. Presidential constitutionalists like Richard Pious contend that the " key to an understanding of presidential power is to concentrate on the constitutional authority that the president asserts unilaterally through the various rules of constitutional construction and interpretation, in order to resolve crises or important issues facing the nation."[31] Presidents can act; and when they do they leave a road map for their successors. President Eisenhower's nationalization of the Arkansas National Guard during the 1957 Little Rock Central High School desegregation crisis made it easier for President Kennedy to do likewise in the 1962 University of Mississippi integration case.

Unilateral action is not without its perils. We have scholars lamenting the Imperial Presidency[32] and others trying to protect the office from overuse. As the presidency grows, so does the size of the staff and the government in general. The presidency is the parasite of the ambition of the permanent government (i.e., bureaucracy). As any successful bureaucrat would agree, crisis is the mother's milk of agency growth. Recurrent racial crises did expand the mission of the government's civil rights agencies. The problem is that racial crises are only episodically available, leaving such created agencies as the Equal Employment Opportunities Commission (EEOC), the U.S. Civil Rights Commission, the Office of the Assistant Secretary for Civil Rights, and the U.S. Department of Justice drifting into routine.[33]

Concerns about Character

The office of the presidency cannot protect its occupants from their character flaws. Once a person becomes president, these imperfections will inevitably affect his or her conduct in the office. Conversely, a president's previously untapped positive attributes may also surface. The task then focuses on detection and prediction. The president's human qualities is the topic of James David Barber's *Presidential Character*.[34] In most textbooks about the presidency, Barber's typology— active-positive, passive-positive, active-negative and passive-negative—reminds the reader of presidential fallibility. The inability of Richard Nixon to avoid self-destruction lent much credence to Barber's psychological analysis of the presidency. Building on the work of Harold Lasswell[35] and Ervin Hargrove,[36] Barber constructed a scenario of presidents limited by their personalities. The president is, after all, a human being with a specific psychological makeup, including both assets and liabilities. All presidents are tested in office; some pass and others fail. Barber's exemplar of a well-adjusted person and thus an active-positive type is Franklin Roosevelt. Active-positive presidents are self-confident and adaptive. His archetype of poorly adjusted personalities are Woodrow Wilson and Lyndon Johnson. Richard Nixon joins them as an active-negative type.

Barber's theory has attracted legions of critics.[37] First, it relies on psychology as a means of predicting behavior; and second, its typology leaves room for discussion; scholars disagree about the assignment of specific presidents to the four boxes in Barber's matrix. There are so many counter-examples that can be cited to prove that specific presidents have been misclassified. Yet the media and the public have embraced Barber's scheme because of its simplicity. To be fair, Barber never claimed that presidents are simple to understand, only that there are behavioral patterns that presidents might follow that will reveal their true selves.

It does not follow from Barber's analysis that a self-confident president would stand foursquare on achieving equality for blacks. According to O'Reilly, Bill Clinton was the least prejudiced person to occupy the White House, but his ruminations and actions did little to change the objective conditions of most blacks. Clinton cannot be considered the second coming of Lyndon Johnson. He neither shepherded through Congress any civil rights bills that could be considered an SIP nor did he expand any Great Society programs.[38]

Concerns about Political Time

Stephen Skowronek's *The Politics Presidents Make*,[39] is arguably the most important book on the presidency since Richard Neustadt's *Presidential Power*. Skowronek attempts to locate presidents within *political time* rather than secular time. He asserts that "Presidential leadership in political time will refer to the various relationships incumbents project between previously established commitments of ideology and interest and their own actions in the moment at hand."[40] This characterization allows Skowronek to compare presidents across generations. He found that presidents elected at certain periods of American history had their fate sealed by either inherited policies or overarching ideologies. The cycle of problematic times can be quicksand for a president. When a president comes into office by default or electoral controversy, he may experience difficulties in office (e.g. John Q. Adams, Rutherford Hayes, and George W. Bush).

What is most interesting about Skowronek's work is his fascination with the capacity of the president to make changes in either direction. The power invested in the office can either reinforce the current political environment or disrupt extant power arrangements. Conversely, it can accommodate time-servers (Eisenhower) or order-preservers (Herbert Hoover). For Skowronek, the presidency works best when it is charged with repudiating the old regime and establishing a new order (Thomas Jefferson, FDR, and Reagan). Skowronek calls this repudiation "reconstruction politics."[41] When such change happens, the president's politics reconfigures the office and then redirects government institutions. In terms of Skowronek's analysis, George W. Bush would appear to be locked into the Reagan/George H. W. Bush approach to race relations. This approach entails making a strong statement against quotas, appointing loyal blacks to highly visible offices, and letting the masses interpret these actions as change. So far Bush, save the compassionate conservative moniker he adopted, has not repudiated this approach.

Race and Presidential Fortunes

Such social issues as race, gender, and family life were not built into the job description of the presidency. These issues are like barnacles attached to the presidential ship. Since the inception of the Republic, race has always been a difficult issue.[42] No president has been able to escape the race issue, although several have ignored it. President Washington brought the first blacks (slaves) into the first White House. Several slave-owning presidents brought their favorite servants to serve them in the White House. Throughout the history of the White House, blacks who worked there did not wear business suits until Eisenhower appointed E. Frederick Morrow to the White House staff. At the time, this act was a quintessential symbol of black initiation into presidential decision making, yet Morrow was isolated and often denigrated.

Few presidents had the political capacity of Dwight D. Eisenhower, the former five-star general and hero of World War II. Eisenhower was president when the *Brown* decision was handled down by the Supreme Court, during the Montgomery bus boycott and the integration of Little Rock Central High School. Given Eisenhower's popularity, he apparently had enough political flexibility to be a great civil rights president,[43] but he never used his political capital on this issue. Did President Eisenhower fear a massive loss of political capital when he gave weak support to the *Brown* decision,[44] or did he increase it with his actions in the Little Rock episode? Edelman describes Eisenhower's passive leadership style as consisting "basically of the avoidance of firm positions on controversial subjects while at the same time posturing as protagonist against an evanescent enemy, thereby retaining political support from large numbers of antagonists on both sides of the controversies."[45] Fred Greenstein's *The Hidden-Hand Presidency*[46] paints a picture of a man doing the right thing behind the scenes and preserving his political capital. But preserving it for what purpose?

At first glance, one would think that Lyndon B. Johnson would be a prototype of Skowronek's reconstruction president. He repudiated the segregation regime that had dominated the South since the Civil War. He was the first and last president to invoke the phrase, "We shall overcome." The nation didn't, but Johnson did become a model of what the president can say and do.[47] Yet Skowronek classifies Johnson as engaging in the politics of articulation because he offered an updated version of the New Deal (that is, the Great Society). The Great Society was viewed as a continuation and consolidation of the New Deal.

Was George H. W. Bush trying to placate the right wing of his party when he vetoed the 1990 Civil Rights Bill? Or did he think that playing the quota card would win him support? What did he gain from signing the 1991 Civil Rights Act, which represented only a minor change from the 1990 edition? Did he know his legacy would be that of the only modern president to veto a civil rights act? Do presidential scholars see him in those terms? In many ways the older Bush is as perplexing as Eisenhower was.

As of the early 2000s, presidents regardless of political party will appoint an African American or sometimes an obligatory second black appointee either to the White House staff or to the cabinet. What do these appointments mean? Is it just throwing what Riley calls "an occasional bone"[48] to black citizens? Have we reached a new era in race relations or do these appointments obscure a larger problem? In an increasingly multiracial society, can the American presidency set the tone for racial inclusion in our society?

Presidents, Political Parties, and Race

In the past, political parties played a critical role in the construction of a concerned but constrained presidency. The Democrats sought to show that white privilege is elastic and that black progress is not a zero-sum game. This approach has generally worked since the 1930s as black voters have become fiercely loyal to the Democrats. The post-Goldwater Republican Party presented itself as the safe haven for disaffected and uncertain whites.[49] This was done primarily through a system of racial code words.[50] The rhetorical flourishes about opportunity and personal responsibility masked the party's seeming indifference to the massive opportunity gap between the races. Yet this message is very effective because it resonates with the economically insecure white middle class, or what St. Clair Drake called the "strainers." These are Americans struggling to make ends meet and resent what they perceive as special privileges for blacks. The scholarship on the presidency fails to flush out these tactics in order to make a closer connection between various theories of the presidency on the one hand and the changing complexion of the nation on the other hand.

Abraham Lincoln, the Great Emancipator, imprinted the Republican Party on the minds of freed slaves. The Republican Party remained the home party of blacks for sixty years. This loyalty changed in the 1930s, when the Republican Party lost black voters to Roosevelt's New Deal Democratic Party. How did this shift happen? Was it a political epiphany on the part of black voters? History shows that the Republican Party elected several presidents who generally ignored their black supporters—even Northern blacks who voted for them. The inept Hoover administration accelerated the disaffection of blacks. Donald Lisio claims that Herbert Hoover's naivety and ignorance of race-oriented politics lured him into a dubious Southern strategy to reform state parties.

> The overriding goals or operating principles of these various southern strategies were his commitment to clean and efficient government and his dream of a southern revolution that would remove race as the traditional basis of southern politics and pave the way for political, economic, and racial progress. However, because he believed that he must outwit the Democrats by a policy of silence and by working behind the scenes, these varied efforts never became publicly known and understood. Instead they remained in the shadow of the more sensational perception of one racist, lily-white southern strategy. In the end, Hoover's diverse, unexplained, and thus confusing southern strategies managed to alienate both blacks and lily-whites.[51]

Hoover's Northern strategy was to use a RAG, i.e., inviting the wife of the newly elected Republican member of Congress from Chicago, Oscar De Priest, to tea at the White House.[52] In 1932 the President invited a delegation of black leaders to the White House.[53] Neither Hoover's Southern nor his Northern strategy worked, as blacks voted for Roosevelt in 1932.[54] Hoover's role as party leader was as bungling as his role as the chief national economist.

The black shift toward the Democratic Party endured through the Roosevelt era.[55] In 1948, Hubert Humphrey introduced the first civil rights plank at a

Democratic national convention, and Truman integrated all branches of the military service several months later. It was Lyndon Johnson who brokered the first Civil Rights Bill of 1957; as President, he moved the major Civil Rights Bills of 1964 and 1965 through Congress. These two laws represented the first serious situational improvement policies (SIPs) since Reconstruction. Black politicians became more ensconced in the Democratic Party at the national level than they ever had been in the Republican Party of the Reconstruction period. The late Ron Brown became the first black to chair the national committee of the Democratic Party. Brown also served as Secretary of Commerce in the Clinton Administration. A black woman, Donna Brazile, served as campaign manager for Al Gore in the 2000 Democratic presidential campaign.

The Republican Party has recently learned to play symbolic appointment politics with blacks. President Nixon appointed William Coleman as Secretary of Transportation. Reagan appointed Sam Pierce as Secretary of Housing and Urban Development (HUD). George H. W. Bush appointed General Colin Powell Chairman of the Joint Chiefs of Staff. His son George W. Bush appointed Condoleezza Rice as National Security Advisor, with Colin Powell as his first-term Secretary of State.[56] The obligatory second is Rod Paige, Secretary of Education. Selecting a black aide is an old story that doesn't get as much attention as it once demanded. Yet it is an effective RAG with which to offset black criticisms and create the effect of having a black counter-elite pool.

RAGs have also been used to titillate the black voters in presidential elections. Black names have been mentioned as possible vice presidential candidates in both major parties; however, none have been actually nominated as of the early 2000s.[57] Presidential candidate Al Gore interviewed Congressman John Lewis prior to the 2000 election. Although no black Americans yet have been asked to run on a national ticket, these RAGs show that white Americans are clearly being primed for a future black vice or presidential candidacy. The Gallup polling organization has tracked attitudes toward the possibility of a black candidate for president since 1958. Gallup asked Americans if they would be willing to vote for a "well-qualified" black for president. Figure 12.1 shows the results:

The 1958 poll found that only 38 percent of respondents answered "yes." This low percentage was rather significant because it came in the middle of the civil rights movement. One could quibble over whether blacks and whites shared a common definition of "well-qualified," but the polling results do show a softening of attitudes toward the idea. In 1958 the idea of a black politician running on a major party presidential ticket was just a supposition. After the passage of the Voting Rights Act of 1965, the percentage of Americans saying they would vote for a well-qualified black candidate rose to 59 percent. Gallup then found that between 1987 and 1997, the percentage in favor jumped from 79 percent to 93 percent. By 1999 the percentage had climbed to 95 percent,[58] declining slightly to 92 percent in 2004.

Americans have supposedly warmed to the idea that if their party nominated a "well-qualified" black presidential candidate, that individual could win their vote. Granted, a willingness to tell a pollster that one would vote for a black candidate is not the same as being faced with that choice. Ironically, the Republican

"If your party nominated a generally well-qualified person for president who happened to be black, would you vote for that person?"

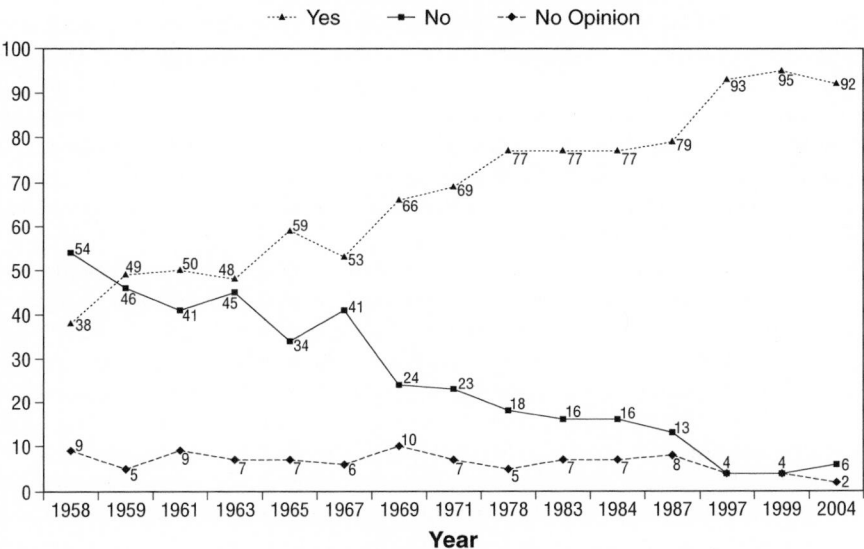

FIGURE 12.1 Respondents' Attitudes toward Black Presidential Candidates, 1999

Party, considered by many as the more conservative of the two major parties, spent time promoting the idea of a black candidate for the 1996 presidential election.[59] For several complex reasons the Republicans may be the first major party to actually put an African American on the presidential ticket.

Notwithstanding that possibility, blacks consider themselves major players in the Democratic Party. In another 2000 poll, it was found that 76 percent of black respondents picked the Democrats as the party that represented their values. Only 13 percent thought that the Republicans represented their values.[60] As I stated earlier, black voters are among the most dependable members of the Democratic coalition.

Most black elected officials are Democrats. Some political scientists hail this change from outsider to insider politics—that is, from protestors to elected officials—as a sign of political incorporation.[61] Others have been more skeptical.[62] In any case the Democratic Party benefits from this deepening sense of ownership.

Nonetheless, this change does raise a series of questions about the meaning of black appointments. Does the presidential appointment of more blacks to high-profile jobs means something more than a RAG? Can perceptions of health and social welfare problems be changed with the appointment of an African American as Secretary of Health and Human Services? Is the symbol worth more than the substance? More importantly, do these appointments hoodwink the supposedly alert media?

Presidents, the Media, and Race

We are told that the ubiquity of the mass media has changed the presidency. The press is the watchdog waiting for the president to act. Scholars debate how powerful the media are or whether they have a liberal bias. Eric Alterman believes that the Washington media have become a punditocracy.[63] Journalists are the new sages who comment on all types of social and political issues on cable television. The growing influence of liberal columnists has spurred the emergence of a counter-group of right-wing commentators. Alterman believes that the losers are the American people, who have not been served by what he considers Orwellian political double-speak.

Other writers worry about the concentration of power in the mass media and how it will affect the airing of diverse political opinions. Fewer people control more and more media outlets. Cities are becoming one-newspaper towns. Most people are getting their news from television. Reagan's aide Michael Deaver asserted that "the picture is everything." If it is, then race progress is measured simply by the dearth of black protests.

In many ways the media have assisted the president in his approach to race conflicts. Most modern presidents have enjoyed a favorable press. The so-called adversarial relationship between journalists and politicians is usually absent when it comes to racial issues. In recent years the White House has institutionalized its relationship to the press. With the establishment of the Office of Communication in the Nixon White House, managing the press has become a full-time job. The Reagan White House demonstrated how easily press management can be accomplished. The staff literally negotiated what was newsworthy—what got covered and how the story was covered. Subsequent administrations have followed that model. Stories about deteriorating conditions in minority communities rarely get covered. And because these topics have gone unreported, presidents can claim they don't know anything about them. Neustadt advises presidents not to use that excuse. He asserts that "To help himself he must reach out as widely as he can for every scrap of fact, opinion, gossip, bearing on his interests and relationships as President."[64] If one carries this advice over to racial issues, Hoover would have wanted to know the details of the trials of the Scottsboro Boys, and Roosevelt would have established a commission to study lynching. Moreover, Eisenhower would have visited the segregated schools in the South. And George H. W. Bush would have visited Rodney King in the hospital.

Because controlling the president's connection with events is as important as controlling the message, Edelman's work on symbols applies here. Presidential actions are instrumental as well as expressive. This symbolic dimension explains why racial events are reflected through partisan ideologies. There is an entire deck of race cards to play, making it relatively easy for a president to define black grievance as a local issue and a protest as a threat to law and order. In 1968 Nixon won the White House partly because he ran on a platform of law and order. As Riley has pointed out, restoring law and order has been a recurrent theme in presidential campaigns. It is both a rationale for action and an excuse for inaction. Most presidents have systematically avoided taking the initiative in race relations. Nation-keeping is a policy legacy that few presidents have been prepared to repudiate.

The media facilitate the process of denial. Because the media, whether television, radio, or newspapers, have a short attention span, they allow presidents numerous opportunities to escape accountability. The Rodney King incident should have been a watershed for American indignation; it was not. President Bush was reported to have said that "watching the King beating made [him] sick."[65] Reporters noted the comment but didn't use their considerable resources to challenge the president's inaction. This, however, did not stop their full coverage of the riot that followed the trial of the police officers. Journalistic outrage was too little and too late. The president got off scot-free.

Another occasion on which the media demonstrated their distractibility was Bill Clinton's National Conversation on Race.[66] After covering the hearings and testimonies, reporters became convinced that this conversation was yet another commiseration enterprise for African Americans. This was a "news hole," (that is, an evanescent event generating no new information) and nothing newsworthy would happen. The Lewinsky scandal provided them with a convenient exit.

Managing Black Expectations

Why has the presidency been so successful in keeping the plight of African Americans off the national agenda? What accounts for relative black acquiescence? First, the president often decides which issues should get the nation's attention and which may be ignored. Presidents who ignore the black experience can count on little reaction from the media or the majority of the public. Such a strategy has guided both Democratic and Republican presidents.

Burman believes that the black experience is "the touchstone for much of the debate in the U.S. public life, one around which ideas of democracy, freedom, justice, and equality take concrete shape."[67] Presidents have not seen it that way. Ronald Reagan was a man who used those terms repeatedly in his speeches, but rarely if ever when discussing black grievances. For Reagan, these ideals were America's inherited entitlements that transcended particularistic objections.

On Tony Brown's television talk show on February 18, 1982, President Reagan seemed genuinely surprised that he had a negative reputation among blacks. He defended himself against such claims. What was so fascinating about this particular appearance is that members of Reagan's staff thought an effort had to be made to disabuse the public of this notion. Allowing the President to appear on a black talk show, albeit on the Public Broadcasting Service (PBS), was seen as a ploy to make the president look like a caring person who might be skeptical of black leaders' partisan claims but not oblivious to the black condition.[68] Besides, Reagan was not afraid to go into the lion's den and answer questions. It was a gesture within the grand spectacle Reagan was constructing. His administration was upfront and forthcoming with blacks. Riley reported a variety of more devious tactics used by other presidents.

Cursory reflection finds Lincoln using the moral authority of his office in attempting to shame prominent black ministers into using their influence to initiate mass black colonization; Cleveland using his rhetorical and symbolic powers to channel support to Booker T. Washington; Wilson sanctioning the political application of federal police powers against Marcus Garvey; Franklin Roosevelt showing the charms of the White House to A. Philip Randolph to stave off an impending march on Washington; the shunning and subsequent embracing by John Kennedy of Martin Luther King Jr. as the perception of King went from radical to moderate in relation to the rise of student insurgency; and Robert Kennedy promising draft deferment for SNCC leaders who ceased demonstrating and moved into voter registration projects.[69]

It is unsettling to discover that so many presidential actions regarding race have been done covertly. This discretion may still be the case in the early 2000s; we don't know. The public was rarely aware in the 1960s and 1970s that deals were being made behind the scenes. Black citizens were never told that their presidents were attempting to avoid taking direct remedial action on their behalf. Yet behind closed doors, presidential staff members worked to keep black grievances off the agenda. Even when presidents indicated that something would be done about racial injustices (e.g. racial profiling), their staff quickly replaced the initiative with other more pressing presidential priorities.

The mechanism of this downgrading of racial issues is facilitated by recurrent racial stereotypes. O'Reilly's book reports that several presidents told jokes about black people.[70] He reports that Reagan often used his stories about playing college football with a black player as evidence he was sensitive to the problems of blacks.[71] Willingness to stand up for a black teammate represented evidence of the President's lack of prejudice. There seems to be an endless supply of jokes and stereotypes that serve presidents who want to avoid taking action. Earl Butz, the Secretary of Agriculture under Presidents Nixon and Ford, came to the public's attention for making an infamous and atrocious joke about the limited aspirations of blacks. Butz was fired, and that supposedly confirmed the forthrightness and determination of President Gerald Ford to stay on top of these issues and not tolerate such behavior. Ford's quick reaction served as a reassurance that people like Butz were aberrations.

In low-balling the race issue, writers help to perpetuate a racial myth. Burman asserts that "Liberal writers cling to the camouflage that the system that has worked to incorporate others will do so for Blacks as well."[72] Blacks will simply have to wait their time in the queue. The reality is that the situation for blacks is not improving in the same way that it has for other groups, tokenism notwithstanding.

Conclusions

We have examined presidential action on racial issues within the context of presidential scholarship. We have separated gestures of racial acknowledgement (RAGs) from situational improvement policies (SIPs) in an attempt to alert students to the confusion often found in the historical literature. Presidential scholars have constructed a fragile office imprisoned by the Constitution and subject to the vicissitudes of politics. The weakness of their approaches lies in their ide-alism. When it comes to race relations, the presidency has rarely been used per-suasively or effectively. A review suggests that both liberal and conservative presidents produced ambivalent records on black civil rights. Only President Johnson's promotion of the Civil Rights Acts of 1964 and 1965 rises above a mere symbol or a racial acknowledgement gesture.

Charles Jones is correct about the nature of the Constitution in that its assign-ment of responsibilities works as a limitation on what presidents can do. Con-gress has not stepped up, however, but has rather abdicated much of its agenda-making role to the president.[73] Skowronek is also correct that most pres-idents inherit policies and that presidents like George H. W. Bush and Bill Clin-ton were preemptive types. Franklin Roosevelt's model of hedging on the race issue, however, or using it as a bargaining tool to save support in the South is no longer creditable.[74] Southern politics has changed, and the "Solid South" has dis-appeared. Southerners no longer dominate Congressional committee chairs, and black people now vote in the South.

Presidents have used the rhetoric of law and order to discourage black protest and to put down demonstrations once they start. Presidents have been reactive rather than proactive. Nation-keeping is not incorporative for blacks. Still, one can find instances in which an apparently small presidential gesture could move white opinion about blacks. These instances speak to the power of the office as an imprimatur in our increasingly secularized society. Clearly, opportu-nities have either been squandered or presidents have not been aware that some-thing could have been done or said.

The image of the president's party affects how racial acknowledgement ges-tures (RAGs) are perceived. Leaders of the Democratic Party have suggested that racial acknowledgement gestures initiated by a Republican president are ephemeral and disingenuous. For the Democratic Party leaders, Republican pres-idents have been forced to make these gestures, but the action does not represent their true attitudes toward blacks; hence, these gestures should be accepted and then safely forgotten. By contrast, a Democratic president's initiated racial improvement gestures are obligatory, authentic and magnanimous, and they should be cataloged and celebrated.

Democratic presidents have insulated themselves from criticism by organiz-ing more symbolic politics like appointing black notables to high-profile jobs, which gives blacks a feeling of incorporation into the party. The Republicans now mimic these tactics and are slowly developing their own cadre of black staffers. They also imitate the old Democratic Party tactics of inviting high-profile black leaders to the White House.

Presidential scholars have aided and abetted this charade by overemphasiz-ing RAGs. In claiming that the presidency is overburdened, they perpetuate the myth of the postmodern presidency. This process is fostered by the view that for-eign policy trumps domestic social policy issues. Constructing this legacy of big issues may be a way in which interest groups manage the presidency.

This essay contends that the imprimatur power of the modern American presi-dency continues to expand, and could be *the* critical facilitator of societal change.

Scholars must acknowledge this social transformation of the presidency. In their writings about the office, they have implicitly advised presidents to regard issues of war and peace as their primary legacy. For them, the battlefield and conference table are where great presidents are made. Presidents have taken their advice and thus have allowed the nation's racial situation to continue to remain precarious.

We need voices that will expand the scope of the presidency rather than counsel temerity. Herein lies the conflict of vision between whites and blacks. Cronin and Genovese point out that Americans are ambivalent about the presidency.[75] They want a powerful leader but are suspicious of centralized leadership. They also want a common man with heroic qualities and uncommon political skills. This is an area in which survey research could be helpful. Is this a white or black vision?

We have seen how presidential scholars have aligned themselves with traditionalists. Presidents have been allowed to ignore one of the nation's most intractable problems. Returning to Madison's notion of the proper role for the president is old-fashioned. Alexander Hamilton was right: African American scholars should join George McGregor Burns and stretch the presidency. This expansion is necessary in order to infuse true accountability into the institution.

Notes

1. See Eric Foner, *The Story of American Freedom* (New York: Norton, 1998); and Celeste Michelle Condit and John Louis Lucaites, *Crafting Equality: America's Anglo-African World* (Chicago: University of Chicago Press, 1993).

2. There are exceptions; see Ruth Morgan, *The President and Civil Rights: Policy Making by Executive Order* (New York: St. Martin's, 1970); Steven Shull, *The President and Civil Rights Policy: Leadership and Change* (New York: Greenwood, 1989); Russell Riley, *The Presidency and the Politics of Racial Inequality* (New York: Columbia University Press, 1999); James Riddlesperger and Donald Jackson, eds., *Presidential Leadership and Civil Rights Policy* (Westport, CT: Greenwood, 1994); and Garth Pauley, *The Modern Presidency and Civil Rights* (College Station: Texas A&M University Press, 2001)

3. Phillip A. Klinkner, *The Unsteady March* (Chicago: University of Chicago Press, 1999); see also Mary I. Dudziak, *The Modern Presidency and Civil Rights* (Princeton, NJ: Princeton, 2000).

4. Stephen Burman, *The Black Progress Question* (Thousand Oaks, CA: Sage, 1995), 6.

5. Peter Bachrach and Morton Baratz, "The Two Faces of Power," *American Political Science Review* 56, no. 4 (December 1962): 947–52.

6. Charles Mills, *Racial Contract* (Ithaca, NY: Cornell University Press, 1997).

7. Riley, *Presidency and the Politics of Racial Inequality*, 10.

8. See Mark Stern, *Calculating Vision* (New Brunswick, NJ: Rutgers University Press, 1992).

9. See Michael R. Gardner, *Harry Truman and Civil Rights* (Carbondale, IL: Southern Illinois University Press, 2002), 106.

10. For an understanding of the use of stories in policy making, see Deborah Stone, *Policy Paradox* (New York: W. W. Norton, 1997), Chapter 6.

11. See Fred Greenstein, *Children and Politics* (New Haven, CT: Yale University Press, 1970).

12. See Mary E. Stuckey, *Defining Americans: The Presidency and National Identity* (Lawrence: University of Kansas, 2004).

13. For a discussion of the presidency by political scientists, see Ray Tatalovich and Thomas S. Engeman, *The Presidency and Political Science: Two Hundred Years of Constitutional Debate* (Baltimore, MD: Johns Hopkins University Press, 2003).

14. Richard E. Neustadt, *Presidential Power: The Politics of Leadership* (New York: John Wiley, 1960).

15. See Thomas E. Cronin and Michael A. Genovese, *The Paradoxes of the American Presidency* (New York: Oxford University Press, 2003), 110–12.

16. See Leon E. Panetta and Peter Gall, *Bring Us Together: The Nixon Team and the Civil Rights Retreat* (New York: Lippincott, 1971).

17. See Steven Shull, *A Kinder, Gentler Racism* (Armonk, NY: M. E. Sharpe, 1993).

18. Murray Edelman, *The Symbolic Uses of Politics* (Urbana: University of Illinois, 1964).

19. An incident in 1906 in which black soldiers were wrongly accused of murder and the President dismissed them without a trial.

20. Edelman, 73.

21. Stephen Skowronek, *The Politics Presidents Make* (Cambridge, MA: Belknap, 2003), 354.

22. Ibid.

23. Bruce Miroff, "The Presidential Spectacle," in *The Presidency and the Political System*, edited by Michael Nelson, 279–80 (Washington: CQ Press, 2003).

24. See Murray Edelman, *Constructing the Political Spectacle* (Chicago: University of Chicago Press, 1988).

25. John David Skrentny believes that Nixon's action still confuses presidential scholars; see John David Skrentny, *Ironies of Affirmative Action* (Chicago: University of Chicago, 1996), 178.

26. Charles O. Jones, *The Presidency in a Separated System* (Washington, DC: Brookings Institution, 1994), 1.

27. Ibid.

28. James MacGregor Burns, *Presidential Government: The Crucible of Leadership* (Boston: Houghton Mifflin, 1965).

29. Harold M. Barger, *The Impossible Presidency: Illusions and Realties of Executive Power* (Glenview, IL: Scott Foresman, 1984).

30. Gerald Ford, "Imperiled, Not Imperial," *Time*, November 10, 1980, pp. 30–31.

31. Richard Pious, *The American Presidency: An Intellectual History* (New York: Basic Books, 1979), 16.

32. Arthur M. Schlesinger Jr., *The Imperial Presidency* (Boston: Houghton Mifflin, 1973).

33. See Hanes Walton Jr., *When the Marching Stopped* (Albany: State University of New York Press, 1988).

34. James David Barber, *The Presidential Character* (Englewood Cliffs, NJ: Prentice Hall, 1972).

35. Harold Lasswell, *Power and Personality* (New York: W. W. Norton, 1948).

36. Ervin Hargrove, *Presidential Leadership: Personality and Political Styles* (New York: Macmillan, 1966).

37. See Michael Nelson, "The Psychological Presidency," in Nelson, ed., *The Presidency and the Political System*, 170–94.

38. Clinton's defenders point to the Earned Income Tax Credit (EITC) as an example of the President's programs to help the poor.

39. Stephen Skowronek, *The Politics Presidents Make*.

40. Ibid., 30.

41. Ibid., 36–38.

42. Kenneth O'Reilly, *Nixon's Piano: Presidents and Racial Politics from Washington to Clinton* (New York: Free Press, 1995).

43. This incident occurred several years before the Goldwater Republicans gained a lot of influence in the party.

44. Eisenhower refused to endorse *Brown*, giving solace to Southerners and unleashing widespread rhetorical attacks on the Warren Court.

45. Edelman, *The Symbolic Uses of Politics*, 81.

46. Fred I. Greenstein, *The Hidden-Hand Presidency: Eisenhower as Leader* (New York: Basic Books, 1982).

47. See Harry Ashmore, *Civil Rights and Wrong: A Memoir of Race and Politics, 1944–1994* (New York: Pantheon, 1994).

48. Ibid., 267.

49. Shull, *A Kinder, Gentler Racism*.

50. See Thomas Edsall and Mary Edsall, *Chain Reaction* (New York: W. W. Norton, 1992).

51. Donald J. Lisio, *Hoover, Blacks and Lily-Whites: A Study of Southern Strategies* (Chapel Hill: University of North Carolina Press, 1985), xvi.

52. Because this act occurred in the 1930s, Lisio assigns a higher degree of political risk to this gesture. Lisio, *Hoover, Blacks, and Lily-Whites*, 135–40.

53. Cited in *Durahn A. B. Taylor, "Black Gotham: Voters, Leaders, and the Political Game in Harlem, 1928–1950,"* (PhD dissertation, Columbia University, 1999), 71.

54. The vote in Harlem shows the growing shift. In 1928 Hoover received 66 percent of the vote, but only 44 percent in 1932. See Taylor, "Black Gotham," 71–72.

55. See Ralph Bunche, *The Political Status of the Negro in the Age of FDR* (Chicago: University of Chicago Press, 1973).

56. After Bush was reelected in 2004, Powell resigned and Rice was appointed Secretary of State.

57. Julian Bond was once nominated from the floor of the convention but declined because he was underage.

58. Bunche, 2

59. See Richard Benedetto, "Color and the 'Litmus Test,' Polls Suggest Many Blacks Are Wary of Powell," *USA Today*, October 10, 1995, p. 9A.

60. Chris Chambers, "Black Americans Maintain Strong Ties to Democratic Party," *Gallup News Service*, August 25, 2000, pp. 1–7.

61. See Martin Kilson's "Report on Black Politics in Comparative Perspective," cited by Gerald D. Jaynes and Robin M. William, eds., *A Common Destiny: Blacks and American Society* (Washington, DC: National Academy Press, 1989), 245

62. See the concluding chapter of Lucius Barker and Mack Jones, *African Americans and the American Political System* (New York: Prentice Hall, 1994).

63. Eric Alterman, *Sound and Fury: The Making of the Punditocracy* (Ithaca, NY: Cornell University Press, 1999).

64. Neustadt, *Presidential Power*, 154.

65. See Richard Lacayo, "For Cops, Fear, and Frustration are Constants," *Time*, April 1, 1991, p. 1.

66. See Wilbur C. Rich, "The Ennobling of Presidential Symbolism: Policy Drift and the Future of Race Relations," *Journal of Public Management and Social Policy* 5, no. 2 (Winter 1999): 37–50.

67. Burman, *Black Progress*, 7.

68. For a revisionist history of Reagan's civil rights history, see Robert Detlefsen, *Civil Rights under Reagan* (San Francisco, CA: Institute for Contemporary Studies, 1991).

69. Riley, *Presidency and Politics of Racial Inequality*, 241.

70. O'Reilly, *Nixon's Piano*.

71. Ibid., 357.

72. Burman, *Black Progress*, 212.

73. See Theodore J. Lowi, *The Personal President* (Ithaca, NY: Cornell University Press, 1985).

74. FDR played the same political game with his former black New York constituency; *see* Taylor, "Black Gotham."

75. See Cronin and. Genovese, *Paradoxes of the American Presidency*, Chapter 1.

PART V

The Subfields

THE SUBFIELDS IN POLITICAL SCIENCE exist in separate universes. Many political scientists do not know the names of people who are outside their subfield. At the annual APSA meeting, members of the the different subfields go to separate panels, talk among themselves, and rarely interact socially. This is true for both black and white political scientists. Not only do they travel in different circles, but they rarely read each other's work. When I began soliciting chapters for this volume, I discovered that I knew very few scholars in international relations, theory, and comparative politics. These subfields have their own APSA sections, journals, and networks. Obviously, they have their own ranking systems. Many of them believe that the APSA and its regional associations are dominated by Americianists.

This separation has taken quite a toll on political scientists of African descent. Because our numbers are so small, it is difficult for us to know each other. There is also the problem that Africans from the continent and Latino and Caribbean political scientists find themselves ensconced in area studies organizations. Although some of them prefer not to be considered African Americans, they are often counted as such by their home universities. Jamaican Americans or Nigerian Americans cannot isolate themselves from the fight for parity.

The good news is that more and more black political scientists are studying international relations, comparative politics, and theory. The essays in Part V reflect this diversity.

CHAPTER THIRTEEN

Comparative Politics and Asia

Contesting Hegemonic Inter– and Intra–Disciplinary Boundaries

GERMAINE A. HOSTON, PHD

All points of view in politics are but partial points of view because historical total-
ity is always too comprehensive to be grasped by any one of the individual points
of view which emerge out of it. Since, however, all these points of view emerge
out of the same social and historical current, and since their partiality exists in
the matrix of an emerging whole, it is possible to see them in juxtaposition and
their synthesis becomes a problem which must continually be reformulated
and resolved.

—Karl Mannheim (1936, 151)

KARL MANNHEIM'S OBSERVATION concerning the constraints on individual views of politics is as valid today as it was nearly three-quarters of a century ago. Forced into exile as Weimar's fragile democracy succumbed to the totalizing ideology of National Socialism, Mannheim was acutely aware of the threat to liberal politics posed by the refusal to accept the legitimacy of a plurality of visions. Preclusion of alternative views of reality and competing images of its immanent potentiality defined the totalizing politics of fascism. It struck the death knell for democracy if such pluralism were not reflected in the pursuit of knowledge as well as in political action. Yet when intellectuals of Mannheim's generation were disheartened by what they saw as the "crisis" or "decline" of Western civilization, it was not only the eclipse of liberalism that they lamented. They also mourned the passing of stable "norms and truths which were once believed to be absolute, universal, and eternal, or which were accepted with unawareness of their implications being questioned" (Wirth 1936, x). Intellectual pluralism is a double-edged sword. If recognizing the legitimacy of diversity and resistance to an imposed "consensus" was the sine qua non of democratic politics, it also seemed to open the door to moral relativism, shaking the very foundations of Enlightenment optimism loose from their positivist moorings.

As the study of politics as a discipline in the United States marks its first centennial, it finds itself on the horns of the same dilemma, particularly with respect
to the study of non-Western societies. It is no trivial matter that the subfield of
comparative politics is generally defined in practice in American academia simply as the study of politics in countries other than the United States—even
though in fact comparative study ought properly to be at the core of any inquiry
purporting to be scientific. The same is true of political theory: Underlying abstract
models and game-theoretic simulations are normative assumptions about the
nature of human beings and relations among them. Such assumptions, even when
largely unacknowledged and uninterrogated, separate the rational choice and
postmodern approaches to politics. The two perspectives barely coexist in the discipline: The latter is largely confined to the subfield of political theory, "a distinctive and often isolated subgroup" (Hollinger 1997) and to area specialists; and
advocates of the two approaches rarely communicate with one another.[1]

Scholars of European and to a lesser extent American politics have made
major advances in drawing intelligible comparisons that combine cross-national
statistical analysis with rich understandings of the cultures in which these political systems are embedded. Nevertheless, the discipline has yet to become sufficiently authentically comparative, incorporating the historically grounded
knowledge of the cultures and languages that mediate political processes that is
required to produce insightful and nuanced comparisons among a diversity of
polities. With advances in computer-facilitated quantitative methodologies, the
study of comparative politics has become bifurcated: Large-n quantitative studies
premised on idealized models mapping American and European politics dominate
the subdiscipline qua "science," while scholarship grounded in a depth of knowledge of other peoples drawing on qualitative as well as quantitative methodologies has been relegated to "area studies," whose practitioners increasingly seek
refuge in the humanities. Ideally, there is no reason that quantitative research
should not incorporate rigorous qualitative analysis and vice versa. In practice,
this incorporation is substantially less likely when foreign language acquisition is
very limited and area studies is devalued as inherently "less sophisticated" research
(Bates 1997, 167–68). As the profile of quantitative analysis has ascended, it has
become more difficult for the average American student to master foreign languages as well as quantitative methodologies and model building. Doctoral candidates who have not already mastered one or more foreign languages before
beginning graduate study increasingly despair of this twofold challenge and resort
to relying exclusively on quantitative skills and abstract models. Lacking the tools
required to discern culturally and linguistically embedded clues to unanticipated
similarity or difference, they risk compromising qualitative rigor.

This language obstacle alone would suffice to relegate the study of the politics of non-Western polities to the periphery of the American academy,[2] leaving
insights gleaned from the study of such societies largely on the margins of mainstream discourse on the broad themes and issues shared across the profession as
a whole. This dynamic has been exacerbated by the tendency for minority scholars to restrict their research agendas to the study of their own groups or of societies in geographical areas associated with their own respective ethnicities.

Historically, such a focus was essential if these groups did not wish to cede the power to define their respective ethnic identities and experiences to colonization, representation, or misrepresentation by others whose scholarship might be (and has been) wielded to advance morally dubious ends.[3] A major strength of centers devoted to East Asian, Latino, and African American studies programs has been their interdisciplinary character, skillfully deploying theoretical insights and methodological approaches from anthropology, sociology, psychology, history, philosophy, and comparative literature alongside the positivist quantitative methodologies of political science. The creation of such ethnic and area studies centers has also functioned as an effective strategy for breaking down the ivy-covered walls of American academia, but it has not been without cost. Ironically, the more frequently such scholars were recruited for ethnic-specific research, the greater the skepticism concerning the quality of their scholarship, devalued precisely because they relied on an intimate knowledge of the languages and subject cultures that are more readily accessible to members of their own groups. Reliance on such programs to recruit minority scholars has thus reinforced their isolation within the university and their de facto segregation from the mainstream of their disciplines. It has also generated conflict among minority groups, pitting them against one another in competition for scarce funds (McClain and Garcia 1993, 269; McClain and Karnig 1990; McClain 1993). Together these trends have reinforced the marginalization of the study of these groups and regions and the ghettoization of its practitioners. As a result, the profession as a whole is deprived of their vital contribution to the plural points of view that Mannheim correctly saw as essential to an accurate, panoptical view of reality.

This essay will identify the major trends in the field of comparative politics of East Asia. It will situate and then assess the contributions that minority perspectives have made or might make to such a panoptical appreciation of East Asia. I argue that the existing hegemonic boundaries within political science, and between that discipline and its sister disciplines, are constitutive of what Foucault called a "rationalization" of knowledge, resulting in power that actually impedes the effort to enhance our understanding of politics. Artificially fragmenting "scientific" inquiry into the subject into barely recognizable constituent parts, these techniques of rationalization mask the true relationships among the different modes of inquiry that are represented in the various subfields and disciplines and their objects. I conclude, then, that minority scholars—indeed all scholars—must expand their research agendas in a manner that will shatter such boundaries and permit their partial perspectives to coalesce to advance scholarship and political action in support of the well-being of all humankind. Because the challenges extend beyond the narrowly political, and their remedies are to be found beyond any one of the narrowly delimited subdisciplines of the profession, scholarly research that contests the frontiers that divide these is essential if the segregation of minority scholars from the main currents of the discipline is to be reversed and the artificial boundaries that inhibit collaboration among these historically subaltern groups are to be lifted to advance shared intellectual and sociopolitical commitments. Such advances promise to unmask and repudiate the hegemonic false logic of politics as a self-defeating, zero-sum game among narrowly construed, undifferentiated individual and group interests in favor of the promotion of universal values to benefit humankind as a whole.

States, Democratization, and Modernity in the Study of East Asian Politics

The study of East Asian politics in the United States has always been highly politicized, the product of the influence of missionary and economic interests collectively known as the China Lobby on United States foreign policy. The country's first research centers established to study East Asian politics were born out of the cold war imperative to study "the enemy"—the Russian Revolution[4]—in order to limit its global influence. The focus on democracy and democratization that has been the hallmark of American political science in general made its impact on studies of the great powers in the region from the outset (Katznelson and Milner 2002, 4–5, 25). The forcible opening of Japan by Commodore Matthew Perry in 1854 was echoed with respect to China in the Open Door Notes, with which American diplomacy opened the new century by claiming the right to acquire any spheres of influence in China that were opened to Europe through gunboat diplomacy. When the cold war resumed after Soviet-American collaboration during World War II, amidst Senator Joseph McCarthy's persecutions, scholars and foreign service officers who were most familiar with China found themselves pursued, accused of being Communists contributing to the "loss" of China, expelled from academia, and shunned for their alleged treason. The research agendas of those fortunate enough to continue in the field were constrained by the political vicissitudes of American foreign policy as long as the remnant regime on Taiwan was granted sole recognition as the legitimate government of China. This policy rendered field work in China virtually impossible for American scholars until the United States adopted a "two-China policy" during the Nixon Administration, dropping its opposition to recognition of the Communist regime on the mainland as the legitimate representative of China while maintaining American support for the defense of authoritarian Taiwan as an island of "democracy." Attention was quickly shifted to Japan, which became the principal outpost of American democracy in the Pacific during its American-led occupation from 1945 to 1952. By the end of the 1950s, academia had registered these cold war imperatives in the notion of *political development*, positing *tradition* and *modernity*, *Communism* and *laissez-faire capitalism*, and *dictatorship* and *democracy* as irreconcilable opposites. The orthodoxy that liberal democracy and economic prosperity went hand in hand was firmly ensconced, and some fifty years later it has persisted (Curtis 1998; Fukuyama 1989; Przeworski et al. 2000), despite the preponderance of evidence to the contrary, especially in East Asia.

This is not to say that the stunning economic success of Japan has made no impact on the field. On the contrary, as the Japanese economic miracle unfolded during the 1960s and 1970s, certain discomfiting realities could no longer be treated without attending to the role that the highly bureaucratic state ruled by a single political party, the Liberal Democratic Party, played in the country's economic development. The conventional wisdom that a powerful activist state apparatus is inherently inimical to economic growth was clearly contradicted by the actual postwar experience in East Asia. Chalmers Johnson's study, *MITI and the Japanese Miracle* (1982), challenged this orthodoxy so long supported by the stagnation of the state Communist societies of the Soviet Union and Eastern Europe. Japan's economically activist state, which dated back to the Meiji Restoration of the mid-nineteenth century, had played a decisive role in the economic growth that enabled Japan to assert military primacy over the former regional powers—China and Russia—by the turn of the twentieth century. Japan then passed on this legacy through colonization to Korea, China, and Taiwan (Hoston 1994; Hoston 1991; Johnson 1987; Johnson 1999; Woo 1991). In terms of democratization, the Japanese experience was especially problematic: Economic growth in Japan was achieved against the backdrop of an alternating sequence of democratizing and authoritarian or militarist tendencies. Even after the conclusion of World War II in the Pacific Theater, when Japan was "forced to be free" under Occupation authorities, for nearly half a century there was no effective parliamentary opposition—which, in a European context, would have been based on labor interests—to the rule of the Liberal Democratic Party (LDP), a party that was neither liberal nor particularly democratic (Pempel and Tsunekawa 1979; Hoston 1987; Deyo 1989). By the time the Asian economic miracle metamorphosed into the Asian crisis of the 1990s, it had engendered a new paradigm explaining how the strong centralized Japanese state had achieved a level of industrial development to rival that of the United States.

Coinciding with studies by scholars "bringing the state back in" (Evans, Rueschemeyer, and Skocpol 1985) after its systematic neglect in studies of politics and government in the United States (long presumed by American scholars to be exceptional in having a government but no "state" as such), the East Asian experience gave rise to a curious paradox. The charge of "revisionism" hurled against Chalmers Johnson brought those influenced by the conservative political "right"[5] and left[6] together to argue for adopting a state-society paradigm to interpret revolutionary change in the context of "late" development. Drawing on Weberian sociology and Marxist-influenced perspectives, new studies elaborated upon Johnson's notion of the "developmental state" (Woo-Cumings 1999a; Johnson 1999) on the basis of first-hand research tracing its trajectory in East Asia (Amsden 1989; Gold 1986; Hoston 1986).

As Johnson described it, the developmental state in Japan was characterized by: its attribution of top priority to economic development for over half a century; an efficient central bureaucratic apparatus; a cultural predisposition to consensus on the part of the population and the willingness of individuals to make personal sacrifices in the interest of the well-being of the community; an analogous readiness on the part of the business community to exercise self-restraint with respect to the particular goals of individual enterprises for the well-being of the economy as a whole; a realistic assessment by Japan's leaders of the obstacles to its development; a history of successful crisis management for most of the twentieth century, beginning with the post–World War I economic recession; a symbiotic relationship between business (*zaikai*) and the state apparatus; and a set of institutional structures and procedures granting sufficient autonomy to the state bureaucracy vis-à-vis the legislative and judicial branches of government for the state to guide economic development. These elements together distinguished Japan's developmental model not only from classic British-style laissez-faire market-dependent development, but also from the state Communist regimes of the Soviet bloc, as well as from the "bureaucratic authoritarian" regimes of Argentina, Brazil, Chile, and Uruguay (Johnson 1982, 305–17; Johnson 1999; Evans 1984).

Variations on the Japanese model emerged as these factors were replicated in Japan's former colonies, specifically (South) Korea and Taiwan (Gold 1986). Political scientists Meredith Woo-Cumings Woo-Cumings (Woo[-Cumings] 1991; Woo-Cumings 1995; Woo-Cumings 1999b) and Atul Kohli have demonstrated how the Korean state's control of finance contributed to its successful industrialization program (Kohli 1999), while economist Alice Amsden cited the Korean state's deliberate price-setting errors as evidence that the Korean example of state collaboration with business offers an alternative model of "late development" (Amsden 1989). The role of the central state's bureaucracy in Japan (Pempel and Muramatsu 1984; Vogel 1994) offered fertile ground for further comparisons with the "neoauthoritarian NICs [newly industrializing countries]"—Indonesia, Vietnam, and Burma (Pei 1998)—and with state-led economic and political development in other parts of the world, including Germany and Latin America (Cumings 1989; Cumings 1998). Meanwhile, the newly available research support drew non-Asia specialists who were applying models based on Western Europe and the United States to the study of East Asia, and Asian politics became the focus of heated political conflict yet again. This time the clash arose on methodological grounds but retraced familiar ideological territory as well. The controversy over the continued value of "area studies," as opposed to models abstracted from Western experiences, quickly rendered the politics of East Asia some of the most hotly contested terrain in the discipline.

The difficulty here has been twofold. The discipline was divided not merely by rival methodological approaches, but also by their competing normative foundations. At issue was not merely a preference for qualitative versus quantitative methodologies and models born of Western societies and applied frequently inappropriately to other societies. Rather, as in the confrontation between "New" and "establishment" political science in the 1960s, at issue were normative biases that rendered an instrumental positivist approach to East Asia premised on Western models suspect to specialists on the region committed to dealing with these societies on their own terms. Deep ideological cleavages divided devotees of an American-inspired institutional approach to politics from those who were convinced that the Asian economic miracle could not be accommodated to the new orthodoxy of political development paradigms. The latter tended to define out of existence the state as such, treating it as a neutral arena in which cost-benefit analyses of particular interests and preferences, largely economic, were conducted, and not as an effective actor endowed with sufficient autonomy from society to promote economic development. Contestation of these issues made East Asia the site of a major bifurcation within area studies itself. Those who sought to treat the region in accordance with Western models on the one hand opposed those who believed that even when the new Western models proved capable of generating plausible accounts of political outcomes, these accounts did not necessarily reflect the dynamics actually at play (Vogel 1999).

The terrain of this contestation extended to post-Mao China, which also refused to comply with the conventional orthodoxy. Recognition of the full implications of the Japanese developmental state coincided with the Chinese Communist Party's (CCP) launch of the "Four Modernizations," intended to lead the country to recovery after the prolonged catastrophe of the Great Leap Forward (1958–1961) and the Cultural Revolution (1966–1976). Here once again a powerful state promoted economic development from above in a manner that diverged dramatically from the Soviet Union's and China's own prior strategies of economic development. China's revolutionary state had penetrated to the roots of Chinese society for nearly half a century, and how that penetration would be affected by the state's new development strategy became a central concern (Shue 1988). The relationship between this state-led industrialization and the prospects for democratization in China became the single most important focus of an entire generation of Chinese students who had been "lost" in the collapse of the country's educational system during the Cultural Revolution and sought to study Chinese development in comparative perspective in American universities. The Tiananmen Square massacre in June 1989 only intensified their resolve to study the relationship between political and economic reform in that country, as such leading dissidents as former head of the Institute of Marxism-Leninism-Mao Zedong Thought Su Shaozhi,[7] joined the debate as new members of the Chinese émigré community. New studies by American-trained Chinese PhDs systematically compared the renewal of political repression in China on the one hand with the rapid and peaceful "velvet" revolutions in East Europe and the changes that marked the bicentennial of the French revolution on the other (Sun 1994; Tong 1994; Tong 1997). The contrast between *perestroika* and *glasnost'* in Mikhail Gorbachev's Soviet Union and developments in China added to the emphasis on the role of the state in economic development that was being brought to bear by specialists on Japan, Taiwan, and Korea (Johnson 1987; Chu 1989; Pempel 1999).

This emphasis on the role of the state did not, however, produce excessive emphasis on the political institutions of the central government either in the case of Japan or in the study of China and other East Asian NICs. The Ministry of International Trade and Industry (MITI), the Ministry of Finance, and the recruitment of suitable candidates through the educational system in Japan all received due attention (Vogel 1994; Schoppa 1991; Hoston 1992). But the vivid contrast with the political liberalization occurring in the Soviet Union and the Eastern bloc illuminated the inadequacy of a focus on institutions that fails to explore the attitudes that those institutions reflect and shape. Just as Hong Kong was preparing for its return to Chinese sovereignty, the devolution of responsibility to the local level and encouragement of individual entrepreneurship produced rapid economic growth on the mainland, drawing attention to local sites of resistance to or support for the reforms (Walder 1995; Walder 1996; Walder 1998; Oi 1989; Oi 1999; Walder and Oi 1999). In China the idealism of Confucius and Mencius had long ago prevailed over its philosophical rivals (Lin 1979; Schwartz 1996); and at the end of the twentieth century, officials and dissidents alike came to agree that the ideational realm and human will or voluntarism—ideas about ideas—were determinative factors in the making of history. Although human action is constrained by much that is beyond the control of men and women, their consciousness is all the more determinative when associated with a state structure that has the capacity to act with relative autonomy from social forces. One might even argue that every state and its institutions reflect an individual or collective consciousness, and that a greater collective consciousness resides in institutions that are representative or democratic in character. This claim, of course, implies that a state that is more fully elaborated ought also to be one that is more democratic in character, yet this aspiration conflicts directly with the mandate for ever more centralized and bureaucratically rationalized state institutions.

This tension within the very notion of modernity itself is evident in the aforementioned accounts of Japan's emergence as a strong modern developmental state. The country had had an abortive series of experiments with democratic institutions prior to World War II, tracing a zigzag course between the dominance of freely contested parliamentary politics and an autocratic imperial system supported by a heavy-handed domestic police force and a military subject to the influence of rogue elements abroad. After the war, the emperor denied his divinity, and the Meiji Constitution that his grandfather had "granted" was replaced by one closely modeled on that of the United States. Yet for nearly fifty years there was no alternation of the party in power in postwar Japan. The prolonged ascendancy of the LDP worked to the advantage of the state's economic strategy, assuring a stable relationship between the state bureaucracy and the business-dominated ruling party. The persistence of this "one-and-one-half" party system presented convincing evidence that Japan's democratization was limited at best.

This shortcoming linked Japan to the other leading actor in East Asia, China. In both cases, the literature on the developmental state has evinced the role played by ideology, by consciousness—including national consciousness—as constitutive, at least partially, of the resolve to achieve industrial modernity and the policies to which it has given rise. The manner in which particular aspects of such consciousness affected the adaptation of such Western notions as liberalism both reflected and affected the trajectories of political development envisaged and implemented by East Asian leaders (Hoston 1992). The work of Nathan (1990; 2002), Su (1993; 1998), Sun (1991; 1995), and Tong (1997) has demonstrated how the relationship between democratization and economic development strategy in Japan, China, and other East Asian countries is mediated by ideas that the actors themselves claim as vital principles to guiding their actions, and by the moral ecology of the local national context in which they seek to implement them. Nihonjin-ron (theories of Japaneseness) in Japan (Befu 1993), Marxist-Leninist and Maoist thought in China, and analogous guiding discourses in other East Asian societies have prevailed over calculation of narrowly construed self-interest by isolated "rational" individuals seeking personal economic gain. These values include ideas concerning private property and property rights (Walder and Oi 1999); what constitutes the moral ecology of the workplace (Walder 1986); public beliefs about the legitimate use of state funds and authority (Sun 1991; Sun 1999); and finally discourses of resistance, views about the circumstances under which resistance to state initiative is considered valid (Su 1993; Su 1994; Walder 1992; Su 1998). Indeed, only by eschewing the thin rationalist view that in fact rests on a rather "thick" account of what ought to go into making policy choices (Pempel 1999; Vogel 1999) can any sense can be made of the relationship between democratization and economic growth in East Asian societies in which the developmental state has been most effective.

This tension between the quest for democratization on the one hand and the need for strong centralized state institutions to be used to protect or advance the interests of the collectivity on the other is by no means unique to the study of East Asian politics. Nor is the siting of political action and initiative at the local level necessarily more beneficial to democratic forces, offering protection from oppression that can only be wielded at the level of the centralized state. Here the centralizing impetus of modernity coupled with nationalistic resistance to perceived inequities in the international system collides with the modern impulses of individuals claiming citizenship rights. This dilemma, as evidenced at the international level with respect to the aspirations of East Asians to be recognized and treated with justice and equality, is mirrored in those who see themselves as members of ethnic groups oppressed in their own lands and abroad. Here East Asian development experiences converge with the aspirations of minority scholars in the United States. It is to the contributions of the latter to the study of Asia that we now turn.

The Comparative Politics of East Asia: In Search of Alternative Voices

The world had barely begun to breathe more easily after the fall of the Berlin Wall and the demise of the Soviet Union, when those whose universe is incomplete in the absence of mortal confrontation resurrected the original East-West divide. Harkening back to Hegel's schema of history as a progressive series of increasingly enlightened civilizations, the thesis of the "clash of civilizations" tidily relegated "Confucian" and "Islamic" societies to the ignominious category of "uncivilized"—or at least less civilized—cultures, condemning the West to a desperate glorious struggle for the sake of its own survival (Huntington 1993a). This language, which fuels the discourse of hatred of and resistance to what Islamic extremists call "the crusaders," has been a self-fulfilling prophesy, one that has found few courageous critics in the United States, especially in the aftermath of the events of September 11, 2001. The ascendancy of this *Weltanschauung* is now complete. Its reflection in American foreign policy and in public discussions of world affairs marks an injudicious return to the "Orientalist" discourse that Edward Said deftly exposed and discredited two decades earlier (1978). As long as the premises of this worldview remain yet again unchallenged, they will undermine serious efforts to understand "the East"—that is, anything that is not "the West"—on its own terms.

It is not fortuitous that the restoration of Orientalist discourse should have coincided with Murray and Herrnstein's revival of racialist discourse in public and scholarly circles (1994). The two arguments are merely two sides—international and domestic—of the same coin (Huntington 1993b; Huntington 1994; Huntington

1993a; Sautman 1995). It would seem self-evident that those who share lineages and cultural ties with the "non-Western" Other also share the same fate and thus the same responsibility to evaluate critically such truth claims and contest the terms of such discourse. They can do so only if they self-consciously breach the hegemonic boundaries within the discipline and between it and related disciplines—boundaries that fragment the totality of the lived experiences of these peoples, shatter their solidarity with contrived and reified distinctions that cloak the ties that bind all humanity from shared origins to common destiny, and segment the interrelated and interdependent aspects of human beings, crippling the ability of those most affected by it to respond effectively.

How, then, have Afro-American[8] and other minority scholars responded to this challenge as it applies to the comparative politics of East Asia? Have they challenged the boundaries scientized by the proponents of racialism to offer alternative voices? Millennium's end augured propitiously enough. The 1990s seemed to mark the decisive emergence of the Afro-American public intellectual through the triumphs of such figures as Henry Louis Gates, Toni Morrison, and Stephen L. Carter, among others. This emergence, however, has not been matched by a significant presence of Afro-Americans in the comparative study of East Asia. The study of African and Caribbean societies is well populated by Afro-American scholars, and the latter have begun to establish a presence in the study of Latin America. Yet despite the East Asian economic miracle that has drawn record enrollments in courses in East Asian languages and cultures across the full range of ethnic groups in the United States, non-Asian minority political scientists have been virtually absent in the study of East Asian politics.

Yet important contributions have been made by such scholars. Interestingly, most of those minority scholars who have worked and published in this field are women. Not surprisingly, gender and other axes of social hierarchy figure heavily in their work. Cheryl Brown, for example, has highlighted the difficulties confronting Chinese women as they seek to realize the Chinese Communist Party's official goal of assuring equality for women (Brown 1994). Her focus on local implementation of policy articulated by central party organizations charged with "women's affairs," primarily the All-China Women's Federation ("an appendage of the Chinese Communist Party"), illustrates the conflict between two desiderata of modernity: an effective central state apparatus on the one hand and the devolution of authority to the local level on the other. While the latter is commonly presumed to be a measure of progress in democratization, localities are often the loci of the most intense resistance to such democratizing measures as the elimination of gender and ethnic discrimination, and only the application of the force of the central government can guarantee their implementation at the local level. This contradiction is a familiar one to Americans, as it was illustrated in the conflict between the claim to states' rights by the Confederate states and the federal government's determination to bring full civil rights to Afro-Americans. The federal government under Abraham Lincoln was forced to resort to war to enforce the abolition of slavery, and federal troops had to be dispatched again to assure integration of educational institutions in Southern states in the mid-1960s. By contrast, in contemporary Japan, the central administration's exploitation of its role in selecting textbooks for kindergarten through high school by approving only those texts that minimize Japan's war guilt has been widely denounced as an anti-democratic force. What if local schools in the former Confederate states had invoked local autonomy to prescribe their own educational content inimical to the interests of Afro-Americans in such a manner? Should elected officials simply parrot views of their constituents that they know to be wrong? It might also be argued that it would be more "faithful" for officials to interpret the vote that brought them to power as a mandate to exercise a more educated and considered judgment even if that judgment diverges from the clearly articulated preferences of the electorate. The introduction of this comparison reframes the problem in terms of such general political theoretic themes as the problem of representation and allows them to be answered more satisfactorily than they would be in the absence of comparison.

Some of the most exciting research in the subfield is the comparative work of Michael Hanchard (1994 and 1999), Melissa Nobles (2000), and Michael Mitchell and Charles Wood (1999), who draw explicit comparisons with respect to Latin America. More recently, Sherry Lynne Martin's study of "Gender, Partisanship, and Political Alienation in Japan and the US" (2002) employs such a comparison between Japan and the United States to illuminate broad differences between male and female attitudes towards politics. Drawing on survey data collected over a twenty-five-year period, the study demonstrates that while both men and women may feel disappointed by the failure of political actors to adhere to behavioral norms, women are more likely than men to feel incapable of doing anything to change this state of affairs. Many of these women express their resulting sense of alienation from the standard operating procedures of traditional, establishment political parties by supporting new parties that presumably offer the promise of an "alternative political process" (2002, Abstract). The significance of this phenomenon is reflected in a dramatic rise in the number of independent voters in a context in which effective choice among the established political parties has historically been limited.

Martin's and Brown's studies highlight the manner in which external events, international events, and developments in other societies expand the range of possibilities for local actors within a single society. Japanese women scored a decisive political victory when Doi Takako rose to the leadership of the second most powerful party in Japan in 1986.[9] They had been heartily encouraged when Doi led a delegation of women to Nairobi, Kenya, in 1985 to participate in the United Nations Conference on the Status of Women, which drew some 15,000 women worldwide. A decade later, in preparation for the fourth event in the series, which drew over 35,000 women to Beijing,[10] the transnational movement extended its impact to Chinese domestic affairs. In order to fulfill China's requirement as host and "as a signatory state to the United Nations Convention on the 'Elimination of All Forms of Discrimination against Women,'" the PRC promulgated a new "Law Protecting Women's Rights and Interests" (Brown 1994, 116–17). Brown's research, however, highlights some of the constraints on such international influences. To assure that the subject of a "previously neglected subfield" be properly situated in the context of its interrelations with other social elements (Brown

1990, 67), it is vital that its agenda be integrated institutionally into existing disciplinary structures, even while drawing on methodologies and conceptual approaches of multiple disciplines.

This admonition does not diminish the tremendous importance of external events in placing such matters as women's rights on a domestic agenda. Such international pressures can constrain as well as expand policy choices, particularly in societies that occupy a subaltern status within a hierarchical world order. Such external pressures were decisive in defining the timing and conditions under which China as well as Japan would make the transition to industrial "modernity." As we have seen, the desiderata associated with this "modernity" were not only defined elsewhere and then received in these societies under duress, but they came into conflict with one another. Western thinkers have commonly described modernity as characterized by "the secularization of society; an increasingly complex division of labor between political and other social functions and in political roles; a sense of nationalist national identity; the presence of a centralized national state providing 'stability and security vis-à-vis internal and external political threats'; increasing levels of popular participation in politics; and a valorization of the state as an appropriate agency for achieving desirable political, economic, and social change" (Hoston 1992, 289). Industrialization and democratization that had previously occurred elsewhere prescribed these objectives, but they also radically proscribed the range of options available to the elites pursuing them in so-called late-developing societies. Moreover, in contrast to the Western European societies that were their examples, in these later-developing societies modernity was not only pursued self-consciously by actors within and outside the ruling leadership, it was also subject to radical reinterpretation as the various aspects of the modernity promoted by Western Europe collided with indigenous values as well as socioeconomic and political structures in East Asia. Teasing out these "competing modernities" and tracing their trajectories in China, Japan, and elsewhere has required scholarship that draws on epistemological and philosophical concepts, theoretical approaches, and methodologies that contest the boundaries among subfields in political science and the frontiers demarcating the disciplines, echoing both factitious distinctions among peoples—most notably the myth of "race"—and the infelicitous compartmentalization of the totality of the human experience into unrecognizable fragments. Transcending these boundaries to enhance our understanding of how these antinomies of modernity have been resolved in Asia in turn leads us to re-interrogate the nature and legitimacy of modernity in the West reflexively.

Transcending Intra– and Inter–Disciplinary Boundaries: The Antinomies of Modernity— The View from Below

The United States has long imagined a "special" relationship with China. This fascination intensified during the twentieth century, and as America's "Manifest Destiny" stretched across the Pacific, it eventually brought a direct confrontation with Japan. The end of World War II, the revival of the cold war, and then the victory of the Chinese Communist Party on the mainland in 1949 conspired to create a new "special relationship" in Asia, this time with Japan. Area studies flourished in support of U.S. foreign policy, and China and Japan drew increasing attention from scholars of political development. Unfortunately, for most of the twentieth century studies of the two countries were somewhat disengaged from the mainstream of a profession that had traditionally focused on Europe and North America. The challenge of attaining fluency in Chinese or Japanese required sufficiently intense effort to discourage the incorporation of the study of these two societies into broader comparative endeavors. This situation began to change in the 1980s and 1990s with the emergence of a new generation of scholars, many of whom had spent part of their lives in the region as U.S. military or diplomatic personnel or their offspring. Coupling a depth of knowledge of East Asia with critical scrutiny of the application of methodologies and theoretical approaches developed in the study of Western Europe, the new studies have explored Chinese and Japanese development through the prism of a range of disciplines, indirectly drawing the two countries into the discourse on the nature and significance of modernity.

Despite the important differences between them, China and Japan have shared common challenges as their leaders sought to define for themselves what *modernity* ought to mean for their peoples. Because their quest for modernity was imposed by external forces, these same forces also constrained the range of options that were feasible for them. Consciousness of these constraints produced strains of thought and programs for action that married aspects of the West European definition(s) of modernity with indigenous philosophico-religious conceptions of the good. Defining that quest inescapably entailed self-conscious reexamination of the received wisdom of indigenous values, even reformulation of national and individual identities, as part of the effort to determine which of the competing visions of modernity would best serve the needs and values of the Chinese and Japanese peoples.

An effective comparison of these judgments must privilege the importance of structures without neglecting the world of thought that has historically been so central to Chinese and Japanese elites. It must allow these leaders to articulate their dilemma in their own terms, capturing the view of the world order from below, so to speak, where that order looks substantially different from its appearance when viewed from atop the global hierarchy. The key here lies in factors that have been highlighted by research in the field of cognitive psychology. As presented vividly in Akira Kurosawa's classic film *Rashōmon* since the 1950s, psychologists have made important advances in understanding how competing, even mutually contradictory, images of a single situation may be held simultaneously by different actors. Led as early as the 1950s by Kenneth Boulding and then by Robert Jervis in the 1970s, American social scientists began to incorporate the results of research on such conceptual images and the result of conflicts among them (termed *cognitive dissonance*) into studies of international relations (Boulding 1956; Jervis 1970; Adelson and Aroni 2002). Two findings of this research are especially noteworthy: (1) conceptual images vary from group to group depending on shared (or different) experiences, values, or culture; (2) when confronted with new information, men and women strive first to incorporate it into their existing paradigms or images of the world. This need for consistency is why a historian of science, Thomas Kuhn, argued that new paradigms arise through "scientific revolutions." Such dramatic paradigmatic shifts emerge only after innumerable attempts have been made to force new information to fit into existing paradigms (Kuhn 1962).

Thus Chinese and Japanese thinkers who confronted the challenges posed by Western definitions of the "new times" (for that is the meaning of *modernity*) first sought to address them within the bounds imposed by their own indigenous values and experiences. In China this tendency resulted in a strained effort to adopt Western technology (*yong*) while maintaining intact the fundamental worldview that was held to define China's national essence (*ti*). To simplify the matter somewhat, one might argue that this effort was ultimately unsuccessful in large part because the key assumptions that supported Western technological development—such as those governing the relationship between man and nature, for example—were in fundamental conflict with traditional Confucian perspectives. It was ultimately impossible to unbundle *ti* and *yong*, and when the (military) supremacy of the technological development forced itself upon China's reluctant elites, the philosophical presuppositions that had resisted it collapsed, taking with them the imperial governance that they had legitimated for two thousand years. The demise of the Qing dynasty at the beginning of the twentieth century thrust the country into revolutionary turmoil from which it had still not recovered a full century later. By contrast, Japan certainly shared much of China's Confucian philosophical heritage, but the frontiers of the values and assumptions that prevailed in Japan were considerably more porous and fluid since Japan had a long history of successful cultural syncretism. By the nineteenth century the Japanese synthesis was such that important elements in Tokugawa culture converged with what Max Weber defined as the ethic that nurtured the development of capitalism in the West (Bellah 1970). The challenge of modernity could be accommodated within Japan's historical pattern of syncretism, enabling Meiji Japan to reinvent itself ingeniously.

But this analysis must be taken a step further, for yet another interaction is at work. There is communication, or interface if you will, between the scholar (with her conceptual images) and the subject of the research—or on the macro level, between the gaze conditioned by the scholar's specific historical situation on the one hand and the society (or unit thereof) that is the object of the former's desire to know it, his "rancorous will to knowledge" (Foucault 1984). The scholar "is not the 'bearer of universal values'" but has a specificity related to her position in her own society and in the world, which in turn has a relationship bringing it closer to or further from the society that is the object of study. "Each society has its regime [or 'political economy'] of truth, its 'general politics' of truth: that is, the types of discourse which it accepts and makes function as true; the mechanisms and instances which enable one to distinguish true and false statements, the means by which each is sanctioned; the techniques and procedures accorded value in the acquisition of truth; the status of those who are charged with saying what counts as true" (Foucault 1984). The closer the situation of the scholar to that of the object of study, the more congruent should be the conceptual images at work, and the more faithfully one can expect the scholar to portray her subject.

In the case of the study of China and Japan, the scholar who recognizes the hierarchical nature of the international system by virtue of her own "view from below" instantly experiences a glimmer of recognition when encountering Chinese and Japanese intellectuals struggling to reconcile their respective indigenous cultural identities with seemingly irresistible external forces. These forces imposed a modernity based on values fundamentally in conflict with indigenous East Asian philosophico-religious perspectives. The dissonance arising out of this confrontation furnished a major impetus for the appeal of Marxist thought to Japanese as well as Chinese reformers and revolutionaries. Marxism, after all, offered an intellectual framework and action program that was based on a radical criticism of the shortcomings of Western bourgeois capitalist modernity. Of course, Marxism was ultimately unable to transcend its own context—its cultural critique of that modernity had been shaped by and reflected its influences (Hoston 1990a, 175ff). For those outside the Western context that gave rise to it, adopting Marxism engendered its own quandaries, the foremost of which I have treated as *the national question*. For here were Chinese and Japanese intellectuals using Marxism to analyze and criticize both their own societies and the Western European capitalist model. They were attracted to this alien system of thought for what it offered to those who would save their countrymen, yet it remained a system of thought that was essentially alien. As if to discourage its advocates from dwelling too long on that difficulty, Marxian socialism repudiated nationalism in theory as a narrow chauvinistic impediment to international unity in socialist revolution. Programmatically, however, Marxism required its proponents to subordinate the interests of the very countrymen one would save in the name of humanism to a higher, more abstract, and thus potentially less human, vision of the good.

By the end of the twentieth century, tremendously rapid political and economic change had repositioned both China and Japan from subaltern status in the mid-nineteenth century to the position of leading economic powers in the global economy. Both China and Japan achieved these gains, however, under the pressures faced by all later-developing societies, undergoing industrialization well after the process had occurred in willy-nilly fashion in Western Europe and had given rise to a continually expanding integrated world economy. The new order was one that carved out exclusive spheres of influence in Asia, Africa, and Latin America; and it compelled leaders of these societies to either accede to the imperative of adopting the West European objectives of "wealth and power," or consign their peoples to economic and political subjugation. This was the first instance in which the national question began to take form. For China, rich in commodities coveted by Western merchants, the encounter with this new order was an especially brutal one. The Qing, itself a foreign (Manchu) but sinified dynasty, had wisely outlawed the opium trade, noting its demoralizing effect on the scholar gentry class that formed its social base. Supported by British gunboat diplomacy, however, by the beginning of the nineteenth century, opium smuggling had become Britain's most potent instrument for offsetting its enormous trade deficit with China. Britain's defeat of China in the Opium Wars in the mid-1800s signaled the end of the classical Chinese view of the world as a moral order in which the culture of the "Middle Kingdom"[11] was presumed to be superior to that of the Western "barbarians," and its emperor was paid tribute by foreign dignitaries in deference to his moral authority. Chinese port cities were suddenly opened to Western residents who would not be subject to Chinese law, and their public parks bore signs indicating, "No Chinese or dogs allowed." Internal economic strains that had been building for two centuries, punctuated by increasingly large-scale peasant rebellions, finally combined with Western pressures to destroy the Qing empire. Japan's experience of cultural syncretism eventually accorded greater esteem to the sword (武) than to the pen (文) and it was the sword that was much better positioned to meet the Western challenge on its own terms. The Meiji leaders nimbly appropriated aspects of Western thought as well as Western technology, adapted them both to their own ends, and by the beginning of the twentieth century had defeated not only China (1895) but tsarist Russia as well (1905).

If Britain took the lead in bringing these challenges to East Asia, the United States played no small part. Indeed, from the Japanese perspective, the American role, for all its disingenuous modesty, was paramount. The United States was completing its rise as a global power, extending its "Manifest Destiny" across the Pacific and directly into confrontation with Japan's rising sun. Domestically, the country's leaders hastened to adopt immigration policies founded on the same racism that legitimated the genocide of the Native American population (whose deepest roots reached back to Asia), as well as the enslavement and continued repression of peoples of African descent. The new measures were intended to prohibit the arrival of still more of those peoples over whose territory the United States was poised to share dominion with Western European powers. The value of China and its civilization as a whole had become the object of derision: "China is the reservoir of cheap labor of the world," opined representatives of the Knights of Labor, including a California congressman. "[S]he has wrought no wonders and performed no service to humanity" (McNeill 1886, 429, cited in Iton 2000, 32). Another Californian complained that "the Chinese were enough to make people wonder that nature and custom should so combine to manufacture so much individual ugliness." The fates of all the nation's "racial" minorities were unambiguously intertwined. "No inferior race of men can exist in these United States without becoming subordinate to the will of the Anglo-Americans. . . . It is so with the Negroes in the South; it is so with the Irish in the North; it is so with the Indians in New England; and it will be so with the Chinese in California" (Saxton 1971, 18, 19, cited in Iton 2000, 32).

Japanese were not exempt from such derision, despite their country's rise in the global order. The anti-Chinese legislation was soon extended to apply to other Asians, while on the international stage the Western powers estimated Japanese military power to be worthy of only three-fifths of their own at the London and Washington Naval Conferences. Such treatment did not pass unnoticed by Japanese and Chinese leaders and activists, whose discourses about their countries' future economic and political development revolved heavily around the problématique of identity, nationalism, and modernity. Marxism-Leninism promoted itself as the most advanced strain of Western thought, confronting these concerns in a manner that was critical of Western capitalism. In addressing the problématique of the *national question,* Chinese and Japanese thinkers fashioned their own, often prescient, understandings of the nature of the international system, and they offered solutions that transcend conventional discourses of "modernity" and "tradition," "East" and "West." Moreover, they did so in ways that asserted normative equivalency between their "East" and the Europe that had fostered the political theoretical framework that guided their work.

Until the 1980s, the cold war cast China and Japan in opposing roles in support of American foreign policy. China was but the first "domino" to succumb to the influence of the Soviet Union, while Japan had become the bastion of democracy in the Pacific. This view held that Japan had been immune to the taint of Marxism. To be sure, Japan too had had a Communist party, but American scholarship on it revealed not an intellectually dynamic indigenized system of thought like that of Mao Zedong's Sinified Marxism, but a mechanistic, uninspired ideology imported from abroad and slavishly followed as the Soviet Communist line in Japan.

Recent scholarship drawing on interviews with the last surviving participants in Japan's left-wing movement has revealed that the true picture was quite different. There was not only a vital indigenous Marxist movement in Japan, but also lively debate that drew its Marxist participants into pioneering comparative scholarly work on the development of capitalism in Japan (Hoston 1986; Hoston 1994). They produced innovative interpretations of Japan and East Asia that anticipated by nearly half a century Immanuel Wallerstein's world systems approach (Wallerstein 1976) and dependency theory. From where these scholars were situated, the global order was clearly hierarchical, and yes, this hierarchy was grounded in racism on the part of the leaders of the Western powers as well as in purely "objective" economic forces. Takabatake Motoyuki, who played a major role in introducing Marxism-Leninism into Japan, cited the Washington Naval Conference to argue that the *tatemae* (façade) of peacemaking through arms control concealed the true objective of the Western powers: to force Japan back into its former inferior position alongside other Asian peoples (Hoston 1984b, 57). "We recognize that the present oppression and exploitation of the colored peoples by white peoples is not to be permitted, and we hope for their complete liberation by the unification of all colored peoples and their formation of a large league of nations," he declared (Hoston 1981, II, 552). His conviction that the international hierarchy was unjust in its racialist character made Takabatake mistrustful of Lenin's prescription of "stateless" internationalism for Japanese revolutionaries. Bolshevik "internationalism" was nothing other than Russian nationalism, he asserted, and if such nationalism was appropriate for the Bolsheviks, so it was for Japan's socialists as well. By 1919 Takabatake invoked his reinterpretation of Marxism-Leninism as authentically "statist" in order to found a Marxian national/state socialist party (Hoston 1984b).

Takabatake's view was not exceptional in Japan. Many Marxian students of Japan's economic development in the global context shared with those conventionally associated with the right-wing righteous indignation at Japan's plight. In an argument heavy with racialist overtones, the influential economic columnist Takahashi Kamekichi deplored the unfairness of the distribution of global resources, which, he claimed, was reinforced by racism on the part of the Western powers. Given its meager natural resource base, Takahashi argued, Japan was obliged to pursue expansion onto the Asian mainland, because the imperialist powers of Europe and America had unjustly appropriated resources that were far out of proportion to the needs of their peoples. Japan was burdened with a population density that was ten times that of the United States and Europe. Yet North America's 6.6 percent of the world's population monopolized 28.7 percent of the world's natural resources and foodstuffs; and adding insult to injury, the United States invoked fear of the "yellow peril" to prohibit the "colored races" from immigrating into its bountiful territory (Hoston 1984a, 15). Takahashi astutely observed that once the West had developed industrial capitalism and built a global economic order thereupon, no other nation could possibly develop industrial capitalism in the same manner again. As Germany had been precluded from building a comparative advantage in textiles because Britain, with its outposts in India, had carved out an exclusive advantage in that industry, so too Japan's options for economic development were constrained not only by British dominance in textiles but by German supremacy in other industries. Given the limitations of its natural resource base, Japan, originally a subaltern power, was in danger of remaining so, particularly in the hostile international order that it confronted (Hoston 1984a, 24).

Not surprisingly, this analysis led Takahashi to join Takabatake in his wariness of the Comintern's strictures on Japanese nationalism. In his view, the new Soviet Union, with its immense natural resource base and legitimate claim to be at least "semi"-European (Baron 1958), shared in the Euro-American domination of the world order. The Bolsheviks' repudiation of Japan's nationalism and military and economic expansion onto the Asian mainland, which he viewed as indispensable to Japan's survival, was suspect as an effort to relegate Japan to a subaltern position alongside by other "enslaved" Asian peoples (Hoston 1984a, 12–15; Hoston 1984b, 57). In the increasingly shrill wartime environment of the 1930s and 1940s, the powerful group orientation of Japanese national identity, represented by an emperor considered divine, intensified. Within just a few years after the Manchurian Incident (1931)[12], virtually the entire Japanese left-wing movement "changed direction" (tenkō) en masse, renouncing ties to the Soviet Union and embracing the national mission to defend the emperor (Hoston 1983).

Because China was the victim of Japanese expansionism as well as of Western imperialism, nationalistic Chinese revolutionaries did not have to make the same excruciating choice as their Japanese counterparts. In both China and Japan, however, the desire to assert moral equivalence with the West gave rise to efforts to reinterpret imported Marxist ideas in terms of indigenous spiritual values (Hoston 1990a; Hoston 1990b). Just as African nationalist and pan-Africanist leaders have done in ensuing decades, Chinese and Japanese reformers and revolutionaries sought to unravel the complex web of structures and values that had been woven by what they saw as the nefarious influences of foreign capital, to "return to the source" (Cabral 1973; Nyerere 1968; Walters 1993, 61ff; Rodney 1972), to recapture a pristine pre-imperialist national essence on the basis of which they could formulate a new, better society for their own peoples.

In East Asia, we know that in the form of the Greater East Asia Co-Prosperity Sphere, Japan's assertion of the nativist claim to support its "younger sisters and brothers of Asia" (Clemons 1995) became little more than an apology for what Orlando Patterson has called "ethnic chauvinism" (Patterson 1977). Half a century later, a similar discourse reappeared to celebrate the Asian economic miracle, this time articulated by such leaders as Lee Kuan Yew in Singapore (Sautman 1995). Such discourse had played a major role in the Pacific War because the Meiji state had had such singular success in reinventing Imperial traditions to unify and reassure its population that in fact nothing had changed, even in the midst of the upheaval of a state-led industrializing revolution from above (Hoston 1991; Fujitani 1993). The Meiji oligarchs artfully manipulated imagery associated with traditional Japanese religious beliefs (Shinto) to invent new traditions centered around the figure of the emperor, who had been eclipsed by regents and shoguns in Japanese political consciousness for centuries. The Meiji Restoration made him visible and immediate in the hearts and minds of his subjects (Fujitani 1996). Elaborate pageantry confirmed the emperor's exceptional position in the re-imaged polity—the new constitution was one he had "granted" to his people. The emperor's spiritual authority as the direct descendant of the Sun Goddess overshadowed the legal positivism associated with the theory of state sovereignty that the new constitution borrowed from German *Staatsrecht* thinkers. The new orthodoxy—the family conception of the state (*kazoku kokka*)—held that all Japanese (*minzoku*) were but a single extended family, of which the emperor was the head (Ishida 1954). If the emperor was divine, then by extension all Japanese were superior to other peoples by virtue of being part of his divine family. This mythology functioned as the quintessential Socratic lie, which Plato describes in the *Republic* as the "noble lie to persuade, in the best case, even the rulers, but if not them, the rest of the city" that the new rulers were legitimate. The Meiji formulation precluded legitimate criticism of this view of the emperor and of nationalistic actions that might flow therefrom. "Absolute values [were] embodied in the person of the Emperor himself, who [was] regarded as 'the eternal culmination of the True, the Good, and the Beautiful throughout all ages and in all places'" (Maruyama 1969, 8). This variety of racialism provided its own justification. In mistreating Chinese or Filipinos during the war, for example, the Japanese "perpetrator [of war crimes] was conscious of the comparative proximity of himself and of his victim to the ultimate value, that is, to the Emperor" (Maruyama 1969, 12).

Since World War II, Japanese racism has been the single most common focus of work by Afro-American scholars. Anthropologist John Russell's research originated with impressive work on anxiety disorders in Japan (1989), deploying a comparative approach to interrogate the social and cultural contingency of the diagnosis and treatment of mental illness. Russell has drawn on his background in psychology to write on racism in Japan specifically with respect to images of

Afro-Americans represented in Japan. "The problem isn't just *Little Black Sambo*," he argues (1991b). Rather, the point is the reflexivity of such an image, how difference contributes to identity. Russell's work demonstrates how images of Afro-Americans—"the black Other"—operate in Japanese society as a transferal mechanism to help the Japanese situate themselves in their own subordination to Europeans and North Americans (Russell 1991a; Russell 1996). Russell's analysis echoes that of Maruyama in its invocation of the psychological device of transferal. Maruyama argued that "by exercising arbitrary power on those who are below people manage to transfer in a downward direction the sense of oppression that comes from above, thus preserving the balance of the whole." This psychological mechanism applied to the anthropomorphized collectivity of the Japanese nation as well: "Since the latter part of the Tokugawa Period Japan had never ceased to be conscious of the close and heavy pressure of the Great Powers, and as soon as the country was unified it used its new strength to stage a small-scale imitation of Western imperialism [what Takahashi Kamekichi termed "petty (bourgeois) imperialism"]. Just as Japan was subject to pressure from the Great Powers, so she would apply pressure to still weaker countries—a clear case of the transfer psychology" (Maruyama 1969, 18). Thus, much as Frantz Fanon once sought to penetrate the racism of the colonist in psychological terms in his *Peau noire, masques blancs* [Black skin, white masks] (1952), Russell describes the roles that images of Afro-Americans play in situating Japaneseness in this global context. For all such indigenous racialist impulses with respect to Chinese and Koreans, Russell argues that the specific negative Japanese imagery of Afro-Americans is almost entirely borrowed from the United States itself. Images of Afro-Americans first began to proliferate in Japan after the arrival of Commodore Perry's "black ships" in 1854. Where previously, the only difference between white and black American figures in Japanese etchings had been in skin color, gradually other stereotypical features were borrowed from American representations of black Americans. Likewise, the offensive remarks made by Japanese Prime Minister Yasuhiro Nakasone in 1986 and by Watanabe Michio, the head of the ruling Liberal Democratic Party's Policy Research Council, shortly thereafter concerning the influence of Afro-Americans upon American society "were heavily indebted to Western discourse on the theme of race and difference" (Russell 1996, 18–19).

Anthropologist Eric Clemons's research on membership and social exclusion of non-Japanese employees moves beyond an initial focus on images of black Americans (1990) to find that in general "the ideal of a collective national identity in Japan is based on modern-day notions of a 'Japanese race.'" Clemons "problematizes the concept of race in Japan to critique nation, race, and ethnicity as malleable (at times competing and other times eliding) theoretical and practical constructs of identity formation that inform a Japanese sense of self" (1999, Abstract). This approach enables Clemons to speak to Japanese images of themselves in terms of a "race" apart, as a people who historically has wished to be placed in the same category as Chinese, Korean, and other Asian peoples only when such placement has served Japan's expansionist ambitions. American social scientists know well that this instrumental use of the notion of "race"—its service to established power—is not unique to Japan or to East Asia. Only in problematizing the illusory notion of "race"—and keeping it firmly between quotation marks wherever we encounter it—can we expose the vacuity of its truth claims and unmask the true social and political functions that its preservation serves. Whenever it is not subjected to such critical scrutiny and repudiated, "race" is endowed with legitimacy, reified, and allowed to replace rigorous analysis in reductionist fashion. It is to this problem that we now turn.

What Is To Be Done?
Beyond the Discourse of "Race"

If throughout its existence, American political science has been, in Charles Lindblom's words, "not . . . a field of conventional scientific inquiry but a continuing debate about specific subjects and claims" (Katznelson and Milner 2002), the debate has been extraordinarily circumscribed. One would have thought that the rise of the multinational corporation and other transnational actors would have opened the discipline to research of new sites of political action. If democracy has been the primary focus of the discipline, then the spread of democratizing movements throughout the postcolonial world should have heralded new voices from a more diverse array of scholars; and an impact on the content and terms of that debate ought to be in fuller evidence half a century later.

Such limitations in discourse about politics in the American polity are manifested in the structural characteristics of the discipline. We have already noted the physical and intellectual segregation of the treatment of "race"—and ethnicity–related concerns from the mainstream of the discipline. Non-Western political philosophers are systematically neglected within the subfield of political theory, and interested students must seek their contributions as relatively minor elements of comparative politics courses on these regions, because their ideas are not included in the standard curriculum in political theory. In American politics, some of the most problematic aspects of the American experiment in democracy, as in the relationship between state power and inequality and injustice in civil society, have risen to prominence largely as a result of the work of scholars trained in other disciplines, notably sociology.[13] The tendency to privilege research questions that can be quantified and emphasize how (well) American institutions operate and apply their (often peculiar) characteristics as the basis for models to be applied to describe politics in general and assess other political systems injects an inherently conservative bias.

Students of "race"-based inequalities have resisted many of these tendencies, but they and their concerns remain on the periphery of the field. A cursory review of previous "state of the discipline" volumes finds virtually no mention of work by Afro-American, Latino, or Asian-American scholars outside the article or two allocated to treating minority politics and "race"—concerns that figure in virtually all issues treated in all the subfields in the discipline. In this respect, the volumes reflect quite accurately the true state of affairs in political science. Minority voices remain muffled in the side corridors, and important claims on which they might make a contribution that is critical to achieving an accurate panoptic of politics in all subfields remain uncontested in the "debate" to which Lindblom refers.

Institutionalized "race"-based barriers persist within and beyond academia, and those who have made them a central focus of their research are redressing a major deficiency in the discipline. Yet one's primary focus need not be racism or the oppression of one's own ethnic group in order to combat these. The "minority" voices that we have examined here make important contributions to global efforts to unveil and redress inequities; but in the study of East Asia there are extraordinarily few such voices. Minority scholars ought to insist on being engaged in the study of all peoples and civilizations, just as their peers have done. The discipline needs to benefit from the perspectives of persons of all ethnic backgrounds on the concerns of all the subfields as they affect all regions of the world. When each group studies only its own group, it isolates itself from others with shared histories and fates, and it risks sacrificing on the altar of particularistic identities the larger truth of the unity of all mankind in the only race there is—the human race.

Scholars of African descent must exercise special vigilance with respect to the consequences of this pattern. Surely as the most privileged of their group(s) globally speaking, they have a moral obligation to use their expertise to help resolve challenges that face their own group(s), but the fate of no group is determined in isolation from that of humanity as a whole. Afro-Americans are diminished by iniquities visited upon any and all other groups, just as the humanity of those who are members of historically hegemonic ethnic groups is impaired by harm done to their neighbors both near and far. This is precisely why it is essential that racism itself not be permitted to limit the research agendas of its victims. This subject is properly the territory of scholars from all backgrounds, and there are finally hopeful signs that the civil rights struggles in the United States are bearing fruit in sensitive treatments of the problem by scholars of increasingly diverse backgrounds (e.g., Appiah and Gutmann 1996; Hochschild 1997; Hochschild 2001; Sautman 1995; and Malcomson 2000). The difficulty arises in that efforts to focus on the problem of racism tend quickly to devolve into discussions of "race."[14] The more ink spilled discussing it, the more readily the tiresome quotation marks that should always bracket it to signal its speciousness fall aside (cf. Gates 1986), and the more the empty notion of "race" is reified, the greater the legitimacy imparted to it. In any event, since every "ethnicity" offers but a partial image of the larger whole of humanity, the quest for social justice requires a sense of that larger whole if the multiethnic coalitions required to attain it are to be forged (Wolfe and Klausen 1997).

We can best approximate that larger whole by contesting the interdisciplinary and intra-disciplinary boundaries that have reinforced the fragmentation and isolation of the various aspects of the whole of human experience, including ethnicity. Such boundaries have contributed to an unwarranted reticence among minority scholars in offering the bold propositions required of decisive contributions to social science theory. A prominent exception is Edward Said, the Palestinian scholar whose devastating critique of orientalism in European literature revolutionized not only the study of the Middle East but the study of the non-Western world here in the West as a whole. Said's work exemplifies how intellectual boundaries must be overcome if we are to revolutionize received understandings that continue to impose hierarchy and cast Asian, Latin American, and African peoples in a subaltern role. One must not be intimidated by the virtual certainty that theoretical insights and tools borrowed from other disciplines will be greeted with mistrust. There is something liberating about erasing the boundary lines that delimit the range of legitimate inquiry. Is not doing so the very essence of the paradigmatic shifts that constitute scientific revolutions?

Key findings of recent scholarship on Asia suggest that such a paradigmatic shift might be timely, even vital, to make sense of the lived experience of most of the world's peoples; they also suggest the directions in which this shift might take us. We have already commented on the notion of the developmental state, but we have yet to consider how its articulation in the area of "late development" in East Asia might influence our understandings of "first world" politics. One problématique that needs to be reformulated in light of these Asian experiences has to do with the relationship between state activism and political and economic democracy. It would be simple enough from the vantage point of the exceptionalist conceit of stateless government in the United States to conclude simply that the activist state is in fundamental conflict with liberal democracy. But a reconsideration of Western trajectories of industrialization and democratization in light of what we have learned in East Asia suggests that this assumption has it wrong.

Part of the problem lies in the relationship between the two components of the notion of "bourgeois democratic revolution" (or in current parlance, "modernization"): the economic transition to industrial capitalism—which Marx conceptualized on the basis of the British model—on the one hand, and the political demise of monarchical autocracy and theocratic power with the rise of liberal democracy, which was based primarily on the French Revolution. If we reverse the geographical referents of the two components by considering the economic development of France alongside the political development of England in the light of the East Asian experience, we find that the relationship between the state and economic development might in fact never have been as it was presumed to be in the West, and that the democratic component of "modernity" was in fact received with far less enthusiasm in the paradigmatic Western cases than we have presumed.

The record shows that the relationship among the state, democratization, and industrialization was not definitively settled with the radical breach of 1789. The ensuing Terror destroyed many of the French Revolution's most democratic architects, and the post-revolutionary order hurtled between Bonapartism and its variants on the one hand and parliamentarian democracy on the other, well into the twentieth century. Nor was a transition to democracy uniformly welcomed enthusiastically by its putative beneficiaries, the working men and women of France. On the contrary, there was an immediate and prolonged backlash against the Revolution, which was reflected not just among the aristocracy but also in the rise of fascist tendencies within workers' parties that one would ordinarily have expected to associate with the political left (Sternhell 1978; Sternhell 1983). Intellectually, this backlash was expressed in an anti-Marxist historiography that finally triumphed two centuries later in the reinterpretations of Cobban and Furet (Cobban 1955; Furet and Richet 1965–66). This backlash, expressed in Britain and Prussia by Edmund Burke and G. W. F. Hegel, contested the view of the

Revolution in 1789 as a progressive, salutary turn in human history. The first centennial of that revolution was greeted with rancorous division within France on precisely this point, when many labor leaders condemned it as the forcible introduction of an artificial and inherently corrupt political order that destroyed what had been a good and authentically French organic polity. The new order rewarded the partial private interests of politicians by introducing schisms among a naturally harmonious population for personal gain. It might be noted that these sentiments were not unlike those that inspired suspicion of competitive party politics in late imperial China (Wakeman 1972).

These sentiments were also echoed subsequently in Hitler's *Mein Kampf*, which invoked the inherent virtue of an organic polity to denounce the machinery of competitive democratic politics. If such sentiments erupted so explosively not only in interwar Germany, Japan, and Italy, but in the very soil of the prototypical "bourgeois-democratic revolution" in France, then perhaps it is erroneous to associate these fascist movements only with "later industrializing societies." We might also need to reexamine them in light of the identity claims made against modernity in still other settings (e.g., Islamic and African societies), as they interact with other social forces resisting industrialization, such as religious movements and sub-state actors.

Such resistance is related to a second set of findings, which can be summarized in a caveat concerning institutional overdetermination. A major trend in comparative politics over the past fifteen years has been an emphasis on institutions. Following the focus on revolutionary change that dominated the 1950s through 1970s, the discipline as a whole seemed to yearn collectively for the stability promised by institutions. Governed by universally applicable, rationally derived "preferences," the installation of structures and procedures that are similar enough from one society to the next seems to assure the predictive power that one ought to expect from a science of politics.

Studies of East Asian politics, however, underscore the danger of presuming that similar institutional configurations will necessarily operate similarly and yield similar results. The advent and persistence of the Asian financial crisis is but one indication of this problem. Even when consciously borrowing from Western institutional models, Asian leaders have consistently adapted these to suit their own indigenous values and requirements, resisting efforts to force the politics of very different societies onto the Procrustean bed of institutionalism. The Meiji oligarchs and their successors, and China's revolution from Mao's time through its succession, vested institutional arrangements that superficially resembled Western and Soviet structures with very different philosophical and cultural content, resulting in dramatically different patterns of political practice. This phenomenon is neither new nor unique to Asia; nor is the plurality of cultures and continual renewal of inventiveness that it signals inherently regrettable. These societies too have contributions to make, not all of them necessarily nefarious simply because they diverge from patterns laid down elsewhere. The new institutionalism, then, may offer a theoretically parsimonious explanation for a set of political outcomes across a specific culturally homogenous landscape, but it may well be less effective in predicting outcomes than in helping to identify how and why the dynamics of politics in action can differ very widely behind the façades of very similar structures.

As the preceding discussion of the vicissitudes of democratic modernization in France underscores, imposing models premised on idealized Euro-American experiences over the past millennium as a standard for evaluating Others is wrong-headed. These trajectories were in fact remarkably bloody, and were greeted with both internal and external resistance that ought to give pause to those who would wield them as examples by which to condemn Others. Perhaps, as Takahashi Kōhachirō has asserted, the paths forged by Western European countries—specifically the collapse of their feudal structures, which triggered these trajectories—were not the norm but rather the exception (Takahashi 1976, 74, 95–96). Perhaps, then, some other standard should be sought, one that affirms difference without relinquishing moral imperatives to assure the primacy of genuinely humane humanism, one that does not excuse inhumanity by reference to particular ends elevated to universal status, one that renounces instrumentalizing the majority of the world's peoples in service to such ends. This is a task to which contributions of scholars from all backgrounds are essential.

Notes

1. See Catherine Zucker's attempt to simulate such an encounter (1995). For a related critique of "the centrality of interest-based explanation" in the discipline, see Blyth (2003).

2. I specify the American academy, for this seems to be less of a problem in Europe, where ordinary citizens often have a working knowledge of two or more languages—although it is rare that one of these would be an Asian or African language.

3. See Edward W. Said's trilogy for a critical discussion of the ways in which such uses have supported the subordination of the Palestinians and other Muslim peoples of the Middle East (Said 1981; 1978; 1993).

4. Harvard's East Asian Studies Center, which quickly became the leading such center in the country, was initially founded under the auspices of the Russian Research Center. The first publications to emerge therefrom, beginning with Benjamin I. Schwartz's *Chinese Communism and the Rise of Mao* (1951), were sponsored by the Russian Research Center.

5. Johnson's other work, on revolutionary change, drew heavily on Talcott Parsons's systems equilibrium approach that understood change, particularly revolutionary change, as exceptional and to be avoided whenever possible (Johnson 1966). Johnson's study of the victory of Communism in China—which he compared to the rise of Tito in Yugoslavia—heavily discounted the appeal of Marxism-Leninism-Mao Zedong thought in favor of a thesis that the Chinese revolution was preponderantly a nationalist revolution (Johnson 1962).

6. Barrington Moore's Marxian typology of three paths to industrial modernity (1966) directly inspired Theda Skocpol's comparison of the role of the state in the French, Russian, and Chinese revolutions (1979) and other studies asserting the relative autonomy of the state vis-à-vis society, particularly in later-industrializing societies (Trimberger 1978).

7. Throughout this essay, Asian names are given in their customary order, with the family (last) name preceding the personal (first) name.

8. I have elected to use the term *Afro-Americans* in preference to "African Americans" or "blacks." Here I am substantially in agreement with Orlando Patterson's rather harsh judgments on the problems posed by the latter two terms. Patterson argues persuasively that, given the "historically and culturally ingrained and dictionary sanctioned meanings of" the term *black* as opposed to *white*—which consistently connotes virtue, purity, and thus moral superiority—it was "linguistically naive, culturally obtuse, socially inept, and politically stupid" for leaders of the Afro-American community and their supporters from other groups in "to insist on a return to" the terms *black*

and *white* as appropriate references for Americans to use in regard to one another during the 1960s. Similarly, *African Americans* "mutes the Americanness of Afro-Americans [. . . which is "politically unwise"]" and "fails to distinguish" this population from "the growing number of immigrants from Africa who . . . are far more culturally different from Afro-Americans than are Afro-Americans from any group of Euro-Americans" (Patterson 1998, xxi-xxii). Finally, this group could also rival Edward Said's claim that the Palestinians constitute a universal class (in the Hegelian sense) because of their experience as an oppressed group (Said 2003), in that Americans of African descent who are not also of Native American (and thus ultimately Asian), Latino, or European descent are rare. The historic dominance of the "one-drop rule" for defining Americans as "black" alone ought to have sufficed to invalidate these labels in the eyes of Americans of African descent. In any case, given the tendency for the members of various ethnic groups to intermarry, the designations *Afro-American*, *Latino*, and *Asian American* promise to be short-lived as mutually exclusive identifiers.

9. Doi was the first female party leader, holding this position as head of the Japanese Socialist Party (Nihon Shakaitō) from September 1986 through mid-1991. After the velvet revolutions in Eastern European and the collapse of the Soviet Union, the party changed its name to the Japanese Social Democratic Party (Shakai Minshutō, or Shamintō) in order to distance itself from the Stalinist past of its alliance with the Soviet Union.

10. http://www.feminist.org/global/beij902p.html (accessed January 20. 2004).

11. "Middle Kingdom" is the literal meaning of the Chinese characters 中国 (*zhongguo*) that represent China.

12. In a plot led by Japanese field officers, a bomb was exploded on the Japanese railway north of Mukden in Manchuria on September 18, 1931, thereby providing a pretext for the launch of full-scale war against Chinese troops in Manchuria.

13. The relatively recent attention to the welfare state has come from scholars trained in sociology. Frances Fox Piven and Richard A. Cloward's extraordinary study, *Regulating the Poor* (1971), Theda Skocpol's work on the welfare state (Skocpol 1982), and even Chalmers Johnson's work on the developmental state are all examples of this trend.

14. Cf. Appiah 1989, 44–46, 48. The point here is not to deny difference. Modern identity is socially constructed, premised on first identifying fundamental similarities with others (men as "men," etc.), then differentiating ourselves from them (Hoston 1987). The elasticity of the term "race" is to be noted here; for it has not always been a black v. white issue. Japanese have long viewed themselves as a special "race," comparable to Jews (Shillony 1991); Anglo-Canadians have viewed French Canadians as a "race," just as Anglo-Saxons have treated the Irish as a separate race (Iton 1994). In each case, clearly "race" is something attributed to someone else, some "Others" regarded as inferior to one's self. As Jeff Spinner has noted, "race" differs from "ethnicity" in that "race" is an "an imposed identity" (1994, 19). Like Sartre, Spinner finds that "racial boundaries . . . are not simply matters of cultural identity but of political and economic power" (Grady 1996, 265–66). Thus, even if the Jew—or the Afro-American—were to minimize evident "racially based" differences, she would still continue to find herself stigmatized by that imposed "racial identity."

References

Adelson, Marvin, and Samuel Aroni. 2002. Differential images of the future. In *The Delphi method: Techniques and applications*, ed. Harold A. Linstone and Murray Turoff. Reading, MA.: Addison-Wesley. Originally published, 1975.

Amsden, Alice H. 1989. *Asia's next giant: South Korea and late industrialization*. New York: Oxford University Press.

Appiah, Kwame Anthony. 1989. The conservation of race. *Black American Literature Forum* 23, no. 1 (Spring): 37–60.

Appiah, Kwame Anthony, and Amy Gutmann. 1996. *Color conscious: The political morality of race*. Princeton, NJ: Princeton University Press.

Baron, Samuel. 1958. Plekhanov's Russia: The impact of the West upon an "Oriental" society. *Journal of the History of Ideas* 19, no. 3 (June): 388–404.

Bates, Robert H. 1997. Area studies and the discipline: A useful controversy? *PS: Political Science and Politics* 30, no. 2 (June): 166–69.

Befu, Harumi. 1993. Nationalism and *Nihonjinron*. In *Cultural nationalism in East Asia: Representation and identity*, ed. Harumi Befu, Research Papers and Policy Studies, no. 39. Berkeley: Institute of East Asian Studies, University of California, 1993.

Bellah, Robert N. 1970. *Tokugawa religion: The values of pre-industrial Japan.* Boston, MA: Beacon. Originally published, 1957.

Blyth, Mark. 2003. Structures do not come with an instruction sheet: Interests, ideas, and progress in political science. *American Political Science Review* 97, no. 4 (December): 695–706.

Boulding, Kenneth E. 1956. *The image: Knowledge in life and society.* Ann Arbor: University of Michigan Press.

Brown, Cheryl L. 1990. Incorporation vs. separation: An assessment of gender and politics in the People's Republic of China. *Women and Politics* 10, no. 1:59–69.

———. 1994. The rights and interests of women in the People's Republic of China: Implementation of a new law. In *Modernizing China*, ed. Dhirendra K. Vajpeyi, New York: E. J. Brill.

Cabral, Amilcar. 1973. *Return to the source: Selected speeches of Amilcar Cabral*, ed. African Information Service. New York: Monthly Review Press.

Chu, Yun-Han. 1989. State structure and economic adjustment of the East Asian newly industrializing countries. *International Organization* 43, no. 4 (Autumn): 647–72.

Clemons, Eric Walton. 1990. The history of blacks in Japan. BA thesis, Amherst College.

———. 1995. Japanese race propaganda during World War II: A comparative analysis of propaganda tactics in Southeast Asia and the West. In *Racial Identities in East Asia*, ed. Barry Sautman, 213–36. Hong Kong: Division of Social Science, Hong Kong University of Science and Technology.

———. 1999. Transcending national identity: Foreign employees and organizational management in corporate Japan. PhD diss., Columbia University.

Cobban, Alfred. 1955. *The myth of the French Revolution: An inaugural lecture.* London: n.p.

Connolly, William E. 1991. *Identity/difference: Democratic negotiations of political paradox.* Ithaca, NY: Cornell University Press.

Cumings, Bruce. 1989. The abortive abertura: South Korea in the light of Latin American experience. *New Left Review* 173 (January–February): 5–32.

———. 1998. The Korean crisis and the end of "late" development. *New Left Review* 231 (September–October): 43–72.

Curtis, Gerald L. 1998. A "recipe" for democratic development. In *Democracy in East Asia*, ed. Larry Diamond and Marc F. Plattner, Baltimore, MD: Johns Hopkins University Press and the National Endowment for Democracy.

Deyo, Frederic C. 1989. *Beneath the miracle: Labor subordination in the new Asian industrialism.* Berkeley: University of California Press.

Evans, Peter. 1984. Class, state, and dependence in Asia: Lessons for Latin Americanists. In *Political economy of the new Asian industrialism*, ed. Frederic C. Deyo, 203–26. Ithaca, NY: Cornell University Press.

Evans, Peter B., Dietrich Rueschemeyer, and Theda Skocpol, eds. 1985. *Bringing the state back in.* Cambridge: Cambridge University Press.

Fanon, Frantz. 1952. *Peau noire, masques blancs.* [Black skin, white masks]. Paris: Seuil.

Foucault, Michel. 1984. Truth and power. In *The Foucault reader*, ed. Paul Rabinow, New York: Pantheon.

Fujitani, Takashi. 1993. Inventing, forgetting, remembering: Toward a historical ethnography of the nation-state. In *Cultural nationalism in East Asia: Representation and identity*, ed. Harumi Befu, Research Papers and Policy Studies, no. 39. Berkeley: Institute of East Asian Studies, University of California.

———. 1996. *Splendid monarchy: Power and pageantry in modern Japan.* Berkeley: University of California Press.

Fukuyama, Francis. 1989. *Have we reached the end of history?* Santa Monica, CA: Rand.

Furet, François, and Denis Richet. 1965–66. *La révolution française* [The French Revolution]. 2 vols. Paris: n.p.

Gates, Henry Louis. 1986. Talkin' that talk. *Critical Inquiry* 13 (Autumn): 203–10.

Gold, Thomas. 1986. *State and society in the Taiwan miracle*. New York: M. E. Sharpe.

Grady, Robert C. 1996. Review of *The boundaries of citizenship: Race, ethnicity, and nationality in the liberal state*, by Jeff Spinner. *Journal of Politics* 58, no.1 (February): 264–66.

Hanchard, Michael George. 1994. *Orpheus and power: The movimento negro of Rio de Janeiro and Sao Paulo, Brazil, 1945–1988*. Princeton, NJ: Princeton University Press.

———, ed. 1999. *Racial politics in contemporary Brazil*. Durham, NC: Duke University Press.

Hochschild, Jennifer L. 1995. *Facing up to the American dream: Race, class, and the soul of the nation*. Princeton, NJ: Princeton University Press.

———. 2001. Making white Americans and excluding nonwhite Americans through immigration laws. Review. Translated by Desmond King. *Journal of Policy History* 13:484.

Hollinger, David A. 1997. The disciplines and the identity debates, 1970–1995. *Daedalus* 126, no.1 (Winter): 333–51.

Hoston, Germaine A. 1981. State and revolution in China and Japan: Marxist perspectives on the nation-state and social revolution in Asia. PhD diss., Harvard University.

———. 1983. *Tenkō*: Marxism and the national question in prewar Japan. *Polity* 16, no.1 (Fall): 96–118.

———. 1984a. Marxism and Japanese expansionism: Takahashi Kamekichi and the theory of "petty imperialism." *Journal of Japanese Studies* 10, no. 1 (Winter): 1–30.

———. 1984b. Marxism and national socialism in Taisho Japan: The thought of Takabatake Motoyuki. *Journal of Asian Studies* 44, no. 1 (November): 43–64.

———. 1986. *Marxism and the crisis of development in prewar Japan*. Princeton, NJ: Princeton University Press.

———. 1987. Between theory and practice: Marxist thought and the politics of the Japanese Socialist Party. *Studies in Comparative Communism* 20, no. 2 (Summer): 175–207.

———. 1990a. *Ikkoku Shakai-Shugi*: Sano Manabu and the limits of Marxism as cultural criticism. In *Culture and identity: Japanese intellectuals during the interwar years*, ed. J. Thomas Rimer. Princeton, NJ: Princeton University Press.

———. 1990b. A "Theology of Liberation"? Socialist revolution and spiritual regeneration in Chinese and Japanese Marxism. In *Ideas across cultures: Essays on Chinese thought in honor of Benjamin I. Schwartz*, ed. Paul A. Cohen and Merle Goldman. Cambridge, MA: Harvard University Press and the Council on East Asian Studies.

———. 1991. Conceptualizing bourgeois revolution: The prewar Japanese left and the Meiji Restoration. *Comparative Studies in Society and History* 33, no. 3 (July): 539–81.

———. 1992. The state, modernity, and the fate of liberalism in prewar Japan. *Journal of Asian Studies* 51, no. 2 (May): 287–316.

———. 1994. *The state, identity, and the national question in China and Japan*. Princeton, NJ: Princeton University Press.

Huntington, Samuel P. 1993a. The clash of civilizations. *Foreign Affairs* 72, no. 3 (Summer): 22–49.

———. 1993b. If not civilizations, what? Paradigms of the post–cold war world. *Foreign Affairs* 72, no. 5 (November–December): 186–94.

———. 1994. Interview. *Asiaweek*, April 6, p. 36.

Ishida, Takeshi. 1954. *Meiji seiji shisōshi kenkyū* [Studies in the history of Meiji political thought]. Tokyo: Mirai-sha.

Iton, Richard. 1994. Gateway blues: Comparative political cultures and the search for the missing American left. PhD diss., Baltimore, MD: Johns Hopkins University Press.

———. 2000. *Solidarity views: Race, culture, and the American left*. Chapel Hill: University of North Carolina Press.

Jervis, Robert. 1970. *The logic of images in international relations*. Princeton, NJ: Princeton University Press.

Johnson, Chalmers A. 1962. *Peasant nationalism and Communist power: The emergence of revolutionary China, 1937–1945*. Stanford, CA: Stanford University Press.

———. 1966. *Revolutionary change*. Boston: Little Brown.

———. 1982. *MITI and the Japanese miracle: The growth of industrial policy, 1925–1975*. Palo Alto, CA: Stanford University Press.

―――. 1987. Political institutions and economic performance: The political economy of the new Asian industrialism: The government-business relationship in Japan, South Korea, and Taiwan. In *The political economy of the new Asian industrialism*, ed. Frederic Deyo, 136–64. Ithaca, NY: Cornell University Press.

―――. 1999. The developmental state: Odyssey of a concept. In *The developmental state*, ed. Meredith Woo-Cumings, 32–60. Ithaca, NY: Cornell University Press.

Katznelson, Ira, and Helen V. Milner. 2002. American political science: The discipline's state and the state of the discipline. In *Political science: State of the discipline*, Centennial Edition, ed. Ira Katznelson and Helen V. Milner. New York: W. W. Norton.

Kohli, Atul. 1999. Where do high-growth political economies come from? The Japanese lineage of Korea's "developmental state." In *The developmental state*, ed. Meredith Woo-Cumings, 93–136. Ithaca, NY: Cornell University Press.

Kuhn, Thomas S. 1962. *The structure of scientific revolutions.* Chicago: University of Chicago Press.

Lin, Yü-sheng. 1979. *The crisis of Chinese consciousness: Radical antitraditionalism in the May Fourth era.* Madison: University of Wisconsin Press.

Malcomson, Scott L. 2000. *One drop of blood: The American misadventure of race.* New York: Farrar, Straus, and Giroux.

Mannheim, Karl. n.d. *Ideology and utopia: An introduction to the sociology of knowledge.* Translated by Louis Wirth and Daniel Shils. New York: Harcourt Brace and Jovanovich, Harvest Books. Originally published, 1936.

Martin, Sherry Lynne. 2002. Gender, partisanship, and political alienation in Japan and the U.S. PhD diss., University of Michigan.

Maruyama, Masao. 1969. *Thought and behavior in modern Japanese politics.* Expanded ed. Translated by Ivan Morris. London: Oxford University Press.

McClain, Paula. 1993. The changing dynamics of urban politics—Black and Hispanic municipal employment: Is there competition? *Journal of Politics* 55:399–414.

McClain, Paula D., and John A. Garcia. 1993. Expanding disciplinary boundaries: Black, Latino, and racial minority group politics in political science. In *Political science: The state of the field II*, ed. Ada W. Finifter. Washington, DC: American Political Science Association.

McClain, Paula D., and Albert K. Karnig. 1990. Black and Hispanic socioeconomic and political competition. *American Political Science Review* 84:535–45.

Mitchell, Michael J., and Charles H. Wood. 1999. Ironies of citizenship: Skin color, police brutality, and the challenge to democracy in Brazil. *Social Forces* 77, no.3 (March): 1001–20.

Moore, Barrington. 1966. *Social origins of dictatorship and democracy: Lord and peasant in the making of the modern world.* Boston: Beacon.

Murray, Charles, and Richard Herrnstein. 1994. *The Bell curve: Intelligence and class structure in American life.* New York: Free Press.

Nathan, Andrew J. 1990. The place of values in cross-cultural studies: The example of democracy and China. In *Ideas across cultures: Essays on Chinese thought in honor of Benjamin I. Schwartz*, ed. Paul A. Cohen and Merle Goldman. Cambridge, MA: Harvard University Press.

―――. 2002. Redefinitions of freedom in China. In *The idea of freedom in Asia and Africa*, ed. Robert H. Taylor, 248–74. Palo Alto, CA: Stanford University Press.

Nobles, Melissa. 2000. *Shades of citizenship: Race and the census in modern politics.* Palo Alto, CA: Stanford University Press.

―――. 2002. Lessons from Brazil: The ideational and political dimensions of multiraciality. In *The new race question: How the census counts multiracial individuals*, ed. Joel Perlmann and Mary C. Walters. New York: Russell Sage Foundation; Annandale-on-Hudson, NY: Levy Economics Institute of Bard College.

Nyerere, Julius K. 1968. *Ujamaa: Essays on socialism.* Oxford: Oxford University Press.

Oi, Jean Chun. 1989. *State and peasant in contemporary China: The political economy of village government.* Berkeley: University of California Press.

―――. 1999. *Rural China takes off: Institutional foundations of economic reform.* Berkeley: University of California Press.

Patterson, Orlando. 1977. Slavery. *Annual Review of Sociology* 3:407–49.

————. 1998. *Rituals of blood: Consequences of slavery in two American centuries.* Washington, DC: Civitas/CounterPoint.

Pei, Minxin. 1998. The fall and rise of democracy in East Asia. In *Democracy in East Asia,* ed. Larry Diamond and Marc F. Plattner. Baltimore, MD: Johns Hopkins University Press.

Pempel, T. J. 1999. The developmental regime in a changing world economy. In *The developmental state,* ed. Meredith Woo-Cumings, 137–81. Ithaca, NY: Cornell University Press.

Pempel, T. J., and Michio Muramatsu. 1984. The Japanese bureaucracy and economic development: Structuring a proactive civil service. In *The Japanese civil service and economic development: Catalysts of change,* ed. Hyung-Ki Kim et al., 19–76. Oxford: Oxford University Press; New York: Clarendon.

Pempel, T. J., and Keiichi Tsunekawa. 1979. Corporatism without labor? The Japanese anomaly. In *Trends toward corporatist intermediation,* ed. Philippe Schmitter and Gerhard Lehmbruch, Chapter 9. Beverly Hills, CA: Sage.

Piven, Frances Fox, and Richard A. Cloward. 1971. *Regulating the poor: The functions of public welfare.* New York: Pantheon.

Przeworski, Adam, Michael E. Alvarez, José Antonio Cheibub, and Fernando Limongi. 2000. *Democracy and development: Political institutions and well-being in the world, 1950–1990.* Cambridge Studies in the Theory of Democracy. Cambridge: Cambridge University Press.

Rodney, Walter. 1972. *How Europe underdeveloped Africa.* Rev. ed. Washington, DC: Howard University Press.

Russell, John G. 1989. Anxiety disorders in Japan: A review of the Japanese literature on *Shinkeishitsu* and *Taijinkyofusho. Culture, Medicine and Psychiatry* 13, no. 4 (December): 391–403.

————. 1991a. Narratives of denial: Racial chauvinism and the black other in Japan. *Japan Quarterly* 38, no. 4:416–28.

————. 1991b. *Nihonjin no kokujin-kan: mondai wa chibi kuro sambo dake de wa nai* [Japanese images of blacks: the problem is not just Little Black Sambo]. Tokyo: Shinhyōron.

————. 1996. Race and reflexivity: The black other in contemporary Japanese mass culture. In *Contemporary Japan and popular culture,* ed. John Whittier Treat. Honolulu: University of Hawaii Press.

Said, Edward W. 1978. *Orientalism.* New York: Routledge.

————. 1981. *Covering Islam: How the media and the experts determine how we see the rest of the world.* New York: Vintage Books.

————. 1993. *Culture and imperialism.* New York: Alfred A. Knopf.

————. 2003. Memory, inequality and power: Palestine and the universality of human rights. Webcast. Berkeley, California, February 19.

Sartre, Jean-Paul. 1948. *Anti-semite and Jew.* Translated by George J. Becker. New York: Schocken.

Sautman, Barry. 1995. Theories of East Asian intellectual and behavioral superiority and the "Clash of Civilizations." In *Racial identities in East Asia,* ed. Barry Sautman, 58–121. Hong Kong: Hong Kong University of Science and Technology.

Schoppa, Leonard J. 1991. Zoku power and LDP power: A case study of the zoku role in education policy. *Journal of Japanese Studies* 17, no.1 (Winter): 79–106.

Schwartz, Benjamin I. 1951. *Chinese Communism and the rise of Mao.* Cambridge, MA: Harvard University Press.

————. 1996. A brief defense of political and intellectual history: The case of China. In *China and other matters,* by Benjamin I. Schwartz, 30–44. Cambridge, MA: Harvard University Press.

Shillony, Ben-Ami. 1991. *The Jews and the Japanese: The successful outsiders.* Rutland, VT: Charles E. Tuttle.

Shue, Vivienne. 1988. *The reach of the state: Sketches of the Chinese body politic.* Palo Alto, CA: Stanford University Press.

Skocpol, Theda. 1979. *States and social revolutions: A comparative analysis of France, Russia, and China.* Cambridge: Cambridge University Press.

————. 1992. *Protecting soldiers and mothers: The political origins of social policy in the United States.* Cambridge, MA: Belknap.

Spinner, Jeff. 1994. *The boundaries of citizenship: Race, ethnicity and nationality in the liberal state.* Baltimore, MD: Johns Hopkins University Press.

Sternhell, Ze'ev. 1978. *La droite révolutionnaire 1885–1914: Les origines française du fascisme* [The radical right 1885–1914: The origins of fascism in France]. L'Univers historique. Paris: Le Seuil.

———. 1983. *Ni droite, ni gauche: L'idéologie fasciste en France* [Neither right nor left: Fascist ideology in France]. Paris: Éditions du Seuil.

Su, Shaozhi. 1993. A decade of crises at the institute of Marxism-Leninism-Mao Zedong thought, 1979–89. *China Quarterly* 134 (June): 335–51.

———. 1994. Problems of democratic reform in China. In *The politics of democratization: Generalizing East Asian experiences,* ed. Edward Friedman. Boulder, CO. Westview.

———. 1998. The prospects for democratization in China: Breakthroughs in economic policy require breakthroughs in political reform. *Harvard Asia Pacific Review* 2, no. 2:52–56.

Sun, Yan. 1991. The Chinese protests of 1989: The issue of corruption. *Asian Survey* 31, no. 8 (August): 762–82.

———. 1994. The Chinese and Soviet reassessment of socialism: The theoretical bases of reform and revolution in Communist regimes. *Communist and Post-Communist Studies* 27, no. 1 (March): 39–58.

———. 1995. *The Chinese reassessment of socialism.* Princeton, NJ: Princeton University Press.

———. 1999. Reform, state, and corruption: Is corruption less destructive in China than in Russia? *Comparative Politics* 32, no.1 (October): 1–20.

Takahashi, Kōhachirō. 1976. A contribution to the discussion. In *The transition from feudalism to capitalism,* ed: Rodney Hilton. London: New Left Books; Atlantic Highlands, NJ: Humanities Press.

Tong, Yanqi. 1994. State, society, and political change in China and Hungary. *Comparative Politics* 26, no. 3 (April): 333–53.

———. 1997. *Transitions from state socialism: Economic and political change in Hungary and China.* Lanham, MD: Rowman and Littlefield.

Trimberger, Ellen Kay. 1978. *Revolutions from above: Military bureaucrats and modernization in Japan, Turkey, Egypt, and Peru.* New Brunswick, NJ: Transaction Books.

Vogel, Steven K. 1994. The bureaucratic approach to the financial revolution: Japan's Ministry of Finance and financial system reform. *Governance, no. 3* (July): 219–43.

———. 1999. When interests are not preferences: The cautionary tale of Japanese consumers. *Comparative Politics* 31, no. 2 (January): 187–207.

Wakeman, Frederic Jr. 1972. The price of autonomy: Intellectuals in Ming and Ch'ing politics. *Daedalus* 101 (Spring): 35–70.

Walder, Andrew G. 1986. *Communist neo-traditionalism: Work and authority in Chinese industry.* Berkeley: University of California Press.

———. 1992. *Popular protest in the 1989 democracy movement: The pattern of grass-roots organization.* Hong Kong: Hong Kong Institute of Asia-Pacific Studies, Chinese University of Hong Kong.

———, ed. 1995. *The waning of the Communist state: Economic origins of political decline in China and Hungary.* Studies on China 21. Berkeley: University of California Press.

———, ed. 1996. *China's transitional economy.* Studies on Contemporary China. Oxford: Oxford University Press.

———, ed. 1998. *Zouping in transition: The process of reform in rural North China.* Cambridge, MA: Harvard University Press

Walder, Andrew G., and Jean C. Oi, eds. 1999. *Property rights and economic reform in China.* Palo Alto, CA: Stanford University Press.

Wallerstein, Immanuel. 1976. A world-system perspective on the social sciences. *British Journal of Sociology* 27:343–52.

Walters, Ronald W. 1993. *Pan Africanism in the African diaspora: An analysis of modern Afrocentric political movements.* Detroit, MI: Wayne State University Press.

Wirth, Louis. N.d.. Preface to *Ideology and utopia: An introduction to the sociology of knowledge*, by Karl Mannheim. Translated by Louis Wirth and Edward Shils. New York: Harcourt Brace Jovanovich.

Wolfe, Alan, and Klausen, Jytte. 1997. Identity politics and the welfare state. *Social Philosophy and Politics* 14, no. 2 (Summer): 231–55.

Woo, Jung-en (Woo-Cumings, Meredith). 1991. *Race to the swift: State and finance in Korean industrialization*. Studies of the East Asian Institute, Columbia University. New York: Columbia University Press.

Woo-Cumings, Meredith. 1995. Developmental bureaucracy in comparative perspective: The evolution of the Korean civil service. In *The Japanese civil service and economic development: Catalysts of change*, ed. Hyung Ki Kim et al. Oxford: Oxford University Press.

———. 1999a. Introduction: Chalmers Johnson and the politics of nationalism and development. In *The developmental state*, ed. Meredith Woo-Cumings. Ithaca, NY: Cornell University Press.

———. 1999b. Slouching toward the market: The politics of financial liberalization in South Korea. In *Capital ungoverned: Liberalizing finance in interventionist states*, ed. Michael Loriaux et al. Ithaca, NY: Cornell University Press.

Yack, Bernard. 1995. Reconciling liberalism and nationalism. *Political Theory* 23, no.1 (February): 166–82.

Zucker, Catherine H. 1995. On the "rationality" of rational choice. *Political Psychology* 16, no.1: 179–98.

CHAPTER FOURTEEN

Race and the Problem of Equity in the Administrative State

Implications for Political Science Theory and Methods

LENNEAL J. HENDERSON JR.

T HE INCREASING COMPLEXITY and power of administrative agencies is one of the hidden crises of American politics. Policy is implemented in an array of bureaucracies at the national and subnational level. In the study of political science and public administration, the role of bureaucracy is to implement public policies. This traditional dichotomy between politics and administration, however, understates the power of bureaucracies. Policies made with good intentions are often transformed, truncated, and revised within and over the life cycle of government bureaucracies.

There is no better example of this dynamic than race and administration. African Americans, Latinos, Native Americans, Asian Americans, and members of other racial and ethnic groups have a monumental stake in the politics of public administration in the United States. Whether at the level of federal, state, or local government, administrative decision making and implementation often represent fundamental public policy issues and challenges for both public policymakers and for nonwhite American elected officials, public administrators, and leaders of most institutions in minority communities. The political scientist Charles V. Hamilton predicted that this would be the case in the 1990s; it is now even more significant in these early years of the twenty-first century. Hamilton argued that in the future, there would be struggles over resources "as well as struggles over rights."[1]

These struggles occur often in public bureaucracies. Given the role of administration in the formulation, implementation, and evaluation of public policy and the centrality of the public sector to the status and fate of nonwhite populations, political scientists, whether black or not, must have the acumen to discern the ways in which policy is modified and influenced by public bureaucracies. These modifications affect minority interests as well as the tendency of bureaucracies to become policy formulators as well as implementers. There is no way to escape what Emmett Redford refers to as "the administrative state." The thickening of government is a central reality in politics and political science. Nonetheless, political scientists often evaluate policy without fully appreciating its impact on dependent minorities. Race and ethnicity do matter in the allocation of economic resources; and bureaucracies are fundamental suppliers of economic resources, particularly to those most needy. Accordingly, these elements must be teased out of the implementation of public policy.

Political science theory and methods are essential in advancing the study of the interplay of race, ethnicity, politics, bureaucracies, and a variety of social, economic, and political resources. This chapter argues that two recurrent issues or problems characterize the relationship of nonwhite populations to public policy and administration in the United States:

The first issue concerns public administration, which is at the center of the ethical debate over resource allocations to nonwhite populations in the United States. How should political scientists fashion appropriate methodological and normative tools for analyzing the reciprocal influences of race and bureaucracy?

The second issue concerns strategies and designs. Given the perennial ethical problem, public administrators have constantly struggled with the most appropriate strategies and designs for administrative intervention and action concerning needs, demands, and status of nonwhites in the United States.

Both problems raise both theoretical and strategic issues for American political scientists. Most scholars in the field have approached these problems through such theories as dominant/*submissive* group theory; pluralist theory; and representative bureaucracy theory; various forms of elite-mass theory; and most recently, through theories of social equity.[2] Yet much is lost in the application of these approaches. For example, a key tenet of pluralist theory is that competing and often conflicting interest groups influence the process of making public policy through lobbying, bargaining, and compromising about political agendas. This bargaining process affects the distribution and redistribution of such key resources as education, health care, employment, and business opportunities. Pluralists recognize that rights provide access to resources. The rights to vote, to hold public office, and to mobilize allow nonwhite Americans opportunities to influence the allocation of public resources: how tax dollars are distributed in public budgets. Because of disproportionate poverty, discrimination, and other historical legacies, nonwhite American politicians and advocacy organizations have fought to make sure that the allocation of resources is fair and equal, whether in terms of taxing and spending, or in the design and development of such longer-term capital-intensive public works as highways, bridges, convention centers, and other parts of the infrastructure. Obviously, this has not been enough because allocation decisions continue to disadvantage nonwhite populations. Consequently, political scientists have and can employ a wide variety of methods in studying the politics of race and bureaucracy. These include history, action research, narrative, phenomenological and other qualitative techniques, and traditional survey and quantitative techniques.

Historical Perspectives

Race has been a salient dynamic in public administration for nearly a hundred and fifty years. Between 1865 and 1900, three major kinds of racially oriented bureaucracies emerged on the American political landscape: the Department of Indian Affairs; the Bureau of Freedmen, Refugees and Abandoned Lands (known as the Freedmen's Bureau); and various immigration agencies. The first two of these bureaucracies were under the jurisdicton of the War Department.

The Department of Indian Affairs was established in 1871 after the general decimation of Indian tribes by war, disease, famine, and relocation. It essentially redefined the Indians as wards of the United States government. Only the federal government had legal authority to deal with Indian land, location, and mobility issues. The Department later assumed some authority over Indian lands controlled by the federal government as a result of the 1887 Dawes Allotment Act. The Department of Indian Affairs was assigned to the War Department because many Indian issues were closely associated with war and because of the residual issues of the Civil War.

The Freedmen's Bureau was also placed within the War Department in 1865. The Bureau was established to distribute food, supplies, protection, and both confiscated and conferred land to former slaves. Although the Bureau eventually collapsed as a result of mismanagement and corruption, at its peak it provided hundreds of primary schools and health centers for former slaves. It also maintained some thirty-six bank branches to accommodate the wills, deeds, and financial instruments of slaves living in tenuous financial and economic conditions.

With regard to the immigration agencies, in the late nineteenth century they performed investigative and adjudicative functions, as Gabriel Chin has indicated. These agencies made both factual and legal determinations in many individual cases involving both Chinese and Japanese immigrants to the United States. Beginning with the Immigration Act of 1875, the federal government preempted state and local governments in defining the Chinese as an immigrant group and formally excluding them as aliens. The Chinese Exclusion Act became law in 1882 and used deportation as well as prohibition of immigration as policy tools to exclude Chinese.

Although these statutes would eventually be repealed in the twentieth century, they established clear racial categories maintained, monitored, and managed by immigration authorities. And although the Department of Indian Affairs Act was eventually replaced in 1933 by the Indian Reorganization Act, the fate of the Indians had already been significantly defined by law and bureaucracy.

Consequently, the most important effects of these racially oriented bureaucracies on blacks, Asians (and later Latinos), and Indians included:

- Definition and labeling in designations used by the Census Bureau and other official agencies
- Use of bureaucratic determinations to *locate* or relocate racial populations to establish correlations among concepts of race, space, and place

- Control of such essential resources as food, water, land, and employment needed by nonwhites
- Administratively determined terms and conditions of interaction between nonwhites and whites in social, economic, and political contexts

Although major policy changes by the courts in *Brown v. the Board of Education of Topeka, Kansas* as well as the 1957, 1960, 1964, and 1968 Civil Rights Acts (including an Indian Civil Rights Act in 1968) and a variety of "Great Society" programs in the Kennedy and Johnson administrations clearly changed the role of government bureaucracy in racial minority communities, earlier administrative precedents continued to affect the living conditions and life chances of nonwhites.

From Bush to Clinton to Bush: Changing Perspectives on Administration as an Instrument of Racial Policy

Given this historical context, if pluralists maintain that government decisions and policies result from the collective efforts of various interest groups conveying their preferences for public resources to public officials, nonwhite Americans perennially confront a cruel paradox in the web of pluralist theory. How can nonwhites achieve success in meeting their emergency fiscal needs in a pluralist political system that favors incremental over comprehensive public policies and distributive over redistributive choices? There is no better indicator of nonwhite political and administrative success than the extent to which they achieve their fiscal preferences in any significant measure. When pluralist theory is applied to nonwhite American politics and fiscal policy, two interrelated hypotheses are posited that guide the discussion in this chapter: First, that most nonwhite Americans continue to be disproportionately dependent on the public sector for their current social and economic vitality and life chances. Second, that fiscal policy—the public financial transactions of government—can and does directly and immediately affect the quality of life issues addressed by most African, Latino, and Native American politicians, interest groups, and institutions.

Given the turbulent early twenty-first century characterized by the troubled presidency of George W. Bush, economic decline, an unprecedented federal budget deficit, the war on terrorism and the war in Iraq, and the catastrophic failure of the Federal Emergency Management Agency (FEMA) in responding to Hurricane Katrina in the Gulf region and New Orleans, there is an inverse relationship between the severity of the challenges nonwhites face and the inclination of federal, state and local policy makers to use public bureaucracy as an instrument of racial equality and delivery of public services. Moreover, Bush is attempting to deal with all these crises while pursing tax cuts beyond those legislated by Congress in 2003.

Even the economic plans developed by President Bill Clinton in the 1990s, including both taxing and spending components, were designed to stimulate

economic growth, reduce the federal deficit, and enhance America's global economic competitiveness. Both the short-term stimulus plan to invest nearly $30
billion in an employment-generating program to repair and rebuild roads, bridges,
tunnels, highways, airports, and other infrastructure, particularly in cities, could
have provided opportunities for millions of nonwhite American individuals,
households, and businesses experiencing continuing financial and management
challenges, particularly in metropolitan areas.

The intense congressional conflicts and compromises regarding the budget,
complicated by macroeconomic and political challenges facing the United
States, significantly reduced President Clinton's aspirations for a substantial
public investment strategy. The final compromise budget program included less
than $4 billion for "empowerment zones"[3] designed to uplift inner-city com-
munities through concentrated investment and development as well as a
retroactive tax provision raising the income tax rate to well over 35 percent for
most Americans.

Enterprise zones, conceptualized by the administrations of Ronald Reagan
and George H. W. Bush, and advocated by Jack Kemp (R-NY), the former representative and secretary of Housing and Urban Development, resembled Clinton's empowerment zones. They were designed to target designated areas of distress
in central cities for intensive and continuous investment, business development,
employment development, and infrastructural repair and rebuilding. Theoretically
speaking, the government was to use tax incentives to attract business investment
in empowerment zones. The intended beneficiaries of the investment were the
residents, business owners, and consumers who reside and operate in these zones.

As the United States made the transition to George W. Bush's administration in 2001, many challenges perennially faced by nonwhite Americans were
increasingly ignored because of macroeconomic changes at the local, regional,
national, and global levels. There were dramatic political and economic changes
in the former Soviet Union, Eastern Europe, Central and South America, and
the Middle East. In addition, the shocking attacks on the World Trade Center
and the Pentagon on September 11, 2001, and the global economic recession that
followed imposed substantial pressures on the United States as a debtor nation
with a federal budget deficit of more than $500 billion and a continuing negative
balance of payments and trade.

Despite evidence of expanding socioeconomic and racial disparities, the central administrative development of the early twenty-first century was the reorganization of the federal government to enhance homeland security. Twenty-two
federal agencies, including the Immigration and Naturalization Service (INS)
and the Customs Service, were reorganized into the new Department of Homeland Security (DHS) in 2003. Perhaps the only central domestic policy initiative
of the Bush administration with significant implications for nonwhites is the 2001
No Child Left Behind Act (NCLB). The most comprehensive statute affecting
federal intervention in education policy since the 1965 Elementary and Secondary School Act, the NCLB imposes strict new standards on public school
accountability for student achievement without significant funding to state and
local agencies providing education.

Ironically, social equity, civil rights, and racial justice had all but disappeared from the policy agenda at the same time that Condoleezza Rice as National Security Advisor and Colin Powell as Secretary of State provided unprecedented bureaucratic leadership roles to African Americans in the Bush administration. Rice eventually became Secretary of State in 2005. These appointments, although substantive, are no substitute for a more equitable allocation of public resources to increasingly difficult conditions in nonwhite communities.

The message for nonwhite Americans is simple: remain politically active, vigilant regarding the nation's fiscal decisions and challenges, and attuned to macroeconomic shifts and changes—or risk being even more disadvantaged in administrative and fiscal policy processes than ever before in history. It is the responsibility of political scientists to alert themselves, policymakers, and racial and ethnic leaders to some subtle and hidden changes in the nation's political agenda and allocation policies.

The task of administrative and fiscal vigilance is complex and arduous. John Mikesell, for example, describes fiscal policy as covering the budget cycle, taxes, charges, and fees; administration of the government debt, bonds, procurement policy, and public enterprise; and the creation and use of various trust accounts earmarked for specific purposes.[4] The average American cannot negotiate this maze of technical, financial, regulatory, and organizational dynamics that characterize the administrative state.

Context of Fiscal Policies and Racial Politics

Clearly, the political connection between race and fiscal decision making is essential. In many respects, fiscal policy combines past, present, and future policy practices and issues. It asks how many past allocation patterns should guide present (usually the current fiscal year) allocation options. Simultaneously, fiscal policy experts ponder and struggle over the short- and long-term consequences of selecting one financial option over another. They debate one method of using budgets and taxes to respond to social priorities over another. Historical, contemporary, and future policies toward blacks, Latinos, and Native Americans are reflected in the fiscal policies adopted by the government, whether these groups are explicitly or implicitly the focus of these policies. This process is further complicated by the various ways in which equity issues and national economic and financial problem underlie budgetary and tax decisions. Such complications imply five interrelated essential points about the relationship between administrative and fiscal policies and the economic and political aspirations of nonwhites.

First, nonwhites continue to be disproportionately dependent on public finance in order to advance their economic and political agenda. This fiscal dependence takes place at three interrelated levels: macroeconomic, institutional, and household. Other socioeconomically disadvantaged populations in the United States share these three interrelated levels.[5]

Second, the politics and economics of deficit reduction and tax policies continue to pose severe challenges for most nonwhite populations, particularly in the current climate of accelerating budget deficit to finance the war on terrorism and the war in Iraq in the Bush administration. Deficit reduction is often employed as a justification for a federal budget rescission (a presidential decision to with-hold funds permanently); a deferral (a presidential decision to withhold funds for a brief period); or reprogramming (taking money appropriated for one program and diverting it to another that has emerged as a higher priority). For example, the 1990 Budget Summit Agreement and eventual deficit reduction package came after one of the most acrimonious, intense, and difficult budget and tax negotia-tions ever to take place. Voters expressed their dismay with both the process and the product of these negotiations in the 1990 elections, particularly at the state and local levels.[6] In the second Bush administration, the use of administra-tive agencies, particularly intelligence agencies within the new Department of Homeland Security mega-bureaucracy, raises questions about the centralization of fiscal resources as well as the erosion of civil liberties associated with the war on terror. The Immigration and Naturalization Service (INS) was among the twenty-two agencies absorbed by the new department. This agency is in a strate-gic position to influence the specific racial or ethnic populations encouraged into or discouraged from immigration to the United States.

Third, the continued shifting of responsibility for financial and public policy to state and local government challenges black and Latino elected officials, who are more numerous at these levels, to maintain existing levels of service for their constituents with declining revenues. The interest of political scientists in the del-icate balance of power involved in federalism includes the use of bureaucracy to accommodate or orchestrate the operations of state and local government.

Black and Latino mayors and county officials are particularly vulnerable to fiscal stress in the public sector. Fiscal stress is here defined as the "gap between the needs and expectations of citizens and government employees for government services and benefits and inability of the economy to generate enough economic growth to expand (or even sustain, in some places) tax-supported programs with-out putting unacceptable demands on taxpayers' take-home pay."[7] Nonwhite may-ors and county officials are vulnerable to fiscal stress because they frequently use the resources of government to improve the quality of life for their constituents, particularly black and Latino constituents, since blacks and Latinos are often more reliant than whites on government for their well-being.

Fourth, African Americans and other nonwhites have a direct and continu-ing stake in fiscal policies because these policies influence lending institutions, hospitals, local and state governments, strategic large and small businesses, non-profit organizations, and other institutions that affect nonwhite populations in sub-stantive and material ways.[8] For example, President Clinton's proposed investment tax credits, particularly for small businesses, that could have assisted thousands of fledgling African American and Latino businesses who were severely chal-lenged in the 1990s by the restrictive lending policies of savings and loan and banking institutions.

Fifth, the impact of fiscal policy on the generic, institutional, and household levels among African Americans and other nonwhites simultaneously affects all Americans. African Americans purchase goods and services from non-African American vendors. The continuing socioeconomic struggles of African Americans challenge metropolitan areas, corporations, places of worship, and nonprofit organizations throughout the country to be more attentive to the African American experience. Consequently, the interdependency of African Americans and other Americans is evident in almost any fiscal decision made by a federal, state or local government.

The Congressional Black Caucus, in its *Quality of Life Fiscal 1991 Alternative Budget*, argued that "a nation's values and concern for social and economic justice are measured by the fiscal priorities established in its national budget."[9] The League of United Latin American Citizens (LULAC) has repeatedly warned tax experts that the failure to incorporate large numbers of unemployed and underemployed Hispanic citizens and aliens represents not only a fiscal but also a moral failure. The rapidly rising number of women entering the work force and becoming subject to rising taxes without benefit of adequate child care makes a telling statement about the nation's value priorities as well as its fiscal dynamics.[10]

Current Dependency of African Americans on Fiscal Policies

All nonwhite American populations depend to some degree on public bureaucracies. African Americans, however, are a salient case study of profound interest to political scientists. To put the relationship of African American interests and fiscal policy in perspective, it is useful to recall the three levels of African American fiscal dependency—macroeconomic, institutional, and household—discussed earlier. At the macroeconomic level African Americans, like all Americans, depend on the provision of such goods and services as roads, tunnels, schools, hospitals, law enforcement, and defense. At the institutional level, however, community-based organizations, national associations, schools, health care organizations, businesses, and institutions owned, operated, or directed to African Americans depend on public money or are affected by tax policies in far more direct ways than are experienced by most Americans. Local Urban League or Opportunities Industrialization Centers depend on federal employment development funding for significant portions of their budgets and missions. African American businesses depend on government contracts, including set-aside programs, to remain viable. In addition to state and local government programs, the Department of Housing and Urban Development (HUD) makes funds available to hundreds of churches and community-based nonprofit organizations to provide affordable housing for thousands of African Americans. At the household level, thousands of African American households depend on Temporary Assistance to Needy Families (TANF), food stamps, the Low-Income Household Energy Assistance Program (LIHEAP), Section 8 housing certificates, and state and local assistance programs to sustain themselves. When welfare reform was instituted in 1996, many nonwhite households were eventual victims of "administrative load shedding" as many came off the rolls under the new rubric of TANF. Without public support, many households are at the mercy of charitable institutions.

The term *dependency* is not used pejoratively in this context. Many of America's largest corporate, nonprofit, and educational institutions are substantially if not predominantly dependent on public monies or tax credits.[11] Some corporations, particularly defense contractors, receive most of their annual gross sales receipts from the federal government. Many smaller businesses sell solid waste management, transportation, telecommunications, health care, and other services to state and local governments.

The absence of diverse and flexible sources of income, however, creates financial vulnerability for any institution or household, particularly given significant fluctuations and changes in the public policy environment. Without steady progress in obtaining contracts, employment, and goods and services from the corporate sector, African Americans' dependency on government resources makes them particularly vulnerable to conservative politicians and interest groups advocating reductions in federal, state, or local support for their households and institutions.

For example, of the more than 4 million businesses owned and operated by nonwhite Americans, more than 90 percent supply or provide services directly to the government. Less than 50 percent of all other businesses are as dependent on government dollars.[12] In addition, black, Latino, and Native American households are more than twice as dependent on some form of federal, state, or local public assistance; and a black student attending college or university is almost three times as likely as other students to receive government support to pay the costs of tuition or room and board.

African Americans and Latino Americans are disproportionately represented in federal, state and local correctional institutions, and increasing public dollars are devoted to the maintenance and expansion of these institutions. Moreover, as the political scientists Georgia Persons, Hanes Walton, Paula McClain, and other experts on black elected officials indicate, black elected officials usually represent congressional, state, or local districts or jurisdictions with large numbers of impoverished, poorly housed populations with health care, day care, education, employment, business, and infrastructural needs that severely strain federal, state and local budgets and taxes.[13] Given rising rates of poverty, homelessness, health care deficiencies, and other social maladies, the dependency of the needy on government will increase.

Paradoxically, much of the recent dependency of nonwhites on public money resulted from the struggles of the civil rights, feminist, and other movements of the 1960s, 1970s, and 1980s. These movements insisted on an ethic of responsiveness by fiscal decision makers that was unprecedented even during the Great Depression of the 1930s. For example, through the Great Society programs of the Kennedy and Johnson administrations, such as the Manpower Development and Training Act of 1962 (employment training), the Economic Development Act of 1964 (poverty programs), and the Cities Demonstration and Metropolitan Development act of 1966 (the Model Cities Program), the alleviation of poverty and racism was placed higher on the public policy agenda than ever before in the nation's history. The result was a great redistributive impulse: a desire to reallocate the country's financial resources through selected fiscal policies.

Professor Walton maintains that federal outlays for civil rights regulatory activities increased from $900,000 in 1969 to $3.5 billion in 1976.[14] In 1968, the Small Business Act of 1953 was amended to create a federal set-aside program for minority businesses. Although the 1968 act was challenged in 1989 by the Supreme Court in *Richmond v. Croson*, many states and localities operate set-aside programs for minority enterprises, particularly African American-owned businesses.[15] But in the early twenty-first century, the real dollar value of many of these programs significantly declined and many programs became the victim of more conservative national, state, or local politics or failed to meet an orientation toward more outcomes-based performance accountability.

Although it is common, however, to be concerned primarily about those government programs earmarked specifically for blacks and other target groups at the household or institutional levels, the generic or macro level of dependency is also critical to African Americans and other nonwhite populations. Three observations are essential about this generic level of dependency. First, like white Americans, nonwhites depend on government for public goods. Support for national defense, the space program, research and development funding, law enforcement, parks and recreation, streets, highways, and bridges represent a generic or macro level of funding for goods and services needed by all Americans. Although nonwhites may receive inadequate quantities or qualities of these goods or services, they are public in the broadest sense of the word. Political scientists emphasize that such public spending and revenue schemes as corporate and individual income taxes, property taxes, sales taxes, excise taxes, trust funds, bonds, and user fees support these public goods.

Generic levels of fiscal policy affect African Americans, Latino and Native Americans in particular ways. These groups depend disproportionately on key components of generic-level spending compared with other citizens. For example, when recommendations are made for overall reductions in military installations, weapons systems, or research and development, nonwhite Americans employed as civilians or enlisted personnel in the armed services suffer more than others because they are overrepresented as employees of military installations.[16] When President Richard Nixon closed or reduced the size of 274 military installations in 1974, many African and Latino Americans lost jobs or were transferred to lower-paying forms of employment. More recent actions of President Bush involving additional base closings include many installations in or near substantial African American and Latino American communities. Although less than $30 billion dollars of defense reductions has been proposed by Congress for fiscal year 2007, many of these reductions will profoundly affect African and Latino American institutions and households. Even the expansion of military spending and homeland security by President Bush in fiscal years 2001 through 2007 does not necessarily translate into immediate economic or employment benefits for nonwhite Americans. Military spending creates jobs: conversely, each $1 billion reduction in Pentagon outlays eliminates thirty-eight thousand U.S. workers.[17]

The peace dividends expected in the late 1990s to result from reductions in military outlays because of democratization in Eastern Europe and the former Soviet Union have yet to materialize. Before the Persian Gulf War, Defense Secretary Dick Cheney, elected to the vice presidency in 2000, instructed the armed forces to consider reductions of up to $180 billion for fiscal years 1992 through 1994.[18] But United States participation in the war temporarily suspended discussions of major defense reductions. Although Cheney's suggested reductions were not substantially incorporated in the federal budget, President Clinton considered defense cuts as part of his deficit reduction strategy and as an opportunity to convert defense spending into domestic investment in human and physical resources. The Bush administration, however, pursued both a war on terrorism following the September 11, 2001 attacks in New York and Washington, and a war in Iraq costing some $155 billion and helping to expand the federal deficit to nearly $600 billion. These policy and administrative decisions had the effect of stalling investments in domestic policy and slowing urban community and economic development initiatives supported by the federal government.

A second observation about the generic level of dependency is its intergovernmental nature. Federal defense, education, space, and infrastructural spending is so inextricably intertwined with the fiscal decisions of states, cities, and counties that any political or economic strategy involving public finance must consider its intergovernmental impact. Table 14.1 illustrates the impact of federal defense spending on goods, services, and research and development in selected metropolitan areas.

In addition to defense, infrastructure—the nation's system of roads, bridges, tunnels, water distribution, transit, highways, airports, gas mains, and other public works—is in severe disrepair. Estimates for infrastructural restoration range from $50 billion to $3 trillion dollars over the next ten years.[19] These cost projections suggest that federal leadership and resources are essential and intergovernmental response is imperative. All Americans, including black Americans, are hindered by a degraded infrastructure.

Poorer infrastructural conditions in black and other nonwhite communities are a glaring reality. They cannot be wished away or ignored. For example, the Commission on Budget and Financial Priorities of the District of Columbia reported in November 1990 that the District of Columbia, whose population is 70 percent black, has not kept pace with its infrastructural maintenance and investment needs for many years and that its backlog of maintenance projects amounts to $1.6 billion. Philadelphia, New Orleans, Oakland (California), Detroit, Baltimore, and Newark (New Jersey), which all have at least 50 percent black populations, report dangerously dilapidated and overutilized streets, tunnels, levees, canals, highways, water and sewer lines, wastewater treatment plants, landfills, gas mains, and other essential infrastructural resources.

A third observation about the generic level of fiscal policy is its frequent lack of racial sensitivity. For example, the Tax Reform Act of 1986 is income-based rather than race-based. The Earned Income Tax Credit (EITC) provides tax assistance to low-income working families to support their children. The assistance is provided without regard to family size, penalizing larger families, like those of blacks and Hispanics.[20] Gramm-Rudman-Hollings sequesters were not sensitive to their adverse impacts on predominantly black institutions like the government of the District of Columbia.[21] These institutions include populations with proportionately higher rates of participation in social services programs, higher rates of dependency on federal or local subsidies or grants, and African American-owned businesses dependent on government procurement because of their inability

TABLE 14.1   Department of Defense Spending for Goods, Services, and Research and Development in Selected Metropolitan Areas (Excluding Military Payroll), 1992

	Share of Total Spending	Share of R & D Spending
Los Angeles, * Long Beach, CA	7.2%	19.7%
Washington, DC*	4.2	5.4
Norfolk-Virginia Beach-Newport News, VA	4.2	0.0
St. Louis, East St. Louis, IL*	3.8	1.1
Nassau and Suffolk Counties, NY	3.0	4.5
Boston, MA	3.1	9.1
San José, CA	2.7	4.5
Fort Worth and Arlington, TX	2.1	2.4
Anaheim and Santa Ana, CA	2.1	3.7
Seattle, WA*	1.7	3.9
Dallas, TX	1.6	1.6
Denver, CO*	1.5	7.8

* Cities with current or recent African American or Hispanic American mayors.

Source: U.S. Department of Defense.

to penetrate markets in the private sector. Consequently, an analysis of the generic level of fiscal dependency is essential for overall nonwhite economic and political development. It facilitates the interface between minority racial and ethnic populations and other populations at the intersection of the broad public use of goods and services. Although the distributional effects on nonwhites of the generic level of fiscal dependency vary, its objectives may be found in broad statements about national, state, or local public needs.

In contrast to the generic level of dependency, the institutional level of nonwhite fiscal dependency more directly and specifically affects institutions that are owned, operated, or influenced by African Americans. Black schools, hospitals, churches, fraternal organizations, professional and occupational organizations, and charitable and community-based organizations depend disproportionately on public finance. This level of dependency includes targeted or earmarked public programs aimed at black institutional development. Black institutions are supported in order to generate more educational, career, employment, and business opportunities for blacks. Several examples of these programs illustrate the point. The Small Business Administration's (SBA) Office of Minority and Small Business manages the minority set-aside program. Of more than four hundred thousand minority-owned firms, just over twenty-five hundred in 1990 (Table 14.2) participated in the sheltered market reserved for them, which consists of working for various federal agencies. Through federal offices for small and disadvantaged business utilization, the minority set-aside program has generated millions of dollars for minority firms that could not have been acquired in the competitive marketplace. In the early twenty-first century, these programs have been sharply curtailed and the scope and scale of operations circumscribed.

Another example of a targeted federal program is the National Energy Act of 1978.[22] The Office of Minority Economic Initiative (OMEI), administratively housed with the Department of Energy (DOE), provides a comprehensive program

TABLE 14.2   Number of Minority Firms Participating in
the SBA's 8(a) Program, 1985–1990

Year	Number of Firms
1985	2,977
1986	3,188
1987	2,990
1988	2,946
1989	3,297
1990	2,500

Source: Small Business Administration, Office of Minority and Small
Business Files, 1989.

of socioeconomic research on the impact of energy prices, supplies, and policies
on minorities; assistance to minority institutions of higher learning for research
and development opportunities; a Minority Energy Information Clearinghouse;
and a Comprehensive Business and Community Development Program.[23] Moreover, OMEI collaborated with the Argonne National Laboratory on the economics of household energy consumption and expenditures and with various
black and Hispanic-oriented colleges and universities. Although small in both
budget and staff (Table 14.3), OMEI is pivotal in both its monitoring of energy
policies for their effects on minorities, and its opportunities for bartering with DOE
for nonwhite institutions. The monies reflected in these minority programs are
minimal, but the impact on the financial well-being and development of the institutions they assist is substantial. Now called the Office of Economic Impact and
Diversity (EID), this small unit is an example of a specialized racial bureaucracy.

The last level of public financial dependency is quite direct. Black households
are sensitive to minute changes in the financial disposition of either black institutions or generic fiscal policies. Taken together, Gramm-Rudman-Hollings, its
1987 amendments, the 1990 deficit reduction packages, and the Tax Reform Act
of 1986 were fiscally regressive for nonwhite households. The minor benefits that
the Tax Reform Act provided to the poorest black households were eliminated

TABLE 14.3   Budget of the Office of Minority Economic
Impacts, U.S. Department of Energy, 1985–1991

Year	Budget (in millions)
1985	$2.4
1986	2.6
1987	2.8
1988	3.8
1989	4.1
1990	3.9*
1991	3.5

*Gramm-Rudman-Hollings sequester.

Source: U.S. Department of Energy, Office of Minority Economic Impact

by real dollars budgeted—deficit reductions and changes in both generic and tar-geted federal programs.[24] Even the tax cuts approved by Congress in 2003 have limited benefits for nonwhite households. Congress approved $350 billion in reductions over ten years. If fully implemented, annual reductions will average a mere $35 billion.

Paradoxically, African Americans and other nonwhites experience generic, institutional, and household dependency on public budgets while experiencing a perennial vulnerability to regressive taxation and revenue policies. Socioeco-nomic retrogression in inner-city and poor rural black communities are unfortu-nately correlated with declines in the levels of federal, state, and local spending in those communities.

A Case Point: 1991 Budget Summit Agreement

A compelling case study of budgets, bureaucracies, and race is the budget for fis-cal year 1991, which led to a budget summit. The 1991 summit agreement had several key provisions. First, in contrast to the original summit proposals of Sep-tember 1990, the final budget legislation adopted by Congress on October 27, 1990, was generally progressive. To reach a deficit reduction target of nearly five hundred billion dollars over the next five fiscal years, reduction in entitlement programs and defense spending were enacted together with increases in federal user fees for government services, various tax increases, and reductions of inter-est payments on the national debt.[25]

More than half the forty-one billion dollars in deficit reductions for fiscal year 1991 were to be generated by direct spending reductions. User fees for some federal services were to be increased by nearly a billion dollars, while entitlement programs were to be reduced by nearly ten billion dollars. These programs—mandated by a statute requiring the payment of benefits to any person or unit of government that met the eligibility requirements established—are particularly sig-nificant to nonwhites.[26] Included among those entitlements at that time were food stamps, Aid to Families with Dependent Children (AFDC), nutrition programs, housing programs, veterans' benefits, Social Security benefits, worker's compensation, and Medicare. Nonwhite participation in these programs ranged from 22.7 percent of Social Security beneficiaries to 53 percent of AFDC recipients.

Real dollar deficit reduction, while important to overall fiscal control, cre-ated hardships for nonwhite beneficiaries in at least three ways: (1) the reduc-tions occurred during an economic recession, thus exacerbating existing crisis conditions, particularly in nonwhite urban neighborhoods and rural settlements; (2) the reductions ignored accelerating needs in nonwhite communities, even then documented through means testing; and (3) reduction in net disposable income in these communities was a negative economic multiplier; that is, land-lords, businesses, churches, local governments, and other institutions dependent on the purchasing power of nonwhites experienced aggregate revenue reductions. These revenue reductions significantly affected the continued capacity of federal, state and local bureaucracies to provide goods and services to African Americans and other nonwhite communities.[27]

President Clinton's fiscal plan, however, sought to balance the impact of spending reductions with some modicum of public investment, particularly in cities. In addition to reductions of more than eight billion dollars in defense spending over fiscal years 1994 through 1998, freezes on civilian and military employee wages, controls on social entitlements, and health care cost reform, Clinton proposed increases in employment-generating public works programs as well as increases in Head Start, college assistance, and community infrastructure programs. Combined with his emphasis on small business support, the impact of these initiatives on nonwhite households and institutions and, most importantly, on their dependency on fiscal policies remain was slight if not negligible.

In contrast, there is little direct administrative support for nonwhites in the twenty-first century Bush administration. The emphasis in the administration is on the war on terror, the war in Iraq, and global economic competitiveness. Health, education, law enforcement and welfare responsibilities have been further devolved to states and localities. States struggle with Medicaid, public assistance, public education, and corrections management. Unfunded or underfunded federal mandates continue to burden state and local government and to circumscribe the distribution of goods and services to all populations, including nonwhite populations.

Revenue Dimensions of Fiscal Policy

Almost eighteen billion dollars in deficit reduction in fiscal year 1991 was to be generated by revenue increases, principally tax increases. These provisions represented a reversal of the "no new taxes" pledge by President George H. W. Bush. These tax provisions raised taxes for most income earners. Tax increases by income group are shown in Tables 14.4 and 14.5. Although people earning incomes of over two hundred thousand dollars experienced a 6.3 percent increase in taxes and constituted 46 percent of the total of all income categories, tax increases were

TABLE 14.4 Percentage Change in Federal Taxes, 1991

Income Level	Final Package (%)	Summit Agreement (%)	House (%)	Senate (%)
Less than $10,000	−2.0	7.6	−1.3	−0.0
$10,000–30,000	3.2	1.9	−1.6	−2.3
$20,000–30,000	1.8	3.3	1.0	2.7
$30,000–40,000	2.0	2.9	1.0	2.8
$40,000–50,000	2.0	2.9	0.8	2.8
$50,000–75,000	1.5	1.8	1.4	1.9
$75,000–100,000	2.1	2.1	1.5	2.5
$100,000–200,000	2.3	1.9	0.7	3.5
$200,000 and over	6.3	1.7	7.4	3.7

*Includes childcare bill with approximately $12 billion in tax credits primarily for working families with children and incomes below $20,000.

Source: Center on Budget and Policy Priorities calculations, based on data from the Joint Committee on Taxation.

Table 14.5 Tax Increase Borne by Various Income Groups, 1991

Income Level	Final Package*	Summit Agreement	House	Senate
Under $50,000	19%	57%	11%	34%
$50,000–100,000	22	22	22	24
$100,000–200,000	13	10	5	18
$200,000 and over	46	11	63	24

*Includes effect of the tax provisions of the child care bill.

Source: Center on Budget and Policy Priorities calculations, based on data from the Joint Committee on Taxation.

fairly well distributed among other income groups. Net increases in taxes over the next five years were projected to be $137 billion.

In addition, this tax program called for five major excise tax provisions, including a five cents per gallon rise in gasoline taxes; increases in cigarette taxes from sixteen cents a pack to twenty cents in 1991 and 24 cents in 1993; higher alcohol taxes; and greater airport and aviation excise taxes, including an increase from 8 percent to 10 percent in the tax on airline tickets. Moreover, the temporary 3 percent excise tax on telephone service became permanent under the law.[28]

In contrast to income tax provisions, these taxes are generally regressive. Given the documented tendency of poorer and larger African American and Latino families to use older, larger, and less fuel-efficient vehicles, the gasoline tax has a disproportionately higher impact on them and their Hispanic and white income counterparts.[29] "Sin taxes" on cigarettes and alcohol also disproportionately and negatively affect blacks. Despite vigorous efforts to discourage smoking and drinking in black communities, smoking and drinking rates are still high. Health and moral issues aside, sales of cigarettes and alcohol support many small business establishments in those communities, such as liquor stores, small grocery stores, and franchises selling alcohol, cigarettes, and other commodities. Those businesses and their customers would be adversely affected by these taxes.

The positive structure of the revenue side of this enactment is best expressed in the Earned Income Tax Credit (EITC) (Table 14.6). The EITC is a tax credit available to working families with children that have incomes below twenty-five thousand dollars. For example, for the tax year 2005, the income cutoff was $25,264; for the tax year 2006, it was about $27,000. The credit is refundable: If an eligible family earns too little income to owe federal income tax, or if the amount of the credit exceeds the income tax owed by the family, the Internal Revenue Service (IRS) sends the family a refund.[30]

President Bush's economic program, however, included direct reductions in income and corporate tax rates as part of his tax reduction program. But federal excise taxes on fuel, telephone service, and other commodities are regressive for nonwhite families and households. Families earning more than $25,000 a year are likely to feel the impact of the new tax program. The program included a new tax on gasoline and home heating fuels, an increase in the individual and corporate income tax from 31 to 36 percent, as well as taxes on various fees.

TABLE 14.6   EITC Benefit Structure, 1993

Tax Year	Families with One Child		Families with Two or More Children		Supplemental Credit for Families with a Child under Age One	
	Credit Percentage	Maximum Benefit ($)	Credit Percentage	Maximum Benefit ($)	Credit Percentage	Maximum Benefit ($)
1990	14% of first $6,810	953	14% of first $6,810	953	—	—
1991	16.7% of first $7,140	1,192	17.3% of first $7,140	1,235	5% of first $7,440	357
1992	17.6% of first $7,440	1,309	18.4% of first $7,760	1,369	5% of first $7,760	372
1993	18.5% of first $7,760	1,436	19.5% of first $7,760	1,513	5% of first $7,760	388
1994	23% of first $8,090	1,861	25% of first $8,090	2,023	5% of first $8,090	405

Note: Dollar amounts for 1991 and beyond are based on current Congressional Budget Offices estimates of inflation, using the consumer price index.

Source: Center on Budget and Policy Priorities, 1990.

Consequently, the fifty-three African American and Latino members of Congress, the more than 600 African American and Latino state legislators, and more than 14,000 African American and Latino local elected officials will closely monitor the combined impacts of these revenue policies and the Bush spending program on both nonwhite Americans and the nation as a whole.

Toward an Ethical Fiscal Strategy

Political scientists examine politics as both an authoritative allocation of values and a process of determining who gets what, why, how much, and how often. Both bureaucracies and ethics are essential to the study of politics. Both the values implied in the struggle of nonwhite Americans seeking fiscal justice and the related criteria of good fiscal policies must somehow be maintained and balanced. At a minimum, good fiscal policies include the principles of productivity, equity, and elasticity. A productive fiscal policy generates sufficient revenues to meet governmental needs on the tax side and makes investments in human needs, economic development, and defense on the spending side. If tax policies fail to generate adequate revenue, more public monies must be spent on borrowing, with a subsequent effect on interest rates and economic growth. An equitable fiscal policy is fair to both taxpayers and specific public constituencies benefiting from public expenditures. In tax policy, economists and political scientists refer to two kinds of equity—horizontal and vertical. Horizontal equity means that taxpayers who have the same amount of income should be taxed at the same rate. Vertical equity implies that wealthier people should pay more taxes than poorer people. A related principle is that tax policies should be proportionate to increases in income. Given strong correlations between race and income, policy and administrative tax strategies have vast racial and socioeconomic implications. Regressive taxes impose greater burdens on nonwhite taxpayers least able to pay.[31]

Although traditionally applied to taxes, notions of progression, proportionality, and regression also have budgetary counterparts. Fiscal policies that cost the poor more and the rich less are inherently regressive and racist. For example, the Gramm-Rudman-Hollings budgets of the 1990s were generally regressive in their effects on blacks and Hispanics because they used budget bases that were already retrenched before 1985 as baselines for cuts mandated by their budget and because needs continued to rise as funding levels declined. Current deficit policies and national debt policies in the Bush administration threaten the social and economic development of nonwhite populations well into the twenty-first century.

In addition, the principle of elasticity suggests that the fiscal system should be flexible enough to address its revenue and spending needs regardless of changes in macroeconomic conditions. Taxes and spending help to stabilize the economy as well as the society. As the Congressional Black and Latino Caucuses and the National Center for Budget Priorities point out, fiscal policies are usually adverse for nonwhite populations. They tend to be fiscally regressive for black and Hispanic households, individuals, and institutions. Strict enforcement of the 2003 tax reduction provisions and extension of the EITC objectives may be generally progressive for nonwhite low-income families and households, but only if accompanied by federal, state and local support for local employment and neighborhood development.

Moreover, consideration of the ethics of good fiscal policy should include the reciprocal relationship between households and institutions. Institutions like charitable organizations; businesses; advocacy organizations; municipal, county, and state government; trade unions, and others provide essential services to their members and constituencies. These institutions are profoundly affected by fiscal policies. If fiscal policies damage institutions, households suffer.

Thus, although President Bush's original fiscal plan seriously challenged the ethics of fair budgets and taxes, congressional political priorities clearly diminished any emphasis on significant urban investment strategies or on the President's investment tax credits and energy taxes. Neither nonwhite American institutions nor most lower income households will benefit directly from these policy initiatives. Nor is it clear that they benefit from any generic short- or longer-term effects of the program without targeted public investment, particularly in the human and physical infrastructure of the inner cities.

Political scientist Aaron Wildavsky's reflections on the implications of normative theories of budgeting are particularly appropriate to analysis of the political implications of the federal budget to nonwhite Americans: "If a normative theory budgeting is to be more than academic exercise, it must actually guide the making of governmental decisions."[32] Wildavsky indicates that the Congressional Black Caucus represents those who envisage "a high-tax, high service state geared to improving the lot of the worst off."[33] The key point is that a normative ethical approach to budgetary politics is required not only in policy formulation and adoption but also in policy implementation.[34]

Summary and Conclusions

The high levels of dependency on public sector funding by nonwhite Americans raise two key questions for pluralist theory: Is racial and ethnic group access to resources solely dependent on the organizational prowess of these groups? Does that access include the distributional and redistributional capacity of public bureaucracies? These questions raise two additional theoretical issues for political scientists: First, is the degree of institutionalized variation of administrative access maintained by various groups in the political system fair and equitable? If group A historically influences public choices more than group B, will government be biased or skewed in its policy making and administrative orientations toward group A? Will that policy bias institutionalize itself enough to require a greater effort by group B to use its rights to influence resource allocation from bureaucracies vis-à-vis group A?

The second theoretical issue centers on the universe of resources available to government and governmental agencies to satisfy the preferences of groups in the political system. Possible outcomes of competition between groups A and B will be influenced by resources (taxes and other revenue sources) generated by groups A and B into the political system and the total resources government has available through the administrative process. Given socioeconomic conditions in nonwhite communities, will dependency on the meager resources of government bureaucracies expand or contract?

These two theoretical issues make the application of pluralist theories and its variants to nonwhite Americans and fiscal politics problematic. Nonwhite Americans have been brought into the political system at a different level from other groups. They begin and sustain competition with those groups for public resources at a much lower level. Specifically, blacks, Latinos and Native Americans are substantially and uniquely dependent on government dollars for their most fundamental needs. History and ongoing discriminatory practice limit their ability to compete at all levels of government.

On the other hand, other groups and institutions in the United States are becoming increasingly dependent on government budgets for their survival: such groups as farmers, the disabled, immigrants, the homeless, those who suffer from acquired immune deficiency syndrome (AIDS), and many others, including such institutions as state and local governments, lending institutions, transitional foreign governments, and declining manufacturing industries. Consequently, nonwhite Americans are competing with an increasingly diverse constellation of the budgetary needy while available budget dollars at all levels of government continue to shrink. This particular context of nonwhite participation in the politics of allocation policies is rarely incorporated in analyses of public policy and administration.

These developments combined to create clouded budgetary scenarios for nonwhites in both the first and second Bush administrations. Equity issues raised by the controversy over President George W. Bush's record on homeland security, civil rights; a badly bungled response and recovery program in New Orleans and the Gulf region following the devastation of Hurricane Katrina in 2005 and throughout 2006; continuing struggles over the implementation of No Child Left Behind in increasingly nonwhite public school systems; and exponential increases in the number of young black men killed and wounded in inner-city drug-related warfare generated serious political skepticism among nonwhite American politicians and political activists. They continue to place federal, state and local bureaucracies in the center of the political maelstrom.

In response, the politics of federal deficit management makes no effective response to any particular group or institutional need. Bush proposals for the overhaul of the Social Security Trust Fund, the Highway Trust Fund, and federal housing programs will continue to raise issues about the role of public bureaucracies in the politics of race and ethnicity. Nonwhites are inextricably intertwined in these spending debates. The prospects of reduced entitlements not only erode the value of food stamps, TANF, Medicare, and other public dollars but also are unresponsive to increases in need resulting from the most recent economic recession. Moreover, tax provisions, particularly the Earned Income Tax Credit, are generally progressive at the income tax level but generally regressive at the excise tax level. Consequently, tax reduction and other fiscal packages proposed by President Bush may be only partially responsive to the fiscal principles of productivity, equity, and elasticity.

The struggle to attain equity and financial choice for blacks, Hispanics, women, and the poor will escalate. Middle- and upper-income white Americans have as great if not a greater stake in the outcome of that struggle as do those who are needy. The ultimate financial beneficiaries of this struggle include white businesses, educational institutions, and public agencies, because those who are needy frequently patronize them.

Formal policy and administrative impact assessments should be used by nonwhite political and advocacy organizations to advance the needs of nonwhite Americans participating in legislative hearings, public rule makings, regulatory processes, and judicial proceedings. All these points underscore the need for nonwhite policy advocates to acquire, utilize, and work carefully with their own and other experts. Policy expertise comes from many disciplines and is the major weapon of interests whose ethical preferences prevail in policy. The new fiscal imperatives are therefore best met by a new and more effective use of expertise.

Because of the budgetary constraints now faced by federal, state, and local governments and the general malaise and morass of problems confronting lending institutions, nonwhites face, at best, an attitude of fiscal indifference from those governments despite the policy and administrative strategies of President Bush. Traditional policy approaches to the resolution of obstinate socioeconomic and institutional problems in nonwhite communities will be largely overlooked by fiscal decision making without linking those resolutions to visible financial and socioeconomic paybacks.

Finally, this analysis links the continuing dependency of many nonwhite American households and most nonwhite American institutions on public sector fiscal decisions to the shortcomings of political science as a discipline. Given the position of people of color in the economy, their lack of well-funded political lobbying groups, and their limited access to the mainstream media, it is easy to overlook their exposure to the vicissitudes of politics and the whims of the economy. Even decisions made in a supposedly race-neutral way have a disparate impact on nonwhite Americans. Moreover, the quality of life issues addressed by most nonwhite American politicians and political activists must increasingly include explicit references to fiscal policy. The former mayor of New York City, John Lindsay, was correct when he said that "a budget is a political document."[35] As a number of political scientists have argued, it is also often a document with hidden beneficiaries.

Offering such alternative budget proposals as the National Urban League's call for a fifty billion dollar urban Marshall Plan for cities in the 1990s, the Small and Minority Business Legal Defense and Education Fund demand for increases in government procurement opportunities for minority businesses, and the demands of many civil rights groups for greater government investment in the education of African American children has not worked, as evidenced in contemporary socioeconomic disparities. The majority of the American public has not rallied to support these programs. Accordingly, nonwhite Americans must engage the politics of fiscal policy more directly, more vigorously, and more explicitly. Otherwise certain interest groups in the political agenda will continue to have their preferences met at the expense of the blacks, Latinos and other substantially poor populations. Indeed, it is the responsibility of political scientists to explicate policy preferences in an increasingly complex public policy process. They must expose the unethical aspects of budgetary decision more cogently. Given that budgets are the resource base of bureaucracies, the potential contributions of the administrative state to racial justice in the United States rests firmly on a vision of public finance that addresses the conditions of the neediest to both advance social justice and to contribute to social, economic and political stability in the nation as a whole.

Notes

1. Charles V. Hamilton, "The Welfare of Black Americans," *Political Science Quarterly* 101 (June 1968): 253. See also Vincent Philip Munoz, "Unreconstructed Democracy: W. E. B. Du Bois and the Case for Reparations," *American Political Science Review* 97, no. 1 (February 2003): 33–44. On the concept of the administrative state, see Dwight Waldo, *The Administrative State: A Study of the Political Theory of American Public Administration*, 2nd ed. (New York: Holmes and Meier, 1983); Gabriel J. Chin, "Regulating Race: Asian Exclusion in the Administrative State," *Harvard Civil Rights–Civil Liberties Law Review* 37, no. 1 (Winter 2002): 1–63; Steven E. Aufrecht and David Case, "Indians 78, Washington State 0: Stories About Indians and the Law," *Public Administration Review* 65, no. 4 (July–August 2005): 450–61; William C. Canby, *American Indian Law in a Nutshell*, 4th ed. (St. Paul, MN: Thomson-West, 2004); and Emmett S. Redford and Roscoe C. Martin, *Democracy in the Administrative State* (New York: Oxford University Press, 1985).

2. Mack Jones, "A Frame of Reference for Black Politics," in Lenneal J. Henderson, *Black Political Life in the United States: A Fist as the Pendulum* (San Francisco, CA: Chandler, 1972).

3. Xavier de Souza Briggs, ed., *The Geography of Opportunity: Race and Housing Choice in Metropolitan America* (Washington, DC: The Brookings Institution, 2005), 310–43.

4. John L. Mikesell, *Fiscal Administration: Analysis and Applications for the Public Sector*, 6th ed. (Belmont, CA: Thomson-Wadsworth, 2003). See also Lawrence C. Howard, Lenneal J. Henderson Jr., and Deryl Hunt, eds., *Public Administration and Public Policy: A Minority Perspective* (Pittsburgh, PA: Public Policy Press of Pittsburgh, 1977); and H. George Frederickson, "The State of Social Equity in American Public Administration," *National Civic Review* 94, no. 4 (November 2004): 31–38; Frank Sacton, "Financing Public Programs under Fiscal Constraint," in *Managing Programs: Balancing Politics, Administration, and Public Needs*, ed. Robert E. Cleary and Nicholas Henry, 147–66 (San Francisco: Jossey-Bass, 1989).

5. Lenneal J. Henderson Jr., "Budget and Tax Strategy: Implications for Blacks," in *The State of Black America, 1990*, ed. Janet Dewart, 53–54 (New York: National Urban League, 1990).

6. John W. Wright, ed., *The Universal Almanac 1991* (New York: Universal Press, 1991), v–vi; Charles H. Levine, ed., *Managing Fiscal Stress: The Crisis in the Public Sector* (Chatham, NJ: Chatham House, 1980), 4. See also Georgia A. Persons, "Blacks in State and Local Government: Progress and Constraints," in *The State of Black America 1987*, ed. Janet Dewart (New York: National Urban League, 1987), 167–92; Georgia A. Persons, "Reflection on Mayoral Leadership: The Impact of Changing Issues and Changing Times," *Phylon* 41 (September 1985): 205–18; Hanes Walton, *Black Politics: A Theoretical and Structural Analysis* (Philadelphia: J. B. Lippincott, 1972); and Frank D. Bean and Stephanie Bell-Rose, *Immigration and Opportunity: Race, Ethnicity and Employment in the U.S.* (New York: Russell Sage Foundation, 1999).

7. Francisco Rodriguez, "Inequality, Redistribution and Rent-Seeking," *Economics and Politics* 16, no. 3 (November 2004): 293.

8. Henderson, "Budget and Tax Strategy," 55. On theories, concepts, and methodologies in political science see Robert E. Goodin and Hans-Dieter Klingemann, eds., *A New Handbook of Political Science* (New York: Oxford University Press, 1998); and Nelson W. Polsby, ed., *Annual Review of Political Science*, vol. 8 (Palo Alto, CA: Annual Reviews, 2005).

9. Congressional Black Caucus, *The Quality of Life, Fiscal 1991 Alternative Budget* (Washington, DC: Government Printing Office, 1989), 1–7. See also Katherine Tate, *Black Faces in the Mirror: African Americans in their Representatives in the U.S. Congress* (Princeton, NJ: Princeton University Press, 2003).

10. Children's Defense Fund, *Children's Defense Fund Budget, Fiscal Year 1989* (Washington, DC: Government Printing Office, 1989), 12. See also Joel Spring, *Conflict of Interests: The Politics of American Education*, 5th ed. (New York: McGraw-Hill, 2005); and Larson and Carlos J. Ovando, *The Color of Bureaucracy: The Politics of Equity in Multicultural School Districts* (Stamford, CT: Wadsworth/Thomson Learning, 2001).

11. For examples, see the Congressional Task Force on Federal Excise Taxes, *Analyzing the Possible Impact of Federal Excise Taxes on the Poor, Including Blacks and Other Minorities* (Washington, DC: Voter Education and Registration Action, 1987).

12. *State of Small Business, 2001* (Washington, DC: Government Printing Office, 2001).

13. Persons, "Blacks in State and Local Government," and "Reflections on Mayoral Leadership."

14. Hanes Walton, *When the Marching Stopped: The Politics of Civil Rights Regulatory Agencies* (Albany: State University of New York Press, 1988), 59. See also Lucius J. Barker, Mack H. Jones, and Katherine Tate, *African Americans and the American Political System*, 4th ed. (Englewood Cliffs, NJ: Prentice-Hall, 1998); Paula McClain and Joseph Stewart, *Can We All Get Along? Racial and Ethnic Minorities in American Politics*, 3rd ed. (Boulder, CO: Westview, 2001).

15. 488 U.S. 469 (1989)

16. Lenneal J. Henderson Jr., "The Impact of Military Base Shutdowns," *Black Scholar* (September 1974): 56–58.

17. "The Peace Economy: How Defense Cuts Will Fuel America's Long-Term Prosperity," *Business Week*, December 11, 1989, p. 51.

18. Ibid., 52.

19. Marshall Kaplan, "Infrastructure Policy: Repetitive Studies, Uneven Response, Next Steps," *Urban Affairs Quarterly* 25 (March 1990): 371–88. See also Harrell R. Rodgers, "Saints, Stalwarts, and Slackers: State Financial Contributions to Welfare Reform," *Policy Studies Journal* 33, no. 4 (November 2005): 497–508.

20. Children's Defense Fund, *Children's Defense Fund Budget, Fiscal Year 1989*, 12.

21. District of Columbia, *Operating Budget, 1990 Fiscal Year*. Gramm-Rudman-Hollings is the informal title for the Balanced Budget and Emergency Deficit Control Act of 1985, which mandated steadily decreasing national government annual budget deficits through fiscal year (FY) 1991, when the deficit was supposed to reach zero. The legislation was amended in 1987 to postpone the target date for a zero deficit to FY 1993. It was amended further in 1993, in effect, by the five-year deficit reduction agreement reached by President George H. W. Bush and the Congress.

22. 42 U.S.C. 7141, Section 641.

23. U.S. Department of Energy, *Functional Interrelationships of the Office of Minority Economic Impact* (Washington, DC: U.S. Government Printing Office, 1989).

24. William W. Ellis and Darlene Calbert, *Blacks and Tax Reform 1985–86* (Washington, DC: Congressional Research Service, 1986).

25. Paul Leonard and Robert Greenstein, *One Step Forward: The Deficit Reduction Package of 1990* (Washington, DC: Center on Budget Priorities, 1990), 5.

26. Mikesell, *Fiscal Administration*, 487.

27. Lenneal J. Henderson Jr., "Fiscal Strategy, Public Policy and the Social Agenda," *Urban League Review* 13 (Summer 1989–Winter 1989–1990), 9–22. See also Paul Posner, *The Politics of Unfunded Mandates: Whither Federalism?* (Washington, DC: Georgetown University Press, 1998). See also Michael Eric Dyson, *Come Hell or High Water: Hurricane Katrina and the Color of Disaster* (New York: Basic Books, 2006).

28. Ibid.

29. Leonard and Greenstein, *One Step Forward*, 12–14.

30. Ibid., 16–17.

31. Henderson, "Blacks, Budgets and Taxes," 84.

32. "Without Sacrifice," *The Economist*, 328, no. 7823 (1993): 25–26.

33. Aaron Wildavsky, "Political Implications of Budget Reform," *Public Administration Review* 21 (January–February 1961): 183–90. See also Barbara S. Romzek and Jocelyn M. Johnson, "State Social Services Contracting: Exploring the Determinants of Effective Contract Accountability," *Public Administration Review* 65, no. 4 (July–August 2005): 436–49.

34. Aaron Wildavsky, "Political Implications of Budget Reform: A Retrospective," *Public Administration Review* 52 (November–December 1992): 594–99; Thomas Dye, *Understanding Public Policy*, 11th ed. (Upper Saddle River, NJ: Pearson-Prentice-Hall, 2004), 241–67. See also Wojciech Olszewski and Howard Rosenthal, "Politically Determined Income Inequality and the Provision of Public Goods," *Journal of Public Economic Theory* 6, no. 5 (December 2004): 707–36; Francisco Rodriguez, "Inequality, Redistribution and Rent-Seeking," *Economics and Politics* 16, no. 3 (November 2004): 287–320; and Lael R. Keiser, Peter R. Mueser, and Choi Whan-Sueng, "Race, Bureaucratic Discretion, and the Implementation of Welfare Reform," *American Journal of Political Science* 48, no. 2 (April 2004): 314–27.

35. Lenneal J. Henderson Jr., "Fiscal Strategy, Public Policy and the Social Agenda," *Urban League Review* 13 (Summer 1989): 14.

CHAPTER FIFTEEN

Race and the City

The View from Two Political Science Journals

MARION ORR AND VALERIE C. JOHNSON

T HIS ESSAY IS an exploratory examination of the ways in which political scientists have covered urban politics. What is the place of the study of urban life among American political scientists? When political science has taken up the issue of urban affairs, what has been its focus? And finally, how have political scientists who study American urban politics handled race and racial issues?

To explore these questions, we systematically examined the articles on urban politics in the two oldest political science journals: the *Political Science Quarterly* and the *American Political Science Review*. Founded in 1886, *PSQ* is the older of the two journals. The *APSR*, founded in 1906, is the official journal of the American Political Science Association (APSA). Both journals are considered to be first-rate publications among political scientists.[1] The *APSR* is regarded by many as the top journal in the discipline. In addition, these journals are national in scope and encourage contributions from all subfields within the discipline of political science. Our research process allows for a systematic longitudinal survey of over a century of scholarship on urban politics.[2]

Urban Affairs Review (formerly *Urban Affairs Quarterly*) and the *Journal of Urban Affairs* are journals dedicated to the specific study of urban issues. They do not allow, however, an in-depth analysis of the place of urban politics in the discipline of political science as a whole. In addition, both of these journals are relatively new in comparison to *PSQ* and *APSR* and do not provide the opportunity for a longitudinal survey of scholarship on urban politics—more particularly, how race has been treated in the urban literature.[3]

Journal articles in the *APSR* from 1906 to 2002 (volumes 1–96) and in *PSQ* from 1886 to 2001 (volumes 1–116) were compiled and downloaded using the online electronic journal archive *JStor*. Articles published after 1999 were identified in the bound copies of the journals located in the libraries of Brown and DePaul Universities respectively. We conducted a systematic and chronological search through each volume of the selected journals to determine the total number of major articles and to identify the number of articles that dealt with urban politics. Our analysis included only research articles; review and bibliographical articles were not included. Articles with a central focus on American cities were selected for inclusion in the analysis.

Academic journals are published for the express purpose of exposing the general membership of the discipline to important scholarly developments in the field. Journals distribute highly specific knowledge and report original research in order to make such information available to members of the discipline. One survey of political scientists found that "scholarly journals were more important than other media for the communication of professional knowledge."[4] Articles featuring cutting-edge research that extends the academic frontiers are found in academic journals, especially the "flagship" journals that are the official publications of their scholarly associations. We can learn a great deal about the methods and concerns of scholars in a particular discipline by examining its premier journals. Of course, there are other published indicators of an academic discipline's understanding and approach to a particular subject matter.[5] To keep the length of this essay manageable, however, we focused on journal articles only. Many academicians are quick to link their prestige and credentials to subjects that are "hot" or just short of revolutionary because they know that editors and reviewers are likely to look favorably on such work. Publishing such work in a premier journal enhances the academicians' prestige among their peers and advances their careers.

General Analysis of Journal Articles on Urban Politics

As Table 15.1 shows, only a tiny fraction of the articles in the selected journals deal with urban subjects. Of the 6,842 articles published in the *APSR* and *PSQ* in the time periods under consideration, only 168 or 2.4 percent covered some aspect of urban politics. The *APSR* and *PSQ* published nearly identical percentages of urban articles. In almost a hundred years of existence, the *APSR* published nearly four thousand major articles, but only 90 (2.2 percent) were urban-related. Among its 2,847 articles, *PSQ* published a slightly higher percentage—2.7 percent—of urban-related manuscripts. As viewed from its oldest and most prestigious journals, urban politics has not had a prominent place in political science.[6]

Cities have always been a feature of the American political scene. The data in Figure 15.1 show that cities began to receive attention in the *PSQ* and *APSR* in the early twentieth century. Nineteen percent of the urban articles in the two

TABLE 15.1 Articles in Two Premier Journals

Political Science Journal	Number of Articles	Number of Urban Articles
Political Science Quarterly	2847	78 (2.7%)
American Political Science Review	3995	90 (2.2%)
Total	6,842	168 (2.4%)

Source: Authors' compilation of articles from the *APSR* (Volumes 1–96) and *PSQ* (Volumes 1–116).

journals appeared between 1900 and 1919. The bulk of these articles appeared in the *PSQ*. Surprisingly, as the United States became an urban nation in the 1920s and 1930s, the number of urban articles in political science journals fell slightly from that of the previous twenty-year period. During the 1950s, as the period of what Rae called "urbanism" began to taper off, the total number of articles in the *PSQ* and *APSR* fell to one and four respectively.[7] The 1960s and 1970s witnessed a significant resurgence in the number of articles on cities published in the two selected journals. Clearly, the protest activities and civil disorders in the central cities of the 1960s captured the attention of social scientists. Over one-third of all the urban articles published in *PSQ* and *APSR* appeared during the 1960s and 1970s. Indeed, nearly a quarter of these articles were published between 1970 and 1979—the largest number of urban-related articles to appear in the two journals during any single decade. The *APSR*, for example, published 23 urban-focused articles during the 1970s. In the 1980s, the number of urban articles returned to the level of the early 1900s, to 22. As we approached the dawn of the twenty-first century, we found that the number of articles tapered off, reaching the lowest number in over three decades.

Major Areas of Interest

In order to discern the patterns and relationships that emerge from the data, we categorized the articles into five substantive areas. *Urban policy* articles examine key laws, judicial decisions, and administrative rules that determine the benefits and constraints that come from federal, state and local governments and impact cities. Articles on *governance and service delivery* analyze governance arrangements,

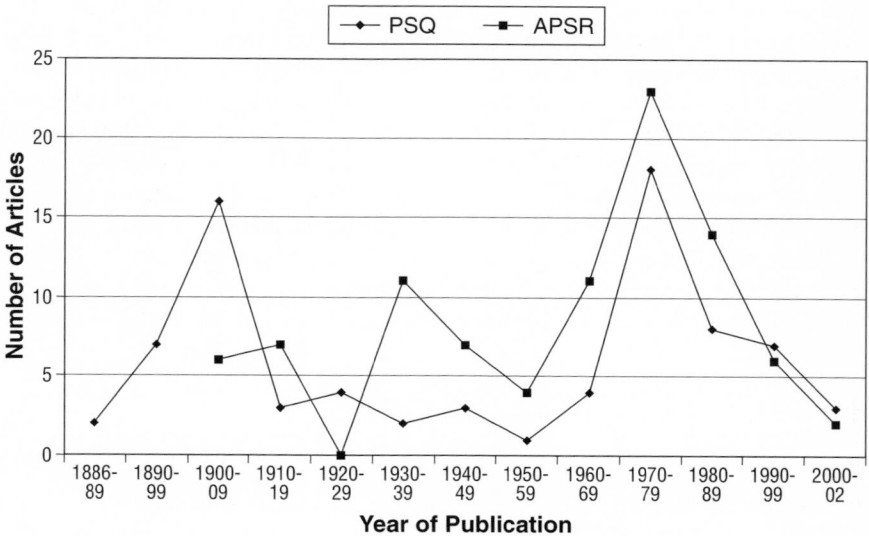

FIGURE 15.1   Urban Articles in *PSQ* and *APSR*, 1886–2002

Source: Authors' compilation of articles from the *APSR* (Volumes 1–96) and *PSQ* (Volumes 1–116).

metropolitan and regional government, and issues related to the provision of urban services. *Theory* refers to studies that provide conceptual approaches to urban politics, including issues of political power and the structure and function of decision making processes. Articles on *political participation* address voting turnout, public opinion, political parties, and electoral behavior in city politics. *Race and racial politics* articles analyze political issues directly concerning African Americans in the city.

Which substantive areas in urban politics have appeared most frequently in the *APSR* and *PSQ*? The data in Table 15.2 show that political scientists have been most interested in issues of governance and service delivery. In *PSQ*, 43 percent of the urban-related articles were in this area; 33 percent of the *APSR* urban articles concerned governance and service delivery. Of the 168 urban articles published in the two journals, 38 percent covered governance and service delivery. A higher percentage (24 percent) of urban policy articles appeared in the *PSQ* than in the *APSR*, in which only 11 percent of the urban articles focused on policy. In the *APSR*, articles on political participation in central cities comprised the second-largest percentage of urban articles. Issues of race and ethnicity received very little coverage among urban articles. Across the two journals, only 11 percent of the articles dealt with race and ethnicity. In the *PSQ*, only 6 percent of the urban articles were focused on race and ethnicity. With 15 percent of its articles on race, the *APSR* did a little better in this substantive area than the *PSQ*. Finally, the lowest number and percentage of urban articles were in the area of theory; the majority of them appeared in the *APSR*.

The remainder of this essay provides an overview of the manner in which race and racial issues were treated in each of the five substantive urban research areas covered in the two journals. Such an analysis is important, as large urban areas are predominately populated by African Americans and Latinos. In short, urban areas have become synonymous with racial politics.

Urban Governance and Service Delivery

The *APSR* and *PSQ*'s formative years were during the Progressive Era (1890s–1920s), when concerns about corruption and the efficient operation of city governments were paramount. It should cause little surprise that the early urban-related articles in the *APSR* and *PSQ* were dominated by discussions of the municipal reforms

TABLE 15.2   Percentage of Articles in Five Substantive Research Areas

Substantive Area	PSQ	APSR	Combined Percentage
Governance and Service Delivery	43%	33%	38%
Urban Policy	24%	11%	17%
Theory	3.8%	13%	9%
Political Participation	19%	26%	22%
Race and Racial Politics	6.4%	15%	11%
Other	2.5%	1%	1.7%

Source: Authors' compilation of articles from the *APSR* (Volumes 1–96) and *PSQ* (Volumes 1–116).

advocated by progressives. Political scientists were among the leading advocates of the reform movement.

What stands out from a reading of these articles is that political scientists clearly took normative positions concerning the challenges facing municipal governance. Throughout the Progressive Era, articles appeared in the *APSR* and *PSQ* supporting the virtues of municipal charter reform, scientific management in city governance, commission plans, city manager systems, referenda, initiatives, and recalls, as well as denunciations of the dominance of political party bosses.[8] In short, the two premier journals in the field of political science became advocates of progressive reforms.

The politics and administration of progressive reforms continued to dominate the scholarship of urban affairs in the *APSR* and *PSQ* through the 1950s and into the 1970s. By the 1980s, however, attention shifted to service delivery and the distribution of services across communities. Essentially, these studies sought to determine the ways in which city governments allocated services and what types of equity characterized service delivery.

The early political scientists who used the academic journals to advocate progressive reforms were guided by the view that values and normative judgments can be eliminated from the administration of policy. In their analysis, there is no substantive discussion of black voters or black leaders' reactions to progressive reform, nor is there any significant attention paid to the potential impact of the reforms on the black community. This oversight is striking, considering that African Americans were present in considerable numbers in many of the major cities during the Progressive Era. Indeed, the first great migration of African Americans from the rural South to the urban North took place during that period. Still, the bulk of the published articles in the area of urban governance and service delivery ignored African Americans.

In some instances, when the presence of blacks confounded analysis, political scientists simply dropped them from the study. This approach was taken by Wolfinger and Field, who tested Banfield and Wilson's "political ethos" theory among "foreign stock" residents in 309 cities with populations over 50,000 according to the 1960 census. "Foreign stock population percentages exclude Negroes," they wrote, because "in most such cities Negroes were scarce and politically unimportant."[9] Although African Americans were excluded from the study, Wolfinger and Field nevertheless speculated that African Americans "might be considered inclined to the private-regarding ethos."

One of the first exceptions to the pattern of ignoring urban blacks was Zeller and Bone's 1948 study of the repeal of proportional representation (PR) in New York City.[10] Zeller and Bone noted that black organizations, including the National Association for the Advancement of Colored People (NAACP) and the *Amsterdam News*, favored the retention of PR. This article made clear that the establishment of proportional representation was a significant reason why New York City voters elected an African American to the city council for the first time in 1941. Black leaders in New York strongly supported PR and opposed the successful effort to repeal it.

As we moved into the 1980s, we noted that journal articles that focused on service delivery and governance often included some discussion of the African American community. By the 1960s, race had become such a salient issue, especially in urban America, that most researchers found it prudent to include race when analyzing urban bureaucracies. Typically, these studies included the race variable to test whether there was evidence of discrimination in the distribution and allocation of municipal services. For the most part, the studies supported the view that the level of services a community receives is not the result of conscious discrimination but is largely determined by decisions or rules made within an agency as it attempts to perform its job. Bryan Jones, for example, found no indication of discrimination on the basis of race in his study of service delivery in Chicago.[11] In fact, Kenneth Mladenka showed that in Chicago, "black demands and protests" were important determinants for the allocation of parks in African American communities.[12] These are interesting findings, for they raise the question that if there is no or little discrimination in the distribution of urban services, why have public opinion polls consistently shown a racial gap in citizens' views about service delivery? Polls usually find white residents indicating a high level of satisfaction with public services and African American residents typically expressing a negative opinion of the quality of the urban service in their communities.

Political Participation, Elections, Campaigns

Elections, campaigns, and political participation are exciting aspects of urban life. The annals of American urban politics are dotted with colorful politicians who appealed to residents for their vote. Early urban-related journal articles that focused on campaigns and elections were critical of the election processes and the political bosses that controlled them. As indicated above, the flagship political science journals were organs for advocacy of progressive reforms and outlets for those who proposed alternatives to boss rule. And as successful challenges to machine rule occurred, political scientists captured them for the readers of their premier journals.[13]

With the 1948 publication of the landmark study *The People's Choice*, American political scientists began a period of long and sustained interest in the individual and systemic determinants of political participation.[14] Political scientists who studied cities joined this "behavioral revolution."[15] In the behavioral approach to political participation, however, resource-poor citizens (read African Americans) were often perceived as powerless. Hence the traditional models used to explain participation were predicated on an inverse relationship between social status and political participation, especially voting.[16]

Early scholarship on urban elections, campaigns, and participation that appeared in the *APSR* and *PSQ* typically ignored African Americans. Although much of this work focused on New York, Philadelphia, Cleveland, and Chicago, where boss rule was prevalent and an emerging concentration of African American residents existed, only in rare cases did the articles capture the African American experience under the heading of machine politics. For

example, none of the articles covering the electoral strength of New York's Tammany Hall paid attention to African Americans. Studies of the Workingmen's
Party's attempt to challenge machine rule in Boston and New York City ignored
the thousands of free African Americans living in those two cities.[17] Roy Peel's
close examination of New York City's Democratic machine made no mention of
African Americans.[18] John Salter mentioned that in the 1930s Philadelphia's
Republican machine had a "negro division," but he tells us nothing about it.[19] In
his examination of political parties in New York, Hugh Bone went a little further
than others, describing the role of "a young Negro," James Pemberton, who was
an important "protégé" of U.S. Representative Vito Marcantonio, a key player in
New York's Tammany Hall.[20] Congressman Marcantonio depended on Pemberton to be his liaison to local political parties. As Bone described it, "through
Pemberton, Marcantonio can always get his view across in Tammany executive
meetings." Bone's description of Pemberton, however, appears only in a footnote.
There is no mention of him in the article's text.

The presence of African Americans often confounded some of the underlying theoretical assumptions and findings of early urban scholars studying elections,
campaigns, and participation. For example, in one statistical study, Ogburn and
Hill found a strong correlation between low economic status and voting for
Franklin D. Roosevelt. These scholars discovered, however, that socioeconomic
status was only weakly associated with African Americans' evaluations of the two
major parties. African American voters did not fit their theory. How did the
authors explain this conundrum? They surmised that low-income blacks' voting
patterns diverged from those of similarly situated whites, "no doubt for historical
reasons."[21] To make their analysis consistent, Ogburn and Hill simply dropped
African American voters from the analysis. As they stated: "Negro precincts were
omitted; they were low rent precincts that voted for Republicans."[22]

Wilson and Banfield's political ethos theory, which bifurcated voters into
those who had a so-called public-regardingness value and those who did not,
caused a great deal of interest in the discipline. Wilson and Banfield's work, however, also highlighted the difficulties of making valid scientific interpretations
with inadequate or incomplete data. For example, the authors claimed that
middle-class and upper-income white voters were "more disposed than others to
rest their [vote] choices on some conception of the 'public interest' or the 'welfare of the community'" than low-income voters.[23] When they sought to test the
extent to which public-regardingness existed among "upper-income home owners," their sample of voting precincts in Cleveland included only whites. As Wilson and Banfield acknowledged, "There are not enough home-owning Negroes
. . . to make a really satisfactory matching of the wards possible."[24] To this extent,
the structural factors that limited African American social and economic mobility rendered this comparison impossible and the analysis incomplete.

Protest has long been a part of the American political landscape. The black
protests of the 1960s were the first participatory activity by blacks that actually
encouraged political scientists to take a different line of research. In the 1960s
political scientists were forced to examine the involvement of African Americans
and other "powerless" groups with unconventional political activities. When the

doors of the voting arena were closed to African Americans, they turned to protest politics. Voting studies conducted prior to the 1965 Voting Rights Act, when systemic and formal restrictions limited black voting, obviously illuminated only a small aspect of black political participation. This situation is not surprising, given that the "most striking and theoretically interesting features of black political behavior have been expressed through unconventional political participation exemplified by sit-in activity and direct action."[25]

The articles that captured the political protest of the 1960s put African Americans front and center. Peter Eisinger, for example, found that during the 1960s, African Americans tended to be more confident than whites about the impact of their particular protest efforts.[26] Michael Lipsky's classic article, "Protest as a Political Resource," was less sanguine about the effectiveness of protest politics.[27] He noted that a critical element in the success of protest is the capacity of powerless groups to activate or gain the support of "reference publics." It is the reaction of these third parties that cause the protest "targets" to address or ignore the concerns raised by the protest constituents. In the final analysis, Lipsky questions whether protest is a viable political resource for powerless groups.

Urban Policy

As noted above, the *PSQ* published a higher percentage of urban policy articles than the *APSR*. Generally speaking, however, the urban policy articles focused on the politics of urban policy at the federal level. Only a small number of urban policy studies that appeared in the two journals focused on policy specifically at the local level.[28]

The articles on urban policy once again reflected limited coverage of African Americans and race. As noted, the bulk of the articles in this area focused on federal urban policy. There is an underlying assumption in these articles that federal programs designed to address the problems of cities would ultimately benefit African Americans. There is no discussion, however, of the role African Americans played in shaping federal urban policy. Historically, African American members of Congress have represented central cities. Their district boundaries typically included blighted inner-city areas struggling with poverty, high unemployment, homelessness, crime, and other indicators of social and economic distress. Black members of Congress and their positions on federal urban programs were not discussed.

By directing their attention primarily to the role of the federal government in formulating urban policy, political scientists missed opportunities to examine the formation and implementation of urban policy at the local level. This oversight left the role of African American mayors and other local black elected officials out of the analysis. In the few articles that focused on urban policy from a local perspective, none of the authors considered race or racial politics.

Urban Theory

Long-time students of urban politics will remember the community power studies of the 1950s and 1960s, and the great debate they generated among political scientists. Over a twenty-year period—from 1958 through 1980—the *APSR* became the primary venue for the battle of ideas between the elitists, pluralists, neo-elitists, and the neo-pluralists. During the height of the community power controversy, the editor of the *APSR* was Nelson Polsby, who had studied under Robert Dahl and worked as a graduate research assistant on his *Who Governs?* book, which challenged Floyd Hunter's findings in *Community Power Structure*.[29] Polsby provided space in the journal not only for major articles like Dahl's 1958 article, "A Critique of the Ruling Elite Model," but also for extensive comments and exchanges between the community power combatants.[30] Interestingly, the *PSQ* did not publish any articles concerning the community power debate.

Floyd Hunter's *Community Power Structure* and Dahl's *Who Governs?* pay very little attention to African Americans or racial politics. Hunter included a separate chapter on the "power structure" in Atlanta's black community but indicated that the African American community was isolated from the city's power center. Dahl's massive study devoted a few paragraphs to blacks in the politics of New Haven, Connecticut. Given that the two major works at the center of the debate about the distribution of power within urban communities paid little attention to race, it is not surprising that subsequent studies in urban political theory included very little analysis of African Americans' role in urban decision making. Moreover, many of these studies were published in the 1960s and 1970s, when African Americans were just beginning to capture political offices. African Americans had long been shut out of positions of authority in the corporate sector. Given the paucity of African Americans in leadership positions in the public and private sectors at the time, it is not surprising that studies of elites did not include them. These studies were more concerned with examining politics from the top down than from the bottom up.

Racial Politics

The first urban-related article to appear in the *APSR* that dealt directly with the politics of the African American community was published in 1934 by Harold Gosnell.[31] *PSQ* published its first article in this category in 1977. Gosnell's article, part of his larger study of "Negro politics" in Chicago, was a unique appraisal of the meetings and rallies designed to encourage the black community toward political action.[32] We learned from this pioneering article about the character of African American urban politics, including the role of religion, the significance of black oratory, and racial group consciousness in African American political life. Gosnell's seminal article appeared nearly thirty years after the founding of the *APSR*. It would be another forty-six years before the *APSR* published another urban-related article in which race and racial politics were central.

In the 1970s the pace of published urban-related articles devoted to race and racial politics quickened. This newfound scholarly attention was engendered by the massive upswing in African American political mobilization and civil disorders in Detroit, Los Angeles, Newark, and other central cities. The articles mentioned above by Eisinger and Lipsky on protest politics were representative of attempts to understand the nature and quantify the individual characteristics of African Americans who participated in the civil disturbances in the central cities. Aberbach and Walker used a public opinion survey of Detroit residents in 1967 to examine the meaning and reaction of black and white respondents to the then-popular slogan "black power." Not surprisingly, they found that the "overwhelming majority of whites are frightened and bewildered by the words *black power*" and that 42 percent of black respondents viewed the term positively, "either as a call for equal treatment and a fair share for Negroes, or as an appeal for racial solidarity in the struggle against discrimination."[33] Miller, Bolce, and Halligan sought to challenge the popular "relative deprivation theory" that posited that the civil disorders were fueled by rising African American expectations combined with the actual decline of their social and economic status.[34] Joel Lieske offered a developmental model of the civil disorders, showing them to be a function of black social class. Lieske argued that the economic progress blacks made during the 1960s might have been the needed social catalyst that ignited the civil rights movement and subsequent unrest.[35]

By the late 1970s, as the full impact of the 1965 Voting Rights Act was being felt, and as African American communities across the nation shifted from "protest to politics," a number of political scientists studying urban politics focused on African American voters. In 1977 *PSQ* published a short article by Charles Hamilton, the first urban-related research published by an African American to appear in either of the two premier journals. Hamilton examined the relationship between voter registration drives and subsequent voter turnout in Harlem. His analysis showed that only about half of the new registrants voted on election day. Harlem's black community apparently responded to the nonprofit organizations that were conducting voter registration. Because of their tax-exempt status, however, the nonprofit organizations could not work to turn out voters on election day, leaving the task to labor unions and party organizations.[36] Hamilton observed that the party organizations in Harlem were particularly weak, failing to mobilize black voters.

In a second article on black politics in New York City, Hamilton argued that the poverty programs of the 1960s and 1970s had a demobilizing impact on blacks. These programs operated within the framework of a "patron-recipient" instead of a "patron-client" relationship. In the former, "the recipient receives from the patron and is asked to do nothing but receive the benefits. The recipient, for the most part, is a passive partner."[37] Hamilton was interested in the impact of poverty programs in determining levels of African American political participation. Other urban scholars looked at a range of factors that could explain black political behavior at the local level. Bobo and Gilliam determined that the presence of black elected officials had a statistically significant positive impact on black political participation. They found that black residents who lived in high "black empowerment" cities (cities with a black mayor) were more likely to participate in politics than blacks who did not.[38] Cohen and Dawson found that living in high-poverty areas led to greater isolation from the social institutions that are most involved in African American politics; a lack of confidence in black group effectiveness; and lower levels of political participation.[39]

African Americans have long shared the expectation that putting blacks in positions of authority in municipal government would lead to policy outcomes more beneficial to the black community. Several scholars tested this proposition, examining the impact of African American mayors, city councilors, and other city officials. Peter Eisinger, and later Kenneth Mladenka, found that the size of the black population had the strongest effect on the level of black municipal employment. Eisinger's research showed that African American mayors were especially significant in appointing African American professionals and administrators who subsequently played a vital role in increasing the percentage of African Americans working for municipal agencies.[40] Mladenka confirmed Eisinger's finding that the size of the minority population provided the "dominant explanation of why some municipal governments hire more blacks and Hispanics than others," but found a weak relationship between the presence of a black mayor and black municipal employment.[41] Instead, Mladenka found that minority city councilors exerted greater impact than minority mayors on black municipal employment. In a 1984 *APSR* article, Meier and England examined the relationship between the presence of black school board members and education policies that affect black students.[42] Using multiple regression analysis, they found that African American access to school board seats was associated with the hiring of black administrators and teachers; and that their presence in turn was associated with such positive policy outcomes as larger proportions of African American students attending college and a reduction in the discriminatory assignment of minority students to dead-end vocational tracks and special education classes. The authors called these discriminatory assignments "second generation segregation."[43] Eisinger, Mladenka, and Meir and England's research suggest a relationship between black political power, African American municipal employment patterns, and municipal policy.

Finally, the influx of Latinos into America's big cities changed the political dynamics and the paradigms that political scientists used to study race and ethnicity in the city. Increasingly, students of urban politics in the early 2000s are shifting toward a multiracial paradigm, raising the question of whether Latinos and African Americans will form electoral coalitions or compete for their fair share of city resources. McClain and Karnig's article showed that the two groups do not always have to compete with each other.[44] Drawing on municipal employment data from a number of American cities, they demonstrated that politics between the two groups is not always zero-sum and that each group could do well when it builds alliances with the other.

Hanes Walton, Cheryl Miller, and Joseph McCormick provide a useful framework for analytical assessment of the urban-related articles that feature race and racial politics.[45] These authors have divided political science studies that focused on race into two categories. "Race relations politics" articles are studies "that emphasize an implementation strategy to obtain peaceful and consensual relations between the two races, even if the result is the domination of one and the subordination of the other."[46] These studies also "value and highlight stability over conflict, gradual and moderate change over strident or disruptive change."[47] Studies in the "African American empowerment" tradition support "parity and "empowerment" and "tend to focus on the analysis and evaluation of the obstacles, limitations, and inadequate delivery of policy outputs/services."[48] These studies also look to African American initiatives to deal with social, economic, and political inequalities.

The studies by Gosnell, Bobo and Gilliam, Cohen and Dawson, Hamilton, and Eisinger all fit within the "African American empowerment" tradition. These studies provide a rich, contextual, and situational examination of the efforts of African Americans to move toward political parity. At the same time, the authors acknowledged the systemic forces that African Americans have had to overcome to gain positions of political authority and to deliver services. The articles dealing with the protest era of the 1960s—Aberbach and Walker; Lieske; and Miller, Bolce, and Halligan—all fall into the "race relations" tradition. These articles emphasized the "individual traits and practices" ("relative deprivation," for example) as barriers to black political participation.

The other important observation to make about the articles in this substantive area is that African American (Bobo, Cohen, Dawson, Gilliam, Hamilton, McClain) scholars wrote several of them. As mentioned, Charles Hamilton's 1974 PSQ article was the first urban-related article published in one of the two major political science journals written by an African American. All of the African American scholars except Cohen came of age during and were influenced by the modern civil rights movement. Hamilton, for example, was directly involved in the civil rights struggle in Tuskegee, Alabama. Dawson was a community activist in Berkeley, California, in the 1970s. The opening of the academy to African American political scientists represented a change, which was reflected in the scholarship on urban politics.

Conclusion

Looking back over the discipline's treatment of urban politics as reflected in its two premier journals, we find that it is limited. As gauged by the number of major articles published in the PSQ and APSR, urban politics has not been one of the major concerns in political science. Only a tiny fraction of the major articles published in the two journals have been urban-related. One obvious conclusion of this exploration is that urban politics is not the preferred field of study in political science. It is not clear to the present authors why this is the case. It could be that many present-day political scientists came of age during the period of increasing suburbanization and have had few relationships with central cities. There may simply be a lack of awareness of the issues that might emanate from an urban-focused research agenda. As the methods employed by political scientists have moved solidly toward survey research and the quantification of political variables, younger political scientists are increasingly trained to seize an existing data set and begin testing theories and hypotheses with mathematical models. Few such data sets exist in urban politics and not many graduate students (or faculty) have the capacity (or desire) to create such data sets.

Perhaps political scientists do not see urban phenomena as central concerns of political life. With the discipline's frequent and persistent focus on Congress, legislative enactment, elections, and political campaigns, anyone reading contemporary political science literature on American politics would be led to forget that much politics and policy take concrete form at the local level. Indeed, a good deal of what Congress does on the domestic front has some links or feedback to urban America. Hence studies of housing, immigration, urban renewal, transportation, education, health disparities, public safety, and much more would be incomplete without a local or urban element. In addition, because implementation is such a large part of policy action, legislative enactment ultimately requires significant buy-ins and follow-throughs at the local level. While we would not make the claim that all politics is local, we think a strong case can be made that urban politics provides a useful lens through which to explore many issues of concern to political scientists.

Much of the scholarship in the subfield of urban politics that appeared in the *APSR* and *PSQ* ignored or had little to say about African Americans, race, and racial issues. Whether it is urban policy, governance or service delivery, elections, campaigns, electoral participation, or urban theory, the African American presence in these journals is limited. During the formative years of the two journals, urban scholars wrote about city life with no mention of African Americans. New York City, for example, is a metropolis in which race has long been a persistent and pervasive element of local politics. Nevertheless, works that looked closely and deeply into the city's machine culture did not discuss the implications of machine politics on New York's African American community. Roy Peel's exhaustive look at New York's party organizations is a prime example. Prior to the 1970s, only Gosnell's article on Chicago's black political machine dealt seriously with race and African American politics. As Lucius Barker observed, American political science has never "squarely faced the dehumanizing conditions suffered by blacks and minorities in American 'democratic' life."[49]

What are we to make of this relative silence? Walton and McCormick maintain that some aspects of academic research may represent a kind of "social danger" that scholars purposely avoid.[50] For example, they argue that political scientists avoid studying the African American political experience because of their own personal need for approval from family, friends, and professional colleagues; their concern that by studying black politics they might have to take a critical view of the American political system; and that professionally, such scholarship would lead to "fewer academic opportunities, lowered professional standing, and greater difficulty in obtaining grants and awards."[51] In other words, Walton and McCormick argue that political scientists avoid researching and publishing on subject matters that are "seen by the larger culture as socially unacceptable and therefore socially dangerous."

There is evidence that the study of urban life can be characterized as "socially dangerous." William Julius Wilson argues that after the angry reaction of many African American scholars to the unflattering depictions of black family life in Daniel Patrick Moynihan's 1965 report, "The Negro Family: The Case for National Action," "serious research on minority problems in the inner city" was curtailed "as liberal scholars shied away from researching behavior construed as unflattering or stigmatizing to particular racial minorities."[52] According to Wilson, liberal researchers avoided studying the urban "underclass" "either because of a fear of providing fuel for racist arguments or because of concern of being charged with 'racism' or with 'blaming the victim.'"[53]

By the late 1970s, however, political scientists conducting research on American cities would find it difficult not to include some aspects of race and the African American political experience in their analyses. Political science simply could not avoid the black protest movement and political mobilization that took place in the 1960s. They could not legitimately ignore the black voter and the subsequent emergence of African American mayors. What is significant, however, is that the increased attention to race and racial politics in the urban-related articles also corresponded with the entrance of African Americans into the discipline. It is no coincidence that the first urban-related article to appear in *PSQ* that dealt directly with African American politics was written by Charles V. Hamilton, a black political scientist.

Although race and racial issues have been central to the American urban experience, urban politics studies in the two premier journals has constrained its coverage, virtually rendering the study of race and racial groups in the city marginal to the discipline. This fact has had a curious effect on the treatment of race and racial issues in the study of urban politics, largely restricting it to publication in second-tier and minor journals, and more recently, to journals dedicated to the study of urban politics. The establishment of the National Conference of Black Political Scientists (NCOBPS) and its official journal, the *National Political Science Review*, is a manifestation of this reality. The NCOBPS was created in 1969 as a professional organization of scholars "committed to the study and practice of black politics."[54] The first edition of the *National Political Science Review* was published in 1989; the journal has served as an outlet for scholars studying various aspects of race and ethnicity. Although there are alternative publication vehicles for the study of race and racial issues in urban politics, it remains that work on race and the city is a tiny component of the articles published in the journals that are considered by many in the discipline as the most prestigious. This fact, no doubt, has had and continues to have an impact on promotion and tenure opportunities for scholars whose work focuses on race and the city.

Notes

1. James C. Garand and Michael W. Giles, "Journals in the Discipline: A Report on a New Survey of American Political Scientists." *PS: Political Science and Politics* 36, no. 2 (April 2003): 293–308.

2. For a similar approach that examines education-related articles see Marion Orr, "Political Science and Education Research: An Exploratory Look at Two Political Science Journals," *Education Researcher* 33, no. 5 (June–July 2004): 11–16. The historian Earl Lewis analyzed articles focused on African Americans in the *American Historical Review*; see Earl Lewis, "To Turn as on a Pivot: Writing African Americans into a History of Overlapping Diasporas," *American Historical Review* 100, no. 3 (June 1995): 765–87. For an examination of coverage of African American politics in political science journals, see Hanes Walton Jr., Cheryl M. Miller, and Joseph P. McCormick, II, "Race and Political Science: The Dual Tradition of Race Relations Politics and African-American Politics," in *Political Science in History*, eds. James Farr, John S. Dryzek, and Stephen T. Leonard (New York: Cambridge University Press, 1995), 145–74.

3. *Urban Affairs Review*, formerly *Urban Affairs Quarterly*, was first published in September 1965. The *Journal of Urban Affairs* was first published in the fall of 1981.

4. William C. Baum, G. N. Griffiths, Robert Matthews, and Daniel Scherruble, "American Political Science before the Mirror: What Our Journals Reveal about the Profession," *Journal of Politics* 38, no. 4 (November 1976): 895–917.

5. For a fascinating pioneering examination of the urban politics literature through the lens of urban textbooks, see Lawrence J. R. Herson, "The Lost World of Municipal Government," *American Political Science Review* 51, no. 2 (June 1957): 330–45.

6. R. T. Daland's 1957 exploration of urbanism and political science came to a similar conclusion. He wrote: "It is the contention of this article that political scientists have been slow to study seriously the impact of urbanization on our governmental institutions and political life." See R. T. Daland, "Political Science and the Study of Urbanism," *American Political Science Review* 51, no. 2 (June 1957): 491–509.

7. Douglas W. Rae, *City: Urbanism and Its End* (New Haven, CT: Yale University Press, 2003).

8. See for example Horace E. Flack, "Municipal Charter Revision: Kansas City, Mo," *American Political Science Review* 3, no. 3 (August 1909): 413–16; and Flack, "Municipal Charter Revision: Boston," *American Political Science Review* 3, no. 3 (August 1909): 410–13; Henry T. Hunt, "Obstacles to Municipal Progress," *American Political Science Review* 11, no. 1 (February 1917): 76–87; Oswald Ryan, "The Commission Plan of City Government," *American Political Science Review* 5, no. 1 (February 1911): 38–56; Herman G. James, "The City Manager Plan: The Latest in American City Government," *American Political Science Review* 8, no. 4 (November 1914): 602–13; and James, "Some Reflections on the City Plan of Government," *American Political Science Review* 9, no. 3 (August 1915): 504–6; L. D. Upson, "City Manager Plan in Ohio," *American Political Science Review* 9, no. 3 (August 1915): 496–550; John R. Commons, "Referendum and Initiative in City Government," *Political Science Quarterly* 17, no. 4 (December 1902): 609–30; and Morris L. Cooke, "Scientific Management of the Public Business," *American Political Science Review* 9, no. 3 (August 1915): 488–95.

9. James Q. Wilson and Edward C. Banfield, "Public Regardingness as a Value Premise in Voting Behavior," *American Political Science Review* 58, no. 4 (December 1964): 876–87; Raymond E. Wolfinger and John Osgood Field, "Political Ethos and the Structure of City Government," *American Political Science Review* 60, no. 2 (June 1966): 311.

10. Belle Zeller and Hugh A. Bone, "The Repeal of P.R. in New York City: Ten Years in Retrospect," *American Political Science Review* 42, no. 6 (December 1948): 1127–48.

11. Bryan D. Jones, "Party and Bureaucracy: The Influence of Intermediary Groups on Urban Public Service Delivery," *American Political Science Review* 75, no. 3 (September 1981): 688–770.

12. Kenneth R. Mladenka, "The Urban Bureaucracy and the Chicago Political Machine: Who Gets What and the Limits of Political Control," *American Political Science Review* 74, no. 4, (December, 1980): 991–98.

13. See for example Roy V. Peel, "The New York Municipal Elections," *American Political Science Review* 27, no. 6 (December 1933): 918–23; George H. McCaffrey, "Proportional Representation in New York City," *American Political Science Review* 33, no.5 (October 1939): 841–52; and Hugh A. Bone, "Political Parties in New York City," *American Political Science Review* 40, no. 2 (April 1946): 272–82.

14. Paul Lazarsfeld et al., *The People's Choice* (New York: Columbia University Press, 1948).

15. See for example W. F. Ogburn and Estelle Hill, "Income Classes and the Roosevelt Vote in 1932," *American Political Science Review* 50, no. 2 (June 1935): 186–93; Robert R. Alford and Harry M. Scoble, "Sources of Local Political Involvement," *Political Science Quarterly* 62, no. 4 (December 1968): 1192–206; and James Q. Wilson and Edward C. Banfield, "Public Regardingness as Value Premise in Voting Behavior," *American Political Science Review* 58, no. 4 (December 1964): 876–87.

16. Hanes Walton Jr., *Invisible Politics: Black Political Behavior* (Albany: State University of New York Press, 1985).

17. See for example Frank T. Carlton, "The Workingmen's Party of New York City: 1829–31," *Political Science Quarterly* 22, no. 3 (September 1907): 401–15; Edward Pessen, "Did Labor Support Jackson? The Boston Story," *Political Science Quarterly* 64, no. 2 (June 1949): 262–74.

18. Roy V. Peel, "The Political Machine in New York City," *American Political Science Review* 27, no. 4 (August 1933): 615.

19. John T. Salter, "Party Organization in Philadelphia: The Ward Committeeman," *American Political Science Review* 27, no. 4 (August 1933): 618–27.

20. Bone, "Political Parties in New York City," 275.

21. Ogburn and Hill, "Income Classes," 186–93.

22. Ogburn and Hill, "Income Classes," 188.

23. Wilson and Banfield, "Public Regardingness," 876.

24. Ibid., 884. Hanes Walton Jr., suggested that had Wilson and Banfield expanded their analysis and examined some Southern cities, their conclusions might have been more reliable. See Hanes Walton Jr., *Invisible Politics: Black Political Behavior* (New York: State University of New York Press, 1985), 293.

25. Ernest Wilson III, "Why Political Scientists Don't Study Black Politics, but Historians and Sociologists Do," *PS: Political Science and Politics* 18 (1985): 600–607.

26. Peter K. Eisinger, "Racial Differences in Protest Participation," *American Political Science Review* 68, no. 2 (June 1974): 592–606.

27. Michael Lipsky, "Protest as a Political Resource," *American Political Science Review* 62, no. 4 (December 1968): 1144–58.

28. Other examples include William H. Brown Jr., and Charles E. Gilbert, "Capital Programming in Philadelphia: A Study of Long-Range Planning," *American Political Science Review* 54, no. 3 (September 1960): 659–68; Heinz Eulau and Robert Eyestone, "Policy Maps of City Councils and Policy Outcomes: A Developmental Analysis," *American Political Science Review* 62, no. 1 (March 1968): 124–43; Herbert Jacob and James Eisenstein, "Sentences and Other Sanctions in the Criminal Courts of Baltimore, Chicago, and Detroit," *American Political Science Review* 90, no. 4 (Winter 1975–1976): 617–35.

29. Floyd Hunter, *Community Power Structure: A Study of Decision Makers* (Chapel Hill: University of North Carolina Press, 1953).

30. Robert A. Dahl, "A Critique of the Ruling Elite Model," *American Political Science Review* 52, no. 2 (June 1958): 463–69.

31. Harold F. Gosnell, "Political Meetings in the Chicago 'Black Belt,'" *American Political Science Review* 28, no. 2 (April 1934): 254–58.

32. See also Gosnell's *Negro Politics* (Chicago: University of Chicago Press, 1935).

33. Joel D. Aberbach and Jack L. Walker, "The Meanings of Black Power: A Comparison of White and Black Interpretations of a Political Slogan," *American Political Science Review* 64, no. 2 (June 1970): 373.

34. Abraham H. Miller, Louis H. Bolce, and Mark Halligan, "The J-Curve Theory and the Black Urban Riots: An Empirical Test of Progressive Relative Deprivation Theory," *American Political Science Review* 71, no. 3 (September 1977): 964–82.

35. Joel A. Lieske, "The Conditions of Racial Violence in American Cities: A Developmental Synthesis," *American Political Science Review* 72, no. 4 (December 1978): 1324–40.

36. Charles V. Hamilton, "Voter Registration Drives and Turnout: A Report on the Harlem Electorate," *Political Science Quarterly* 92, no. 1 (Spring 1977): 43–46.

37. Charles V. Hamilton, "The Patron-Recipient Relationship and Minority Politics in New York City," *Political Science Quarterly* 94, no. 2 (Summer 1979): 211–27.

38. Lawrence Bobo and Franklin D. Gilliam Jr., "Race, Sociopolitical Participation and Black Empowerment," *American Political Science Review* 84, no. 2 (June 1990): 377–93.

39. Cathy J. Cohen and Michael C. Dawson, "Neighborhood Poverty and African American Politics," *American Political Science Review* 87, no. 2 (June 1993): 286–302.

40. Peter K. Eisinger, "Black Employment in Municipal Jobs: The Impact of Black Political Power," *American Political Science Review* 76, no. 2 (June 1982): 380–92; Kenneth R. Mladenka, "Blacks and Hispanics in Urban Politics," *American Political Science Review* 83, no. 1 (March 1989): 165–91.

41. Mladenka, "Blacks and Hispanics," 173.

42. Kenneth Meier and Robert England, "Black Representation and Educational Policy: Are They Related?" *American Political Science Review* 78 (December 1984): 392–403.

43. Ibid.

44. Paula D. McClain and Albert K. Karnig, "Black and Hispanic Socioeconomic and Political Competition," *American Political Science Review* 84, no. 2 (June 1990): 535–45.

45. Walton, Miller, and McCormick, "Race and Political Science."

46. Ibid., 150.

47. Ibid.

48. Ibid..

49. Lucius J. Barker, "Political Scientists as Gatekeepers: Overcoming Inequality in Our Own Backyard," *Perspectives on Politics* 3, no. 2 (June 2005): 328.

50. Hanes Walton Jr., and Joseph P. McCormick, II, "The Study of African-American Politics as Social Danger: Clues from the Disciplinary Journals," *National Political Science Review* 6 (1997): 229–44.

51. Ibid., 231.

52. William Julius Wilson, *The Truly Disadvantaged* (Chicago: University of Chicago Press, 1987), 4–6.

53. Ibid., 5.

54. NCOBPS Web page, http://www.ncobps.org/about_ncobps.htm. Accessed June 7, 2005.

* We would like to thank Larry Bennett, Richard Snyder, Clarence N. Stone, and Hanes Walton Jr., for their comments and suggestions on earlier drafts of this essay.

CHAPTER SIXTEEN

Navigating the Muddy Waters of the Mainstream

Tracing the Mystification of Racism in International Relations

ERROL A. HENDERSON

Introduction

THE FIRST AFRICAN AMERICAN male and female PhDs in political science, the diplomat and Nobel laureate Ralph Bunche, and the disarmament specialist Merze Tate, both chose to focus on international relations (IR, or world politics) as their area of expertise. Interestingly, many newly minted black PhDs today opt for American politics rather than IR as their chief area of specialization. This focus is in obvious ways understandable, considering the salience of domestic politics in general to citizens of the United States—including academics. The focus also reflects the more prominent role of blacks in contemporary electoral politics than in Bunche and Tate's era, which makes it possible for black political scientists to directly study the impact of blacks in the political arena in a way that was less available in the past. This focus is further intensified by the ever-increasing specialization of political scientists, which encourages newer PhDs to concentrate on niches even within subfields like American politics, such as race and ethnicity, religion and politics, urban politics, voting, the presidency, the legislature, and the like. This specialization is also evident in the other primary fields of political science such as comparative politics, political theory, methodology, and of course, world politics. But the relatively reduced concentration of black scholars in world politics compared to the interests of Bunche and Tate has to my mind clear effects on the focus and subsequently the quality of research in the field. In particular, the relative lack of black voices in world politics in the academy seriously affects the breadth and depth of scholarship in the field. This absence—to my mind— has resulted in, among other things, insufficient engagement of the impact of racism in world politics, which might be informed by the insights of African American political scientists grounded in a research tradition appreciative of racial dynamics in the United States.

This essay addresses the centrality of racism in the origins of the major paradigms of world politics and its continued influence today. I argue that both realism and idealism (liberalism) are grounded in racist precepts that provided the foundation of world politics as an academic field of inquiry. I maintain that this orientation continues to inform analyses derived from the major paradigms, such as the clash of civilizations and democratic peace theses. The silence of Western authors on the racist foundations of their theses leave them complicit in the furtherance of an inegalitarian version of IR and imbues the policies that derive from their theses with a white supremacist logic that both undermines their empirical accuracy and generates resistance on the part of the nonwhite majority peoples who face the policies that are derived from such theses. The persistence of racism in world politics has been facilitated by a process whereby its dominant form, white supremacism, has been mystified and morphed over time and across academic fields. I maintain that it is important to recognize how the contorted logic that allows the perpetuation of white supremacism is "normalized" and made to seem "natural" and thereby allowing it to not only become acceptable but also to lend itself as an intellectual anchor to important precepts in world politics as a field, and important practices in the foreign policies of those who find their interests in consonance with such orientations. The latter is especially evident in the foreign policy practices of Western states. In order to appreciate the seminal and enduring impact of racism in world politics, one should reconsider the origins of the field and the major paradigms that have come to dominate it.

Racism, Anarchy, and Commonalities in Paradigms of World Politics

Of the major paradigms of world politics, realism and idealism (liberalism), and their assorted variants, are the most prominent. Today realism—or neorealism—is the dominant paradigm in the field. Realists assert that the international system is basically anarchic and that states are the dominant actors in the system. Given the anarchical system of states, security is the basic objective of international actors; power is essential to achieving one's aims and resisting those of others. Realists argue that states seek to balance power to ensure their security. They note that morality and ethics are secondary to such concerns. Warfare is the ultimate expression of state power and is the primary arbiter of conflicts of interest among states. With homage to Niccolò Machiavelli (1469–1527)—who is viewed by the seminal political realist, E. H. Carr, as the prototypal realist—scholars and policymakers who advocate these assumptions insist that states should pursue foreign policies that ensure relative gains compared to others. This approach accepts a perpetual competition among states largely as a result of the security dilemma. The security dilemma describes the basic source of friction in an international system of sovereign states in pursuit of their individual security in a system in which there is no superordinate authority. In such a system, ironically, each state's pursuit of its own security leads ultimately to greater insecurity. What results is a war-ridden global system in which power—especially military power—is the ultimate arbiter of conflicts of interest.

At the heart of the realist preoccupation with power and war is the conceptualization of the global system as fundamentally anarchic. This characterization of the system as anarchic is essential to understanding realist (and subsequent neorealist) assumptions regarding power and war, since anarchy is a fundamental aspect of the system's structure, which necessitates the pursuit of power and in turn the prosecution of war. The anarchic structure of an international system dominated by sovereign territorial states (and the nonsovereign territories they control) necessitates a self-help orientation among the states, because absent an authority above them, each individual state must ensure its own security. But it is not only realism that asserts the centrality of anarchy among its core precepts; idealism (and neo-idealism)—the paradigmatic counterpoise of realism—is similarly grounded in a preoccupation with anarchy in the global system.

Idealists accept the view that the global system is anarchic and that anarchy may lead to security dilemmas, balance of power politics, and interstate war. Unlike realists, however, they do not maintain that these problems are the inevitable outcomes of international interactions. Instead, grounded in the Enlightenment belief in the perfectibility of the individual, they transfer this view of domestic politics to the international realm and argue that conflict and warfare are largely a result of such corrupt institutions as authoritarian regimes. Idealists argue further that by reforming such regimes, in this case making them more democratic, and interposing international institutions above the state level to coordinate international behavior—especially free trade—one may encourage "good" or "cooperative" behavior among states and enshrine this behavior in international law. In the idealist view, states are not destined to be predators as a result of anarchy, the myopic pursuit of national interests defined in terms of power, and the conflict-laden repercussions of the security dilemma as realists argue. Instead, idealists believe that there is a real prospect of reorienting state behavior to reflect such collective interests as global peace. Simply put, idealists argue that democratization among states, liberal international trade policies, and the institutionalization of international law—each buttressed by transnational organizations that help coordinate interstate interactions—will allow states to overcome the security dilemma and facilitate international cooperation. Implicit in these idealist assumptions is the view that a state's foreign policy derives from its domestic policy. Therefore, states that observe the rule of law at home (e.g., democracies) are more likely to accept the principles of international law in their foreign affairs, while those that are more violent domestically (e.g., non-democracies) are more likely to be violent abroad. In essence, states with a domestic predisposition to norms of peace and justice should be similarly disposed in their foreign policies.

One of the key idealists of the twentieth century, who is also regarded as one of the progenitors of the field of international relations, was a former professor, Woodrow Wilson, who became President of the United States on the eve of World War I. Confronting the issue of the United States' involvement in what was then called the Great War, Wilson articulated and at the war's end attempted to institutionalize these idealist premises in the postwar order established at Versailles in 1919. Some analysts, such as Ray argue that "Wilson can be seen as the founder of idealism and, in a way, as the founder of the field itself" (1995, 7). But the view that Wilson established the scholarly field of International Relations is more accepted wisdom than actual fact; it actually obfuscates less salutary but more significant factors that contributed to the emergence of world politics. Clearly,

IR at its birth was concerned with anarchy and power; however, this anarchy was largely assumed to result from the lack of cohesion in the primitive polities of the inferior races—especially those in the tropical domains of what we would now consider the third world. At the same time, the power that was wielded by the "civilized" white races through their "modern" states and the mechanism of "efficient" and "rational" colonial administration could insure that "anarchy" did not spread to the modern world and contribute to violence among the major (white) powers. These notions, while informed to some extent by Woodrow Wilson's (1887) work, emerged more directly from such scholars of world politics as Paul Reinsch, whose *World Politics at the End of the Nineteenth Century* (1900) is considered the first work in the intellectual field of world politics. Reinsch's *Colonial Government* (1902) and *Colonial Administration* (1905) placed him among the leading experts on colonial administration. Olson and Groom (1991, 47) note that Reinsch's work "suggests that the discipline of international relations had its real beginnings in studies of imperialism, not in world order, as has so often been suggested."

Reinsch (1900, 14) argued that the emergent force of "national imperialism" was transforming the landscape of international relations as European states sought "to control as large a portion of the earth's surface as their energy and opportunities will permit." For him, national imperialism was the attempt "to increase the resources of the national state through the absorption or exploitation of undeveloped regions and inferior races" without attempting to "impose political control upon highly civilized nations." Reinsch attempted to reconcile the interests of colonizer and colonized in his conceptualization of effective colonial administration, which led him to criticize United States policy in the Philippines following the Spanish-American War. Reinsch, however, also justified expansion in the name of the "white man's burden" (Schmidt 1998, 72).

Some scholars, such as Philip Kerr in his *An Introduction to the Study of International Relations* (1916), argued that "one of the most fundamental facts in human history" is that "mankind is divided into a graduated scale" ranging from the civilized to the barbarian, which necessitated colonization of the latter by the former (163). Still others, such as Giddings, invoked "survival of the fittest" logic to rationalize the subjugation or "governing" of "the inferior races of mankind" as the duty of the civilized. These scholars drew on Kidd's *The Control of the Tropics*, which stated that the tropical regions were "existing [in] a state either of anarchy, or of primitive savagery . . . in which no attempt is made or can be made to develop the natural resources lying ready to hand" (1898, 15). For Kidd, the superior races had a responsibility to overcome the anarchy of the tropics so that the riches of the "third world" could be cultivated. The competition for these resources might engender conflict among the civilized states, as Hobson, Angell, Du Bois, Lippmann, and subsequently, Lenin, would more famously argue. It follows that world politics as a field of inquiry in political science emerges from the comparative study of colonial administration in the context of concerns with anarchy, power, and race.

So the discussions of anarchy among both realists and idealists are grounded in a discourse concerned with the obligations of "superior peoples" to impose order on the anarchic domains of "inferior peoples" in order to prevent the chaos endemic in the tropics from spilling over into the superior peoples' territories, possessions, or spheres of interest. Similarly, both realist and idealist concerns with power are grounded in a racist discourse concerned largely with the power of whites to subjugate the tropics and then put themselves in charge of the administration of the societies of the colonized "others." Therefore, the roots of realism—the dominant paradigm in world politics—are grounded in a rationalization for constructing a hierarchical racial order to be imposed upon the anarchy alleged to arise from the "tropics," an anarchy that begs for rational administration from whites. That is, realism is little more than an intellectual justification for colonialism and imperialism in the guise of the "white man's burden." In addition, the roots of idealism are found less in idealized versions of classical liberal precepts regarding the perfectibility of humanity; the primacy of "God-given" individual rights; and the institutionalization of democracy, free trade, and the rule of law (which in actuality were never intended for the nonwhite peoples of the world) than with the imposition of a racist order on indigenous peoples throughout Africa and Asia and the administration of that racist order for the benefit of white people. Thus realism and idealism have common roots in their shared racist conception of anarchy as a condition inherent in the societies of the "inferior races" and the corresponding necessity for whites to use power to impose "order" on the anarchical societies. This order would be imposed to prevent the anarchy from spilling over into the lands of the civilized whites and threatening their security.

Given imperatives for "progress" and "development," and the reality that the unspoiled lands were not being sufficiently exploited by the indigenous peoples, realists and idealists agreed that the incentive to imperialism in this regard is so great that it might lead to conflict among whites. Therefore, there must be a rational distribution of territory and its appropriate administration by colonial agencies. Realists and idealists disagreed regarding the implications of a global system thus structured on the interactions of white peoples and their political institutions, but such disagreements were not evident when these theorists considered nonwhite people and their societies. It follows that realism and idealism converge on a white supremacist logic that has been evident since the establishment of the field of world politics.

> The centrality of race in the analysis of world politics can be documented in the origins of the most venerable international relations journal in the US, *Foreign Affairs*. It became the house organ of the Council of Foreign Relations in 1922, having been renamed that year from its previous title, the *Journal of International Relations* from 1919–1922. However, from 1910–1919 it bore its original title, which suggests its dominant orientation: the *Journal of Race Development*.

I contend that white supremacism was not only present at the creation of the field but also that it continues to inform the arguments derived from each paradigm today. To better appreciate the enduring impact of racism in world politics, one should understand how racism as a concept has been transformed, mystified, and eventually turned on itself even as the effects of racism have consistently accrued advantages to whites and disadvantages to nonwhites—especially blacks—in both the United States and abroad. In the next section we will address these issues.

Racism and World Politics: Mystification

The academic field of international relations had two birth mothers: the United States, one of the most prolific enslavers; and Great Britain, one of the most prolific colonizers. At the heart of the domestic politics of both regimes was a legacy of racism operationalized as white supremacy, which was practiced in politics, economics, culture, education, and law within both countries and throughout the domains they subjugated. At the same time, both regimes articulated some of the most profound notions of individual freedom while they enslaved and colonized great swaths of human beings. They rationalized the subjugation of these peoples through the propaganda of their societies, including their educational systems. A key manifestation of such rationalization was evident in the international relations scholarship that they promulgated. While the impact of racism in international affairs has been noted previously by diplomatic historians (e.g., Lauren 1996; Hunt 1987; Furedi 1998; Dudziak 2000; Anderson 2003), for many IR specialists in the discipline of political science it is often assumed to be a relic of a bygone colonial era. Theses generated from the racist policies of that period are thought to have little relevance to post–cold war world politics. But such a view represents a basic misunderstanding of the centrality of racism in the field and the enduring impact of racism in current IR scholarship. The relative silence of IR authors and their unwillingness to engage the issue forthrightly and in an informed manner are the result of willful perversions of the historial record of white racism in political science, which has assisted in the construction of a deracialized intellectual history of world politics. This disjointed and misleading view has become ingrained in the catechism of primary, secondary, undergraduate, and graduate students throughout the West.

At the center of this mythified version of history is either the neglect of issues of racism altogether, the marginalization of racism as a matter of domestic—as opposed to international—politics, or the assumption of the irrelevance of racism in the postcolonial era. This mythification was largely effected by U.S. and British scholars and policymakers as they sought to rationalize their racist foreign policies. The formation of this myth required the promulgation of an assemblage of euphemisms to camouflage the egregious history of white supremacy that both societies pursued, as well as the denigration or silencing of antiracist challenges to the systems of oppression that these societies instituted and spread abroad.

Prior to World War I, Western political leaders and scholars celebrated their imperialist projects and the racism that underlay them. As noted above, the field of IR emerged largely in response to the need to provide more efficient colonial administration of the subjugated peoples of Africa and Asia. As Western elites began to draw on their colonial subjects to assist in the fighting of their increasingly horrific wars, these subjects petitioned for racial equanimity in the domestic and diplomatic affairs of states. As the international system globalized, information, media, and military technology spread throughout many states; meanwhile, resistance to colonialism became better coordinated and more widespread. Subjugated peoples began to make progress in drawing out the contradiction between the West's advocacy of democratic ideals and the reality of the West's white supremacist practices as they increasingly organized to overturn the institutions of domination that facilitated their subjugation on an international scale.

As indigenous resistance to Euro-American dominance became increasingly apparent around the time of World War I, Western leaders attempted to contain the growing discontent. Their academics provided them with pseudo-scholarly justifications to rationalize the simultaneous pursuit of democratic ideals for some and the denial of human rights to others. Woodrow Wilson's call to "make the world safe for democracy" was seemingly at odds with white perceptions prior to WWI, which cast imperialism as a glorified, vaunted, and even religiously ordained pursuit. Euro-American imperialist wars were often viewed as race wars justified by a religious obligation to bring the heathen to Christ or as vindications of the social Darwinist tenets of the survival of the fittest. For example, Theodore Roosevelt celebrated imperialist war and "lashed out at those who would apply the 'rules of international morality' to 'savages' and 'beasts'." For him, "a war with savages, though it is apt to be also the most terrible and inhuman" was "the most ultimately righteous of all wars" because "the rude, fierce settler who drives the savage from the land lays all civilized mankind under a debt to him." He adds that "the victor, horrible though many of his deeds are, has laid deep the foundations for the future greatness of a mighty people" (Lauren 1996, 68). Roosevelt thought it inevitable that the lands of the indigenous peoples should pass to the more powerful Western states, and his successor in the presidency, William Howard Taft, similarly justified imperial conquest in the name of "our superior race" (68).

Although these views occupied a prominent place in public discourse, it was Taft's successor, Woodrow Wilson, who appeared to provide a transition between those who lauded imperial slaughter and subjugation and those who proffered a more egalitarian foreign policy acknowledging the rights of the subjugated to self-determination and the promotion of the principles of democracy. Wilson had made positive statements regarding the need for equality among nations during WWI; in his view, "Only a peace between equals can last. Only a peace the very principle of which is equality and a common participation in a common benefit. The right state of mind, the right feeling between nations, is as necessary for a lasting peace as is the just settlement of vexed questions of territory or of racial and national allegiance. The equality of nations upon which peace must be founded, if it is to last, must be an equality of rights" (Lauren 1996, 87). Wilson had even made convincing overtures to African Americans regarding their domestic and international concerns—which led the dean of black scholars, W. E. B. Du Bois, to pen an essay, "Close Ranks," to encourage black support for the war effort and Wilson's promises for redress of blacks' concerns. But in actuality Wilson was as steeped in white supremacist precepts as his predecessors. A Southerner himself, he was an apologist for Southern racism and once excused objections to black voting rights on the basis that blacks' "minds are dark; . . . they are ignorant, uneducated, and incompetent to form an enlightened opinion" (Patler 2004, 76). As president of Princeton, he advised a black seminary student interested in attending the school that "it is altogether inadvisable for a colored man to enter Princeton" and he suggested Harvard, Brown, or Dartmouth as alternatives, as Princeton retained its policy of excluding blacks for several more decades (77). In 1889 he had argued in *The State: Elements of Historical and Practical Politics*, that in order to understand the origins of modern government, "one should not study the 'savage' traditions of 'defeated' primitive groups but rather the contributions of the 'survived fittest,' primarily the groups composing the Aryan race" (Oren 2003, 35). As U.S. president, Wilson rejected entreaties of blacks, whose support he solicited prior to the war in his "New Freedom" platform, and implemented and expanded segregation in several departments of the federal government. He once remarked to black representatives protesting segregation that "Segregation is not humiliating but a benefit, and ought to be so regarded by you [colored] gentlemen" (Lauren 1996, 89). He accepted the racist fiction of the pro-KKK film, *Birth of a Nation* (which he screened in the White House), as historical fact (Patler 2004, 39–40, 76). It is difficult "to reconcile Wilson's treatment of blacks with his often expressed noble sentiments of justice, liberty, and equality" given that "he not only failed to uplift African-Americans, but he enabled forces to crush them even further, . . . all this as he preached to the world the importance of serving humanity" (78). Wilson was intent on institutionalizing his racist policies internationally through his Kantian-inspired League of Nations, which was also oriented by his racist logic.

Wilson's true colors on the issue of racial equality were revealed in his response to the Japanese proposal at the Paris Peace Conference to include a clause in the League of Nations Covenant recognizing racial equality. The Japanese amendment stated that "equality of nationals being a basic principle of the League of Nations, the High Contracting Parties agree to accord as soon as possible to all alien nationals of State members of the League, equal and just treatment in every respect, making no distinction, either in law or in fact, on account of their race or nationality." The Japanese delegation's expectations were buttressed by Wilson's earlier comments on the importance of equality in the construction of a postwar peace; but they would have done better to heed Wilson's statements regarding the Japanese in the domestic politics of the United States. On the question of Japanese immigration he opined, "I stand for the national policy of exclusion. We cannot make a homogeneous population out of a people who do not blend with the Caucasian race" (Lauren 1996, 89). This view Wilson cast abroad in his dealings with the Japanese delegation on the issue of the racial equality clause. So while the Japanese felt that international diplomacy would prevail and their request would be supported, to their surprise and consternation, the United States, Britain, and Australia voiced strong and pointed opposition to the proposed amendment. William Hughes, the prime minister of Australia, "denounced the principle of racial equality as dangerous nonsense" and openly articulated his beliefs in white superiority (Furedi 1998, 42). Lord Robert Cecil, a British representative at the negotiations, "saw the amendment as a challenge to the management of the Empire" (42), while Harold Nicholson, another British diplomat present at the conference, opposed the idea of a clause in the League Covenant that "implied the equality of the yellow man with the white man," or worse, "might even imply the terrific theory of the equality of the white man with the black" (90). But it was Wilson, the president who argued for the United States' entry in the war in order to make the world safe for democracy, who personally orchestrated the rejection of the racial equality clause.

Not only did Wilson personally reject the principle of racial equality; he, along with the other American diplomats, was concerned about the consequences such a policy might have on the relations of blacks and whites within the United States. Wilson had rejected the original clause, but even when the reference to "race" was deleted in an amended proposal, he still sought to kill it. Wilson tried to avoid taking an official vote on the clause, but the Japanese delegate, Baron Nobuaki Makino, pressed the issue. The vote was 11 of 17 in favor of the Japanese proposal. Wilson, however, "declared from the chair that the amendment had failed" because it didn't secure unanimous support—although majority votes had been sufficient in the past for acceptance of amendments that Wilson supported (Furedi 1998, 99). Nevertheless, with the promise of equality of peoples ignored, the framers of the postwar peace vacated the promise of democracy and self-determination by rejecting the rights of indigenous peoples in the colonies of the defeated powers—especially those of Africa and Asia—not to mention those in the colonies of the victors. Instead they underwrote the imperialism of its members, including Japan, who lined up in queues to gorge themselves on the spoils of Germany's defeated empire. The dismemberment of the colonies belonging to the Central Powers was facilitated by a mandate system that allowed for the continuation of white domination in most of the colonial areas of the world. One analyst observed that in effect, the League remained essentially "an all white and predominantly European affair" (Gardiner 1968, 21). Central to the maintenance of the façade of freedom and democracy was the racism that in a manner increasingly distinct from discourse at the turn of the century was less stridently proclaimed, though continually practiced.

Discussions of "race relations" and "race consciousness" emerged in the nascent field of world politics in the interwar era. Since colonial administrators faced continued challenges among colonized people organizing around issues of self-determination, these academic discussions were "characteristically alarmist and had a tendency to inflate the significance of every manifestation of anti-Western sentiment" (Furedi 1998, 123). The concerns raised in the metropole (i.e., the capital of the colonizing country) were no doubt magnified as a result of the view that those who had been for so long oppressed and exploited would seek revenge against their transgressors. Those who displayed such an orientation came to be viewed by many whites as "race conscious." Race consciousness was neither a characteristic of white peoples pursuing racist policies in the colonies nor was it even a reflection of white racism, but it came to be seen as a condition that afflicted indigenous (i.e., nonwhite) peoples that at times compelled them to seek "racial revenge." It was increasingly evident that "the Western sense of race could only interpret the aspiration for independence and equality in a racial form" (123), which casts the victims as potential perpetrators of racist acts—like throwing off the colonial yoke. Furedi notes that "it is not clear to what extent officials were conscious of their evasion of responsibility for the legacy of racial domination. During the 1930s they seemed to elide the distinction between the action of the oppressor and the oppressed." In such a context, "demands for civil rights were seldom greeted as legitimate aspirations, but as attempts to change the existing balance of racial power" (127–28).

The challenges to the assertions of freedom and independence did not rely on sentiment alone. In the United States, national and local law enforcement agencies, including the Federal Bureau of Investigation (FBI), targeted individuals branded as "racially conscious," such as those involved in Marcus Garvey's Universal Negro Improvement Association (UNIA) and African Communities League (ACL). It also targeted black newspaper editors implicated in the vile act of "drawing attention to acts of racism," such as publishing articles about lynching, leading the FBI to target them "as a threat to social harmony" (Furedi 1998, 128). Similar actions were evident in Britain. For example, the West India Royal Commission "indirectly blamed local newspaper editors for stirring up race consciousness" (128). The British mentality on the subject reflected greater scorn for those who complained about the "colour bar" than for the "colour bar" itself. Revolts against the imperialist status quo were often attributed to "race consciousness." From the perspective of the British, racism "was associated with movements against Western domination," but less evident as a characterization of Western imperialist rule. It was a "term [that] might be applied to the contemporaneous Nazi movement, but certainly not to the British" (129–30).

Alarmist sentiments in the interwar era augured a race war that would result from the teeming masses of nonwhite peoples who were becomingly increasingly assertive (i.e., "race conscious"). Figures on demographic growth in the colonial world were brought to bear to justify the growing fear of "race war" during the period before World War II. Furedi notes that "these interwar contributions were characteristically incoherent and unfocused. Allusions to racial competition and unspecified hints about growing resentment against the white race were the usual fare" (Furedi 1998, 48). He adds that "racial fears were seldom engaged openly and the object of anxieties was usually vague. This lack of specificity was based in part on the relative dearth of experience to substantiate such pessimism. These were unsubstantiated fears, which said more about those who suffered from them than about any clearly defined dangers" (48). Part of the concern was intensified by a rise in the popularity of literature about the decline of civilizations, epitomized in Oswald Spengler's *Decline of the West* as well as Lothrop Stoddard's *The Rising Tide of Color against White World Supremacy*. These works reflected in part the view that the moral standing of the West had been undermined by its prosecution of World War I, the most destructive war in recorded history up to that time. The war was largely viewed in the colonial world as the result of disputes over imperial acquisitions as W. E. B. Du Bois had argued in "The African Roots of the War" in 1915, prior to publication of Lenin's more famous tract, *Imperialism: The Highest Stage of Capitalism*. Moreover, Spengler's and other works heightened the sense of impending racial warfare. Nonetheless, "The threat was very much an imagined one. It had the character of expectations. Sometimes empirical evidence was ignored in favour of the presentiment of racial danger" (57). One result was that "every Western setback" from the defeat of Russia by the Japanese in 1905 to the Turkish defeat of the Greeks in 1923 "was a direct boost to anti-white consciousness" and augured greater conflicts to come (58). These sentiments were echoed in the arguments of such prominent social scientists as Bronislaw Malinowski, but they also resonated in the arguments of such prominent sociologists as Ernest W. Burgess and Robert E. Park.[1]

> Voices of reason challenging these portents of impending race war included political scientists such as Ralph Bunche in his *A World View of Race* (1936); however, his commentary that what appeared to be inter-racial conflicts were actually rooted in social, political, and especially economic conflicts that were inherently resolvable was lost in a cacophony of prophesies of an imminent racial maelstrom.

In sum, "the race agenda that emerged in the interwar period was strongly influenced by apprehensions concerning differential fertility, racial deterioration, and race war. These anxieties were based on the premise that any impending conflicts would be at the expense of the prevailing balance of power (Furedi 1998, 79). The major implication of this view was that "public displays of white racial superiority had become dangerous since they invited an explosion of racial resentment" (79). To be sure, "this new racial pragmatism did not fundamentally question the assumption of superiority as such. Indeed it was even critical of those who promoted the radical idea of race equality" (79). Fundamentally, "this was an approach that self-consciously ignored the fundamental question of racial oppression and focused its concern on the etiquette of race relations" (79). It was a replacement of Rudyard Kipling's and Cecil Rhodes's celebration of imperialism and white supremacism with Frederick Lugard's assertion of the "rights" of indigenous peoples within a colonial arrangement of indirect rule, which, though no less white supremacist in practice, at least seemed to make some rhetorical overture to native rights—as long as the natives stayed in their place. In effect, it was the intellectual rationalization of the separate but equal doctrine of apartheid or Jim Crow. Nonetheless, these sentiments shaped the discourse on race and were embraced by such cultural relativists as Malinowski. Furedi notes that "the new racial pragmatism presented itself as an alternative to racial supremacist philosophy," and in that context "Malinowski was as scathing of Nordic supremacist theories as he was of ideas of race equality" (93). In effect, cultural relativism was quite compatible with white supremacist tenets, and the move to cultural relativist arguments on the issue of race relations simply represented the most recent morphing of white supremacist discourse without any real change in the effect of white supremacist practices and white power in the global system.

Toward the outbreak of World War II there was a rise in anticolonial sentiment that began to change the contours of world politics. Most obviously, it was becoming increasingly unacceptable to proffer patently supremacist foreign policy statements, especially in light of the racist claims of Nazi Germany—less so those of Imperial Japan—that ostensibly generated opprobrium in the West. This was so even though such important aspects of Nazism as eugenics found support in the United States and other Western countries as applied to blacks. One result was that racism "continued to influence Anglo-American policy decisions and political life, but more and more covertly," while "the silencing of racial concerns became public policy" (Furedi 1998, 163). Engagement in World War II against the Nazi regime was to some extent a civil war among the leadership of the international order, which was compelled to disassociate itself at least superficially from the doctrine of the regime that it had just defeated. Nevertheless, Du Bois (1946 [1987], 23) situated the condition of white supremacy following World War II in its historical context in his assessment that "there was no Nazi atrocity—concentration camps, wholesale maiming and murder, defilement of women or ghastly blasphemy of childhood—which the Christian civilization of Europe had not long been practicing against colored folk in all parts of the world in the name of and for the defense of a Superior Race born to rule the world." Subsequently, the international order would not substantively alter the racist status quo; instead, it would silence attempts at racial redress and even cast those who opposed racist practices as racist themselves.

The Western powers had learned from the failures of the League of Nations and sought to create a much more powerful international organization following World War II. They also learned to be much subtler in accommodating calls for racial equality without fundamentally changing the racist status quo. The role of Japan in the Paris Conference was taken up by China at the Dumbarton Oaks Conference in 1944. The official Chinese proposal for the new organization's fundamental principles included the following: "The principle of equality of all states and all races shall be upheld" (Lauren 1996, 158). The response of the United States was to attempt to separate issues of racial equality in the international sphere from issues of racial equality in the domestic sphere. In this way it was hoped that Jim Crow laws could be maintained, and the contradictions between the American creed of freedom, justice, and equality and the American practice of segregation, lynch law, and inequality would not affect the United States' newfound status as a superpower in the global arena. Although Article 1 of the United Nations (UN) Charter advocates human rights and fundamental freedoms "for all without distinction as to race, sex, language, or religion," it was clear that "countries might have been willing to consent to the inclusion of words and statements of principle," but "few were prepared to commit themselves to practical or effective means of implementation" (166). U.S. officials at first resisted the inclusion of statements regarding racial equality and consistently rejected notions of economic equality as Communist inspired, but they were ultimately assuaged by the inclusion of a domestic jurisdiction provision that would effectively check enforcement of the UN ideals with respect to the domestic affairs of member states. The impact of this provision was so great that "when John Foster Dulles wondered aloud among his U.S. colleagues in the delegation whether the human rights and nondiscrimination provisions might not create difficulties for 'the Negro problem in the South,' he was told that the inclusion of a domestic jurisdiction provision would preclude this possibility. . . . In the words of Senator Tom Connally on the U.S. delegation, this article 'was sufficient to overpower all other considerations'" (167).

These positions were not the specific domain of any particular political per-suasion. George Kennan, the architect of the United States' containment strat-egy, argued against the inclusion of a Declaration of Human Rights in the UN Covenant since it might generate charges of hypocrisy on the part of the United States, given its own domestic policies (Anderson 2003, 132). One of the most prominent critics of the extension of human rights protections to blacks in the United States through stipulations in the UN Covenant was the liberal former First Lady, Eleanor Roosevelt. Anderson (133) notes that "she made sure that the proposed Declaration and, especially the Covenant, contained no viable imple-mentation mechanisms"; moreover, "Roosevelt worked to ensure that neither individuals nor nongovernmental organizations would have any authority to petition the UN for redress of human rights violations." She threatened to resign from the board of the National Association for the Advancement of Colored People (NAACP) if it pursued efforts to include the "negro problem" under the rubric of human rights issues that would fall under the purview of the UN Covenant. At one point, she "emphasized three key, important areas in which the current balance of federal-state power would be sacredly preserved. The fed-eral government, she promised, would never interfere in 'murder cases,' investi-gate concerns over 'fair trials,' or insist on 'the right to education.' In essence, Eleanor Roosevelt had just assured the Dixiecrats that the sacred troika of lynch-ing, Southern justice, and Jim Crow schools would remain untouched, even with a Covenant on Human Rights" (201). Roosevelt's actions contributed to W. E. B. Du Bois's charge that she was one of the most implacable foes of African Amer-icans' struggle for human rights (141).

Facing a cold war imperative, in which U.S. officials beginning in the Tru-man administration found themselves in geopolitical as well as ideological bat-tles with the USSR as both superpowers sought to form alliances with the many new nations that were emerging from the collapse of colonial regimes, succes-sive presidential administrations asserted the greater desirability of the United States' politico-economic system as compared to the Soviet Union's, given the greater freedom in the former. But in order to make this argument, the United States had to engage its serious domestic problem of racial discrimination. Pres-ident Truman's Secretary of State, Dean Acheson, acknowledged that "racial discrimination in the United States remains a source of constant embarrassment to this Government in the day-to-day conduct of its foreign relations; and it jeopardizes the effective maintenance of our moral leadership of the free and democratic nations of the world" (Dudziak 2000, 101). In light of such concerns, Truman issued his Executive Order 9981, which stated that it was "the policy of the President that there shall be equality of treatment and opportunity in the armed services without regard to race, color, religion, or national origin" (86). The order did not mention desegregation, however, nor did it state when the objective of equality was to be achieved. In practice the armed forces remained segregated until the Korean War (1950–1953), when military commanders in need of reinforcements realized that segregation was under-mining their ability to achieve their military objectives on the ground. It was these wartime imperatives instead of appeals to norms of equality that compelled the military to begin to challenge its long-held racist view of accept-able military service.

Meanwhile the emergent anticolonial struggles in the third world—especially following the Mau Mau rebellion in colonial Kenya (1954–1956)—were recast as hysterical epidemics of anti-white resentment expressed in "pathological ide-ologies" of anticolonial nationalism. Western experts "insisted that this was a negative reaction, driven by jealousy and hatred of the white race," which was rooted in "an inferiority complex" among colonial subjects (Dudziak 2000, 208). Clearly, then, "it was the feeling of inferiority rather than the reality of racial dom-ination that provoked anti-colonial revolts" (209). Subsequently, this racist psy-chobabble, "the pathology of anti-racist resentment," became "a catch-all explanation of events" in the independence struggles in Africa and Asia and "provided an important theme for official reports" (208). In this view, "the prob-lem was not so much the impact of imperialism or of racism as the failure to adjust" (134). Prominently implicated was the so-called "marginal man," the colonial subject who was either racially mixed or had received some Western education and found himself "between two worlds." It was these marginal men who had the greatest difficulty in "adjusting" and it was opined that "those who could not adjust became racially conscious, anti-white or unstable" (Furedi 1998, 134). It followed that "it was not so much racism as the overreaction to it that constituted the problem. It was not idealism, conviction or political passion, but a psychological overreaction which drove Marginal Man's anti-imperialism" (148). In the final analysis, "this stress on adjustment left the colonial reality as unprob-lematic," meanwhile "the focus on the psychology of anti-Western sentiment invariably distracts from the wider social and historical structures of Western domination" (148–49).

Racism in world politics was reconceptualized again to accommodate the changed realities on the ground, with only superficial adjustments to the façade of white supremacy. At this point, "racial inferiority became a subject of study in its own right. Accordingly, the standard model of analysis used to explain anti-colonial nationalism began with the premise that the source of the problem was frustration, resentment and a feeling of inferiority. It was held that these nega-tive sentiments led to a virulent type of reaction against the West, which invari-ably took on an anti-white racist form" (Furedi 1998, 208). Therefore, "the very rejection of the West was held to be the defining feature of racial prejudice" (208). The strained, perverted, but nonetheless prevailing logic of this contention suggested that "anti-colonial nationalism was the product of a disturbed state of mind, which was invariably susceptible to racist emotions," creating a state of mind marked by a "highly infectious" hysteria that magnified grievance towards whites out of all proportion to its actual degree. Africans and Asians, the argu-ment went, were highly susceptible to this irrational hatred of white people; therefore making them just as racist as they claimed whites to be. The result was that "precisely at a time when scientific racism was under attack and when ideas of race equality were gaining currency, a rearguard action was successfully dis-crediting the reaction to racism" (149). Antiracist movements "were interpreted as the irrational action of the psychologically frustrated" whose main problem was hypersensitivity to perceived slights. Therefore, "it was not so much racism as the overreaction to it that constituted the problem," which stressed the need for greater "adjustment" on the part of the natives while leaving the oppressive colonial apparatus blameless (148).

Further, if all peoples could harbor these racist feelings, then surely everyone was guilty of racism to some degree. As Furedi notes, "In the post-war period there was a gradual shift from the focus on race consciousness to one that portrayed racism as a problem for which everyone bore responsibility. The logic of this representation was at once to implicate everyone and no one in particular. This discourse was rooted in the discussions of the interwar period, but in the 1950s it was systematically developed into a powerful theory of race relations. It provided a coherent defence for the negative argument that suggested that the West should not be singled out since everyone else was also racist" (Furedi 1998, 226). As a result, racism in world politics had become thoroughly mystified. Race consciousness was linked to common problems of interracial relations in which it was assumed that there was a constant potential for conflict. "The implication was that the international conflict of colour possessed an autonomous dynamic" and that "this was a problem which transcended particular societies and circumstances" (116–17). Racism in world politics was not particular to white people or the white nations that dominated the globe and subjugated most of the world's non-white people. Such a "reduction of racism to a generic concept of conflict led many writers to conceptualise racism as a universal problem." Consequently, their conclusions invariably implied that Western societies bore no greater responsibility for racism than others." In fact, it was "a sin afflicting the whole of humanity" (229).

But such a misinterpretation of history rests on a mystification of the definition of racism in world politics and a willful attempt to minimize the practice of racial domination and exploitation. It seeks to remove power from our conception of racism, reducing it to some form of ubiquitous ethnocentrism that may or may not affect the life chances of peoples who encounter it. It ignores the institutional apparatus of white supremacy in place in the governance of the world for at least the last two centuries. This mystification could not be accomplished internationally had it not been firmly established domestically. It was a concomitant of similar processes at work within Western societies that housed sizable black minorities. Nowhere was it more evident or more influential than in the United States. This situation has put African Americans in a pivotal position insofar as they experience a domestic form of racial oppression that has been extended abroad; therefore, the extent to which they can effectively challenge this dominant form of racial oppression, the greater their ability to provide a blueprint for others similarly situated. Moreover, the degree to which blacks might transform U.S. society through the transformation of its racist institutions— including its foreign policy institutions—the greater the likelihood of a transformation of international relations itself, structured as it is around the political, economic, military, and cultural hegemony of the United States. To appreciate this viewpoint, we need to turn to demystifying racism in the United States.

Demystifying Racism in the United States

There is an immediate challenge when one attempts to define racism in U.S. society because a system of white racism persists in the United States that acts to prevent those within it from recognizing it, confronting it, indicting it, and therefore changing it. Scholars analyzing racism in the United States are often confronted with the task of defining the concept in ways that do not offend extant racist sensibilities and institutions. In this context racists themselves have defined their racism out of existence through the creation of a "nonracist" discourse that obscures racist practices that persist in the society and instead targets relatively powerless expressions of bigotry among minority communities as more appropriate targets of state action. In such a context, mainstream scholars and policymakers willfully pervert definitions of such terms as racism in order to deracialize, naturalize, and marginalize white supremacism, which is at the core of U.S. society, while often indicting as racists those who call this racist order into question.

The post–civil rights era has witnessed the mystification of white supremacism that has resulted from *misdefining* the concept of racism and *mystifying* the practice of racism. For example, Omi and Winant's widely touted text (1994) focuses on racism as a "sociohistorical process" by which racial categories are created, inhabited, transformed, and destroyed, which they refer to as "racial formation." They define racism as "a fundamental characteristic of social projects which create or reproduce structures of domination based on essentialist categories of race" (Omi and Winant 1994, 162). They add that "we should think of race as an element of social structure rather than as an irregularity within it; we should see race as a dimension of human representation rather than as an illusion." Race should be understood in its social context, which varies across time and space. It "signifies and symbolizes social conflicts and interests by referring to different types of human bodies" (55). They accept that race as a category is not biologically defined; nevertheless, they agree that it has an enduring impact on social relations. They maintain that theory should explain the enduring significance of race, and this is what they set out to do. They eschew what they consider two limited views of race, either as (1) an essence, or something "fixed, concrete, and objective"; or another view of race as (2) mere illusion, or "a purely ideological construct which some ideal non-racist social order would eliminate" (54). Their attempt to transcend these bipolar conceptualizations of race leads them to aver that race is an "unstable and 'decentered' complex of social meaning constantly being transformed by political struggle" (55).

Feagin (2000, 21) maintains that Omi and Winant's thesis places far too much emphasis on "the ideological construction of race or the formation of racial meanings and identities" and far too little on "the concrete advantages whites have gained, unjustly, over several centuries of slavery, segregation, and contemporary racism." He argues that while racial formation is an aspect of racism, it is hardly the most important one. He is emphatic that white supremacism, which he characterizes as "systemic racism," is "not just about the construction of racial images, attitudes and identities," but "it is even more centrally about the creation, development, and maintenance of white privilege, economic wealth, and sociopolitical power over nearly four centuries" (21). That is, "it is about hierarchical interaction." (29) Feagin adds that "the past and present worlds of racism include not only racist relations at work but also the racist relations that black Americans and other Americans of color encounter in trying to secure adequate housing, consumer goods, and public accommodations for themselves and their families. Racism reaches deeply into family lives, shaping who has personal relations with whom, and who gets married to whom. Racism shapes which groups have the best health, get the best medical care, and live the longest lives" (21). Feagin concurs with Cornel West's sentiment that "'Categories are constructed. Scars and bruises are felt with human bodies, some of which end up in coffins. Death is not a construct'" (21).

Feagin is essentially correct, but beyond his critique it is clear that Omi and Winant's turn to "racial formation" largely abandons the enterprise of conceptualizing and confronting racism. That is, in arguing that race is a construct that is largely wedded to specific and shifting social milieu, Omi and Winant conflate the origins and dynamics of the manipulation of races by elites with the definition of the term itself. While it is true that race is "constructed" and reflects certain "social conflicts," this generalization can be made about many socioeconomic or political categories such as gender, class, or sexuality. In addition, Omi and Winant's recognition does not uncover the deleterious impact of policies and practices geared toward the oppression of people who are denigrated through these constructs. Moreover, even as a construct, race is not subsumed by gender, class, or sexuality but incorporates these lines of cleavage within it. Often analysts ignore this obvious inclusiveness in order to insinuate and camouflage their actual focus on white women, white workers, and white homosexuals (and as an afterthought, "other" minorities in these categories) in order to artificially narrow a focus on black people as one that ignores other lines of cleavage that the category "black" obviously subsumes. Race in important ways is much simpler than Omi and Winant suggest. It has a clear history in the United States, and it has enduring precepts and straightforward, if hardly scientific, denotations. The most fundamental denotation across time and space is white supremacy. Specifically, race has been clearly grounded in a classificatory scheme that places those who are white and associated with whiteness in the superior position and those who are nonwhite or associated with nonwhites—especially blacks—in the inferior position. Regardless of the context, since the establishment of the United States race has consistently meant this: white supremacism.

Similarly, racism is not the mélange that Omi and Winant suggest; instead, racism as it has been actualized, experienced, and propagated in U.S. society is the belief, practice, and policy of domination based on the specious concept of race. Racism is not simply bigotry or prejudice but a public policy supported by institutional power, primarily state power. The functional or most persistent and dominant form of racism in the United States is white supremacy. It is this form of racism in the U.S. that is responsible for the genocide against the Native Americans, the human and cultural destruction and debasement of African enslavement, the denial of the humanity and citizenship rights of blacks after enslavement, Jim Crowism, de jure and de facto segregation, and the establishment of ideologies and institutions to rationalize and perpetuate the subjugation of nonwhite peoples. It also involves the privileging of white peoples and their interests, opportunities, and life chances by granting them differential access to the major life-giving and life-sustaining institutions of the society. Racism provides concrete advantages for those viewed as whites and concrete disadvantages for those viewed as blacks. As Lipsitz (1998, viii) reminds us, whiteness has a "cash value" as well as an emotional value; and this is evident domestically and internationally. Among the cash values is "a system for protecting the privileges of whites by denying communities of color opportunities for asset accumulation and upward mobility." One of the main instruments of the maintenance of this distorted system of privilege and privation is racist discrimination in the distribution of land following manumission and racist discrimination in home ownership, which is the major vehicle for the transmission of wealth across generations and persists today. Government and local policies promoting housing discrimination (and financial support for mortgages) against blacks have been a major and persistent impediment to black socioeconomic development in the U.S. It has repercussions for education opportunities from kintergarten through high school and into college, as well as access to insurance and health care. It also plays a role in the feminization of black poverty through its differential and deleterious impact on black women who suffer under both the racism and sexism of many of these discriminatory policies.

Thus white supremacism in the U.S. is hardly the same conceptually, in practice, or in effect, as a black person using a racial slur against a white person or voicing the black supremacist tenets of Nation of Islam members. To be sure, black supremacist pontifications are not institutionalized in any major life-giving or life-sustaining institutions. It is not black supremacist policy that redlines districts for insurance or mortgages. White people do not fear going to black supremacist hospitals where without insurance they cannot afford to get sick. Nor does any racist doctrine other than white supremacism find solace and support in the institutions of the United States armed forces, its local police forces, or its courts, prisons, and jails. Nor is white employment, housing, or education affected in even a minuscule way by notions of black supremacy. Such arguments are a subterfuge and meant to distract attention from and opprobrium for the major functional form of racism in past and present U.S. society: white supremacism—nothing else comes close, and to argue otherwise is to engage in the absurd. Therefore, definitions of racism in the United States that do not focus primarily on white supremacism are abstractions with little relevance to U.S. social dynamics. This view is more historically accurate and is consistent with the experience of U.S. society than Omi and Winant's mystification. The failure to situate racism in its historical and most prevalent manifestation leads to a mystification of the concept and leaves us unprepared to challenge it or even to articulate it in terms that are clear: the fundamental form of racism in the United States is white supremacism.

In attempting to apply the "racial formation" thesis to world politics, Winant (2001) again errs in his assessment of the phenomenon. Although he is correct that a racial hierarchy persists even against claims to the contrary; that it correlates very well with worldwide and national systems of stratification and inequality;

that it corresponds to glaring disparities in labor conditions; and that it reflects differential access to democratic and communicative instrumentalities and life chances, he still succumbs to the façade of change in the functional form of racism. That is, he asserts that "what remains of racial discourse has a new tone," such that "Race talk today presents itself as egalitarian, respectful of 'cultural difference,' and, above all, humane. The appearance and consolidation of such post-racial sentiments is a recent phenomenon; it has reshaped contemporary understanding and debates over race" (1–2). But the reality of racism as white supremacism has not changed. Further, discussions of social Darwinism, the white man's burden, *mission civilisatrice*, all took on an "ethical" dimension, albeit dualist ones that suggested one form of conduct for civilized, Christian, and evolved whites and another for uncivilized, heathen, and unevolved blacks. What is most important is not the superficially varied propaganda of white supremacist proponents, but the underlying hierarchy that white racism supports and the distribution of concrete advantages across races that it ensures. It is clear that today as for the last two centuries, this hierarchy is ordered by white supremacist precepts. In that way, the essence of racism as a system of power has not changed, although some of the language related to present racist policies clearly has.

Having defined racism clearly, we can demonstrate its influence in world politics through its impact on the dominant paradigms of the field. Pursuant to this, we analyze two theses arising from the two prominent paradigms in the field. First, I examine one of the most recent but influential theoretical arguments from the realist school, Samuel Huntington's clash of civilizations thesis, which posits that cultural difference leads to international conflict. Second, I examine one of the most influential theses in the idealist tradition, the democratic peace thesis, which posits that democratic states are less likely to fight each other. I will attempt to show how racism inheres in the assumptions of the two theses to the extent that it challenges and confounds their empirical assumptions even as they are utilized to guide international relations research and to inform U.S. foreign policy.

Realism: Racism and the Clash of Civilizations

While a critique of realism could usefully begin with a discussion of balance of power theorists dating from the Enlightenment (see Henderson 2005), here I will focus on more recent formulations in order to demonstrate the persistence of racism in more recent realist theses. For example, in the 1990s an extensive literature emerged in world politics that focused on the impact of cultural identity conceived as shared religious or ethnolinguistic characteristics (e.g., Chay 1990; Mazrui 1990; Davis and Moore 1997; Henderson 1997). This literature was epitomized in studies focusing on "ethnic conflicts" (Ryan 1990; Gurr 1994, 2000), and many of these began to explicate these events through an application of realist frameworks such as found in the study of "ethnic security dilemmas" as precipitants of "ethnic conflicts" (Posen 1993), and most prominently in Huntington's (1993a, 1993b, 1996, 1999) cultural realist "clash of civilizations" thesis, which suggests that shared civilization membership is the fulcrum upon which post–cold war era world politics rests. Huntington's initial essay (1993a) on the clash of civilizations is one of the most frequently cited articles to have appeared in *Foreign Affairs*, while the book-length version of the article has become an international bestseller and has been translated into several languages while becoming increasingly influential in policy circles. Decision makers in the West have evoked "clash of civilizations" explanations to account for the attacks on the United States of September 11, 2001 and to suggest Huntington's thesis as a guidepost to orient U.S. and Western foreign policy in both the war on terrorism and in post–cold war international relations more generally. In this way, both the literature on the increasing role of culture in international relations generally, and Huntington's "clash of civilizations" thesis in particular, have become prominent points of departure in analyzing world politics in the post–cold war era.

Huntington's (1993a, 1993b, 1996) "clash of civilizations" (hereafter, CoC) thesis posits that conflict is more likely to occur between states of different civilizations. His basically realist formulation insists on the primacy of states as the major actors in international relations, however, he maintains that whereas ideological differences framed cold war era international relations, in the post–cold war era cultural identities—civilization identities—are increasingly salient. Moreover, he insists that for the first time in history the global system is both multipolar and multicivilizational. He is concerned—like realists in general—that the balance of power among these poles is shifting in such a way as to decrease the power of the West and to increase that of "the Rest." Therefore, Huntington's thesis should be viewed as providing a cultural façade over a clearly realist foundation.

For Huntington (1996, 43), a civilization is "the highest cultural grouping of people and the broadest level of cultural identity people have short of that which distinguishes humans from other species." He maintains that a civilization "is a culture writ large" (41) and the "central defining characteristic" of a civilization is its religion (47); hence, "the major civilizations in human history have been closely identified with the world's great religions" (42). These civilizations include the Sinic, Japanese, Hindu, Islamic, Orthodox, Western, Latin American, (apparently) Buddhist, and "possibly African" civilizations (47–48). Huntington (1996, 126) is clear that "people rally to those with similar ancestry, religion, language, values, and institutions and distance themselves from those with different ones." For Huntington, shared religion is the single most important indicator of a civilization; therefore, he avers that clashes of civilizations are usually conflicts "between peoples of different religions" (253). For him, "Civilizations are the ultimate human tribes, and the clash of civilizations is tribal conflict on a global scale" (207). Huntington (1996, 289–90) implies that culturally dissimilar decision makers are likely to employ a "civilizational realpolitik" (i.e., a cultural realist) strategy in their inter-civilizational disputes, which, in his view, increases the probability of escalation to a fault-line war.[2] Moreover, since membership in a civilization is rooted primarily in religious identity, this factor further reduces the likelihood of compromise. In fact, it intensifies the likelihood of conflict in inter-civilizational disputes because the exclusivity of religion is far more pervasive than that of race or ethnicity. He notes that "A person can be half-French and half-Arab and simultaneously even a citizen of two countries"; however, it "is more difficult to be half-Catholic and half-Muslim" (Huntington 1993, 27).

The popular version of Huntington's (1993a, 22) thesis asserts that in the post–cold war era the most prevalent form of global conflict will occur at the fault lines of the major civilizations. According to Huntington (1996), the CoC emerged in the post–cold war era as a result of: (1) the heightened interaction of peoples from different civilizations; (2) the de-Westernization of elites in non-Western states; (3) increased economic regionalization; (4) a global resurgence of religious identity; and (5) a demographic and economic shift in the balance of power toward non-Western states—especially Asian and Islamic states—in ways that challenge Western hegemony. The interaction of these factors has resulted in the increased salience of civilization membership in global politics. Since civilizational characteristics are basic and essential, differences among civilizations are increasingly likely to generate conflict. For Huntington, the result is that cultural factors have replaced ideological ones as the major source of conflict in world politics in the post–cold war era. But systematic analyses of Huntington's empirical claims have consistently failed to support his thesis for international wars (Henderson and Tucker, 2001), militarized interstate disputes (Russett, Oneal, and Cox 2000; Henderson 2004a), and international crises (Chiozza 2002). With respect to civil wars, one finds that drawing on data that includes observations through the year 1999, there is no support for Huntington's thesis in the post–cold war era (Henderson 2006). In fact, where there have been changes in the incidence of clashes of civilizations in the post–cold war era, we find that their number has actually *declined*, if only marginally. Similarly, if we consider the proportion of clashes of civilizations to all intrastate armed conflicts, we find that if anything the proportion of clashes of civilizations has declined since the end of the cold war (Henderson 2006).

While many post–cold war conflicts are disputes crossing ethnic, linguistic, or religious lines, they do not cross civilizational lines as designated by Huntington; therefore they do not constitute clashes of civilizations. For example, the conflicts in Rwanda and Burundi—which are included in most lists of "ethnic conflicts" in the post–cold war era—are not clashes of civilizations but are clashes *within* the African civilization as defined by Huntington. Similarly, the conflicts between the Krahn and Gio in Liberia are clashes within the African civilization as defined by Huntington. The armed conflicts involving Kurds and Iraqis in Iraq; Pashtun, Uzbeks, and Tajiks in Afghanistan; and Shia and Sunnis in Iraq—as well as Somali clans in Somalia—are not clashes of civilizations but clashes *within* the Islamic civilization as defined by Huntington. By the same token, the conflict between Catholics and Protestants in Northern Ireland and the conflict between Basque separatists and the Spanish government are clashes *within* Western civilization. Even the conflicts in the Middle East involving Israel and its Arab neighbors are not clashes of civilizations according to Huntington since he does not recognize Judaism as a major civilization. These conflicts and many others like them involve disputes that cross cultural lines, but they are not clashes of civilizations according to Huntington's definition. Thus, even where it appears that interethnic or interreligious conflicts have proliferated in the post–cold war era, most of these are not "clashes of civilizations," nor do they originate from or portend the supposed transformation of warfare in the post–cold war era that Huntington's thesis suggests.

The empirical evidence does not support the clash of civilizations thesis, or by implication the policy recommendations that Huntington derives from it. These recommendations advocate, among other things, the "cultural containment" of non-Western civilizations—especially the presumed impending Islamic-Sinic threat to Western hegemony internationally and the crippling of multicultural initiatives within Western states (especially the United States) domestically. Instead, Huntington's thesis represents a simplistic conceptualization of world affairs that is for the most part unrelated to the reality that it attempts to explain. His view of the post–cold war political landscape as one checkered by the impending threat of cultural "others" conceived as "clear and present strangers" is more likely to provide succor to those already predisposed towards ethnocentric and even xenophobic foreign policies. The implementation of policies founded on Huntington's assumptions is likely to antagonize rather than ameliorate difficulties across cultural divides in our highly interdependent international system. In this way, the clash of civilizations thesis may become a self-fulfilling prophecy for those following its recommendations because it encourages policies that generate strong opposition among cultural "others" who resist their marginalization across political, economic, social, and cultural dimensions.

The main problem is that Huntington's thesis relies largely on anecdote and selective attention to the historical record. Throughout his text, Huntington appears to have little problem taking the remarks of government leaders at face value when they provide support for his thesis while ignoring what these leaders actually do in pursuit of their presumably civilizational interests. As a case in point, Walt (1997, 185) challenges Huntington's (1996, 246–52) depiction of the Gulf War as a harbinger of the civilizational clashes that are presumed to prevail in the post–cold war era. First, Walt reminds us that the Gulf War did not begin as a dispute between states of different civilizations but as an intracivilizational dispute between two Islamic states, Iraq and Kuwait. In this "clash of civilizations," Western states (with tacit support from Israel) allied with one Islamic state, Kuwait, and repulsed another Islamic state, Iraq. Undeterred by these peculiarities, Huntington (1996) attempts to salvage his thesis by focusing on the sentiments of select individuals and groups within Islamic populations that, he argues, favored Iraq. Second, Walt (1997, 185) counters that "even if this were true, it merely underscores the fact that state interests mattered more than loosely felt and politically impotent loyalties to a particular 'civilizational' entity."

Turning toward another post–cold war "clash of civilizations," Walt (1997, 185) points out that although the war in the former Yugoslavia manifests some of the trappings of a fault line war, it ultimately fails as an intercivilizational conflict because the more than 50,000 U.S.-led troops that were deployed to Bosnia in 1996 were not there to defend Western interests, represented by Croatia, but Muslims. This is also evident in the North Atlantic Treaty Organization (NATO) intervention in Kosovo, which is aimed at protecting ethnic Albanians, who are predominantly Muslim. Further, Walt contends that while modest sums of aid for the Bosnian Muslims were sent by Islamic countries, the lion's share of support was provided by Western states. "Similarly, Russia offered some rhetorical support to the Serbs, but it backed away from its 'Orthodox' brethren when Serbian bellicosity made Belgrade an unappealing ally. Even the Western states failed to lineup according to cultural criteria, with Britain and France being more sympathetic to the Serbs, Germany backing the Croats, and the United States reserving most of its support for the Muslims." Even Huntington's (1996, 313–16) hypothetical case of an intercivilizational World War III in 2010 begins as a conflict between China and Vietnam, both of which Huntington includes in the Sinic civilization; therefore, even this hypothetical "clash of civilizations" is a clash *within* civilizations.

The major critique of the CoC thesis is that it ignores the persistent role of nationalism in world politics. Clearly, although nationalist conflict may resemble intercivilizational conflict at times, as in independence struggles or colonial wars, national interests often work at odds with civilizational ones, leading to such intracivilizational wars as the wars of Italian and German unification in the nineteenth century. For example, Walt (1997, 183–84) states that "being part of some larger 'civilization' did not convince the Abkhaz, Armenians, Azeris, Chechens, Croats, Eritreans, Georgians, Kurds, Ossetians, Quebecois, Serbs, or Slovaks to abandon the quest for their own state." Contrary to Huntington's thesis, the nation, and not the civilization, appears to be the largest identity group to which people consistently swear fealty in the post–cold war era. While Huntington is correct that states continue to be the major actors in world politics—and will be for the foreseeable future—he seems to have ignored the reason that their influence persists: the enduring salience of nationalism in international relations. This "neglect of nationalism," for Walt (187) "is the Achilles Heel of the civilizational paradigm." Since civilizations are more or less ideational constructs rather than political agents, they are devoid of decision-making power or control over political or economic resources. By comparison, states "can mobilize their citizens, collect taxes, issue threats, reward friends, and wage war; in other words, states can act. . . . Nationalism is a tremendously powerful force precisely because it marries individual cultural affinities to an agency—the state—that can actually do something" (187). To be sure, nationalist struggles may engender conflicts; however, cultural differences in the future as in the past are likely to remain one of several factors, including political, military, economic, and demographic considerations, that give rise to international conflict.

While Huntington's thesis has the "merit of simplicity, and it seems to make sense of some important contemporary events" (Walt 1997,181, 188–89), its allure appears to rest more on a "call for new enemies" and its partial resemblance to classical realist tenets (Rubenstein and Crocker 1994) than its empirical evidence. But not only should Huntington's (1996) foreign policy recommendations be viewed as questionable, his domestic policy prescriptions, which center on an attack on multiculturalism in the United States (Huntington 1996, 304–7), appear to be similarly misguided and essentially racist. According to Huntington (1993b, 190), multiculturalists "reject the idea of a 'color-blind' society of equal individuals and instead promote a 'color-conscious' society with government-sanctioned privileges for some groups." He contends that "Such claims run directly counter to the underlying principles that have been the basis of American political unity." Huntington's view ignores the clear historical fact that the framers of the United States Constitution had every intention of creating a country rooted in "government-sanctioned privileges for some groups": specifically, whites. The framers institutionalized and provided constitutional protections of the liberty of whites and de jure and de facto subjugation of nonwhites. To suggest that "color blindness" is somehow an article of faith or a centerpiece of American political philosophy or practice—as Huntington does—ignores centuries of constitutionally supported white supremacism in the United States.

Huntington's (1993b, 1996) thesis also seems to imply that one cannot be simultaneously multiculturalist and Western; this is clearly incorrect. To be Western does not suggest that one must be a Western chauvinist. His argument that multiculturalism rejects Western constructs appears to rely on an erroneous conflation of Western culture and white racism such that attacks on white racism by multiculturalists become in his mind synonymous with attacks on Western culture. Multiculturalists primarily contend that the Western features of American society have been melded from a quite remarkable amalgamation of diverse races, cultures, and peoples that provide the various threads of its social tapestry. Fundamentally, multiculturalists assail racist depictions of American history—not its Western heritage per se—and remind us that America since its inception has been multicultural in composition but has been dominated by whites who sometimes confuse their hegemony with the state's homogeneity.

Huntington's domestic policy prescriptions also give succor to those who blame intercultural disputes in the United States on the diversity of American society and the failure of divergent groups (especially African and Latino Americans) to assimilate themselves into a generally Western and evidently white cultural mold, while ignoring the historic and ongoing impact of white racism in the United States and the context of intergroup relations that it has created. A domestic policy that targets these historically marginalized culture groups alone instead of the institutions that buttress white racism will ensure the continuation of interracial and intercultural conflict in the United States. In its temper and substance, Huntington's analysis appears to suggest that nonwhites in the United States— just as nonwhites abroad—represent a "clear and present danger" to the state; and as such they should be contained domestically just as their cultural kin should be contained abroad. It is this rationale that would justify the preemptive attack of the United States on an Arab state—any Arab state—after the attacks on the United States in 2001, even though there was no evidence that Iraq posed an imminent threat to the United States.

Huntington's domestic policy prescriptions also fail to recognize that the manner in which the United States and other states promote interracial and intercultural cooperation within their own borders can fulfill the best ideals of Western (and many non-Western) societies while providing a blueprint for other culturally heterogeneous states. This point is especially significant in light of the fact that the modal composition of states or nations is one of territorially bounded political units housing culturally heterogeneous communities within them. Therefore, it is incumbent upon most, if not all, states to effectively integrate (not assimilate) the diverse groups in their heterogeneous societies in a manner that respects both the sovereignty of the state and the cultural pluralism of its inhabitants; or, on the other hand, to facilitate the autonomous development of culturally separate societies in their midst.

In sum, by focusing on theoretical and empirical blind spots in the CoC thesis as noted in the critiques cited earlier, we are better equipped to respond to Huntington's (1993b) query, "If not civilizations, what?" Evidently it is not civilizations, therefore, we should proceed in a systematic way toward uncovering the actual correlates and causes of war so that we can employ more effective strategies to prevent them. Rather than trying to simply "build new bogeymen" as Walt suggests that Huntington endeavors to do, we should build on extant research on the causes of war and peace and put forward empirically grounded and rigorously substantiated theoretical models to inform foreign policy. The fundamental problem with racist discourses in IR—or those that are silent with respect to white supremacism—is that they are empirically inaccurate and untethered to the reality they propose to explain. The clash of civilizations thesis is largely a rehash of the civilizationist arguments of the pre–World War I and interwar eras; it shares the alarmism that viewed the "teeming uncivilized masses" of Africa and Asia as the greatest threat to Euro-American global dominance, which is replicated in Huntington's thesis concerning the Asian "affirmation" and the Islamic "resurgence" (the latter fueled largely by the Muslim "youth bulge" and other demographic factors auguring the decline of Western civilization in Huntington's view). This early twentieth-century alarmism predicted a race war that would threaten the racial balance of power with little credence given to empirical evidence to support this view and little effort put forth to alter the system of white supremacy to ameliorate the conditions in the colonies that were giving rise to organized resistance. Similarly, the clash of civilizations thesis augurs a world where the black, brown, and yellow peoples—especially those embracing Islam—are a clear and present danger to Western power internationally and to white American power in the United States. It does not address the system of white supremacy either internationally or domestically but instead calls for cultural containment abroad and culturally hegemony (and its corollary, cultural repression) domestically. It demurs—following G. W. F. Hegel and Arnold Toynbee—on the existence of an African culture, as well as on the contributions of African and other nonwhite minorities' cultures to American society. Its ongoing popularity is a testament to the persistence of white supremacism in world politics. And like white supremacist theses of the last two centuries its strength lies in its proffer of a rationale for the maintenance and "naturalization" of an international status quo of white domination, however, its weakness is also emblematic of earlier white supremacist thesis and is its empirical inaccuracy. Hopefully the absence of empirical support for its claims suggests that Huntington's *Foreign Affairs* article of 1993, in which he first promulgated his clash of civilizations thesis, will not be viewed as the post–cold war equivalent of Kennan's "Long Telegram"[3]; instead, it should be seen as resembling a post–cold war Schlieffen Plan[4] that, if followed, is likely to provide the same result in the future as its namesake provided for Imperial Germany in 1914.

Idealism: Racism and the Democratic Peace Thesis

Having examined a major realist argument in world politics, at this point we turn to a prominent idealist thesis. In fact, idealism has provided one of the most important arguments to emerge from recent research in world politics, namely, the view that democracies are less likely to fight each other, and the related argument that democracies are more peaceful than nondemocratic states (Oneal and Russett 1997; Oneal and Ray 1997; Russett and Oneal 2001). The supportive evidence for this "democratic peace" thesis is allegedly so extensive that this central claim of Wilsonian idealism has been hailed as virtually an "empirical law" of world politics (Levy 1988). It compelled U.S. President Bill Clinton (1996, 9) to promulgate his post–cold war grand strategy of "democratic enlargement." President George W. Bush, while giving less credence to the Wilsonian idealism that undergirded Clinton's assessment, nonetheless has described his "war on terrorism" as an attempt in part to assist more democratic elements to assume control of such states as Afghanistan and Iraq. The strategy is based on the explicit assumption that once transformed, these states will be more peaceful and less likely to support forces aligned against Western democracies.

The democratic peace thesis is rooted in the philosopher Immanuel Kant's view that republics requiring the consent of the governed to both support and do the actual fighting in war would be less bellicose because their citizens would not visit upon themselves all the calamities of war if given a choice. Woodrow Wilson regarded Kant's republics as analogous to the democratic republics of the early twentieth century; Wilson consequently enshrined the notion of "democratic peace" in his vision of the post–World War I global order. The democratic peace thesis today argues that democratic states apply the shared norms of peaceful conflict resolution that inhere in their domestic politics to their international relations. Variants of this argument suggest that democratic institutions, which rely on checks and balances, require coordination of foreign policy before the state may take action, as opposed to the institutions of autocratic states, which often require only an edict from the ruler to embark on foreign conflict. Given that mobilization takes more time in democracies, in the interim democracies may pursue mediation or third-party arbitration of their conflicts. These relationships are assumed to be evident in instances in which democracies face off against other democracies, but they are less likely to be apparent when democracies confront nondemocracies (Russett 1993). Implicit in both versions of the democratic peace thesis is that a state's foreign policy derives from its domestic policy. That is why, for Wilson, peace in international relations required a concert of nations committed to peace in their domestic relations: namely, democracies. But the version of democracy that informs the post-Wilsonian democratic peace thesis is not a race-neutral concept. To be sure, the notion of peace between democracies was not meant to include nonwhite peoples. Much of the evidence for the "democratic peace" proposition rests on the definition of democracy that is used as well as the types of wars one analyzes. What is more, the roots of the notion of democratic peace are found in the white supremacist notions of *Herrenvolk* democracy[5] that undergirds many Enlightenment-inspired precepts of classical liberalism and the idealist paradigm of world politics that borrows heavily from this tradition. An appreciation of racism in the democratic peace thesis requires that we confront the seedier side of the democratic peace literature and some of its historic advocates such as Hegel, Kant, and Wilson, since Africa and Africans in their minds constituted a realm and a group of peoples for whom principles that were observed for Western nations were not deemed desirable or thought practicable.

For example, Hegel, whom Ray (1995, 4) acknowledges as a "generally under-appreciated . . . inspiration for contemporary work on the democratic peace proposition," noted that the consciousness of blacks "has not yet attained to the realization of any substantial objective existence . . . in which the interest of man's volition is involved and in which he realized his own being." Hegel added that "the Negro . . . exhibits the natural man in his completely wild and untamed state," and that "among the Negroes moral sentiments are quite weak, or more strictly speaking, non-existent." Further, he argues that they lack self-control and that "the only essential connection between the Negroes and the Europeans is that of slavery. . . . The gradual abolition of slavery is therefore wiser and more equitable than its sudden removal." He is emphatic that Africa "is no historical part of the World; it has no movement or development to exhibit. . . . What we properly understand by Africa is the unhistorical, undeveloped spirit, still involved in the conditions of mere nature" (Hegel 1944, 91–93). Hegel's racist historiography informed Toynbee's (1934, 233), which insisted that "the only one of the primary races, . . . which has not made a creative contribution to any of our twenty-one civilizations is the Black race," and, in turn, informs Huntington's thesis which demurs on whether Africans possess a civilization at all.

Since Hegel is only indirectly associated with the democratic peace thesis, perhaps Ray's silence on his racism can be attributed to that fact. Kant's philosophy, however, provides "an important symbolic as well as substantive source of inspiration for advocates of the democratic peace proposition," according to Ray (1995, 3). Kant is for Doyle (1997, 302) the author whose thesis "lays a special claim to what world politics is and can be: a state of peace." Kant is the theorist whose thesis "claims a special property right in what shapes the politics of Liberal states—liberty and democracy" (302). It is Kant, whose focus on "republican constitutionalism" is for Russett (1993, 4) "compatible with basic contemporary understandings of democracy." It is Kant (1960, 113), the intellectual godfather of the democratic peace thesis, whom these advocates and others extol profusely, who suggested that nonwhite human beings are not full persons whose rights are bound to be respected, protected, and defended by the very democracy that advocates of the democratic peace so persistently associate with his name.

According to Kant, blacks are inferior to whites. He is clear that "so fundamental is the difference between these two races of man (whites and Negroes), and it appears to be as great in regard to mental capacities as in color" (Kant 1960, 111). For Kant "talent" was an "'essential,' natural ingredient for aptitude in higher rational and moral achievement" and talent was unequally distributed across races with whites possessing the greatest "gift" of talent and blacks largely lacking it (Eze 1995, 227). Whites occupy the highest position in Kant's "racial rational and moral order," "'followed by the 'yellow,' the 'black,' and then the 'red'" and this rank reflected their relative "capacity to realize reason and rational-moral perfectibility through education" (218). Therefore, "it cannot . . . be argued that skin color for Kant was merely a physical characteristic" but rather "evidence of an unchanging and unchangeable moral quality" (218–19). Mills (1999, 71) agrees that "in complete opposition to the image of his work that has come down to us and is standardly taught in introductory ethics courses, full personhood for Kant is actually dependent on race." Take for example, Kant's (1960, 113) discussion taken from his *Observations of the Feeling of the Beautiful and Sublime* where he affirms that "this fellow was quite black from head to foot, a clear proof that what he said was stupid." He adds that "the Negroes of Africa have by nature no feeling that rises above the trifling" (110). For Kant they are incapable of achieving the level of rationality required of moral agents.

Kant asserted that negroes "can be educated but only as servants (slaves); that is, they allow themselves to be trained" (Eze 1995, 215). Such training does not require reason but only repetition. Cognitive inabilities of blacks require of their masters a stern disposition and informed instruction in their catechism that Kant does not hesitate to supply in providing guidance on the proper method of punishment for blacks: use "a cane but it has to be a split one, so that the cane will cause wounds large enough that prevent suppuration underneath the 'negro's' thick skin" (215). Neugebauer (1990, 264) points out that Kant's advice to use a split bamboo cane instead of a whip was intended to ensure that the slave suffered—"because of the 'negro's' thick skin, he would not be racked with sufficient agonies through a whip"—without actually dying. Only if the black person is not fully human can one reconcile this instruction with Kant's imperative that we "always treat humanity whether in your own person or in the person of any other, never simply as a means, but always at the same time as an end." Blacks do not meet the minimal requirements for moral agency and thus of personhood for Kant. Personhood, for Kant, is circumscribed by his white supremacism. The republicanism he espouses—in contrast to Russett's claims—is quite a distance from democracy popularly conceived: it is a *Herrenvolk* democracy for whites that provides for "perpetual peace," but democratic peace advocates are silent about this core precept of their "universalist" thesis. Mills (1995, 72) explains that "*the embarrassing fact for the white West (which doubtless explains its concealment) is that their most important moral theorist of the past three hundred years is also the foundational theorist in the modern period of the division between* Herrenvolk *and Untermenschen, persons and subpersons, upon which Nazi theory would later draw. Modern moral theory and modern racial theory have the same father*" [emphasis in original]. The democratic peace literature is silent on this particular impact of Kant's writing and its implications for his "perpetual peace."

Woodrow Wilson, who is generally considered among the leading theorists of democratic peace, inherited Kant's notion about the benevolence of democracy and was no less a student of Kant's white supremacism, which Wilson helped to institutionalize both in the United States and abroad. In world affairs, the architect of the "democratic peace" had little patience for democracy that would include people who were not white. While Wilson is said to have helped to usher in a new era in world politics by institutionalizing the core precepts of classical liberalism and making an ostensible departure from the *Realpolitik* that guided international relations in the previous era, he also perpetuated the white supremacism of the earlier epoch, as discussed above. Wilson provides an excellent example of the liberal or idealist notion that a state's foreign policies reflect its domestic policies; in this case the white racism of Wilson's domestic policies translated into the white supremacism of his foreign policies. His "idealism" is revealed for the *Herrenvolk* foreign policy that it is, justifying, as it does, imperialism and the subjugation of nonwhite peoples. Democratic peace advocates too readily ignore the persistent role of these notions in their present enterprise to embark on a crusade to remake the world in the image of these self-same Western *Herrenvolk* democracies.

With white supremacism an inherent aspect of the historic logic of democratic peace arguments, it seems for most democratic peace theorists today that pervasive white racism in the domestic and foreign policies of Western imperialist states neither disqualifies these states from being classified as democratic in their domestic politics, nor does it encourage the simple straightforward imputation of the liberal ideal that links a state's foreign policy to its domestic policy. The latter would lead most unbiased analysts to conclude that democracies are likely to pursue racist or imperialist wars. Hunt (1987, 91) reminds us that decision-makers in the United States—one of the most enduring democracies—"fixed race at the center of their world view." Hunt (91) is clear that U.S. political elites share "a loyalty to race as an essential category for understanding other peoples and as a fundamental basis for judging them." But democratic peace advocates such as Weart (1998) and Russett (1993) argue that even given their biased perceptions of certain peoples, democratic leaders have not prosecuted international warfare against other democracies. Such a view ignores imperialist wars between Western democracies and potentially egalitarian polities that they were attempting to subjugate. For example, the conflicts related to the Belgian subjugation of the indigenous societies of the Democratic Republic of Congo may provide candidate cases of joint democratic conflict, especially in light of the research by such African scholars as Ernest Wamba dia-Wamba, who have been documenting such indigenous representative institutions as *palaver* which are found in several societies in Africa's interlacustrine region (see also Nzongola-Ntalaja 2002). Conflicts involving indigenous egalitarian states in the region and the agents of imperial Belgium, which is coded as a democracy from 1830 on by quantitatively oriented democratic peace scholars—with the exception of the few years when it was occupied by Germany—could readily inform democratic peace research and allow us to determine its accuracy in light of Africa's political history.

The African cases with respect to Belgium and other Western colonizers is even more instructive given that the Belgian king, Leopold II, committed what Hochschild (1998, 3) labels "one of the great mass killings of recent history" in the "Rubber Terror" in the Belgian Congo. An estimated ten million Africans were killed between 1880 and 1920, in what Hochschild characterizes as a holocaust in Central Africa (225). Hochschild maintains that the scale of the killing subsided only when the "democratic" Belgian government took over control of the colony. Hochschild adds that democratic France followed similar policies in their equatorial African territories with indigenous population losses estimated at roughly 50 percent, but little research has been conducted on the extent to which the polities of Africa who resisted colonial subjugation were egalitarian. Similarly, Britain's colonial subjugation of African and Asian peoples neither affects her democratic standing among democratic peace researchers nor does it seem to warrant much research on the extent to which the British fought indigenous egalitarian politics.

In addition, by excluding colonial and imperial wars from their analyses, democratic peace advocates ignore the loathsome record of Western involvement in colonial and imperial wars. Some democratic peace researchers accomplish this feat at the same time that they laud the impact of peace-generating norms in inhibiting democratic states from the pursuit of bellicose foreign policies (e.g., Russett 1993; Weart 1998). If there are any consistent examples where such "norms" did not inhibit Western democracies, it is in the bloody record of the West's colonial and imperial wars (e.g., see Rodney 1980; Hochschild 1998). Only recently have democratic peace scholars returned to systematically analyzing these wars, and the results are modest at best. None of these studies, however, has attempted to determine the relative egalitarian nature of indigenous regimes in a way in which dyadic relationships can be determined. Nevertheless, it is clear that Western democracies are *most likely* to be involved in extrastate wars (Henderson 2002). Moreover, a review of Correlates of War data reveals that among extrastate wars involving democracies in the Correlates of War data set, roughly half (16 of 33) involved African states. Nevertheless, discussion of these types of candidate cases is noticeably absent from most democratic peace research, including Russett (1993), Ray (1995), Russett and O'Neal (2001), and Weart (1998). Weart's study claims to have documented the entire population of approximate cases of joint democratic war. Lost to the empirical record of democratic peace researchers are most of the armed conflicts associated with colonial subjugation of peoples—especially African and Asian peoples.

Russett (1993, 14) offers a rationale for his exclusion of "'colonial' wars fought for the acquisition of territory inhabited by 'primitive' people without recognized states, as practiced by nineteenth century imperialism, or for the twentieth-century liberation of those people." He argues that since he is interested in "interstate" warfare, which requires that both entities are in fact states, these types of wars do not qualify for inclusion. Russett seems to have overlooked that in Chapter 5 of the same volume he provides an analysis of the democratic peace in "nonindustrial societies"—not states, but "societies, each of which is a population that more or less contiguously inhabits a geographical area and speaks a language (or lingua franca) not normally understood by people in neighboring societies" (Russett 1993, 99). With different definitions of warfare and democracy, he nonetheless proclaims the democratic peace thesis vindicated with respect to this class of cases. In light of this, the rationale Russett provides for excluding imperialist wars, noted above, seems disingenuous. Moreover, what is implicit in his exclusion of these wars is the view that the behavior of democracies with respect to them are not inconsistent with the causal logic of the democratic peace thesis-but this is an empirical question that Russett's research design cannot possibly address. Therefore, Russett's rationalization for ignoring these wars seems self-serving.

Nevertheless, such rhetorical sleights of hand are really not surprising given the extent to which democratic peace advocates wax eloquent on—and largely root their theoretical models in—the pronouncements of "democratic" theorists who clearly espoused white supremacism, especially Kant and Wilson, while remaining strangely silent on these authors' racist views and the implications of these views for the arguments they put forward. One implication of this silencing is that analysts rarely pose the question that in cases in which racism is a central component of a state's domestic and foreign policy, perhaps those states are not really democracies? Such a view has received relatively short shrift among democratic peace advocates, especially when the focus is on Western states in the postwar era. On the other hand, Du Bois ([1903] 1961; 1915; [1946] 1987) wrote voluminously on both the merits of democracy and the hypocrisy of its Euro-American form guided by a white supremacism that justified in particular the denial of the rights of citizens of African and Asian extraction domestically and the colonization and subjugation of Africans and Asians abroad. Martin Luther King Jr. ([1968] 1986) made a similar point repeatedly with respect to U.S. foreign policy during the Vietnam War, which he viewed as an imperialist extension of the country's racist domestic policies toward its racial minorities. This rather obvious relationship between a state's domestic and foreign policy—a centerpiece of classical liberalism—is too often minimized in the Wilsonian idealist preoccupation with the sanguine impact of democratic domestic politics on a state's foreign policy. When ignored, however, it leaves the democratic peace thesis cut off from the reality that it seeks to explain: namely, how democracies that ostensibly recognize freedom as a basic human right pursue the subjugation of other people and the prosecution of war against them in order to effectuate their subjugation. The theoretical inconsistency evaporates once we appreciate that the "founding fathers" of the democratic peace advocated a *Herrenvolk* democracy, and following the logic of classical liberal theses of world politics, one would expect a *Herrenvolk* democracy to practice a *Herrenvolk* foreign policy. It is this white racist democracy that we observe in the discourse of democratic peace, about which democratic peace advocates remain largely silent. This silence is most pronounced in the case of Africa.

African examples receive little more than silence since they are often invisible to democratic peace advocates and therefore do not even warrant rationalization (South Africa is the exception that proves the rule). The case of Western complicity in the assassination of Congo's first democratically elected leader, Patrice Lumumba, provides the most glaring example of such silences. In this case, the democratic forces of Belgium and the United States, operating within the context of a UN peacekeeping mission, made use of Belgian mercenaries, Katangan secessionists, and armed forces loyal to Colonel Joseph Mobutu to assassinate Prime Minister Patrice Lumumba, Senate Vice President Joseph Okito, and Sports Minister Maurice Mpolo on January 17, 1961. But the murder of Lumumba, and with him, the nascent democratic movement of the former Belgian Congo, had been orchestrated from Washington and Brussels long before the murders were carried out in the Brouwez villa near Lubumbashi, Congo (Nzongala-Ntalaja 2002). On August 18, 1960, the Eisenhower White House hastily called a meeting of the National Security Council (NSC) and in that meeting "the tenor of Eisenhower's remarks about Lumumba was strong enough for two officials at the meeting [NSC executive member Robert Johnson and Eisenhower's Special Assistant for National Security Affairs, Gordon Gray] to conclude that the President had authorized Lumumba's assassination" (Mahoney 1983, 40–41). The next day, CIA Director Allen Dulles cabled CIA Station Chief in Leopoldville and emphasized that "in the view of 'high quarters here,' Lumumba's 'removal must be an urgent and prime objective" (41). De Witte (2000) charges that Belgian Prime Minister Gaston Eyskens was at the head of the assassination conspiracy, which also involved Minister for African Affairs, Count Harold d'Aspremont Lyndon, as well as Foreign Affairs Minister Pierre Wigny who informed his subordinates in Brazzaville to "render Lumumba harmless" leading Colonel Louis Marliere, Colonel Mobutu's Belgian advisor, to make preparations for Lumumba's murder in October 1960.

Apparently, the United States and Belgium, two stalwart democratic states, somehow were not able to invoke the requisite democratic norms to prevent them from orchestrating the assassination, dismemberment, and disposal (by acid) of an African democratic leader. Not only did these democratic states strangle Congolese democracy in its cradle, the agents of these Western democracies wreaked havoc and devastation throughout the country and laid the basis for over thirty years of rapine, kleptocracy, and despotism by Joseph Mobutu, which was underwritten by the United States, France, and Belgium. Such policies did not end with the cold war but persist well after. Discussion of these African cases are largely absent from the discussion of democratic peace. Further, discussion of the policy implications of the replication of Western democracies throughout the globe rarely engages the issue of Western democratic states' treatment of nascent democracies in Africa and Asia. Nor does it deal with the likelihood of the repetition of some of the most egregious foreign policy pursuits of Western democratic states that might be occasioned by the proliferation of Western democratic forms.

In sum, Oren (1995, 151) is correct that "the democratic peace proposition is not about democracy per se; rather, it should be understood as a special case of an argument about peace among polities that are similar relative to some normative benchmarks." What is "special" about the benchmarks that indicate "democracy," for Oren, is that they represent "our kind." The designation of "our kind," in my view, often transcends regime type and may draw instead on the cultural characteristics of the rival society (Henderson 1998). Therefore, the conflict-dampening impact of democracy that democratic peace advocates ascribe to liberal regimes often rests on whether members of the political elite perceive the adversary as similar to themselves. Specifically, among culturally dissimilar disputants, the reduction of conflict occasioned by joint democracy may be undermined by racist or ethnocentric animus on the part of decision-makers. Since democratic peace analysts largely ignore or dismiss issues of white racism in their analyses, the impact of such factors are left unexplored or simply assumed to play little role in the phenomenon. Interestingly, recent empirical work reveals that even if one accepts the basic research design utilized by democratic peace advocates, the democratic peace phenomenon does not appear to be operative outside the West (Henderson 2004b). This finding undermines previous empirical results that suggest the universality of the phenomenon, which, as in the case of the clash of civilizations thesis, reveals that theses that do not attend to issues of racism are simply untethered to the reality they attempt to explain.

Conclusion

In this essay, I have attempted to address the centrality of racism in the origins of the major paradigms of world politics and their continued influence today. I argued that both realism and idealism are grounded in similar white supremacist precepts that provided the foundation of world politics as an academic field of inquiry. I maintain that this seminal racist orientation continues to inform analyses derived from such major paradigms as the clash of civilizations and democratic peace theses. Beyond the specific evidence that I provide to support my claims, it should be evident that both theses reinforce each other. When combined, they provide a powerful rationale for continued mobilization of the West against the "Rest"; that is, the clash of civilizations thesis reinforces a hierarchy of humanity that identifies and objectifies selected nonwhite peoples as enemies to be confronted on battlefields of politics, economics, and culture. Only overwhelming power can withstand the forces of these "cultural others" whose teeming masses are exploding as a result of their "demographic bulges" and are threatening to expand, inter alia, "Islam's bloody borders" to our shores. Even as Huntington argues that the West should absent itself from conflicts involving other civilizations, at the same time he calls for "cultural containment" on the part of the West-especially against a presumed Sinic-Islamic connection. But if "cultural containment" is anything like its predecessor that formed the basis of the cold war grand strategy, then it should be clear that this is hardly a nonviolent or noninterventionist policy orientation. It will require the prosecution of wars, political assassinations, the undermining of elected governments, and the almost blind support for what most states in the international community consider excessive and indiscriminate military actions by the Israeli regime that promise to be "for us" and "against them." It justifies no less than a "crusade" against cultural "others."

Providing a rationale for attacking these "others" is hardly required, since the issue will largely turn on who they are instead of what they have done." So Muslims collectively become synonymous with "terrorists" with little more of a rationale for opposing U.S. policies than the "fact" that they "hate freedom." Beyond the pale are considerations that allies of the U.S.—or the U.S. itself—could employ "terrorism" or that many Muslims—and non-Muslims—may have a rational basis for their opposition to the U.S. rooted in their abhorrence of U.S. leaders' often blind support for the state sponsored terrorism of the Israeli regime, especially that which is carried out in the Occupied Territories against Palestinians and more recently in Lebanon. In many Western conceptualizations, Muslims simply are placed lower on the "civilization" scale; thus their "barbarism" is to be expected and should be met with unbridled power. It follows that responses to attacks on the United States should occasion the conservative Bush administration to launch a preemptive invasion of Iraq by U.S.-led forces even in the absence of evidence linking Iraq to the attacks on the United States of September 11, 2001.[6] The "clash of civilizations" logic of Huntington's thesis suffices as a rationale for the linking of Muslim terrorists with Muslims in general (Mamdani 2004). Similarly, the Clinton Administration not only failed to intervene in the civil war that spawned the horrific genocide in Rwanda in 1994, but it appears to have even forbade its diplomats from using the word "genocide" to describe the event in case it might obligate the United States to provide more than lip service to stop the slaughter. Instead the liberal Clinton regime rationalized its inaction on the basis that the genocide was the result of "tribal" or "ethnic conflict" that was allegedly endemic among Africans. In actuality, the genocide was more a result of political rather than ethnic cleavages (Destexhe 1994; Lemarchand 1995) and the Hutu *genocidairres* targeted Tutsi's as well as moderate Hutus in a program of mass killing that was facilitated by France, and Mobutu's Zaire, which remained a U.S. ally in the region (Ntalaja-Nzongola 2003). Nevertheless, simplistic hierarchical caricaturizations of international relations are granted succor and support throughout the United States, among policymakers and public opinion alike, where white supremacism continues to be the norm, and analyses that suggest an inherent hierarchy of race, culture, or civilization are readily embraced by political leaders and a jingoistic populace.

If the clash of civilization thesis provides the logic for delineating potential enemies, the democratic peace thesis provides the gloss to justify the slaughter and sacrifice of war. That is, since democracies are more peaceful than non-democracies, and our enemies "hate freedom" and clearly are not democratic, then by attacking our enemies and reconstructing their states along the lines of the procedural (and *Herrenvolk*) democracies of the West, then warfare itself becomes the mechanism to ensure peace. Constructed in this way, the democratic peace thesis justifies warfare in order to ensure peace in an almost Kafkaesque fashion. The present "war on terrorism," as articulated and prosecuted by the Bush and Blair administrations, largely follows this logic. The view of the Bush administration, in particular, is that by "democratizing" Iraq, the United States diminishes the likelihood that Iraq will fight its neighbors or support international terrorism against the United States. Ignoring for the moment the dubious nature of each of these claims, it is evident that the Bush administration does not apply this requirement to the Saudi regime, which continues to have one of the most authoritarian regimes in the world, especially in its treatment of women. Ironically, Iraq's policies toward women under Hussein's regime were more progressive than those of the Saudi regime. Nor is democracy an important objective justifying war for the myriad non-democratic and oppressive regimes in the Caribbean, in Latin America, and throughout the Middle East, Africa, and Asia that the Bush administration continues to support.

Convinced of U.S. exceptionalism, few mainstream commentators in academia, policy circles, or the general public in the United States challenge the persistent inegalitarianism of U.S. foreign policy and the international relations that it dominates. This exceptionalism often blinds adherents of this view to the long history of American imperialism and the racism that has undergirded it and

persists to this day. Vitalis (2000) is correct that there is a "norm against notic-
ing" white supremacism throughout the field of international relations. The failure to appreciate this bedrock aspect of the field leaves analysts ill-equipped to
address the reality of world politics as it shapes the concrete reality of people's
lives, their opportunities, their aspirations, and the movements among them to
shape a better future for themselves. But even those who might want to engage
the issue of racism in world politics rarely successfully navigate the labyrinth of
mystification that surrounds the term in order to see it for what it is: white
supremacism. Instead it is often (mis)understood as simple bigotry and prejudice
with little consideration of the power dynamic that is at its core. Scholars today
pursue faddish intellectual contrivances such as "globalization" and "Empire" in
order to comprehend a global system that continues to be dominated by white
supremacist logic. Neither phenomenon is new. By some accounts the present
phase of globalization is the third, and not even the most extensive one (Hirst
2000). Moreover, Hardt and Negri's highly touted treatise, *Empire*, is largely a neo-
Marxist rehash of dependency (Frank 1967; Dos Santos 1970) and neocolonial-
ist arguments (Nkrumah 1965).[7] Their study appears to be just as myopic on issues
related to black peoples as current neorealist and neoidealist frameworks, as suggested by Moore's (2001) critique entitled "Africa: The Black Hole at the Middle of Empire?" Intellectual faddism continues to color much of the "progressive"
or "radical" discourse in world politics, leaving the core issues of white supremacism largely unchallenged by systematic analysis or informed policy prescriptions.
Therefore, in world politics today the 800–pound elephant in the middle of the
room that few want to talk about in an informed and straightforward fashion is
white supremacism. Without this meaningful engagement with the subject, policy prescriptions to eradicate it are not likely to be forthcoming. The dearth of
African Americans in IR undoubtedly is the main source of this problem. Moreover, the unwillingness of mainstream white academics, who dominate the field,
to appreciate the foundational and enduring impact of racism in world politics
contributes to its persistence. In such an environment it is little wonder that
racist precepts continue to play a prominent role in the major paradigms of world
politics and the policies that derive from them.

Notes

1. Malinowski would provide a rationalization for the support of the "colour bar" in his "A
Plea for an Effective Colour Bar" in 1931. Burgess proferred a white supremacist hierarchy of races
and discussion of their propensity for political development in his major work, The Foundations
of Political Science, which also compelled him to support the "civilizing mission" mythology of
Western imperialism in his "The Ideal of the American Commonwealth" in 1895, and later in
his Reminiscences of an American Scholar in 1934. Park's social contact thesis portended racial
conflict as a result of contact between races.

2. A fault-line war is an armed conflict between groups or states of different civilizations that
occurs on the borders of the two civilizations.

3. Also published in *Foreign Affairs*, Kennan's essay promulgated the "containment" strategy
that would guide U.S. foreign policy in the cold war era.

4. The war plan of the German Imperial Army prior to World War I.

5. A "master race" democracy, in which the privileged race in a country enjoys democracy as it subjugates those of a different race within its state. This is most evident in apartheid era South Africa or in the Jim Crow United States.

6. One of the ironies of "September 11th" is that prior to the attacks on the United States of 2001, the most prominent foreign-policy incident occurring on that day was the U.S.-sponsored overthrow of the democratically elected Allende regime in Chile, which ushered in decades of oppression and state sponsored terrorism of the U.S.-allied Pinochet regime in that South American country.

7. Interestingly, the thesis outlined in Empire is also convergent with many of the notions espoused by Black Panther Party leader, Huey Newton's (1980), theses on "revolutionary intercommunalism," first articulated almost three decades before publication of Empire.

References

Anderson, Carole. 2003. *Eyes off the prize: The United Nations and the African American struggle for human rights, 1944–1955*. Princeton, NJ: Princeton University Press.

Bunche, Ralph. 1936. *A world view of race*. Albany, NY: J.B. Lyons.

Chay, Jongshuk, ed. 1990. *Culture and international relations*. Westport, CT: Praeger.

Chiozza, Giacomo. 2002. Is there a clash of civilizations? Evidence from patterns of international crisis involvement 1946–97. *Journal of Peace Research* 39, no. 6:711–34.

Clinton, William. 1996. *A national security strategy of engagement and enlargement*. Washington, DC: U.S. Government Printing Office.

Davis, David, and Will Moore. 1997. Ethnicity matters: Transnational ethnic alliances and foreign policy behavior. *International Studies Quarterly* 41:171–84.

Destexhe, Alain. 1994. The third genocide. *Foreign Policy* 97 (Winter): 3–17.

De Witte, Ludo. 2000. *L'assassinat de Lumumba*. Paris: Karthala.

Dos Santos, Theotonio. 1970. The structure of dependency. *American Economic Reivew* 60 (May): 231–36.

Doyle, Michael. 1997. *Ways of war and peace*. New York: W. W. Norton.

Du Bois, W. E. B. 1903. *The souls of black folk*. New York: Vintage.

———. 1915. The African roots of the war. *Atlantic Monthly* 115 (May): 707–14.

———.1987. *The world and Africa*. New York: International Publishers. Originally published in 1946.

Dudziak, Mary. 2000. *Cold war civil rights*. Princeton, NJ: Princeton University Press.

Eze, Emmanuel. 1995. The color of reason: The idea of "race" in Kant's anthropology. In *Anthropology and the German Enlight*enment, edited by Katherine Faull. Lewisburg, PA: Bucknell University Press.

Feagin, Joe. 2000. *Racist America*. New York: Routledge.

Frank, Andre Gunder. 1967. *Capitalism and underdevelopment in Latin America: Historical studies of Chile and Brazil*. New York: Monthly Review Press.

Furedi, Frank. 1998. *The silent war, imperialism and the changing perception of race*. New Brunswick, NJ: Rutgers University Press.

Gardiner, Robert. 1968. Race and color in international relations. In *Color and race*, edited by John Hope Franklin, 200–241. Boston: Houghton Mifflin.

Giddings, Franklin. 1898. Imperialism? *Political Science Quarterly* 13, no. 4:585–605.

Gurr, Ted. 1994. Peoples against states: Ethnopolitical conflict and the changing world system. *International Studies Quarterly* 38:347–77.

———. 2000. *Peoples vs. states: Ethnopolitical conflict and accommodation at the end of the 20th century*. Washington, DC: U.S. Institute of Peace.

Hardt, Michael, and Antonio Negri. 2000. *Empire*. Cambridge, MA: Harvard University Press.

Hegel, Georg Wilhelm Friedrich. 1944. *Philosophy of history*. Translated by J. Sibree. New York: Willey. Originally published in 1840.

Henderson, Errol. 1997. Culture or contiguity: "Ethnic conflict," the similarity of states, and the onset of war, 1820–1989. *Journal of Conflict Resolution* 41, no.5:649–68.

———. 1998. The democratic peace through the lens of culture, 1820–1989. *International Studies Quarterly* 42 (September): 461–84.

———. 2002. Democracy and war: The end of an illusion? Boulder, CO: Lynne Rienner.

———. 2004a. Mistaken identity: Testing the clash of civilizations in light of democratic peace claims. *British Journal of Political Science* 34:539–54.

———. 2004b. Disturbing the peace: Evaluating the Universality of Democratic Peace Claims for African States. Paper presented to the annual conference of the International Studies Association, Montreal, Canada, March.

———. 2005. Hidden in plain sight: Racism in IR theory. Paper presented to the annual conference of the International Studies Association, San Diego, CA, March.

———. 2006. Not letting evidence get in the way of assumptions: Testing the clash of civilizations thesis with more recent data. *International Politics* 42:458–69.

Henderson, Errol, and Richard Tucker. 2001. Clear and present strangers: The clash of civilizations and international conflict. *International Studies Quarterly* 45:317–38.

Hirst, Paul. 2000. The global economy: Myths or reality. In *The ends of globalization*, edited by Don Kalb et al., 107–23. Lanham, MD: Rowman and Littlefield.

Hochschild, Adam. 1998. *King Leopold's ghost: A story of greed, terror, and heroism in colonial Africa.* New York: Houghton Mifflin.

Hunt, Michael. 1987. *Ideology and U.S. foreign policy.* New Haven, CT: Yale University Press.

Huntington, Samuel. 1993a. The clash of civilizations? *Foreign Affairs* 72:22–49.

———. 1993b. If not civilizations, what?—Paradigms of the post–cold war world. *Foreign Affairs* 72, no. 5:186–94.

———. 1996. The *clash of civilizations and the remaking of world order.* New York: Simon and Schuster.

———. 1999. The many faces of the future: Why we'll never have a universal civilization. In *Annual editions: Global issues 99/00*, edited by R. Jackson, 15–18. Guilford, CT: Dushkin/McGraw-Hill.

———. 2000. Try again: A reply to Russett, Oneal and Cox. *Journal of Peace Research* 37, no. 5:609–10.

———. 2004. *Who are we?* New York: Simon and Schuster

Kant, Immanuel. 1930. *Lectures on ethics (1780–1781).* Translated by Louis Infield. London: Methuen.

———. 1960. Observations *on the feeling of the beautiful and the sublime.* Translated by John T. Goldthwait. Berkeley: University of California Press.

———. 1964. Groundwork *of the metaphysics of morals.* Translated by H. J. Payton. New York: Harper Torchbooks.

Kerr, Philip Henry, Marquis of Lothian. 1916. Political relations between advanced and backward peoples. In *An introduction to the study of international relations*, edited by A. J. Grant, Arthur Greenwood, J. D. I. Hughes, P. H. Kerr, and F. F. Urquhart, 141–82. London: Macmillan.

Kidd, Benjamin. 1894. *Social evolution.* New York: Macmillan.

———. 1898. *The control of the tropics.* New York: Macmillan.

King, Martin Luther, Jr. (1986) Remaining awake through a great revolution. In *A testament of hope: The essential writings and speeches of Martin Luther King*, edited by J. Washington, 268–78. San Francisco: HarperCollins. Originally published in 1968.

Lauren, Paul. 1996. *Power and prejudice: The politics and diplomacy of racial discrimination.* 2nd ed. Boulder, CO: Westview.

Lemarchand, Rene. 1995. Rwanda: The rationality of genocide, *Issue: A Journal of Opinion* 23, no. 2:8–11.

Levy, Jack. 1988. Domestic politics and war. *Journal of Interdisciplinary History* 18:653–73.

Lipsitz, George. 1998. *The possessive investment in whiteness.* Philadelphia: Temple University Press.

Mahoney, Richard. 1983. *JFK: Ordeal in Africa.* New York: Oxford University Press.

Mamdani, Mahmood. 2004. *Good Muslim, bad Muslim.* New York: Pantheon.

Mazrui, Ali. 1990. *Cultural forces in world politics*. London: James Currey.

Miller, Stuart. 1995. Racism and military conquest: The Philippine-American War. In *Major problems in American foreign relations*, edited by Thomas Paterson and Dennis Merrill, 431–42. Lexington, MA: D. C. Heath.

Mills, Charles. 1997. *The racial contract*. Ithaca, NY: Cornell University Press.

Moore, David. 2001. Africa: The black hole at the middle of empire? *Rethinking Marxism* 13, no. 3/4:100–118.

Neugebauer, Christian. The racism of Kant and Hegel. In *Sage philosophy: Indigenous thinkers and modern debate on African philosophy*, edited by H. Odera Oruka, 259–72. New York: Brill, 1990.

Newton, Huey. 1980. *War against the Panthers: A study of repression in America*. New York: Harlem River Press.

Nkrumah, Kwame. 1965. *Neo-colonialism: The last stage of Imperialism*. London: Panaf.

Nzongola-Ntalaja, Georges. 2002. The *Congo from Leopold to Kabila: A people's history*. London: Zed Books.

Olson, William, and A. J. R. Groom. 1991. *International relations then and now: Origins and trends in interpretation*. London: HarperCollins.

Omi, Michael, and Howard Winant. 1994. *Racial formation in the United States*, 2nd ed. New York: Routledge.

Oneal, John, and James Lee Ray. 1997. New tests of democratic peace: Controlling for economic interdependence, 1950–1985. *Political Research Quarterly* 50, no. 4 (December): 751–75.

Oneal, John, and Bruce Russett. 1997. The classical liberals were right: Democracy, interdependence, and conflict, 1950–1985. *International Studies Quarterly* 41:267–93.

Oren, Ido. 1995. The subjectivity of the democratic peace: Changing U.S. perceptions of imperial Germany. *International Security* 20 (Fall): 147–84.

———. 2003. *Our enemies and U.S.: America's rivalries and the making of political science*. Ithaca, NY: Cornell University Press.

Patler, Nicholas. 2004. *Jim Crow and the Wilson administration*. Boulder: University of Colorado Press.

Posen, Barry. 1993. The security dilemma and ethnic conflict. In *Ethnic conflict and international security*, edited by M. Brown, 103–24. Princeton, NJ: Princeton University Press.

Ray, James. 1995. *Democracy and international conflict*. Columbia: University of South Carolina Press.

Reinsch, Paul. 1900. *World politics at the end of the nineteenth century, as influenced by the oriental situation*. New York: Macmillan.

———. 1902. *Colonial government: An introduction to the study of colonial institutions*. New York: Macmillan.

———. 1905. *Colonial administration*. New York: Macmillan.

Rodney, Walter. 1980. *How Europe underdeveloped Africa*. Washington, DC: Howard University Press.

Rubenstein, R., and J. Crocker. 1994. Challenging Huntington. *Foreign Policy* 96 (Fall): 113–28.

Russett, Bruce. 1993. *Grasping the democratic peace*. Princeton, NJ: Princeton University Press.

Russett, Bruce, and John Oneal. 2001. *Triangulating peace*. New York: W. W. Norton.

Russett, Bruce, and Harvey Starr. 2000. From democratic peace to Kantian peace: Democracy and conflict in the international system. In *Handbook of war studies*. Vol. 2, edited by Manus Midlarsky, 93–128. Ann Arbor: University of Michigan Press.

Russett, Bruce, John Oneal, and Michaelene Cox. 2000. Clash of civilizations, or realism and liberalism déjà vu? Some evidence. *Journal of Peace Research* 37, no. 5:583–608.

Ryan, Stephen. 1990. *Ethnic conflict and international relations*. Brookfield, VT: Dartmouth University Press.

Schmidt, Brian. 1998. *The political discourse of anarchy: A disciplinary history of international relations*. Albany: State University of New York Press.

Tinker, Hugh. 1977. *Race, conflict, and the international order*. London: Macmillan.

Toynbee Arnold. 1934. *A study of history*. Vol 1. London: Oxford University.

Vitalis, Robert. 2000. The graceful and generous liberal gesture: Making racism invisible in American international relations. *Millennium* 29, no. 2:331–56.

Walt, Stephen. 1997. Building up new bogeymen. *Foreign Policy* 106 (Spring): 177–89.

Weart, Spencer. 1998. *Never at war: Why democracies will not fight one another.* New Haven, CT: Yale University Press.

Wilson, Woodrow. 1887. The study of administration. *Political Science Quarterly* 2:202–17.

———. 1889. *The state.* Boston: DC Heath.

Winant, Howard. 2001. *The world is a ghetto.* New York: Basic Books.

CHAPTER SEVENTEEN

A Critical Review of American Political Institutions

Reading Race into the Constitutional "Silence" on Race

KATHERINE TATE, KEVIN L. LYLES,
AND LUCIUS J. BARKER

"But what is government itself but the greatest of all reflections on human nature? If men were angels, no government would be necessary. If angels were to govern, neither external nor internal controls on government would be necessary. In framing a government which is to be administered by men over men, the great difficulty lies in this: You must first enable the government to control the governed; and in the next place oblige it to control itself."

—James Madison, *The Federalist Papers*

CLEARLY THE CONSTITUTION was not "silent" about race, nor could that "silence" be seen in the political social system that evolved from it. The compromises ratified in the original Constitution of the United States both recognized and protected slavery. Slavery and racial injustice were thus accommodated and written into the Constitution. And these compromises were inherent in the origin and development of American political institutions. Consider, for example, that through strong-state federalism and the creation of the Electoral College, slave owners felt that they had obtained reliable mechanisms that would protect their share of the power in the national government. Slavery could never be banned without the slave owners' explicit consent. Ridding the country of the institution of slavery would necessitate a civil war and the adoption of the Thirteenth Amendment. It would take even longer to secure a political system that at least *legally* granted blacks their equal rights. The question remains, in fact, whether this system has completely purged itself of mechanisms that keep blacks in a subordinate political position.

To be sure, the United States is the oldest constitutional democracy in the world and is the world's leading economic power. The United States Constitution drafted at the Constitutional Convention in 1787 and ratified by the thirteen original states provided for a basic governmental structure that continues to exist and function today. The American Constitution is considered by many as a model for aspiring democratic states. But as the saying goes, "all that glitters is not gold." While emerging democracies may express keen interest in the basic structure of the U.S. Constitution and its intricate system of checks and balances, one must be aware that the original Constitution, ratified in 1788, was flawed in many respects—key among them are issues of race and gender. After all, the men present at the Constitutional Convention were not in fact angels, and universalistic or egalitarian wisdom was not the overriding norm.

In this chapter we review the institutions that make up the American political system. In the United States, race, notably the divisions between blacks and whites, has always been a fundamental political fault line. Following this review, we contend that until political scientists develop a scholarship that examines more critically the ways in which our political institutions were designed to maintain the racial dominance of the white majority, we will not be able to effectively address and resolve through conventional politics the economic and social inequalities that exist among racial and ethnic groups in the United States.

Political scientist at times have described the motives of the founding fathers as both idealistic and pragmatic. These analyses tended to conclude that the founding fathers' success resulted from enlightened debate and compromise. These framers, as the story goes, were deeply influenced by the writings of the English philosopher John Locke (1632–1704) and the French writer Charles-Louis de Secondat, Baron de Montesquieu (1689–1755) when they argued for separation of powers among three branches of government (including one Supreme Court), popular sovereignty, the right of rebellion against oppression, and the guarantees of life, liberty, and private property. In six articles, the framers of the Constitution spelled out the respective powers of the federal government and the states, and established a republican form of government. Without the Great Compromise (also known as the Connecticut Compromise of 1787) that created a bicameral Congress, the Constitution would never have won ratification. The compromise of course created a two-house Congress where states would have and equal vote in the Senate but where representation would be based on population in the second house.

This focus on governmental structure, however, tends to obscure the role that race has played in the founding and development of this nation. This role indicates that the intentions of the framers were deeply influenced by their interest in preserving slavery and the subordination of black citizens. While some rightfully point out that the original Constitution enshrined the institution of slavery, they fail to note that slavery was a primary motivation behind the basic institutional arrangements that were adopted.

American Political Culture

Understanding the political philosophy of a people is one key to understanding their political system, because generally political systems originate within the context of a political philosophy. In turn, the political philosophy shapes the growth and development of the political system. After all, as James Madison wrote, "What is government itself but the greatest of all reflections on human nature?" (*The Federalist Papers* 1961, 322) The American political system was founded on the principles of political equality, individualism, and freedom. The Declaration of Independence penned by Thomas Jefferson in 1776 declared that "all men are created equal," because they are "endowed by their Creator with certain inalienable rights." These are rights which the government should not take away. And thus the notion of individualism—namely, that individuals have certain rights which no state government, national or state, should abridge or deny—becomes the bedrock principle of the United States. Indeed, it is the very purpose of the government to protect these rights. The Declaration of Independence also enunciates the noble concept of equality, one that Americans have found difficult to put into practice. Political equality is best expressed, at least in more recent times, as the "one person, one vote" principle. Legal equality means that no person is above the law; all are subject to the law; and every individual is equal under the law. Social equality means that no individual should be treated badly because of their station in life or the circumstances of their birth. Each person should enjoy an equal chance to succeed in life and to develop their full potential within the limits of the human and material resources available to them.

These values so dominant in American political culture made the United States exceptional in fact. Writers from Alexis de Tocqueville (1805–1859) to Gunnar Myrdal (1898–1987) would characterize America as embodying a universal and unique belief in the essential dignity of human beings, the fundamental equality of people, and the inalienable right to freedom, justice, and fair opportunity. The uniqueness of American values in Louis Hartz's (1955) seminal publication, *The Liberal Tradition in America*, was attributed to the fact that Americans lacked a "feudal past." Americans founded this country as a unique population of human beings who were "born equal." Hartz's characterization of American political culture as profoundly egalitarian and shaped by laissez-faire individualism has stood for decades as unquestionable until it was challenged by Rogers Smith (1997).

Smith argued that American political culture really consists of two separate value systems: the liberalism that Hartz describes on the one hand, and what Smith calls illiberal principles that support racism and patriarchy on the other. Smith showed in his analysis of America's citizenship laws how white males maintained their dominance over women, blacks, Indians, and immigrant groups. "Racial, ethnic, and gender restrictions were blatant, not 'latent,'" Smith wrote. "For these people, citizenship rules gave no weight to how liberal, republican, or faithful to other American values their political beliefs might be" (Smith 1997, 15). He contended that the dichotomy between America's liberal values and its racist practices are not moral lapses, as Gunnar Myrdal had argued, but represented the dominance of these alternative values that have existed from the beginning of the republic.

Barker, Jones, and Tate (1999) characterized American political culture as one that has sought since its founding as a nation to maintain and preserve white racial dominance. This model is an extension of power theory as defined by Bobo and Blumer (Bobo 1983; Blumer 1958). Lawrence Bobo (1983) characterized the politics over racial programs and policies as rooted in realistic group conflict, in which whites are opposed to affirmative action not because of racial prejudice or principles but because such programs threaten their privileged place in the competition for valued social resources and status. As Bobo (2000, 163) states: "Race, at least in terms of the traditional black-white divide, has long been the axis along which full and genuine membership in the polity was established and which set the boundaries for determining what constituted appropriate or inappropriate treatment of individuals. . . . Race has been so profoundly implicated in American politics that it played the central role in reshaping national partisan political identities and party alignments in the post–World War II period."

Whites as the politically dominant actors in this democracy invariably act in ways to preserve their position of political dominance and hegemony. Barker, Jones, and Tate write: "Thus, rather than conceptualizing black politics as a process through which black people, propelled by some unseen hand, move inexorably to a position of equal status, it is more appropriate to conceptualize it as a power struggle between two groups, one bent on maintaining its position of dominance and the other struggling for liberation" (1999, 9).

Smith's alternative thesis, that racist values are an embedded part of American political culture, changes the way in which we should review and interpret American political history. Understanding that a primary goal of the white majority was the preservation of white dominance throws open anew the questions of how and why the country designed the institutions it did at the Constitutional Convention of 1787 and the adoption of the Constitution in 1789. "The history of the modern state and racial definition," as David Theo Goldberg points out in *The Racial State* (2002), "are intimately related." As states acquire their constitutional powers, these powers are both expressions of race relations within the society as well as the ability to define and shape the boundaries of race in society.

Drafting the American Constitution: Explicit and Implicit Political Agendas

The framers at the 1789 Constitutional Convention came with two explicit goals. As Thomas E. Patterson writes in his textbook on American government (2003), these goals were (1) protecting popular liberty through the establishment of a limited government; and (2) creating a government powerful enough to act on the people's behalf and therefore achieving "self-governance." The structure that had been previously created under the Articles of Confederation had failed because the Articles had not given the federal government enough power to meet the country's economic needs both internally and abroad. The masterful concept of the separation of powers, proposed by James Madison, served as the foundation through which a tyrannical government could be constrained. Separation of powers is the doctrine through which the powers of the national government are divided among three branches: legislative, executive, and judicial. Functions are allocated accordingly: the legislature makes laws, the executive enforces the laws, and the judiciary interprets the laws. At the same time, the Constitution provides for three independent branches, their authorities commingled, so that the branches are interdependent rather than independent. The overriding purpose of the separation of powers and the system of checks and balances is to prevent any one group of government officials from becoming too powerful.

The system of checks and balances, however, did not solve the real fears that many of the framers brought with them to the Constitutional Convention. Clearly, the delegates feared the creation of a strong federal government that would become tyrannical in the same way as King George III had done with his abusive taxation polices. The framers also feared, however, that a more powerful federal government would ban slavery in the states. Thus, while the explicit agenda was indeed the creation of a more powerful federal government that pro-tected the individual liberties of citizens [white males], the implicit agenda was the preservation of slavery and patriarchy. Federalism, in which the centralized federal government would be powerful—but not more powerful than the states—granted legal authority to the states to keep their own laws regarding the insti-tution of slavery. Still, federalism obviously did not afford enough protection for slaveholders, as the slave states sought greater guarantees at the Constitutional Convention for the preservation of slavery.

According to Winthrop Jordan, "the Convention could not consider even the eventual termination of domestic slavery; propositions on this head would have sent half the delegates packing" (1968, 323). In the end, the Constitution that was ratified in 1788 not only recognized but *protected* slavery in several of its pro-visions. Legal historians, most notably William Wiecek, have cited numerous instances in which the Constitution refers to "other Persons" and "Person[s] held to Service of Labour," and argue that at least ten other clauses in the document were influenced by slavery (1991, 187). Consider the following: One of the first provi-sions protecting slavery—article 1, section 2, cl. 3—embodies one of the most famous compromises of the Constitutional Convention: the determination that each slave amounted to three-fifths of a person for purposes of taxation and appor-tionment: "Representatives and direct taxes shall be apportioned among the sev-eral States . . . according to their respective numbers, which shall be determined by adding to the whole number of free persons, including those bound to service for a term of years, and excluding Indians not taxed, three-fifths of all other persons."

In short, the term "three-fifths of all other persons" meant three-fifths of all slaves (Corwin 1968, 6–8). According to Garry Wills (2003), the states were to be taxed on the basis of their wealth, and a head tax was the most reliable method for assessing a state's wealth. Essentially, the compromise arose after the conven-tion delegates had agreed to a system of proportional representation for the House of Representatives. The obvious question that arose was whether to count slaves as people or property. Some Northerners wanted to count slaves as full persons, possibly because this stipulation would penalize slave owners who would have to pay more in taxes, but the proposal sparked a debate. Southerners objected because the Northerners' proposal was "taxation without representation." On the other hand, counting slaves as persons would also increase the political representation of the Southern states. Consider, for example, the majority-minority status of slaves in South Carolina at the time. To consider slaves as people would have effectively doubled South Carolina's representation in the House of Representa-tives. The Northern delegates predictably objected. Other Northerners believed that counting slaves was tantamount to counting horses because slaves were property; thus these delegates opposed a head tax. The contemporary reader should consider also the irony of this debate: the Southern states, where dehumanizing chattel slavery was flourishing, wanted to count slaves as whole persons for purposes of representation. On the other hand, the Northern states, which had fewer slaves and an ongoing process of abolition, wished to count slaves as merely property. In the end, the delegates agreed to the three-fifths compromise; that is, five slaves equaled three people for purposes of taxation and determining the number of congressional representatives. For the slaves, it meant that the Constitution of the United States had determined each of them to be equal to only three-fifths of a whole person without any political representation.

Historians claim that this compromise was the only way the Constitution could be ratified because of the South's determination to protect the institution of slavery at all costs. "South Carolina and Georgia were inflexible" on the point of slaves, according to James Madison (Wills 2003). The Southern states would pay higher taxes as a consequence of having their slaves counted, but they gained a tremendous political advantage over the free states through this compromise.

With the South having won this advantage, a few delegates left fully outraged at the major concessions made to the slave states. Maryland's representative at the Constitutional Convention in Philadelphia, Luther Martin, refused to sign the new Constitution, stating: "To have a provision not only putting it out of its power to restrain and prevent the slave trade, but even encouraging that most infamous traffic, by giving states power and influence in the union in proportion as they cruelly and wantonly sport with the rights of their fellow creatures, ought to be considered as a solemn mockery and insult to the God whose protection we had then implored" (quoted in Wills 2003, 60). The three-fifths compromise had major enduring ramifications that Wills spells out. First, the slave states had one-third more seats in Congress than their free population warranted (2003, 6). Moreover, this compromise led to the fact that ten of the fifteen presidents elected before the Civil War were slave owners. Between 1789 and 1850, slave owners controlled the American presidency for over half a century, and they controlled the position of Speaker in the U.S. House of Representatives for forty-one years. Finally, eighteen out of thirty-one Supreme Court justices were slaveholders. The three-fifths rule, as Wills points out, gave the South a "permanent advantage." This curious formula for representation granted to the slave states explains much by way of the preservation of the status quo. Abolitionists at the time that the new Constitution was drafted accepted the compromise over slavery, hoping that over time it would fade away as an institution. But it was not made unconstitutional until the 13th Amendment was ratified in 1865.

A second provision in the Constitution protecting slavery is art. 1, sec. 9, cl. 1, which refers to the African slave trade: "The migration or importation of such persons as any of the States now existing shall think proper to admit, shall not be prohibited by the Congress prior to the Year one thousand eight hundred and eight, but a tax or duty may be imposed on such importation, not exceeding ten dollars for each person." Not only did this provision protect the African slave trade for a period of twenty years and impose a tax on the importation of each slave, it also reveals that the framers of the Constitution believed that Congress, under its power to regulate commerce, might in fact have had the authority to end slavery. Not wanting to risk the chance that Congress would act to do so, the framers constitutionally protected the slave trade for a minimum of twenty years. This constitutional provision for all intents and purposes stalled the African American quest for freedom for the first twenty years of the United States' existence.

Yet another constitutional provision protecting slavery is in art. 4, sec. 2, cl. 3—the fugitive slave clause: "No person held to service or labor in one State, under the laws thereof, escaping into another, shall, in consequence of any law or regulation therein, be discharged from such service or labor, But shall be delivered up on claim of the party to whom such service or labor may be due." In theory, this clause provided for the lawful return of fugitive slaves and prohibited states from passing laws that freed escaped slaves. In practice, however, it provided constitutional authority for decades of bounty hunting for fugitive slaves and the nightmarish atrocities that often accompanied such actions.

In a fourth measure, the framers were also careful to guarantee the provisions protecting slavery by writing into the original document a prohibition against amending the Constitution involving the slave trade before 1808—twenty years from the date of ratification. "No amendment which may be made prior to the Year One thousand eight hundred and eight shall in any manner affect the first and fourth Clauses in the Ninth Section of the first Article."

On the whole, the compromises adopted in the original Constitution of the United States recognized and protected slavery. Slavery was thus accommodated and given constitutional status. James Madison of Virginia, writing in *Federalist* 42, defended the slavery compromises in the following terms:

> It ought to be considered as a great point gained in favor of humanity, that a period of twenty years may terminate forever . . . a traffic which has so long and so loudly upbraided the barbarism of modern policy; that within that period, it will receive a considerable discouragement from the federal government, and may be totally abolished, by a concurrence of the few States which continue to unnatural traffic, in the prohibitory example which has been given by so great a majority of the Union. Happy would it be for the unfortunate Africans, if an equal prospect lay before them of being redeemed from the oppressions of their European brethren! Attempts have been made to pervert this clause into an objection against the Constitution, by representing it on one side as a criminal toleration of an illicit practice, and on another as calculated to prevent voluntary and beneficial emigrations from Europe to America (*The Federalist Papers* 1961, 266).

Of course, it may be difficult for many to adopt Madison's perspective. After all, given the average life span at the time, it was certainly shortsighted (or ridiculous) for Madison to characterize one additional day—much less a span of twenty years—of forced servitude, every manner of sexual exploitation, and sadistic brutality and mutilation, to represent "a point gained in favor of humanity."

In all, these constitutional provisions augmented the political and economic power of the slave states by giving them additional representation in Congress and the executive branch, and in maintaining the economic efficiency of slavery by keeping labor costs low through the continuation of the slave trade and the complicity of free states by forcing them to return fugitive slaves. One must be careful, however, when measuring the effects of constitutionalized slavery in purely economic terms. Theoretically, there are two major competing arguments that seek to explain the impact and interrelationships of slavery in colonial America: racism and white supremacy versus marketplace economics and capitalism (Morris 1996, 8–14). There is an abundance of scholarly literature debating the merits of either argument or a combination thereof. Though many have attempted to justify slavery in largely economic terms, for many scholars, however, race is the "driving explanation" (Tannenbaum 1946; Tushnet 1975).

In fact, some scholars, Winthrop Jordan, for example, have noted that racism existed long before slavery. According to Jordan, the British had deep-rooted beliefs about the supremacy of whiteness (as well as Christianity) and a corresponding belief in the de facto inferiority of blacks (Jordan 1968, 4–11, 24). The "colonist subsequently used racial differences to justify slavery. In turn, slavery reinforced their racist perceptions" (Morris 1996, 10). As such, many of the laws that developed in colonial America and later across the United States reflected first and foremost a firm belief in the supremacy of whiteness and second, a developing legal process designed to dehumanize blacks for marketplace gain. Both of these goals were cemented in the new Constitution and are inherent in various elements of American political institutions even in the early 2000s.

A. Leon Higginbotham and Anne E. Jacobs (1992) have argued that ten "basic underlying precepts" permeated the law of slavery. Consider the following four:

1. Inferiority: Presume, preserve, protect, and defend the idea of the superiority of whites and the inferiority of blacks.
2. Property: Define the slave as the master's property, disregard the humanity of the slave except when it serves the master's interest, and deny slaves the fruits of their labor.
3. Powerlessness: Keep blacks—whether slave or free—as powerless as possible so that they will be submissive and dependent in every respect, not only to the master but to whites in general. To assure powerlessness, subject blacks to a secondary system of justice with fewer rights and greater punishments than those assigned to whites.
4. Racial purity: Draw an arbitrary racial line and preserve white purity as thus defined. Tolerate sexual relationships between white men and black women; severely punish sexual relations between white women and nonwhite men.

In the main, the combination of white supremacist ideology with developing laws and political institutions that made black slaves completely powerless and dehumanized, facilitated the marketplace demand for slave labor. It is important for the reader to appreciate the significance of this debate throughout this chapter. De jure segregation and forms of racial discrimination in the twentieth century, for example, certainly resulted in part from economic and marketplace demands and competition for jobs. After all, to deny African Americans employment or access to education or membership in labor or trade organizations unquestionably benefited whites—that is, white privilege. Such policies then might support economic explanations of contemporary racial discrimination as merely extensions of marketplace competition. On the other hand, other twentieth-century laws, such as those denying blacks equal access to public accommodations; laws prohibiting blacks and whites from drinking from the same water fountains, using the same washrooms or swimming pools, sitting in the same section of a theater or lunch counter, or riding in the same railroad car; and particularly antimiscegenation laws, make arguments based on economic or marketplace competition tenuous if not ridiculous. Accordingly, many of the issues that must be addressed by our political institutions in the early twenty-first century deal increasingly with *race* and forms of white supremacy.

In sum, the discussion above describes the setting at the time of the drafting of the Constitution in 1788. A delegate from Connecticut, Oliver Ellsworth, foresaw the initial position that the Supreme Court would later take regarding slavery. Ellsworth, who himself would later serve as the third Chief Justice of the United States Supreme Court from 1796 to 1800, stated that the "morality and wisdom" of slavery, "are considerations belonging to the states themselves." Every state, argued the future chief justice, "should import what it pleases."[1]

The Judiciary

Powers assigned to the federal judiciary were vague and not fully enumerated as those allocated to the legislative branch, nor deliberately left as undefined as those granted to the President. To ensure their political independence, federal judges, were granted lifetime tenure on the bench under article 3 of the Constitution for as long as they remain on "good Behaviour." The right of the Supreme Court to review and overturn the decisions of the federal government through judicial review was established by its own ruling in *Marbury v. Madison* (1803). In *Marbury*, Chief Justice John Marshall (who held the office from 1801 until 1835) established and defined enormous powers for the Supreme Court, including judicial review. In Marshall's own words: "[I]t is emphatically the province and duty of the judicial department to say what the law is."[2]

This right of judicial review significantly expanded the power of the Supreme Court vis-à-vis the other two branches of government. Though such an assumption of power by the Court did trigger some debate, perhaps it did not stir as much discord as might be expected. In the main, judicial review then and now is more or less considered as consistent with the judicial function. But lack of debate should not suggest the absence of conflict, especially when the Court's use of judicial review is examined within the broader contexts of race, gender, and American political institutions.

Indeed, the Court positioned itself so as to further delineate the rights and privileges of African Americans, Indians, and women—those abandoned by the framers of the original Constitution. Initially, however, history records that the Supreme Court—armed with its newly proclaimed power of judicial review—would use its authority to accommodate and perpetuate racial discrimination and the dehumanization of African Americans for the next 150 years. Time and again, the Court used its power of judicial review to uphold the violence of slavery and de jure segregation. For example, the Supreme Court used judicial review to strike down an act of Congress in the 1857 *Dred Scott* case, where the Court under Chief Justice Roger Taney, Marshall's successor, invalidated the provisions of the Missouri Compromise that *restricted* slavery.

Over time, however, judicial review as exercised by the Supreme Court became both a curse and a blessing for African Americans and other political minorities, including women.[3] On the one hand, the Supreme Court after 1803 was armed with the means and the authority to strike down racially discriminatory laws as unconstitutional, as it did in the 1954 *Brown* school desegregation decision a century and a half later. On the other hand, during the roughly 150 years between 1803 and 1954, the Supreme Court for the most part used its power of review to confer legitimacy on racially discriminatory and dehumanizing state and federal laws. These actions, viewed within the context of the African American experience, help to reveal the dual nature of the Supreme Court as an American political institution.

Theoretically, there are two major arguments concerning the role of the Supreme Court in the American political system. One view, often associated with Martin Shapiro (1966), is that the Court's special function is the representation of potential or unorganized interests or values that are unlikely to be represented—or adequately represented—elsewhere in government. In this role the Court might well serve as a protector of minority rights against majority tyranny (Ely 1980, 135; Shapiro 1964). This view was articulated in then Associate Justice Harlan Stone's famous footnote four in *United States v. Carolene Products Co.*[4], which suggests that the Court should be concerned with what majorities do to minorities, especially regarding laws "directed at" religious, national, and racial "discrete and insular" minorities and those infected with prejudice against them (Ely 1980, 76).

A second view suggests, however, that Supreme Court policymaking and interest representation most often mirror the views of the dominant lawmaking majorities. For example, Robert Dahl argued that the Supreme Court's main function is to confer legitimacy on the policies of the majority coalition in power (Dahl 1957). Moreover, Dahl suggested that the role of the Court as a defender of minority rights is "rare and transitory" and that only during periods of upheaval or transition from one electoral coalition to another might we expect to find the Court in a position to block a particular policy. Dahl concluded that the policy views dominant on the Court "are never far out of line with the policy views dominant among lawmaking majorities."[5]

Today the Court's policymaking role might be viewed as a combination of these two roles. Accordingly, given our attention to American political institutions in this essay, we should recognize that judicial policymaking is one of the major institutionalized forms of group and interests conflict resolution. Put another way, the institutional operation of courts and judges continue to hold importance for African Americans in their continual quest for freedom, equality, and justice. American courts are critical and may prove pivotal among the conflicting interests and forces in American law and politics, especially with regard to such enduring matters as race and gender.

With regard to major rights issues such as those involving race, gender, criminal justice, reapportionment and voting rights, considerable attention is perennially given as to whether particular courts or judges are engaged in what some view as "judicial activism" or exercising what is labeled as "judicial self-restraint." While such terms continue to be used in social and scholarly discourse, they are of little value in terms of conceptualizing the role of the judiciary in the policy/political process. For as political scientist Jack Peltason put it, "courts are in the political process ...not as a matter of choice but of function"(Peltason 1955, 3). Certainly the position of courts and judges with respect to their exercise of *judicial review* as well as *statutory interpretation* can prove crucial even determinative at any given time in the outcome of interest and policy conflict.

Moreover, scholarly analyses are not furthered in associating "judicial activism" or "judicial self-restraint" with "liberal" or "conservative" courts and judges. This is especially salient in examining certain court decisions. Clearly *Plessy v. Ferguson* (1896) and *Bush v. Gore* (2000) did not result in "liberal" outcomes but they did arguably represent examples of judicial activism if such "activism" is defined—as some do—as the Court's application of a "broad interpretation" of the U.S. Constitution to make public policy. Public concern over "judicial activism" grew as a consequence of the Warren Court, which greatly expanded the rights of criminal suspects.[6] "Legislating from the bench," has triggered controversy because as some view it, judicial activism invariably leads to liberal public policies, as in the case of *Roe v. Wade* (1973), which guaranteed the right of women to seek abortions. But judicial activism may also lead to conservative public policies and outcomes, as we have seen in *Plessy* and *Bush v. Gore*.

Critics of judicial activism argue that public policies should be advanced in legislative bodies precisely because justices are unelected political actors. This criticism is also based on a strict interpretation of the Constitution as an immutable document that does not support broad interpretation. Proponents of judicial activism argue that broad interpretation was expected by the founders, and that a broad interpretation is in fact necessary to protect civil rights and equal protection under changing social conditions and circumstances.

To us as political scientists the notion that courts can reliably exercise judicial restraint and have virtually no consequential impact on the continuous interest and policy conflicts involved beyond their affirmation of existing public policy is unrealistic. Whether or not Courts or judges enter or refuse to enter into the "political fray" or "political thicket," or refuse to hear or not hear a particular case (issue a writ of certiorari) such decisions promote and advantage certain interests and retard and disadvantage others. Whatever the case, however, whether viewed as activist or restrainist, American courts by their very nature are political institutions, and their rulings matter politically. As political scientist and Supreme Court scholar David O'Brien put it:

> [t]he Court, regardless of its composition, has increasingly asserted its power. The ideologically conservative Burger and Rehnquist Courts, for example, have been as activist as the liberal Warren Court. Their differences lie in the directions in which they have pushed constitutional law and politics. (O'Brien 2003, 30)

Indeed, while a great deal of attention has focused on liberal "judicial activism," as in *Roe v. Wade*—a decision which occurred during the Burger Court—the Supreme Court has also powerfully reinforced conservative policies beyond the "confines" of the U.S. Constitution. The Court, for example, made the Southern *states'* racial policies *national policy* in recognizing the states' authority to circumvent the Fourteenth Amendment in *Plessy v. Ferguson*.

Similarly, some suggest that the Supreme Court's 1954 ruling in *Brown v. the Board of Education of Topeka, Kansas* is a prime example of the Court going beyond the "confines" of the Constitution. And in any case, *Brown* exemplifies that the Court at the time was not acting in concert with the elected branches of the government. That the Court did not do so, was monumental in deconstitutionalizing government-sponsored de jure segregationist practices in the United States. Some contend that it was the unexpected death of the racially conservative Chief Justice Fred Vinson that allowed for the *Brown* decision. Chief Justice Earl Warren, who orchestrated the unanimous ruling in *Brown*, was appointed to the Court to fill the vacancy and chief justiceship only after Vinson's sudden death.

Even more, some contend that the Court's ruling in *Brown* came about because racial segregation was an embarrassment during the nation's propaganda war with Communism. (See generally Dudziak, 2000) As a national policy, however, *Brown* remains poorly implemented in contrast to the rapid and full implementation of Jim Crow under *Plessy*. States' rights under federalism as well as the national government's unevenness or unwillingness to intervene are important factors in fully understanding the reasons why racial integration (e.g., school desegregation) since *Brown*, even in 2006, has not been effectively achieved. One must keep in mind, however, that the Court's rulings in *Heart of Atlanta* (upholding the 1964 Civil Rights Act) and in *South Carolina v. Katzenbach* (upholding the 1965 Voting Rights Act) moved the country beyond the symbolism of *Brown*. The Court, by giving constitutional status to those legislative initiatives, confirmed that Congress, if spurred by protests and demonstrations and with clear presidential support (of President Lyndon Johnson), could in fact pass laws to protect and expand the constitutional rights of all American citizens; including African Americans and women. Moreover, the Court confirmed that such rights, including public accommodations (Title II), fair employment practices (Title VII), and the various measures adopted to secure and protect the right to vote in the 1965 Voting Rights Act, could constitutionally be supported by Congress.

Even more, at times the Supreme Court has been effective in conferring legitimacy on affirmative action policy. In addition to legitimating the Civil Rights Act of 1964 and the Voting Rights Act of 1965, the Court has also played a crucial role in defining the constitutional limits on legislative measures adopted to redress the vestiges of past racial and gender discrimination. This role, however, continues to be a source of conflict and dissent among the Justices as well as in the country generally. This is exemplified dramatically in the 1978 *Bakke* decision, where the Court both struck down the use of racial quotas as such but held that the *race* of applicants to the medical school at the University of California, Davis could be used as a factor in determining admission. Since *Bakke*, however, battles over affirmative action continue to be fought in the individual states.

For example, in 1996 California voters passed Proposition 209, which ended all state affirmative action programs, including those at the University of California. Earlier, the state of Texas eliminated affirmative action programs at its state universities. Washington State and Florida followed suit and ended their state affirmative action programs as well. Although the Supreme Court reaffirmed its *Bakke* ruling in 2003 in a case involving an affirmative action program at the University of Michigan's law school, in a companion case the Court simultaneously limited the tools by which universities could increase minority enrollment. Specifically, the University of Michigan could not systematically assign extra points to applicants of color seeking admission to its undergraduate program (*Grutter v. Bollinger* and *Gratz v. Bollinger* respectively).

Clearly, one could list a number of Supreme Court cases including the landmark 1954 *Brown* decision that expanded the life chances for African Americans. Simultaneously, however, the Court has also issued rulings (for example *Dred Scott* or *Plessy* and the affirmative action case of *Richmond v. Croson* (1989) that have served to limit opportunities for African Americans. The larger point, however, is that the Court's posture with regard to slavery, segregation, affirmative action, and other civil rights issues was, and continues to be, influenced by institutional as well as political constraints under which courts and judges must operate within the American political system.

Chief among these influences is the nomination and selection process for federal judges. As such, there is strong empirical support for the view that "who sits on the courts, determines what decisions come out of the courts." All federal judges, including Supreme Court justices, are nominated and appointed to the bench for life by the President and must be approved with the "advice and consent" of a simple majority of the Senate. Under the Constitution, all federal judges hold office for life "during good behavior." The essential constitutional provision regarding judicial selection is the Appointments Clause (art. 2, par. 2, cl. 2): "[The President] shall nominate, and by and with the advice and consent of the Senate, shall appoint . . . judges of the Supreme Court, and all other officers of the United States . . . but the Congress may by law vest the appointment of such inferior Officers, as they think proper, in the President alone, in the Courts of Law, or in the Heads of Departments." As detailed by many scholars, however, these *general* procedures and guidelines have been variously interpreted and tailored by different presidential administrations.

Arriving at formal selection procedures was a difficult task for the framers. The selection of federal judges was included in the many matters debated and negotiated at the Constitutional Convention in 1787 (Harris 1953). But of course, like many issues debated there, the delegates to the convention strongly disagreed on the best way to appoint the justices of the Supreme Court. Briefly, this dis-agreement concerned two polarized camps, each advocating a different method of judicial selection. In the first camp were those delegates who opposed the con-centration of power in the executive branch and endorsed the appointment of justices and other judges by the Senate, the House, or both. Those who favored legislative appointment of judges feared the potential of monarchical tyranny. They maintained that the legislature would be better positioned to know the pool of qualified nominees. Luther Martin argued that the Senate, "being from all the States . . . would be best informed of the characters and most capable of making a fit choice" (Hickok 1990). Roger Sherman echoed Martin, saying that the Senate "would have more wisdom. They would bring to their deliberation a more diffusive knowledge of characters. It would be less easy for candidates to intrigue with them than the Executive Magistrate."

In the other camp were those delegates—notably James Wilson, Alexander Hamilton, and James Madison—who favored a strong executive branch and feared judicial appointments made by members of the legislature; they promoted the investment of the power to appoint in the executive branch alone. In an early speech at the Constitutional Convention, James Wilson argued that "experience showed the impropriety of such appointments by numerous bodies. Intrigue, par-tiality and concealment were the necessary consequences. A principal reason for unity in the Executive was that officers might be appointed by a single responsi-ble person" (Hickok 1990). One of the most persistent advocates of executive appointment during the Constitutional Convention was Nathaniel Gorham of Massachusetts. Gorham challenged those in favor of legislative appointment: "As the executive will be responsible in point of character at least, for judicious and faithful discharge of his trust, he will be careful to look through all the states for the proper characters. The Senators will be as likely to form their attachments at the seat of government where they reside as the Executive. If they cannot get the man of the particular state to which they may respectively belong, they will be indifferent to the rest. Public bodies feel no personal responsibility, and give full pay to intrigue and cabal" (Hickok 1990, 8).

Also defending the need for executive control of judicial appointments was Alexander Hamilton. Writing in *the Federalist Papers* 76, Hamilton said: "One man of discernment is better fitted to analyze and estimate the peculiar qualities adapted to particular offices, than a body of men of equal, perhaps even superior discernment. The sole and undivided responsibility of one man will naturally beget a livelier sense of duty and a more exact regard to reputation. He will on this account feel himself under stronger obligations, and more interested to inves-tigate with care and impartiality the persons who may have the fairest preten-sions to them. He will have fewer personal attachments to gratify than a body of men." (*The Federalist Papers* 1961, 455–56).

Because neither group could muster enough support for their respective posi-tions, the delegates adopted a method of appointment proposed in part by James Madison. This compromise provided that the executive would nominate and appoint Supreme Court justices, among other officers, but subject to the *advice and consent* of the Senate. One of the strongest and perhaps most noted defenses of the compromise appointment process was provided by Alexander Hamilton in *the Federalist Papers* (66): "It will be the office of the President to nominate and with the advice and consent of the Senate, to appoint. There will, of course, be no exertion of choice on the part of the Senate. They may defeat on choice of the Executive, *and oblige him to make another*; but they cannot themselves choose—they can only ratify or reject the choice of the President" (Hamilton 1961, 405).

In the modern context, however, one flaw has become apparent in Hamilton's argument. Presidents in the twenty-first century want to avoid being "obliged to make another," as the defeat of a nomination today signals a weakened administration. While there is wide agreement that modern presidents would rather avoid this type of political battle, they nonetheless continue to occur. Consider, for example, the intense controversy that accompanied President Reagan's failed nomination of Robert Bork in 1987 (Lyles 1994, 133–60). Even more, consider the bitter controversial confirmation hearings over President George H. W. Bush's appointment of Clarence Thomas in 1991. Further consider the appointments to the Court of President George W Bush (II) in 2005 of Appeals Court Judge Samuel Alito, and of D. C. Court of Appeals Judge John G. Roberts Jr. to the Supreme Court as well as appointing Roberts to fill the vacancy left by Chief Justice William Rehnquist. Overall, the bottom line is that presidents in general do indeed attempt to appoint persons on the Court who are, or are believed to be in agreement or sympathetic with the President's overall political ideology and position on issues that matter most to the President.

In sum, a Supreme Court justice is appointed when the President makes a nomination and it is confirmed by a simple majority of the senate. Key institutionalized actors in federal judicial selection include the President, the Senate Judiciary Committee, the Department of Justice and the Attorney General, the Standing Committee on the Federal Judiciary of the American Bar Association (ABA), and various other interest groups and organizations. Despite the variety of participants, however, it is apparent that presidents can affect public policy through their judicial appointments—at times even achieving victories that would be nearly impossible through legislative channels (Fried 1991). And it is this power, both potential and realized, for judicial policymaking that highlights the key institutional and crucial role that the Court and courts generally can play in dealing with the multifaceted problems of race in our overall politics and society.

To reiterate as stated earlier what Jack Peltason wrote some fifty years ago, only one year after the Court's landmark decision striking down de jure segregation in public schools (*Brown v. Board of Education*), "A judge is in the political process and his [or her] activity is interest activity not as a matter of choice but of function" (1955, 3). Essentially, Peltason challenged the traditional perception of judges as merely applying the law—mechanical jurisprudence—as ideologically based and failing to describe actual judicial behavior. Moreover, the very "function of judges and the conditions under which they do their assigned tasks are determined by and are not above the group struggle" (Peltason 1955, 8; see also Barker 1967; and Vose 1959). The point here is that there is increased attention on the dual role of courts as both enunciators of legal doctrine and instruments for the resolution of political conflicts. This is the nature of the courts as American political institutions.

One must be careful, however, to not allow the complexities of this dual role to be used as an excuse to avoid moral realities and humane principles, especially with regard to the construct of race in the United States. The dual nature of courts, especially the Supreme Court, often leads to ambiguity and inconsistency—especially regarding African Americans and the Supreme Court. Our constitutional and legal history is fraught with contradictions between principles and policy, and inconsistencies between doctrines and decisions. Harry Kalven stated succinctly in his *The Negro and the First Amendment*, that "the law has a great capacity to tolerate inconsistencies; perhaps the most difficult thing for the beginning law student to grasp is the sense of tolerable inconsistency" (1965, 4–5). Nowhere is this tolerance more necessary than when examining the role of the courts as American political institutions while simultaneously exploring the position of race and gender in American politics and society.

In sum, when viewing the courts as American political institutions, we must recognize that the key actors in American courts are individual judges. The judges who are selected by the President—based on a number of factors including their individual ideologies—are those who will exercise judicial review in carrying out their policymaking function in the political process. And for the most part, judges are selected from those who come from the "haves" or who are otherwise well-connected with those who have standing and influence in the public and private sectors; in short our judges are mostly white males. This is the institutional nature of the judiciary in American politics, and these factors condition or impact on the extent to which courts and judges have been willing to respond to the call for racial justice and equality over time.

The Legislative Branch

The problem of how best to represent the American people in an elected government was so controversial that it nearly defied political solution. Under the Articles of Confederation, the states were politically equal, each having two representatives in the national government. Large states then wanted legislative seats to be based on population. The Great Compromise of 1787 resulted in a bicameral Congress to which each state would send two senators and different numbers of representatives to the lower house based on the state's population.

The allocation of an equal number of seats in the U.S. Senate to each state makes it one of the most unusual as well as undemocratic features of the American political system. Most other countries with federal systems that accord regional units significant political autonomy do not grant the regional units equal representation in the federal legislature, as in the case of the United States (Lee and Oppenheimer 1999). Antifederalists were critical of the composition of the Senate, whose members would be indirectly elected by state legislatures and serve exceptionally long terms of six years. For these two reasons, the antifederalists feared that an American aristocracy would emerge from the Senate. Frances Lee and Bruce Oppenheimer (1999) question whether the Senate was created to express the federal nature of the American political system. They argue that clearly the Senate represents a "symbol" of the federal system, but does not function as such (1999, 23–26). One way in which a federal role for the Senate was undercut was by according equal legislative authority to the lower chamber. Both houses, including the People's House, the House of Representatives, must agree to identical versions of legislation before it can become law. A stronger federal system would accord the Senate more veto authority over the House. The historical record suggests, however, that the Senate was to function as a "cooler" to the lower house to block unwise or intemperate legislation passed in the House. In reality, as Sarah Binder's scholarship (2003) shows, this has not been the case, at least in the modern era. The two houses have exhibited an equal propensity to block legislation originating in the other house.

The problem of casting the debate over the representation of the states in the new American Congress as a conflict between small-population and large-population states has minimized the negative and direct consequences that the creation of the unrepresentative Senate has had for African Americans. As Lee and Oppenheimer (1999) show, the allocation of two seats to states in the upper chamber accorded blacks and other minorities significantly less political representation than whites. One can demonstrate this point effectively by comparing the median state's black population to the nation's black population. In 1996, the median state's black population was 7.1 percent in contrast to the nation's black population of 12.5. For all minorities, specifically blacks, Latinos, Asians, and American Indians, the median state's minority population is 18.1 percent, in contrast to the nation's minority population of 26.8 percent (Lee and Oppenheimer 1999, 20–22). If seats in the Senate were allocated in proportion to the population, minorities would be able to vote for a higher percentage of the seats in such a Senate. Lee and Oppenheimer conclude: "In sum, rather than protecting racial and ethnic minorities, Senate apportionment underrepresents these groups' presence in the nation as a whole. With all the controversy over racial gerrymandering in the House, it is surprising that the impact of Senate apportionment on the representation of minorities has drawn so little attention" (1999, 23).

An electoral system that makes it difficult for blacks to win seats in Congress has important political consequences. Scholarship clearly demonstrates that African Americans serving in the House of Representatives advance agendas that speak directly to the interests of black Americans (Canon 1999; Tate 2003; Whitby 1998). Because so few blacks have served in the Senate, which remains virtually a "lily-white" branch of government, analysis has focused primarily on the activities of blacks serving in the lower chamber, the House of Representatives. Black members of the House of Representatives have been more consistent spokespersons for and champions of black interests. Other research has found that blacks feel that they are more adequately represented by a black in Congress (Tate 2001; Tate 2003). Black constituents also expressed higher levels of political knowledge about their representative in the House when he or she was black rather than white, Asian, or Latino. Blacks were no more likely, however, to vote or express higher levels of trust in the institution of Congress when represented by a member of their own race than were blacks represented by a member of a different race (Gay 2001; Tate 2003). There was no consistent "political empowerment" effect associated with being represented by a person of one's own race in the House for African Americans. Black office holding at the congressional level has important symbolic consequences, however. The long absences of blacks from the U.S. Senate, for example, still conveys an image of black inferiority, suggesting that blacks are not able or fit to serve in the upper house. Only a few blacks have served in the U.S. Senate. Two served in the Senate during Reconstruction: Hiram R. Revels (R-Miss.), 1870–1871 and Blanche K. Bruce (R-Miss), 1875–1881 (Barker, Jones, and Tate 1999, 257–58). Even with the adoption of the 17th Amendment in 1913 (which called for the popular election of senators), it was only toward the end of the twentieth century, however, that blacks regained seats in the Senate, notably Edward W. Brooke (R-Mass.) 1967–1979 and notably Carol Moseley-Braun, who became the first black female and first black Democrat to win in 1992. Braun lost her reelection bid in 1998. Barack Obama, a black Democrat was elected in 2004. Like Braun, Obama was elected from the state of Illinois. Both are well-qualified politicians, having previously held office and crafted biracial campaigns that appealed to many whites.

The absolute number of blacks elected to the House of Representatives is significantly higher than that for the Senate because most blacks elected to the House represent majority-black districts. During Reconstruction twenty blacks served in the House, in the Forty-first and Fifty-sixth Congresses (Tate 2003, 27). After George White's election in 1898, no black person was elected to Congress until 1928, when Oscar De Priest won a House seat. The numbers of blacks in the House remained at about two through 1953 and increased to seven in 1967. The numbers rose sharply during the late 1960s through the 1990s, as blacks mobilized politically in the aftermath of the civil rights movement and because of the effectiveness of the 1965 Voting Rights Act. Blacks formed electoral majorities in rural counties in the South and urban areas in the North, but without legislative and judicial protection through the Voting Rights Act, they often found state legislatures gerrymandering districts in order to cancel out black electoral majorities. Having majority-black districts is important to the political advancement of blacks. Few majority-white districts have elected black candidates (Davidson and Grofman 1994; Lublin 1997). The Supreme Court, which has the final say on the extent to which minority voters are protected under the Fourteenth Amendment and the Voting Rights Act, has increasingly moved to the political right on such matters. In *Allen v. State Board of Elections*, the Supreme Court ruled in 1969 that the Voting Rights Act should be given "'the broadest possible scope'" (Parker 1990, 97). In 1982, Congress amended Section 2 of the Voting Rights Act to provide minorities with additional voting rights protection.

In its 1993 ruling in *Shaw v. Reno*, the Court signaled its intention to refuse to accept historical evidence that minorities are afforded fewer opportunities than whites to hold elective office. The Court instead suggested that majority-minority and majority-black districts might now violate the Fourteenth Amendment rights of white citizens. Furthermore, the key provisions of the Voting Rights Act, which were extended in 1970, 1974, and 1982, are set to expire in 2007 unless Congress acts to extend them again. The political environment that granted the 1965

Voting Rights Act does not exist today. Significant barriers to black voting remain, including the disenfranchisement of black felons. Because the states having the worst records on minority voting rights, such as Mississippi, now have large numbers of blacks serving in their state legislatures and representing them in Congress, conservative groups are set to challenge provisions that would target states that have necessitated voting rights litigation in the recent past. The Voting Rights Act is likely to be renewed in 2007 because of its historical and symbolic significance, but it may be extended in a form that may not provide minorities with enough protection to expand their presence in Congress. To design a system in which blacks and other minorities lack sufficient descriptive representation in contrast to whites has political consequences. As shown through a national survey, black Americans feel that they are better represented in government when represented by a fellow black (Tate 2003). A majority of blacks also would endorse changing the electoral system to advance their descriptive representation in government (Tate 2003, 169). At the same time, blacks are not likely to withdraw from politics and revolt if even fewer numbers of blacks are elected to Congress as a result of the diminished protection of their voting rights through legislation (i.e., the Voting Rights Act) or Supreme Court rulings. Would more blacks be elected to Congress under a different electoral system that abolished the undemocratic Senate and instituted a proportional representation system? The answer is yes, but the country remains only dimly aware of the electoral disadvantages that plague African Americans and other minority groups. The political environment is not conductive to either electoral reform at present.

The Executive Branch, the Electoral College, and Presidential Power

According to Robert Dahl (2003), the Electoral College remains high on the list as one of the most "undemocratic" features of the American political system. Yet it is the institution by which we elect our presidents. Textbooks tell us that the framers chose this system because of their fears of a popular vote that could be manipulated by a candidate to erect a new "monarchy." Candidates for the Presidency receive votes in the Electoral College for each state in which they have won a majority of the popular vote. As of 2006, candidates need 270 Electoral College votes to win the White House. Analysts have labeled the institution undemocratic because candidates can secure a majority of votes in the Electoral College while actually losing the popular vote. In addition, the Electoral College confers significant power on the states. The electors—a number equal to the sum of their state's members in the House and the Senate—would be selected by state legislatures. The unequal weight of states based on the Senate makes the electoral college unrepresentative of the people. As in the case of the Senate, minorities are underrepresented in the Electoral College as well.

This feature of the American system has given the Southern states an enormous advantage in presidential elections. Candidates must pursue and win the "Solid South," and Republicans have a tremendous edge over Democrats in the early twenty-first century because of their conservative racial policies. During the 1980s,

Republicans won impressive victories in the South, suggesting that they had a "lock" on the region (Lublin 2004). Because of state laws that kept most blacks in the South from voting until 1965, for much of American history presidents—including liberal Democrats—have been coldly uninterested in the plight of blacks. Franklin Delano Roosevelt, who is widely perceived as a champion of the poor and downtrodden, had a dismal record on racial issues. Although some New Deal legislation was beneficial, most blacks continued to be victimized in the 1930s by both private and state-sponsored racial discrimination. President Roosevelt himself remained reluctant to support legislation on behalf of blacks. For example, until 1936 Roosevelt refused to support antilynching legislation, fearing that it would infuriate Southern legislators in Congress and thus impede the passage of his New Deal programs. John Davis has reported in an evaluation of the New Deal that blacks were in many cases worse off than they were before, and even where there were benefits, they were dispensed in grossly discriminatory fashion (Davis 1935, 141–45).

The inherent defects of the Electoral College are several, including, as Robert Dahl points out (2003), that it can declare an election in favor of candidates who lose the popular vote. It can also produce outcomes in which no candidate wins the majority in the college that is necessary to win the presidency. Both outcomes have happened in American history. In 2000, the Democratic presidential candidate, Al Gore, led the Republican candidate, George W. Bush, by a slim margin in the popular vote, but still lost the election as Bush won a majority of votes in the Electoral College. The 2000 presidential election raised the issue of racial bias in the electoral process, as it was revealed through statistical analysis that a significantly higher percentage of black voters failed to have their ballots counted in Florida's Palm County. Florida's ballots were at the center of the controversy over the outcome of the 2000 presidential race. Because of uncertainty over Florida's balloting results, neither candidate had achieved the 270 votes necessary to win in the Electoral College. Gore had 267 votes, while Bush had only 246. Thus Florida's 25 electoral votes decided the outcome.

In Florida, Bush led Gore in the initial tallies by a mere 1,784 votes out of six million cast. By state law, such a narrow margin of victory necessitated a machine recount, which then cut Bush's lead over Gore even further to just 327 votes. The absentee ballots from overseas had not yet been counted, and they were expected to give Bush a final victory over Gore. Yet Gore demanded a hand tabulation in order to include ballots that the machines hadn't been able to count, because the card either had not been fully punched through or had been marked for more than one candidate for president. Florida's Secretary of State, Katherine Harris, refused to provide the counties with enough time to complete a recount by hand, maintaining that state law required certification of a final vote one week after the election.

In addition to the 2000 election, the Electoral College failed to elect a president on three previous occasions—in 1800, 1824, and 1876. In the event that no candidate obtains a majority in the Electoral College, the House of Representatives decides on the winner. In 2000, however, the controversy spilled over into the courts. Eventually, in a 5–4 decision issued in *Bush v. Gore*, the U.S. Supreme Court blocked further hand counts. With no hand counts to challenge the narrow victory of Bush over Gore in the state of Florida, Florida's electoral votes went to Bush. Gore conceded the election to Bush on December 13, 2000.

The five justices who made up the majority in the *Bush v. Gore* decision were nominated by Republican presidents and considered politically conservative. The majority opinion was based on the Equal Protection Clause in the Fourteenth Amendment, which was originally adopted to provide black former slaves with the full protection of the law. The conservative majority on the Court, however, argued that since the method of hand counting was unreliable and even arbitrary and partisan, it was a violation of the equal protection clause. Gore's supporters saw it as quite the opposite; the fact that ballots were not counted because a tabulation machine had rejected them was itself a denial of equal protection under the law. The state should have been given the time to count all ballots for which the voter's intent could be readily identified; anything less than a full count constituted voter disenfranchisement.[7]

The 2000 election reopened old wounds and accusations. The history of the South includes blatant denials of black voting rights. Furthermore, since the 2000 election statistical evidence has emerged revealing that blacks often cast a disproportionate number of missing and uncounted ballots or "nonvotes" in elections. The reasons why black voters cast a higher rate of spoiled ballots are debated. While some analysts believe that Florida officials deliberately assign old and error-prone balloting machines to majority-Democratic and majority-black precincts to negate their votes, some still believe that the fault lies principally with mistakes made by black, minority, and elderly (mostly Jewish) voters. Determining the real reason why blacks in particular go the polls and cast a disproportionately higher percentage of spoiled ballots than other voters is important because of its electoral implications. One set of scholars maintains that based on their statistical analysis of the votes cast in Florida, perhaps erroneously for Buchanan, or rejected as spoiled in the machine tabulation, "Al Gore would have won a majority of the officially certified votes in Florida" (Wand et al. 2001, 803). Thus Al Gore and not George W. Bush would have been elected president in 2000. This outcome has significant policy ramifications for black and minority voters, as Republican presidents generally support an economic and social policy agenda antagonistic to black interests.

Article 2 of the U.S. Constitution vests executive power in the president. Similar to the judicial and legislative branches, the executive branch of government and the constitutional powers inherent in the institution have been instrumental in constructing and maintaining race and gender as "American dilemmas."[8] In brief, the institution of the American presidency is often divided into two differing spheres of influence: foreign policy and domestic policy. The constitutional and institutional powers of the presidency provide the incumbent with unparalleled power and world influence. The President of the United States is often considered the chief of state; i.e., he or she is the symbolic embodiment of the entire country. Under the Constitution the president is the chief executive, directing the cabinet and the executive branch of government. The Constitution specifically gives the president the authority to make treaties and to appoint cabinet officers, federal judges, and ambassadors. The president is also a political leader, directing the operations of his party and serving as leader of its members in Congress. In practice, modern presidents also play a key role in setting the national agenda. In addition, the president is also the commander-in-chief of the armed forces. With these broad institutional powers, the office of the presidency is well positioned to address the enduring dilemma of race in the United States. And of course, one should note that the president is elected by the citizens (via the Electoral College, discussed below) and is limited to two terms in office. On this account, throughout history several presidential elections have proved to be critical, even determinative, junctures in the African American experience.

For example, one certainly cannot ignore the significance of the Great Compromise of 1877. In the main, as part of the political maneuvering and bargaining that accompanied the resolution of the disputed 1876 presidential election in favor of the Republican candidate, Rutherford B. Hayes, the Republican Party struck deals with Southern Democrats and agreed to pull all federal troops *out* of the Southern states in exchange for electoral votes and support. Thus under the Compromise of 1877, Hayes became president; federal troops abandoned African Americans in the South, and the era of Reconstruction ended (Woodward 1974, 69–70). Immediately, the Southern states began passing laws that restricted every single aspect of black participation in the political, social, and economic life of the South. The political maneuverings in 1876 and 1877 resulted in complete abrogation of the right to vote guaranteed by the Fifteenth Amendment for nearly all blacks in the South.

To summarize, the Compromise of 1877 resulted from the disputed Hayes-Tilden presidential election in 1876. At the time, according to article 2 of the Constitution, presidential electors were to be selected under state laws and to cast votes for the president. The electors are then certified to the President of the Senate. Specifically, article 2 states:

> Each State shall appoint, in such manner as the legislature thereof may direct, a number of electors, equal to the whole number of Senators and Representatives to which the State may be entitled in the Congress. . . .
>
> The electors shall meet in their respective States, and vote by ballot . . . [and] shall make a list of all the persons voted for, and of the number of votes for each; which list they shall sign and certify, and transmit sealed to . . . the President of the Senate. . . .
>
> The President of the Senate shall, in the presence of the Senate and House of Representatives, open all the certificates, and the votes shall then be counted. The person having the greatest number of votes shall be the President.

A dispute arose in 1876, however, over conflicting vote counts from four states: Florida, Louisiana, South Carolina, and Oregon. The first three, Florida, Louisiana, and South Carolina, were Republican strongholds and certified their electors for Rutherford B. Hayes. The Democrats, however, claimed fraud and accused the Republicans of stealing or disallowing thousands of Democratic votes.

Consequently, the Democrats sent a separate set of electors to Washington. In Oregon, Hayes received a majority of the votes; however, one of the state's three electors was disqualified because he was a federal officer. Pursuant to this disqualification, the governor of Oregon certified the two other original Republican electors and the Democrat who had initially lost to the disqualified Republican elector (the federal officer). The two Republican electors, however, selected a third Republican elector as a replacement and certified the election results to Oregon's Secretary of State.

Congress established an Electoral Commission in 1877 to resolve the disputed electoral count.[9] The commission comprised ten members of the House and Senate, equally divided by chamber and party, and four Supreme Court justices, two from each party. Additionally, these four justices were to select a fifth justice; they chose Associate Justice Joseph P. Bradley, a Republican.[10] As history documents, the Electoral Commission divided along strict party lines; Justice Bradley's vote helped to ensure an eight-to-seven Republican victory in Hayes's favor. Hayes was declared the winner two days before his inauguration.

With the withdrawal of federal troops, African Americans in large measure fell victim to even harsher violence, disenfranchisement, and other vestiges of slavery than had existed before the withdrawal. The 1877 compromise and the withdrawal of federal troops brought about the end of Reconstruction and established the "let alone" policy with regard to blacks (Logan 1965, 26). In short, the Compromise of 1877 ushered in a period of widespread Jim Crow laws, disenfranchisement and the erosion of the guarantees of the Fifteenth Amendment (Franklin 1957, 241–48). With the conclusion of Reconstruction, the Southern states enacted legislation and instituted practices that required the complete segregation of blacks and whites. As stated elsewhere, "the segregation was designed to express in thousands of ways white society's judgment of the inferiority of blacks and superiority of whites." Virtually no aspect of life in the South, and eventually in the North, was exempted.[11]

A brief look at twentieth-century presidents—John F. Kennedy to George W. Bush—is also instructive in reviewing the institutional powers of the presidency and their relations to race in America. The reader should keep in mind, however, that a president's agenda is far more than an itemized list.[12] The issues (or choices between alternatives) that a given president selects to support are not arbitrary policies but pointers to what the president considers to be the most important issues facing his administration (Light 1986, 2–3). Presidents concentrate on issues that match their personal and political goals (Light 1986, 62).

For example, On June 25, 1941, President Franklin Delano Roosevelt signed Executive Order 8802 creating the Fair Employment Practices Committee to enforce a nondiscrimination policy in defense programs, but he did so in response to a threat that blacks were planning to organize a mass march on Washington. John F. Kennedy, too, seemed determined to ignore blacks' demand for civil rights until 1963 when he took his first decisive stand in favor of civil rights (Carmines and Stimson 1989, 31; Nieman 1991; 139–40; Tate 1994, 51–53). [13]A closer look at Kennedy's presidential record on civil rights, however, highlights one of the key institutional powers of the American presidency and its relation to race, namely the executive order.[14] For example, in March 1961 President Kennedy issued Executive Order No. 10926, which combined the committees on Government Contracts and Government Employment Practices into the President's Committee on Equal Employment Opportunity.[15] This order marked the first instance of an official requirement that contractors "*actively* pursue equal employment rather than settling simply for passive nondiscrimination." Other examples of Kennedy's use of executive directives include the use of federal marshals and the federalizing of Mississippi's National Guard in September 1962 to assist in registering James Meredith at the University of Mississippi,[16] and the use of federal marshals and the Alabama National Guard to desegregate the University of Alabama in June 1963.[17] But consider also that Kennedy used the institutional powers of the presidency— such as the executive appointment of federal judges—to reward staunch racial segregationists with lifetime federal judgeships (Lyles 1997, 84–85).

President Johnson also issued executive orders to address issues of race directly. It was Johnson's initiatives in the form of executive orders that put the teeth in affirmative action programs (Lyles 1997, 86–90). Johnson's Executive Order No. 11197 issued February 5, 1965, established the President's Council on Equal Opportunity, which was charged with finding ways to "more effectively" implement the 1957 and 1964 Civil Rights Acts.[18] In September of the following year, Johnson issued the capstone of affirmative action, Executive Order No. 11246, requiring all federal contracts to include clauses agreeing "not to discriminate against any employee or applicant for employment because of race, color, religion or national origin" (Benokraitis and Feagin 1978, 11–12; see also Glazer 1975, 46). Two years later, in October 1968, Johnson issued Executive Order No. 11375. This order also included a ban on discrimination in employment on the basis of sex. For example, it prohibited "separate seniority rosters for men and women, discrimination based on a woman's marital or child bearing status, and, separate columns of help wanted advertisements in newspapers" (Benokraitis and Feagin 1978, 12). This order also included a requirement that contractors develop "written *affirmative action* plans to remedy the effects of past discrimination" (Benokraitis and Feagin 1978, 12). And, commensurate with his support for the Civil Rights Act of 1964, Johnson directed the U.S. Commission on Civil Rights in 1965 to conduct a nationwide study of segregated school systems.[19] Johnson's vocal support for African American voting rights put the issue at the forefront of the national agenda; that is, he used the institutional powers of the presidency to restore blacks' civil rights and to promote voting rights as a national policy.[20] It is well documented that Johnson also used the institutional powers of the presidency to promote both his policy and partisan agenda in the selection of judicial nominees; he attempted to select judges with progressive civil rights views while simultaneously remaining sensitive to party considerations, especially those involving Democratic senators (Lyles 1997, 90–92).

A brief look at the Nixon presidency also reveals the Nixon administration was well aware of its potential to influence national policy on race under the institutional powers of the presidency. In fact, Nixon gained the presidency in 1968 at least in part because of his "Southern strategy," which was designed to reduce federal pressure on the South to comply with civil rights laws (Lyles 1997, 92–97).

Nixon "pledged to take a more cautious, slow approach to [civil rights laws] enforcement" (Bullock and Lamb 1984, 27). This caution included condemning busing, promising to terminate cutoffs of federal aid designed to impose desegregation, criticizing parts of the Voting Rights Act, and pledging to appoint "strict constructionists" to the Supreme Court (Orfield 1986). Nixon's overall policy on civil rights was, in the words of Thomas and Mary Edsall, to develop "a strategy of staying within the letter of the law, while making abundantly clear wherever possible his reluctance to aggressively enforce it" (1991, 81). With regard to judicial appointments; however, the institutional checks and balances inherent in the advice and consent clause frustrated Nixon's agenda. The reader should recall that Nixon did suffer major defeats in his Supreme Court nominations. Although he experienced little difficulty winning confirmation for Warren Burger as Chief Justice in 1969, he was defeated in the nominations of both Clement F. Haynsworth (a Southerner who had ruled against school desegregation and in favor of segregated hospitals receiving federal funds) and G. Harold Carswell (also attacked by civil rights groups).

President Gerald Ford also utilized the powers of the presidency and the influence of his presidential candidacy to influence national policy on race (Lyles 1997, 99–103). For example, during the 1976 campaign, President Ford was adamant in his condemnation of busing in numerous speeches.[21] The 1976 GOP platform also endorsed an antibusing amendment. As chief executive, President Ford attempted to curb busing through Congress. For example, in 1976, after an eight-month study by the Justice Department, President Ford directed the department to draft a legislative proposal captioned as the School Desegregation Standards and Assistance Act, primarily an antibusing bill (McDowell 1988, 161; Orfield 1988, 267). The proposal stood to practically nullify the implementation of busing by barring it in cases of de facto segregation. Although Ford's proposal received no action in Congress (it died in committee), his willingness to use the institutional powers of the executive branch to frustrate racial integration are instructive.

A brief look at the presidencies of Jimmy Carter and Ronald Reagan also reveals the enormous power afforded the executive branch under the institutional powers and constraints outlined in the Constitution. For example, the fundamental thrust of the Carter administration's developments in the area of civil rights was in making enforcement mechanisms more effective, particularly in enforcing equal opportunity laws and regulations, and prohibiting discrimination in federally assisted programs (Amaker 1988, 25–28). An essential element of this enforcement—and a utilization of an enumerated constitutional power—included the executive appointment of unprecedented numbers of women, African Americans, and other minorities to positions in which they might aggressively promote and enforce such laws (Lyles 1997, 117–28).

During his two terms in office, President Reagan also used the institutionalized appointment powers of the executive branch to affect race and civil rights issues generally. It is also common knowledge that President Reagan firmly opposed affirmative action and used the institutional powers and position of the presidency to promote his attack on programs geared toward achieving racial balance in the workplace. Reagan's attacks on affirmative action could be seen in several institutional areas, such as policy guidelines in the bureaucracy, legislation, and legal challenges. In August 1981, for example, Reagan's Secretary of Labor, Raymond Donovan, issued new guidelines for the Office of Federal Contract Compliance Programs (OFCCP), effectively limiting its jurisdiction to government contractors with 250 or more employees and a federal contract of one million dollars or more.[22] Donovan himself admitted that these new guidelines would exempt almost 75 percent of all federal contractors from affirmative action requirements.[23] Later that month, on August 20, William Bradford Reynolds, the head of Reagan's Justice Department's Civil Rights Division, announced that "in the area of civil rights he would restrict remedies to the aggrieved party, rather than impose remedies to benefit an entire class of persons."[24] Acting through Reynolds, the Reagan administration attacked affirmative action repeatedly. A case in point: following the Supreme Court's 1984 attack on racial quotas in *Firefighters v. Stotts*,[25] which Reagan's first Solicitor General, Rex E. Lee, called "one of the greatest victories of all time," (Witt 1986, 126) Reynolds affirmed that he would "order the review and assess the validity of hundreds of court-ordered affirmative action programs where the courts had employed racial quotas and goals in hiring to effectuate appropriate relief" (*New York Times*, February 17, 1983).[26]

Nonetheless, these actions clearly reflected the Reagan administration's general hostility to affirmative action. The administration's posture could also be seen in other actions, including the appointments of two anti-affirmative action African Americans, Clarence Pendleton to head the Civil Rights Commission and Clarence Thomas, now Associate Justice Thomas, to head the Equal Employment Opportunities Commission (EEOC). In general, as political scientist Michael Preston put it, "No administration since the inception of the affirmative action program . . . has reacted more negatively to it [affirmative action] than has the Reagan Administration" (Preston 1986, 165–67).

A brief review of the administrations of George H. W. Bush, Bill Clinton, and George W. Bush also supports the view that the institutional powers of, and constraints on, the executive branch afford modern presidents many opportunities to either support or retard racial equality in the United States. For example, with regard to institutional powers, the first President Bush's veto of the 1990 Civil Rights Act is instructive. Although President Bush did sign the Civil Rights Act of 1991, he vetoed an earlier 1990 version, labeling it a "quota bill."[27] In the same year Bush also nominated Federal Court of Appeals Judge Clarence Thomas to the Supreme Court. Thomas is an African American who is generally conservative and hostile to the judicial protection of civil rights for women and minorities.

The Civil Rights Act of 1990 was introduced to reverse a series of civil rights decisions issued by the Supreme Court during its 1988–89 term, as well as some other conservative civil rights decisions that the Court had issued since 1985 that eroded equal employment opportunities for minorities and women.[28] President Bush, however, consistently warned that he would not sign any law that might lead to hiring quotas. "I want to sign a civil rights bill," said Bush at a White House Rose Garden ceremony on May 17, 1990, "but I will not sign a quota bill."[29] Bush wrote to key senators on October 16, 1990, before their vote, that he believed the 1990 bill would cause businesses to adopt hiring and promotion quotas. Bush wrote, "It will also foster divisiveness and litigation rather than conciliation and do more to promote legal fees than civil rights. If the bill is presented to me, I will be compelled to veto it."[30] Despite Bush's warning, the 1990 bill passed the Senate, 65–34, on July 18, 1990, and the House, 227–157, on August 3, 1990. And as promised, on October 22, President Bush vetoed the 1990 legislation after a battle with Democratic sponsors over whether the 1990 bill would establish quotas for minorities and women and thereby discriminate against whites[31]— even though the bill explicitly forbade quotas.[32]

The Senate failed to override the president's veto by only one vote, thus marking the first defeat for a civil rights bill since the Eisenhower administration. In addition to realizing Bush's opposition to quotas, the president's proposal also set lower limits on damages than the vetoed bill passed by Congress.[33] About four months later, in January 1991, the Civil Rights Act of 1991 was introduced in the House and passed in June of 1991 after numerous compromises were reached between President Bush and Senate Republicans who supported the legislation.[34] Bush eventually gave his endorsement to the compromise bill at a news conference held on October 25, 1991, stating the new agreement "does not resort to quotas. . . . I wanted a non-quota civil rights bill that I could sign. And assuming there are no changes in the bill as agreed to last night . . . I will enthusiastically sign this bill." [35] The Civil Rights Act of 1991 was signed into law by Bush on November 21, 1991.[36]

President Clinton, like his predecessors, was also keenly aware of the nexus between the institutional powers of presidency and issues of race in America. In practice, however, Clinton played on both sides of the fence (Lyles 1997, 172–77) While opposing racial quotas, Clinton nonetheless made comments on affirmative action like "mend it." It is notable, however, that President Clinton also used the institutional powers of the presidency to dramatically increase the number of women and racial minorities on the benches of federal courts. In fact, the overall number of women appointed to the district courts during Clinton's *first term* (both in terms of proportion as well as in raw numbers, 30.2 percent and 51 respectively) was the largest number of women appointed in history for any administration. Clinton also appointed historic numbers of African Americans to the federal courts. The point here, of course, is that the constitutional and institutionalized parameters of the power of appointment, with the advice and consent of the Senate, affords the executive branch frequent opportunities to shape judicial policy via the selection and nomination of federal judges.

Conclusion

Federalism, a bicameral Congress, the Electoral College, and the American presidency, as well as the federal judiciary, are institutions that have in many ways protected and preserved slavery, its vestiges, and the exploitation and subordination of African Americans in the United States. As it took four years of civil war, and a constitutional amendment, to free black slaves, it would take a political movement for blacks to win their civil rights. The founders of the United States wanted a system that protected liberty but also stability, which is necessary for people to enjoy property rights. The vast majority of blacks entered this country as property. Understanding the desire for white domination in the construction of this country's political system explains the longevity of black oppression. Undoing the evils of black oppression therefore requires a thorough reexamination of the virtues and costs of the institutional structure of this country.

The very design of the political institutions that make up the American political system has delayed the realization of equal rights for blacks. It took a movement outside of routine politics in order for blacks to win many of the basic civil liberties and civil rights enjoyed by other citizens. And it is doubtful whether without this resort to protest politics that the system would permit blacks such basic rights in the early twenty-first century. The black civil rights movement made it possible for other groups that have suffered discrimination in this country, chiefly American Indians, women, Asian Americans, and Latinos, to seek equal protection of their rights.

Could the United States have a political system that gives blacks and minorities more political equality with whites? The answer is yes. Scrapping the Electoral College, creating a proportional representation system as opposed to single-member districts, and abolishing the Senate are radical proposals, but reforms that would very likely increase the representation of minorities in government. Prospects for such reforms are dim. Robert Dahl flatly states, "The likelihood of reducing the extreme *inequality of representation in the Senate* is virtually zero" (2003, 154). There is a slightly higher but not significant chance that the country would change to proportional representation for its national legislative elections and abolish the Electoral College, granting the people the right to vote for the president directly. Major reforms come about only in the most drastic of times. While the 2000 election controversy did raise the possibility that the Electoral College might be abolished, the fact of the matter is that the High Court's ruling was peacefully accepted by the American public. When terrorists attacked America on September 11, 2001, the crisis also served to divert attention from the inherent problems of the Electoral College. Still, a number of political scientists have made strong arguments that the College should be abolished, if only to provide what Americans mistakenly think they have already, the right to vote for president directly through a popular election (Keyssar 2003).

Thus America's political system is far from perfect. Its roots expose how cunningly the framers sought to create a democracy that still permitted slavery and the subjugation of racial minorities and women. These design flaws are exacerbated by the unwillingness of individual leaders to use what institutional powers they do possess to redress the enduring vestiges of slavery in the United States. The Supreme Court, for example, rather than using its power of judicial review to promote racial equality, has most of the time instead acted to affirm the will of the dominant lawmaking majorities in power. Congress, staffed through an electoral system that makes it difficult for blacks to win seats, has also historically legislated away the rights of minorities and women. This is especially true of the Senate, given its undemocratic nature. Modern presidents enjoy enormous power to shape the national agenda on race and gender equality. Moreover, through executive orders and their selection of federal judges they can affect minority issues for decades to come. Regrettably, however, even the most pedestrian analyses reveal that modern presidents have failed to address these issues in a meaningful way. In fact, there is ample evidence to support the view that modern presidencies have all but ignored racial and gender inequality. This is the knowledge that should and must be transmitted by political scientists as well as appropriate glorification of our system as the first and most enduring democratic state in the world. It is a necessary part of the story as we reflect on its virtues, namely its fairness, and its weaknesses, the biases that are inherent in the American political system.

Notes

1. *The Debates in the Federal Convention of 1787* reported by James Madison, Tuesday, August 21, 1787. For the accompanying remarks on this day of the debates, see "The Avalon Project at Yale Law School." The debate from Tuesday August 21, 1787 was accessed on September 23, 2006 at http://www.yale.edu/lawweb/avalon/debates/821.htm.

2. *Marbury v. Madison*, 1 Cranch 137.

3. Early decisions of the Supreme Court indicated that the Court would find "reasonable" justifications to conclude that women could be treated differently from men, especially in such matters as job opportunities and conditions of employment. For discussion see generally Lucius J. Barker, Twiley W. Barker, Michael W. Combs, Kevin L. Lyles and H. W. Perry, *Civil Liberties and the Constitution: Cases and Commentaries* (Upper Saddle River, NJ: Prentice Hall, 1999), 707–52. Hereafter cited as Barker et al., *Civil Liberties and the Constitution*.

4. *United States v. Carolene Products Co.*, 304 U.S. 144 (1938). On its face, this case was merely one of numerous instances wherein the Supreme Court upheld federal economic policies. Its significance was generated from a footnote in which Justice Harlan Stone argued that the Court was justified in holding a "tolerant" view of government economic policies, while it gave "more exacting judicial scrutiny" to policies that transgressed civil liberties.

5. Dahl's view of the Supreme Court's role in the policy process has been broadly debated by judicial scholars (Adamany 1973; Canon and Ulmer 1976; Casper 1976; Funston 1975; Handbag and Hill 1980).

6. For a Discussion of the Warren Court's expansion of the rights of persons accused of crime, see generally Barker et al., *Civil Liberties and the Constitution*, 321–454.

7. For a discussion that supports the Supreme Court decision, see Posner (2001). For a critical review of the ruling, see Dershowitz (2001).

8. The use of the phrase "American dilemma," in this context was coined by Gunnar Myrdal.

9. Stat. 227 (1877).

10. As detailed by Bernard Schwartz, initially it was expected that the four Justices would have selected Justice David Davis, who was considered nonpartisan. Justice Davis resigned from the Court, however, after his election to the Senate by the Illinois legislature. Justice Bradley was "supposedly the least partisan among the remaining Republicans on the Court," Bernard Schwartz, *A History of the Supreme Court* (New York: Oxford University Press, 1993), 172.

11. See Barker et al., *Civil Liberties and the Constitution*, 463. Also, see generally pp. 463–64.

12. As explained by E. E. Schattschneider some two decades ago, "The definition of the alternatives is the supreme instrument of power. . . . He who determines what politics is about runs the country, because the definition of alternatives is the choice of conflict, and the choice of conflict allocates power" (1975, 66).

13. For example, it was not until eighteen months later that Kennedy effected a "timid executive order covering very little of the country's housing" (Fishel 1985, 2). Kennedy also issued executive orders that prohibited discrimination in federally aided libraries and hospitals, in the armed forces, in the training of civil defense workers, and in the off-base treatment of military personnel (Berman 1987, 242).

14. In addition to executive orders regarding employment and nondiscriminatory grants-in-aid policies, the Kennedy administration also sought changes through executive action in the areas of housing and transportation. (*Congressional Quarterly Almanac* 1961, 393).

15. By this order the vice president was appointed chairman of the committee and the Secretary of Labor was instructed to implement equal employment practices in hiring federal employees and government contractors. Executive Order No. 10925, 3 C.F.R. 86 (Supp. 1961), 6 R.R.L.R. 9 (1961). Among other requirements, the order required contractors to publicize their antidiscrimination policies in their help-wanted ads and their requests to employment agencies; it also required contractors to "make every effort to obtain agreements with their unions that the unions would not practice discrimination" (*Congressional Quarterly Almanac* 1961, 392). Consider also that it was President Franklin Delano Roosevelt who issued the first executive order that dealt with equal opportunity in employment. This order forbade employment discrimination on the basis of race, creed, color, or national origin by employers who held Defense Department contracts. As explained by political scientist Michael B. Preston, however, it was not until twenty years after Roosevelt's 1941 order that "the idea of affirmative action became interwoven with the discrimination ban" (Preston 1986, 167). Under Presidents Truman and Eisenhower, further executive orders were issued, extending the ban on discrimination by government contractors and setting up various bodies to oversee and enforce it (Glazer 1975, 44–46).

16. For a thorough account of the integration of the University of Mississippi, see Meredith (1966) and Fleming (1965).

17. John F. Kennedy, Proclamation No. 3497, September 30, 1962; Code of Federal Regulations, 1959–1963 Compilation, 225. For an informative yet condensed summary of the Meredith case, see Bardolph (1970, 473–91), see also Barker (1967, 41–69), and Amaker (1988, 17)

18. Executive Order No. 11197, 3 C.F.R. 278 (1964–65 comp.), revoked by Executive Order No. 11247.

19 The commission's 1967 report, *Racial Isolation in the Public Schools*, called attention to increasing racial segregation in the nation's urban schools and recommended national legislation outlawing such practices. See U.S. Commission on Civil Rights (1967).

20. The 1964 March on Selma provides a poignant example and commentary on Johnson's commitment to voting rights. For a well-developed discussion of the relationship between the Selma-Montgomery March and the eventual passage of the 1965 Voting Rights Act, see Garrow (1978). President Johnson's early and personal support of the march was clearly expressed in a news conference on February 4, 1965: "All of us," said the President, "should be concerned with the efforts of our fellow Americans to register to vote in Alabama. . . . I intend to see [that the right to vote] is secured to all of our citizens (Sobel, *Civil Rights*, 1960–1966, 293–294.)." Moreover, only one week after the marchers were assaulted and brutally beaten on a bridge outside Selma on March 15, 1965, Johnson proposed the enactment of the 1965 Voting Rights Act to a joint session of Congress in a speech that was broadcast to the entire country (President Johnson, "State of the Union Message," Public Papers of the Presidents of the United States. (Washington, DC: Government Printing Office, 1965, 1–9). "It is wrong," said President Johnson, "deadly wrong to deny any of your fellow Americans the right to vote in this country. [I]t is not just Negroes, but really it is all of us, who must overcome the crippling legacy of bigotry and injustice. . . . And we shall overcome" (Amaker 1988, 20).

21. *New York Times*, August 20, 1975; *Education Daily*, August 21, 1975; *Washington Post*, September 17, 1975.

22. The OFCCP's previous guidelines had specified any federal contractor with fifty or more employees and contracts worth $50,000.

23. See "Affirmative Action Assailed in Congress: Administration," *Congressional Quarterly Weekly Report* 39, no. 37 (September 1981): 1749–53.

24. Ibid.

25. Reagan's first Solicitor General, Rex E. Lee, argued the administration's case opposing affirmative action in the joint claims *Firefighters Local Union No. 1784 v. Stotts* and *Memphis Fire Department v. Stotts* (467 U.S. 561, 1984). In 1981, a federal judge had ordered the Memphis fire department to implement "budget-dictated" layoffs by dismissing senior white firefighters; thus enabling more recently hired African Americans to keep their jobs. The appeals court upheld the order against the city and the Reagan administration backed the city when the issue was appealed to the Supreme Court. The Assistant Attorney General for Civil Rights, William Bradford

Reynolds, joined Lee in the administration's amicus curiae (friend of the court) brief. Essentially, the brief argued that the lower court judge's action was illegal; that is, affirmative action plans are unconstitutional when they are adopted to benefit any persons or groups who were not themselves the victims of discrimination (Lyles 1997, 133–36).

26. For a discussion of the ways in which Reagan used the federal courts for his objectives, see Charles Fried, *Order and Law*.

27. For a thorough examination of the shifting patterns of partisan voting and leadership in Congress, as well as President Bush's shifting positions, see Stern (1995).

28. The overturned decisions included, for example, *Patterson v. McClean Credit Union* (491 U.S. 164 [1989]), in which the Supreme Court ruled that the 1866 Civil Rights Act did not protect employees from blatant race discrimination once they have been hired; *Wards Cove Packing Co., Inc. v. Atonio* (490 U.S. 642 [1989]), in which the Supreme Court overturned an earlier ruling, *Griggs v. Duke Power Company* (402 U.S. 424 [1971]), and shifted the burden to employees of proving that an employer's hiring practices are discriminatory; and *Martin v. Wilks* (490 U.S. 755 [1989]), in which the Supreme Court allowed "white" firefighters to challenge an affirmative action settlement that had been in effect for eight years (Eskridge 1991).

29. "Bush Shifts on Job-Rights Bill, but Differences Remain," *Congressional Quarterly Weekly Report* 48, May 19, 1990, p. 1563.

30. "Expected Bush Veto Looming over Civil Rights Measure," *Congressional Quarterly Weekly Report* 48, October 20, 1990, p. 3519.

31. For a discussion of these "last-second" negotiations over the bill, including the enlistment of a former Transportation Secretary, William T. Coleman, called in by the White House on October 19, see "Expected Bush Veto," 3518.

32. For the text accompanying President Bush's October 22 veto of the civil rights bill (S. 2104), see "Bush Vetoes Rights Bill, Objects to 'Quotas,'" *Congressional Quarterly Weekly Report* 48, October 27, 1990, p. 3654.; also see Steven A. Holmes, "President Vetoes Bill on Job Rights; Showdown is Set," *New York Times*, October 23, 1990, p. A1.

33. For a discussion of Bush's veto of the 1990 bill, see Wasby (1992).

34. Bush nonetheless continued to vigorously attack the measure well into 1991, denouncing it as a quota bill. The House of Representatives passed the revised 1991 bill, 273–158, knowing that members might be subjects of racial scare advertising about whites losing jobs to blacks, like the advertising used by Senator Jesse Helms (R-NC) in his 1990 campaign. See *New York Times*, May 31, 1991; *New York Times*, June 6, 1991.

35. *New York Times*, October 26, 1991.

36. Civil Rights Act of 1991, by the Committee of Federal Legislation, reported in the Record of the Association of the Bar of the City of New York 48 (1993), 75–124.

References

Adamany, David. 1973. Legitimacy, realigning elections, and the Supreme Court. *Wisconsin Law Review* 3:790–846.

Amaker, Norman C. 1988. *Civil rights and the Reagan administration*. Washington, DC: Urban Institute Press, 1988.

Bailyn, Benard. 1993. The debate on the Constitution: Federalist and Antifederalist speeches, articles, and letters during the struggle over ratification: Part 1, September 1787–February 1788. 2 vols. New York: Library of America.

Bardolph, Richard. 1970. *The civil rights record: Black Americans and the law, 1849–1970*. New York: Thomas Y. Crowell.

Barker, Lucius J., Twiley W. Barker, Michael W. Combs, Kevin L. Lyles, and H. W. Perry. 1999. *Civil liberties and the Constitution: Cases and commentaries*. 8th ed. Upper Saddle River, NJ: Prentice Hall.

Barker, Lucius J., Mack Jones, and Katherine Tate. 1999. *African Americans and the American political system*. 4th ed. Upper Saddle River, NJ: Prentice Hall.

Benokraitis, Nijole V., and Joe R. Feagin. 1978. *Affirmative action and equal opportunity: Action, inaction, reaction*. Boulder, CO: Westview.

Berman, Larry. 1987. *The new American presidency*. Boston: Little, Brown and Company.

Binder, Sarah A. 2003. *Stalemate: Causes and consequences of legislative gridlock*. Washington, DC: Brookings Institution.

Bobo, Lawrence. 1983. Whites' opposition to busing: Symbolic racism or realistic group conflict? *Journal of Personality and Social Psychology* 45:1195–210.

———. 2000. Race and belief about affirmative action. In *Racialized politics: The debate about racism in America*, edited by David O. Sears, Jim Sidanius, and Lawrence Bobo. Chicago: University of Chicago Press.

Blumer, Herbert. 1958. Race prejudice as a sense of group position. *Pacific Sociological Review* 1:3–7.

Bullock, Charles S., III, and Charles M. Lamb, eds. 1984. *Implementation of civil rights policy*. Monterey, CA: Brooks/Cole.

Canon, Bradley C., and S. Sidney Ulmer. The Supreme Court and critical elections: A dissent. *American Political Science Review* 70 (December 1976): 1215–18.

Canon, David T. 1999. *Race, redistricting, and representation: The unintended consequences of black majority districts*. Chicago: University of Chicago Press.

Carmines, Edward G., and James A. Stimson. 1989. *Issue evolution*. Princeton, NJ: Princeton University Press.

Casper, Jonathon. 1976. The Supreme Court and national policy making. *American Political Science Review* 70 (March): 50–63.

Congressional Quarterly Almanac. 1961. Washington, DC: Congressional Quarterly.

Congressional Quarterly Weekly Report. Bush shifts on Job-Rights Bill, but differences remain, 48, May 19, 1990.

Congressional Quarterly Weekly Report. Expected Bush veto looming over civil rights measure, 48, October 20, 1990.

Corwin, Edwin S. 1969. *The Constitution and what it means today*. New York: Atheneum.

Dahl, Robert A. 1957. Decision-making in a democracy: The Supreme Court as a national policy-maker. *Journal of Public Law* 6: 293–95.

———. 2003. *How democratic is the American Constitution?* New Haven, CT: Yale University Press.

Davidson, Chandler, and Bernard Grofman, eds. 1994. *Quiet revolution in the South: The impact of the Voting Rights Act, 1965–1990*. Princeton, NJ: Princeton University Press.

Davis, John. 1935. A black inventory of the New Deal. *Crisis* 43, no. 3:141–45.

Dershowitz, Alan 2001. *Supreme injustice: How the High Court highjacked Election 2000*. New York: Oxford University Press.

Dudziak, Mary L. 2000. *Cold war civil rights: Race and the image of American democracy*. Princeton, NJ: Princeton University Press

Edsall, Thomas, and Mary Edsall. 1991. *Chain reaction: The impact of race, rights and taxes on American Politics*. New York: W. W. Norton.

Ely, John Hart. 1980. *Democracy and distrust: A theory of judicial review*. Cambridge, MA: Harvard University Press.

Eskridge, William M. 1991. Reneging on history? Playing the Court/Congress/President civil rights game. *California Law Review* 79:613–17.

Fishel, Jeff. 1985. *Presidents and promises: From campaign pledge to presidential performance*. Washington, DC: CQ Press.

Fleming, Harold. 1965. The federal executive and civil rights: 1961–1965. *Daedalus* 94, no. 4 (Fall 1965): 921–48.

Franklin, John Hope. 1957. Legal disfranchisement of the Negro. *Journal of Negro Education* 26 (Spring): 241–48.

Fried, Charles. 1991. *Order and law*. New York: Simon & Schuster.

Funston, Richard. 1975. The Supreme Court in critical elections. *American Political Science Review* 69 (September): 795–811.

Garrow, David L. 1978. *Protest at Selma: Martin Luther King Jr. and the Voting Rights Act of 1965*. New Haven, CT: Yale University Press.

Gay, Claudine. 2001. The effect of black congressional representation on political participation. *American Political Science Review* 95, no. 3:589–602.

Glazer, Nathan. 1975. *Affirmative discrimination*. New York: Basic Books.

Goldberg, David Theo. 2002. *The racial state*. Malden, MA: Blackwell.

Hall, Kermit L., William M. Wiecek, and Paul Finkelman. 1991. *American legal history: Cases and materials*. New York: Oxford University Press.

Hamilton, Alexander. 1961. Federalist 66. In *The federalist papers*, by Alexander Hamilton, James Madison, and John Jay. Edited by Clinton Rossiter. New York: New American Library. Originally published in 1788.

Hamilton, Alexander, James Madison, and John Jay. 1961. *The federalist papers*. New York: New American Library.

Handbag, Roger, and Harold F. Hill Jr. 1980. Court curbing, court reversals, and judicial review: The Supreme Court versus Congress. *Law and Society Review* 14 (Winter): 309–22.

Harris, Joseph P. 1953. *The advice and consent of the Senate*. Berkeley: University of California Press.

Hartz, Louis. 1955. *The liberal tradition in America: An interpretation of American political thought since the Revolution*. New York: Harcourt, Brace, and World.

Hickok, Eugene W., Jr. 1990. Judicial selection: The political roots of advice and consent. In *Judicial selection: Merit, ideology, and politics*, edited by Henry J. Abraham, with Griffin B. Bell, Charles E. Grassley, Eugene W. Hickok Jr., John W. Kern III, Stephen J. Markman, and William Bradford Reynolds. Washington, DC: National Legal Center for the Public Interest.

Higginbotham, A. Leon and Anne F. Jacobs. 1992. "'The law only as enemy': The legitimization of racial powerlessness through Ccolonial and antebellum criminal laws of Virginia. *North Carolina Law Review* 70:969–1070.

Holmes, Steven A. 1990. President vetoes bill on job rights: Showdown is set. *New York Times*, October 23, 1990.

Johnson, Lyndon B. 1965. State of the Union Address. Public Papers of the Presidents of the United States. Washington, DC: Government Printing Office, 1965.

Jordan, Winthrop. 1968. *White over black: American attitudes toward the Negro, 1550–1812*. Baltimore, MD: Penguin.

Kalven, Harry, Jr. 1965. *The Negro and the First Amendment*. Chicago: University of Chicago Press.

Keyssar, Alexander. 2003. Shoring up the right to vote for president: A modest proposal. *Political Science Quarterly* 118, no. 2:181–205.

Lee, Frances E., and Bruce I. Oppenheimer. 1999. *Sizing up the Senate: The unequal consequences of equal representation*. Chicago: University of Chicago Press

Light, Paul C. 1982. *The presidential agenda*. Baltimore, MD: Johns Hopkins University Press.

Logan, Rayford W. 1965. *The betrayal of the Negro*. New York: Collier.

Lublin, David. 1997. *The paradox of representation*. Princeton, NJ: Princeton University Press.

———. 2004. *The republican South*. Princeton, NJ: Princeton University Press.

Lyles, Kevin L. 1994. The bork nomination and black america. In *African-Americans and the American political system*, 3rd ed., by Lucius J. Barker and Mack Jones. Upper Saddle River, NJ: Prentice Hall.

———. 1997. *The gatekeepers: Federal district courts in the political process*. Westport, CT: Praeger.

Madison, James. 1961. Federalist 42. In *The federalist papers*, by Alexander Hamilton, James Madison, and John Jay. Edited by Clinton Rossiter. New York: New American Library. Originally published in 1788.

McDowell, Gary L. 1988. *Curbing the courts: The Constitution and the limits of judicial power*. Baton Rouge: Louisiana State University Press.

Meredith, James. 1966. *Three years in Mississippi*. Bloomington: Indiana University Press.

Morris, Thomas. 1996. *Southern slavery and the law, 1619–1860*. Chapel Hill: University of North Carolina Press.

Nieman, Donald G. 1991. *Promises to keep: African Americans and the constitutional order, 1776 to the present*. New York: Oxford University Press.

O'Brien, David M., 2003. *Storm Center: The Supreme Court in American Politics*. New York: W. W. Norton.

Orfield, Gary. 1978. *Must we bus? Segregated schools and national policy*. Washington, DC: Brookings Institution.

———. 1988. Nixon and the assault on civil rights. In *The politics of social policy in the United States*, edited by Margaret Weir, Ann Shola Orloff, and Theda Skocpol, 347–51. Princeton, NJ: Princeton University Press.

Parker, Frank R. 1990. *Black votes count*. Chapel Hill: University of North Carolina Press.

Patterson, Thomas E. 2003. *The American democracy*. 6th ed. Columbus, OH: McGraw-Hill.

Peltason, Jack W. 1955. *Federal courts in the political process*. New York: Random House.

Posner, Richard A. 2001. *Breaking the deadlock*. Princeton, NJ: Princeton University Press.

Preston, Michael B. 1986. Affirmative action policy: Can it survive the Reaganites? In *Affirmative action: Theory, analysis, and prospects*, edited by Michael W. Combs and John Gruhl. Jefferson, NC: McFarland.

Schattschneider, E. E. 1975. *The semisovereign people*. 2nd ed. Hinsdale, IL: Dryden.

Schwartz, Benard. 1993. *A history of the Supreme Court*. New York: Oxford University Press.

Shapiro, Martin. 1964. *Law and politics in the Supreme Court*. New York: Free Press.

———. 1966. *Freedom of speech: The Supreme Court and judicial review*. Englewood Cliffs, NJ: Prentice Hall.

Smith, Rogers. 1997. *Civic ideals: Conflicting visions of citizenship in U.S. history*. New Haven, CT: Yale University Press.

Sobel, Lester. 1967. *Civil Rights, 1960–66*. New York: Facts on File.

Stern, Mark. 1995. Party alignments and civil rights: Then and now. *Presidential Studies Quarterly* 25:413–27

Tannenbaum, Frank. 1946. *Slave and citizen: The Negro in the Americas*. New York: Vintage.

Tate, Katherine. 2003. *Black faces in the mirror: African Americans and their representatives in the U.S. Congress*. Princeton, NJ: Princeton University Press.

Tushnet, Mark. 1975. The American law of slavery, 1810–1860: A study in the persistence of legal autonomy. *Law and Society Review* 10:119–84.

U.S. Commission on Civil Rights. 1967. *Racial isolation in the public schools*. Washington, DC: Government Printing Office.

Vose, Clement. 1959. *Caucasians only: The Supreme Court, the NAACP, and the restrictive covenant cases*. Berkeley: University of California Press.

Wand, Jonathon N., Kenneth W. Shotts, Jasjeet S. Sekhon, Walter R. Mebane Jr., Michael C. Herron, and Henry E. Brady. 2001. The butterfly did it: The aberrant vote for Buchanan in Palm Beach County, Florida. *American Political Science Review* 95, no. 4:793–810.

Wasby, Stephen L. 1992. Epilogue to *The affirmative action controversy*, edited by Ronald J. Fiscus and Stephen L. Wasby. Durham, NC: Duke University Press.

Whitby, Kenny J. 1998. *The color of representation: Congressional behavior and black constituents*. Ann Arbor, MI: University of Michigan Press.

Wiecek, William M. 1991. *The sources of antislavery constitutionalism in America, 1760–1848*. Ithaca, NY: Cornell University Press.

Wills, Garry. 2003. *"Negro president": Jefferson and the slave power*. Boston: Houghton Mifflin.

Witt, Elder. 1986. *A different justice: Reagan and the Supreme Court*. Washington, DC: Congressional Quarterly Press.

Woodward, C. Vann. 1974. *The strange career of Jim Crow*. 3rd rev. ed. New York: Oxford University Press.

CHAPTER EIGHTEEN

Political Science Confronts Afro-America

A Reconsideration

JERRY G. WATTS

A S AN ACADEMIC DISCIPLINE, American political science has historically relegated to the margins issues pertaining to Afro-Americans, race, and anti-black white racism.[1] Ralph Bunche, the first Afro-American president of the American Political Science Association, once complained about the lack of interest in academic political science in publishing articles on the political behavior of black Americans. In 1941, Bunche stated: "In some field[s] this [publishing] is relatively easy. Anthropologists deal with the Negro as a respectable topic, and the journals of anthropology take such articles without hesitation. In respect to my own field, which concerns the status of the Negro, except insofar as papers having to do with colonial problems and the like are involved, there isn't a very cordial reception for papers dealing with the Negro."[2] Rogers M. Smith has shown that explicit anti-black prejudice, or white racism, saturated the scholarship of political science from its founding through the early 1920s. This white supremacist ethos was explicitly concerned with race and racial hierarchies. Following the demise of the white supremacist ethos, the discipline ignored or devalued the study of Afro-American politics in much the way that it ignored and devalued the study of race in American politics. This disregard for the issue of race perplexes Smith. He is baffled by the unwillingness of political science to study race during the early decades of the twentieth century. "The puzzle is the ensuing disregard of racial topics in a country that was seeing the spread of Jim Crow segregation, race-based immigration restrictions, legislative battles over anti-lynching and civil rights bills, court cases dealing with racial voting and jury exclusions, the growth of a huge separatist movement, the Universal Negro Improvement Association, in the 1920s, followed by the growth of the older NAACP into a mass-based organization, the formation of racially exclusive black labor and then protest movements, and so much more."[3]

Smith argues that the marginalization of the study of race within political science in the 1920s and 1930s, following the demise of the white supremacist ethos, stems from the widely held belief that "races came from our genomes or economic systems or our historical and present social and cultural practices and the psychic needs they express—anywhere but from our formal politics. And scholars have also thought race mattered most in social and cultural contexts though they have acknowledged that race has, some of the time, *affected* politics as an exogenously generated independent variable."[4] Political scientists evidently believed that race was a subject better treated in cultural anthropology or sociology. Unfortunately, traces of this parochialism continue within the very center of political science.[5] When one thinks of those social sciences that have attempted to confront their racist pasts or their historical and contemporary embrace of Eurocentric biases, political science does not come to mind.

During the past thirty years, the status and recognition given to scholarship on race, racism, and Afro-American politics has gradually improved.[6] Of the many reasons for this progress, most stem from the impact of the civil rights movement of the 1960s on American academia. First, the civil rights movement made it analytically ridiculous for the discipline to continue to disregard the political plight of Afro-Americans. Whether political science scholars supported or opposed the movement, its significance was self-evident. The discipline could no longer "play ostrich" with the race question, though it momentarily tried to do so. As such, change was neither immediate nor drastic. For instance, fifteen to twenty-five years after the demise of the civil rights movement, political science journals still generally ignored the study of Afro-American politics.[7] A second result of the civil rights movement and its accompanying era of black political agency—that is, the Black Power movement—was an intensified focus on training a larger number of Afro-American political scientists. This too proved be a slow process. Ultimately, these black political scientists helped in varying degrees to push the discipline to broaden the range of issues deemed significant. As a final offshoot of the civil rights movement, a cadre of white political scientists emerged who believed that it was morally problematic to devalue the study of American racism. Along with an older generation of black political scientists, these progressive and liberal white scholars helped to mentor subsequent generations of political scientists, both black and white, who contested the discipline's marginalization of the study of the political ramifications of race and racism within the discipline.

This nurturance has culminated in a virtual explosion of scholarship on race, racism, and Afro-American politics during the last fifteen to twenty years. This scholastic expansion in the scope and study of race and racism is undoubtedly worthy of celebration. Yet the conceptual influence of this expansive new body of literature on political science scholarship as a whole remains questionable, insofar as "race scholarship" has been frequently confined to a residual corner of the discipline.[8] Whereas an earlier generation of students of Afro-American politics confronted a pervasive and relatively explicit racial parochialism that defined the subject matter as inconsequential or relatively minor, contemporary scholars engaged in the study of race and racism or Afro-American politics are at least recognized as engaging in a valid field of study. Nevertheless, this recently validated subfield of study remains pigeonholed, incapable of generating conceptual insights or theories that demand incorporation or contestation within other subfields of political science. This compartmentalization has hindered the development of political science as an intellectually cosmopolitan enterprise.[9]

During the last twenty-five years, students of race and racism or Afro-American politics have attained appointments in many leading political science departments. The political science departments of Harvard, Yale, the University of Chicago, the University of Michigan, Duke, Columbia, the University of Virginia, the University of Southern California, Princeton, the University of Illinois, Washington University in St. Louis, Northwestern, Stanford, and the University of California, Los Angeles, have all been home to scholars whose primary research and teaching focus centered around the study of the Afro-American political experience. Though indicative of progress, these appointments should not be cause for celebration. It might be shocking to discover that the same individual scholar was the only scholarly presence in Afro-American politics within several of the different departments listed above, through moving from one high-status institution to another. In far too many instances, those scholars of American race and racism or Afro-American politics found that their host departments considered one scholar in this area sufficient for the department's entire course and research offerings. As such, it has been rare to have several scholars of race and racism or Afro-American politics present in the same department at the same time. Incredibly, there are still political science departments at major universities that have not recognized Afro-American politics as a fundamental component of their curriculum. Somewhat related to this dismal record is the horrendous fact that many departments of political science have never been racially integrated. Moreover, those departments that have hired a black scholar during the past twenty-five years have usually been more than content to hire only one. In American academic political science, the era of Jackie Robinson is still with us. The ramifications of the racially parochial hiring practices of political science departments dovetail with the racist devaluation of the scholarly study of Afro-American politics. In both instances, black bodies and the subjectivities that they embody are deemed inconsequential.

Note the 1990 roundtable discussion, "The Nature of Contemporary Political Science," which was published in *PS*.[10] It was obvious that all of the participants in the discussion were white. I will quote Benjamin Barber at length.

> The central question for political science as a discipline concerns not the nature of our discipline's "core" but how and why it continues to reflect the inequalities and disparities of power and influence found in the society we affect objectively to study. . . . If we look at the larger society rather than our own little society, it seems apparent that we are at once affected by its inequities without being moved to examine them critically. Why are there so few blacks, so few women, in the political science discussions we conduct on the themes of race and gender? Look around this room, and ask yourselves whether our subject matter is really as white and male as we are?. . . Perhaps the question we need to ask is whether we are a discipline or a club?[11]

While Barber's statement is sufficiently eloquent and to the point, one can only wonder why he continued to participate in a so-called public dialogue that was restricted to whites once he saw that it was restricted to whites? It is akin to claiming that one abhors segregation while dining at a whites-only restaurant. Moreover and more importantly, one wonders if Barber ever actively fought to substantively desegregate the political science department at Rutgers, the institution where he spent most of his academic career. Perhaps he had engaged in such a struggle, but experience has taught me and other blacks to be wary of whites who protest rhetorically against racial exclusion but find themselves repeatedly in whites-only environments.

While racial parochialism in the staffing of political science faculties remains an important issue, it is not a primary concern of this essay. Similarly, this essay will not chronicle the discipline's historical devaluation of scholarship pertaining to Afro-Americans. Instead, I intend to confront some of the theoretical and conceptual problems that plague the burgeoning scholarship on race and racism and Afro-American politics.

One of the central problems in the discipline of political science as it pertains to the study of American race relations is that political science has paid little attention to theory in Afro-American politics. Throughout its history, political science as a collective project has invested very little intellectual energy in conceptualizing the meaning of race and racism—or for that matter, the meaning of blackness and whiteness within American society and politics. Too often one confronts scholarly texts in the area of Afro-American politics that assume the political behavior of black Americans is sufficiently self-evident that theory would only get in the way of understanding. The utter weakness of political science in conceptualizing black politics and the meaning of race and racism within American society has been simultaneously a cause and a result of the marginality of a critical interpretive approach to the study of politics.[12] But first we must trace some of the historical origins of the problematic status of the study of Afro-American politics within the discipline of political science.

Historical Marginalization of Afro-American Politics

During the first six decades of the twentieth century, too many political scientists believed that they had an implicit mandate to describe American politics as the politics of a functioning democracy. Rarely questioning whether the United States is democratic, these scholars sought increasingly novel ways of valorizing the workings of the very thing they assumed, American democracy.[13] Of the social sciences, political science, along with economics, has been the most committed to ideological defenses of the United States' social order. Nowhere can the theoretical costs of the capitulation of political science to hegemonic American ideologies be seen more clearly than in political scientists' track record on the study of Afro-Americans or white racism. Had the condition of black Americans been taken seriously by scholars working in American political science, the entire edifice of the discipline would have had to be rethought, reformulated, and revised. Instead, during the first six or seven decades of the twentieth century, most American political scientists writing about the United States chose to ignore the situation of blacks. This omission was true for both empirical studies of American politics (i.e., urban politics) and thematic discussions of American political thought. Even a great deal of normative theorizing about the good society did not take into account the problem of a resilient white anti-black racism.

How do we explain the discipline's astounding conformity to the dominant ideological discourses, including racism, prior to the civil rights movement? Perhaps the answer lies in the many ways that the cold war influenced the discipline. Among the social sciences, political science may have been the discipline most saturated by the ideological currents of the cold war.[14] In assuming the responsibility of scholastically legitimating the United States and its western European allies as beacons of light against the totalitarianism of the Soviet Union, China, and the Eastern European communist bloc, American political science became intellectually and morally compromised by its willingness to serve the raw interests of American power.[15] During the cold war, most American students of political development or modernization presupposed that the ideal end game of progress for third world societies lay in approximating social orders that looked a great deal like those of the United States or western Europe.[16] Gabriel Almond and Sidney Verba's *The Civic Culture*, a highly influential study of comparative political development, was premised on American society as the unstated but ever-present ideal type.[17] An idealized version of American society was the normative standard for the theories of modernization or political development that proliferated in political science for almost twenty-five years. Within this ideal type, there was little room for a discussion of white supremacy as practiced in the United States.

One does not have to engage in conspiratorial thinking to grasp the reasons behind the willingness of the discipline of political science to align itself with the superpower interests of the American state in the aftermath of World War II.[18] First, there was a great deal of research funding that led to collusion between the American state and American political science researchers. The Carnegie Corporation, which funded the research behind Almond and Verba's *Civic Culture*, "worked very closely with national security agencies in the 1940s and 1950s."[19] By the 1950s, Harvard University's Russian Research Center, as well as other area studies research centers on that campus, were directly tied to Central Intelligence Agency (CIA) funding.[20] The historian Bruce Cumings notes that during this period, the Carnegie, Rockefeller and Ford Foundations not only worked with the state to fund projects but in some cases actually laundered CIA funding for "scholarly" research.[21]

Second, American political scientists in their roles as citizens of the United States were subjected to a pervasive form of national socialization that valorized the United States as the primary beacon of light in a world poisoned by the rise and expansion of totalitarianism. Unsurprisingly, pro-American biases infiltrated their scholarly work. By the late 1950s and mid-1960s, the United States was in competition with the Soviet Union for the allegiances of the third world. Not only was American political science as a discipline involved in projecting the United States as a normative ideal for the emerging third world, but American political science was committed to devising ways to regulate and steer the newly independent countries of the world into alignment with—read: subservience to— the interests of the United States. "*The Civic Culture* and, more generally, the 'political culture' approach of which the book became a leading classic can be seen as the culmination of a trajectory of preoccupation with winning and controlling the minds of people. It was a trajectory in which political science scholarship and the politics of national security shaded into and fed each other, beginning with the issue of civilian morale during World War I, through research on 'civic training' and 'propaganda' in the 1920s and 1930s, through renewed concern with morale and propaganda during World War II and the early Cold War, leading to the issue of winning the minds of the peoples of the emerging nations."[22]

Winning the minds of third world peoples might have been important to American foreign policy planners, but one should not assume that their ambitions towards third world countries necessarily rested on the benign support of democracy for indigenous populations.[23] The United States was not involved in a competition with the Soviet Union merely for the hearts and minds of newly independent nations. The United States was in need of information about societies and regions of the world that were seen as essential to the nation's economic expansion.[24] The proper political information could facilitate control, and departments of political science attempted to provide that knowledge. Ellen Herman writes, "It was partly because of the blueprint it offered for engineering political change in the third world—a primary concern of much U.S. foreign and military policy—that the political culture perspective became a dominant one by the mid-1960s."[25] Much like area studies and international relations, the study of American politics after World War II within academic American political science was saturated with cold war ideologies.[26]

It was during this period that pluralism became the dominant paradigm to describe and interpret American domestic politics. Furthermore, within political science, pluralism became the ubiquitous normative ideal for American society, an ideal that made American-style democracy the prototype for the developing world. Though it probably cannot be proven that the cold war sensibilities in this country led to the creation of pluralism, it can be argued that pluralism successfully played a propagandistic role during the cold war. Commenting on the interrelationship between the cold war and the pluralism of Robert Dahl, Douglas Rae, a Yale political scientist, stated that Dahl's *Preface to a Democratic Theory* and *Who Governs?*, two foundational texts of pluralism within American political science, "portrayed capitalist democracy in a favorable light and gave it a little theoretical apparatus which discriminated nicely between this system and other systems with which we as a nation were in rivalrous relations. His intuitions corresponded closely to those of national political elites and I think that had something to do with the Cold War and with Bob's fleshing out of a kind of open society story."[27] In *Our Enemies and Us*, Oren states: "The significance of the classic studies of American politics published in the 1950s, most notably David Truman's *The Governmental Process* and Robert Dahl's *A Preface to Democratic Theory*, derived in large part from their unqualified acceptance of interest-group pluralism as a normative thesis."[28]

Pluralism in political science became entangled in the "end of ideology" intellectual movement that arose during the mid- to late 1950s.[29] The end of ideology movement captured the allegiances of centrists and liberal Western intellectuals, as it centered around the belief that the American or European versions of welfare state capitalism had resolved all fundamental ideological conflicts in modern society. As a result, the "isms," whether the left (Communism and socialism) or the right (Fascism) had supposedly become obsolete. Seymour Martin Lipset, an advocate of the end of ideology, could state that "the fundamental problems of the industrial revolution have been solved: the workers have achieved industrial and political citizenship; the conservatives have accepted the welfare state."[30] The influence of the end of ideology movement on pluralism meant that the latter would be grounded in a belief that only minor reforms were necessary for the smooth functioning of American democracy. In many respects, the affiliation between the end of ideology movement and pluralism in political science resembled the alliance between the end of ideology movement and consensus historiography within American academic history.[31]

Pluralism succeeded in silencing many of the most pervasive conflicts and problems within American society. Racism was no exception. In his classic pluralist text of 1956, *Preface to Democratic Theory*, Dahl could write "the full assimilation of Negroes into the normal system already has occurred in many northern states and now seems to be slowly taking place even in the South."[32] That Dahl could write such nonsense in 1956 indicates a phenomenal ignorance of American racial realities. I suspect, however, that Dahl was not ignorant of such matters but instead chose to be conspicuously dishonest about the American racial problem—dishonest in the service of maintaining the continuity of his theory. In discussing David Truman's pluralist classic, *The Governmental Process*, Ira Katznelson notes that Truman not only virtually ignored racism in American society but alluded to the emerging civil rights movement in the South only to express his fears that Southern blacks, in seeking to change "the rules of the game," threatened the political stability of the American democratic system.[33] Katznelson states, "For Truman and his colleagues it followed implicitly . . . that it is far better for the excluded to remain apolitical than challenge the dirty secrets of the regime. Their fear of mass politics and political disorder had become integral to their anti-totalitarian program. Their theories treated disruption and protest as standing outside the normal process of legitimate political participation."[34]

The impact of the cold war on American political science was particularly devastating to the study of race and racism in American politics.[35] The ubiquity and resilience of American racism brought into doubt two of American social science's most sacred cold war cows: 1) *that modern societies like the United States are no longer significantly influenced by ascriptive allegiances; and 2) that the United States is a pluralist society.*

If there was any single public issue that should have generated skepticism about the supposed decline of ascriptive behaviors in so-called modern societies, it was the pervasiveness and resilience of racism in American life. After all, modernization theory presupposed that traditional societies are premised on ascriptive status for groups and individuals, while modernity rests on rational group and individual status. Racism is presumably a premodern trait, but it is one that exists in the most modern of societies. During the 1950s and early 1960s, an era of intense international competition with the Soviet Union, the viciousness and resilience of white American anti-black racism became highly embarrassing to the United States government as it tried to convince colored peoples throughout the colonized and recently decolonized worlds of the good intentions of the United States.[36] Serious analyses of white anti-black racism could not buttress the image of American egalitarianism that the superpower of the free world wanted to disseminate throughout the world. For the most part, political science as a discipline complied with this national ideological objective.

Contemporary Conceptual Pitfalls in the Study of Afro-American Politics

The historical distortions of the race problem that stemmed from the American academy's desires to be of service to the national state during the cold war are no longer necessary. At some point during the decolonization of Africa, the American government realized that it could not successfully hide its domestic race problem. The international coverage given to the civil rights movement undermined that strategy. Moreover, it became apparent that newly independent African countries were far more invested in obtaining United States foreign aid than in criticizing America's domestic racial politics. In order to appear attractive to the recently decolonized states of the world, the United States no longer needed to project itself as the normative society. As a result, scholarship depicting America's race problem was no longer deemed embarrassing or antithetical to the international interests of the United States.

The historical devaluation of Afro-American politics as a subject worthy of study is no longer the norm within the discipline. Yet the mere presence of a large quantity of scholarly literature does not in and of itself signal the maturation of this subfield. Now that it is considered a valid arena of study, students of the politics of race, racism, and Afro-American politics must engage in the torturous task of conceptual and theoretical development. One of the crucial steps on this journey is to question many of the assumptions about the nature of politics that linger from the period when Afro-American politics was deemed a marginal arena of study. It is undoubtedly a highly subjective enterprise to list the conceptual pitfalls that have been retained from this earlier moment in contemporary political science. The conceptual problems that I believe must be confronted are undoubtedly a reflection of my particular scholarly interests. Furthermore, I do not claim that the conceptual problems that I discuss constitute a novel grouping. Other scholars have certainly engaged in this reflective enterprise. Yet I believe that my list is worthy of serious consideration.

This essay highlights six problematic arenas that need to be rethought and reconceptualized in order to make the study of Afro-American politics a more reflective and informative enterprise:

1. nonexistent theorization of black subjugation or white domination;
2. an overly narrow conceptualization of " political";
3. fetishization of electoral politics;
4. reification of blacks and race in general;
5. refusal to discuss blacks as subjugators; and
6. discussion of blacks only as parentheticals.

Nonexistent Theorization of Black Subjugation and White Domination

One of the most striking weaknesses in American political scientists' approach to the study of race and racism in American politics and Afro-American politics lies in the under-conceptualization or lack of theorization of the racial subjugation of black Americans. Conceptualizing Afro-American subjugation and white domination is an extraordinarily difficult enterprise but one that must be undertaken. For instance, in what ways did white anti-black racism impact the economic, social, and political opportunities of black people? In what ways did this racism grant a privileged status to whites within the economic, social, and political arenas? How did white anti-black racism impact the psychological makeup of whites and blacks in a given locale during specific periods of history?

In order to construct a viable thick description of black racial subjugation one must take into account historical changes in American society and the ways in which those changes have determined race relations during a given period. For instance, Michael Dawson and Cathy Cohen have utilized the historical periodization of different racial orders created by the historian Thomas Holt.[37] In synopsizing Holt, Dawson and Cohen write:

> Holt divides the history of the United States into three periods, each characterized by a modal organization of the nation's political economy. Fairly typically, he divides U.S. history into three modal periods: pre-Fordist, Fordist, and post-Fordist. During the pre-Fordist period, slavery and its immediate aftermath, marked by Reconstruction, forged the dynamics and structural logic of the racial order. Jim Crow racism, where blacks were partly integrated into the bottom of the industrial economy but were neither full participants in either the polity or civil society, predominated during most of the Fordist era. It was during this era that Holt identifies organized industrial manufacturing as the central dynamic motor and organizing principle within the economy. A much more complicated racial dynamic has evolved alongside the service and high-tech centered economy of the post-Fordist era.[38]

A different periodization of American racial orders was provided by Joel Kovel in his pathbreaking study, *White Racism: A Psychohistory*.[39] Kovel divides American racism into three types, each of which was dominant during different historical moments. *Dominative racism*, the first distinctive phase of American racism, was premised on the direct domination of blacks. Its ideal form in the United States was slavery, a form of domination premised on the objectification and commodification of black bodies. Unlike dominative racism, *aversive racism* was premised on distancing whites from degraded and immoral black bodies. As the predominant form of racism in the North (while dominative racism was the pre-eminent form in the antebellum South), aversive racism gave rise to racial seg-regation. In some respects, it constituted racial "progress" over dominative racism. The third form of racism, *metaracism*, is the hegemonic form of racism in con-temporary America. It is a form of racism that does not depend on active white hatred of blacks but on white acceptance of the bureaucratic rationalizations and logics of modern society that systematically produce and reproduce black infe-riority. Kovel argues that these three types of racial domination can be pres-ent at any given time, so that in many respects his periodization is more fluid than Holt's.

Whether or not one finds the Holt or Kovel periodizations compelling is of little concern. What is significant is that some type of historical contextualiza-tion is necessary in order to discuss the situation of Afro-American politics with any degree of rigor or sophistication. In addition, the student of Afro-American politics must be able to discuss and analyze differences in the treatment of blacks that have been determined by the particular socioeconomic histories of different geographical regions in the United States. The scholar must also be able to dis-cuss the ways in which alterations in the national economic order have affected race relations, as well as the ways that regional differences in economic structure have affected blacks and whites. Finally, the student of Afro-American politics should consider the ways that gender, class, and social status intersect with and reinforce or subvert black racial subordination.

One major roadblock to the development of sophisticated conceptualizations of black subjugation is the lingering traces of behaviorism in American political science, as well as contemporary attempts to reinvigorate a scientific political sci-ence. It is not clear that the contemporary vogue in political science of utilizing survey data to explore beliefs and preferences can decipher the complex realities of the *weltanschauung* of blacks or whites in a racist society. What has been miss-ing within the study of Afro-American politics is an analysis and discussion of Afro-Americans akin to what Frantz Fanon and Albert Memmi attempted to do for the colonized of the world.[40] In the absence of such a discussion, black Amer-icans are usually depicted as possessing the same subjectivities as white Americans, though with fewer material resources and confronting more barriers to political agency. But, I ask, were there not costs to blacks of being dominated that have influenced and perhaps distorted their views of the world and life's possibilities? Did different forms of white domination affect blacks differently? And what effect did white domination have on the mentalities of whites of varying classes? Are there still psychosocial and cultural costs to racial subjugation for contemporary blacks? To address these questions one must utilize a fluid notion of black subju-gation that allows for historical contexts, social contexts, class differences, and gender differences. This is no easy task, but until it is completed, a major under-conceptualized elephant lingers in the room.

One example of the absence of theorization of black subjugation is V. O. Key's *Southern Politics in State and Nation*.[41] Many people consider *Southern Poli-tics* a classic study of American politics and one of the most influential political science books ever written. While Key has been essential reading for generations of students trying to understand the uniqueness of Southern politics, the book suffers from numerous conceptual shortcomings. First, at no point in the book does Key offer an adequate description of the subjugation of black Americans within the South. Consider the following inadequate definition of white supremacy offered by Key. "' White supremacy' is a watchword of no exact meaning. Broadly it includes the practice of residential segregation, the custom of social separation, the admonition of sexual isolation, the reality of economic subordination, and the habit of adherence to the caste etiquette of black deference toward white. When applied to politics white supremacy in its more extreme formulation simply means that no Negro should vote"[42]

The power and brutality of white Southern anti-black racism is completely omitted from Key's definition of white supremacy. There is no reference to coercion or the threat of coercion in Key's description of the subservient behavior of Southern blacks towards Southern whites. Moreover, Key's thoroughly faulty description of white supremacy is also somewhat disingenuous. After all, the most extreme formulation of white supremacy in the arena of Southern politics remained the lynch mob, not the disenfranchisement of blacks. Without a sophisticated notion of black subjugation, Key writes as if the primary articulation of white racist behavior focused on keeping blacks out of the voting booths. This is utterly simplistic.

One can read *Southern Politics* and never know that there was a full-scale authoritarian subsystem in the American South centered around the domination of black Americans.[43] Astonishingly, Key stated: "Yet, it is far from the truth to paint a picture of southern politics as being chiefly concerned with the maintenance of white supremacy of white over black. The dominance is an outcome, but the observer must look more closely to determine which white and which black gives southern politics its individuality."[44] Key spends a great deal of time arguing that those black belt counties in the South, the counties with the highest percentage of black residents, were the counties in which the whites were most mobilized in support of white supremacy. He asserts that this mobilization stemmed from a fear of blacks getting the vote and voting as a racial bloc. This assertion seems completely naive. Might it not have been the case that larger numbers of blacks being forced to live under dehumanizing conditions led to a level of white paranoia about acts of rebellion and thus the need for white social control of the Negroes?

While minimizing black voting participation was a goal of Southern white elites—as well as of many common Southern white folk—the issue of racially circumscribed voting rights cannot be divorced from the totality of the social existence of blacks in the white supremacist South. After all, within white supremacist logic, the primary function of blacks in the South between the 1880s and the 1940s was to serve as low-wage laborers in white households and white-owned agricultural fields. The exploitation of black agriculture workers lay at the center of the Southern economic order. The vicious legal and civil repression to which blacks were subjected in the South was linked to the need to keep these people working for very low wages and very long hours in the fields. One could argue that the lack of legal rights and decent schooling for blacks were also a function of the economic role assigned to blacks in the South. Disenfranchisement was but one facet of an entire social system predicated on maintaining white supremacy. The quest to maintain black disenfranchisement could never explain why the white South endorsed such brutal normalities as dehumanizing prisons like Mississippi's Parchman Prison;[45] the neo-slave-like vagrancy laws; the hyper-exploitative system of convict lease labor;[46] or the existence of peonage.[47]

In *An American Dilemma*, which was published in 1944, Gunnar Myrdal commented on the threats of wanton violence that all Negroes had to face in the South. He wrote: "It is the custom in the South to permit whites to resort to violence and threats of violence against the life, personal security, property and freedom of movement of Negroes. . . . There is a wide variety of behavior, ranging from a mild admonition to murder, which the white man may exercise to control Negroes. . . . Any white man can strike or beat a Negro, steal or destroy his property, cheat him in a transaction and even take his life without much fear of legal reprisal."[48] But in *Southern Politics*, which was published a mere six years after *An American Dilemma*, Key ignores the social, cultural, and structural reinforcements of black subjugation and writes as if black Southerners follow orders from whites merely out of a tradition of always having done so. Key writes: "A basic principle of the social system is that the black man does what the white man says. This ingrained habit undoubtedly gives the Negro vote (not so much as it is, but as it might be on a larger scale) a high degree of organizability which would probably be more marked in rural rather than in urban communities. The problem of transforming the Negro's habit of obedience into a capacity for independent and responsible exercise of the suffrage appears far simpler when viewed from Boston than when seen from Atlanta."[49]

Why would Key construct a thoroughly vacuous narrative about the reasons behind black acceptance of and adherence to the racial status quo in the South? As a white Southerner, he had experienced the nature of institutionalized white supremacy. As a scholar, he certainly had access to scholarship that could have given him insight into the authoritarian repression of black Southerners. He must have known of Hortense Powdermaker's *After Freedom*, John Dollard's *Caste and Class in a Southern Town*, Allison Davis's *Deep South,* and even Myrdal's *An American Dilemma*.[50] How, for instance, could Key not recognize the importance of lynching or the threat of lynching in controlling Southern blacks?[51] Evidently, lynching was outside the purview of Key's understanding of politics. In regards to race, Key was concerned only about the role that blacks or the idea of blacks played in shaping the electoral behavior of white Southerners. Key was laboring under a conception of politics that was too narrow to take into account issues other than voting.

Without conceptualizations of black subjugation and a white supremacist authoritarian subsystem in the South, Key had no way of describing or examining the *weltanschauung* of racist Southern whites. Why and how were white Southerners invested in white supremacy? Had their anti-black racism distorted their lives in significant ways? Was racism a therapeutic balm utilized by whites to compensate for some other injury? Unlike Key, contemporary scholars of race and racism in Southern politics have at least arrived at the point at which blacks are no longer treated as mere objects of white attitudes and behaviors. Yet the absence of a thorough conceptual analysis of black subjugation remains endemic to the scholarly literature on Southern politics and, for that matter, most political science literature on the politics of Afro-Americans.[52]

One possibility that might enrich the study of Afro-American politics—and I assume there are numerous others—in regard to conceptualizing subjugation can be found in the co-authored work of the political psychologists Jim Sidanius and Felicia Pratto. Sidanius and Pratto have devised a fertile theoretical framework on subjugation. Attempting to construct a cross-national theory of intergroup conflict and group oppression, Sidanius and Pratto have formulated what they call *social dominance theory*.[53] Although I cannot offer a abridgement of their theory in this paper, I will outline some of the major conceptual components of social dominance theory. I warn the reader that the theory is sufficiently nuanced to warrant a full reading of their textual exposition.

Social dominance theory (SDT) assumes that all societies "tend to be structured as systems of group-based social hierarchies."[54] Group-based social hierarchy, unlike individual-based social hierarchy, "refers to that social power, prestige, and privilege that an individual possesses by virtue of his or her ascribed membership in a particular socially constructed group such as a race, religion, clan, tribe, lineage, linguistic/ethnic group, or social class."[55] In complex social systems, individual-based and group-based hierarchies will not be completely divorced from each other. The authors then assert that there are three generic systems of group stratification. The first is an age stratification system, in which adults have power over children and adolescents. The second is a gender stratification system, in which men have more social and political power than women. The third and final grouping is called an arbitrary-set system, which can account for hierarchies based on clan, ethnicity, nation, race, caste, religion, social class or any other imagined socially relevant group distinctions. Age- and gender-based systems of stratification have at times been very brutal; however, the authors state that the arbitrary-set system of group hierarchies has been by far associated with the greatest degree of violence, brutality, and oppression. While age and gender systems of social hierarchy appear to have been present in all human societies, arbitrary-set hierarchies seem to arise only in those societies that produce economic surplus.[56]

Social dominance theory is premised on three assumptions. 1) Although age and gender hierarchies exist in all societies, those social systems that produce sustainable economic surpluses will give rise to arbitrary-set hierarchies; 2) Most forms of group conflict and oppression are manifestations of the human predisposition to form group-based social hierarchies. Consequently, prejudice, racism, and discrimination cannot be understood outside the conceptual framework of group-based social hierarchy; and 3) "Human social systems are subject to the counterbalancing influences of hierarchy-enhancing forces, producing and maintaining ever higher levels of group-based social inequality, and hierarchy-attenuating forces, producing greater levels of group-based social equality."[57]

The authors believe that group-based social hierarchies are driven by three practices: *aggregated individual discrimination; aggregated institutional discrimination; and behavioral asymmetry.* Aggregated individual discrimination refers to such individual acts of discrimination as the refusal of a store manager to hire a Latino worker because he is Latino. Aggregated institutional discrimination refers to the rules and procedures of various social institutions (e.g., schools, churches, lending institutions, courts) that produce and reproduce the subordination of one group or the dominance of another. Institutional discrimination may be conspicuous or inadvertent. Aggregated institutional discrimination also includes *systematic terror*, the systematic use of violence or threats of violence against subordinates. There are three types of systematic terror: 1) *official terror*: the public and legally sanctioned violence carried out by organs of the state and directed against subordinate groups; 2) *semiofficial terror*: violence directed against subordinates by officials of the state but which are not publicly, overtly, or legally sanctioned by the state; and 3) *unofficial terror*: violence perpetrated by private individuals of dominant groups against subordinates. Examples of the third form include the lynching of black Americans by white mobs. Behavioral asymmetry refers to the differences "in the behavioral repertoires of individuals belonging to groups at different levels of the social power continuum . . . these behavioral differences will both contribute to and be reinforced by the group-based hierarchical relationships within the social system."[58] The concept of behavioral asymmetry allows the researcher to confront the ways that subjugated people participate in the reproduction of their own subjugation. While there are many other aspects of social dominance theory, I offer this brief glimpse of the theory only to suggest that it potentially offers one mechanism for dynamically situating Afro-American political behavior and thought within broader analytical contexts

Another potentially rich source for conceptualizing aspects of black American subjugation can be found in the work of James C. Scott.[59] Scott, a political scientist who has integrated ethnography and anthropological theories into his analyses of political domination, has enriched the study of dominated groups via interrogations of the "internalized" lives of the subjugated. Scott argues that subjugated peoples create internalized discourses that are hidden from their subjugators but keep alive, at least in their own minds, an affirmative sense of themselves as valid and valuable human beings. In addition, Scott notes how these intra-subjugated, publicly muted discourses constitute "hidden transcripts" that contain repressed but existent oppositional beliefs. In some respects, Scott wanted to understand how subjugated peoples could appear at one moment to be completely acquiescent to the dominant order and yet "suddenly" engage in revolts against that status quo. For students of Afro-American politics, Scott's discussion compels us to devise research strategies that uncover these hidden transcripts among black Americans. Perhaps a more complex question centers around the political functions of hidden transcripts. While hidden transcripts might keep alive rebellious energies, they can also provide the subjugated with a psychological balm that allows them to more easily tolerate their subjugation. In most instances, the subjugator is not concerned with the internalized beliefs of the subjugated provided that these beliefs do not lead to insubordination. Hidden transcripts may simultaneously embody oppositional energies and acquiescence.

In utilizing the theories of Sidanius and Pratto or those of James C. Scott, students of Afro-American politics may be able to situate black political behavior and thought within a macrotheoretical framework that allows for multivariate analyses. In effect, such theories allow researchers to recognize that the "normalized" political behavior of blacks (such as voting or running for office) may be only one facet of an entire web of black political behaviors, some of which are not recognizable through the normalized channels of political inclusion and exclusion.

Narrow Conceptualization of the Political

The political science scholarship on Afro-American politics has been afflicted with a narrow conceptualization of " political." American political science has been caught in a cul-de-sac of viewing black political agency through a lens that presumes the political behavior of whites as not only normative but inherently rational. Historically, American social science has tended to label black social and political behavior as pathological whenever it does not correspond to the behavior of whites. Ironically, the practice of white supremacy has rarely been labeled as an expression of pathology among American whites. Within political science, the mere fact that white Americans go to the polls to elect senators insinuates that blacks should also go to the polls to elect senators. In granting rationality to similar behaviors on the part of whites and blacks in voting for senators, political scientists may conceal differences in the degree to which each group is represented or feels that they are substantively represented by their senators. Given the myriad historical ways that the votes of blacks have been compartmentalized as being those of a "special interest group" or utterly ignored, nonvoting blacks may be acting in a manner that is quite rational and quite different from that of nonvoting whites. The point here is that rationality should not be invested in the behavior of whites because of their whiteness. Nor for that matter, should rationality be invested in the behavior of the subjugators merely because they occupy a higher rank in the American social hierarchy. It would be akin to making male behavior normative in regards to women simply because men occupy a superior sociopolitical status to that of women in our sexist society. At times, whites can be and have been irrational political actors. To view black mimicry of whites as an indication of black political maturation is to reproduce ideological deference to whiteness.

The issue before students of Afro-American politics is that a narrow conception of the political precludes the possibility that there are forms of political engagement employed by the subjugated that do not mirror the forms of political engagement embraced by the subjugator. As previously mentioned, the work of James Scott on hidden transcripts might be fruitfully employed in discovering some alternative notions of political engagement for black Americans.

Numerous scholars now argue that the American political system is less of a democracy than an oligarchy.[60] Right now voting may be one of the least efficacious ways to influence national policies. If this is true, scholars who focus primarily on elections may be guilty of embodying an instrumental rationality that valorizes procedures over substantive self-government. As the dominant corporate infra-structure becomes increasingly free to act without government regulation, fewer and fewer issues of importance are even brought before the electorate for con-sideration. Issues brought before the broader polity by the corporate media are often commodified into trivial sound bites and sensationalized controversies that prohibit reflective engagement. As such, enlightened discourse and debate, a pre-requisite for a democratic society, are increasingly relegated to the fringes of American society. The mere fact that black voters are now able to elect black can-didates who also utilize the mind-numbing practices of Madison Avenue-style campaigns does not by itself contest the decreasing space for democratic self-governance in the United States.

This is not a call to discard all analyses of black participation in established political processes of political inclusion. After all, the differential exclusion of blacks from participating in established American political processes is one major way of assessing the degree and scope of black subjugation. Moreover, the estab-lished political channels of voting and running for office are not only the primary way that the average American citizen of any race articulates political agency but also the primary nexus through which public policy is influenced by the mass pub-lic, however ineffectually.

The emergence of a black electorate in the South following the civil rights movement denoted a significant racial change in American society. The exclu-sion of blacks from participation in the political process in the South during the first half of the twentieth century, however, when coupled with the inability of political science as an academic discipline to conceptualize politics in terms broader than merely voting or running for office, helps to explain why academic American political science (with a few exceptions) has produced such a sparse and uneven literature on black politics in the South before the civil rights era. In the absence of voting data, American political science has been and contin-ues to caught in a vise in which black Southerners appeared to be without a pol-itics or political agency of any type.[61] American historians have produced a scholarly literature concerning black political life in the pre–civil rights South that is far richer than the scholarly literature produced by political science stu-dents of the American South. Foremost, historians have intricately analyzed the white Southern domination of black Southerners. Historians of the South were not burdened with a conception of the political that began and ended with vot-ing. Compare Key's *Southern Politics*, which was published in 1950, with C. Vann Woodward's *The Origins of the New South, 1877–1913*, which was published in 1951.[62] Woodward does not pretend that the primary aim of the highly developed socio-politico-economic system of white supremacy in the South was to under-mine black voting strength.

Scholarly evidence suggests that there is significant mass black political oppo-sition to the status quo of American society that cannot be gauged through stud-ies of election returns.[63] Given the mirror imaging of the dominant two-party system, black oppositional political beliefs are either squashed or channeled into a far tamer electoral consensus. Students of Afro-American politics need to devise analytical strategies to capture black political identities and sensibilities that have no outlet through established political channels. Any analysis of black political beliefs that is premised upon interpreting black political preferences after they have been funneled into an "acceptable" consensus or coalition runs the risk of silencing black oppositional convictions. While the willingness of many black Americans to engage in consensus politics is worthy of study, it is also important to research those popular beliefs held by many blacks that are discarded or devalued in the consensus-making process.

Another mistaken assumption governing a great deal of scholarship on Afro-American politics is that black elected officials are by definition the representative embodiments of the oppositional energies of black voters. Some of this misperception stems from the racial reification that is so prevalent in political science scholarship—a phenomenon that I will discuss shortly.

The problem of a narrow conceptualization of "the political" can also be seen in the numerous studies that construct urban elections and city governance as discrete entities defined solely by geographical boundaries. Just how many studies can be written on the elections of black mayors? While some of these studies are engaging and raise significant issues, the mere election of a black mayor after a city has attained a majority or near-majority black electorate may be of negligible scholarly value in and of itself. Perhaps the more important questions have to do with the impact of the administrations of these black mayors on life in these cities. Have black mayors made a significant difference in the lives of those blacks who voted for them? As scholars, we cannot presume an affirmative answer.

For instance, the city of Hartford, Connecticut, recently elected its first Puerto Rican mayor. Admittedly, it might be a worthy scholarly enterprise to study the ways in which this candidate succeeded in attracting the votes of blacks, who constitute a larger percentage of the city's population and electorate than Puerto Ricans. But what is the significance of such an election? Any mayor of Hartford is probably destined to fail when trying to develop the city economically. The two black mayors in Hartford's recent past were not able to stimulate the city's economy. Many of the reasons for Hartford's economic decline stem from policies generated at the state level. The state of Connecticut has pursued policies that have economically crippled the city. Foremost was the decision to allow the building of several large suburban shopping malls just outside the Hartford city limits. These malls signaled the death knell for Hartford's downtown, which is now a ghost town. It may well be the case that no city with a population smaller than Washington, DC, can absorb the economic drain of suburban malls. Hartford has only 130,000 residents. Moreover, during the 1950s the state of Connecticut eliminated its counties as legal and governmental jurisdictions. Thus there is no mechanism in place for Hartford to share resources with its wealthy suburbs. The same can be said for two other impoverished Connecticut cities, New Haven and Bridgeport. The latter is located in Fairfield County, one of the nation's richest counties in terms of per capita income. In effect, the most important decisions affecting Hartford are not made by Hartford's elected officials. Variations on this phenomenon are at work in urban areas throughout the United States.[64] Yet students of Afro-American urban politics continue to treat any and all urban elections involving black candidates as if they are tremendously significant events, even in instances when they matter little to the life chances of the people residing in the specific city. Why do we participate in this charade?

It might well be the case that many students of Afro-American politics are too enamored of the mere presence of black elected officials. For some of us, black mayors and city council officials are still novelties. We remember the days when there were few if any black mayors of big cities. As a result, we become analytically captivated by what we think of as a celebration of American democracy for the downtrodden. In valorizing the mere election of a black official, however, many students of urban Afro-American politics often fail to discuss the declining significance of urban electoral offices.

This narrow construct of "the political" becomes even more glaring in this era of globalization of the work force and industry. Decisions fundamentally altering the lives of urban residents are increasingly made in corporate boardrooms by persons who have no allegiances to the city. One might plausibly conclude that the study of Afro-American politics in cities should forego the typical focus on urban electoral returns in behalf of analyses of corporations and the political ramifications of their policies. In the case of Hartford, one cannot really discuss the declining economic fortunes of the city without addressing the departure of large sectors of the insurance industry. Now that some insurance companies have scaled down their operations in Hartford and others have moved elsewhere, the imminent threat of relocation by those remaining insurance companies casts an unacknowledged veto power over any attempt of the city to extract more tax revenues from them.

A similar process was at work in Gary, Indiana, during the 1960s and 1970s.[65] Yet too many scholars write as if the 1967 election of Richard Hatcher as Gary's first black mayor constituted the defining political moment for Gary's black citizenry. Had scholars been less celebratory of the election of one of the nation's first black mayors, they might have foreseen that Hatcher would not be able to reverse the economic decline of Gary. Though some scholars now blame the lack of an economic revival on Hatcher, I do not think that any mayor could have succeeded in revitalizing Gary.[66] The issues dictating Gary's decline were beyond the authority of the mayor's office.

Though political scientists need to broaden our understanding of the political, I do not believe that all novel discussions of political engagement are of equal value. Borrowing from the work of the political scientist James C. Scott, some cultural historians and many scholars in cultural studies have broadened the concept of oppositional political agency to include any and all acts that appear to either affirm the lives of the subjugated or register opposition to the homogenizing tendencies of a white-dominated society. Supposedly, there is a great deal of black opposition to the present social order that is articulated through dress styles, music (such as rap), and other forms of popular culture. These cultural acts of opposition are presumed to be the Afro-American embodiments of what Scott referred to as hidden transcripts. I for one think that these scholars have bastardized Scott's concept by extending it too far, but that is a debate for another essay. What is significant is that according to these scholars, the black community is brimming with political agency, albeit disjointed and ineffectual. But as a political scientist interested in questions of power, I must always question the form that such agency appropriates. When these energies are not or cannot be channeled into forms of protest that are potentially efficacious, the energies are wasted. Besides, the belief that political opposition can be registered via one's consumption habits (e.g., wearing Nike tennis shoes) or tastes in hair styles, strikes me as somewhat absurd and utterly naive. The capitalist economy does not care if we all dress up like Fidel Castro in fatigues as long as we are buying the outfits—which, ironically, may well be made in sweatshops in China. Also troubling is the idea that a mass populace acting as solitary agents (consumers) can engage in political opposition that sidesteps the need for collective action. Dialectically, it seems just as likely that this cultural studies notion of political agency could be describing a consumerist balm that functions as a form of vicarious opposition, thus further insulating the political status quo from challenge.

Extending our conceptualization of "the political" will allow us to better address Afro-American subjugation; black opposition to the status quo that takes unorthodox forms; and the limitations of the American political system in regard to democratic self-governance. It will also compel us to better integrate the economic, the global, and the psychological into our understanding of politics.

Fetishization of Voting

The literature of Afro-American urban politics often suffers from the absence of a serious discussion of local, national, and international economic structures. The same criticism can be leveled against most contemporary discussions of American national electoral politics within political science. One can easily document the fact that many of the most significant decisions affecting the lives of Americans do not now come before the electorate, if they ever did. Hegemonic American ideologies do not consider "private" corporate decisions such as the decision to relocate a plant to Mexico as constituting public political acts. Political scientists need not, in fact, should not, let hegemonic ideological rhetorics determine the ways in which we conceptualize the issue of factory relocation. We cannot adopt the rationales and rhetorics of the state and then use those rationales to analyze state policies.

Though hegemonic ideologies also construct the American political system as reasonable and responsible, this construction should not dictate our perceptions. After all, during the worst moments of white supremacy in the United States, the dominant ideologies in the society at large, as well as those within the discipline of political science, viewed the American political order as reasonable and rational.

When voting is discussed and analyzed without contextualizing the declining scope and influence of the body politic over political decisions, voting is divorced from its supposed original intent—democratic self-governance. In such instances, voting has become fetishized. It behooves students of Afro-American politics not to continue to participate in the myth that the United States is fundamentally a democratic nation except in regard to blacks and a few "others." Such claims erroneously assume that the United States is democratic in regard to white folks. Furthermore, the phrase "except in regard to blacks" constitutes a parenthesis that essentially erases blacks from the American political landscape. In other words, if it is not true in regard to blacks, than it cannot be true of America.

Putting aside that myth, one might well regard voting as more often a ritual of democratic inclusion than a substantive articulation of it. If that is true, then voting becomes the means by which the populace is symbolically wedded to the prevailing political order. For the black electorate, a black mayor often becomes the symbol through which they feel included in the social order. That same black mayor can also function as a therapeutic mechanism through which the black populace becomes attached to antagonistic public policy outcomes. Consider the case of Maynard Jackson, the first black mayor of Atlanta. During his first term in office, Mayor Jackson fired two thousand sanitation workers who had gone out on strike. The overwhelming majority of these fired workers were Afro-Americans, but there was little protest from the residents of Atlanta.[67] Might it not have been the case that Mayor Jackson was able to get away with such a repressive political act because of the symbolic investment of black Atlantans in his blackness? Had a white mayor fired the striking sanitation workers, there might well have been a great deal of black public protest against what would undoubtedly have been framed as a racist act. Contrary to the assumptions made by numerous scholars of Afro-American politics, black elected officials may simultaneously retard and stimulate black empowerment. Moreover, they may do both either intentionally or unintentionally.

But what does it mean when blacks vote? Do blacks vote with the same expectations of political efficacy as white voters? Do black voters view the American political system as theirs to the same degree that white American voters claim ownership of the political system? If in the minds of blacks, the act of voting means something quite different from the act of voting for whites, then one could conclude from a phenomenological perspective that voting for blacks is a fundamentally different act from voting for whites, even though they look like similar behaviors. It is akin to Geertz's discussion of the need to create a cultural context in order to decipher the difference between an eye wink and an eye blink.[68] Once again, I wonder: is it rational to utilize the same criteria for assessing the political behavior of both the subjugated and the subjugator, given the significantly different opportunity structures in which they act politically? Though somewhat rhetorical, this question is an important one.

For the sake of argument, let us for a moment pretend that we have entered the realm of black electoral nirvana. In this fictitious world, the number of black elected officials is equal to the number of blacks in the represented population. In such a world, the Connecticut state legislature will have as many black members as the percentage of blacks in the state. The same holds true in other states. Blacks will occupy city council seats in Connecticut towns and cities in proportion to their populations in those towns and cities. The same holds true for all cities and towns throughout the United States. Finally, the United

States Congress will have as many black members as the percentage of blacks in the national population. That might equal fifteen black United States Senators and between seventy and eighty members of the House of Representatives.

Under such conditions a political scientist might reasonably assume that the black mass public would obtain a greater share of public policy resources from their local, state, and federal governments. But our assumption might be premature without first assessing the condition and structure of the national economy as well as the hegemonic ideologies. Because of the economic order and the configurations of the contemporary capitalist state, the number of black elected officials might have very little influence on the scope and outcome of decisions made within the supposedly "private" economic arena. For instance, would proportional black representation provide more public control over private corporations? Would the election of numerous blacks to office indicate a more rational political arena—that is, one governed less by Madison Avenue campaigns? I think not!

In our present electoral configuration, white Americans as whites are clearly over represented in our national and state legislative bodies. All but two or three members of the United States Senate are white Americans. Questions beg to be asked. Can we deduce from this that the white mass public is substantively represented in these legislative bodies? Do these numbers mean that the American political system is democratic for white voters? Do whites feel democratically empowered simply because the overwhelming majority of our political leaders are also white? Perhaps, but not necessarily so. Polls continue to indicate a reduced sense of political efficacy among middle-class whites even though the overwhelming majority of American elected officials are white. One could also surmise, however, that white middle-class perceptions of political efficacy would decrease dramatically if the majority of those individuals occupying positions of political power in America were nonwhite. Racial similarity with one's elected officials is an insufficient gauge by which to assess substantive representation, but it cannot be dismissed entirely. Too many students of Afro-American politics continue to treat the shared racial identity of a black elected official and her majority black constituency as constituting necessary and sufficient proof of substantive representation.

Reification of Race

One of the major conceptual problems that haunts the study of race and racism as well as Afro-American politics lies in the frequent reification of race. For our purposes reification will be defined as: "The act (or result of the act) of transforming human properties, relations and actions into properties, relations and actions of man-produced things which have become independent (and which are imagined as originally independent) of man and govern his life. Also transformation of human beings into thing-like beings which do not behave in a human way but according to the laws of the thing-world. Reification is a 'special' case of alienation, its most radical and widespread form characteristic of modern capitalist society."[69]

Race—or better yet, our investment in racial identity—assigns to individuals who possess certain qualities an identity that is deemed similar to others who possess those same qualities. What may need explanation is why human beings in the United States and other parts of the world have such an investment in racial identities. Of course, much of the answer to this question will lie in the ways that racial identities have been used to create hierarchies in various societies. Some people embrace racial identities because certain identities grant them privileged existences. For those whose racial identities function as social stigmas, they may be embraced because of a sense of historical memory and pride that goes with those identities. Needless to say, it is not even clear that most individuals believe that they have the power to choose to embrace or not embrace a racial identity. It is also not clear that they have such power, given that one's racial identity may rest on physical characteristics as determined and evaluated by persons and social processes outside the individual's control. In effect, racial identity may be socially determined. The point remains, however, that racial identity is invented and controlled by human beings as they interact with other human beings.

In the case of the study of Afro-American politics, black racial identity is often reified into something akin to an object—known henceforth as American blackness—which is possessed by all those deemed black. In this sense, racial identity, though a reification, is predicated on an essentialist logic. Take a worst-case scenario for example. Suppose one reads an article in which the authors state that certain blacks voted for Candidates X and Y but opposed Candidate Z because Candidates X and Y were black and Candidate Z was white. In effect, a characteristic that itself demands interrogation is now employed to explain other behavior. Unless it could be proven that all blacks would have voted for Candidates X and Y but not Z, it seems rather difficult to explain this voting behavior by referencing racial identities. After all, how would we explain the voting behavior of a person who chose Z over X and Y and yet claimed to be black? Did she vote for Z because she is black? Or did she vote for Z despite the fact that she is black? And who determines just how a true and authentic black would have voted?

Most contemporary students of race relations or Afro-American politics do not reify blacks in such a blatant manner, but some do. Frequently, political scientists embrace milder forms of race reification. Take, for example, an important scholarly work, *Black Presidential Politics in America: A Strategic Approach*, written by Ronald W. Walters, a well-known Afro-American political scientist. Though Walters offers some perceptive comments on the behavior of the majority of black voters during recent presidential elections, racial reification of blacks runs throughout the book. There is an unstated but ever-present assumption throughout the book that there is a definable black political interest. Now it is certainly true that poll data have consistently shown that a majority of blacks favors liberal welfare-state government interventions as opposed to, say, Reagan small-government conservatism. It is not clear, however, that support for these positions constitutes support for a "black agenda." After all, how do we label those blacks who hold views opposed to the welfare-state liberalism supported by most black voters? Are such people advocates of a less-black agenda or even a white agenda? Can whites support and embrace a black agenda?

The willingness of Walters to reify black people into an objectified entity called *blacks*—the black vote, the black political agenda, and similar expressions—is evident throughout his study. Take, for instance, Walters's discussion of a phenomenon he calls "black political integration": "Thus, we proceed beyond an analysis of registration and voting strategies in this chapter in an effort to both describe and analyze the political behavior of Blacks within the Democratic party as they have attempted to establish a beach-head which could lead to sustained power."[70] An initial reading of the foregoing might not generate any controversy insofar as most American political scientists and most Americans in general are used to reifying racial identities. The blacks that Walters refers to as striving to create a beachhead in the Democratic Party are individual black political elites (or groups of black political elites) working within the Democratic Party hierarchy. Walters assumes, however, that the black political elites who bargain within the Democratic Party are the organic embodiments of the blacks who have registered and voted. He presumes that these black individuals have the interests of the majority of blacks in mind whenever they act and whatever they do. Whence comes the claim that the inclusion of black political elites within the leadership of the Democratic Party will ipso facto represent the broader interests of all blacks, if there is such an entity as the common interests of all blacks? Worse, and more importantly, why does Walters write as if all blacks participate in this back-room bargaining merely because some blacks are present?

Walters is guilty of utilizing within his study the same rhetoric and myths invoked by the very black political elites that he is supposedly analyzing. These black political elites utilize the imagery of a staid and reified black community to stimulate their political mobility within predominantly white elite political circles. Black political figures have become quite skillful at marketing themselves as ipso facto representatives of a black mass public even if they have no direct ties to that public. Who, for instance, was organically embodied by an un elected power broker in the Democratic Party like Ron Brown? Though his racial identity remained constant, did his represented constituency change when he evolved from a bargainer for Jesse Jackson's primary candidacy to the position of chairman of the Democratic National Committee?

Adolph Reed criticizes the reification of blacks in commenting on the distortions invoked by the term "black community": "This idea of community is a mystification, however, and an anti-democratic one at that. All social units are comprised of discrete individuals whose perspectives and interests and alliances differ, and every unit's members are bound together through a combination of negotiation and coercion."[71] The imagery of the aroused or dormant black horde (depending on political needs) that lies beneath a great deal of the rhetoric of black politicians concerning "black America" is frequently hidden, according to Reed, because it often emerges within a protest discourse directed against oppression. But Reed further perceptively comments: "Because whites by and large don't see black Americans as a complex population of differentiated individuals, the organic community imagery seems reasonable and natural to them. . . . Within black politics, of course, hustlers of one sort or another, high-toned and low, have always been willing to exploit that fundamentally racist mind-set, usually by giving whites with resources authentic-sounding doses of what they want to hear."[72]

Utilizing Reed's insight, one could argue that black voter support for Jesse Jackson's Democratic primary bids in 1984 and 1988 constituted a coalition. *But who ever writes as if the so-called black vote constitutes a coalition in and of itself?* Many recent studies of black political incorporation are premised on this racial reification of blacks. Why, for example, would the emergence of a cadre of black political elites in a specific town or city signal the political incorporation of all those people who share a racial identity with these elites? Did the election of David Dinkins as Mayor of New York City mean that blacks were now incorporated in New York City politics, as if Dinkins issued referenda to all blacks in New York before he made a decision? Those who choose not to differentiate blacks beyond race also ignore differences within the black population based on sexual preference, religion, class, gender, status and ideology . Many examples of racial reification are benign, but they point to a broader problem that must be addressed.

There were numerous examples of racial reification in the articles concerning minority political incorporation that were collected in *Racial Politics in American Cities*.[73] Rufus P. Browning, Dale Rogers Marshall, and David H. Tabb, the editors *of Racial Politics*, were also the authors of *Protest is Not Enough*, one of the most influential studies of race and urban politics written during the last twenty-five years.[74] In *Racial Politics in American Cities*, Browning and his colleagues asked other urban scholars to utilize their ideas about political incorporation presented in *Protest Is Not Enough* in an examination of the plight of blacks and Latinos in other cities. An article on minority mobilization in ten northern Californian cities states: "Blacks in Oakland might have been able to form an alliance with Latinos and liberal whites and take control of city government years before they did, but they were badly split."[75]

When do blacks as a collectivity "take control of city government"? But of course, when a black individual is the mayor! Certainly racial reification is a common phenomenon in American politics. Whites tend to think that they can be represented only by a white person. Blacks tend to think that a black person will automatically represent them better than a white person. What becomes problematic is when we as political scientists reproduce within our analyses the very thing that we are studying.

One can see racial reification at work in many of the studies of what is termed "deracialized" black politicians. A deracialized black political figure is one who runs for office utilizing a platform and political style that supposedly minimizes his identification with black people. Usually he or she is running for office within a predominantly white electorate. Examples of this phenomenon include the two unsuccessful campaigns for a seat in the United States Senate run by Harvey Gantt in North Carolina; the successful gubernatorial campaign of Doug Wilder in Virginia; the five mayoral campaigns of Tom Bradley in Los Angeles, four of which he won; and the senatorial campaigns of Carole Moseley-Braun in Illinois, one of which she won. In the case of Wilder, or for that matter Edward Brooke of Massachusetts, they ran as blacks who were "unlike other" black politicians. It was not so much that they tried to appear "race-less"—whatever that might mean—but that they appeared to not have any special ethnic affinity for blacks. In some ways they accepted a stereotyped image of the black politician and did everything in their power to act as if that racial image had nothing to do with them as individual candidates. This is why it became so important for them to do something that indicated difference and distance from the image of the black community.

Unlike other black politicians, Edward Brooke would be a post–New Deal Republican. Brooke essentially would "sit out" the entire busing crisis in Boston. He did not want to be seen as too closely identified with the pro-integration forces, nor did he want to intensify the existing racial acrimony of the anti-busing forces.

Wilder ran for governor of Virginia on a platform of fiscal conservatism and law-and-order, two issues not normally associated with black candidates. In addition, he conspicuously divorced himself from the idea and image of Jesse Jackson, the preeminent national figure of black protest.

Brooke and Wilder ran as "exceptional blacks," not as nonblacks. As exceptional blacks, their campaigns rested on being seen as unlike other black candidates. They reinforced stereotypes of black politicians by acting as if the stereotyped images are valid for other black politicians but invalid for themselves. Because of their unstated but ever-present willingness to shadow racial stereotypes and thus keep them alive, it remains uncertain whether the electoral successes of Brooke and Wilder created an expansive opportunity structure for future black candidacies in the psyches of whites.

Using this faulty logic, one could conclude just the opposite: within black electoral politics, those campaigns for office that appear most deracialized occur when two blacks challenge each other within a predominantly black electorate. In such instances, the significance of blackness for either candidate is reduced because it is universalized. It would be erroneous to conclude from this, however, that two blacks running for office in a predominantly black jurisdiction remove race as a factor in the election, provided that *a black racial identity is an unstated prerequisite for winning the election*. Similarly, the exclusion of black voters and black candidates from Southern electorates during the pre–civil rights era did not remove race as an issue in Southern elections, insofar as whiteness remained an unquestionable prerequisite for winning and holding elected office.

Clearly some racial groups in American society are more reified than others. A blatant case of this phenomenon is the willingness of many scholars to assign blacks a racial identity without making a similar assignment to whites. If I were attending a political science conference and announced that I am researching racial politics in America, many if not most of the listeners would assume that I am a student of the political behavior of blacks or other nonwhites. In fact, I could well be studying the political behavior of white New Englanders. In a similar vein, many commentators have little trouble saying that Clarence Thomas occupies the "black seat" on the Supreme Court. How many of them would subsequently say that other seats on the Supreme Court are "white seats"? It is far more respectable to claim that Thomas was appointed because he is black than to claim that David Souter or Sandra Day O'Connor were appointed because they are white. *But once one black person was appointed to the Supreme Court, whiteness became one of the criteria for the appointment of the other justices*.

Nevertheless, the issue of racial reification is not easy to dismiss in the world of *Real politik* . When the President makes appointments to the cabinet, the federal bench, and regulatory commissions, even I believe that he or she should take racial diversity into account. Seeing diverse faces in positions of power not only helps to create a public perception that we are all Americans but also makes historically underrepresented peoples feel increasingly included. What is more, people of diverse racial and ethnic backgrounds should have access to such appointments. Having said this, I recognize that the reasons such appointments make diverse groups of people feel included lie within the mystifications of reification. Though the authentic representation of diverse peoples can only exist when procedures are in place to ensure representative accountability, in the absence of authentic representation, we are stuck with reification. As political scientists, however, we must begin to address the interrelationships among race, reification, and political representation.

Refusal to Discuss Blacks as Subjugators

Students of Afro-American politics are most comfortable with analytical and moral depictions of Afro-Americans as an oppressed people. While it is true that racial domination has been the defining characteristic of Afro-American life since the founding of the nation, it is also true that black Americans have on occasion occupied social positions other than that of subjugated. Among the most understudied phenomena in Afro-American politics are those beliefs and practices of blacks that are oppressive to others and to themselves. Given the history of Afro-Americans as one of the two most subjugated groups in American history, Native Americans being the other, students of Afro-American politics often invest an inherent moral quality in black political activities. Although the black American quest for political inclusion and political empowerment is worthy of support, the scholar of Afro-American politics must be vigilant against granting an ethical carte blanche to any and all forms of black political agency.

Take the issue of sexism in the black community. Why is sexism so understudied within the subject area of Afro-American politics? Sexism has been a devastating force in Afro-American life, for it systematically devalues and distorts the lives and talents of a large portion of the community. Throughout American history, all major Afro-American political and social institutions have embraced sexism and devalued black females. Is it surprising that the NAACP and the National Urban League have never had a black female president?[76] The so-called "black church" is even worse. Discrimination against women is openly practiced in most predominantly black denominations. The largest black Pentecostal group, the Church of God in Christ, does not ordain women as of the early 2000s. The overwhelming majority of black Baptist churches do not support the ordination of women. In those rare instances when black women have been ordained within the Baptist church, it is highly unlikely that they will ever become the senior pastor of a Baptist congregation—unless they break off and start a church of their own. In black Baptist churches, ordained women have been usually confined to positions of secondary authority and importance. These female leadership positions include the superintendent of the Sunday school and head minister for home and hospital visitations. The devaluation of black females is so intense in many black Pentecostal and Baptist churches that women are even not allowed to stand within the pulpit area.[77] The African Methodist Episcopal (AME) Church is not much better. Most ordained AME women will never serve as the senior pastor of a church. It is only within the last five years that the AME Church appointed its first female bishop. The African Methodist Episcopal Zion (AMEZ) Church has yet to have a black female bishop. Coincidentally, the predominantly white United Methodist Church (UMC) had and continues to have more black female bishops than the AME and AMEZ churches combined. The irony of the blatant sexism practiced in the black churches is that the majority of black church goers are females.[78]

Another subject that needs to be more intensively studied is the presence of homophobia within Afro-American communities. The issue of concern is not whether there is a unique form of homophobia among blacks, but rather the ways in which homophobia influences discourse and debate among blacks. For instance, numerous groups of blacks were mobilized during the summer of 2004 in support of a federal marriage amendment to the United States Constitution. This amendment would have limited the legal recognition of marriage to unions between one man and one woman. President Bush and numerous conservative Republicans in the House of Representatives and the Senate announced their support for this amendment. It soon became clear, however, that many conservatives were not eager to actually summon a constitutional convention, so despite their rhetoric, they did not support the amendment. The amendment failed to obtain the necessary number of votes.

The Reverend Walter Fauntroy, a Democrat and the former nonvoting delegate to Congress from Washington, DC, has been a key player in several of these black organizations opposed to same-sex marriage. Although Fauntroy is liberal on many social issues, he has joined forces with the utterly reactionary Sun Myung Moon, the founder and leader of the Unification Church and publisher of the *Washington Times* newspaper, in the effort to eliminate legal recognition of same-sex marriage. Moon has utilized his considerable financial resources to fund various black organizations that espouse conservative viewpoints. Through their shared homophobia, the white Right has coalesced with some black Christians and made new inroads into black America. Once again, large segments of the black church are in the forefront of trying to deny people (including other blacks) an equal status. As explicit advocates of homophobia, these black churches conspicuously devalue the lives of gays and lesbian s. One can only hope that the track record of the black church in the arenas of sexism and homophobia might finally put to rest those romantic depictions of the black church as a bearer of emancipatory values.

When discussing the issue of blacks acting in the guise of subjugators, we must also confront the class biases that exist within Afro-American politics. Do more affluent blacks actively support policies that are beneficial to the black poor? Are they favorably disposed to helping the white poor? Do they support these policies when there are costs to themselves? I have witnessed several instances when members of black middle-class communities mobilized to keep low-income housing from being built in their neighborhoods. In these instances, these black middle-class residents were acting in a manner similar to their white peers. But that is precisely my point. When affluent or middle-class blacks have the opportunity to make use of their class privileges, they often do so. In this regard, it would be informative to read a study about the response of black doctors and their National Medical Association to various national health care proposals. It would be interesting to discover if these doctors gave primacy to the needs of the uninsured or tried to protect their class privileges as doctors. It would be equally informative to see analyses of the black middle-class response to President Clinton's draconian policy towards welfare recipients. Did his reactionary attitudes toward welfare undermine his support among the black middle classes?

Numerous scholars have argued that the centrality of affirmative action as an issue championed by black political leaders is the result of a middle-class bias. These scholars argue that affirmative action is disproportionately beneficial to the black middle class. Furthermore, they claim that issues more pertinent to lower- and working-class blacks, such as the creation of living-wage jobs, public school improvement, and prison reform, are not given their rightful priority. While I contend that affirmative action as a public policy has had a beneficial impact on blacks in all social classes, I also maintain that the black middle class and stable working classes have benefited more from the policy than the black poor.

Political Theory and the Treatment of Blacks as Parentheticals

Political theory as a subfield of American political science has a rich history of normative theorizing about democracy in general and the American political experience in particular. Generations of American political philosophers and students of American political philosophy have tried to capture the governing dynamics or the core philosophical underpinnings of the American political experience. The founding documents of this nation, particularly the Declaration of Independence, the Articles of Confederation, the Constitution (with particular emphasis on the Bill of Rights), and the ancillary though utterly important *Federalist Papers*, have been the focal points of this reflective enterprise. Twentieth-century students of American political thought have often situated these founding documents within narratives that proclaim the new nation either a democracy or at least beholden to a democratic teleology. While some of these reconceptualizations of American political thought have been quite creative and provocative, many if not most of them have utterly marginalized the history of American slavery and white supremacy. The historical contradiction between this nation's founding commitment to freedom for whites (particularly white men) and its equal commitment to chattel slavery for blacks has created a tumultuous dilemma for all political theorists who desired to construct an overarching thematic discussion of American political values. Unfortunately, many students of American political thought crafted arguments that ignored this dilemma. Some chose to write books that simply ignored slavery as a major determinant of American political thought. Other scholars crafted works that considered slavery and other forms of white supremacy as minor aberrations in a democratic landscape.

The inability to confront slavery and white supremacy lies at the very center of Louis Hartz's classic work, *The Liberal Tradition in America: An Interpretation of American Political Thought since the Revolution*.[79] Insofar as the issue of slavery was not granted a centrality in Hartz's discussion of American political culture, he was a modern-day disciple of Alexis de Tocqueville.

De Tocqueville had argued that American ideals were premised on the egalitarian ideas and relatively equalized material conditions that existed when the country was founded. Although he viewed slavery as a doomed institution, he predicted that slavery's aftermath would give rise to heightened white hatred of blacks. He foresaw a growing racial conflict between whites and blacks that would ultimately culminate in a genocidal debasement of the black population.

Hartz provides a rather convoluted argument to support his thesis that American political ideals were fundamentally liberal. Following de Tocqueville, he argued that the absence of a history of feudalism with its rigid class structure gave rise to the rather free social conditions in the United States. Hartz was critical of what he viewed as the widely accepted consensus of matter-of-fact American liberalism. What bothered Hartz was that Americans championed a liberalism that was not forged out of conspicuous ideological struggles but appeared to be the only "natural" response to American social conditions.

Hartz recognized that the vehement forms of anti-black racism that were popularly held by whites during the antebellum period were not liberal in character. Yet he could not successfully reconcile slavery with the claim that Americans were seemingly "naturally" liberal. Instead, Hartz argued that this vehement racism was necessary "if slaveholders were to avoid embracing feudalism for all and 'keep democracy for whites.'"[80] Because white slaveholders desired to maintain democracy for themselves, Hartz viewed them as being committed to liberalism. Rogers M. Smith comments: "Hartz treated this desire as evidence of their commitment to democracy *among* whites, and so it is. But it is equally evidence of southern whites' insistence on confining democracy to *whites*, while they assigned to blacks statuses that should not have existed in a liberal democratic society."[81]

Even when Hartz confronted late nineteenth-century American white supremacist beliefs and practices, he concluded that these beliefs were "alien to the national liberal spirit" and had limited impact on American democratic ideals. Smith calls Hartz's evasion of the centrality of racism to American political ideals *grotesque*.[82] Reading *The Liberal Tradition*, the contemporary scholar perceives that Hartz was not going to allow his theory of American liberalism to be undone by the annoying existence of slavery and the persistence of white supremacist ideals and ideas. The historical treatment of blacks in the United States was not sufficiently momentous to compel Hartz to reformulate his argument—an argument that could be made only by excluding Afro-Americans from consideration.[83] Hartz's *The Liberal Tradition in America* embodies one of the central strategies employed by political philosophical commentators on American life. Blacks are treated as exceptions to the rule. Yet blacks constitute a unique kind of exception to the rule: they are an exception that does not have the authority to bring the rule into question. I refer to this tradition as the black-as-parenthetical tradition in American political thought.

Perhaps the most blatant example of the black-as-parenthetical tradition is Seymour Martin Lipset's *The First New Nation*. In the introduction to *The First New Nation*, Lipset wrote:

When I say that we value equality, I mean that we believe all persons must be given respect simply because they are human beings; we believe that the differences between high and low-status people reflect accidental, and perhaps temporary, variations in social relationships. This emphasis on equality was reflected in the introduction of universal suffrage in America long before it came in other nations; in the fairly consistent and extensive support for a public school system so that all might have a common educational background. . . .

> The value we have attributed to achievement is a corollary to our belief in equality. For people to be equal, they need a chance to become equal. Success, therefore, should be attainable by all, no matter what the accidents of birth, class, or race. . . .
>
> America's key values—equality and achievement—stem from our revolutionary origins. The United States was the first major colony successfully to revolt against colonial rule. In this sense, it was the first "new nation."[84]

At the very end of this study, Lipset includes an epilogue. There he states:

> American egalitarianism is, of course, for white men only. The treatment of the Negro makes a mockery of this value now as it has in the past. During the early nineteenth century, when European leftists and liberals were pointing to the United States as a nation which demonstrated the viability of equality and democracy, America was also the land of slavery. . . . The contradiction between the American value system and the way in which the Negro has been treated has, if anything, forced many Americans to think even more harshly of the Negro than they might if they lived in a more explicitly ascriptive culture. There is no justification in an egalitarian society to repress a group such as the Negroes unless they are defined as a congenitally inferior race.[85]

How is it that Lipset can state, without any sense of contradiction, that the treatment of black Americans by whites does not embody the values of equality and yet still proclaim equality as one of America's key values? Describing eighteenth- and nineteenth-century America as committed to egalitarianism is akin to describing Nazi Germany as an egalitarian political culture except for Jews. Ironically, in the above quotation, Lipset criticizes de Tocqueville for treating blacks as parentheticals in *Democracy in America* and yet Lipset's argument is an updated version of that same treatment.

The willingness of Hartz and Lipset to treat blacks as parentheticals may be seen by some observers as an advance over the writings of political theorists who simply ignored black subjugation as if it had never existed in America. Yet whether blacks are ignored entirely or treated as parentheticals, their racial devaluation is clear. Harley Fogg-Davis has written: "Many social scientists argue that models of white ethnic pluralism fail to capture the anomalous historical trajectory of black Americans. Instead of using this anomaly to rethink liberalism, many political theorists simply relegate African Americans to a footnote or overlook them altogether."[86] Although my examples of Hartz and Lipset may appear dated, these texts have retained their scholarly importance for many contemporary scholars. Besides, prominent contemporary political theorists are no strangers to the devaluation of blacks. Take the case of political philosopher Michael Walzer, a purported democratic socialist. In an infamous footnote to a discussion of "What it means to be an American," Walzer wrote: "A historical and empirical account of the place of blacks in the 'system' of American pluralism would require another essay, a different book."[87] Why, one wonders, did Walzer think it appropriate to except blacks from his discussion of "what it means to be American"? Moreover, why did he think that his mere mention of the erasure of blacks from the American landscape would render that exclusion acceptable? Evidently, Walzer assumed that the invocation of blacks-as-parentheticals was more intellectually compelling than merely ignoring their existence entirely. He must have known that he could have ignored blacks without receiving scholarly condemnation from most of his readers. This example speaks to the presumed acceptability of continuing to devalue blacks in American political theory.

Walzer's erasure of blacks from the American landscape would merely constitute a case of racial parochialism had the erasure not fundamentally distorted his entire discussion. After all, there is nothing more constitutive of being American than our racial identities; and racial identities in America are fundamentally centered around the presence of blacks. The entire edifice of whiteness, an edifice that undergirds the construction of American politics from the days of the Continental Congress through yesterday, is premised on being nonblack or non black-like. Upon this edifice of whiteness, generations of immigrants from diverse European nations became "Americanized." Given the centrality of blacks and the black historical experience to all aspects of American identity formation, the black-as-parenthetical arguments of Dahl, Hartz, Lipset, and Walzer are not only morally bankrupt but empirically shallow and analytically erroneous.

The time is ripe for students of political philosophy who have a decided interest in the Afro-American question (or students of Afro-American politics who have an interest in political philosophy) to construct arguments that place Afro-Americans in the foreground as *the paradigmatic case* for interrogating American political realities. Reading American political thought through the lens of Afro-American subjugation might generate radically enriched interpretations.

Afterword

Certainly, there are other conceptual problems that students of Afro-American politics must confront. If we take seriously the six issues discussed above, however, we will go a long way toward making the subfield far more conceptually sophisticated and analytically enriching. We may also be able to offer a beacon of light to a discipline that appears to be increasingly divorcing itself from the study of politics in the real world.

Notes

1. For a provocative discussion of the marginalization of the study of black politics within political science, see Ernest J. Wilson III, "Why Political Scientists Don't Study Black Politics, but Historians and Sociologists Do," *PS* 18, no. 3 (Summer 1985): 600–607.

2. The quote is from Paula D. McClain and John A. Garcia, "Expanding Disciplinary Boundaries: Black, Latino and Racial Minority Group Politics in Political Science," in *Political Science: The State of the Discipline*, 2nd ed., ed. Ada W. Finifter (Washington, DC: American Political Science Association, 1993), 247. Also see Matthew Holden Jr., *The Politics of the Black "Nation"* (New York: Chandler, 1973), 34.

3. Rogers M. Smith, "The Puzzling Place of Race in American Political Science," *PS* 37, no. 1 (January 2004): 43.

4. Ibid., 44.

5. See Michael C. Dawson and Ernest Wilson III, "Paradigms and Paradoxes: Political Science and African-American Politics," in *Political Science: Looking to the Future*, vol. 1, ed. William Crotty (Evanston, IL: Northwestern University Press, 1991); and Hanes Walton Jr., Cheryl M. Miller, and Joseph P. McCormick, II, "Race and Political Science: The Dual Traditions of Race Relations Politics and African-American Politics," in *Political Science in History: Research Programs and Political Traditions*, ed. James Farr, John Dryzek, and Stephen T. Leonard (New York: Cambridge University Press, 1995).

6. Elevation of the status of scholarship on race, racism, and Afro-American politics within political science has been most acute during the past fifteen years.

7. Between 1984 and 1993, only 1.5 percent of the articles published in the *American Political Science Review*, the *American Journal of Political Science*, *Comparative Politics*, *World Politics*, and the *British Journal of Political Science* unambiguously addressed issues of race or ethnicity. I think we can assume that topics of race and ethnicity offer a broader pool of potential articles than articles focused solely on Afro-American politics. Thus the number of articles on Afro-American politics must have been even smaller. See Rupert Taylor, "Political Science Encounters 'Race' and 'Ethnicity,'" *Ethnic and Racial Studies* 19 (1996): 891–92.

8. There have been three "state of the discipline" volumes commissioned by the American Political Science Association. Comparing the volumes issued in 1983 and 1993 with the most recent one in 2002, one finds clear evidence of the rising status of studies of race and racism within the discipline. The initial state of the discipline volume in 1983 did not contain a single full chapter devoted to a review of the literature on race and racism or Afro-American politics, although there was a short discussion of the intersection of race and political beliefs in Donald Kinder's chapter on "Diversity and Complexity in American Public Opinion." The 1993 state of the discipline volume contained a chapter on "Expanding Disciplinary Boundaries: Black, Latino and Racial Minority Group Politics in Political Science," written by Paula D. McClain and John A. Garcia. The most recent volume (2002) contains a comprehensive and perceptive discussion of the literature on race, racism, and Afro-American politics written by Michael C. Dawson and Cathy Cohen. In addition to the essay by Dawson and Cohen, the volume contains several other chapters in which issues pertaining to race and racism are discussed. The inclusion of a chapter on the literature concerning the politics of race in both the 1993 and 2002 volumes must be considered a major improvement over the silence on the issue in the 1983 volume. Yet there are numerous fields of study discussed in the 2002 volume in which race or racism is not mentioned or discussed to the extent it should have been. I still dream of the day when all fields of study within political science become cognizant of the ways that race and racism impact their arenas of study. When such a moment arrives, there may be less need for a separate chapter on the literature on race and racism.

9. For a thoughtful discussion of the limitations of political science in regards to studying Afro-American politics, see Walton, Miller, and McCormick, "Race and Political Science,"145–74.

10. Benjamin Barber, *PS* 23, no. 1 (March 1990): 34–44.

11. Barber, *PS* 23, no. 1 (March 1990): 40.

12. A discussion of a critical interpretive strategy for political science can be found in David M. Ricci, *The Tragedy of Political Science: Politics, Scholarship, and Democracy* (New Haven, CT: Yale University Press, 1984). One example of a critical interpretative strategy for the social sciences can be found in Bent Flyvbjerg, *Making Social Science Matter: Why Social Inquiry Fails and How It Can Succeed Again* (Cambridge: Cambridge University Press, 2001).

13. For a somewhat early but perceptive critique of the acquiescence of academic political science to the interests of the American status quo, including American participation in the Vietnam War, see Lewis Lipsitz, "Vulture, Mantis, and Seal: Proposals for Political Scientists," *Polity* 3, no. 1 (Fall 1970): 3–21.

14. For a thoughtful commentary on the impact of the cold war on American political science see Ido Oren, *Our Enemies and Us: America's Rivalries and the Making of Political Science* (Ithaca, NY: Cornell University Press, 2003).

15. Another major impact of the cold war on American political science was that the discipline never intellectually engaged the Marxist intellectual tradition. Simply put, within American political science, Marxism was erroneously seen as coterminous with Soviet Communism. Unlike their European colleagues, who often wrestled with questions and insights originating in Marxism, many American social scientists never understood that Communism and Marxism are not necessarily synonymous.

16. For a discussion of the impact of the cold war on modernization theory, see P. Preston, *Development Theory: An Introduction* (Oxford: Blackwell, 1996), particularly Chapter 9, "Decolonization, Cold War and the Construction of Modernization Theory," 153–78.

17. Gabriel A. Almond and Sidney Verba, *The Civic Culture: Political Attitudes and Democracy in Five Nations* (Princeton, NJ: Princeton University Press, 1963).

18. For a different view of the impact of the cold war on American political science, see S. M. Amadae, *Rationalizing Capitalist Democracy: The Cold War Origins of Rational Choice Liberalism* (Chicago: University of Chicago Press, 2003). Amadae argues that rational choice liberalism was a cornerstone of the American ideological front during the cold war.

19. Oren, *Our Enemies and Us*, 146.

20. See Sigmund Diamond's *Compromised Campus: The Collaboration of Universities with the Intelligence Community* (New York: Oxford University Press, 1992).

21. Bruce Cumings, "Boundary Displacement: Area Studies and International Studies during and after the Cold War," in *Universities and Empire: Money and Politics in the Social Sciences during the Cold War*, ed. Christopher Simpson (New York: New Press, 1998), 165.

22. Oren, *Our Enemies and Us*, 146.

23. See Irene L. Gendzier, *Managing Political Change: Social Scientists and the Third World* (Boulder, CO: Westview, 1985).

24. Irene L. Gendzier, "Play It Again, Sam: The Practice and Apology of Development," in *Universities and Empire: Money and Politics in the Social Sciences during the Cold War*, ed. Christopher Simpson (New York: New Press, 1998), 71.

25. Ellen Herman, *The Romance of American Psychology: Political Culture in the Age of Experts* (Berkeley: University of California Press, 1995), 145.

26. Immanuel Wallerstein provides an excellent discussion of the influence of cold war politics on the development of area studies within American academia. Political science was one of the core contributing disciplines to the growth of area studies. See Immanuel Wallerstein, "The Unintended Consequences of Cold War Area Studies," in *The Cold War and the University: Toward an Intellectual History of the Postwar Years* (New York: New Press, 1997), 195–231.

27. Richard M. Merelman, *Pluralism at Yale: The Culture of Political Science in America* (Madison: University of Wisconsin Press, 2003), 50–51.

28. Oren, *Our Enemies and Us*, 95.

29. Daniel Bell, ed., *The End of Ideology: On the Exhaustion of Political Ideas in the Fifties* (Boston: Free Press, 1960). For a contextualization of the movement, see Christopher Shannon, *A World Made Safe for Differences: Cold War Intellectuals and the Politics of Identity* (Lanham, MD: Rowman and Littlefield, 2001).

30. Seymour Martin Lipset, *Political Man: The Social Bases of Politics* (Garden City, NY: Doubleday, 1960), 406.

31. In regard to consensus historiography, see Peter Novick, *That Noble Dream: The "Objectivity Question" and the American Historical Profession* (Cambridge: Cambridge University Press, 1988), particularly Chapter 11, "A Convergent Culture."

32. Robert A. Dahl, *Preface to Democratic Theory* (Chicago: University of Chicago Press, 1956), 138–39.

33. Ira Katznelson, "The Subtle Politics of Developing Emergency: Political Science as Guardianship," in *The Cold War and the University: Toward an Intellectual History of the Postwar Years* (New York: New Press, 1997), 254.

34. Ibid., 255.

35. Some contemporary discussions of the historical development of American political science as a discipline continue to ignore the inability of political science and pluralism to deal with the "race question." Witness the virtual erasure of the issue of race and racism in John G. Gunnell's *Imagining the American Polity: Political Science and the Discourse of Democracy* (University Park: Pennsylvania State University Press, 2004). Given the centrality of racism in American life, Gunnell's omission of a discussion of it borders on the absurd.

36. A wonderful body of literature now exists that discusses the connection between domestic American racial politics and American foreign policy during the cold war. See Brenda Gayle Plummer, *Rising Wind: Black Americans and U.S. Foreign Affairs, 1935–1960* (Chapel Hill: University of North Carolina Press, 1996); Penny M. Von Eschen, *Race Against Empire: Black Americans and Anticolonialism, 1937–1945* (Ithaca, NY: Cornell University Press, 1997); Azza Salama Layton, *International Politics and Civil Rights Policies in the United States, 1941–1960* (New York: Cambridge University Press, 2000); Mary L. Dudziak, *Cold War Civil Rights: Race and the Image of American Democracy* (Princeton, NJ: Princeton University Press, 2000); Thomas Borstelmann, *The Cold War and the Color Line: American Race Relations in the Global Arena* (Cambridge, MA: Harvard University Press, 2001); James H. Meriwether, *Proudly We Can Be Africans: Black Americans and Africa, 1935–1961* (Chapel Hill: University of North Carolina Press, 2002); and Carol Anderson, *Eyes Off the Prize: The United Nations and the African American Struggle for Human Rights, 1944–1955* (New York: Cambridge University Press, 2003).

37. Thomas C. Holt, *The Problem of Race in the 21st Century* (Cambridge, MA: Harvard University Press, 2000).

38. Michael Dawson and Cathy Cohen, "Problems in the Study of the Politics of Race," in *Political Science: The State of the Discipline*, ed. Ira Katznelson and Helen V. Milner (New York: W. W. Norton, 2002), 492.

39. Joel Kovel, *White Racism: A Psychohistory* (New York: Columbia University Press, 1984).

40. I am particularly speaking of Fanon's *The Wretched of the Earth* (New York: Grove, 1963) and *Black Skin, White Masks* (New York: Grove, 1967); and Memmi's *The Colonizer and the Colonized* (Boston: Beacon, 1991) and *Dominated Man: Notes Toward a Portrait* (Boston: Beacon, 1968), among other works.

41. V.O. Key Jr., *Southern Politics in State and Nation* (New York: Alfred A. Knopf, 1950).

42. Ibid., 646.

43. Thirty years ago, Martin Kilson expressed unease with Key's *Southern Politics*. Kilson wrote: "Nowhere in this seminal work is it ever apparent that Key grasped the ultimate existential character of Southern politics: that underlying what he analyzed as the intricate modalities of balancing-off the one-party politics of the South with the competitive politics of the nation was a norm gap of great moral gravity. To treat this norm gap, as Key did, merely as an incidental variable is to contribute to the vulgarization of the pragmatic-consensus tradition in the American political culture and process." Martin L. Kilson, "Political Science and Afro-Americans: Normative Problems of American Politics," in *Teaching Political Science: The Professor and the Polity*, ed. Vernon Van Dyke (Atlantic Highlands, NJ: Humanities Press, 1977), 168.

44. Key, *Southern Politics*, 5.

45. David Oshinsky, *Worse Than Slavery: Parchman Farm and the Ordeal of Jim Crow Justice* (New York: Free Press, 1996).

46. Alex Lichtenstein, *Twice the Work of Free Labor: The Political Economy of Convict Labor in the New South* (New York: Verso, 1996).

47. Pete Daniel, *Shadow of Slavery: Peonage in the South, 1901–1969* (Urbana: University of Illinois Press, 1972).

48. Gunnar Myrdal, *An American Dilemma: The Negro Problem and Modern Democracy* (New York: Harper and Brothers, 1944), 558–59.

49. Key, *Southern Politics*, 655.

50. Hortense Powdermaker, *After Freedom: A Cultural Study in the Deep South* (New York: Viking, 1939); John Dollard, *Caste and Class in a Southern Town* (New Haven, CT: Yale University Press, 1937); Allison Davis, Burleigh B. Gardner, and Mary R. Gardner, *Deep South: A Social Anthropology of Caste and Class* (Chicago: University of Chicago Press, 1941). Note that Powdermaker and Dollard studied the same town in Mississippi.

51. For two contemporary discussions that highlight the centrality of lynching in the Southern racist authoritarian order, see Leon F. Litwack, *Trouble in Mind: Black Southerners in the Age of Jim Crow* (New York: Alfred A. Knopf, 1998), particularly Chapter 6, "Hellhounds"; and Philip Dray, *At the Hands of Persons Unknown: The Lynching of Black America* (New York: Random House, 2002).

52. For an insightful commentary on research pertaining to blacks in Southern politics, see Charles D. Hadley, "Blacks in Southern Politics: An Agenda for Research," *Journal of Politics* 56, no. 3 (August 1994): 585–600.

53. Jim Sidanius and Felicia Pratto, *Social Dominance: An Intergroup Theory of Social Hierarchy and Oppression* (Cambridge: Cambridge University Press, 1999).

54. Ibid., 31.

55. Ibid., 32.

56. Ibid., 36. It should be noted that Sidanius and Pratto have not created an "optimistic" theory, for they unequivocally assert that arbitrary-set hierarchies are quite stable (e.g., the Indian caste system, which has been around for at least three thousand years, or the four centuries of white supremacy in the United States).

57. Sidanius and Pratto, *Social Dominance*, 38.

58. Ibid., 43.

59. Among other works, see James C. Scott, *Weapons of the Weak: Everyday Forms of Peasant Resistance* (New Haven, CT: Yale University Press, 1985); and particularly *Domination and the Arts of Resistance: Hidden Transcripts* (New Haven, CT: Yale University Press, 1990).

60. See Robert Dahl, *On Political Equality* (New Haven, CT: Yale University Press 2006); Morris Berman, *Dark Ages America: The Final Phase of Empire* (New York: Norton, 2006); Kevin Phillips, *Wealth and Democracy: A Political History of the American Rich* (New York: Broadway, 2002); Michael Graetz and Ian Shapiro, *Death by a Thousand Cuts: The Fight over Taxing the Rich* (Princeton, NJ: Princeton University Press, 2005) and Cornel West, *Democracy Matters: Winning The Fight Against Imperialism* (New York: Penguin, 2005).

61. Commenting on Key's *Southern Politics*, Hanes Walton Jr. has written, "The basic flaw of the Key classic is its failure to treat systematically the political efforts and activities of Southern blacks." Hanes Walton Jr., "Black Southern Politics: The Influences of Bunche, Martin, and Key," in *Black Politics and Black Political Behavior: A Linkage Analysis*, ed. Hanes Walton Jr. (Westport, CT: Praeger, 1994), 34. Walton justifiably criticizes Key for ignoring black participation in the Agriculture Adjustment Act cotton and tobacco referenda that were held in rural counties to ascertain farmer support for various federal agricultural policies. Yet Walton, like Key, is guilty of utilizing a conception of politics that accentuates only voting patterns. Walton's complaint against Key is that Key did not take account of the limited voting opportunities presented to black Southerners. Walton does not, however, differ from Key in his narrow conceptualization of "the political."

62. C. Vann Woodward, *The Origins of the New South, 1877–1913* (Baton Rouge: Louisiana State University Press, 1951).

63. For an ambitious and discerning discussion of black oppositional beliefs, see Michael C. Dawson, *Black Visions: The Roots of Contemporary African-American Political Ideologies* (Chicago: University of Chicago Press, 2001).

64. One recent study that attempts to step outside the geographical borders of cities in order to conceptualize issues pertaining to cities is Peter Dreier, John Mollenkopf, and Todd Swanstrom,

Place Matters: Metropolitics for the Twenty-first Century (Lawrence: University Press of Kansas, 2001).

65. For a discussion of the declining economic fortunes of Gary, Indiana, linked to the decline of the U.S. Steel Company, see Edward Greer, *Big Steel: Black Politics and Corporate Power in Gary, Indiana* (New York: Monthly Review Press, 1979).

66. One scholar who puts the blame for Gary's economic failure on Hatcher is Jon C. Teaford. See Teaford's "'King Richard' Hatcher: Mayor of Gary," in *Journal of Negro History* 77, no. 3 (Summer 1992): 126–40.

67. Adolph Reed Jr., Class Notes: Posing as Politics and Other Thoughts on the American Scene (New York: New Press, 2000), 3.

68. Clifford Geertz, "Thick Description: Toward an Interpretive Theory of Culture," in *The Interpretation of Cultures*, by Clifford Geertz (New York: Basic Books, 1973), 3–30.

69. Tom Bottomore, ed., *A Dictionary of Marxist Thought* (Cambridge, MA: Harvard University Press, 1983), 411.

70. Ronald Walters, *Black Presidential Politics in America: A Strategic Approach* (Albany: State University of New York Press, 1988), 53.

71. Reed, *Class Notes*, 11.

72. Ibid., 11–12.

73. Rufus P. Browning, Dale Rogers Marshall, and David H. Tabb, eds., *Racial Politics in American Cities* (White Plains, NY: Longman, 1990).

74. Rufus P. Browning, Dale Rogers Marshall, and David H. Tabb, *Protest Is Not Enough: The Struggle of Blacks and Hispanics in Urban Politics* (Berkeley: University of California Press, 1984).

75. Browning, Marshall, and Tabb, *Racial Politics*, 19.

76. The NAACP had a black female chairman of the board in Myrlie Evers Williams.

77. For a discussion of some blatant forms of sexism present in the black church, see Traci C. West, "Religious Intellectuals, Social Change, and Women's Bodies," in Harold Cruse, *The Crisis of the Negro Intellectual Reconsidered*, ed. Jerry G. Watts, 203–21 (New York: Routledge, 2004).

78. For an informed discussion of the sexism present in black churches, see Fredrick C. Harris, *Something Within: Religion in African-American Political Activism* (New York: Oxford University Press, 1999), particularly Chapter 9. Harris's sound study could have been improved had he woven his discussion of sexism throughout his analysis of the black church and not confined it to its own separate chapter.

79. Louis Hartz, *The Liberal Tradition in America: An Interpretation of American Political Thought Since the Revolution* (New York: Harcourt, Brace and World, 1955).

80. Rogers M. Smith, "Beyond Tocqueville, Myrdal, and Hartz: The Multiple Traditions in America," *American Political Science Review* 87, no. 3 (September 1993): 554. For the extended version of Smith's "multiple traditions" argument, see his magisterial study, *Civic Ideals: Conflicting Visions of Citizenship in U.S. History* (New Haven, CT: Yale University Press, 1997).

81. Ibid., 554.

82. Ibid.

83. As mentioned earlier in this chapter, Robert Dahl similarly marginalizes blacks in his reconsideration of American political thought, *Preface to a Democratic Theory*.

84. Seymour Martin Lipset, *The First New Nation: The United States in Historical and Comparative Perspective* (Garden City, NY: Doubleday Anchor, 1967), 2.

85. Lipset, *First New Nation*, 379–80.

86. Hawley Fogg-Davis, "The Racial Retreat of Contemporary Political Theory," *Perspectives on Politics* 1, no. 3 (September 2003): 555–64.

87. Michael Walzer, *What It Means to Be an American: Essays on the American Experience* (New York: Marsilio, 1996), 44–45.

CONTRIBUTORS

LUCIUS J. BARKER is William Bennett Munro Professor Emeritus of Political Science at Stanford University. His publications include a number of books, articles, and essays; including co-author of a leading constitutional law textbook. His most recent publication is "Political Scientists as Gatekeepers: Overcoming Inequality in Our Own Backyard," in *Perspectives in Politics* (June 2005). Professor Barker retains an active career in research and writing, and is presently co-authoring with Kevin Lyles a biographical type study entitled *Taking on the System: Thurgood Marshall, Warrior for Justice.*

LORRIE A. FRASURE (PhD, University of Maryland–College Park) is a Postdoctoral Associate at Cornell University. Her fields of study include American politics and urban political economy, with specialties in immigrant and ethnic minority politics, suburbanization, urban politics, public policy, as well as research design and methods. She is working on a book manuscript examining post-1980 immigrant and ethnic minority migration patterns and suburban local governance. Frasure was a Ford Foundation Dissertation Fellow as well as a Southern Regional Education Board (SREB) Doctoral Scholar.

BARBARA L. GRAHAM (PhD, Washington University–St. Louis, 1984) is Associate Professor of Political Science at the University of Missouri–St. Louis. Graham's areas of research are in judicial politics and critical race theory. Her most recent publication is "Toward an Understanding of Judicial Diversity in American Courts" (2004). She is currently working on a manuscript on judicial selection and racial and ethnic diversity in federal and state courts.

MELISSA HARRIS-LACEWELL (PhD, Duke) is Associate Professor of Politics and African American Studies at Princeton University. She is author the award-winning book, *Barbershops, Bibles, and BET: Everyday Talk and Black Political Thought* (Princeton University Press, 2004). Her academic research has been published in scholarly journals and edited volumes and her interests include the study of African American political thought, black religious ideas and practice, and social and clinical psychology. She is at work on a new book, *For Colored Girls Who've Considered Politics When Being Strong Wasn't Enough.* It is an examination of the connections between shame, sadness, and strength in African American women's politics.

ERROL A. HENDERSON (PhD, University of Michigan) is Associate Professor of Political Science and African/African American Studies, Penn State University. His most recent book is *Democracy and War: The End of an Illusion.*

LENNEAL HENDERSON is currently Distinguished Professor of Government and Public Administration and a Senior Fellow in the William Donald Schaefer Center for Public Policy at the University of Baltimore, as well as the Daniel T. Blue Endowed Professor of Political Science at North Carolina Central University in Durham. He has edited *Black Political Life in the U.S., authored Administrative Advocacy: Black Administrators in Urban Bureaucracy,* and co-edited *Public Administration and Public Policy: A Minority Perspective* and *The New Black Politics: The Search for Political Power.* He is working on a forthcoming book on bureaucracy and developing nations.

GERMAINE A. HOSTON (PhD, Harvard University) is Professor of Chinese and Japanese Politics and Philosophy at University of California–San Diego. The author of numerous articles and several books on comparative Chinese and Japanese and European political philosophy and political economy (Princeton University Press), she has been Vice President of the American Political Science Association, Co-Chair of the North East Asia Council of the Association for Asian Studies, and Chair of the Competing Modernities in 20th Century Japan Conference Series. She is currently completing a comparative study of liberation theologies in East and West.

OLLIE A. JOHNSON III received his PhD from the University of California at Berkeley and now teaches Africana Studies at Wayne State University. He is the author of *Brazilian Party Politics and the Coup of 1964* and co-editor of *Black Political Organizations in the Post–Civil Rights Era.* He is currently researching *Black Politics in the United States and Latin America.*

VALERIE C. JOHNSON (PhD, University of Maryland–College Park, 1995) is Assistant Professor of Political Science at DePaul University and the author of *Black Power in the Suburbs: The Myth or Reality of African American Suburban Political Incorporation,* as well as numerous articles and book chapters.

VERNON D. JOHNSON (PhD, Washington State University, 1985) is Professor and Director of Graduate Studies in the Department of Political Science at Western Washington University. He has authored several scholarly and popular articles on issues ranging from revolution in Africa to race and identity in American politics. His two books are *The Structural Origins of Revolution in Africa* (Edwin

Mellen Press, 2003) and *Walkin' the Talk: An Introduction to African American Studies* (Prentice-Hall Publishers, 2002), edited with Bill Lyne.

MARTIN L. KILSON (PhD, Harvard University) is Frank G. Thomson Professor of Government (emeritus) at Harvard University. His publications include *Political Change in a West African State* (1966), *Apropos of Africa: American Negro Leadership Sentiments toward Africa, 1850s–1950s* (1969), *Key Issues in the Afro-American Experience* (1970), *New States in the Modern World* (1975), *The African Disapora: Interpretive Essays* (1976), and *The Making of Black Intellectuals: Studies on the African American Intelligentia* (2007).

KEVIN L. LYLES (PhD, Washington University–St. Louis, 1991) is Associate Professor of Political Science and Associate Professor of African American Studies at the University of Illinois–Chicago. His scholarship centers on constitutional law with a special focus on African American legal history. Lyles is author of *The Gatekeepers: Federal District Courts in the Political Process*, is co-author of a leading constitutional law textbook, and is presently co-authoring with Lucius Barker a biographical type study entitled *Taking on the System: Thurgood Marshall, Warrior for Justice*.

MARION ORR is Fred Lippitt Professor of Public Policy, Political Science, and Urban Studies at Brown University. He is the author of *Black Social Capital: The Politics of School Reform in Baltimore* and *The Color of School Reform: Race, Politics and the Challenge of Urban Education*.

WILBUR C. RICH (PhD, University of Illinois) is Professor of Political Science at Wellesley College. His most recent book is *David Dinkins and New York Politics: Race, Image and the Media*.

EVELYN M. SIMIEN (PhD, Purdue University) is Assistant Professor of Political Science at the University of Connecticut, where she teaches courses on black leadership and civil rights, as well as black feminist theory and politics. A nationally recognized teacher, she was awarded the 2006 Anna Julia Cooper Teacher of the Year Award from the National Conference of Black Political Scientists (NCOBPS). She is the author of *Black Feminist Voices in Politics* (State University of New York Press, 2006).

ANDREA Y. SIMPSON is Associate Professor of Political Science at the University of Richmond in Virginia. Her first book, *The Tie that Binds* (New York University Press, 1998), won the "Best Book of 1998 on Racial Identity" award from the Race, Ethnicity, and Politics section of the American Political Science Association. Her current project involves research on women activists in the environmental justice movement. In addition to several book chapters on environmental justice, a book manuscript on gender and social movements is forthcoming from Oxford University Press.

ROBERT C. SMITH (PhD, Howard University, 1976) is Professor of Political Science at San Francisco State University and the author most recently of the *Encyclopedia of African American Politics* (Facts on File, 2004).

KATHERINE TATE (PhD, University of Michigan) is Professor of Political Science at the University of California–Irvine, where she also holds a courtesy appointment in African American Studies. Tate is the author and co-author of several books, including most recently *Black Faces in the Mirror, African Americans and Their Representatives in the U.S. Congress* (Princeton University Press, 2003).

HANES WALTON JR. (PhD, Howard University, 1967) is Professor of Political Science at the University of Michigan and the author of the forthcoming *Remaking the Democratic Party: Lyndon B. Johnson as a Native Son Presidential Candidate*, the third in a series of southern native sons presidential candidates.

JERRY G. WATTS, political scientist, is Professor of English at the CUNY Graduate Center. He is a student of the politics of Afro-American intellectuals and has most recently edited Harold Cruse's *The Crisis of the Negro Intellectual Reconsidered* (Routledge, 2004).

KENNY J. WHITBY is Professor of Political Science, at the University of South Carolina where he specializes in the areas of legislative behavior, electoral and minority politics. He is the author of *The Color of Representation* (Ann Arbor: University of Michigan Press, 1997), and his published articles have appeared in political science journals such as *American Politics Research, British Journal of Political Science*, and *Journal of Politics*.

ERNEST J WILSON III is Professor in the Departments of Government and Politics and of African American Studies at the University of Maryland–College Park. Educated at Harvard and Berkeley, he has written on blacks and the energy crisis and blacks and the information revolution. He is the author of *Diversity and US Foreign Policy* (Routledge, 2004) and "Why Political Scientists Don't Study Black Politics, but Historians and Sociologists Do" (*PS*, Summer 1985).

INDEX

Aberbach, Joel, 110, 317
Abney, Glenn, 111
Abramson, Paul, 114
academic heavens, 46
Adelson, Marvin, 265
Afrodiaspora, 65
Alex-Assensoh, Yette, 212, 225
Alianza Estrategica, 56
Alice in Wonderland, 38
Allen v. State Board of Elections, 381
Almond, Gabriel,79, 80, 402
Alterman, Eric, 244
Altman, Andrew, 216
Amadiume, Ife, 97–98
American Council of Learned Society, 25
American Economic Review, 12
American Historical Review, 12, 22n7, 31n2
American Journal of Political Science, 12, 13, 18
American Journal of Sociology, 12
American National Election Study (ANES), 11, 122, 124
American Negro Academy, 189
American Political Science Association (APSA), 2, 21, 24, 25, 26, 28, 30
American Political Science Review (APSR), 11, 13, 14, 18, 28, 30, 308
American Sociological Review, 12
Amsden, Alice, 257
Anderson, Barbara, 1, 14
Anderson, Bendict, 95
Anderson, Carole, 320
Andrews, George, 55, 58
Annales School, 82
Annals of the American Academy of Political and Social Science, 181, 183

Annual Review of Political Science, 34
Appiah, Anthony, 274
Applebaum, Nancy, 55
Ard, Sheila, 37
Aroni, Samuel, 265
Augelli, Enrico, 88
Austin, Regina, 151
Aylward, Carol, 223

Banfield, Edward C., 312
Barber, Benjamin, 400
Barber, James David, 238
Barger, Harold, 237
Baritz, Loren, 38
Barker, Lucius, 10
Barnett, Majorie R., 201
Baron, Samuel, 270
Barr, Campbell, 72
Bates, Robert, 254
Beckwith, Karen, 138, 139
Befu, Harumi, 260
Bell, Derrick, 214–15, 219
Bellah, Robert, 266
Bello, Alvaro, 59
benign neglect, 233
Benokraitis, Nijole, 387
Black Cultures Research Center, 57
Black Women's House of Culture, 59
Bledsoe, Tim, 114
Blumer, Herbert, 366
Bobo, Lawrence, 10, 109, 366
Bone, Hugh, 312, 314
Boulding, Kenneth, 265
Bowen, William G., 22n5
Brady, Henry, 138, 139

Braudel, Fernand, 82
Brent, William, 71
Brooke, Nigel, 68
Brown, Cheryl, 263
Brown, Ronald, 112
Brown, Tony, 245
Brown v. Board of Education, 240, 288, 373, 375, 378
Browning, Rufus, 118
Bullock, Charles, 387
Bunche, Ralph, 32, 33, 169, 172, 177, 325, 398
Burdick, John, 60
Burman, Stephen, 233, 245
Burns, James McGregor, 37
Bush, George H. W., 110, 289
Bush, George W., 120, 206, 242, 288, 303, 386, 389, 390
Bush v. Gore, 374, 384

Cabral, Amilcar, 271
Cameron, Charles, 198, 202
Campbell, Angus, 139
Campbell, Barr, 72
Canon, David, 196, 199, 201, 203
Carbado, Devon, 83
Cardenas, Osvaldo, 62
Carr, E. H., 326
Carroll, Lewis, 38
Castaneda, Jorge, 55
Centeno, Miguel, 62
Champagne, Richard, 196
Chapman, Valeria, 207
Chatterjee, Partha, 84, 95–96
Chay, Jongshuk, 343
Cho, Sumi, 217
Chu, Yun-Han, 259
Civil Rights Act of 1964, 236
Civil Rights Act of 1991, 390
Claque, Monique, 44
Clawson, Roselea, 134, 137, 146
Clay, William, 201
Clemons, Eric W, 271
Clinton, Bill, 70, 110, 122, 235, 237, 239, 242, 245, 247, 249n38, 288–89, 291, 295, 299, 350, 358, 389, 390, 425
Cobban, Alfred, 275
Cohen, Cathy 9, 11, 19, 114, 117, 121, 151, 159 317, 319, 406
Collins, Patrica, 117
Combs, Michael, 114
Committee on Political Research, 29
Committee on Political Science, 34
Congressional Black Caucus, 195, 292
Conniff, Michael, 58

Cook, Samuel DuBois, 34
Corwin, Edwin, 368
Council for the Development of Social Science in Africa, 91
Cowater International, Inc., 57, 58, 59
Cox, Oliver, 82
Cox, Robert, 83
Crenshaw, Kembele, 138, 151
Critical Race Theory (CRT), 212–14, 217, 219, 222, 224, 226
Cronin, Thomas, 248
Crotty, William, 27, 28, 33
Cumings, Bruce, 258
Curtis, Gerald, 256

Dahl, Robert, 316, 373, 382, 383, 404
Davis, Darren, 112, 116
Dawson, Michael, 8, 11, 19, 109, 110, 111, 113–16, 136, 317, 406
De la Fuenta, Alejandro, 62, 63
Delgado, Richard, 216, 219, 220
Departmeto Administrativo Nacional de Etadistica (DANE), 57
Dependency Theory, 81
De Silva, Benedita, 60
Deyo, Frederic, 257
Diop, Cheik Anta, 96
Dominant/Submissive Theory, 286
Dos Santos, Theotonio, 359
Drake, St. Clair, 113, 214
Du Bois, W. E. B., 92, 189, 218, 328, 331, 334, 336, 337, 355
Dudziak, Mary, 219, 330, 337, 338
Dunbar, Leslie, 108
Dunleavy, Patrick, 2
Dzidzienyo, Anani, 58

Economic Commission for Latin America, 81
Edelman, Murray, 236, 244
Ekins, Paul, 87–89
Ely, John H., 373
Epps, Edgar, 40
Equal Opportunity Commission (EEOC), 218, 238
Escober, Arturo, 84, 86, 94, 95
Eulau, Heinz, 205
Evans, Peter, 83, 258
Executive Order 8802, 181–82, 386
Executive Order 11063, 236

Fair Employment Practices Committee (FEPC), 180–85
Fanon, Frantz, 272
Farber, Daniel, 222

Feagin, Joe, 340–41, 387
Fenno, Richard, 195–96, 203, 206, 207
Finifter, Ada, 25
Firefighters v. Stotts, 389
Foner, Eric, 232
Fontaine, Pierre-Michel, 56, 59
Foreign Affairs, 329, 343–44, 349, 359n3
Foucault, Michel, 85, 266, 267
Frank, Andre Gunder, 81, 83, 84
Franklin, John Hope, 386
Frazier, E. Franklin, 113
Freeman, Alan, 215
Fried, Charles, 278
Fujitani, Takaski, 271
Fukuyama, Francis, 256
Fulenwider, Claire, 132
full-length articles (FLAs), 12–18
Furedi, Frank, 334, 335, 339
Furet, Francois, 275

Gaines, Kevin, 154
Galli, Rosemary, 87
Garand, James, 19
Garcia, John, 8, 108, 255
Gardiner, Robert, 333
Gartner, Scott, 120
Gates, Henry Louis, 262, 274
Gay, Claudine, 131, 146, 152–53, 38
Geddes, Barbara, 80
Geertz, Clifford, 417
Geiger, Shirley, 36
General Social Survey, 11, 122
Genovese, Michael, 248
Gerber, Elizabeth, 119
Gidding, Franklin, 328
Gile, Roxanne, 201
Gilliam, Frank, 10, 110, 319
Gilroy, Paul, 117
Givens, Sonja, 151
Globetti, Suzanne, 111
Gold, Thomas, 257
Goldberg, David T., 367
Gosnell, Harold, 30, 33, 198, 316
Gotanda, Neil, 218–19
Got It Goin' On Foundation (GIGO), 157
Gouldner, Alvin, 48
Gratz v. Bollinger, 376
Greenstein, Fred, 26, 240
Grofman, Bernard, 199, 381
Groom, A. J. R., 238
Grutter v. Bollinger, 376
Guimaraes, Antonio, 58
Guinier, Lani, 196, 200, 205
Gunning, Isabella, 223

Gurr, Ted, 343
Guterbock, Thomas, 139
Gutman, Amy, 274

Hacker, Andrew, 228n11
Haddow, Anna, 25
Hadley, Charles, 109
Hall, Arnold Bennett, 36n17
Hamilton, Charles, 108, 285, 317, 319
Hanchard, Michael, 55, 59, 67, 263
Handley, Lisa, 199
Haney-López, Ian, 223
Hannan, Michael, 83
Hardy-Fanta, Carol, 22n10
Harris, Angela, 222
Harris, Frederick, 113, 138
Harris, Joseph, 376
Harris-Lacewell, Melissa, 112
Hartz, Louis, 366, 426
Hasenbalg, Carlos, 55
Hastie, William, 173
Hawkin, Denise, 159
Hayes, Rutherford, 386
Helg, Aline, 63
Henderson, Errol, 343, 345
Henry, Charles, 113, 172
Heringer, Rosana, 60
Herr, Phillip, 328
Herrnstein, Richard, 261
Herval, Tara, 157
Hetherington, Marc, 111
Hickok, Eugene, 377
Higginbotham, A. Leon, 371
Hill, Estelle, 314
Hill, Kevin, 202
Historical Black Colleges and Universities (HBCUs), 42
HIV/AIDs, 156–59
Hochschild, Adam, 353–54
Hochschild, Jennifer, 116, 274
Holden, Matthew, 108
Hollinger, David, 254
Hollingshead, A. B., 42
Holt, Thomas, 406
hooks, bell, 138
Hoston, Germaine, 257, 259, 260, 264, 267, 269, 270
Howell, Susan, 111
Htun, Mala, 60
Huckfeldt, Robert, 116
Hunter, Floyd, 316
Huntington, Samuel, 80, 261, 343–49, 351, 357, 358
Hurricane Katrina, 303
Hutchings, Vincent, 34

Hutchinson, Darren, 222
Hutchison, Harry, 224

Ilchman, Norman, 80
Inkeles, Alex, 79
Inter-Agency Consultation on Race in Latin American (IAC), 72
International Monetary Fund, 80
Ishida, Takeshi, 271
Iton, Richard, 268

Jackson, James, 125n2
Jackson, Jesse, 110, 112–13, 125n2
Jacoby, Russell, 41
Jervis, Robert, 265
Johnson, Chalmers, 257
Johnson, Kevin, 221
Johnson, Lyndon, 235
Johnson, Ollie, 60
Jones, Byran, 313
Jones, Charles 237, 247
Jones, Mack, 10, 366–67
Journal of Politics, 12, 13, 14, 15, 16, 17, 18
JSTOR, 12, 15, 16, 17, 18

Kalven, Harry, 379
Kant, Immanuel, 350–52, 355
Karnig, Albert, 255
Karps, Paul, 205
Katznelson, Ira, 7–8, 256, 273, 404
Kennan, George, 337, 349
Kennedy, John F., 236, 237
Kerr, Phillip, 328
Key, V. O., 30, 32, 108, 408–9, 413
Khor, Martin, 90
Kidd, Benjamin, 328
Kilson, Martin, 49
Kim, Claire, 118
Kinder, Donald, 109
King, Deborah, 137
King, Desmond, 183
King, Mae, 137
King, Martin Luther, Jr., 120, 218, 237, 355
Kirsey v. Board of Supervisors of Hinds County Mississippi, 208n
Klein, Ethel, 141
Kohli, Atul, 258
Kousser, Morgan, 197
Kovel, Joel, 406
Kuhn, Thomas, 266

Lai, James, 224
Lamb, Charles, 387
Lasswell, Harold, 238
Lauren, Paul, 330, 331, 332, 336

Lawrence, Charles, 219
League of United Latin American Citizens (LULAC), 292
Lee, Frances, 379, 380
Lemarchand, Rene, 358
Leonard, Stephen, 31
Levine, Lawrence,113
Levy, Arthur, 201
Lewis, Shelby, 51
Lien, Pei-Te, 119
Lin, Yu Sheng, 259
Lincoln, C. Eric, 113
Lipset, Seymour Martin, 404, 427
Lipsitz, George, 342
Lipsky, Michael, 315
Liso, Donald, 241
Lublin, David, 195, 202, 381, 383
Lyles, Kevin, 378, 387, 388, 390

Mackie, Diane, 44
MacPherson, Anne, 55
Madron, Thomas, 113
Malcomson, Scott, 274
Mander, Jerry, 90
Mannheim, Karl, 253
Manor, James, 87
Mansbridge, Jane, 152, 197, 207
Marbury v. Madison, 372
Marshall, Dale, 118
Marshall, Thurgood, 179
Maruyama, Masao, 271
Marx, Anthony, 60
Matsuda, Mari, 221, 222
Matthews, Donald, 108, 206
Maveety, Nancy, 27, 33
Mayhew, David, 206
McAdam, Doug, 128
McClain, Paula, 8, 108, 255, 257, 293
McClelland, David, 79
McCormick, Joe, 8, 19, 318, 320
McGarrity, Gayle, 62
McGrew, Tony, 99n2
McLemore, Leslie Burl, 36
Meekison, J. Peter, 28
Meier, Kenneth, 318
Merriam, Charles, 29, 31–32
Messick, David, 44
Meyer, John, 83
Micheaux, Elder, 173
Miller, Binny, 222
Miller, Cheryl, 8, 318
Miller v. Johnson, 199
Million Man March, 162
Mills, Charles, 233
Mills, C. Wright, 43

Mills, Gisele, 698
Milner, Helen, 7–8, 256, 273, 404
Miroff, Bruce, 236
Mitchell, Clarence, 181–82, 186
Mitchell, Michael, 263
Mkwandawie, Thandika, 91–92
Mladenka, Kenneth, 313, 318
Moore, Carlos, 63, 64
Moore, Will, 343
Morris, Aldon, 51
Morrison, Judith, 72
Morrison, Renee, 162
Moseley, K. P., 87
Mosquera, Juan de Dios, 64
Moynihan, Daniel Patrick, 233, 320
Murphy, Craig, 88
Murray, Charles, 261
Myrdal, Gunnar, 108, 366, 409

Nakanishi, Don, 224
Nascimento, Elisa, 58, 63, 64, 67, 69
Nathan, Andrew, 260
Nathan, Richard, 260
National Association for the Advancement of
    Colored People (NAACP), 10, 155–57, 174,
    178, 181, 214, 312, 398
National Black Election Studies, 11, 122, 138,
    203, 207
National Black Feminist Study, 131, 135, 136
National Black Politics Study, 11, 122, 136
National Coalition of 100 Black Women of
    America, 159
National Conference of Black Political Scien-
    tists (NCOBPS), 1, 2, 21, 23, 321
National Conference on Science of Politics, 30
National Election Studies (NES), 138
National Political Science Review, 13, 321
National Science Foundation, 8, 21
National Survey of Latinos, 11
National Urban League, 157, 305
Neustadt, Richard, 234–35
New Negro Alliance (NNA), 171, 177–78, 189
New Negro Alliance Yearbook, 171–72
Nie, Norman, 111, 138
Nieman, Donald, 386
Nkrumah, Kwane, 81
Nobles, Melissa, 55, 57, 263
No Child Left Behind Act (NCLB), 289
North American Free Trade Agreement
    (NAFTA), 235
Nyerere, Julius, 271

O'Brien, David, 375
O'Donnell, Guillermo, 83

Office of Minority Economic Initiative,
    296–97
Ogburn, W. F., 314
Oi, Jean, 259
Olson, William, 328
Omi, Michael, 340, 341, 342
Oneal, John, 345, 350
Oppenheimer, Andres, 62
Oppenheimer, Bruce, 379, 380
O'Reilly, Kenneth, 239, 246
Oren, Ido, 332, 356, 403
Orfield, Gary, 388
Orientalism, 85
Orum, Anthony, 113
Overby, L. Marvin, 202

Pacifico, Michele, 174–75, 179–80
Parsons, Talcott, 79, 233
Patler, Nicholas, 332
Patterson, Orlando, 271
Patterson, Thomas E., 367
Pattillo-McCoy, Mary, 118
Pei, Minxin, 258
Peltason, Jack, 374, 378
Pempel, T. J., 257, 261
Perea, Juan, 220
Perestroika, 11, 20, 259
Perez, Sarduy, 62
Persons, Georgia, 293
Perspectives, 123
Phillips, Anne, 207
Pinderhughes, Dianne, 51
Pinkey, Alphonso, 110
Pious, Richard, 238
Pitkins, Hanna, 196
Plessy v. Ferguson, 374
Podunk U, 46
Political Science in American Colleges
    and Universities, 1636–1900, 26
Political Science Quarterly (PSQ), 8, 28, 308
Polsby, Nelson, 26, 33, 316
Pratto, Felica, 410
Prebisch, Raoul, 81
Prestage, Jewel, 8
Preston, Michael, 389
Programa de Desarrollo de los Pueblos Indigenas
    y Negros del Ecuador (PRODEPINE), 61
Prothro, James, 108
Przeworski, Adam, 256
PS, 7, 400
Putnam, Robert, 110

Quality of Life Fiscal 1991 Alternative Budget, 292
Quarterly Journal of Economics, 12

Racial Acknowledge Gestures (RAGS), 232, 241, 242, 243, 246 247
Reagan, Ronald, 110, 235, 289
Redford, Emmett, 285
Reed, Adolph, 113, 420, 421
Reichmann, Rebecca, 59
Reinsch, Paul, 328
Reitan, Ruth, 70
Rice, Condoleezza, 290
Richmond v. Croson, 294, 376
Riley, Russell, 233
Roberts, Dorothy, 151
Robertson, Roland, 83
Robnett, Belina, 160
Rodgers, Harrel, 110
Rodney, Walter, 271
Roe v. Wade, 374
Romany, Celina, 223
Roosevelt, Franklin D., 180–81, 233, 238
Rosenblatt, Karin, 55
Rosenstone, Stephen, 138, 139
Ross, Malcolm, 183
Rostow, W. W., 79
Roth, Benita, 132
Rout, Leslie, 56
Rubenstein, R., 347
Rudman, Lauri, 153
Rueschemeyer, Dietrich, 257
Russell, John 271, 272
Russett, Bruce, 345, 350, 351, 353, 354
Ryan, Stephen, 343

Said, Edward, 85, 261, 274
Salter, John, 314
Santo, Helios, 60
Sarduy, Perez, 62
Sautman, Barry, 262, 274
Schein, Edgar, 40
Schmidt, Brian, 328
Schoppa, Leonard, 259
Schuman, Howard, 109
Schwartz, Benjamin, 259
Schwartz-Shea, Peregrine, 21
Scott, James, 411, 412, 415
Segura, Gary, 120
Shapiro, Martin, 373
Shaw, Todd, 152–53
Shaw v. Reno, 199, 381
Shingles, Richard, 112
Shipler, David, 110
Sigelman, Lee, 119, 145–46
Silberman, Charles, 113
Simien, Evelyn, 132,133
Singh, Robert, 206

situational improvement policies (SIPs), 232, 242, 246
Skocpol, Theda, 257
Skowronek, Stephen, 239, 247
Skrentny, John David, 249n24
Smith, Richard, 116
Smith, Robert,196, 224
Smith, Roger, 366, 398
So, Alvin, 77
social dominance theory (SDT), 410
Social Forces, 12
Social Science Research Council, 30
Soludo, Charles, 91
Sonenshein, Raphael, 118
South Carolina v. Katzenbach, 375
Spann, Girardeau, 230
Special Office for the Promotion of Racial Equality, 60
Spengler, Oswald, 334
Spinner, Jeff, 278
Stanford, Karin, 69
Staples, Robert, 134
Stark, Andrew, 39
State of the Discipline, 1, 24, 25, 26, 27, 28, 33
Steele, James, 21
Steeth, Charlotte, 109
Stefancic, Jean, 219
Sternhell, Ze'ev, 275
Su, Shaozhi, 261
Sun, Yan, 260, 261
Swain, Carol, 195, 197

Tabb, David, 421
Takahashi, K., 270
Tannenbaum, Frank, 371
Tate, Katherine, 125, 152, 196, 203, 381, 382
Tate, Merze, 325
Thernstrom, Abigail, 201
Thernstrom, Stephen, 201
Thomas, Clarence, 130–131, 134, 389
Thornburg v. Gingles, 208n5
Thorne, Eva, 55
Timpone, Richard, 138
Tong, Yangi, 259, 260
Torres, Arlene, 55
Truman, David, 403
Truman, Harry S., 234
Tsunekawa, Keiichi, 257
Tucker, Richard, 345
Tushnet, Mark, 371
Twine, France, 55
Tyson, Tim, 70

Unified Black Movement, 59

United States v. Carolene Products Co., 373
Uphoff, Warren, 80
Upson, Lent, 36
Urban Affairs Review, 308
U.S. News & World Report, 47

Valdes, Francisco, 222
Valentino, Nicholas, 34
Van Maanen, John, 40
Verba, Sidney, 111, 138, 402
VisBrasil, 69
Vogel, Steven, 259, 261
Voting Rights Act of 1965, 108, 198, 206, 375, 381, 382

Wade, Peter, 59
Wahlke, John, 207
Wakeman, Frederic, 276
Walder, Andrew, 259, 260, 261
Walker, Sheila, 59
Wallerstein, Immanuel, 81–82, 83
Walt, Stephen, 346, 347, 349
Walters, Ronald, 68, 419
Walton, Hanes, 8, 35n, 108, 224, 293, 318
Walzer, Michael, 428
Wand, Jonathon, 384
Warren, Dorian, 21
Washington, Booker T., 187–88, 235
Washington: Magazine of the Historical Society of Washington, DC, 173
Washington Times, 424
Waters, Mary, 117
Watson, Denton, 181
Weart, Spencer, 353, 354
Weber, Max, 79
Weisberg, Herbert, 27
Weiss, Nancy, 109

Welch, Susan, 109, 114, 119, 145–46
West, Cornel, 85, 341
Westie, Frank, 49
Whitby, Kenny, 199, 201
White, Aaronette, 131
White, Stephen, 85
Whitten, Norma, 55
Wickham, DeWayne, 110
Wildavsky, Aaron, 302
Wilkins, David, 224
Williams, George, 41
Williams, Patricia, 222
Williams, Robert, 70
Wills, Garry, 368, 369
Wilson, Earnest, 7, 8, 10, 11
Wilson, James Q., 312
Wilson, William Julius, 320
Wilson, Woodrow, 327, 328, 350, 351, 352, 353, 355
Winant, Howard, 340, 341, 342
Wing, Adrien K., 222
Wirth, Louis, 253
Witoshynsky, Mary, 68
Witt, Elder, 389
Witt, Linda, 160
Wolfe, Alan, 274
Wolfinger, Raymond, 139, 312
Woo-Cumming, Meredith, 257, 258
Wood, Charles, 263
Woodward, C. Vann, 413
World Trade Organization (WTO), 91

Yamamoto, Eric, 225
Yelvington, Kevin, 55
Yokley, Raytha, 113

Zeller, Belle, 312